Medical Negligence Case Law

Medical Negligence Case Law

Second edition

Rodney Nelson-Jones MA (Oxon)
Partner, Field Fisher Waterhouse, Solicitors

Frank Burton BA, PhD
Barrister

Butterworths
London, Dublin & Edinburgh
1995

United Kingdom	Butterworths a Division of Reed Elsevier (UK) Ltd, Halsbury House, 35 Chancery Lane, LONDON WC2A 1EL and 4 Hill Street, EDINBURGH EH2 3JZ
Australia	Butterworths, SYDNEY, MELBOURNE, BRISBANE, ADELAIDE, PERTH, CANBERRA and HOBART
Canada	Butterworths Canada Ltd, TORONTO and VANCOUVER
Ireland	Butterworth (Ireland) Ltd, DUBLIN
Malaysia	Malayan Law Journal Sdn Bhd, KUALA LUMPUR
New Zealand	Butterworths of New Zealand Ltd, WELLINGTON and AUCKLAND
Puerto Rico	Butterworth of Puerto Rico, Inc, SAN JUAN
Singapore	Reed Elsevier (Singapore) Pte Ltd, SINGAPORE
South Africa	Butterworths Publishers (Pty) Ltd, DURBAN
USA	Butterworth Legal Publishers, CARLSBAD, California and SALEM, New Hampshire

A CIP Catalogue record for this book is available from the British Library.

First edition 1990

ISBN 0 406 03601 2   2019 1146

Typeset by Kerrypress Ltd, Luton
Printed by Clays Ltd, St Ives plc

Preface

Since the preface to the first edition was written, now over five years ago, the growth in medical malpractice cases has continued to rise. In 1991/1992 over 2,000 cases were settled for a total cost of approximately £58,000,000. The Medical Protection Society has estimated that compensation for medical negligence is expected to cost the National Health Service more than £125,000,000 in 1995 and contends that claims have doubled within the past four years (The Times, Monday 10 April 1995). Important new developments such as the introduction of Crown indemnity for hospital practitioners and more recently the setting up of the Clinical Negligence Scheme for NHS Trusts illustrate the ways in which hospital authorities and the Government have attempted to deal with this increase in litigation.

A further significant development has been the increase in the quantity and quality of case reporting with respect to medical negligence actions such as that illustrated in the Medical Law Reports. The growth in the number of cases and the increasing likelihood that a case will be reported has enabled us to add a further 290 cases to the 320 reported in the first edition. We have also included in this edition more cases from other jurisdictions principally the United States of America, Canada and Australia in recognition of the increasing frequency with which such cases are cited.

In addition the text has been substantially rewritten to deal with important developments in the law concerning consent, access to medical records, structured settlements and limitation.

Many people have worked with great industry to produce this second volume. We are indebted to the valuable comments of Dr Robin Rudd and the research work of Deborah Nadel, Conrad Mewton and Dr Matthew Lohn. Michelle Kinkaid provided tireless secretarial assistance. The law is stated as at 30 June 1995.

Rodney Nelson-Jones, Field Fisher Waterhouse
Frank Burton, 12 Kings Bench Walk

Contents

Table of statutes

References in this Table to *Statutes* are to Halsbury's Statutes of England (Fourth Edition) showing the volume and page at which the annotated text of the Act may be found

Table of cases

PAGE

Case report glossary

AC	Appeal Cases
All ER	All England Law Reports
BMJ	British Medical Journal
BMLR	Butterworths Medical Law Reports
Bing N Cas	Bingham's New Cases
Bulst	Bulstrode's King's Bench Reports
CCLT	Canadian Cases on the Law of Torts
CLY	Current Law Yearbook
C&P	Carrington & Payne's Nisi Prius Reports
Ch	Law Reports, Chancery
DLR	Dominion Law Reports
ER	English Reports
East	East's Term Reports, King's Bench
F	Fraser, Session Cases
F 2d	Federal Reporter – 2nd Series
FCR	Family Court Reporter
FTSB	Frenkel Topping Structures Briefing
F&F	Foster & Finlayson's Nisi Prius Reports
HLR	Housing Law Reports
H Bl	H Blackstone's Common Pleas Reports
HCRR	Health Care Risk Report
H & C	Hurlston & Coltman's Exchequer Reports
ICR	Industrial Court Reports
IR	Irish Reports (Eire)
The Independent	The Independent
KB	King's Bench (Law Reports)
Kemp & Kemp	'The Quantum of Damages', by Kemp & Kemp
LGR	Local Government Reports
LJKB	Law Journal Reports, King's Bench
LR Ex	Law Reports, Exchequer
LS Gaz	Law Society's Gazette
LTJ	Law Times Journal
Lloyds Rep	Lloyds List Report
Med LR	Medical Law Reports
Medical Law Monitor	Medical Law Monitor
MLJ	Medico-Legal Journal
MLR	Modern Law Review

NE	North Eastern Reporter
NI	Northern Ireland Law Reports
NLJ	New Law Journal
NLP	New Law Publishing
NZLR	New Zealand Law Reports
P 2d	Pacific Reporter, 2nd Series
PIQR	Personal Injury and Quantum Reports
PMILL	Personal and Medical Injuries Law Letter
Pa	Pennsylvania Supreme Court Reports
Price	Price's Exchequer Reports
QB	Queen's Bench (Law Reports)
Qd R	Queensland Reports
SASR	South Australian State Reports
SC	Session Cases
Sc LR	Scottish Law Reporter
SJ	Solicitors' Journal
SLT	Scots Law Times
TLR	Times Law Reports
The Times	The Times
WLR	Weekly Law Reports
WN	Weekly Notes (Law Reports)
WWR	Western Weekly Reports
Wils KB	Wilson's Kings Bench Reports

Bibliography

Brazier, M	*Medicine, Patients and the Law* (2nd edn, 1992) Penguin
Capstick, B	*Patient Complaints and Litigation* (1985) National Association of Public Health Authorities
Giesen, D	*International Medical Malpractice Law* (1988) Mohr and Martinus Nijhoff
Jones, M	*Medical Negligence* (1991) Sweet & Maxwell
Jackson, R & Powell, J	*Professional Negligence* (3rd edn, 1992) Sweet & Maxwell
Kennedy, I & Grubb, J	*Medical Law: Text and Materials* (2nd edn, 1993) Butterworths
Lewis, C	*Medical Negligence, a Plaintiff's Guide* (2nd edn, 1992) Tolley
Leahy-Taylor, J	*The Doctor and Negligence* (1971) Pitman Medical
McGregor, H	*Damages* (15th edn, 1988) Sweet & Maxwell
Nathan, P C & Barrowclough, A R	*Medical Negligence* (1957) Butterworths
Nelson-Jones, R & Stewart, P	*Product Liability: The New Law under the Consumer Protection Act 1987* (1987) Fourmat
Nelson-Jones, R & Burton, F	*Personal Injury Limitation Law* (1994) Butterworths
Powers, M & Harris, N	*Medical Negligence* (2nd edn, 1994) Butterworths

PART I

General principles of law

Section A

Causes of action

Chapter 1

Liability in tort

Medical malpractice may give rise to two common law actions in tort. The first, that of trespass to the person, or battery, is of limited significance. The second, that of negligence, forms the basis of most malpractice claims and is the foundation of the modern law determining a medical practitioner's liability to a patient.

1. Battery

1.1 DEFINITION

Battery is the unlawful application of force to another person without his consent and if done intentionally or recklessly, as opposed to negligently, is a crime as well as a tort at common law. The attempt to apply what is frequently thought of as a criminal doctrine to the act of a physician in the course of treatment of a patient has been strongly criticised by the judiciary. Theoretically all procedures which a doctor performs are batteries such as injections, surgery, or manipulations, if done without the consent of the patient. This is so no matter how benign the physician's intentions are or how curative, non-invasive or routine the treatment is. The touching of a person by a doctor without consent violates an individual's right to self determination, breaches the basis of trust in the doctor/patient relationship and constitutes an act of trespass to the person. The attraction for a litigant to sue in battery is that liability for this tort is strict, and accordingly the difficulties of establishing negligence would be circumvented. Moreover, proof of damage is not an essential part of the cause of action, and liability can be established in those cases where a patient either suffers no physical harm or suffers harm which is not a direct cause of the tort. The quantum of damages would, however, reflect the actual harm done although exemplary and aggravated damages are in principle recoverable for the tort of battery/trespass to the person. For example, a woman may consent to relatively minor gynaecological surgery and during the course of the operation the surgeon may find a disease or complication which requires major surgery and may result in sterilisation. The subsequent sterilisation may in fact result in the woman regaining her health. She would, however, be able to sue for battery if she could demonstrate that she gave no consent to the sterilisation.

1.2 INADEQUATE INFORMATION

The question of what constitutes consent has accordingly been inextricably connected with the tort of battery. Where litigants have sought to argue that their

5

consent for an operation or a mode of treatment was given on the basis of inadequate information either of the risks of the treatment or of the extent of the treatment, they have sought to sue in battery (cf *Chatterton v Gerson* (1980) (p 275); *Sidaway v Board of Governors of Bethlem Royal Hospital and the Maudsley Hospital* (1984) (p 554); *Hills v Potter* (1984) (p 380)). The courts, however, have been intolerant of this approach which has been seen as a device to side-step the difficulties in sustaining an action for negligence based on failures to communicate proper information.

In *Hills v Potter* (above) the plaintiff sued in negligence and in battery following the failure of an operation to relieve symptoms caused by a deformity of her neck known as spasmodic torticollis. The operation, although performed with skill and competence, resulted in a severe deterioration so that the plaintiff became paralysed from the neck downwards. The plaintiff alleged that she had not been properly informed about the risks inherent in the surgery and that her consent was therefore vitiated by lack of information that paralysis could result. Hirst J found in relation to the action in battery:

> 'As to the claim for assault and battery, the plaintiff's undoubted consent to the operation which was in fact performed negatives any possibility of liability under this head, see *Chatterton v Gerson*. I should add that I respectfully agree with Bristow J in deploring reliance on these torts in medical cases of this kind, the proper cause of action, if any, is negligence' ([1984] 1 WLR at 653d/e).

In *Chatterton v Gerson* (above) Bristow J had acknowledged that:

> 'It is clear law that in any context in which consent of the injured party is a defence to what would otherwise be a crime or civil wrong the consent must be real' ([1980] 3 WLR at 1012d).

However, consent was judged to be real as long as the patient was informed in 'broad terms' of the nature of the intended procedure and no action for trespass to the person would lie. Alternatively, where information was withheld in bad faith the consent could be vitiated by fraud and a cause of action could be sustained. Bristow J also gave a further example in the course of his judgment concerning an unreported case in which a boy was admitted for a tonsillectomy and was in fact circumcised. The judge indicated that in such circumstances an action in trespass would be appropriate. He went on, however, to say:

> 'But in my judgment it would be very much against the interests of justice if actions which are really based on a failure of a doctor to perform his duty adequately to inform were pleaded in trespass' ([1980] 3 WLR at 1013b/c).

The Master of the Rolls in *Sidaway v Board of Governors of Bethlem Royal Hospital and the Maudsley Hospital* (above) adopted a similar position on consent when he expressed the view:

> 'I am wholly satisfied that as a matter of English law a consent is not vitiated by a failure on the part of a doctor to give a patient sufficient information before the consent is given. It is only if the consent is obtained by a fraud or by a misrepresentation of the nature of what is to be done that it can be said that an apparent consent is not a true consent. This is the position in the criminal law (R v. Clarence (1888)) and the cause of action based upon trespass to the person is closely analogous' ([1984] 2 WLR at 790a/b).

Similarly, Lord Scarman in the House of Lords in *Sidaway v Board of Governors of Bethlem Royal Hospital* (above) concurred with the general disdain in relying on the tort of battery although he was in a minority on seeking to extend the principles of informed consent and the law of negligence:

'The doctrine (of informed consent) is new ground insofar as English law is concerned. Apart from the judgment of Bristow J in *Chatterton v Gerson*, I know of only one case prior to the present appeal in which an English court has discussed it. In *Hills v Potter* Hirst J followed Skinner J in this case, adding a comment with which I respectfully agree, that it would be deplorable to base the law in medical cases of this kind on the tort of assault and battery' ([1985] 2 WLR at 489d/e).

Lord Diplock also remarked in the same case:

'That as long ago as 1767 in *Slater v Baker* (2 WILS 359) (p 558) a suggestion where injury was caused by surgery a form of action lay in trespass vi et armis was rejected with scant sympathy by the Court of King's Bench' (at 497h).

Those cases alleging improper disclosure of risks inherent in modes of treatment are accordingly discussed in further detail in Chapter 8 which is concerned with actions for negligence or breach of contract in failing to inform a patient of the possible consequences of medical decisions and choices.

1.3 NO CONSENT

It would therefore appear that the tort of battery is limited principally to those cases where consent is vitiated by fraud or misrepresentation, and to those cases where although there is no misrepresentation there is no consent at all. For example, in *Cull v Butler* (1932) (p 296) the defendant was held liable for a trespass to the person in circumstances where the plaintiff's specific refusal to consent to a hysterectomy was ignored. Liability was admitted in the cases of *Hamilton v Birmingham Regional Board* (1969) (p 367) and *Devi v West Midlands Regional Health Authority* (1981) (p 308), where sterilisations were undertaken without the consent of the patients. There is no requirement for the touching in question to be hostile as was indicated by the Court of Appeal in *Wilson v Pringle* (1987). Lord Donaldson, the Master of the Rolls, applied Lord Justice Goff's reasoning in *Collins v Wilcock* (1984) when he stated in *F v West Berkshire Health Authority* (1989) (p 327):

'In the absence of consent all, or almost all, medical treatment and all surgical treatment of an adult is unlawful however beneficial such treatment might be. This is incontestable' ([1989] 2 WLR at 1034g/h).

Lord Goff further indicated in the House of Lords in the same case that:

'It has recently been said that the touching must be 'hostile' – see *Wilson v Pringle* (1987). I respectfully doubt whether this is correct. A prank that gets out of hand, an over-friendly slap on the back, a surgical treatment by a surgeon who mistakenly thinks that the patient has consented to it – all these things may transcend the bounds of lawfulness without being characterised as hostile' (at 1083c/d).

Accordingly, whether the touching is hostile (as in *Barbara v Home Office* (1984) (p 237)) or, as is much more likely to be the case, the medical intervention is done in the supposed interests of the patient the absence of consent will found a cause of action in battery. (See also the transatlantic examples of *Marshall v Curry* (1933); *Allan v Mount Sinai Hospital* (1980) (p 224); *Malette v Shulman* (1988) (p 450) where a doctor was found to have committed a battery upon a Jehovah's Witness by transfusing her blood in circumstances where her consent was not given and it was clear she would have objected if able to do so; *Nicoleau v*

Brookhaven Memorial Hospital (p 481); *Raleigh Fitkin–Paul Morgan Memorial Hospital v Anderson and Anderson* (p 516); *Jefferson v Griffin Spalding City Hospital* (p 402) and *Mulloy v Hop Sang* (p 464).)

1.4 VALID CONSENT

For consent to be valid it must be voluntarily given and by a patient capable of understanding the nature of the treatment, its purposes and effects. In competent adults the threshold of comprehension need only be based on information and knowledge in broad terms of what the proposed procedures entail. For example in *Davis v Barking Havering and Brentwood Health Authority* (1993) (p 302) a plaintiff sued in trespass in respect of a leg disability arising out of a non-negligently performed local anaesthetic in the form of a caudal block. Mrs Davis alleged that she had not been informed that she would be given a local as well as a general anaesthetic although the written consent she signed referred to both forms of anaesthesia. The trial judge dismissed her action on the basis that the test to be applied was whether the plaintiff had consented to a procedure the nature and effect of which had been explained to her in broad terms. The judge was of the view that to impose any higher test would not only encourage actions in trespass rather than in negligence but would also lead to the imposition of so-called sectional consent whereby practitioners had to ensure that all component parts of a procedure such as injections, drugs, or manipulations were separately consented to. (See also *Chatterton v Gerson* (p 275)).

1.5 VOLUNTARY CONSENT

Because the validity of consent requires voluntariness the courts on occasions have had recourse to analyse whether the patient did in fact exercise an independence of will. The most authoritative statement on voluntariness is to be found in the case of *Re T* (1992) (p 572) which concerned the validity of a refusal of treatment by a 20-year-old woman who had been raised as a Jehovah's Witness but who had never been accepted into the faith by baptism or otherwise. Miss T was injured in a road traffic accident at a time when she was 34 weeks pregnant. The baby was delivered by Caesarian section but was stillborn. Miss T indicated that she did not want a blood transfusion and she signed a form of refusal of consent to blood transfusion although it was not explained to her that it might be necessary to give her a transfusion so as to prevent injury to her health or even to preserve her life. T's condition deteriorated and the treating consultant wished to administer a blood transfusion and sought an order from the court, which was granted, that it would not be unlawful to administer the transfusion notwithstanding the patient's refusal. The Court of Appeal upheld the decision to allow the transfusion to be performed on the bass that T was not in a fit state physically or mentally to reach a valid decision to refuse and moreover her will had been sapped by the influence of her mother who was a practising Jehovah's Witness. In these circumstances the court held that T's refusal was not of her own volition and there had been no valid refusal. Lord Donaldson MR emphasised that although every adult had the right to decide whether to undertake medical treatment the presumption of a capacity to decide was rebuttable.

A patient may be deprived of their capacity to decide by long-term mental incapacity or retarded development or physical matters such as fatigue, shock, pain or drugs. If an adult patient did not have the capacity to decide at the time of the purported refusal it was the duty of the treating physicians to exercise their clinical judgment in the patient's best interest:

'In all cases doctors will need to consider what is the true scope and basis of the refusal. Was it intended to apply in the circumstances which have arisen? Was it based on assumptions which in the event have not been realised? A refusal is only effective within its true scope and is vitiated if it is based on false assumptions ... in cases of doubt as to the effect of a purported refusal of treatment where failure to treat threatens the patient's life or threatens irreparable damage to his health doctors and health authorities should not hesitate to apply to the courts for assistance' (above p 572).

In the Canadian case of *Beausoleil v La Communauté des Soeurs de la Charité de la Providence* 1964 (p 241) a patient's will was held to be overborne by the effects of pre-operative sedation. Where a doctor is acting in the capacity of a prison physician the courts have recognised the potential for the patient/prisoner's will to be overborne by the powerful role the practitioner has (see *Freeman v Home Office* 1984 (p 334)). In *Re C* (1994) (p 267), however, a prison inmate at Broadmoor successfully obtained an injunction preventing any practitioner from undertaking a below-knee right amputation without his written consent. C had a history of schizophrenia but the trial judge was satisfied that he understood the nature, purposes and effects of the treatment which he refused, notwithstanding that his prospects of survival without the operation were limited.

Particular difficulties may arise in those cases where a patient is unable to consent because of his or her physical or mental condition. The law has therefore evolved certain specific principles with reference to consent in the cases of minors, mental patients, and those persons rendered unconscious and requiring emergency treatment.

1.6 CHILDREN

(a) Consent

Consent for medical treatment to a child may come in certain circumstances from the child itself or from the parent or guardian or others who are lawfully exercising parental responsibility. Firstly, a minor is lawfully competent to give consent pursuant to the provisions of s 8(1), Family Law Reform Act 1969 when the age of 16 has been attained and, accordingly, if consent to dental, surgical or medical treatment is given it is unnecessary to obtain the consent of the parent or guardian. Secondly, a child may give consent below the age of 16 if he has, as a matter of fact, reached a sufficient understanding and intelligence to be capable of making up his own mind concerning what treatment is proposed. This principle was espoused in the House of Lords ruling in *Gillick v West Norfolk and Wisbech Area Health Authority* (1983) (p 353) which determined that a minor under 16 did not, merely by virtue of age alone, lack the legal capacity to consent to medical advice and treatment. Provided that a person under 16 was capable of understanding the proposed treatment and of expressing his own wishes, a valid consent could be given notwithstanding parental opposition. This particular case concerned the lawfulness of giving contraceptive advice, but the general principle applies to all forms of medical treatment. Each case would therefore turn upon the specific capacity of the child's comprehension.

In assessing whether a child is so-called *Gillick* competent the doctor, or the court, will need to be satisfied that the minor comprehends the nature and consequences of the treatment in more than the broad terms required to make consent valid in respect of an adult. Lord Scarman in *Gillick* specified that a doctor when prescribing contraception to a girl under 16 would need to be satisfied that the patient grasped amongst other matters the health implications of sexual intercourse, the emotional impact of pregnancy and abortion and the likely effect on the relationship of the minor with her parents. Lord Fraser also thought that the doctor should be satisfied that it was in the best interest of the patient to give contraceptive advice or treatment without parental consent.

(b) Refusal

The Children Act 1989 has recognised the concept of Gillick competence in preserving the right of a child, for example, to refuse to submit to a medical examination if he or she has sufficient comprehension to make an informed refusal in circumstances where medical evidence is required for the determination of an emergency protection order or a supervision order (s 44 (7), Sch 3, para 4(4)(*d*) and 5(5)(*e*)).

Even when a child is, however, Gillick competent both the court and those exercising parental responsibility have a concurrent authority. The court retains a power to override both consent and refusal whereas those exercising parental responsibility appear to have a residual authority to override a refusal only. In *Re R (a minor) (wardship: medical treatment)* (p 515) a 15-year-old with a history of mental health problems cogently refused, during a period of mental lucidity, to submit to the administration of anti-psychotic drugs. The Court of Appeal held that in the exercise of its wardship jurisdiction the court had power to consent to medical treatment on behalf of a minor who was competent to consent but who had refused. Further the wardship jurisdiction also bestowed on the court the power to forbid treatment even when a minor, albeit Gillick competent, had refused. The court was of the view that it was in the child's best interest. Lord Donaldson MR also indicated that a doctor can lawfully administer treatment to a child who is not a ward of court and who is competent to and does refuse consent if the parent nevertheless consents. However in the converse case where a competent child consented to treatment there was no right for the parents to veto the minor's decision:

> 'In a case in which the "Gillick competent" child refuses treatment, but the parents consent, that consent *enables* treatment to be undertaken lawfully, but in no way determines that the child shall be so treated. In a case in which the positions are reversed, it is the child's consent which is the enabling factor and against the parents' refusal of consent is not determinative. If Lord Scarman (in *F v West Berkshire Health Authority*, above) intended to go further than this and to say within the case of a "Gillick competent" child, the parent has no right either to consent or to refuse consent, his remarks were obiter, because the only question in issue was Mrs Gillick's alleged right of veto. Furthermore I consider that they would have been wrong ... Both in this case and in Re: E the judge treated Gillick's case as deciding that a "Gillick competent" child has a right to refuse treatment. In this I consider they were in error. Such a child can consent, but if he or she declines to do so or refuses, consent can be given by someone else who has parental rights and responsibilities. The failure or refusal of the "Gillick competent" child is a very important factor in the doctor's decision whether or not to treat, but does not prevent the necessary consent being obtained from another competent source' (p 185f-g, 186c-f).

In *Re R* (1991) the court found that the minor was not in fact Gillick competent and that the application of the competency test was not, in any event, appropriate in those cases where due to mental illness the child's understanding and capacity could vary on a daily basis (see also *Re E* (1994) (a minor) (p 317)). In *Re J* (1992) a minor) (medical treatment) (p 398) the court further determined that it retained inherent powers under its *parens patriae* jurisdiction to consent to medical treatment on behalf of a minor who although aged 16, and statutorily competent under the Family Law Reform Act 1969, had refused treatment. J, who was in the care of the local authority, suffered from *anorexia nervosa* and required feeding through a nasogastric tube to which initially she had consented. Subsequently the local authority wished to move J to a different treatment unit and to continue nasogastric feeding and J refused and her life became endangered. The Court of Appeal held that s 8 of Family Law Reform Act 1969 gave a minor who had reached the age of 16 a right to consent but did not give an implied corresponding right to refuse medical treatment. The minor's refusal was an important consideration in determining whether treatment should be afforded but no minor had the power to veto any consent to treatment given by someone who had parental responsibility for the minor. The treatment was therefore permitted against the consent of the child on the court's determination that it was in her best interest. As wardship was no longer available to the local authority the court exercised its inherent powers which were said to be theoretically limitless. The Master of the Rolls recognised the potential conflict this could cause but anticipated that medical ethics would act in tandem with the court's paramount concern to act in the best interests of the child:

> 'Hair-raising possibilities were canvassed of abortions being carried out by doctors in reliance upon the consent of parents and despite the refusal of consent by 16 or 17 year olds. While this may be possible as a matter of law, I do not see any likelihood of it, taking account of medical ethics, unless the abortion was truly in the basic interests of a child. This is not to say it could not happen. That is clear from the facts of *Re D* (1976) (a minor) (wardship: sterilisation) [1976] Fam 185, where the child concerned had neither the intelligence nor understanding either to consent or refuse ... Despite the passing of the Children Act 1989, the inherent jurisdiction of the court could still be invoked in such a case to prevent an abortion which was contrary to the interests of the minor' (at p 323).

(c) Summary

In summary (per Lord Donaldson MR, above 324–325) where a child has a right to consent under s 8 of the Family Law Reform Act 1969, such a consent cannot be overridden by those with parental responsibility for the minor but it can be overridden by the court. A minor of any age who is Gillick competent has a right to consent to treatment which similarly cannot be overridden by those with parental responsibility but can be overridden again by the court. However no minor has power by refusing consent to treatment to override a consent to treatment by someone who has parental responsibility or to override a court consent. The effect of consent to treatment of the minor by someone else with authority acts as a protection to the practitioner from an action based on trespass to the person.

(d) Incompetent minors

In the cases of minors who are incompetent and therefore incapable of consenting to medical treatment consent may be provided by the parent or those exercising parental responsibility. If the local authority has parental responsibility it may exercise a power to consent to treatment on behalf of the child (s 33(3), Children

Act 1989). The natural parents of a child who is subject to a care order do not forfeit the right to consent to treatment on the child's behalf but in the event of a difference of opinion the local authority may take steps to restrict the degree of parental responsibility (s 33(3)(*b*)). A person who has care of the child but who does not have parental responsibility may in certain circumstances consent to medical treatment on the child's behalf (s 3(5)).

(e) Best interests

In all circumstances the exercise by those with parental responsibility, of consent to medical treatment or of refusal to consent to treatment must be done in the best interests of the child (*Gillick*, above). Where there is dispute over what course of treatment is in the best interest of the child the court will determine the dispute. So, for example, in *Re L* (1992) (*a minor*) (p 422) a pregnant 12-year-old, the putative father and the local authority all sought a termination but the child's mother objected. The court considered what the best course was for the welfare of the child and a termination was ordered. A similar position was adopted in *Re P* (*a minor*) (1981) (p 486) where a 15-year-old unmarried mother was allowed to undergo a termination of her second pregnancy notwithstanding her father's opposition to abortion.

In *Re A* (1992) (p 217) the court, being satisfied that a 19-month-old child was brain-dead following non-accidental injury, made a declaration the child was dead and if the medical practitioners thought it appropriate to disconnect the baby, contrary to the parents' wishes, from a ventilator providing life support they would not be acting unlawfully. Because the court was of the view that the child was in fact dead it no longer had any jurisdiction to ward the child nor any inherent jurisdiction and so accordingly made a declaration of death and further indicated that it was not in the child's best interest for him to be subjected to further medical intervention. Conversely in *Re B* (1990) (p 232) the parents of a severely disabled child suffering from Downs Syndrome came to a decision that they did not wish their child to undergo surgery for an intestinal blockage without which she would die within days. The local authority warded the child and at first instance the parents' withholding of consent was authorised by the judge. However, the Court of Appeal reversed the decision holding that it was not for the court to extinguish the life of a mongoloid child notwithstanding that her life would be characterised by severe mental and physical handicap.

(f) Parental religion

Cases where it is more easy to anticipate what the child's best interests are concern parental refusals of consent to treatment based upon religious convictions. In *Re A* (a minor) (blood transfusion) (1992) (p 217) the parents of a 10-month-old child with leukaemia objected to the child receiving blood products because they were Jehovah's Witnesses. The court overrode the parental prohibition on the basis that the child's need for blood was so overwhelming it was in his best interests to receive it. A similar attitude was adopted by the court in *Devon County Council v S* (p 309) and *Re O* (1993) (*a minor*) (*medical treatment*) (p 482) where although great weight was attached by the court to a family's religious principles the court had to determine the child's best interest by acting as a judicial reasonable parent. Further in *Re S* (p 538) a hospital was granted a declaration permitting it to carry out a Caesarian section on a born again Christian who was opposed to anything other than natural childbirth on the basis that it was necessary to preserve the life of the unborn child (see also the transatlantic cases of *Jefferson v Griffin Spalding City Hospital* 1981 (p 402) and *Raleigh Fitkin–Paul Morgan Memorial Hospital v Anderson and Anderson*) 1964 (p 516)). In *R v Harris and Harris* 1993 (p 505) a parent's refusal to consent to insulin treatment on religious grounds until after it was too late to save the life of their 9-year-old-daughter was the basis of a conviction for manslaughter.

(g) Sterilisation

Parental consent to the sterilisation of a girl under 18 was considered incompetent by Lord Templeman in *Re B* (*a minor*) (1988) (p 232). In *Re E* (*a minor*) (p 317) Sir Stephen Brown held that the parents could give a valid consent to a medical sterilisation on a minor done for therapeutic reasons whose primary object was to relieve symptoms rather than to effect a sterilisation. Cases of non-therapeutic sterilisation continue to require a declaration by the High Court that it is in the best interests of the child for the sterilisation to take place (see the current *Practice Note, Official Solicitor: Sterilisation* [1993] 4 Med LR at 302, *Re M* (*a minor*) (*wardship: sterilisation*) [1988] 2 FLR 497, *Re HG* (*specific issue order: sterilisation*) [1993] 1 FLR 587 and *Re D* (*a minor*) (*wardship sterilisation*) [1976] 1 All ER 326).

(h) Procedure

As a matter of procedure the determination of a dispute concerning the proposed treatment or refusal of treatment on a minor who is not in care can be determined by private wardship proceedings. Where a child is in the care of the local authority the wardship jurisdiction cannot be used (s 100(2), Children Act 1989) but the court retains an inherent jurisdiction to oversee the welfare interests of a minor (s 100, Children Act 1989, *Devon County Council v S*, above). In *Re O* (p 482) Johnson J considered the procedural framework best suited to determine the refusal of parents, who were Jehovah's Witnesses, to consent to a blood transfusion in respect of their child who had been made the subject of an emergency protection order (s 44(1), Children Act 1989). The judge considered various options potentially open to the court under the Children Act 1989 and rejected the use of an interim care order, a prohibitive steps order and a specific issue order in favour of the inherent jurisdiction of the High Court. However, in *Camden London Borough Council v R* (*a minor*) (*blood transfusion*) Booth J held that such matters could properly be determined either by use of an application for a specific issue order under s 8 of the Children Act 1989 or through the inherent jurisdiction of the High Court pursuant to s 100(3) of the 1989 Act.

1.7 MENTALLY INCOMPETENT ADULTS

In cases of adults who are incompetent to give or withhold consent for medical treatment and who are not subject to be compulsorily detained under the Mental Health Act 1983 there is no statutory power or inherent jurisdiction through which consent or refusal can be given on their behalf. However, in *F v West Berkshire Health Authority* (1989) (p 327) the House of Lords determined that the court had a common law power to declare the lawfulness of any proposed operation on a mentally incompetent adult. This case concerned a 36-year-old voluntary in-patient of a mental hospital who was incapable of giving consent because she had a mental age of approximately four and a verbal capacity of a two-year-old. Those caring for her determined that it would be in her best interests if she underwent a sterilisation, because it was most likely that she was having sexual relations and she was not able to co-operate with any form of contraception. The House of Lords concurred with both the first instance judge and the Court of Appeal that the sterilisation in question would not be unlawful if it was necessary in the patient's best interests. The legal justification for determining that such medical treatment without consent on a person who was mentally incompetent did not constitute an assault was argued by analogy with the emergency cases. Where a patient is presented to a medical practitioner in a state of unconsciousness and is accordingly unable to give consent to any medical treatment, the courts have recognised that the care given to the unconscious patient would not constitute an assault. This justification was previously deemed to have been based on a notion of implied consent or because it fell into a category of a generally acceptable form of touching in everyday life (see *Collins v Willcock* (1984)). The true basis was, however, determined in *F v West Berkshire Health Authority* (above) to be a mixture of necessity and public interest. The doctor is immune from prosecution for trespass in emergency circumstances because he is acting in the best interests of patients in attempting to save their lives or to ensure improvement or prevent deterioration in their physical or mental well-being ([1989] 2 WLR at 1067 d–e, per Lord Brandon).

The House of Lords deemed there to be no difference in principle between those cases concerning emergency treatment and those cases arising out of mental incapacity, provided that the medical practitioners were acting in the best interests of the patient (per Lord Goff at 1086a–h). It is, however, likely that in respect of emergency cases the treatment has to be orientated towards the specific emergency. If a medical practitioner deems that there ought to be a further treatment for long-term future well-being, then he will be under a duty to seek consent when the patient is able to provide it. The House of Lords affirmed that the test as to what was in the best interests of the patient was to be the same test in respect of whether any particular form of treatment was or was not negligent, namely whether the doctor acted in accordance with the properly held views of a responsible and competent body of practitioners in the field in question (the so-called Bolam test established in *Bolam v Friern Hospital Management Committee* (1957) (p 250). Lord Bridge gave the following reason for the same test being applied:

> 'Moreover it seems to me of first importance that the common law should be readily intelligible to and applicable by all those who undertake the care of persons lacking the capacity to consent to treatment. It would be intolerable for members of the medical, nursing and other professions devoted to the care of the sick that, in caring for those lacking the capacity to consent to treatment they should be put in the dilemma that, if they administer the treatment which they believe to be in the patient's best interest, acting with due skill and care, they run the risk of being held guilty of trespass to the person, but if they withhold that treatment they may be in breach of a duty of care owed to the patient. If those who undertake responsibility for the care of incompetent or unconscious patients administer curative or prophylactic treatment which they believe to be appropriate to the patient's existing condition of disease, injury or bodily malfunction or susceptibility to such condition in the future, the lawfulness of that treatment should be judged by one standard not two. It follows that if the professionals in question have acted with due skill and care judged by the well known test laid down in *Bolam v Friern Hospital Management Committee* (1957), they should be immune from liability and trespass, just as they are immune from liability in negligence' ([1989] 2 WLR 1064c–f).

14

See also *T v T* [1988] 1 All ER 613; *Re D (a minor)* [1976] 1 All ER 326 and *Re T* (above).

In *F v West Berkshire Health Authority* (above) the court held that in the absence of any inherent power to consent on behalf of an incompetent adult, because the parens patriae jurisdiction was no longer available to adults, it nevertheless remained good clinical practice to seek the court's approval that a proposed sterilisation was in the best interests of the patient. Such approval remains necessary for non-medical sterilisation but in the cases of *Re GF* (1992) (p 344) and *F v F* (1991) (p 326) the President, Sir Stephen Brown, indicated in those cases concerning therapeutic sterilisation no declaration was needed from the court. In *Re GF* (1992) a 29-year-old with a mental age of 5 was incapable of undertaking her own menstrual care and sanitary hygiene. The President held that when two doctors were satisfied that a sterilisation operation was necessary for therapeutic reasons and it was in the patient's best interest and there was no less intrusive means of treating the condition, the operation could be carried out even though the incidental effect was sterilisation (also reported as *F v F* p 326) (see also *Re C* [1990] FCR 716, sub nom *JVC*; [1990] 1 WLR 1248 and *Practice Note Official Solicitor: Sterilisation* [1993] 4 Med LR).

In the case of compulsorily detained patients and in respect of their psychiatric treatment only, the Mental Health Act 1983 enacts special provisions concerning the requirements of consent and in certain circumstances treatment without consent and treatment in the face of refusal by the patient. When a patient is compulsorily detained, consent is not required for medical treatment for his psychiatric condition provided the treatment is given by or is under the direction of the responsible medical officer (s 62, Mental Health Act 1983). Where, however, certain treatments as indicated in the Mental Health (Hospital, Guardianship and Consent to Treatment) Regulations 1983 such as electro-convulsive therapy are proposed, a patient's veto cannot be overridden unless an independent practitioner has certified in writing the treatment as being appropriate. A patient also retains the right to withdraw consent, unless the responsible medical officer considers that failure to give the treatment would cause serious suffering to the patient (s 62(2)). Further safeguards are to be found concerning treatment consisting of operations to destroy brain tissue or the functioning of brain tissue also as specified in the 1983 Regulations. For such treatment, consent is required by the patient and further an independent practitioner together with two non-medical persons have to certify that the patient is capable of comprehending the nature, purposes and effects of the operation. In addition, an independent practitioner has to be of the view that the treatment is warranted (s 57 and s 58; Mental Health Act 1983). These safeguards, however, do not apply in the case of certain urgent treatments as specified in s 62 of the Act.

These provisions of the Mental Health Act 1983 do not apply except to those patients liable to be detained and the general rule is that in the absence of clear statutory power to the contrary any patient with a mental disorder whether detained, voluntarily in hospital, or residing in the community must not be subject to medical treatment without consent. In *R v Hallstrom, ex p W* [1986] QB 1090, McCullough J found unlawful treatment given to two schizophrenic patients who were not liable to be detained:

' . . . Unless statutory authority to the contrary exists, no-one is to be detained in hospital or to undergo medical treatment or even to submit himself to a medical examination, without his consent. This is as true of a mentally disordered person as of anyone else'.

In *Re C (adult: refusal of treatment)* (p 267) a 68-year-old serving a sentence for wounding who was subsequently diagnosed as suffering from schizophrenia was transferred to Broadmoor. In 1993 he was diagnosed as suffering from gangrene and was advised that a below-knee amputation was required without which his chances of survival were small. C refused to consent and the hospital administration reverted to conservative measures but refused to undertake that it would not amputate at a later date. C sought an injunction, which was granted, prohibiting the amputation by the hospital or any other hospital without C's written consent. Thorpe J applied the principles as set out by the Master of the Rolls in *Re T* (above) and by the House of Lords in *Airedale National Health Service Trust v Bland* (1993) (p 222) which required an analysis as to whether the patient's capacity to consent had been deprived or reduced by his long-term mental disorder. In assessing C's capacity the judge adopted the approach of a consultant psychiatrist who gave evidence:

' . . . The question to be decided is whether it has been established that C's capacity is so reduced by his chronic mental illness that he does not sufficiently understand the nature, purposes and effects of the proffered amputation. I consider helpful Dr Eastman's analysis of the decision-making process in three stages: first comprehending and retaining treatment information, second, believing it and, third, weighing it in balance to arrive at choice. The Law Commission has proposed a similar approach in paragraph 2.20 of Law Commission Consultation Paper No 129 "Mentally Incapacitated Adults and Decision-making". Applying that test to my finding on the evidence, I am completely satisfied that the presumption that C has the right of self-determination has not been displaced. Although his general capacity is impaired by schizophrenia, it has not been established he does not sufficiently understand the nature, purposes and effects of the treatment he refuses. Indeed I am satisfied that he has understood and retained the relevant treatment information, that in his own way he believes it and that in the same fashion, he has arrived at a clear choice' (p 275b–e).

1.8 PERMANENT UNCONSCIOUSNESS

In cases of emergency where a patient is rendered unconscious and is temporarily incapable of giving consent a doctor may afford treatment if it is in the best interests of the patient in order to save life or to ensure improvement or prevent deterioration in the patient's physical or mental health (*F v West Berkshire Health Authority* above, *Marshall v Curry* (1933) (p 455)). Such treatment would not extend to procedures known to be contrary to the patient's informed and rational instructions nor would it cover officious or convenience measures found to be desirable, as, for example, during the course of an operation, but which were not strictly necessary (per Lord Goff *F v West Berkshire Health Authority* above, p 327).

A different consideration, however, applies concerning the management of patients who are permanently unconscious. In *Airedale National Health Service Trust v Bland* (1993) (p 222) the court was concerned with determining the management of a 17-year-old victim of the Hillsborough Football Stadium Disaster whose injuries had rendered him catastrophically brain damaged and left him in a condition known as persistent vegetative state from which all experts agreed recovery was impossible. The hospital sought a declaration that in the absence of the patient, now over the age of majority, being unable to give consent it would be lawful to disconnect all life-sustaining treatment and medical support resources designed to keep him alive including food and water save that which was required to allow him to die peacefully and with the minimum of pain. The President of the Family Division made the declaration. The Court of Appeal ruled that any doctor in those circumstances who discontinued such treatment in pursuance of a conscientious and proper judgment that such discontinuance was in the patient's best interest was guilty of no crime and was not in breach of his duty of care to the patient. (See in particular the powerful judgment of Hoffman LJ which analyses the conflict of two ethical principles, that of the sanctity of human life and that of the right of self-determination.) The House of Lords affirmed the Court of Appeal's decision and re-affirmed that the answer to the question as to whether a patient should be kept on a life supporting system is to be considered through the legal test of what is in the best interest of the patient having regard to established medical practice:

'In *Re F* [1990] 2 AC 1 it was stated that, where a doctor provides treatment for a person who is incapacitated from saying whether or not he consents to it, the doctor must when deciding on the form of treatment, act in accordance with a responsible and competent body of relevant professional opinion, on the principles set down in *Bolam v Friern Hospital Management Committee* [1957] 1 WLR 582. In my opinion, this principle must equally be applicable to decisions to initiate, or to discontinue, life support, as it is to other forms of treatment. However in a matter of such importance and sensitivity as discontinuance of life support, it is to be expected that guidance will be provided for the profession and on the evidence in the present case such guidance is for such a case . . . to be found in a discussion paper on "Treatment of Patients in Persistent Vegetative State" issued in September 1992 by the Medical Ethics Committee of the British Medical Association. . . . (which include) . . .

(1) Every effort should be made at rehabilitation of at least six months after the injury;
(2) The diagnosis of irreversible PVS should not be considered confirmed until at least 12 months after the injury, with the effect that any decision to withhold life prolonging treatment will be delayed for that period;
(3) The diagnosis should be agreed by two other independent doctors; and
(4) Generally the wishes of the patient's immediate family will be given great weight.

In fact, the views expressed by the Committee on the subject of consultation with the relatives of PVS patients are consistent with the opinion expressed by your Lordships' House in *Re F* [1990] 2 AC 1 that it is good practice for the doctor to consult relatives. . . . but the Committee is firmly of the opinion that the relatives' views cannot be determinative of the treatment. Indeed, if that were not so, the relatives would be able to dictate to the doctors what is in the best interests of the patient, which cannot be right' (p 61).

The House of Lords also confirmed that for the time being procedurally such decisions to discontinue life support systems should be the subject of applications to the President of the Family Division. (See also *Frenchay Health Care NHS Trust v S* (p 339).

Active intervention to cause death by, for example, the administration of drugs, no matter how humanitarian the intention is on the part of a practitioner, and irrespective of the patient's consent, remains unlawful and such euthanasia is to be distinguished from decisions not to provide or continue to provide treatment or care which might prolong life (see *R v Cox* (p 503)).

1.9 SUMMARY

In summary it is a civil wrong and may in certain circumstances be a crime to impose medical treatment on an adult of sound mind without consent. A medical practitioner must comply with instructions given by a competent adult, irrespective of whether the instructions may cause a deterioration in the well-being of the patient or even result in death. The presumption of capacity to consent and to consent voluntarily is however rebuttable. Where the patient is a minor aged 16 or where a child is Gillick competent a consent may be given or refusal withheld. If, however, such a minor refuses then those with parental responsibility or the court can override the refusal in the best interests of the minor's welfare. In addition the High Court through its wardship jurisdiction or through its inherent jurisdiction can override a minor's consent. In all cases, the court will consider what the best interests of the minor are and will use a form of substituted judgment taken from the assumed point of view of the patient. In cases of adults who are mentally incompetent no-one, including the court, can give consent on their behalf but treatment may be lawfully given or withheld by a doctor acting in the best interests of a patient in accordance with respected, competent and relevant professional opinion. In cases of dispute the court will give a declaration or occasionally an injunction to that effect. In cases of non-medical sterilisation and in cases concerning persistent vegetative state, the court requires that declarations are made. In determining mental capacity the court will consider to what extent the patient's disorder has rendered him unable to comprehend the nature, purposes and effects of the intended treatment and whether his right of self-determination has not been displaced.

2. Negligence

Negligence is the breach of a legal duty of care owed by a defendant to a plaintiff which results in damage caused by the defendant to the plaintiff. That such a legal duty of care is owed by a medical practitioner to the patient has long been recognised in common law (cf *Pippin v Sheppard* (1822) (p 496), *Pimm v Roper* (1862) (p 495), *Edgar v Lamont* (1914) (p 318), *Gladwell v Steggall* (1839) (p 354)). This duty attaches to all those who hold themselves out as skilled in medical, nursing and paramedical matters and arises independently of any contractual relationship. A litigant may therefore sue concurrently in contract and in tort. The duty of care is imposed even when a practitioner acts gratuitously in a voluntary capacity (cf the Australian case of *Goode v Nash* (1979) (p 355).

The internal structure of the tort of negligence is simple and has proved to be a pragmatic cause of action which has had a flexibility in adapting to changing social circumstances. Its internal component parts require a plaintiff to show first that a legal duty of care was owed to him by the defendant. This normally imposes little difficulty in medical malpractice cases where duties are clearly owed by doctors, nurses, dentists, psychiatrists, radiologists, pharmacists et al directly to the patient. To establish the existence of a duty of care the courts have held that there must be three, interconnected, characteristics. Firstly there must be the foreseeability of harm, secondly a relationship of proximity between the plaintiff and the defendant and thirdly that it is fair, just and reasonable that a duty of care is imposed as a matter of policy (*Caparo Industries plc v Dickman* [1990] 2 AC 605). These features are axiomatic in the doctor/patient relationship. They are not, however, enough to impose a duty of care on a doctor to treat a stranger or to act as a rescuer. The practitioner has no duty in law to act as a good samaritan, because the stranger in need is deemed not to have a relationship of proximity to the doctor. A general practitioner is required to treat all patients on his list (see National Health Service (General Medical and Pharmaceutical) Regulations 1974, SI 1974/160 and 1989/1897). Further in *Barnes v Crabtree* (1955) *Times* 1/2 November it was conceded through a general practioner's counsel that a general practitioner had a duty to treat anyone presenting in an emergency. Once a doctor starts to administer to a patient the duty of care is imposed, even when the doctor acts without remuneration and for example on a patient who might be unconscious.

Further a duty of care may be owed to certain third parties who are sufficiently proximate to a doctor's acts or omissions in circumstances where it is thought just to impose such a duty. In 1937 in the case of *Holgate v Lancashire Mental Hospitals Board* (p 384) liability was established against doctors who had granted a licence to a patient who had been detained at His Majesty's pleasure so that he could visit his brother and be taken on holiday. The patient subsequently attacked Mrs Holgate, causing her severe injury and the jury found that the defendants had failed to take reasonable care in granting the licence. A question-mark, however, was placed over the validity of this decision by Lord Diplock in *Home Office v Dorset Yacht Co Ltd* [1970] AC 1004. Even more difficult questions concerning the extent of a practitioner's duty of care with respect to third parties arise in circumstances where a doctor has knowledge that a patient has a potentially fatal contagious disease such as HIV/Aids or where it is known that a patient has during the course of a consultation expressed threats of violence against a known or an identifiable individual (see *Tarasoff v Regents of the University of California* (p 575)).

The duty of care is also frequently owed by the treating institution such as a hospital. Institutional liability can arise through a failure in respect of a direct duty owed, such as failing to provide a sufficient number of staff, or failing to exercise care in selecting staff, or monitoring the quality of the staff or in supervising the staff, or failing to provide a safe system of health care, or providing dangerous equipment or premises. The institution's duty of care may also be direct in the sense of being a non-delegable primary duty assumed by the hospital when a patient is admitted for treatment. Furthermore, an employing health authority or hospital may be vicariously liable for the negligent acts of its servants and agents (cf *Cassidy v Ministry of Health* (1951) (p 272) and *Roe v Minister of Health* (1954) (p 531).

Secondly, after establishing a duty of care a plaintiff must then demonstrate a breach of that duty. Breach of duty is analysed by examining whether the defendant has fallen below the standard of care deemed appropriate by the courts. Such carelessness has consistently been evaluated by the courts in medical malpractice actions as that which departs from the standard practised and accepted by a responsible body of medical persons skilled in the particular area of medicine in question. The court will be concerned to decide as a matter of fact whether a practitioner has fallen below the ordinary skill of an ordinary practitioner exercising and professing to have the particular skill in issue (*Bolam v Friern Management Committee* (1957) (p 250)). This criterion is determined in most cases by the courts hearing the expert opinion of medical witnesses giving their views on current modes of accepted practice and the particular level of skill exercised by the practitioner in question. This approach is adopted irrespective of whether the alleged lack of care concerns diagnosis and treatment, failure to furnish sufficient information in respect of various forms of treatment, negligent advice, or failure to establish proper communication between practitioners and between the patient and practitioner. Whether there has been a breach of the standard care is a matter of fact which requires careful analysis in each case.

Thirdly, the plaintiff must prove that he has suffered damage which was caused by the defendant's negligence. If no damage is proved, there is no cause of action because this is an essential part of the tort. Cases appearing to indicate gross failures on the part of practitioners, such as failing to attend to a patient despite requests can often fail at this hurdle (see the striking facts in *Barnett v Chelsea & Kensington Hospital Management Committee* (1969) (p 238)). Similarly, it will not avail a patient to prove that a diagnosis made would not have been made by any competent practitioner or that the treatment received was manifestly substandard unless the patient can go on to prove that his health deteriorated, or that he suffered some other damage directly caused by the negligence. Often a patient will be faced with evidence that the progress of his disease would have occurred even if the diagnosis and treatment had been competent. In consent cases the patient also has to establish that, if the warning of the risk had been made clear, the operation or treatment would not have been agreed to. These elements of duty and standard of care, breach, proof and causation give rise to their own particular body of principles and will be analysed separately in the following chapters.

3. Vicarious liability

Vicarious liability arises when the law holds one person or institution responsible for the tortious actions of another even though there is no misconduct or blame on that person or institution. The prime example of vicarious liability is that of an employer being held liable for the torts of an employee. In very limited circumstances, the courts will hold employers liable for the torts of independent contractors and agents employed by them. However, the predominant principle is that an employer is not to be held liable for the acts of an independent contractor. A practitioner is obviously responsible in law for his own actions and will be liable personally if found to have caused damage by negligence. From the viewpoint of a plaintiff there are advantages in suing an employing authority. In the case of a hospital, a patient may be unable precisely to define which member of the medical team was in fact responsible for the particular negligent act or acts. In suing the employer who is responsible for the acts of all the team, this difficulty no longer arises. Moreover, until 1990 hospital doctors were required by the terms of their contract to be insured and were insured with either the Medical Defence Union or the Medical Protection Society, but many paramedical practitioners in hospitals and most nurses were not required to be insured.

The current provision of so-called 'crown indemnity' which came into force in respect of claims lodged on or after 1 January 1990 (HC(89)34, HC(FP)22) requires health authorities to assume responsibility for medical negligence actions arising out of the acts of their employees including all medical and dental staff. Prior to this arrangement the health authorities had a private arrangement (HM(54)32) through which they funded payments to plaintiffs through agreed proportions with the medical defence societies and, in the absence of any agreement, the health authorities and defence societies paid the damages equally. Crown indemnity extends to include agency staff and research workers but not to doctors engaged in private work, those acting as good samaritans, or general practitioners undertaking activities within hospitals but not under a contract with the hospital. General practitioners are excluded from the scheme. National Health Trust Hospitals which first came into existence on 1 April 1991 do not fall within the crown indemnity system, but by paragraph 30 in Appendix A to HC(89)34 confirmation is given that the trusts will be responsible for the negligence of their medical and dental staff and will make their own arrangements for providing financial cover to pay damages including the right to contract with insurance companies for liability insurance. Under s 21 of the National Health Service and Community Care Act 1990 the Secretary of State has power to establish a scheme to include both health authorities and National Health Trust Hospitals concerning the payment of damages in medical negligence actions. This central fund scheme was given approval by the Minister of Health in November 1994 and regulations are to be made with the intention of the scheme commencing in April 1995. The scheme is voluntary but it is anticipated that many trusts and some commissioning authorities will wish to join. It is likely that a special Health Authority will be set up to run the scheme.

There is nothing to stop a plaintiff suing more than one party such as the health authority and a hospital doctor, although there is no clear benefit in doing this. It can be beneficial in some circumstances to sue two parties who are both good for the damages as this can increase the prospects of a settlement. However, naming the hospital doctor in the action against the hospital authority can possibly increase his determination to defend what he is likely to perceive as an assault on his reputation. One employee is not vicariously liable for the acts of another, and accordingly a consultant is not vicariously liable for the acts of his registrars (cf *Rosen v Edgar* (1986) (p 533)).

With regard to general practitioners, there is little scope for bringing in another party because the general practitioner is not the employee of the Family Health Services Authority (formerly the Family Practitioner Committee). The GP is deemed to be employed on a contract for services, not a contract of service, and no vicarious liability arises in this situation (*Roy v Kensington and Chelsea and Westminster Family Practitioner Committee* [1990] 1 Med LR 328). The general practitioner is an independent contractor to this extent. If, however, a doctor practises in partnership, his partners will also be liable for the torts of a fellow partner (s 10, Partnership Act 1890). The liability of each partner for the other's negligence also extends to the negligence of the partnership's staff. A general practitioner and his partners will therefore be liable for the acts of their employees, such as receptionists and other members of staff who provide auxiliary services (*Lobley v Going* (1985)) (p 431). It is unlikely that a general practitioner would be held liable for the negligent acts of a locum general practitioner unless it could be demonstrated that there was negligence in appointing the locum or in failing to provide him with proper information (see the Canadian case of *Rothwell v Raes* (1988) 54 DLR (4th) 193 (Ont HC)). In such a case the liability would be primary not vicarious.

Initially the courts sought to refrain from imposing liability on hospitals for negligent acts done by skilled personnel, which included nursing and medical staff, during the course of their employment. The hospitals were successful in putting forward an argument that they themselves did not undertake to perform the treatment but only to put the patient into the hands of employees with particular skills. Surgeons and other skilled personnel were deemed to exercise their calling independent of any control by any hospital and were accordingly employed on a contract for services but not of services (cf *Strangways-Lesmere v Clayton* (1936) (p 569), *Davis v LCC* (1914) (p 303), *Evans v Liverpool Corpn* (1906), *Marshall v County Council of Lindsey, Lincolnshire* (1937) (p 454)).

In 1942 the courts began to accept the principle of vicarious liability more readily in the area of health care. In *Gold v Essex County Council* (1942) (p 354), an infant plaintiff represented by AD Denning KC (later Master of the Rolls), brought an action for damages arising out of a facial injury due to the negligence of a radiographer in failing to screen the child properly. At first instance, the judge held that the authority was not liable for the radiographer who fell into the same category as nurses who exercised their skills independently of the direct control of the hospital. The Court of Appeal accepted the arguments of counsel for the plaintiff that the radiographers and nurses were in fact acting under contracts of service, and the employing health authority was held liable.

With the nationalisation and reorganisation of health care in 1948 came an extension of the vicarious liability of a hospital and health authority to cover that of doctors and surgeons. In *Cassidy v Ministry of Health* (1951) (p 272), a hospital employing two doctors on contracts of service was found vicariously liable for their negligent care which led to a severe deterioration in the plaintiff's condition of Dupuytren's contracture. Lord Justice Denning traced the judicial reluctance to impose liability on hospital authorities and explained it partly as an attempt to prevent charities being burdened with liabilities they could not afford. He went on to express these views:

> ' ... When hospital authorities undertake to treat a patient and themselves select and appoint and employ the professional men and women who are to give the treatment they are responsible for the negligence of those persons in failing to give proper treatment, no matter whether they are doctors, surgeons, nurses or anyone else. Once hospital authorities are held responsible for the nurses and radiographers, as they had been in *Gold's* case (1942) (p 354), I can see no possible reason why they should not also be responsible for the house surgeons and resident medical officers on their permanent staff. It has been said, however, by no less an authority than Goddard LJ in *Gold's* case, that the liability for doctors on the permanent staff depends "on whether there is a contract of service and that must depend on the facts of any particular case". I venture to take a different view. I think it depends on this: who employs the doctors or surgeons, is it the patient or hospital authorities? If the patient himself selects and employs the doctor or surgeon as in *Hillyer's* case (1909) the hospital authorities are of course not liable for his negligence because he was not employed by them. Where however the doctor or surgeon, be he a consultant or not, is employed and paid not by the patient but by the hospital authorities, I am of the opinion that the hospital authorities are liable for his negligence in treating the patient. It does not depend on whether the contract under which he is employed is a contract of service or contract for services. This is a fine distinction which is sometimes of importance but not in cases such as the present where the hospital authorities are themselves under a duty to use care in treating the patient' ([1951] 1 All ER 586d–h).

The basis of this responsibility was explained as partly being determined by the law of agency in the case of *Roe v Minister of Health* (1954) (p 531). This case concerned consolidated actions by two plaintiffs who had both been rendered paraplegic as a consequence of a spinal anaesthetic administered by a visiting anaesthetist for minor operations on 13 October 1947. No negligence was established in this case but the Court of Appeal held that in principle there was a relationship giving rise to vicarious liability. Denning LJ said:

> ' ... I think that the hospital authorities are responsible for the whole of their staff, not only for the nurses and doctors, but also for the anaesthetists and the surgeons. It does not matter whether they are permanent or temporary, resident or visiting, whole time or part time. The hospital authorities are responsible for all of them. The reason is because, even if they are not servants, they are the agents of the hospital to give the treatment. The only exception is the case of consultants or anaesthetists selected and employed by the patient himself' ([1954] 2 QB at 82).

Since crown indemnity, the doctrine of vicarious liability through the law of agency is of greater significance in cases of negligent private hospital treatment. A private hospital or clinic will clearly be liable for the acts of its negligent employees. Where, however, the doctor is not employed but engaged as an independent contractor some doubt as to the hospital's liability for the negligent acts of that doctor still arise. If as in *Roe*, the doctor is considered an agent then vicarious liability will arise. In addition, the plaintiff will probably have a separate contractual cause of action against the hospital.

NON DELEGABLE DUTY

It is, however, possible to see in the judgments of Lord Justice Denning a clear attempt to impose a direct non-delegable duty of care on the hospital or health authority which is personal to them and not dependent upon the doctrine of vicarious liability. In *Cassidy v Ministry of Health* (1951) (p 272) the argument was by analogy with the duty owed by the general practitioner:

'If a man goes to a doctor because he is ill, no one doubts that the doctor must exercise reasonable care and skill in his treatment of him and that is so whether the doctor is paid for his services or not. If, however, the doctor is unable to treat the man himself and sends him to hospital, are not the hospital authorities under a duty of care in their treatment of him? I think they are. Clearly, if he is a paying patient, paying them directly for their treatment of him they must take reasonable care of him and why should it make any difference if he does not pay them directly, but only indirectly through the rates which he pays to the local authority or through insurance contributions which he makes in order to get the treatment? I see no difference at all. Even if he is so poor that he can pay nothing, and the hospital treats him out of charity, still the hospital is under a duty to take reasonable care of him just as the doctor is who treats him without asking a fee. In my opinion, authorities who run a hospital, be they local authorities, government boards, or any other corporation, are in law under the self same duty as the humblest doctor. Whenever they accept a patient for treatment, they must use reasonable care and skill to cure him of his ailment. Hospital authorities cannot, of course, do it by themselves. They have no ears to listen through the stethoscope, no hands to hold the knives. They must do it by the staff which they employ, and, if their staff are negligent in giving the treatment, they are just as liable for that negligence as anyone else who employs others to do his duties for him. What possible difference in law, I ask, can there be between hospital authorities who accept a patient for treatment and railway or shipping authorities who accept a passenger for carriage? None whatever. Once they undertake the task, they are under a duty to use care in the doing of it and that is so whether they do it for reward or not. It is no answer for them to say that their staff are professional men and women who do not tolerate any interference by their lay masters in the way they do their work. The doctor who treats a patient in a Walton hospital can say, equally with a ship's captain who sails his ship from Liverpool and with a crane driver who works his crane at the docks: "I take no orders from anybody". That "sturdy answer" as Lord Simmonds described it in *Mersey Docks and Harbour Board v Coggins and Griffiths (Liverpool) Ltd* (1946), only means in each case that he is a skilled man who knows his work and will carry it out in his own way. It does not mean that the authorities who employ him are not liable for his negligence. The reason why the employers are liable in such cases is not because they can control the way in which the work is done – they often have not sufficient knowledge to do so – but because they employed the staff and had chosen them for the task and have in their hands the ultimate sanction of good conduct – the power of dismissal' ([1951] 1 All ER at 584h, 585a–f).

This view was also expressed in *Roe v Ministry of Health* (p 531) and *Jones v Manchester Corpn* (p 406) (see also the Australian cases of *Ellis v Wallsend District Hospital* (1989) 17 NSWLR 553, and the Canadian case of *Yepremian v Scarborough General Hospital* (1980) 110 DLR (3d) 513 (ONT CA)).

The argument that the hospital authority has a personal non-delegable duty of care coupled with the doctrine of vicarious liability for servants and agents has been instrumental in establishing the main action in medical malpractice as an action in negligence. Even where there is a direct contractual relationship, as with a private hospital, it is most likely that the hospital will be liable for the actions not only of its employed staff but also for those independent contractors whom it selects and chooses. As indicated, apart from the contention that the hospital will owe this personal duty of care, the hospital clearly owes a direct duty of care concerning such matters as patient surveillance (*Selfe v Ilford and District Hospital Management Committee* (1970) (p 551), *Thorne v Northern Group Hospital Management Committee* (1964) (p 584), *Knight v Home Office* (1990) (p 419); dangers from infection (*Evans v Liverpool Corpn* (1906), *Heafield v Crane* (1937) (p 375), *Lindsey County Council v Marshall* (1937) (p 454); the provision of proper and safe equipment (*Clarke v Adams* (1950) (p 279)); a system for administering drugs (*Collins v Hertfordshire County Council* (1947) (p 283)); the provision of expert back-up obstetric cover (*Bull v Devon Area Health Authority* (1994) (p 264) and the supervision of junior doctors (*Jones v Manchester Corpn* (1952) (p 406)).

In *Wilsher v Essex Area Health Authority* (1987) (p 609) the Court of Appeal also expressed the view that a health authority which conducted a hospital so that it failed to provide doctors of sufficient skill and experience to give treatment offered at the hospital could be directly liable in negligence to the patient. There was no reason why in principle the health authority should not be liable if its organisation is at fault. Lord Justice Mustill ([1987] 2 WLR at 437) indicated that such liability might arise where junior doctors without sufficient skill or experience were wrongly appointed and were not given sufficient training to be able to comprehend the significance of a monitor giving misleading and dangerous results. The Vice-Chancellor, Sir Nicholas Browne-Wilkinson, said this:

> 'In my judgment, a health authority which so conducts its hospital that it fails to provide doctors of sufficient skill and experience to give the treatment offered at the hospital may be directly liable in negligence to the patient. Although we were told in argument that no case has ever been decided on this ground and it is not the practice to formulate claims in this way, I can see no reason why, in principle, the health authority should not be so liable if its organisation is at fault: see *McDermid v Nash Dredging and Reclamation Co Ltd* [1986] QB 965 especially at pp 978–979' ([1987] 2 WLR 465e–g).

It may accordingly be expected that actions based upon a personal non-delegable duty similar to that owed by an employer to his employees and premised upon failures analogous to failing to provide a safe system of work may feature in future proceedings.

Those actions, however, which are framed in terms of a failure to provide sufficient resources for certain types of health care are likely to fail on the basis that the allocation of resources is a matter of public policy. The courts have persistently held that the duty espoused under s 3 of the National Health Service Act 1977 to meet all reasonable requirements in respect of medical, dental, nursing and ambulance requirements must be interpreted within the constraints of resources available. (*R v Secretary of State for Social Services, ex p Hincks*

(1979), *R v Central Birmingham Health Authority, ex p Walker* (1987) (p 502), *R v Central Birmingham Health Authority, ex p Collier* (1988) (p 502) and *R v North West Thames Regional Health Authority, ex p Daniels* (1993) (p 509).

In Re HIV Haemophiliac Litigation) (1990) (p 394) the Court of Appeal was concerned with an interlocutory appeal over the discovery of documents, which also raised an issue as to whether there was any statutory cause of action or any action in negligence sustainable against the Secretary of State arising out of the National Health Service Act 1977. The Court of Appeal expressed a view that in principle an action in negligence could lie in respect of acts or omissions against the Department of Health in respect of the performance or functions under the Act. Lord Justice Gibson indicated:

> 'It is obvious that it would be rare for a case in negligence to be proved having regard to the nature of the duties and the 1977 Act, and to the fact that, in the law of negligence, it is difficult to prove a negligent breach of duty when the party charged with negligence is required to exercise discretion and to form judgments upon the allocation of public resources. That, however, is not sufficient, in my judgment to make it clear ... that there can in law be no claim in negligence' (page 36 of the transcript).

Both Lord Justice Gibson and Bingham LJ shared the trial judge's doubt, however, as to whether or not the National Health Service Act 1977 could be construed as imposing on the Secretary of State any statutory duty which would be enforceable by a member of the public in private law for damages as opposed to the potential public remedy of judicial review. It is therefore likely that actions founded upon allegations concerning a lack of resources are unlikely to succeed unless it can be demonstrated that the particular fault in question lay in the hospital's managerial negligence in the distribution of its resources (see *Knight v Home Office* (p 419)).

In *R v Cambridge District Health Authority, ex p B* (p 501) the Court of Appeal refused to intervene by way of judicial review in respect of a health authority's decision not to fund further chemotherapy and an allogenic bone marrow transplant on a 10-year old girl with an expectation of life of 6–8 weeks. The cost of the treatment was £15,000 for the transplant. The court, in allowing the defendant's appeal, was satisfied that proper measures had been taken in coming to the decision not to spend limited resources in circumstances where the child's prospects of benefiting from the treatment were in the order of 15–20%. The court stated that it was not an arbiter as to the merits of the medical judgements of this type and was restricted to ruling on the lawfulness of the decision. The authority had not exceeded its powers or acted unreasonably and in these circumstances it was not open to the court to substitute its own decision for that of the authority making it.

Chapter 2

Liability in contract

Actions for medical malpractice are primarily actions based on the tort of negligence. This is firstly because for the majority of patients there is only a weak factual basis for suing in contract. Most patients receive treatment under the National Health Service scheme and there is probably no direct contract entered into between the National Health Service patient and his general practitioner, his treating hospital or his dispensing pharmacist. In *Pfizer Corpn v Ministry of Health* [1965] AC 512 it was held that an NHS patient receiving medication from a pharmacist after paying a prescription charge did not receive the contents of the prescription under a contract of sale but through the chemist's statutory duty to dispense. By analogy it is likely that similar reasoning would apply to the NHS dental patient who pays dental charges. It is arguable that a general practitioner enters into a contract with a patient when the doctor accepts the patient on to the practitioner's list and the practice sees an increase in remuneration. However, the consideration moves indirectly because it is not paid for by the patient except through taxation (see *Appleby v Sleep* (1968) (p 229)). The contract of a general practitioner is in fact with the Family Health Services Authority (previously the Family Practitioner Committee) in his area and is defined and controlled by the National Health Service (General Medical and Pharmaceutical Services) Regulations 1974 (SI 1974/160) as amended 1989/1897. These regulations do not define any contractual terms between a doctor and a patient and the patient cannot sue upon them. They do, however, have significance in defining the general practitioner's duties towards a patient such as requiring the GP to provide a personal service to the patient. In *Hotson v East Berkshire Health Authority* (1987) (p 389) the Court of Appeal's discussion on the difference between suing in contract and in tort appears to have accepted that there is no contract between a patient and the National Health Service or its staff. This particular action, however, was not initiated in contract.

Secondly, any private patient is entitled to sue concurrently in tort and in contract, and usually will. Often a private patient has not entered into a strictly defined contract with expressly written terms governing the agreement for medical care. The courts have therefore had to construe what the implied obligations were in any given private agreement. In fact, the courts have construed the implied contractual duty of care as identical to the duty of care owed in tort. Causes of action based upon medical mishap are accordingly exempt from the general movement against the imposition of concurrent liabilities in tort and contract precisely because they do not seek to claim that there are higher tortious duties over lower contractual ones. Accordingly, the true nature of medical malpractice actions can realistically be described as medical negligence cases.

There are, however, and will continue to be, differences between the two causes of action. If a doctor expressly agrees to undertake an operation or a course of treatment in a particular way and departs from this agreement then an action for breach of contract on the express term will arise. The litigant will not then be required to prove that the doctor departed from the implied obligation to use reasonable care and skill. In *La Fleur v Cornelis* (1979) 28 NBR (2d) 569 (NBSC) a plastic surgeon entered into a contract to perform an elective operation on the plaintiff's nose, having made a representation that the plaintiff would be very happy with the outcome. The plaintiff successfully sued for breach of contract when he was left with a scarred and misshapen nose because the Court was satisfied that on the facts of the case there had been a warranty that the operation would be guaranteed successful.

However, for a court to find that a doctor did agree to guarantee a result or to refrain from a specific procedure, the term of the contract must be explicit and unequivocal. So an operation performed privately for sterilisation will not be construed in the absence of any express agreement as a contract to render the patient infertile. In *Thake v Maurice* (1986) (p 579) the plaintiff sued for breach of contract, collateral warranty and misrepresentation seeking damages for the fathering of a child after having a vasectomy. The surgeon in counselling the plaintiff had emphasised the irreversible nature of the operation, but had neglected to warn the plaintiff that there was a small risk of the operation being naturally reversed. The judge at first instance (Peter Pain J) had held that the agreement was to render the plaintiff irreversibly sterile. The Court of Appeal reversed this finding. The operation, which had been competently performed, was not based upon a guarantee to make the plaintiff infertile but was an agreement to perform a vasectomy using reasonable skill and care (Kerr LJ dissenting). Neill LJ inclined to the view that:

'I do not consider that a reasonable person would have expected a responsible medical man to be intending to give a guarantee. Medicine, though a highly skilled profession, is not, and is not generally regarded as being, an exact science. The reasonable man would have expected the defendant to exercise all the proper skill and care of a surgeon in that speciality: he would not in my view have expected the defendant to give a guarantee of 100 per cent success' ([1986]2 WLR at 354d).

Similarly, Nourse LJ found that to imply such an agreement effectively cuts across the universal warranty normally implied in such cases, that of using reasonable skill and care, and quoted with approval Slade LJ in *Eyre v Measday* (1986) (p 325), an action concerning an unsuccessful sterilisation on a female:

' ... but in my opinion, in the absence of any express warranty, the court should be slow to imply against a medical man an unqualified warranty as to the results of intended operations, for the very simple reason that, objectively speaking, it is most unlikely that a responsible medical man will intend to give a warranty of this nature' ([1986] 2 WLR at 355f).

There is therefore no question of any contractual presumption that because an accident happened in the course of treatment, or a misdiagnosis was made, or a person's expectation from an operation had been dashed by poor results, that any breach of contract has occurred. A litigant must demonstrate a breach of an express term, or else it is most likely that the court would imply the normal obligation common to the breach of duty in tort and in contract in medical malpractice actions (cf *Worster v City and Hackney Health Authority* (1987) (p 612)). Lord Templeman in *Sidaway v Board of Governors of the Bethlem Royal Hospital and the Maudsley Hospital* (1985) (p 554) expressed the view that this obligation was originally contractual:

> 'The relationship between doctor and patient is contractual in origin, the doctor performing services in consideration for fees payable by the patient. The doctor, obedient to the high standards set by the medical profession impliedly contracts to act at all times in the best interest of the patient ... At the end of the day, the doctor bearing in mind the best interests of the patient and bearing in mind the patient's right of information which will enable the patient to make a balanced judgment must decide what information should be given to the patient and in what terms that information should be couched' ([1985] 2 WLR at 508e, 509d).

Whether the implied contractual terms between a doctor and patient are expressed as acting in the best interest of the patient or not, in fact they amount to no more than that which is now implied by statute under the provisions of s 13, Supply of Goods and Services Act 1982. This section provides that in a contract for the supply of goods and service where the supplier is acting in the course of a business, it is an implied term that the supplier will carry out his service with reasonable care and skill. This is in effect a position which has long been recognised at common law (see *Morris v Winsbury-White* (1937) (p 462) and *Shiells & Thorne v Blackburne* (1789)). From the doctor's perspective, it is not possible to contract out of such a duty where personal injury has been caused by the doctor's negligence; see s 2, Unfair Contract Terms Act 1977.

Where, however, a product is supplied and used in the course of private medical treatment, stricter duties of care may be implied. A term will be implied by s 4(5), Supply of Goods and Services Act 1982 or under the provisions of the Sale of Goods Act 1979 (as amended by the Sale of Goods Act 1994) that the goods supplied are fit for their purpose and are of 'satisfactory' quality (see s 1 of the 1994 Act). Such articles might include valves, artificial limbs, blood or blood products, contraceptive aids and drugs (see *Davidson v Connaught Laboratories* (1980) (p 298)). In *Samuels v Davis* (p 544) a dentist sued in 1943 for his 12 guinea fee for providing dentures. His claim failed on the basis that the dentures could not be worn and were not fit for their purpose and accordingly a breach of contract was established. This was so even though the dentist was acquitted of negligence. This highlights the significance of suing for breach of contract, because the duty is strict. It will be no defence to a claim that a product was not fit for its purpose or of a satisfactory quality that all proper skill and care was used in choosing or supplying the article. However, much of the significance of a strict contractual liability has been affected by the application of the Consumer Protection Act 1987 which does not require privity of contract and which is discussed in the following chapter.

There must, of course, be privity of contract as is illustrated in the old Canadian case of *Smith v Rae* (p 561). Mrs Rae sued both in contract and in tort following the death of her first child who was stillborn. The birth had been unattended by Dr Smith notwithstanding an agreement he had made with Mrs Rae's husband that he would manage the confinement. The doctor's failure to attend was held not to have been negligent in circumstances where he reasonably gave priority to other appointments acting on information that indicated the birth was not imminent. Mrs Rae's claim failed in tort but also failed in contract on the technical ground that it was her husband rather than herself who had entered into the contract with the practitioner.

Certain terms in a contract for medical care do not concern the duty to take reasonable skill and care and may give rise to a cause of action. In *Morris v*

Winsbury-White (1937) (p 462) a surgeon contracted with the plaintiff to give his personal attention to the case. The surgeon did in fact personally carry out the main operation and did attend to his patient on a number of visits. However the plaintiff was also attended to by other practitioners who were performing their ordinary hospital duties. In the circumstances a breach of contract was not established. It is likely, however, that if a practitioner delegated an operation to a colleague after agreeing to do it personally he would be liable in contract as the contractual duty to perform is not delegable. The contracting doctor would therefore be liable for any fault of the sub-contracting doctor made in the course of the operation. Moreover, even if the operation was a success the patient would still be entitled to nominal damages for breach of contract. Similarly, if consent is given in contract to a specific doctor to undertake a particular operation a sub-contracting doctor without a separate consent undertaking the operation would do so unlawfully (*Michael v Molesworth* (1950) 2 BMJ 171). National Health Service consent forms specify that no assurance has been given that an operation will be undertaken by a specific practitioner.

Occasionally an action in contract may have a significance because it does not require, as an action in negligence does, proof of damage as an essential ingredient in its cause of action. However, although this could be crucial in, say, the question of costs at the end of an action, as the then Master of the Rolls indicated in *Hotson v East Berkshire Health Authority* (1987) (p 384):

'Even in contract, if more than a bare right of action is to be established, the plaintiff must prove a loss of substance and once again, this must be proved on the balance of probabilities' ([1987] 2 WLR at 295d).

It may also be possible to sue for damages for breach of contract in cases where a doctor has breached the patient's right to confidentiality. Such a cause of action in tort is doubtful (see Jones 9.71, *Breach of Confidence* (1981 Law Com no 110)). However, in the absence of actual damage compensation would be nominal (see *W v Egdell* [1989] 1 All ER 1089).

Similarly, Lord Donaldson has indicated (cf *Hotson*, above) that the distinction between contract and tort may give rise to practical importance in the time limitation imposed by law in bringing certain actions. In some cases a cause of action arising in tort, when damage occurs, can arise significantly later than the cause of action in contract which arises immediately on breach. In fact most medical malpractice actions consist of or include claims for damages arising out of personal injury and accordingly will be subject to the three year time limit contained in sections 11 and 14 of the Limitation Act which starts time running from the accrual of the plaintiff's cause of action or from the plaintiff's date of knowledge. All such actions, whether in contract or in tort, will also be subject to a discretion contained in s 33 of the Limitation Act 1980 to allow a time-barred action to proceed. In *Walkin v South Manchester Health Authority* (1994) (p 597) the court held that the plaintiff's claim for the financial effects of a failed sterilisation were in fact time-barred, because even though there was no claim for personal injury the cause of action was one which consisted of or included personal injury namely the unexpected birth. The court made the distinction that there would not be a personal injury element in a failed vasectomy. However, under s 2 of the Limitation Act 1980 whether in contract or in tort a six year limitation period would apply. It would therefore appear that the differences between contract and tort in respect of limitation in medical malpractice claims is of limited significance.

In *Hotson v East Berkshire Health Authority*, the Court of Appeal (see Dillon LJ [1987] 2 WLR at 298g) dismissed the contention that the loss of a chance (in that case the chance of avoiding avascular necrosis) which was capable of being valued should not sound in damages in tort just as much as it could in contract. The Court of Appeal accordingly rejected the argument that there was any significant distinction between the two causes of action in this respect.

In *Lee v South West Thames Regional Health Authority* (1985) (p 428) the then Master of the Rolls, Lord Donaldson, expressed the view, albeit obiter, that a patient has an implied contractual right to ascertain what treatment he did in fact receive and accordingly may bring an action for specific performance of that implied term as a way of circumventing discovery and possibly the problems that arise when a defendant claims privilege in respect of certain documents. The case of *Lee* concerned an application for a report which probably indicated that a mishap had occurred during an ambulance trip which resulted in serious injury to an infant plaintiff. The Court of Appeal held that in the particular facts of that case the document was privileged, but the Master of the Rolls went on to say this:

> 'We reach this conclusion with undisguised reluctance, because we think that there is something wrong with the law if Marlon's mother cannot find out what exactly caused this brain damage. It should never be forgotten that we are here concerned with a hospital-patient relationship. The recent decision of the House of Lords in *Sidaway v Board of Governors of the Bethlem Royal Hospital and the Maudsley Hospital* (1985) affirms that a doctor is under a duty to answer his patient's questions as to the treatment proposed. We see no reason why this should not be a similar duty in relation to hospital staff. This duty is subject to the exercise of clinical judgment as to the terms in which the information is given and extent to which in the patient's interest, information should be withheld. Why, we ask ourselves, is the position any different if the patient asks what treatment he has in fact had? ... If the duty is the same, then if the patient is refused information to which he is entitled, it must be for consideration whether he could not bring an action for breach of contract claiming specific performance of the duty to inform. In other words, whether the patient could not bring an action for discovery, albeit upon a novel basis' ([1985] 1 WLR at 850g–851c).

However, in *Naylor v Preston Area Health Authority* (1987) (p 478) the Master of the Rolls sought to explain that this was not a specific right limited to contract:

> 'In this context I was disturbed to be told during the argument of the present appeals that the view was held in some quarters that whilst the duty of candid disclosure, to which we there referred, might give rise to a contractual implied term and so benefit private fee-paying patients, it did not translate into a legal or equitable right for the benefit of NHS patients. This I would entirely repudiate. In my judgment, still admittedly and regretfully obiter, it is but one aspect of the general duty of care arising out of the patient-medical practitioner or hospital authority relationship and gives rise to rights both in contract and in tort' ([1987] WLR at 967g–h).

In summary, except in rare cases where a contract to effect a cure or guarantee an outcome or to follow or refrain from a certain method of treatment can be expressly construed, a breach of a contractual duty of care will amount to a breach of a tortious duty of care (cf *Gordon v Goldberg* (1920) (p 357), *Ruddock v Lowe* (1865) (p 537), *Walton v Lief* (1933) (p 598), *Shallard v Arline* (1939) (p 553) and *Hodson v Mellor* (1911) (p 382)). Given that there may be technical benefits deriving from a contractual cause of action, even in the absence of express warranties or representations, it will continue to be prudent to sue, if possible, concurrently in contract and tort. Moreover, with the continued growth in private health care, the construction of written contractual agreements is likely to be of increasing relevance.

Contractual relationships between parties other than the actual patient can, of course, give rise to specific duties of care affecting that patient. Such duties will arise, however, in tort not in contract because the patient is not a party to the contractual arrangement. If, therefore, a doctor agrees to write a medical reference to a prospective or actual employer or to furnish a report for insurance purposes, the doctor will owe the subject of that report a duty of care in tort. (Cf *Hedley Byrne and Co Ltd v Heller and Partners Ltd* [1964] AC 465, HL(E) and *Spring v Guardian Assurance plc* [1994] 3 WLR 354, HL(E).)

Chapter 3

Statutory liability

Product liability

Many products used in medicine particularly drugs but also blood and blood derivatives, heart valves and contraception devices have been the subject of worldwide litigation concerning allegations that their use has given rise to significant personal injury. Such injuries may result from a defect in the construction or the manufacturing of the product, where the allegation concerns a defect particular to the actual product used or consumed. In such cases it is not contended that the product in general is unsafe but only that a manufacturing defect has produced a specific fault which has injured a plaintiff (cf *Grant v Australian Knitting Mills Ltd* [1936] AC 85). More frequently, however, the defect alleged is one of design where the product generally is alleged to be defective. This is particularly so in drug-induced injuries where significant side effects occur to a whole population of users or particular groups of users. The traditional forms of action based on contract and tort have historically made little inroad into allegations based on design defect. In the case of an action based in contract, although a litigant would be able to rely upon implied terms as to fitness for purpose or satisfactory quality (Sale and Supply of Goods Act 1994, Sale of Goods Act 1979), very few patients will be in a contractual relationship with the supplier of, for example, a drug because of the organisation of health care within the United Kingdom (cf *Pfizer Corpn v Ministry of Health*). In so called manufacturing defects, a plaintiff suing in tort may have a less onerous task because a court may be willing to infer negligence collateral to some employee during the system of production.

However the vast majority of product liability actions in fact concern design defects principally against the manufacturers of drugs (cf Opren: *Nash v Eli Lilly* (p 466), Myodil: *Chrzanowska v Glaxo Laboratories* (1990) (p 278), Benzo-diazepine (Valium, Ativan, Halcion): *AB v John Wyeth* (pp 218–219), Thalidomide: *Distillers Co (Biochemicals) Ltd v Thompson* (p 309), Neomycin: *Mann v Wellcome Foundation Ltd* (1989), unreported and DES (Diethyl-stilboestrol): *Enright v Eli Lilly and Co* (p 322) and *Sindell v Abrot Laboratories* (p 556)). Such claims when litigated in England have never resulted in a judgment against drug manufacturers as the cases have either settled with damages believed to be lower than that recoverable at common law or have been discontinued. The general difficulty that plaintiffs have in establishing negligence against the manufacturers of drugs is the requirement to prove that the risks which materialised were reasonably foreseeable and could have been avoided with the exercise of reasonable skill and care. The overwhelming difficulty that plaintiffs have in proving this on a balance of probabilities was largely the impetus behind the enactment of two forms of statutory liability in the form of the Consumer Protection Act 1987 and the Vaccine Damage Payments Act 1979. These statutory causes of action provide limited inroads into the fault principle inherent within actions for damages based on negligence and breach of contract. The statutory causes of action are in addition to any other cause of action a plaintiff may have in contract or in tort.

1. The Consumer Protection Act 1987

Part I of the Consumer Protection Act 1987 represents the British interpretation of the EC Product Liability Directive (95/374/EEC), and is predominantly the culmination of pressure largely arising out of the extensive legal difficulties that the victims of the thalidomide disaster had in sustaining actions against the pharmaceutical manufacturers of the drug. The often insuperable problems for plaintiffs in establishing the tort of negligence in matters of defective products have long been recognised and particularly with reference to drugs (see *Liability for Defective Products* (1977 Law Com no 82), the Pearson Report, the *Royal Commission on Civil Liability and Compensation for Personal Injury* (1978 Cmnd 7054) and the *Strasbourg Convention on Products Liability in regard to Personal Injury and Death* (1977)). These reports recommended that a manufacturer's liability for injury caused by defective products should be strict, that is not dependent upon proof of any fault (whether breach of contract or negligence). The implementation of strict liability would obviate the complex, lengthy and expensive enquiries into whether the product in question was foreseeably hazardous, whether the damage that resulted could reasonably have been discovered, whether adequate testing and monitoring had been undertaken, whether the incidence of the defects either in design or in manufacturing would be impracticable or too expensive to alter, and whether there should be different criteria if a litigant sued in contract or in tort.

Some of these difficulties have theoretically been minimised by the provisions of the Consumer Protection Act 1987 which came into force on 1 March 1988 (SI 1987/1680). In practice, however, it is unlikely that the provisions of the Consumer Protection Act 1987 will make much of an inroad into the difficulties of establishing liability against manufacturers of products with design faults, principally because of the difficulty of establishing precisely when a drug is 'defective', and because the Act preserves the so-called development risks defence. In addition, plaintiffs will continue to have difficulty in establishing causation, namely that the drug is capable of causing the type of injury concerned, and the plaintiff's particular injury is attributable to the drug in question and not to some other cause such as an underlying condition or complex interaction between various drugs.

DEFECTIVE PRODUCTS

Section 1 of the Act (see Appendix) defines what a product is and includes standard consumer goods as well as raw materials; the definition includes many products encountered in medical treatment processes, whether they be surgical instruments, intra-uterine devices, or drugs. Blood and blood-based materials are probably included in the definition of a product, because by s 1(2)(*b*) a producer in relation to a product is defined as:

'In the case of a substance which has not been manufactured but has been won or abstracted, the person who won or abstracted it.'

Moreover, by s 45 of the Act, a substance is defined as meaning any natural or artificial substance, whether in solid, liquid or gaseous form or in the form of a vapour, and includes substances that are comprised in or mixed with other goods. It is therefore arguable that blood and blood-based materials are abstracted products for which, if they are defective (for example, if the blood is contaminated and caused acquired immune deficiency syndrome (Aids)) the producer or supplier might be strictly liable. This might have been of significant importance for haemophiliacs and their partners who contracted Aids following transfusions of infected blood products, had the supply taken place after the coming into force of the Act (*Re HIV Haemophiliac Litigation* (p 394)). Legislation in the United States of America has determined that the provision of blood should be a service rather than a product and accordingly outside certain American strict liability legislation. The Pearson Commission did, however, recommend that human blood and organs should be treated as products and the distributors should be liable as the producers (see 1978 Cmnd 7054, paragraph 1276).

Section 2 imposes strict liability against the producers of this product and also certain suppliers. Section 2(1) states:

'Subject to the following provisions of this Part, where any damage is caused wholly or partly by a defect in a product every person to whom sub-section (2) below applies shall be liable for the damage.'

Section 2(2) includes as a producer a person who holds himself out as the producer of the product by putting his name on the product or using it as a trademark, which would cover retailers who put their own brand name on products. In addition, importers of a product are liable if they imported the product from a place outside the European Community into a member state in the course of business.

Section 2(3) also imposes a strict liability upon the supplier of a product, where the injured person requests the supplier to identify who the producer of the product was and the supplier is unable to do so within a reasonable time. This liability is not a vicarious liability and, therefore, if the supplier can name the producer, the supplier will escape liability even if the producer is a company in liquidation, or a person who is dead or bankrupt or cannot be traced. This provision can have serious consequences for pharmacists, doctors, nurses and other practitioners who are often the last link in the chain of supply of medicines, drugs and medical aids to the patient. In the case of a hospital, the supplier will be deemed to be the health authority and not the particular member of staff. However, general practitioners and dentists and pharmacists may be directly liable. A pharmacist who mixes his own medicines or drugs before he supplies them would be liable, if he could not name the manufacturer of the component parts. A general practitioner, who gives a drug to a patient to help alleviate symptoms before the patient can get to a chemist, would again be liable for any defect in the product if he could not name the manufacturer or his suppliers. The dispensing of so-called generic drugs may provide particular difficulty. This particular provision of the Act therefore imposes considerable burdens on practitioners to keep very detailed records over a wide range of products. Practitioners not only need to be able to identify drugs and medicines but also a whole gamut of medicinal equipment such as needles, syringes, catheters, catgut, dacron grafts, screws, plates, surgical instruments, cardiac pacemakers and even the cement used for artificial joint replacement. Such records will need to indicate the name of the manufacturers and/or the practitioners' suppliers, the date of manufacture and/or supply, the batch number of each item and the date received and dispensed or used.

Section 3(1) of the Act defines a defect and does so in terms of safety:

'Subject to the following provisions of this section, there is a defect in a product for the purposes of this Part if the safety of the product is not such as persons generally are entitled to expect; and for those purposes 'safety', in relation to a product, shall include safety with respect to products comprised in that product and safety in the context of risks of damage to property, as well as in the context of risks of death or personal injury.'

The Department of Trade and Industry, in an explanatory note, has indicated in this respect that:

'The safety which a person is entitled to expect raises particularly complex issues in respect of medicinal products and adverse reactions to them. Establishing the existence of a defect in a medicine administered to a patient is complicated by the fact that not only is the human body a highly complex organism but at the time of treatment is already subject to an adverse pathological condition. In order to avoid an adverse reaction a medicine will have to be able to cope successfully with already faulty organs, disease and almost infinite variations in individual susceptibility to the effect of medicines from person to person. The more active the medicine, and the greater its beneficial potential, the more extensive its effects are likely to be, and therefore the greater the chances of an adverse effect. A medicine used to treat a life threatening condition is likely to be much more powerful than a medicine used in the treatment of a less serious condition, and the safety that one is reasonably entitled to expect of such a medicine may therefore be correspondingly lower.' (Department of Trade and Industry, Implementation of EC Directive on Product Liability: An Explanatory and Consultative Note' 1985).

It can therefore be reasonably anticipated that what constitutes a defect is likely to be a matter for complex litigation. A drug designed to combat cancer with a known serious side effect in ten per cent of cases might be safe, whereas, a similar incidence of adverse reaction would be unsafe in a drug designed for minor pain relief. Clearly a drug that is harmful only to a foetus would not be defective if proper and adequate warning was given so that no pregnant woman would ever take it. Again a warning might be adequate to make a drug safe in circumstances where it was known that a small percentage of users would have an allergic reaction.

Section 3(2) provides that all the circumstances shall be taken into account when determining what persons generally are entitled to expect in respect of safety. These matters include how the product has been marketed, what instructions and warnings have been given, how the product might reasonably be expected to be used, the time when the product was supplied; in particular, a defect cannot be inferred from the fact alone that the safety of a product supplied after the initial supply in question is greater. In respect of drug related injuries, this will involve an assessment of the so-called risk/benefit ratio concerning the drug's adverse reactions and contra-indications in relation to its therapeutic value. Commentators have rightly emphasised that determining whether a drug is defective is in some measure analogous to the assessment at common law as to whether negligence has occurred (cf R Nelson-Jones and P Stewart pp 48–52, M Brazier pp 175–178, M Jones p 318).

Statutory liability

CAUSATION

By s 2(1), liability is imposed when a plaintiff suffers any damage caused wholly or partly by a defect in the product concerned. A plaintiff has to prove that the particular product in question had a defect, that the plaintiff suffered damage, and that that damage was caused by the defect. Accordingly, those particularly difficult questions of causation which can arise when a plaintiff is attempting to prove that he is the victim of the side effects of drugs will still occur. Such drug-affected plaintiffs will have to prove that it was the drug that caused the injury or the exacerbation and not the constitutional disease. An infant plaintiff suing for damage occasioned to it as a foetus will also have to prove that it was the drug rather than a congenital defect which has caused the abnormality (cf *Kay's Tutor v Ayrshire and Arran Health Board* (1987) (p 410)). However, on the wording of the Act, it does not appear to be required that the damage was reasonably foreseeable. Also, given the wording of the Act, there would appear to be no impediment to the reasoning of *McGhee v National Coal Board* (1973) being applied to the extent that if the product's defect, on the balance of probability, materially contributed to or materially increased the risk of injury, causation will be proved in the absence of clear proof as to what did cause the disease or abnormalities. Before, however, *McGhee* can apply the plaintiff must establish whether the drug in question can in fact cause the particular reaction the plaintiff contends for. Unless this hurdle is overcome questions of material contribution do not arise. (See *Wilsher v Essex Area Health Authority* (p 609), *Loveday v Renton* (p 435) and *Reay v British Nuclear Fuels* [1994] 5 Med LR 1.) It is to be further noted that the specific wording of s 2(1) allows the plaintiff to prove that his damage was either caused wholly or partly by the defect and presumably this would establish liability to compensation on the part of a producer even when there had been fault on the part of another party.

DEFENCES

Section 4 of the Act provides for six specific defences which taken together have emasculated much of the strict liability imposed under s 2. The most significant of these defences is that provided by s 4(1)(*e*) the so-called 'development risks defence' which provides:

> 'In any civil proceedings by virtue of this Part against any person ... in respect of a defect in a product it shall be a defence for him to show ... (e) that the state of scientific and technical knowledge at the relevant time was not such that a producer of products of the same description as the product in question might be expected to have discovered the defect if it had existed in his products while they were under his control.'

The relevant time (defined in s 42(2)) is when the product was supplied and not when it was manufactured, so that a producer has a duty to act on knowledge that becomes available in the interim. Obviously the product has to be under the defendant's control. The incorporation of this development risks defence, against the advice of the Pearson Commission and contrary to the position in a number of EC countries, probably means that plaintiffs damaged by pharmaceutical products suing under the Act will not be in a much better position than the plaintiffs in the thalidomide, opren or debendox litigation. What the Act does do, however, is to reverse the burden of proof and imposes on the defendant the task of making out the defence. This may well be a benefit, as it requires the defendants to make the running in proving the state of knowledge and research and that the defect was undiscoverable at the time in question. Furthermore, if the defect was in fact discoverable it will be no defence that the cost of discovery would have been disproportionate:

'So far as discovery of a defect is concerned, s 4(1)(e) effectively preserves the principles of negligence law. Only the onus of proof is different. Once a defect is or might be expected to have been discovered, however, the strict liability of s 2(1) applies. The producer cannot plead how difficult or expensive it would have been to have eliminated the defect. If he ought to have discovered it, it will not assist him to show that he manufactured the product to an accepted national or international safety standard. Nor can he rely on traditional practice by others in his industry' (Nelson-Jones and Stewart *Product Liability* (Fourmat, revised edition, 1988), p 68).

A further important defence with respect to pharmaceutical products is contained within s 4(1)(a), namely that the defect is attributable to compliance with any requirement imposed by or under enactment or with any community obligations. It might therefore be argued by pharmaceutical manufacturers that because all drug products are licensed under the Medicines Act 1968, any defect may be attributable to compliance with their licence. The Medicines Act 1968 was enacted in response to the thalidomide tragedy, and it entrusts the licensing of drugs to the Ministry of Health (s 7 and s 35) which acts on advice given by specialist committees principally the Medicines Commission, the Committee on the Safety of Medicines and the Committee on the Review of Medicines. The Act is therefore designed to control the safety, efficacy and quality of a drug product. Even if a drug company could not invoke the mere fact of its licence as a defence under s 4(1)(a) the fact of the licence would be persuasive evidence in maintaining a development risks state of knowledge defence under s 4(1)(e). Further it is as yet undecided as to whether the regulatory bodies themselves in the case of drugs, the Department of Health or the Committee on the Safety of Medicines, owe a duty of care to individually affected consumers of products licensed by them. In *Department of Health and Social Security v Kinnear*, Stuart-Smith J held that there was no cause of action for an individual against the Department in respect of the implementation of a policy to promote vaccination against whooping cough where it was exercising its statutory discretion under the National Health Service Act 1946. A subsidiary claim, however, in the pleadings concerning so-called operational negligence was not struck out as disclosing no reasonable cause of action. Similarly in *Re HIV Haemophiliac Litigation* (p 394), the Court of Appeal concurred that there was no action for breach of statutory duty under the National Health Service Act 1977 in respect of the provision of HIV contaminated blood products but there was an arguable case that the Department of Health and the regulatory authorities owed a duty of care so that an action for damages could lie for negligent acts or omissions in the performance of its functions under the National Health Service Act 1977. It is to be noted that by s 133(2) of the Medicines Act 1968 there is an express provision that the Act does not confer a civil right of action. The recent tendency in English law is not to impose a duty of care on regulatory and statutory authorities when they are exercising their public statutory functions (see *Murphy v Brentwood District Council* [1990] 2 All ER 908). The position may be different in respect of actions based on personal injury rather than economic loss, and it is yet to be decided whether regulatory bodies established under the Medicines Act 1968 do in fact owe a duty of care to patients concerning the licensing procedure of drugs.

By s 4(1)(d), a manufacturer or supplier is afforded a defence based upon the fact that the defect did not exist within the product when manufactured or supplied.

Defects can, of course, arise out of the mishandling or storing of products, and hospitals and practitioners may be vulnerable in this respect particularly in connection with, for example, blood and blood-based products. The Act concerns products supplied after 1 March 1988 only (s 50(7)).

By s 6(3), the Consumer Protection Act 1987 applies to the provisions of the Congenital Disabilities (Civil Liability) Act 1976 and therefore affords protection to the unborn child. The Act limits a product's liability to a ten year period from the relevant time of supply. This time limitation has serious consequences for injuries caused by drugs which have a long latency period and in such cases the common law remedy in tort would have to be reverted to. Any injured person must sue within three years of the accrual of the cause of action or from the date of knowledge that he had a cause of action, subject to the court exercising its discretion within s 33 of the Limitation Act 1980 (see Chapter 13).

2. The Vaccine Damage Payments Act 1979

Although vaccination is not compulsory, the health ministries throughout the United Kingdom have long advocated that children should be vaccinated against certain diseases, particularly tetanus, whooping cough, diphtheria, poliomyelitis, measles, tuberculosis and, in the case of females, rubella. The Department of Health has frequently offered detailed advice to general practitioners with respect to the vaccination programme. In the early 1970s serious concern arose about the safety of the whooping cough (pertussis) vaccine, both from general practitioners and from a group of parents who formed the Association of Vaccine-Damaged Children. Evidence was then emerging that serious and permanent brain damage could follow vaccination and may have been caused by it. As a result of this publicity, the number of children vaccinated for whooping cough fell from 79% to 38% in 1976.

The Pearson Committee considered the question of vaccine-damaged children and emphasised the almost hopeless position a victim was in if he attempted to sue in tort. The general practitioner would have a good defence that he was acting in accordance with Government advice and, of course, within the orthodox accepted normal practice of the overwhelming majority of general practitioners. Similarly suing the manufacturers in negligence involved dislodging the argument that the vast majority of children and, accordingly, the whole of society derived benefit. Suing the Department of Health is equally fraught with difficulty.

In *Loveday v Renton* (1988) (p 435) an infant plaintiff who suffered from permanent brain damage after a whooping cough vaccination sued her general practitioner, and on a preliminary hearing on the question of causation failed to establish that the vaccine could cause permanent brain damage in young children. Stuart-Smith LJ found that all four of the suggested biological mechanisms by which the plaintiff sought to explain the link between the vaccine and the brain damage were improbable. The trial judge also went on to indicate that even if there had been a finding of causation in the plaintiff's favour, she would face insuperable difficulties in proving negligence on the part of the doctor or nurse who administered the vaccine.

In *Department of Health and Social Security v Kinnear* (1984) (p 308), Stuart-Smith J indicated that no cause of action could arise out of a policy adopted in good faith on the part of the department, pursuant to the provisions of s 26, National Health Service Act 1946, to make arrangements regarding the immunisation of people against diseases. This action was, however, allowed to proceed on the basis that there were further allegations of an operational nature concerning the Department of Health and Social Security's giving negligent and misleading advice as to the manner and circumstances in which the immunisations were to be performed. When this matter came on for trial, the plaintiff's case collapsed because legal aid was withdrawn following certain advice given to the Law Society.

The Pearson Report (above) had recognised the difficulty that plaintiffs would have in establishing causation, namely whether the febrile convulsions occurred naturally or as a result of the vaccine. The Report recommended that where vaccine damage can be proved to have followed from medical procedures, advocated by the Government, then the child should have the right to bring an action in tort on the basis of strict liability against the Government. The Vaccine Damages Payments Act 1979 was a compromise which provided for a lump sum payment of £10,000 to be paid to any person who the Secretary of State was satisfied had suffered severe disablement as a result of vaccine damage. The claimant must have suffered at least eighty per cent disablement from the nominated vaccines contained in s 1 of the Act and must have been injected after 5 July 1948 (when the Health Service came into existence). The claimant must have been vaccinated when he or she was under eighteen, except in the cases of rubella or polymyelitis. The Act also protects an unborn child whose mother had been so vaccinated. The claimant must, however, satisfy the Secretary of State on the balance of probabilities that the damage was caused by the vaccine, and difficult problems of causation can arise. If a claimant is turned down, he has the right to have the case heard by an independent tribunal.

The lump sum payment of £10,000 was increased to £20,000 in July 1985. The obvious criticism of this Act is that such damages bear little comparison to those which would be awarded at common law for an eighty per cent disablement case. The reasoning behind this small incursion into the principle of fault liability was justified on the basis that this particular group of disabled people had acted mainly through their parents on advice from the State in respect of a benefit which was intended for the whole of society. It was thought appropriate, therefore, that the State should be the bearer of the consequences of the risks involved.

Just how difficult the problem of causation can be, even within a no-negligence system of strict liability, is illustrated in the difficulty of the infant plaintiff in *Loveday v Renton* (above) with her application for compensation under the Vaccine Damage Payments Act. The child's first application was refused, and on appeal the tribunal did not accept that on the balance of probabilities the vaccination was the cause of her brain damage. The tribunal's decision, however, was quashed by the High Court who ordered a differently constituted tribunal to re-hear the application on the grounds that the tribunal had not given proper reasons and had not considered the possibility that any pre-existing brain damage the infant applicant suffered from may have been aggravated by the PTP vaccine. The second tribunal also refused an award. The High Court again quashed this decision on the grounds of certain evidential and procedural irregularities, but refused to make an order that the tribunal be directed to find a causative link between the vaccine and the damage. The Court of Appeal concurred with this refusal, indicating that there was not sufficient evidence for the court to conclude that the child's condition resulted inevitably from vaccination. The court, however, did express the view that it would not rule out the possibility of directing a tribunal on causation in different cases (*R v Vaccine Damage Tribunal* (1985) (p 514)).

Conversely, in the Scottish case of *Bonthrone v Millan* (1985) (p 252) a child was awarded compensation for damage that the vaccine tribunal found was caused by the second dose of a PTP vaccine. The applicant subsequently brought an action in negligence alleging a want of care on the part of the doctor and health visitor in failing to appreciate the adverse reactions of the child following the first PTP vaccination. Lord Jauncey dismissed the action in negligence and in addition indicated that there was no proved causal link between the damage that had occurred and the pertussis vaccine. (See also *R v Legal Aid Area No 8 (Northern) Appeal Committee, ex p Angell* (p 506).)

Finally in *Best v Wellcome Foundation Ltd and others* (p 245) the Irish Court of Appeal found both negligence and causation established in respect of the plaintiff's contraction of encephalopathy following his first immunisation of DTP vaccine from batch BA 3741 on 17 September 1969. This specific batch had a potency of nearly eight times the minimum dose required by British Standards. The case settled on the subsequent trial on damage for £2.75 million.

Section B

Medical malpractice: general principles

Chapter 4

The duty of care

1. Negligence and contract

Whether a litigant sues in contract or in tort or in both concurrently for damages arising out of alleged medical malpractice, the duty of care imposed by the law of tort will be identical to that implied, in the absence of express terms, in the law of contract. The duty of care adheres to any person who holds himself out as a medical practitioner and is owed not only to patients but also to certain classes of third parties recognised by the law as being so closely and directly affected by treatment or advice that the doctor or other practitioner ought to have had them in mind and it is just and reasonable to do so (*Caparo Industries plc v Dickman* [1990] 2 AC 605 and *M v Newham London Borough Council* (p 438). In medical malpractice actions, such third parties may be children, for example, whose mothers when pregnant received treatment which resulted in the so-called wrongful birth of the child, such as in cases of failed sterilisation. In some such cases the child may also be born with disabilities. Where a child suffers a disability due to a tortious act committed on his parents, the common law duty of care has been replaced by a statutory duty of care contained in the Congenital Disabilities (Civil Liability) Act 1976. These duties of care owed to patients and to third parties will be examined separately.

2. The duty owed to patients

It is hardly surprising that a duty of care independent of contract has long been recognised as owed by a medical practitioner to his patient. In *Pippin v Sheppard* (1822) (p 496) Baron Garrow had no reservation in finding that a wife whose husband had employed a surgeon to treat her had in law a cause of action against the doctor directly:

'To hold to the contrary, would be to leave such persons in a remedyless state. In cases of the most brutal inattention and neglect, patients would be precluded frequently from seeking damages by course of law, if it were necessary, to enable them to recover, that there should have been a previous retainer, on their part, of the person professing to be able to cure them. In all cases of surgeons by any of the public establishments, it would happen that the patient would be without redress, for it could hardly be expected that the Governors of an infirmary should bring an action against the surgeon, employed by them to attend the child of poor parents who may have suffered from his negligence and inattention' ((1822) 11 Price at 409).

A similar duty was accepted as owed to a 10-year old girl whose mother had contracted with a clergyman, who also practised medicine, to attend upon her daughter's injured knee (*Gladwell v Steggall* (1839) (p 354)). In *Edgar v Lamont* (1914) (p 318), Lord Salvesen recognised a similar duty in Scottish law when he held:

> 'It seems to me that the clear ground of action is that a doctor owes a duty to the patient, whoever has called him and whoever is liable for his bill, and it is for breach of that duty that he is liable, in other words, that it is for negligence arising in the course of the employment, and not in respect of the breach of contract with the employer' (1914 SC at 279–80).

A woman was accordingly allowed to sue in respect of the loss of her finger allegedly due to the defendant's negligence while treating her under a contract made with her husband.

The modern law of negligence has extended this duty to all categories of medical practitioners. It is not necessary for a plaintiff to show that his case falls into an already proven category of successful actions. All the plaintiff need establish is that there is a sufficient degree of proximity between the medical practitioner and the injured or affected person, that the practitioner ought reasonably to have foreseen the risk of that injury or damage to that person and that as a matter of public policy it is just and reasonable to impose a duty of care which would be an incremental development from an established category (*M v Newham London Borough Council* (p 438)). Such a duty of care will arise to all those who are treated. Reported cases cover a wide range of medical services: casualty officers (*Barnett v Chelsea and Kensington Hospital Management Committee* (1969) (p 238)); nurses (*Cassidy v Ministry of Health* (1951) (p 272), *Selfe v Ilford and District Hospital Management Committee* (1970) (p 551), *Sutton v Population Services Family Planning Programme Ltd* (1981) (p 570)); physiotherapists (*Clarke v Adams* (1950) (p 279)); pharmacists (*Collins v Hertfordshire County Council* (1947) (p 283)); radiographers (*Gold v Essex County Council* (1942) (p 354)); psychiatrists (*Bolam v Friern Hospital Management Committee* (1957) (p 250)); *Landau v Werner* (1961) (p 425)); pathologists (*Crivon v Barnet Group Hospital Management Committee* (1958) (p 293)); gynaecologists (*Clark v MacLennan* (1983) (p 279)); dentists (*Fish v Kapur* (1948) (p 332), *Edwards v Mallan* (1908) (p 319)); anaesthetists (*Jones v Manchester Corpn* (1952) (p 406)); general practitioners (*Chapman v Rix* (1960) (p 274), *Coles v Reading and District Hospital Management Committee* (1963) (p 283)); surgeons (*Collins v Hertfordshire County Council* (1947) (p 283), *Ashcroft v Mersey Regional Health Authority* (1983) (p 229)) and first-aiders (*Cattley v St John's Ambulance Brigade (*1988) unreported).

In addition, hospital authorities owe certain duties of care directly to patients in respect of supervising them so that they do not come to harm (*Hyde v Tameside Area Health Authority* (1981) (p 396), *Gravestock v Lewisham Group Hospital Management Committee* (1955) (p 358), *Gauntlett v Northampton Health Authority* (1985) (p 349)).

The hospital authority must also properly supervise its own staff (*Jones v Manchester Corpn* (1952) (p 406), *Wilsher v Essex Area Health Authority* (1988) (p 609)). It must also provide a proper system of organisation and co-ordination of skilled staff and a proper system of medical care (*Wilsher* (above), *Cox v Carshalton Group Hospital Management Committee* (1955) (p 291)). Such a system would include a duty to take reasonable care not to injure the *doctor's* health by requiring him to work so many hours that his health is undermined (*Johnstone v Bloomsbury Health Authority* (p 404)).

Further duties of care are owed to patients to protect them from the risk of infection while in an institution (*Heafield v Crane* (1937) (p 375)).

The duty of care that is owed obtains throughout all stages of advice and treatment and for certain types of practitioners, such as general practitioners and casualty officers, frequently includes a duty to take on a patient. A general practitioner under the terms of service with the Family Health Service Authority is required to administer to anyone on his list, those who he has agreed to accept onto his list, temporary residents and those on whose behalf he is required to give treatment which is immediately required owing to an accident or other emergency at any place in his practice area (The National Health Service (General Medical Services) Regulations 1992, paragraph 4, pages 40–4, *Barnes v Crabtree* (p 238)). Similarly a casualty officer is required to see a patient who presents with complaints of illness (*Barnett v Chelsea and Kensington Hospital Management Committee* (p 238)). *Giesen, International Medical Malpractice Law*, Mohr and Martinus Nijhoff, 1988 summarises the medical practitioner's duty of care in the following manner:

'Thus a person who is a medical professional, or holds himself out as ready to give medical advice or treatment, impliedly undertakes that he is possessed of skill and knowledge for the purpose, and when consulted by a patient will owe him a duty of care, namely in deciding whether to undertake the case, in taking a proper case history, in making a careful diagnosis, in properly informing his patient about any proposed treatment or operation and inherent risks of treatment and no treatment, in obtaining the patient's consent to such treatment and in his administration of that treatment or performance of that operation and, at all stages, in answering questions where he knows or ought to know that the patient intends to rely on his answer' (p 81, para 118).

It is also most likely that a practitioner owes a patient a duty to inform him of what treatment he actually did receive as opposed to the treatment he expected to receive (*Lee v South West Thames Regional Health Authority* (1985) (p 428), *Naylor v Preston Area Health Authority* (1987) (p 478)). In both these cases the Master of the Rolls, Sir John Donaldson, indicated that a patient probably had an actionable right to find out what actually did occur during any mishap. Certainly part of the duty of care will be to inform a patient if there has been any product left in the patient such as a needle (*Gerber v Pines* (1935) (p 531)), or where part of a tooth was inhaled by an unconscious patient during dental treatment (*Cooper v Miron* (1927) (p 287)).

The subject of a medical reference commissioned by a third party such as a prospective employer or an insurer might also be owed a duty of care by the practitioner in the compilation of the report (cf the Access to Medical Reports Act 1988 which provides a right for the subject of such reports to have access to them). If a report is commissioned for the legal purpose of assessing damages in a personal injury action, then the doctor who compiles the report will owe the subject a duty of care (*McGrath v Kiely and Powell* (1965) (p 446), *Hughes v Hay* (1989) (p 392)). The position is less clear where a patient is seen in a therapeutic context and is given certain advice which he then acts upon, and under-settles a claim against a third party for damages. In *Stevens v Bermondsey and Southwark Group Management Committee* (1963) (p 566), Paull J held that in such circumstances, unless there were special reasons, a doctor was not required to contemplate or foresee any question connected with a third party's liability to his patient. In certain circumstances such advice may become immune from suit (see *Landall v Dennis Faulkner and Alsop* (p 423)).

Such claims would now be determined by the principles espoused in *Hedley Byrne and Co Ltd v Heller & Partners Ltd* [1964] AC 465 which may impose a duty of care in certain circumstances in respect of economic loss arising out of negligent statements (see in particular the speech of Lord Devlin at page 517 for an example he cited concerning a doctor who wrongly advised a man to give up work on account of his medical condition which in fact turned out to be unnecessary). Unless the court were to find as a matter of policy that it was not appropriate to impose such a duty of care there would appear to be nothing in principle to prevent such a duty being imposed on doctors for economic loss arising out of negligent statements. However certain remarks made by the Court of Appeal in *M v Newham London Borough Council* (p 438) specify an exclusion of the duty of care where a doctor is commissioned to report on an individual by a third party. In *M* the Court of Appeal, by a majority with the Master of the Rolls Sir Thomas Bingham dissenting, held that where a local authority employed a psychiatrist to ascertain whether a child had been sexually abused the psychiatrist owed no duty of care directly to the child. Lord Justice Staughton in the course of his judgment also excluded certain other categories of patients:

> 'In particular, I do not consider that the child was, in law and for all purposes the patient of the psychiatrist in the Newham case. No doubt the medical profession would regard the child as the patient for some purposes, such as the duty of confidentiality. But the child has not sought the psychiatrist's services, nor had her mother as the person with parental responsibility on her behalf; those services have been thrust upon them. The child was no more the patient than an applicant for life insurance who is examined by the company's doctor, or the errant motorist who is deprived of a small quantity of blood by the police surgeon. In all those cases the medical personnel without doubt owes *some* duty to the person to being examined or treated. We have been asking the wrong question, whether *any* duty is owed. The right question is *what* duty. It is a duty to use reasonable skill and care so as not to cause harm in the course of examination or treatment. But the general duty to perform the task allocated with reasonable skill and care–whether it be 'diagnosing' the name of the abuser, or assessing the expectation of life, or producing a blood sample for analysis–is in my opinion owed to the person who engages the doctor to perform that task. That is the health authority or the local council in the first case, insurance company in the second and the police authority in the third' ([1994] 2 WLR 554 at 582 c–f).

In the House of Lords Lord Browne-Wilkinson confirmed that the Court of Appeal drew a correct analogy with the doctor instructed by an insurance company indicating the doctor was under a duty not to damage the applicant during the course of examination but beyond that his duties were owed only to the insurance company. (cf *Walker v Semple* (1993) (p 596) where a duty of care was assumed in respect of an occupational health physician and an employee who he was examining on behalf of employers.)

3. The limits of the duty owed to patients

A medical practitioner is not under a duty to act gratuitously or voluntarily, and accordingly is not required by law to come to the aid of an injured person who is not his patient or who is not presented to a hospital. If, however, a doctor does freely give his services a duty of care will be imposed upon him, as happened in the Australian case of *Goode v Nash* (1979) (p 355) where a doctor engaged in charity work was required to pay damages for negligent treatment (see also *Everett v Griffiths* (1920) (p 325)). Conversely, non-qualified persons who hold themselves out as qualified, or claim to have a particular medical or healing skill, owe a duty of care to the person they treat (*Ruddock v Lowe* (1865) (p 537), *Markham v Abrahams* (1911) (p 452), *Brogan v Bennett* (1955) (p 262) and *Sones v Foster* (1937) (p 563)).

No liability would attach to practitioners who failed to treat or feed competent adults who refuse to give their consent. In certain circumstances a patient can obtain an injunction against a practitioner who might want to provide such services in the patient's best interests (*Re C (adult: refusal of treatment)* (p 267)). Similarly a declaration can be obtained in appropriate cases that it would be lawful to refuse to provide treatment or sustenance in circumstances where a competent patient has insisted upon it (*Secretary of State for the Home Department v Robb* (1994) (p 550), *A-G of British Colombia v Astaforoff*). When the patient is a minor or of unsound mind entirely different considerations apply (see Chapter 1, *B v Croydon Health Authority* (1995) (p 234)).

Financial and health policy decisions made by the Secretary of State and the health authorities impose in effect a limit on the duty of care by determining priorities which may affect, for example, the length of waiting lists for operations. The courts have held that although in principle the decisions of the National Health Service authorities are amenable to judicial review, the remedy would only be rarely available. Accordingly, in *R v Secretary of State for Social Services and Others, ex p Hincks* (1979) orthopaedic patients sought a declaration against the Secretary of State and the hospital authorities that they were in breach of their duties under s 1, National Health Service Act 1977 to promote a comprehensive health service designed to secure improvement in health and to prevent illness because they had been obliged to wait for periods longer than was medically advisable for operations. The court held that it would not interfere with the Secretary of State's duty under the National Health Act 1977 unless he had acted in a manner which no reasonable minister would have done. Again, in *R v Central Birmingham Health Authority, ex p Walker* (1987) (p 502), an applicant whose child needed an operation was refused leave to judicially review the allocation of resources within the health authority's area because there was no prima-facie basis for saying that the authority had acted irrationally within the meaning of *Associated Provincial Picture Houses v Wednesbury Corpn* (1948). The Court of Appeal expressed similar views in *R v Central Birmingham Health Authority, ex p Collier* (1988) (p 502), where the father of a child sought leave to judicially review the health authority's failure to operate on his son who was desperately ill and needed surgery. The child was in fact at the top of the waiting list but due to shortage of intensive care beds and nurses he was left for months without an operation. The court emphasised that it had no power to allocate financial resources and there had been no breach of public duty on the part of the authority. Again in *R v North West Thames Regional Health Authority, ex p Daniels* (1993) (p 509) an attempt to judicially review the closure of a bone marrow transplant unit at Westminster Hospital failed on the grounds that there was no evidence to show that the decision to close the unit was irrational even though the court was of the view that there had been a failure by the health authority to consult the Community Health Council. (See also the case of *Child B, R v Cambridge District Health Authority, ex p B* (p 501)).

Attempts to prosecute private civil actions against government ministries or regulatory bodies have also proved to be fraught with difficulty. In *Department of Health and Social Security v Kinnear* (1984) (p 308) the court struck out a cause of action brought in respect of the Department's policy to promote vaccination against whooping cough under the National Health Service Act 1946. A secondary claim concerning an allegation of negligence in the operation of carrying out of the policy was allowed to proceed on the basis that it was arguable that a duty of care in negligence arose. The case subsequently failed. Similarly in *Re HIV Haemophiliac Litigation* (1990) (p 394) a cause of action based on a breach of statutory duty under the National Health Service Act 1977 in respect of the provision of HIV contaminated blood products was held to be legally untenable. The Court of Appeal refused to strike out a subsidiary claim in negligence against the Department and against certain regulatory bodies which alleged negligent acts or omissions in the carrying out of the policy. An arguable duty of care was held to exist but the Court of Appeal expressed the view that the demonstration of a breach of that duty would be difficult to establish (see Chapter 1).

In *M (a minor) v Newham London Borough Council* (p 438) the Court of Appeal unanimously held that no private law claim for breach of statutory duty under the Child Care Act 1980 against a local authority was enforceable. Somewhat surprisingly the Court of Appeal went on to hold (Sir Thomas Bingham MR dissenting) that there was no enforceable claim at common law against a psychiatrist for negligence in respect of a report on a child where the psychiatrist had been commissioned by the local authority in the exercise of its statutory powers. In *M* the child was examined by a psychiatrist appointed by the local authority to ascertain whether she had been sexually abused and if so by whom. The psychiatrist formed the view that the child had been abused and named the abuser as the mother's co-habitee. It subsequently transpired that the psychiatrist and the social worker had mistakenly identified the abuser because the actual abuser had the same name as the co-habitee and once this error had been ascertained the child was reunited with her mother having been separated and placed in foster care for one year. Both the child and the mother sued for personal injuries namely anxiety neurosis suffered as a result of their separation. The Court of Appeal found that the child was not in fact the patient of the psychiatrist for the purposes of establishing a duty of care in law largely on the basis that the child had not sought the psychiatrist's services and it was never intended that the psychiatrist should give advice to the child or to the mother. The Court of Appeal in considering whether the damage that the psychiatrist might do was foreseeable, whether there was a proximity of relationship and whether it was just and reasonable that the law should impose a duty appeared to be heavily swayed by the last question of policy. Staughton LJ indicated:

'If a new duty of local authorities is established in these appeals, I do not doubt that many claims will be brought, placing further strain in an already stretched system (which will be provided with no more resources). I do not doubt that many claims with little or no prospect of success will be financed by the legal aid fund. Nor that many will be delayed for years perhaps until the plaintiff is 21. Nor that many claims will be settled or even decided in favour of the plaintiff whose misfortunes attract sympathy, although there has been no more than an error of judgment. When Lord Keith of Kinkel in *Rowling v Takaro Properties Ltd* [1988] AC 473 spoke of the danger of overkill, he may have had in mind primarily defensive practices, such as requiring foundations from buildings which are quite unnecessarily elaborate. Certainly that danger is very important in medical negligence cases: high standards of duty and vast awards of damages result in unnecessary tests and other procedures at great expense as experience in the United States has shown. This is 'the exercise of a function being carried on in a detrimentally defensive frame of mind' (see *Hill v Chief Constable of West Yorkshire* [1989] AC 53, 63 by Lord Keith). ... The law of negligence has travelled some way beyond affording a remedy for injury in shops or factories and on railways or roads. Medical negligence, for example is now a substantial and significant category. But I would not go so far as to impose a private duty on local authorities performing their public law function of caring for children in need. Nor would I impose a general duty of the same nature on doctors and health authorities participating in the same process. I recognise that in the Newham case the mother is entitled to feel a sense of outrage that her child was wrongly taken from her for a year, the more so that was done negligently; and the child may indeed be scarred by this trauma. I doubt whether money is the appropriate remedy for either of them ... ' (pp 583f–584f).

In a powerful dissenting judgment the Master of the Rolls Sir Thomas Bingham dealt in terms with the arguments based on public policy against the imposition of a duty of care and gave eight reasons as to why the duty of care should exist in respect of the psychiatrist and the child and mentioned in passing that he was not surprised that in the court below the existence of a duty of care was conceded. In the House of Lords the psychiatrists' immunity from suit was upheld on two grounds. Firstly on the basis that it was not just and reasonable to superimpose a common law duty of care on a local authority in relation to the performance of its statutory duties to protect children. This was because the system of child protection was interdisciplinary and it would not be right to single out the local authority, and its servants or agents such as a psychiatrist, as capable of being sued but not other participating bodies such as the police. In addition, the protection of sexually abused children was a delicate matter and if a local authority was not immune from suit it might make it too cautious and defensive in carrying out its duties. Secondly the House of Lords found that the psychiatrist had a witness immunity because her interview with the child was likely to be relevant evidence in any care proceedings the authority instigated (per Lord Browne-Wilkinson).

As a matter of public policy the courts have also struck out causes of action which are based upon so-called 'wrongful life' (*McKay v Essex Area Health Authority* (1982) (p 447). A similar refusal to allow a cause of action on policy grounds is to be found in the case of *Rance v Mid Downs Health Authority* (1990) (p 517). This case concerned an action for alleged negligence in failing to diagnose that a plaintiff was carrying a baby suffering from spina bifida, notwithstanding a query raised on a scan by a radiographer on the 9 June 1983 when the mother was thought to be 25 weeks pregnant. The plaintiff sued on the basis that if the diagnosis had been made at $25^1/_2$ weeks she would have consented to an abortion at any time up to 28 weeks. Expert evidence was given, which the judge accepted, that as of the 9 June 1983 the baby was in fact a little over 26 weeks and any abortion which could have been carried out would have taken place a little over 27 weeks. Brooke J considered the interaction of The Infant Life (Preservation) Act 1929 with the Abortion Act 1967 and found that the abortion in this case had it taken place would have been unlawful, because it would have involved the destruction of the life of 'a child capable of being born alive' contrary to s 1 of the 1929 Act. Therefore because the judge found as a matter of fact the baby, albeit disabled, was capable of being born alive the action was bound to fail as a matter of public policy because the abortion itself would have been unlawful:

'I have no difficulty in detecting in the 1929 Act a policy decision by Parliament that the sanctity of the lives of children capable of being born alive is to be respected by the law: see *McKay v Essex Area Health Authority* [1982] QB 1166 per Lord Justice Stephenson at page 1180A), even if the foetus, before being born alive, has no directly enforceable rights itself (see *Paton v British Pregnancy Advisory Services Trustees and Another* [1979] QB 276 and in *Re F (Utero)* [1988] Fam 122). I also have no difficulty concluding that in 1967 Parliament did not intend to change that policy when it made major changes in the law relating to abortion. In my judgment, once the court was satisfied that the plaintiffs could only have turned their lost opportunity to value by terminating the life of a child who on the balance of probabilities was capable of being born alive it would be the duty of a court on policy grounds to deny them relief' (at pages 44–5).

In *Landall v Dennis Faulkner and Alsop* (1994) (p 423) a consultant orthopaedic surgeon was held to be immune from suit as a matter of public policy in respect of a report prepared for trial on behalf of a litigant bringing a personal injury action (see also *M v Newham Borough Council* (p 438).

4. The duty owed to third parties

In addition to patients, the practitioner would also owe a duty of care to all those persons who come within the so-called 'neighbour principle' espoused in the famous dictum of Lord Atkin in *Donoghue v Stevenson* (1932):

'The rule that you are to love your neighbour becomes in law, you must not injure your neighbour; and the lawyer's question, who is my neighbour? receives a restricted reply. You must take reasonable care to avoid acts or omissions which you can reasonably foresee would be likely to injure your neighbour. Who then in law is my neighbour? The answer seems to be–persons who are closely and directly affected by my act that I ought reasonably to have them in contemplation as being so affected when I am directing my mind to the acts or omissions which are called in question' ([1932] AC at 580).

The most important qualification on the ambit of the duty of care since *Donoghue v Stevenson* (above) has been the court's insistence that the categories of negligence should be extended incrementally, pragmatically and by analogy rather than by massive extensions to new categories of cases. The court will require not only a foreseeability of harm and a sufficient degree of proximity between the tortfeasor and the victim but also will closely analyse whether as a matter of policy it is just and reasonable that a duty is imposed (see *M (a minor) v Newham London Borough Council* (p 438).

Such a duty will be owed to a paid volunteer who takes part in medical trials (*Halushka v University of Saskatchewan* (1985) (p 367)). Such a duty was conceded in *G v North Tees Health Authority* (1989) (p 344) as owed to the mother of a child in circumstances where the child had been processed as a victim of sexual abuse because of the negligent contamination of the child's vaginal swab with an adult's. This had led to the child suffering distress and disturbance and also to a nervous reaction in the mother. However as seen in the case of *M v Newham London Borough Council* no duty of care was held to be owed to either the child who was the subject of a psychiatric interview commissioned by the local authority or to the mother who suffered harm as a result of the child being placed in the care of foster parents due to the psychiatrist mistakenly identifying the mother's co-habitee as a person who had sexually abused the child.

A general duty is possibly also owed to the public at large as well as to the inmates of prisons in respect of potentially violent patients, to ensure that they are properly segregated or supervised (*Holgate v Lancashire Mental Hospitals Board* (1937) (p 384), *Ellis v Home Office* (1953) (p 321)).

However in 1970, in *Home Office v Dorset Yacht Co Ltd* [1970] AC 1004, Lord Diplock questioned whether *Holgate* was correctly decided (see pages 1062–3). In *Holgate* a prisoner detained at His Majesty's pleasure was allowed on home leave so that he could go on a holiday with his brother. While out on licence he attacked the plaintiff, and the jury found that both the granting and the extension of his licence had been done negligently. Given the views of the Court of Appeal and the House of Lords in the case of *M (a minor) v Newham London Borough*

Council (p 438), it is likely that any practitioner, whether exercising directly or indirectly some statutory power such as occurs under the Mental Health Act 1983, is likely to be immune from suit.

A duty of care will also be imposed in so-called nervous shock cases where a third party suffers an identifiable psychiatric injury through witnessing a trauma or its immediate aftermath caused by the defendant's negligence. In *McLoughlin v O'Brian* [1983] 1 AC 410 and more recently in *Alcock v Chief Constable of South Yorkshire* [1992] 1 AC 310 and in *Page v Smith* 11 May 1995 the House of Lords has limited this cause of action to those who can satisfy the tests of relational, temporal, and spatial proximity to the trauma or its immediate aftermath. To recover damages, a plaintiff must show that he has suffered a psychiatric illness due to the shock of seeing or hearing a horrifying event and that he was proximate in terms of time and space to the event or its immediate aftermath, that such an injury was foreseeable and that there is a sufficient degree of proximity in respect of the relationship between the victim and the plaintiff. In *Taylor v Somerset Health Authority* (p 577) a widow failed to establish liability in circumstances where she had suffered an illness after viewing her husband's body in a hospital mortuary. The defendants conceded primary liability for the death of the plaintiff's husband in respect of a failure to diagnose his heart condition which led to his premature death. The plaintiff's nervous shock was, however, contested on the basis that there had been no external traumatic event in that the husband had had a heart attack at work and was then taken to hospital and that the reason for the plaintiff visiting the mortuary was to satisfy her disbelief that her husband had in fact died. The court was not satisfied that there had been any significant trauma or if there had been, that the plaintiff came within its immediate aftermath. Similarly in *Sion v Hampstead Health Authority* (1994) (p 556) the Court of Appeal struck out a claim for nervous shock on the basis that it disclosed no cause of action in circumstances where a father sued in respect of his development of a mental illness following the death of his son whom he watched slip into a coma over a period of 14 days after a road traffic accident before. The father contended that the hospital had been negligent in failing to diagnose internal bleeding from a kidney. The Court of Appeal held that there was no shocking or horrifying event and in the absence of that there could be no cause of action based on nervous shock.

Conversely in *Tredget and Tredget v Bexley Health Authority* (1994) (p 585) substantial damages were awarded to a couple who successfully prosecuted an action for nervous shock occasioned to them both following the negligently handled birth of their son who died two days old after a complex and traumatic delivery. Both parents obviously satisfied the criteria of relational proximity to their deceased child, the father was present at the birth, and the judge was satisfied that the birth characterised as it was by chaos and pandemonium fell within the category of an external and horrifying event.

A further duty of care would be likely to be imposed when a plaintiff acts as a rescuer as in the Canadian case of *Urbanski v Patel* (1978) (p 590). A duty of care was found to be owed to a father who donated one of his own kidneys to his daughter who had her only kidney negligently removed instead of an ovarian cyst. The father was allowed to recover in respect of his own losses on the basis that it was reasonably foreseeable that he or some other rescuer would come to the assistance of the patient who had suffered on account of the practitioner's negligence.

In *Tarasoff v Regents of the University of California* (1976) (p 575), a duty of care was imposed upon psychotherapists with respect to the potential victim of one of their patients. The court determined that in circumstances where the patient

51

had told the psychotherapists of his intention to kill an unnamed girl, who was in fact easily identifiable, then a duty of care was owed to warn the potential victim of the threat. The patient did in fact murder the girl. The psychotherapists' defence that to inform the victim would cut across their duty of confidentiality to the patient was rejected by the court. It was held that the protective function of the privilege of confidentiality ended where the public peril began. In *Gillick v West Norfolk and Wisbech Area Health Authority* (1986) (p 353), the House of Lords recognised the duty of confidentiality imposed upon a medical practitioner not to disclose information about the patient without consent. There are, however, a number of statutory inroads into this principle whereby practitioners are required by law to give varying degrees of information concerning infectious diseases, drug dependency, abortion, drivers involved in accidents, and persons believed to be engaged in terrorism (see the Public Health (Control of Disease) Act 1984, AIDS Control Act 1987, the Abortion Act 1967, the Misuse of Drugs Act 1971, the Road Traffic Act 1972 and the Prevention of Terrorism (Temporary Provisions) Act 1984).

Whether *Tarasoff* would be followed in UK jurisdictions would turn on the issues of proximity and public policy. If the doctor knew that another of his own patients was at risk from threats made by a patient of his, then it is difficult to see how the condition of proximity would not be established. In *W v Egdell* [1990] 1 All ER 835, the Court of Appeal considered the circumstances in which a medical practitioner might disclose confidential information on the grounds of public interest. That case concerned a psychiatrist who had been asked to produce a report by solicitors acting on behalf of the patient in a secure hospital following the manslaughter of five of his neighbours. Dr Egdell formed a view that the patient was suffering from a paranoid psychosis and treatment was less effective and there would be a risk in releasing the patient. As a result of the content of the doctor's advice the solicitors did not proceed with an application to seek a transfer to another unit with the intention of obtaining release. Dr Egdell sent his report to the hospital and requested that a copy was sent to the Home Secretary. The patient's solicitors sought an injunction restraining the use of the report, but the Court of Appeal held that the public interest in disclosing the report outweighed the patient's interest.

5. Duties owed to the unborn: The Congenital Disabilities (Civil Liability) Act 1976

This Act implements the recommendations of the Law Commission Report on Injuries to Unborn Children (Cmnd 5709) and was intended to clarify the position as to whether at common law a child had a cause of action for personal injuries sustained to it before its birth. Before the implementation of this Act, there was no direct English authority which had extended the duty of care owed by a medical practitioner or other person to a pregnant woman and to her unborn child. In the thalidomide litigation, such a cause of action was assumed in the case of *Distillers Co (Biochemicals) Ltd v Thompson* (1971) (p 309). However, in the substantive litigation concerning allegations that severe deformities were occasioned to children as a result of their mothers being prescribed thalidomide while pregnant, the issue was not resolved, as only a forty per cent settlement between the parties was reached (see *S v Distillers Co (Biochemicals) Ltd* (1969) (p 540)).

In *Williams v Luff* (1978) liability was conceded at common law with respect to a child, aged six at the date of trial, who sustained injuries whilst en ventre sa mère when his mother was involved in a car accident. Similarly, in *McKay v Essex Health Authority* (1982) (p 447), the duty owed to the unborn child was conceded.

Section 1 of the Congenital Disabilitites (Civil Liability) Act 1976, which came into force on 22 July 1976, establishes the right of a disabled child to claim compensation from a person responsible for his disabilities which were caused via a tortious act perpetrated on the child's parent or parents. The tortious act of the mother herself is explicitly excluded by s 1(1), except that a mother is liable to her own disabled child in cases where she committed a tort whilst driving a motor car (s 2).

The Act applies to all births after 22 July 1976 and the cause of action arises only when the child was born alive. The child, suing by his next friend, must prove that the disability he suffers from, whether a disease, deformity, or abnormality, which may be in the nature of a future pre-disposition, resulted from an 'occurrence' as defined in the Act. This occurrence is effectively a tortious act which:

(a) affected the capacity of the child's mother or father to produce a healthy child; or

(b) affected the mother's capacity whilst pregnant to produce a healthy child; or

(c) affected either the mother or the child during birth itself.

The Act retains the fault principle, and therefore the occurrence causing the disability must have been produced by a tortious act against the parent or parents. Such an act could be the negligent prescription of a drug unsuitable for a woman whilst pregnant or, in the case of a father, negligent exposure to substances that caused mutations in the father's sperm. The tort against the parent is to be considered without reference to time limitations imposed by the Limitation Acts, and there is no requirement that the parent suffered any actionable injury. The child's cause of action is extinguished, if either or both parents knew in cases where the tort occurs before conception that there was a pre-conception risk of any child conceived being born with disabilities. If, however, the father is the defendant and only he knew of the risk of pre-conception disablement, the cause of action does survive for the child. Therefore a couple knowingly taking a risk of conceiving and bearing a handicapped child as a result of a third party's tort exclude the possibility of their offspring suing the tortfeasor. However, in circumstances which are reasonably difficult to envisage, where the father is the tortfeasor and he alone knows of the risk and does not tell the mother, the child is able to sue the father.

Section 1(5) gives statutory approval to the common law standard of care in ordinary medical negligence actions by providing for a statutory defence, in effect for the medical practitioner, who may have treated the parents:

'The defendant is not answerable to the child, for anything he did or omitted to do when responsible in a professional capacity for treating or advising the parent, if he took reasonable care having due regard to the then received professional opinion applicable to the particular class of case, but this does not mean that he is unanswerable only because he departed from received opinion.'

This is almost precisely the test laid down in *Bolam v Friern Hospital Management Committee* (1957) (p 250) as the proper criterion for the standard of care in medical malpractice actions.

Section 1(6) is now probably otiose in that it provided for liability to the child being excluded or limited by a contract made with the parent. This provision falls foul of s 2, Unfair Contract Terms Act 1977 which precludes any person excluding or restricting liability for death or personal injury resulting from negligence in contractual relationships. Section 1(7) provides a further partial or complete defence equivalent to contributory negligence by allowing a child's award to be reduced to such an extent as the court thinks just and equitable having regard to any share the parents have in the responsibility for their child being born disabled.

The Human Fertilisation and Embryology Act 1990 inserted s 1A into the 1976 Act and thereby extended a child's cause of action to disabilities arising out of damage caused to an embryo or to gametes during the course of infertility treatment.

It is settled law that just as a mother may sue at common law for damage sustained to her in respect of negligence causing damage to her child as a developing foetus, so too may the living child sue for damages under the statutory cause of action in the 1976 Act in respect of his disabilities. A child's claim, however, of so-called 'wrongful life' would not be allowed either at common law or under the Act. In *McKay v Essex Area Health Authority* (1982) (p 447), a mother and her daughter sued the area health authority's laboratory and a doctor in respect of their joint responsibility which led to the mother being wrongfully informed that she had not been infected with German measles during her pregnancy. The infant plaintiff was born disabled before the Congenital Disabilities (Civil Liability) Act 1976 was passed and the matter was considered at common law, although the Court of Appeal expressed their views on the likely effect of the Act with respect to the cause of action in issue. The case concerns only that part of the infant's claim for damages based on the allegation that but for the defendant's negligence she would not have been born at all. This claim was premised on the likelihood that had Mrs McKay been properly tested and properly informed that she had contracted rubella she would have had an abortion. The court struck out that part of the infant plaintiff's claim for damages based upon the fact that she had been born. The child's allegations in this respect were held to be essentially that although she had been born with deformities caused by rubella the defendants were negligent in allowing her to be born alive at all. The Court of Appeal held that although it was lawful for a doctor to help and to advise a pregnant woman with respect to having an abortion in these circumstances, there was no legal duty to the foetus to terminate its life. Such a claim was thought to be contrary to public policy as being an affront to the sanctity of life. It was also thought to pose insuperable problems in quantifying damages as it required the court to indulge in a metaphysic of establishing the value of non-existence over existence. Stephenson LJ said this about the 1976 Act:

> 'That enactment has the effect explained by Ackner LJ of depriving any child born after its passing on July 22 1976 of this cause of action. Section 1(2)(*b*) repeats the same clause of the draft bill annexed as an appendix to the Law Commission Report on Injuries to Unborn Children 1974 (Law Com No 60) (Cmnd 5709), and was intended to give the child no right of action for 'wrongful life' and to import the assumption that but for the occurrence giving rise to a disabled birth, the child would have been born normal and healthy, not that it would not have been born at all (see pages 46 and 47 of the report).

Section 1(2) requires the tortious occurrence to have the effect 'so that the child is born with disabilities which would not have otherwise been present' and this, as Ackner LJ indicated, rules out any future claim based upon any right not to be born at all (at pages 1186 h–1187 c). In *C v S* (1987) (p 268) and in *Paton v British Pregnancy Advisory Service Trustees* (1979) (p 441), the court held in a different context that a foetus could not be party to an action as no right of its own could arise until it was born and had a separate existence from its mother. In both these cases the prospective fathers who sought to restrain in one case a girlfriend and in the other a wife from having an abortion were not permitted to bring such an application in the name of the foetus. In addition, the application brought directly on behalf of the prospective fathers was dismissed. In *C v S*, the prospective father sought an order restraining his ex-girlfriend from having an abortion on the basis that the pregnancy would constitute a criminal offence. This was dismissed. In *Paton*, the court held that the Abortion Act 1967 gave no right to a father to be consulted in respect of an abortion or termination of a pregnancy.

The question as to whether at common law a child born alive with disabilities caused by negligence whilst en ventre and unborn could sue for damages remains relevant to those who were born before the coming into force of the 1976 Act on 22 July 1976. In *Burton v Islington Health Authority* (1993) (p 267) and in *De Martell v Merton and Sutton Health Authority* (p 307) the Court of Appeal held that such a claim could be brought. Both cases concerned negligence to the pregnant mothers, in *Burton* the carrying out of a D and C whilst the mother was pregnant and in *De Martell* negligence during the course of labour. The Court of Appeal affirmed that a foetus whilst still a foetus has no independent legal status and could not sue or be made a ward of court. However it drew upon, inter alia, the Canadian authority of *Montreal Tramways v Léveillé* [1933] 4 DLR 337 to establish the proposition that once a child was born and viable the child became clothed with all the rights of action which it would have had if actually in existence at the date of the accident to the mother.

Third generational claims would not fall to be compensated under the 1976 Act, such as, occurred in the American case of *Enright v Eli Lilly and Co* (1991) (p 322). In *Enright*, a 9-year-old sued in respect of damage to her, allegedly arising out of her grandmother taking DES (diethylstilboestrol) whilst pregnant, which in turn led to her own mother to be born with defects in her reproduction system. These in turn it was claimed caused her own cerebral palsy.

The court's denial of a cause of action based upon a duty owed to the foetus of a right not to be born follows the predominant tendency in other jurisdictions to prohibit such a cause of action (cf *Giesen*, para 120). The striking out of this cause of action left to be determined the infant plaintiff's claim in *McKay* for damages based upon the pleaded allegations that her injuries would in fact have been less severe had the general practitioner injected the mother with globulins to arrest the damage that had already, and irreversibly, been caused by the rubella. It also left for determination the mother's claim based upon her having to rear a child burdened with serious disabilities. These causes of action and heads of damage for so-called wrongful birth, often arising from failed sterilisations, are recognised in law and are considered in the chapters on causation (Chapter 6) and on damages (Chapter 12) (cf *Emeh v Kensington and Chelsea and Westminster Area Health Authority* (1985) (p 321), *Scuriaga v Powell* (1980) (p 548), *Udale v Bloomsbury Area Health Authority* (1983) (p 589), *Thake v Maurice* (1986) (p 579)).

Chapter 5

The standard of skill and care

1. Introduction

To prosecute successfully an action for medical malpractice either in tort or in contract, a litigant must establish that the practitioner was in breach of his duty of care. The setting of this standard by the courts has been one of the most crucial legal determinants in deciding the prospects of plaintiffs succeeding in proving that the conduct in question amounted to negligence. The courts have set what is essentially a pragmatic standard of care which is flexible to the extent that it mirrors developments within medical knowledge and caters for alterations in modes of acceptable practice. It is also a standard which recognises that medical treatment is consubstantial with risk, that beneficial guaranteed outcomes cannot be provided, and that the practitioner is not an insurer of success. The judicial formulation and refinement of the standard of care has openly conceded that there are public policy limitations insinuated into the criterion of acceptable practice set by the courts. The natural sympathy to find for a plaintiff who may be seriously disabled and who is most frequently an innocent victim is held in check by the requirement to demonstrate fault to the degree of culpability required. Any substantial inroads upon the fault principle have been seen as requiring legislative and not judicial decisions, creating, as they would, marked effects on the structure of the finance of the insurance markets and the health authorities' budgets. Judicial reservations have also articulated that a raising of the standard of care required would possibly inhibit research and produce modes of treatment which were orientated towards minimising litigation risks rather than being in the best therapeutic interests of the patient and the community at large. The courts have further frequently recognised the low margin for error in many aspects of medical care where the delicacy and complexity of treatment may mean that even minor lapses can produce calamitous consequences incapable of rectification. It is also likely that there are other unarticulated factors which have had an effect in determining the particular criterion of care required by the courts. Commentators have detected on occasions a certain judicial reluctance to cast aspersions on the high esteem of the medical profession acknowledging the adverse consequences that a finding of negligence may have on a medical career. A more realistic approach may be found in the words of the then Master of the Rolls when, as Donaldson LJ in *Whitehouse v Jordan* (1980) (p 604), he said:

> 'There are very few professional men who will assert that they have never fallen
> below the high standard rightly expected of them. That they have never been
> negligent. If they do, it is unlikely that they should be believed. This is as true of

lawyers as of medical men. If the judge's conclusion is right, what distinguishes Mr Jordan from his professional colleagues is not that on one isolated occasion his acknowledged skill partially deserted him, but that damage resulted. Whether or not damage results from a negligent act is almost always a matter of chance and it ill-becomes anyone to adopt an attitude of superiority' ([1980] 1 All ER at 666).

2. Normal orthodox practice

The standard of care that has been the basis of the modern law of medical malpractice was formulated by McNair J in *Bolam v Friern Hospital Management Committee* (1957) (p 250) in a judgment which continues to be relevant a generation later. The case concerned ECT treatment given to a patient suffering from depression, and the action raised allegations that the doctor had failed to administer a relaxant drug before the electric shock treatment was given, had failed to control the plaintiff's bodily movements during the administering of the shocks and had failed to warn the plaintiff of the risks inherent in the process. The plaintiff suffered fractures as a result of spasms caused by his body. Evidence was adduced at the trial that different doctors adopted different methods and techniques in administering the treatment; some would use a variety of restraining sheets, some would use manual controls and some would use relaxant drugs. The risk of a fracture occurring was perhaps in the order of one in ten thousand. The jury found for the defendants after McNair J had directed them on negligence in the following way:

'The test is the standard of the ordinary skilled man exercising and professing to have that special skill. A man need not possess the highest expert skill; it is well established law that it is sufficient if he exercises the ordinary skill of an ordinary competent man exercising that particular art ... negligence means failure to act in accordance with the standards of reasonably competent medical men at the time ... there may be one or more perfectly proper standards; and if he conforms with one of these standards, then he is not negligent ... he is not guilty of negligence if he has acted in accordance with the practice accepted as proper by a responsible body of medical men skilled in that particular art ... putting it the other way round, a man is not negligent, if he is acting in accordance with such a practice, merely because there is a body of opinion who would take a contrary view ... it is not essential for you to decide which of two practices is the better practice, as long as you accept that what the defendants did was in accordance with a practice accepted by responsible persons' ([1957] 1 WLR 586–7).

The House of Lords has affirmed this approach in a number of leading cases, whether they concern questions of treatment (*Whitehouse v Jordan* (1981) (p 604), *Wilsher v Essex Area Health Authority* (1988) (p 609)); diagnosis (*Maynard v West Midlands Regional Health Authority* (1984) (p 456)); disclosure of information and consent (*Sidaway v Governors of Bethlem Royal Hospital and the Maudsley Hospital* (1985) (p 554)); or in determining the best medical interests of the patient where a person is mentally incompetent to consent (*F v West Berkshire Health Authority* (1989) (p 327), *Airedale National Health Service Trust v Bland* (p 327)). Further the Court of Appeal in *Bolitho v City and Hackney Health Authority* (p 251) have extended the Bolam test to the issue of causation where a court is required to determine whether a negligent failure to attend the patient would have made any difference had the attendance taken place. The court is required to ascertain what the treating physician would have done had the attendance been made and to thereafter decide whether the practitioner's treatment or absence of treatment could be justified by considering whether it accorded with any proper and responsible body of medical opinion.

The accepted legal criterion is the average yardstick of the ordinary skilful and competent practitioner conforming to a practice accepted as proper by a responsible body of medical opinion skilled in the relevant areas of patient care in issue. A practitioner is not to be found negligent merely because there is a body of responsible professional opinion who would adopt a different approach. An important consequence of this standard is that the court will not be concerned in adjudicating upon conflicts of medical opinion in respect of accepted modes of practice. Moreover, except in very plain cases, it will be for medical experts to give evidence to determine whether a practitioner acted within any one of such accepted modes.

McNair J was justified in indicating to the jury in *Bolam's* case (p 250) that the degree of skill in issue had been well established as that of the average ordinary professional and not that of the highest specialist. In *Seare v Prentice* (1807) (p 550), Lord Ellenborough CJ held that:

'An ordinary degree of skill is necessary for a surgeon who undertakes to perform surgical operations, which is proved in the case of *Wilson*, and indeed by all analogous authorities; in the same manner as it is necessary for every other man to have it in the course of his employment' ((1807) 8 East at 352).

In *Lanphier v Phipos* (1838) (p 426), Tindal CJ expressed the matter particularly cogently when he stated to the jury:

'What you will have to say is this, whether you are satisfied that the injury sustained is attributable to the want of reasonable and proper degree of care and skill in the defendant's treatment. Every person who enters into a learned profession undertakes to bring to the exercise of it a reasonable degree of care and skill. He does not undertake, if he is an attorney, that at all events you shall gain your case, nor does he undertake to use the highest possible degree of skill. There may be persons who have a higher education and greater advantages than he has, but he undertakes to bring a fair, reasonable and competent degree of skill, and you will say whether in this case the injury was occasioned by the want of such skill in the defendant' ([1838] 8 C & P at 479).

The historic evolution of this standard of care is also to be found in the cases of *Hancke v Hooper* (1835) (p 368) and *Rich v Pierpont* (1862) (p 522). (See also Jackson and Powell *Professional Negligence* (Sweet & Maxwell, 2nd edn, 1987) and Nathan and Barrowclough *Medical Negligence* (Butterworth, 1957)).

McNair J in *Bolam* quoted with approval the opinion of the Lord President, Lord Clyde, in *Hunter v Hanley* (1955) (p 396):

'In the realm of diagnosis and treatment there is ample scope for genuine differences of opinion and one man clearly is not negligent merely because his conclusion differs from that of other professional men, nor because he has displayed less skill or knowledge than others would have shown. The true test is whether he has been proved to be guilty of such failure as no doctor of ordinary skill would be guilty if acting with ordinary care ... the standard seems to be the same in England' ([1955] SC at 204–5).

(See also *R v Bateman* (1925) (p 500); *Akerele v R* (1943) (p 223).)

Bolam is also instructive for the further direction which McNair J gave to the jury quoting Lord Denning in *Roe v Minister of Health* (1954) (p 531). The Court of Appeal in *Roe* had affirmed the first instance decision of McNair J. In *Bolam*, McNair J warned the jury that finding for the plaintiff out of sympathy without fault on the part of the practitioner could lead to defensive medicine, by introducing to them Lord Denning's view:

> 'One final word. These two men have suffered such terrible consequences that there is a natural feeling that they should be compensated. But we should be doing a disservice to the community at large if we were to impose liability on hospitals and doctors for everything that happens to go wrong. Doctors would be led to think more of their own safety than of the good of their patients. Initiative would be stifled and confidence shaken ... we must insist on due care for the patient at every point, but we must not condemn as negligence that which is only misadventure' ([1957] 1 WLR at 595 in Bolam, and [1954] 2 QB at 85–86 in *Roe*).

It was not, therefore, surprising that it was Lord Denning in *Whitehouse v Jordan* (1980) (p 604) who came to emphasise that an error of clinical judgment by a medical practitioner did not of itself amount to negligence. The then Master of the Rolls insisted that the law allowed for errors of judgment which of themselves did not amount to negligence in medical malpractice cases. He warned that there were dangers in imposing too high a standard on doctors, such as juries did in America, causing insurance premiums to soar to meet colossal damages and resulting in increased premium fees for doctors and the deterring of persons entering certain branches of the profession:

> 'In the interest of all we must avoid such consequences in England. Not only must we avoid excessive damages, we must say, and say firmly, that in a professional man, an error of judgment is not negligent. To test it, I would suggest that if you ask the average competent and careful practitioner: "Is this the sort of mistake that you yourself might have made?" If he says "Yes, even doing the best I could, it might have happened to me", then it is not negligent. In saying this, I am only reaffirming what I said in *Hatcher v Black* (1954) (p 372) (a case I tried myself), *Roe v Minister of Health* (1954) (p 531) and *Hucks v Cole* (1968) (p 392)' ([1980] 1 All ER at 658 d–e).

The House of Lords, though affirming the Court of Appeal in allowing the defendants' appeal, disapproved of the interpretation made by the Master of the Rolls on the standard of care, and reaffirmed the *Bolam* test. Lords Edmund-Davies, Fraser and Russell expressed the view that to say a surgeon committed an error of judgment was ambiguous and did not indicate whether the surgeon had been negligent or not because some errors were consistent with the due exercise of professional skill while others were so glaringly below proper standards they made a finding of negligence inevitable. The proper test was whether a surgeon had failed to measure up in any respect, in clinical judgment or otherwise, to the standard of the ordinary skilled surgeon exercising and professing to have the special skill of a surgeon. Lord Edmund-Davies was particularly emphatic in his rejection of the 'error of judgment' test:

> 'The principal questions calling for decision are:
>
> (a) In what manner did Mr Jordan use the forceps? and
> (b) Was that manner consistent with the degree of skill which a member of his profession is required by law to exercise?
>
> Surprising though it is at this late stage in the development of the law of negligence, counsel for Mr Jordan persisted in submitting that his client should be completely exculpated were the answer to question (b), "Well, at the worst he was guilty of an error of clinical judgment". My Lords, it is high time that the unacceptability of such an answer be finally exposed. To say that a surgeon committed an error of clinical judgment is wholly ambiguous, for, whilst some such errors may be completely consistent with the due exercise of professional skill, other acts or omissions in the

course of exercising "clinical judgment" may be so glaringly below proper standards as to make a finding of negligence inevitable ... doctors and surgeons fall into no special category, and to avoid any future disputation of a similar kind, I would have it accepted that the doctrine was enunciated, and by no means for the first time, by McNair J in *Bolam* ... in the following words, which were applied by the Privy Council in *Chin Keow v Government of Malaysia* (1967) (p 276):

" ... where you get a situation which involves the use of some special skill or competence, then the test as to whether there has been negligence or not is not the test of a man on the top of the Clapham omnibus because he has not got this special skill. The test is the standard of the ordinary skilled man exercising and professing to have that special skill".' ([1981] 1 All ER at 276g–277b).

The degree of skill of a practitioner is to be judged objectively and it is not therefore pertinent that because of lack of experience, ability or knowledge the standard could not in fact have been reached by any particular practitioner (*Jones v Manchester Corpn* (1952) (p 406)). A novice must recognise his limitations, and seek instructions or refuse to undertake work he is not competent to do. In certain cases it may well be negligent not to obtain a second opinion (*Payne v St Helier Group Hospital Management Committee* (1952) (p 493)). See also *Bova v Spring* (1994) (p 254).

The then Vice-Chancellor, Sir Nicholas Browne-Wilkinson, in *Wilsher v Essex Area Health Authority* (1987 (CA) (p 609)) expressed a different view suggesting that in certain circumstances the standard ought to be subjective. The Vice-Chancellor maintained that a houseman, for example, in his first year after qualifying did not have the skill and experience that he was seeking to learn and gain. Lack of experience could lead to mistakes which could not properly be described as arising out of personal fault but arose out of simply being a novice. The Vice-Chancellor thought that it was a requirement within the law of negligence that there had been some personal fault. The view was obiter and a minority opinion. The subjective view has the obvious disadvantage of limiting the rights of a patient to the particular experience of a doctor. Moreover the court would be faced with the difficulty in establishing any one practitioner's particular degree of skill. It is submitted that any failure to live up to an objective standard should not be premised upon any personal fault or moral blameworthiness. To put it otherwise would make the law of medical negligence capriciously dependent on the subjective skills of any one practitioner and cuts across the principle of objective standards clearly settled in other areas of the law of negligence (cf *Nettleship v Weston* (1971), *Roberts v Ramsbottom* (1989)).

An objective standard, therefore, makes no allowance for any particular practitioner being either physically or mentally ill (*Crompton v General Medical Council (No 2)* (1985); *Nickolls v Ministry of Health* (1955) (p 480)). The standard of care is to be construed in the light of the status of the position held and not the personality holding it. It is therefore reasonable to invoke a higher standard for a specialist over and above a general practitioner and for a consultant over a house surgeon (*Junor v McNicol* (1959) (p 407), *Langley v Campbell* (1975) (p 425)). A specialist is to be judged by the standards of that speciality (*Maynard v West Midlands Regional Health Authority* (1984) (p 456), *Sidaway v Board of Governors of the Bethlem Royal Hospital and the Maudsley Hospital* (1985) (p 554)). The more skilled a position that a person holds, the more that will be demanded of him (*Ashcroft v Mersey Regional Health Authority* [1983] 2 All ER at 247 c–e) (p 229)). A hospital specialising in tropical diseases will be judged by the standards expected in tropical medicine generally but not necessarily in specific modes of infection (*Redmayne v Bloomsbury Health Authority* (p 520)).

In *Knight v Home Office* (p 419), an action was brought by the personal representatives of a deceased who had committed suicide whilst held on remand in Brixton Prison pending removal to hospital following a sentence for detention under s 60 of the Mental Health Act 1959. Because the patient was violent the prison authorities put him in a cell where he was subjected to observations every 15 minutes rather than putting him in a ward where he would be constantly supervised. In the interval between observations the deceased hanged himself. The court held that the standard of care required in a prison hospital did not have to be as high as that which was required in a psychiatric hospital. Pill J held that:

> 'There may be circumstances in which the standard of care in a prison falls below that which would be expected in a psychiatric hospital without the prison authority being negligent ... psychiatric hospitals perform specialist functions in treating mental illness and where possible effecting a cure. Interaction with skilled staff is on the evidence a vital part of the treatment in cases such as the present. The prison's central function is to detain persons deprived of their liberty by operation of law. The prison authorities have a duty to provide medical care where physical or mental illness is present. That includes a duty to protect a mentally ill patient against himself. I bear in mind the statutory provisions but in my judgment the law should not and does not expect the same standard across the entire spectrum of possible situations, including the possibility of suicide, as it would in a psychiatric hospital outside prison. The duty is tailored to the act and function to be performed' ([1993] All ER 237 at 243 d–g).

The standard invoked at the trial is the standard that obtained at the time of the consultation or treatment and therefore is without consideration of developments in practice and knowledge during the interval between the incident and the trial. Denning LJ in *Roe v Minister of Health* (1954) (p 531) expressed the view that:

> 'We must not look at the 1947 accident with 1954 spectacles' ([1954] 2 QB at 84).

Similar principles governed the finding of negligence in *Hopley v British Transport Commission* (1960) (p 387) and the finding of no negligence in *Gale v Cowie* (1965) (p 345). It will be incumbent upon a practitioner to keep abreast of advances in knowledge and technique within his area of expertise as they become disseminated through the medical journals. The standard of care would not however require him to be cognisant with every such article, and it is likely that a reasonable time would be allowed for the dissemination and acceptance of knowledge and techniques (*Crawford v Board of Governors of Charing Cross Hospital* (1953) (p 293)).

It is, therefore, most unlikely that adherence to an orthodox mode of practice would result in a practitioner being found to have been negligent. The courts have indicated that in principle the orthodox practice must be a proper practice, but in fact there has been a judicial reluctance to impinge upon areas which are seen as essentially matters of medical competence. In *Sidaway v Board of Governors of the Bethlem Royal Hospital and the Maudsley Hospital* (1984) (p 554) the Master of the Rolls accepted that the *Bolam* test was applicable in cases such as Mrs Sidaway's when the court was concerned to examine a failure of a surgeon to mention a one to two per cent risk that an operation could result in spinal cord damage. Evidence was adduced that not alerting a patient to this risk and therefore not warning the patient was in fact in accord with accepted medical practice. The Master of the Rolls expressed a caveat to the *Bolam* test after noting that *Bolam* had, in effect, been codified with s 1, Congenital Disabilities (Civil Liability) Act 1976. This section stipulates the need to have 'due regard' to received professional opinion:

' "Due regard" involves an exercise in judgment, inter alia, whether "received professional opinion" is engaged in the same exercise as the law. This qualification is analogous to that which has been asserted in the context of treating a trade practice as evidencing the proper standard of care in *Cavanagh v Ulster Weaving Co Ltd* (1959) and in *Morris v West Hartlepool Steam Navigation Co Ltd* (1956) and would be equally infrequently relevant. In my judgment Skinner J was right to reject the approach of Professor Logue, which was not to refer to small risks if he thought that, in his hands, they were trivial. While it is true that he did so on the basis that none of the other medical witnesses adopted the same approach, I think that, in an appropriate case a judge would be entitled to reject a unanimous medical view if he were satisfied that it was manifestly wrong and the doctors must have been misdirecting themselves as to their duty in law. Another way of expressing my view of the test is to add just one qualifying word (which I have emphasised) to the law as Skinner J summarised it, so that it would read:

> "The duty is fulfilled if the doctor acts in accordance with a practice *rightly* accepted as proper by a body of skilled and experienced medical men" ' ([1984] 1 All ER at 1028 b–c).

It is interesting to note that the Master of the Rolls thought that this approach would be 'infrequently relevant'. Lord Bridge in the House of Lords came close to affirming this view when he attempted to meet the criticism expressed in the Canadian case of *Reibl v Hughes* (1980) (p 521), that to allow the medical profession itself to determine what risks it should disclose to a patient handed over the court's jurisdiction to practitioners:

> 'It would follow from this that the issue whether non-disclosure in a particular case should be condemned as a breach of the doctor's duty of care is an issue to be decided primarily on the basis of expert medical evidence, applying the *Bolam* test. But I do not see that this approach involves the necessity "to hand over to the medical profession the entire question of the scope of the duty of disclosure, including the question whether there has been a breach of that duty". Of course, if there is a conflict of evidence, whether a responsible body of medical opinion approve of non-disclosure in a particular case, the judge will have to resolve that conflict. But, even in a case where, as here, no expert medical witnesses in the relevant medical field condemn the non-disclosure as being in conflict with accepted and responsible practice, I am of the opinion that the judge might in certain circumstances come to the conclusion that disclosure of a particular risk was so obviously necessary to an informed choice on the part of a patient that no reasonably prudent medical man would fail to make it' ([1985] 1 All ER at 663 a–c).

Accordingly the standard of care is one which the law determines, and the court reserves the right to itself to condemn an accepted practice as negligent. Examples of this judicial condemnation are limited (cf Singleton LJ's quotation from the trial judge in *Jones v Manchester Corpn* [1952] 2 All ER at 129 b–c (p 406), *Clarke v Adams* (1950) (p 279). In *Hucks v Cole* (p 392)), a case concerning the failure of a doctor to give penicillin to a woman suffering from puerperal fever, Lord Justice Sachs recognised the role of the court in scrutinising whether a common professional practice was a proper one to hold or whether in fact although accepted by a responsible body of medical opinion it still amounted to negligence. The approach he took concerned an analysis of the risks facing the patient:

> 'When the evidence shows that a lacuna in professional practice exists by which risks of grave danger are knowingly taken, then, however small the risk, courts must anxiously examine that lacuna – particularly if the risks can be easily and inexpensively avoided. If the court finds, on an analysis of the reasons given for not taking those precautions that, in the light of current professional knowledge, there

is no proper basis for the lacuna, and that it is definitely not reasonable that those risks should have been taken, its function is to state that fact and where necessary to state that it constitutes negligence ... despite the fact that the risk could have been avoided by adopting a course that was easy, efficient and inexpensive, and would have entailed only minimal chances of disadvantage to the patient, the evidence for the four defence experts to the effect that they and other responsible members of the medical profession would have taken the same risk and in the same circumstances has naturally caused me to hesitate considerably on two points. The first, whether the failure of the defendant to turn over to penicillin treatment during the relevant period was unreasonable. On this, however, I was in the end fully satisfied that in the light of the omissions made by the defendant himself and by his witnesses ... that failure to do this was not merely wrong but clearly unreasonable. The reasons given by the four experts do not to my mind stand up to analysis ... secondly as to whether in the light of such evidence as to what other responsible medical practitioners would have done, it can be said that even if the defendant's error was unreasonable, it was not negligent in relation to the position as regards practice at that particular date. On the second point ... it appears to be more a case of doctors who said in one form or another that they would have acted or might have acted in the same way as the defendant did for reasons which on examination do not really stand up to analysis.'

The Court of Appeal in the circumstances upheld the finding of negligence.

Just how difficult it is, however, to persuade a court that an accepted mode of practice was in fact negligent is illustrated in the case of *Bolitho v City of Hackney Health Authority* (p 251). In *Bolitho* the defendants accepted that they were negligent in failing to ensure attendance on a two-year old in hospital when a request was made by nursing staff at 12.40 pm. At 2.30 pm the child collapsed and sustained a cardiac arrest following an obstruction to his breathing caused by a mucus plug. The defendants further agreed that had the child been intubated before 2.35 pm then the cardiac arrest would have been averted. The defendants however contended that if the treating doctor had in fact attended she would not have intubated as she would not have considered it an appropriate mode of treatment given the child's history and presenting condition. Medical expertise called by the plaintiffs indicated that intubation was mandatory in these circumstances but expert opinion called by the defence indicated that it was not. The plaintiffs' case therefore failed on causation on the basis that because the child would not have been intubated the cardiac arrest would not have been avoided. The Court of Appeal affirmed the trial judge's finding that the plaintiffs had failed to demonstrate that no responsible body of medical practitioners would have failed to intubate the child. Counsel for the plaintiff sought to rely upon the judgment of Lord Justice Sachs in *Hucks v Cole,* arguing that there was no logical reason why intubation should not have been undertaken given the circumstances. The court dealt with that submission in the following way:

'Mr Brennan ... points out that measuring up to the standard of the competent practitioner does not excuse the court from examining the question where the patient is still at risk. He relies on an unreported case *Hucks v Cole* where Sachs LJ said (at page 11 of the transcript):

"On such occasions the fact that other practitioners would have done the same thing as the defendant practitioner is a very weighty matter to put on the scales on his behalf: but it is not conclusive. The court must be vigilant to see whether the reasons given for putting a patient at risk are valid in the light of any well known advance in medical knowledge or whether they stem from a residual adherence to out of date ideas".

'Mr Brennan relied on this authority to support a further attack on Dr Dinwiddey's evidence (the defence medical expert witness) he contends that a responsible paediatric doctor should, when faced with a patient with the same condition as Patrick was that afternoon have done what counsel describes as a risk/benefit analysis of intubation. If the responsible paediatrician had made such an analysis in this case counsel argues he would inevitably have concluded that it was right to intubate. The risk to Patrick was slight, even though he would have had to have been anaesthetised, whereas the corresponding risk of not intubating bearing in mind the two life-threatening episodes during the afternoon was great. Mr Brennan says that in those circumstances the judge should have rejected the evidence of Dr Dinwiddey as not being representative of a responsible medical opinion. He claims that Dr Dinwiddey fails the test referred to by Lord Scarman in *Maynard's* case supra. There is of course no inconsistency between the decisions in *Hucks v Cole* and *Maynard's* case. It is not enough for the defendant to call a number of doctors to say that what he had done or not was in accord with accepted clinical practice. It is necessary for the judge to consider that evidence and decide whether that clinical practice puts the patient unnecessarily at risk. For my part I cannot see that that particular issue arises in this case. The findings by the judge are inconsistent with the suggestion that the approach of Dr Dinwiddey put Patrick unnecessarily at risk. The judge clearly concluded that Dr Dinwiddey's evidence did constitute "a responsible body of medical opinion" for the reasons already given' [1993] 4 Med LR, pp 386–37).

This judicial reticence is always apparent when two or more modes of accepted practice are put before the court with each side's protagonist saying that the position of the other party is wrong. (See, for example, *De Freitas v O'Brien* (1995) Times, 16 February, CA.) The courts have taken a view that medical knowledge and medical science is characterised by controversy and it is not for the courts to determine the current status of the development of medical debate. To this extent the court will decline to enter the affray between various proponents within detailed specialisms, each putting forward various theories and positions (*Moore v Lewisham Group Hospital Management Committee* (1959) (p 460)). No negligence can be established, if all that a plaintiff can demonstrate is that there is a responsible body of medical opinion which takes the view that the mode of treatment in issue was wrong, but is unable to refute the defendant's evidence that there is a body of responsible practitioners who maintained that it was right (cf *Maynard v West Midlands Regional Health Authority* (1985) (p 456) applying the dicta of the Lord President Clyde in *Hunter v Hanley* (1955) (p 396)). See also *De Freitas v O'Brien* (p 305), *Ratty v Haringey Health Authority* (p 518) and *Hughes v Waltham Forest Health Authority* (p 393).

Attempts therefore to weaken the dominance of the 'accepted mode of practice' defence by imposing a risk-benefit approach are unlikely to succeed in the current judicial climate. Such a defence can only be met by persuading the tribunal that the opinion of the defence experts is not as a matter of fact one held by a responsible body of opinion or alternatively that it is not a proper and responsible one to hold.

3. New forms of treatment and deviating from the norm

The Lord President Clyde in *Hunter v Hanley* (above) expressed the view that deviation from normal practice was not itself evidence of negligence:

'To establish liability by a doctor where deviation from normal practice is alleged, first of all it must be proved that there is a usual and normal practice; secondly it must be proved that the defender has not adopted that practice; and thirdly (and this is of crucial importance) it must be established that the course the doctor adopted is one which no professional man of ordinary skill would have taken if he had been acting with ordinary care' ([1955] SC at 206).

The Lord President thought that to take any different view would be disastrous as it would destroy inducements to progress. In 1957 Nathan and Barrowclough *Medical Negligence* (Butterworth) expressed the following view still applicable today concerning deviation from accepted modes of practice and the ethics of new treatment research and experimentation:

'The practitioner who treads the well worn path, however, will usually be safer, as far as concerns legal liability, than the one who adopts a newly discovered method of treatment (*Crawford v Board of Governors of Charing Cross Hospital* (1953) (p 293)). Further medical men cannot be permitted to experiment on patients: they ought not in general to resort to a new practice or remedy until its efficacy and safety had been sufficiently tested by experience (*Slater v Baker and Stapleton* (1767) (p 558)). On the other hand the courts will not press this proposition to a point where it stifles initiative and discourages advances in techniques ... a line must be drawn between the reckless experimentation with a new and comparatively untried remedy or technique, and the utilisation of a new advance which carries with it wholly unforeseen dangers and difficulties'.

Generally speaking, deviation from accepted practice is likely to result in a finding of negligence if the practitioner cannot establish a cogent reason for adopting the practice he did (*Holland v Devitt and Moore Nautical College Ltd* (1960) (p 385), *Landau v Werner* (1961) (p 425), *Stokes v Guest, Keen and Nettleford (Bolts and Nuts)* (1968) (p 568), *Robinson v Post Office* (1974) (p 528), *Hotson v East Berkshire Health Authority* (1987) (p 389), *Chin Keow v Government of Malaysia* (p 276)).

Nevertheless a balance has to be struck between therapeutic innovation and therapeutic conservatism. In *Sidaway v Bethlem Royal Hospital Governors* (p 554) Lord Diplock warned of the dangers of so-called defensive medicine:

'Those members of the public who seek medical or surgical aid would be badly served by the adoption of any legal principle that would confine the doctor to some long-established, well-tried method of treatment only, although its past record of success might be small, if he wanted to be confident that he would not run the risk of being held liable in negligence simply because he tried some more modern treatment, and by some unavoidable mischance it failed to heal but did some harm to the patient. This would encourage "defensive medicine" with a vengeance' ([1985]) 1 All ER 643 at p 657).

The further a practitioner moves from unorthodox practice towards frank experimentation the more likely the court is to impose a higher standard of care requiring the practitioner to justify his actions as reasonable (see the Canadian case of *Coughlin v Kuntz* (p 289), cf *Zimmer v Ringrose* (p 615), *Halushka v University of Saskatchewan* (p 367)).

In *Clark v MacLennan* (1983) (p 279), the significance of departing from an approved mode of practice was treated by the trial judge, Pain J, as having the effect of reversing the burden of proof so that once the plaintiff established a deviation the defendant had to disprove an inference of negligence. The case concerned the failure of an operation intended to relieve the stress incontinence of a mother following the birth of her daughter. Evidence was adduced that it was normal practice to delay the operation in question until three months after birth, whereas the plaintiff in this case had been operated on approximately one month after the birth of her child. Pain J, interpreting the principles espoused in the case of *McGhee v National Coal Board* (1973), came to the view that:

'Where there is a situation in which a general duty of care arises and there is a failure to take a precaution, and that very damage occurs against which the precaution is designed to be a protection, then the burden lies on the defendant to show that he was not in breach of duty as well as to show the damage did not result from his breach of duty. I shall therefore apply this approach to the evidence in this case' ([1983] 1 All ER at 427 g–h).

The judge went on to find that the defendant had failed to establish that it was justified to perform the operation after only four weeks.

This approach with respect to the burden of proof was explicitly disapproved by the House of Lords in *Wilsher v Essex Area Health Authority* (1988) (p 609). In *Wilsher*, a case also tried by Pain J, the trial judge had applied the reasoning in *Clark v MacLennan* and had determined that the defendants in *Wilsher* were faced with the onus of proof in rebutting negligence. Lord Bridge, with whom the other four law lords agreed, said:

'*McGhee v National Coal Board* (1973) laid down no new principle of law whatever. On the contrary it affirmed the principle that the onus of proving causation lies on the pursuer or plaintiff' ([1988] 2 WLR at 569e).

Lord Bridge went on to express the view that the reasoning of Lord Wilberforce in *McGhee*, which give clear support to Pain J's views both in *Clark v MacLennan* and in *Wilsher v Essex Area Health Authority*, was no more than a minority opinion which had no support from the other speeches in *McGhee*. It must therefore be accepted that *Clark v MacLennan* is not an authority for the proposition that in medical negligence cases, where a deviation from the accepted norm is proved, the defendant has the burden of proof in demonstrating that the treatment was not negligent. The plaintiff will always be required to prove negligence on the balance of probabilities in such cases. Deviation from accepted modes of practice, once proved, is, however, likely to impose a severe tactical evidential burden on a defendant even if, as a matter of law, the onus has not shifted on to the defendant.

Chapter 6

Causation

1. Introduction

If damages are to be recovered in tort or to be substantial in contract the plaintiff must, after having proved breach of duty, go on to prove that the harm and loss complained of were caused by the breach of duty. Just as the plaintiff is required to prove on the balance of probabilities that the acts or omissions complained of were a breach of the legal standard of care owed to him, he must also establish on the balance of probabilities that the resulting damage was occasioned by the breach. In law, linking the damage to the breach is considered as a question of causation. Even if a plaintiff establishes causation in this sense, to have a complete cause of action the damage alleged must be of a type of damage which the law recognises as recoverable. Generally speaking, damage is recoverable if (a) it is considered as being of a type which is reasonably foreseeable as likely to flow from the injury and (b) is not considered too remote to be recoverable. This chapter concentrates on the first question of causation since in cases of medical malpractice it is more frequently an issue. Questions of remoteness and fore-seeability are not considered in any depth because they do not typically arise as difficulties in such cases.

2. The burden of proof, cause and material contribution

Most cases in personal injury litigation pose no factual or conceptual difficulty in relating the injury to a direct consequence of a negligent event. In such cases a simple lineal concept of cause is common-sensically obvious. If a previously healthy plaintiff damages a finger in an unguarded machine he need only prove negligence or breach of statutory duty on the part of the defendant, and the question of causation, the negligence leading to the loss, is self-evident. If the same injured plaintiff attends a casualty department or visits his general practitioner and receives negligent treatment, to found a cause of action against the doctors the plaintiff must be able to demonstrate that because of their negligence he suffered further injury. It is therefore more likely to be a problem for a plaintiff in a medical malpractice action to establish causation because he will usually be suffering from some symptoms or disease before he receives or fails to receive advice and treatment. The litigant will therefore have to rebut the argument that his post-negligent condition was not in fact aggravated by the tortious act but was an inevitable development of his presenting problems. In *Barnett v Chelsea and*

Kensington Hospital Management Committee (1969) (p 238), Mrs Barnett received nothing in respect of the negligent treatment afforded to her husband because he would have died in any event irrespective of whether proper treatment had been afforded to him or not. The casualty officer should have examined Mr Barnett but his failure to do so given the volume of arsenic the patient had inadvertently drunk meant that no known antidote could have had a beneficial effect even if administered some five hours earlier. In *Robinson v Post Office* (1974) (p 528), Mr Robinson failed to establish negligence against Dr McEwan because even if the doctor had not been negligent in the manner in which he administered the anti-tetanus injection, proper administration of the drug would not have resulted in Mr Robinson's adverse reaction becoming known in any event.

Similarly, in actions where a plaintiff alleges there has been a negligent failure to inform the patient of risks inherent in treatment, the plaintiff must go on to persuade the trial judge that had he been appraised of the risks inherent in, say, an operation, he would then have declined to have had the operation. Accordingly in *Chatterton v Gerson* (1980) (p 275), Bristow J found that the plaintiff was a woman desperate for pain relief and even if she had been informed of all the risks in the nerve block operation she would still have had the operation. In *Gregory and Gregory v Pembrokeshire Health Authority* (1989) (p 361), Mrs Gregory gave birth to a mongoloid child following an amniocentesis test which had failed to take. The hospital negligently failed to tell Mrs Gregory of the failure of this test until she was very well advanced into her pregnancy. Rougier J found that had the plaintiff been informed earlier she would have accepted the advice that would have been given to her, namely not to proceed with a repeat test because any abortion that may have been subsequently required could only have been carried out more than twenty-four weeks into her pregnancy.

In *Smith v Barking, Havering and Brentwood Health Authority* (1989) (p 559), Miss Smith's damages were severely curtailed because of a failure to prove causation in this respect. The plaintiff suffered from a condition which was likely to cause her to become tetraplegic within one year if a certain operation was not carried out. However, the operation itself carried an inherent risk of up to twenty-five per cent of causing immediate tetraplegia. The surgeon negligently failed to disclose to the plaintiff the inherent risks in the operation. However, the trial judge, Hutchison J held that there was a strong possibility that even if the plaintiff had been properly informed she would have agreed to the operation in any event. Accordingly the plaintiff was limited to damages to represent her shock and depression upon discovering, without prior warning of the prospect, that following the operation she had been rendered tetraplegic.

Similar principles were applied in *Goorkani v Tayside Health Board* (p 356) where a plaintiff sued in respect of a failure to warn that the immuno-suppressant drug Chlorambucil could cause sterility. Mr Goorkani, an Iranian, was prescribed the drug to prevent the progression of Behcet's disease which had already caused near-blindness in his right eye and which was now affecting the left eye. The drug successfully reduced the symptoms in the left eye but it left the plaintiff infertile. The court found that notwithstanding the cultural stigma attached to infertility the plaintiff, had he known of the risk of becoming sterile, would still have consented to taking the drug. His damages were limited to £2,500 awarded in respect of the distress, anxiety, shock and anger at discovering his infertility.

For further examples see *Burridge v Bournemouth and East Dorset Hospital Management Committee* (1965) (p 266), *Gauntlett v Northampton Health*

Authority (1985) (p 349), *Hayward v Curwen* (1964) (p 373), *Hegarty v Tottenham Hospital Management Committee* (1976) (p 376), *Hulse v Wilson* (1953) (p 394), *Vernon v Bloomsbury Health Authority* (1986) (p 593), *Cowton v Wolverhampton Health Authority*, *Kitchen v McMullen* (p 418) and *Stockdale v Nicolls* (p 567).

These cases for the most part do not necessitate any significant departure from the simple lineal concept of cause. However, other types of actions may involve a more complex interrelationship of a number of causes, each operating simultaneously, and the court has to determine whether the tortious act is part of the combination of causes contributing to the plaintiff's condition. Often with the existing state of medical knowledge it is not possible to be precise as to whether a cause is operating or not.

What tends to categorise medical negligence actions is the often extended and intricate analyses that are required to investigate the medical and statistical basis of causation. (See for example *Hughes v Waltham Forest Health Authority* (p 393) where the issue was raised of whether a death caused by necrotising pancreatitis could have been prevented had a fistula been located by a specialist endoscopy, *Sellers v Cooke* (p 551) which concerned an issue as to whether a foetus would have survived in any event even if an allegedly negligent diagnosis leading to an abortion had not been made). A plaintiff has to show in certain classes of case that the injury sustained was in fact generically capable of being caused by the act or omission of the practitioner. This difficulty is frequently manifest in drug cases (see *Loveday v Renton* (p 435), *Kay's Tutor v Ayrshire and Arran Health Board* (p 410) and *Best v Wellcome Foundation Ltd and Others* (p 245)). A plaintiff then has to demonstrate that his injury was in fact caused by the act or omission as opposed to a number of other competing causes (see for example *Matthews v Waltham Forest Health Authority* (p 456), a case which concerned the causation of cerebral palsy through anoxia).

Frequently all the plaintiff can demonstrate is a temporal association with the injury and the negligence, but has great difficulty in establishing supportive epidemiological evidence or a plausible biological explanation. The result is that the plaintiff's case will fail on causation. In *McAloon v Newcastle Health Authority* (p 443), the Court of Appeal upheld a trial judge's finding that neither the plaintiff's nor the defendants' explanation of damage that occurred following the removal of a wisdom tooth were probable and in those circumstances the plaintiff had failed to discharge the burden of proof upon her. (See also *Howard v Wessex Regional Health Authority* (p 391).)

In attempting to deal with the more complex class of case, the courts in medical malpractice actions have endeavoured to utilise those concepts of cause which have been developed in non-medical personal injury litigation concerned with the contraction of disease. If a plaintiff, for example, suffers a disease, say cancer or dermatitis or pneumoconiosis, it is often difficult to establish whether the disease is constitutional in origin or whether it results from exposure to substances which may cause the disease such as asbestos, brick dust or silica dust. Sometimes a substance which may cause a disease only becomes known as harmful at a later date, and the courts have to decide whether exposure to the substance before or after the date of knowledge when it was realised it was dangerous was the cause of the plaintiff's disease. If the exposure that caused the disease was before this date of knowledge, it may well not be negligent, if it was due to exposure after the date of knowledge then it possibly would be negligent; Similarly, some exposure to certain substances is lawful providing it is within certain threshold limits, and an issue may arise as to whether a disease could be contracted even below such limits of exposure. A victim of lung cancer may have to prove that it was the negligent exposure to asbestos that caused his disease and not merely his smoking habits, or that his breathlessness is due to asbestos-caused pleural disease rather than constitutional bronchitis. In dealing with these types of problems the courts have developed a concept of cause which does not rely simply on the 'but for' lineal notion that had it not been for the accident the injury would not have occurred, or even if there had been no tort the injury would have occurred in any event. The courts have determined that in certain factual circumstances it will be enough to establish causation if the plaintiff can establish on the balance of probabilities that the negligent act materially contributed to or materially increased the risk of his injury or disease.

In *Bonnington Castings Ltd v Wardlaw* (1956) a steel dresser who was exposed to silica dust during the course of his employment contracted pneumoconiosis. The dust he inhaled came from two sources in the factory where he worked, one of which was due to a breach of statutory duty but the other source was from a non-negligent consequence of the production process. Some dust was therefore 'tortious' and some was not. The question arose whether the 'guilty' dust or the 'innocent' dust caused his disease. The medical evidence was unable to determine this issue and could go no further than saying that both sources of dust contributed to the disease. This was so even though the greater amount of dust came from the innocent source. Lord Reid held that the 'guilty' dust did cause the disease because it materially contributed to the disease process:

> 'What is a material contribution must be a question of degree. A contribution which comes within the exception *de minimis non curat lex* is not material, but I think that any contribution which does not fall within that exception must be material' ([1956] AC at 621).

The case affirmed that it was for the plaintiff to prove on the balance of probabilities that there had been a material contribution to the disease from the tort.

In *McGhee v National Coal Board* (1973), the plaintiff contracted dermatitis allegedly due to the failure of his employers to provide him with washing facilities after the completion of his work which exposed him to brick dust. The defendants, on appeal, did not deny that the failure to provide washing facilities was a breach of duty but they denied causation. Again the medical evidence was inconclusive. This evidence could not establish that had the plaintiff been able to wash he would not have contracted the disease, but neither could the defendants prove that the effect of the brick dust and the absence of washing facilities did not materially increase the risk of the plaintiff contracting dermatitis. The House of Lords held that there was no difference between material contribution as in *Bonnington* (above) and materially increasing the risk of injury. The plaintiff accordingly succeeded. Lord Reid said:

> 'It has always been the law that a pursuer succeeds if he can show that the fault of the defender caused or materially contributed to his injury. There may have been two separate causes but it is enough if one of the causes arose from the fault of the defender' ([1973] 1 WLR at 4 c-d).

Lord Wilberforce went further and suggested that in cases where neither the plaintiff nor the defendant could prove the precise causes of a disease and where the plaintiff had established that breach of duty involved an increase of risk of disease then it was for the defendant to prove that the damage was in fact caused by some other mechanism:

'My Lords, I agree with the judge below to the extent that merely to show that a breach of duty increases the risk of harm is not, in abstracto, enough to enable the pursuer to succeed. He might, on this basis, still be met by successful defences. Thus, it was open to the respondents, while admitting or being unable to contest that, their failure had increased the risk, to prove, if they could, as they tried to do, that the appellant's dermatitis was 'non-occupational'. But the question remains whether a pursuer must necessarily fail if, after he has shown a breach of duty, involving an increase of risk of disease, he cannot positively prove that this increase of risk caused or materially contributed to the disease while his employers cannot positively prove the contrary. In this immediate case there is an appearance of logic in the view that the pursuer on whom the onus lies should fail – a logic which dictated that judgment below. The question is whether we should be satisfied in factual situations like the present, with this logical approach. In my opinion, there are further considerations of importance. First, it is a sound principle that where a person has, by breach of a duty of care, created a risk, and injury occurs within the area of that risk, the loss should be borne by him unless he shows that it had some other cause. Secondly, from the evidential point of view, one may ask, why should a man who is able to show that his employer should have taken certain precautions, because without them there is a risk, or an added risk, of injury or disease, and who in fact sustains exactly that injury or disease, have to assume the burden of proving more: namely, it was the addition to the risk caused by the breach of duty, which caused or materially contributed to the injury? In many cases, of which the present is typical, this is impossible to prove, just because honest medical opinion cannot segregate the causes of an illness between compound causes. And if one asks which of the parties, the workman or the employers, should suffer from this inherent evidential difficulty, the answer as a matter of policy or justice should be that it is the creator of the risk who, ex hypothesi must be taken to have foreseen the possibility of damage, who should bear its consequences' ([1973] 1 WLR at 6 c–g).

In *Wilsher v Essex Area Health Authority* (1988) (p 609), the House of Lords affirmed the principle of causation that a plaintiff could in certain circumstances establish causality by demonstrating a material contribution and to this extent has confirmed the law as demonstrated in *McGhee* and *Bonnington*. The House of Lords however distinguished Lord Wilberforce as expressing a minority opinion on the question of the onus of proof and reversed the trial judge's ruling in law that it was for the defendants in this particular case to rebut causation. The plaintiff in *Wilsher* was born prematurely and was placed in a baby care unit and had oxygen administered to him. The oxygen required monitoring by a catheter which should have been located within an artery. A hospital doctor put the catheter into a vein and accordingly received from the monitor low gas readings. The mistake was repeated and on account of these errors the child was saturated with excess oxygen. The plaintiff developed an eye condition which resulted in near-blindness. This condition, retrolental fibroplasia (RLF) could be caused by a number of conditions which affect premature babies; and the infant plaintiff in fact suffered from all of these conditions (apnoea, hypercarbia, intra-ventricular haemorrhage, patent ductus arteriosus). The condition could also be caused by raised PO^2 levels in the blood which in turn could be caused by certain volumes of excess oxygen. The House of Lords, in analysing the judgment, held that there had been no clear finding of fact by the trial judge that the volume of excess oxygen administered to the plaintiff in this particular case was of such volume that it caused or materially contributed to the plaintiff's virtual blindness. Accordingly, the matter was sent for re-trial. It was not open as a matter of law to shift the onus to the defendants to show that the excess oxygen did not cause or materially contribute to the blindness. The expert evidence on this issue at the trial was contradictory and there was no finding of fact as to whether the amount of oxygen administered through the negligence of the doctors was capable of having caused or materially contributed to the injury. Lord Bridge quoted extensively from Lord Wilberforce's reasoning in *McGhee* (above) and concluded:

> 'My Lords, it seems to me that both these paragraphs, particularly the words I have emphasised, amount to saying that in the circumstances the burden of proof of causation is reversed and thereby to run counter to the unanimous and emphatic opinions expressed in *Bonnington Castings Ltd v Wardlaw* (1956) to the contrary effect. I find no support in any of the other speeches for the view that the burden of proof is reversed and in this respect I think Lord Wilberforce's reasoning must be regarded as expressing a minority opinion' ([1988] 2 WLR at 567 bc).

Lord Bridge refused to see any esoteric principle which altered the nature of the burden of proof of causation in cases where a relevant breach of duty had been established. He went on to quote the minority opinion of Sir Nicholas Browne-Wilkinson in the Court of Appeal in *Wilsher* ([1987] QB at 779):

> 'To apply the principle in *McGhee v National Coal Board* (1973) to the present case would constitute an extension of that principle ... In the present case the question is different. There are a number of different agents which could have caused the RLF. Excess oxygen was one of them. The defendants failed to take reasonable precautions to prevent one of the possible causative agents (eg excess oxygen) from causing RLF. But no one can tell in this case whether excess oxygen did or did not cause or contribute to the RLF suffered by the plaintiff.'

It therefore remains necessary for a plaintiff to prove on the balance of probabilities that his injury was either directly caused by or was materially contributed to because of the act of negligence or breach of duty alleged. (See *Murray v Kensington and Chelsea and Westminster Area Health Authority* (1981) (p 466), *Kay's Tutor v Ayrshire and Arran Health Board* (1987) (p 410)). Causation can be proved even when there are several so-called concurrent causes as long as the tortious act is proved to be one of the causes contributing to the injury and provided that the degree of its contribution is not so small that it ought to be dismissed as being so minimal that the law should take no account of it.

Wilsher (above) was never subsequently re-tried and in practice the House of Lords' reasoning in *Wilsher* has not contributed to further clarity as to when precisely the principles in *McGhee* and *Bonnington* (above) will apply either in medical negligence actions or generally in the law of tort. In *Fitzgerald v Lane* [1987] 3 WLR 249, a non-medical case, the Court of Appeal held that *McGhee* was not restricted to those cases concerned with the limitation of medical or scientific knowledge but also applied to cases of other factual uncertainty. Some commentators have sought to draw a fine distinction between those cases where the defendant's negligence has increased a general risk to a plaintiff, when *McGhee* applies, and those cases where the defendant's negligence has added a further discrete risk or possible cause where *McGhee* will not apply. Jones expresses scepticism about such reasoning:

> 'It is not entirely clear why the courts should want to make such fine distinctions when dealing with different types of factual uncertainty. It may be pure chance whether a defendant's negligence enhances an existing risk or adds a new risk factor, even if it is possible to distinguish between such risks. In some cases it may simply be unknown whether an illness is the result of a cumulative effect or of a single event the risk of which has been enhanced by the defendant. In the face of such uncertainty

it would seem strange to attach much significance to the distinction between cumulative and discrete causes, although it may be conceded that in practice, if not in logic, it may be easier to infer that 'there must have been some contribution' in cases of cumulative causes and/or the enhancement of the single risk factor. The decisions in *McGhee, Wilsher* (in the Court of Appeal) and *Fitzgerald v Lane* were quite explicitly based upon policy considerations of fairness to plaintiffs faced with otherwise insuperable problems of proof. On the other hand, in *Wilsher*, Lord Bridge considered that the forensic process would be rendered "still more unpredictable and hazardous by distorting the law to accommodate the exigencies of what may seem hard cases' (Jones 1991 p 174).

Further doubt has been thrown upon the applicability of the principles laid down in *McGhee* by the Court of Appeal's apparent extension of the principles in *Bolam* to the issue of causation in *Bolitho v City and Hackney Health Authority* (p 251). In *Bolitho* a two-year-old suffered a cardiac arrest at 2.35pm on the 17 January 1994 due to respiratory difficulties which had caused a ward sister to summon a doctor at 12.40pm. The child was not attended to by any doctor and the defendants admitted that was negligent. The defendants contested, however, that even if a doctor had attended the child the particular doctor in question would not have intubated the child which it was agreed would have averted his respiratory collapse. The Court of Appeal held that because the action consisted of a negligent omission it was for the plaintiff to prove that if the doctor had attended, the respiratory collapse would have been averted because he would have been intubated. The particular doctor in question gave evidence that had she attended the child she would not have intubated and in those circumstances the Court of Appeal further found that if the plaintiff was to succeed he had to demonstrate that such a decision not to intubate would have been one contrary to accepted medical practice so that no responsible body of medical opinion could have supported the decision not to intubate. The plaintiff's counsel contended that the so-called *Bolam* test was not applicable to a pure question of causation where the correct legal test was to apply those principles set out in *McGhee, Bonnington*, and *Wilsher*. Lord Justice Farquharson recognised that that was a powerful argument but indicated the judge was bound to rely on the evidence of experts in dealing with the question of causation. This view was supported by Lord Justice Dillon. However, Lord Justice Simon Brown in a dissenting minority judgment considered that the matter of causation ought to have been dealt with under the normal principles of probability associated with establishing causation:

'I proceed therefore to Mr Brennan's (the plaintiff's counsel) second argument, that the judge should have applied the probability test rather than the *Maynard* test to the issue of causation. Although this argument lies at the heart of the appeal I do not propose to spend long on it. Frankly it seems obviously right. The *Maynard* test following as it does the well recognised jurisprudential path marked out by such decisions as *Hunter v Hanley* ... and *Bolam v Friern Hospital Management Committee* ... was forged specifically in context of liability, of negligence, not of causation. And one can readily detect and accept the underlying principle: that differences of medical opinion do exist and where each is shown to be respectable, it would be quite wrong to brand as negligent those who choose to adhere to one rather than another's such body of opinion.

But, as it seems to me, quite different considerations come into play when the issue is one of causation, arising in the particular way that issue arises in the present case. This case does not involve a doctor adhering to one body of responsible medical opinion rather than another. No doctor in this case ever took a decision whether or not to intubate. The plain fact here is that no doctor ever arrived at Patrick's bedside.

It is that want of attention that constitutes the undoubted negligence in the case ... '
[1993] 4 Med LR 381 at 388).

Simon Brown LJ then reviewed the principles of causation in the cases of *McGhee, Bonnington, Wilsher* and *Hotson v East Berkshire Area Health Authority* (p 389) and concluded that the ultimate question for decision was not whether it would have been unreasonable and negligent for an attending doctor not to intubate Patrick but should and would an attending doctor probably have intubated Patrick. The judge went on to draw from *Wilsher* the approach that when a court's knowledge of all the material facts was not complete it was legitimate to adopt a robust and pragmatic approach and to infer from those facts whether the defendant's negligence did cause or contribute to the plaintiff's injury.

Lord Justice Simon Brown's approach to causation apart from being in apparent accord with existing authority has also the benefit of leaving with the court the function of drawing inferences from facts rather than having them resolved by the expert opinion of medical witnesses. A doctor who has admitted negligence is likely to be disinclined to agree that the negligence caused damage. Moreover, a plaintiff is placed in a very difficult position because he will not know until after the exchange of witness statements whether it is going to be alleged that the particular practitioner concerned would or would not have adopted a certain course of treatment had they complied with their duty to attend a patient.

3. Loss of a chance

The application of these legal concepts of causation appear to rule out an approach which would merely estimate the chances of a patient recovering from a disease or mishap had he been given the correct treatment. In *Kenyon v Bell* (1953) (p 411) the father of a sixteen-month-old girl who suffered an eye accident sued a casualty officer for allegedly negligent treatment and diagnosis he gave to the child. The doctor instructed a nurse to put drops into the eye and to powder the eye and advised that it was not necessary to return to the hospital or to consult a general practitioner. Approximately three months later the eye began to water and it was found that there was a severe internal haemorrhage, a detached retina and a bulged iris. The child lost the eye and the action included a claim for damages on the basis that the doctor's negligence either led to the loss of the eye or, alternatively, materially increased the chance of the eye being lost. At an interlocutory judgment, Lord Guthrie refused to incorporate the principles in the case of *Chaplin v Hicks* (1911), in which a model who was deprived of an opportunity to compete in a contest was awarded damages commensurate with her prospects of the chance of her winning the competition. Lord Guthrie held that the loss of a chance of saving the eye was not of itself a matter which could sound in damages. To found a cause of action the pursuer must prove facts from which the reasonable inference was that the eye would have been saved:

' ... now the pursuer has repeatedly used the word "material" to qualify the chance of saving the eye by proper treatment. The significance of that word can only be assessed upon a consideration of expert evidence after proof. It may be that the chance of saving the eye by proper treatment was so material that the natural and reasonable inference is that its loss was due to the absence of such treatment' ([1953] SC at 129).

The views of Lord Guthrie in resisting any cause of action based upon less than such an inference were given specific approval in the House of Lords in the case of *Hotson v East Berkshire Health Authority* (1987) (p 389). When the plaintiff was thirteen he fell twelve feet from a rope he had been swinging on at school and suffered a serious hip injury which was not diagnosed until five days later. This failure, the defendants admitted, amounted to negligence. The plaintiff suffered from a condition known as avascular necrosis which the trial judge, Simon Brown J, found was seventy-five per cent likely to have occurred even if the defendants had diagnosed and treated the injury promptly. The trial judge found for the plaintiff on the basis that he had been deprived of a twenty-five per cent chance of recovering without the serious complications that had developed. He awarded him a quarter of the total damages, allowing therefore for the seventy-five per cent likelihood that the complications would have occurred in any event. The trial judge took the view that where a loss of a chance or risk was proved on the balance of probabilities, and provided that that loss was substantial, the plaintiff could recover even if the loss of that chance was below fifty per cent. The judge expressed the opinion that this finding was open to him because in effect he was concerned not with the question of causation and therefore liability, but only with the question of damages and was therefore in a position which courts routinely find themselves in, in cases of personal injury, where they have to quantify in monetary terms the chances of a plaintiff developing, for example, epilepsy or contracting osteo-arthritis in later life.

A very strong Court of Appeal (Sir John Donaldson MR and Dillon LJ and Croom-Johnson LJ) affirmed the persuasive reasoning of Simon Brown J in his careful analysis of the leading cases, including *McGhee* (above), and came to a view that where a plaintiff proved on the balance of probabilities that as a result of a failure to treat a patient timeously the patient lost a benefit of a substantial chance of avoiding long-term disability, the plaintiff was entitled to be compensated for the loss of that chance evaluated in terms of the percentage loss. The Master of the Rolls, Sir John Donaldson, said:

'As a matter of common sense, it is unjust that there should be no liability for failure to treat a patient, simply because the chances of a successful cure by that treatment were less than fifty per cent, nor by the same token can it be just that if the chances of a successful cure only marginally exceed fifty per cent, the doctor or his employer should be liable to the same extent as if the treatment could be guaranteed to cure. If this is the law, it is high time it was changed, assuming that this court has the power to do so. Equally I am quite unable to detect any rational basis for a state of the law, if such it be, whereby in identical circumstances doctor A who treats a patient under the National Health Service, and whose liability therefore falls to be determined in accordance with the law of tort, should be in a different position from doctor B who treats a patient outside the Service and whose liability therefore falls to be determined in accordance with the law of contract, assuming of course, that the contract is in terms which imposes upon him neither more nor less than the tortious duty' ([1987] 2 WLR at 294).

The Master of the Rolls went on to analyse the plaintiff's loss in this case as the loss of the benefit of timely treatment which he proved was of value. Dillon LJ thought nothing offensive in principle in allowing a loss of chance to sound in damages in tort as it already did in damages in contract as in *Chaplin v Hicks* (1911) and other leading cases. It was, however, offensive to common sense to limit a patient's cause of action to those cases where it could be proved that there was a fifty per cent chance or more, that is on the balance of probabilities, that the non-negligent treatment would have prevented the damage. Croom-Johnson LJ, thought, inter alia, that the case could be encompassed within the ordinary forms of the assessment of damages which were routinely subject to quantifying matters of chance.

The House of Lords allowed the defendant's appeal, reversing the trial judge and the unanimous opinions of the Court of Appeal. Moreover the House of Lords did so both on the question of causation and on the principle of the assessment of damages being proportionate to the percentage loss of chance. The House of Lords held that the proper application of the principles in *Bonnington* and *McGhee* (above) required the plaintiff to establish on the balance of probabilities that the delay in treating him at least materially contributed to the development of his avascular necrosis. Therefore, because the trial judge had found as a fact that it was more likely than not (that is, seventy-five per cent likely) that the avascular necrosis would have occurred in any event, there had been a manifest failure to prove causation on the question of liability. Further, where a plaintiff did establish a material contribution and thereby established causality, he was entitled to the whole of the damages and not a proportion. Lord Bridge indicated that the trial judge:

' ... reached the conclusion that the question was one of quantification and thus arrived at his award to the plaintiff at one-quarter of the damages appropriate to compensate him for the consequences of avascular necrosis. It is here, with respect, that I part company with the judge. The plaintiff's claim was for damages for physical injury and consequential loss alleged to have been caused by the authority's breach of their duty of care. In some cases, perhaps particularly medical negligence cases, causation may be so shrouded in mystery that the court can only measure statistical chances. But that was not so here. On the evidence there was a clear conflict of what caused the avascular necrosis. The authority's evidence was that the sole cause was the original traumatic injury to the hip. The plaintiff's evidence, at its highest, was that the delay in treatment was a material contributory cause. This was a conflict like any other about some relevant past event, which the judge could not avoid resolving on the balance of probabilities. Unless the plaintiff proved on a balance of probabilities that the delayed treatment was at least a material contributory cause of the avascular necrosis he failed on the issue of causation and no question of quantification could arise. But the judge's finding of facts ... are unmistakenly to the effect that on the balance of probabilities the injury caused by the plaintiff's fall left insufficient blood vessels intact to keep the epiphysis alive. This amounts to a finding of fact that the fall was the sole cause of the avascular necrosis' ([1987] 3 WLR at 237 c–g).

The appeal was allowed on this narrow basis and is not authority for the wider proposition that in a claim for personal injury it is never appropriate for the plaintiff to show that he has a statistical chance less than even that but for the breach of duty he would not have had the injury. An interesting illustration of the artificiality of preventing a plaintiff from bringing an action in medical malpractice based upon the loss of a chance is to be found in *Gascoine v Ian Sherridan & Co and Latham* (p 348). Mrs Gascoine initiated an action against a health authority in respect of an allegation that a decision to carry out external radiotherapy was negligent. No statement of claim was ever served and the health authority successfully struck out the action for want of prosecution. The plaintiff then sued her solicitors and her counsel who conceded primary negligence but contested that no damage had been occasioned by their negligence because the plaintiff's claim was statute barred and negligence by the hospital authority could not have been established. The trial judge Mitchell J found that the first action was not statute barred and that the plaintiff had a 60% chance of establishing negligence against the treating physicians. In those circumstances the plaintiff was entitled to 60%

of her damages as this reflected the chance of her succeeding in the medical negligence action. This mode of analysis is usual in so-called professional negligence claims where a plaintiff sues a solicitor on the basis that their failure to prosecute an action has resulted in the loss of a chance of them recovering damages (cf *Kitchen v Royal Air Force Association* [1958] 1 WLR 563).

Lord McKay's speech in *Hotson* averred to the outcome in *Kenyon v Bell* (1953) (p 411). In an unreported decision on the case that went on to proof, Lord Strachan held that the child's eye had been irreparably damaged at the initial injury. In Lord McKay's opinion it was proper to apply the same approach to the case of *Hotson*: it was more probable than not that the initial trauma caused the avascular necrosis. The Lord Chancellor's speech involved an interesting analysis of the differing approaches taken on the loss of a chance case in the United States of America (cf *Herskovits v Group Health Co-operative of Puget Sound* (1983) (p 378), *Hamil v Bashline* (1978) and *Hicks v United States* (1966)). He expressed the view that:

> ' ... unless and until the House departs from the decision in *McGhee* your Lordships cannot affirm the proposition that in no circumstances can evidence of a loss of chance resulting from a breach of a duty of care found a successful claim of damage.'

Lord Ackner further emphasised ([1987] 3 WLR at 248a) that where liability is established, the loss which the plaintiff sustained is payable in full and is not discounted by reducing the claim by the extent to which the plaintiff has failed to prove his case with one hundred per cent certainty. Accordingly:

> 'The decision of Simon Brown J in the subsequent case of *Bagley v North Herts Health Authority* (p 234), reported only in [1986] NLJ Rep 1014, in which he discounted an award for a stillbirth, because there was a five per cent risk that the plaintiff would have had a still born child even if the hospital had not been negligent was clearly wrong.'

It must therefore follow that the manner in which Pain J reduced damages in *Clark v MacLennan* (1983) (p 279) was also wrong. In that case the trial judge heard evidence that if the operation to prevent the plaintiff's stress incontinence had been undertaken at the right time the general chance of it succeeding was approximately sixty-six per cent. Therefore, wrongly, he gave judgment for sixty-six per cent of the full value of the claim.

SUMMARY

In establishing causation in terms of material contribution, a plaintiff must show on the balance of probabilities that the breach of duty materially contributed to the injury. In other words it must be established that it was more than fifty per cent likely to have operated as a cause. This is an entirely different issue to the question of proving the percentage degree of the causative effect of the tort vis-à-vis other concurrent non-tortious causes. If the saturation of oxygen, negligently administered to a child, materially contributed to a state of blindness it will be held to be a cause. This is assuming that the state of medical knowledge is unable to say precisely what did cause the blindness. As long as the medical evidence establishes that the tortious act amounts to a cause, it is not necessary for a plaintiff to have to be able to establish that it was *the* cause. All the plaintiff has to show is that the causative power was material, that is not de minimus.

Conversely, and perhaps perversely, when analysing a plaintiff's prospects of the loss of a chance, the question appears to be not whether on the balance of probabilities the plaintiff lost a chance of recovery but whether on the balance of probabilities there was at least a fifty per cent prospect of him suffering as he did, even if the correct treatment had been afforded to him. For example, in *Mitchell v Hounslow and Spelthorne Health Authority* (1984) (p 458) an infant plaintiff sued in respect of spastic cerebral palsy caused by birth anoxia due to compression of the umbilical cord. The umbilical cord had prolapsed and the midwife had failed to apply pressure to the foetus in accord with normal standard practice. Kenneth Jones J accepted the expert evidence that if pressure had been applied to the foetus there was a sixty per cent chance that brain damage would have been avoided and therefore held the hospital authority liable for the midwife's negligence which was the probable cause of the plaintiff's condition. (See also *R v Vaccine Damage Tribunal, ex p Loveday* (1985) (p 514) and *Loveday v Renton* (1988) (p 435).)

Causation is established if the tort caused or materially contributed to the injury. Moreover, as long as a plaintiff proves causation through material contribution, he will be entitled to one hundred per cent of his damages. Where, however, a plaintiff sues in respect of a chance that but for the tort the injury might not have occurred, he has to demonstrate that there was a prospect of more than fifty per cent of the injury not occurring but for the tort. If a plaintiff establishes the chance was over fifty per cent, he will be entitled to the whole of his damages.

4. Foreseeability, remoteness and breaking the chain of causation

For a plaintiff to recover damages, the court must be satisfied not only that there has been negligence or breach of duty and that negligence or breach of duty caused the loss, but also the damage occasioned must be of a type which is recognised in law as recoverable. Whether a type of damage is recoverable or not turns predominantly on the question whether the damage was a reasonably foreseeable consequence of the negligent act or whether it is held to be too remote. These concepts of reasonable foreseeability and remoteness have given rise to relatively complex legal debates. Part of the complexity no doubt arises because the concepts are used in very different contexts. Both remoteness and foreseeability are concepts which are applied to the question of whether there is a duty of care owed by one person to another. Similarly, the question of remoteness is used in analysing the question of causation of an accident or incident as well as looking at the question whether the damage caused is too remote. When remoteness is applied to the question of causation, it is often found in conjunction with another concept which affords defendants a defence concerning the matter of causation, namely where a supervening event occasioned by the plaintiff or a third party is said to have broken the chain of causation and thereby relieved the defendant of the consequences of his breach of duty. A supervening force which is held to break the chain of causation is often known by the phrase novus actus interveniens.

These concepts have on occasions been of significance in certain medical malpractice actions. Often the logic of these essentially legal concepts clearly interrelates with questions of public policy. As long ago as 1954, Lord Denning in *Roe v Minister of Health* (1954) (p 531) recognised the manner in which the concepts interrelated:

'The first question in every case is whether there was a duty of care owed to the plaintiff and the test of duty depends, without doubt, on what you should foresee. There is no duty of care owed to a person when you could not reasonably foresee that he might be injured by your conduct: see *Hay* (or *Bourhill*) *v Young* (1943), *Woods v Duncan* (1946) per Lord Russell and per Lord Porter. The second question is whether the neglect of duty was a "cause" of the injury in the proper sense of that term; and causation, as well as duty, often depends on what you should foresee. The chain of causation is broken when there is an intervening act which you could not reasonably be expected to foresee, see *Woods v Duncan* per Lord Simon, Lord McMillan and Lord Simmonds. It is even broken when there is an intervening omission which you could not reasonably expect. For instance in cases based on *Donoghue v Stevenson* (1932) a manufacturer is not liable if he might reasonably contemplate that an intermediate examination would probably be made. It is only when those two preliminary questions – duty and causation – are answered in favour of the plaintiff that the third question, remoteness of damage, comes into play. Even then your ability to foresee the consequences may be vital. It is decisive when there is intervening conduct by other persons: see *Stansbie v Troman* (1948), *Lewis v Carmarthenshire County Council* (1953). It is only disregarded when the negligence is the immediate or precipitating cause of the damage, as in *Re Polemis* (1921) and *Thurogood v Van den Berghs and Jurgens Ltd* (1951). In all these cases you will find that the three questions, duty, causation and remoteness run continually into one another. It seems to me that they are simply three different ways of looking at one and the same problem. Starting with the proposition that a negligent person should be liable, within reason, for the consequences of his conduct, the extent of his liabilities to be found by asking the one question: Is the consequence fairly to be regarded as within the risk created by the negligence? If so, the negligent person is liable for it, but not otherwise' ([1954] 2 QB 84–85).

In medical malpractice actions, the question of remoteness is normally concerned with the question of negligence or breach of duty rather than with the foreseeable nature of the type of damage. In *Hothi v Greenwich Health Authority* (1982) (p 389), a plaintiff, who presented with a serious head injury, was given phenobarbitone and as a result developed a severe rash and symptoms known as Stevens-Johnson syndrome. The plaintiff sued on the basis that the phenobarbitone should not have been prescribed and that sensitivity tests should have been carried out beforehand. Croom-Johnson J held that it was a proper procedure to prescribe an anti-convulsant drug such as phenobarbitone and the chance of Stevens-Johnson syndrome occurring was so remote that no doctor could be negligent because of the very slight risk that some hypersensitive person might have an adverse reaction.

In *Hyde v Tameside Area Health Authority* (1981) (p 396), a hospital patient suffered severe paralysis following a suicide attempt brought on by depression based upon an erroneous belief that he had cancer and was going to die. The plaintiff sued on the basis that proper care and attention would have led nurses and doctors to have noticed his depression and a psychiatrist should have been brought in. The trial judge found the defendants liable and awarded £200,000 damages. The Court of Appeal reversed the trial judge's decision and found that the nurses and doctors had used proper care. The appeal judges went on to say that, even if they were wrong, any error which might have been made did not amount to negligence. Further, Lord Denning suggested that the plaintiff's suicide attempt was in any event too remote a consequence of any error to be made the subject of damages.

However in *Kirkham v Chief Constable of the Greater Manchester Police* the dictum of Lord Denning in *Hyde* was doubted. In *Kirkham*, the plaintiff's husband committed suicide whilst in custody at a remand centre. The trial judge found that the defendants had been in breach of their duty of care in failing to act upon the notice they had of the deceased's mental state and that he was a suicide risk and that breach of that duty of care was the effective cause of the deceased's death. The Court of Appeal affirmed the trial judge's decision and expressed the view that the defence of volenti non fit injuria did not apply to the facts of the accident because the deceased being depressed was not acting truly voluntarily. Further the claims was not barred by reasons of public policy under the defence of ex turpi causa non oritur actio because the changing public attitude towards suicide meant the act was not an affront to the public conscience nor would it shock the ordinary citizen. Lord Justice Lloyd commenting on Lord Denning's views expressed in *Hyde* said:

> 'In the end it comes down to Lord Denning MR's view that to allow such an action as the present would be unfitting. I have respect for that view. But I do not share it. The court does not condone suicide. But it does not in Bingham LJ's graphic phrase in *Saunders v Edwards* [1987] 2 All ER 651 at 667 ... "draw up its skirts and refuse all assistance to the plaintiff". I notice that neither Watkins LJ nor O'Connor LJ expressed agreement with that part of Lord Denning MR's judgment which I have quoted. Indeed O'Connor LJ clearly contemplated the possibility of a success claim arising out of a suicide. So I would not regard Lord Denning MR's judgment in *Hyde v Tameside Area Health Authority* as standing in the way of a view that I have formed' ([1990] 3 All ER 246 at 252H–253A).

In *Prendergast v Sam & Dee Ltd* (1989) (p 497), the plaintiff sued in respect of brain damage resulting from the dispensing of an erroneous prescription. The plaintiff's general practitioner had written out a prescription for three drugs including Amoxil tablets. This word was written in a manner that was difficult to read. The dispensing chemist, who was also sued, misread the prescription and dispensed Daonil. The Court of Appeal upheld the finding that the poor handwriting did constitute negligence. It also confirmed the reasoning that although other aspects of the prescription should have put the pharmacist on enquiry as being inconsistent with Daonil, the chain of causation was not broken and it was reasonably foreseeable that Daonil would be prescribed.

In *De Freville v Dill* (1927) (p 306), the plaintiff sued a medical practitioner for negligently certifying her under the provisions of the Lunacy Act 1890. Dr Dill signed a statement saying the plaintiff was a person of unsound mind and a proper person to be taken charge of and detained for care and treatment. She was taken to a Justice of the Peace who, without examining her or calling in any other doctor, made a reception order. The jury found that Dr Dill had not acted with reasonable care and, notwithstanding the fact that the Justice of the Peace had ordered the detention, it was Dr Dill's certificate which was the cause of the plaintiff's detention. (See also *Edler v Greenwich and Deptford Hospital Management Committee and Another* (1953) (p 319).)

In *Emeh v Kensington and Chelsea and Westminster Area Health Authority* (1985) (p 321), the interrelationship of these concepts was particularly well illustrated. Mrs Emeh gave birth to a child with congenital abnormalities, despite the fact that she had purportedly been sterilised approximately a year before. Park J held that the operation for sterilisation had been performed negligently but that the plaintiff was limited to damages which had accrued before she discovered her subsequent pregnancy. He took the view that the plaintiff's failure to have an abortion when she knew she was pregnant constituted a novus actus interveniens so as to eclipse the negligence of the surgeons. The Court of Appeal held that the plaintiff's refusal to have an abortion neither broke the chain of causation nor constituted a failure to mitigate her damages. The trial judge held that the plaintiff had acted in such an unreasonable way that the defendant's negligence could no longer be said to have been the cause of her damage. To this extent he dissented from the view expressed by Watkins J in *Scuriaga v Powell* (1979) (p 548). Slade LJ held that the judge had applied the correct test, namely whether the plaintiff had acted so unreasonably as to eclipse the defendant's wrongdoing, but he found himself in profound disagreement with the judge's view of the plaintiff's conduct. He went on to say:

'The judge, in saying that her failure to obtain an abortion was so unreasonable as to eclipse the defendants' wrong doing was I think really saying that the defendants had the right to expect that, if they had not performed the operation properly, she would procure an abortion, even if she did not become aware of its existence until nearly 20 weeks of her pregnancy had elapsed. I do not, for my part, think that the defendants had the right to expect any such thing. By their own negligence, they faced her with the very dilemma which she had sought to avoid by having herself sterilised. For the reasons which I have attempted to give, I think they could and should have reasonably foreseen that if, as a consequence of the negligent performance of the operation she should find herself pregnant again, particularly after some months pregnancy, she might well decide to keep the child. Indeed for my part I would go even a little further. Save in the most exceptional circumstances, I cannot think it right that the court should ever declare it unreasonable for a woman to decline to have an abortion in a case where there is no evidence that there were any medical or psychiatric grounds for terminating the particular pregnancy' ([1985] QB at 1024 f–h).

The defendants also argued that it was not reasonably foreseeable that the child would have been born with congenital abnormalities. Waller LJ dealt with this argument shortly:

'The next question which arises for consideration is the remoteness of the various things which then happened. In my view it is trite to say that if a woman becomes pregnant, it is certainly foreseeable that she will have a baby, but in my judgment, having regard to the fact that in a proportion of all births – between 1 in 200 and 1 in 400 were the figures given at the trial – congenital abnormalities might arise, makes this risk clearly one that is foreseeable, as the law of negligence understands it. There are many cases where even more remote risks have been taken to be foreseeable' ([1985] QB at 1019 f–g).

Finally, the defendants argued that as a matter of public policy a part of the damages which the plaintiff sought should not be recoverable. The argument suggested that once the child is born, on assumption in the first instance that it is a healthy child, damages should not take into account the question of looking after such a child. The Lord Justices reviewed the cases of *Scuriaga v Powell* (1979) (p 548), *Udale v Bloomsbury Area Health Authority* (1983) (p 589) and *Thake v Maurice* (1986) (p 579) and concluded that there were no objections in law to damages in cases of so-called wrongful birth. Waller LJ quoted with approval the view of Lord Scarman in *McLoughlin v O'Brian* (1983) concerning the interrelationship of the judiciary and Parliament on questions of public policy:

'The distinguishing feature of the common law is this judicial development of formation of principle. Policy considerations will have to be weighed: but the objective of the judges is the formulation of principle. And, if principle inexorably requires a decision which entails a degree of policy risk, the court's function is to adjudicate according to principle, leaving policy curtailment to the judgment of Parliament. Here lies the true role of the two law making institutions in our constitution. By concentrating on principle the judges can keep the common law alive, flexible and consistent, and can keep the legal system clear of policy problems which neither they, nor the forensic process which it is their duty to operate, are quick to resolve. If principle leads to results which are thought to be socially unacceptable, Parliament can legislate to draw a line or map out a new path' ([1985] QB at 1021 in *Emeh*, and [1983] AC at 430 in *McLoughlin*).

Once a plaintiff establishes that the type of damage that occurs is reasonably foreseeable and is not considered too remote or against public policy, it does not matter that the extent of the injury was not reasonably foreseeable or that the injury occurred in an unforeseen manner. Accordingly, in *Robinson v Post Office* (1974) (p 528) Mr Robinson was entitled to the whole of his damages from his employers, the Post Office, because of their original negligence causing the laceration to his shin. This negligent act gave rise to a reasonably foreseeable need for a tetanus injection. Although Dr McEwan had been negligent in the way in which he administered the injection, his negligent act was not causative because if he had waited the proper time before giving the injection in question, the plaintiff's particular susceptibility to the serum would not in any event have been made known. Therefore the doctor's negligence could not be considered a novus actus interveniens because it had no causative effect. Although the employers could not have foreseen that Mr Robinson had a particular susceptibility or allergy, the necessity for the injection was occasioned by their negligence and the plaintiff was entitled to recover (cf *Smith v Leech Brain and Co* (1962), a non-medical negligence case illustrating this principle). Had Dr McEwan's negligence been causative, the outcome may well have been different.

In *Hogan v Bentinck West Hartley Collieries (Owners) Ltd* (1949), for example, it was held by the House of Lords that an employer's liability in respect of an injury sustained at work by the plaintiff ceased after an unnecessary operation was undertaken which resulted in amputation. The doctor's negligence in that case was held to have broken the chain of causation. Negligence, however, by a practitioner in such circumstances may not always break the chain of causation (cf *Price v Milawski* (1977) 82 DLR (3d) 130 (Ont CA), *Knightley v Johns* [1982] 1 WLR 349, *Muirhead v Industrial Tank Specialities Ltd* [1985] 3 All ER 705).

5. Contributory negligence

A partial defence to an action for damages arising out of medical malpractice is in principle afforded by the doctrine of contributory negligence. The Law Reform (Contributory Negligence) Act 1945 provides that where a person suffers damage, partly as a result of his own fault and partly as a result of another's fault, then the compensation received may be reduced in a proportion which the court thinks just and equitable having regard to his share in the responsibility for the damage. Fault is defined by s 4 of the Act as: 'negligence, breach of statutory duty or other act or omission which gives rise to a liability in tort or would, apart from this Act give rise to the defence of contributory negligence'. It is likely in the context of medical care that a partial defence of contributory negligence is available, no matter whether a plaintiff sues in tort or for breach of contract.

There is no reported UK medical malpractice case where an allegation of contributory negligence has succeeded. This absence may reflect the fact that in many cases the victim of a medical mishap is innocent. It may also reflect recognition that patients often have little knowledge or control over their treatment programme. Nevertheless, there are many situations in the context of medical care where allegations of contributory negligence may be made. The basis of the doctrine of contributory negligence arises not from any duty that a patient may owe to a doctor but from a generalised duty of self-care. The patient may be partly to blame for a mishap or for the degree of damage that follows from a mishap if he fails to take reasonable care for his own health and safety. Breach of duty of self-care must give rise to a foreseeable risk of damage, and the plaintiff's fault must be causative of some of the damage. In other words, the negligence on the part of the plaintiff must materially contribute to the injury. It is for the defendant to establish on the balance of probabilities that there has been contributory negligence. Once this is established, the percentage of fault held against the plaintiff will in practice be determined by looking not only at the causative effect of the behaviour but also at the relative degrees of blameworthy conduct. The standard of self-care will be what is reasonable in all the circumstances. Accordingly, a lower standard of care will be appropriate for those who are of tender or advanced years and for those are sick or disabled.

In cases of medical malpractice, allegations of contributory fault could be made against a patient who, for example, failed to co-operate with a practitioner in fully answering questions designed to obtain a proper history. Equally, failures to keep appointments or leaving hospital against medical advice, or ignoring warnings, or failing to take heed of instructions concerning prescriptions or diet may in principle amount to contributory negligence. Failing to seek further help after a mishap has occurred or unreasonably refusing the treatment designed to mitigate the effect of a mishap may also result in a plaintiff's damages being reduced.

The Canadian case of *Crossman v Stewart* (1977) (p 295) is a good illustration. The partial defence of contributory negligence succeeded against a plaintiff who suffered irreversible eye damage from prolonged usage of a drug, known as Chloroquine, originally prescribed by the defendant for a facial skin disorder. The plaintiff continued to use the drug without prescription by obtaining it from a salesman who visited her employer's medical practice. On the facts of the case, the defendant was held liable for failing to appreciate from material available to him that the plaintiff had been using the drug without prescription. However, the plaintiff was found to have been two-thirds to blame. Anderson J found the plaintiff negligent because she had obtained the drugs without obtaining prescription renewals and had not consulted a physician about them for almost two years. He went on to say:

> 'In my view, this is not a case where the apportionment of blame is so difficult that liability should be apportioned on a fifty-fifty basis. I hold that if the plaintiff had acted with any reasonable degree of prudence the permanent damage to her eyes would not have resulted. The defendant's failure to take the high standard of care was one of the causative factors but not the major cause. In those circumstances I hold the plaintiff was two-thirds to blame and the defendant one-third to blame.'

Further examples of Canadian cases where contributory negligence has been found against a patient include *Robitaille v Vancouver Hockey Club Ltd* (p 530) where damages were reduced by 20% on the basis that a professional hockey player failed to take proper steps to protect himself and played hockey whilst injured, *Brushett v Cowan* where again 20% damages were deducted on the basis of the plaintiff's failure to ask advice about the proper use of a crutch and *Fredette v Wiebe* (p 337) where a 50% reduction was made because a plaintiff had failed to arrange for a post-operative check up which would have alerted her to the fact that an abortion had been unsuccessful.

Conversely, allegations of contributory fault failed in the Alberta case of *Bernier v Sisters of Service (St John's Hospital, Edson)* (1948) (p 244) where a patient suffered burns to her heels from hot-water bottles put into her bed during a recovery period from an appendicectomy. The defendants alleged that the plaintiff was partly to blame because she did not call for help in time, failed to disclose a possible vulnerability in her feet through having previously suffered from frost-bite, and left the hospital against medical advice. The judge dismissed all these allegations, indicating that the reason why she did not call for help was because her feet was de-sensitised due to the anaesthetic. Moreover, the failure to disclose the history of frost-bite was not unreasonable given the purpose of her visit to hospital, and the premature discharge was not causative of any damage.

Chapter 7

Res ipsa loquitur

In certain classes of injury or mishap, the fact that the accident happened in the way it did is held to be so redolent of negligence as in effect to require the defendants to rebut a presumption that they were in breach of their duty. Obviously this presumption can be of great assistance to plaintiffs, even though the ultimate onus of proving negligence remains with them (*Ng Chun Pui v Lee Chuen Tat* (1988)).

If the maxim applies, defendants can be in substantial difficulty in rebutting the evidential presumption that they were not in fact negligent. In this very limited class of cases, the mishap is said to speak for itself. The classical exposition of the principle was laid down by Erle CJ in *Scott v London and St Katherine Docks Co* (1865):

> 'There must be reasonable evidence of negligence. But where a thing is shown to be under the management of the defendants or his servants, and the accident is such as in the ordinary course of things it does not happen if those who have the management use proper care, it affords reasonable evidence, in the absence of explanation by the defendants, that the accident arose from want of care' ((1865) 3 H & C at 601).

In medical cases, particularly where the treatment or operation is complex and the plaintiff may be unconscious at the time, this doctrine can be of particular significance. However, for the presumption to arise the accident must be more consistent with an act of negligence than any other explanation. In effect, this means that res ipsa loquitur is pertinent only in those cases where the plaintiff cannot prove what did cause the accident. Once there is evidence of what caused the accident, it becomes a question of legal judgment rather than presumption as to whether the act or omission amounted to negligence. The maxim is probably not strictly a doctrine of law creating a presumption but:

> ' ... a rule of evidence affecting onus, based on common sense, and its purpose is to enable justice to be done when the facts bearing on causation and on the care exercised by the defendants are at the outset unknown to the plaintiff and are or ought to be within the knowledge of the defendant' (per Lord Normand in *Barkway v South Wales Transport Co Ltd* (1950)).

The maxim therefore applies when the circumstances of the occurrence are without further explanation more consistent with negligence than with any other cause. A plaintiff needs to demonstrate that the injury happened in an unexplained way, that the injury would not have happened in the ordinary way without negligence and the circumstances point to the liability of the defendant rather than any other person, that is, the incident causing the damage was in the management and control

85

of the particular defendant sued. (See Charlesworth and Percy *Negligence* (Sweet & Maxwell, 8th edn, 1990) pp 421–433.) Where the maxim is held to apply, the defendants have the tactical or evidential onus of proving that they in fact were not negligent, and they may do this even though they cannot explain how the act occurred. The prime way in which defendants typically rebut this presumption is to adduce evidence that the act could have reasonably occurred without negligence. It is accordingly more accurate to state that the defendants need not disprove negligence; what they need to do is rebut the inference by indicating that other non-tortious reasonable causes exist and are just as, or more likely, to have caused the plaintiff's injury (*Moore v R Fox and Sons* (1956)).

In *Barkway v South Wales Transport Co Ltd* (above), Asquith LJ expressed the issue of rebutting the inference of negligence in the following way:

'(i) If the defendants' omnibus leaves the road and falls down an embankment, and this without more is proved, then res ipsa loquitur there is a presumption that the event is caused by negligence on the part of the defendants, and the plaintiff succeeds unless the defendants can rebut this presumption.

(ii) It is no rebuttal for the defendants to show, again without more, that the immediate cause of the omnibus leaving the road is a tyre-burst, since the tyre-burst per se is a neutral event consistent, and equally consistent with negligence or due diligence on the part of the defendants. When a balance has been tilted one way, you cannot redress it adding an equal weight to each scale. The depressed scale will remain down ...

(iii) To displace the presumption, the defendants must go further and prove, or it must emerge from the evidence as a whole either (a) that the burst itself was due to a specific cause which does not connote negligence on their part but points to its absence as more probable, or (b) if they can point to no such specific cause, that they used all reasonable care in and about the management of their tyres ... ([1948] 2 All ER at 471). (See also *Ng Chun Pui v Lee Chuen Tat* (1988).)

Before the development of the doctrine of vicarious liability, the maxim had less force within hospital settings because the act, for example, of leaving a swab in a body could point to more than one person being negligent, such as occurred in *Morris v Winsbury-White* (1937) (p 462). In this case, a portion of tube was left in the plaintiff's bladder. This tube may have been left in by either the contractual visiting surgeon or by a resident surgeon or resident nurses of the hospital. The tube may have been left in after the operation on 27 November 1933 or at any time up until the plaintiff's discharge on 10 February 1934. The plaintiff sued the contractual surgeon (as a matter of law at that time, the resident surgeons and the nurses were not deemed agents of the contractual visiting surgeon). Tucker J held that the maxim did not apply, because the plaintiff was not in the control or charge or power of the defendant throughout the whole of the period in question.

Inroads were made on this restriction in *Mahon v Osborne* (1939) (p 449) where the Court of Appeal held by a majority that the maxim did apply in a case where a packing swab had been left in the patient's body. Scott LJ, in a dissenting judgment, did not think the maxim applied because the ordinary experience of mankind had no knowledge about the complications that can arise in emergency operations and therefore it would be unsafe to infer that such an event does not happen without negligence. He went on to say:

'How can the ordinary judge have sufficient knowledge of surgical operations to draw such an inference, or to apply the phrase in the judgment of *Scott v London and St Katherine Docks Co* (1865)? What does he know of the "ordinary cause of things" in a complicated abdominal operation?" ([1938] 2 KB at 23).

McKinnon LJ disagreed and thought that the act of leaving the swab raised an inference both against the surgeon and the chief nurse:

> 'Five persons were concerned in the operation on 4 March: Mr Osborne (the surgeon), the anaesthetist, Nurse Ashburner (as chief or theatre nurse), Nurse Edmunds and Nurse Callaghan. The plaintiff, having no means of knowing what happened in the theatre, was in the position of being able to rely on the maxim res ipsa loquitur so as to say that some one or more of these five must have been negligent, since the swab was left in the abdomen in the deceased' ([1938] 2 KB at 38).

Goddard LJ concurred that the maxim applied, but did so on the narrow grounds that it was applicable to the surgeon because he was in command of the operation and therefore had overall control.

In *Roe v Minister of Health* (1954) (p 531), McNair J at first instance held the maxim was not applicable because the treatment and operation in question were under the joint control of the anaesthetist and the theatre staff who were not responsible for each other's acts and the defendants were not responsible for the anaesthetist. The Court of Appeal held that the maxim did, in effect, apply. The judge's objections were undermined by the Court of Appeal finding that the hospital authorities were vicariously liable for the acts of the anaesthetist. Lord Denning went further and suggested that even in cases where the negligence points to two persons possibly being at fault, the plaintiff could require each to rebut the inference:

> 'I do not think that the hospital authorities and Dr Graham (anaesthetist) can both avoid giving an explanation by the simple expedient of each throwing the responsibility onto the other. If an injured person shows that one or other or both of two persons injured him, but cannot say which one of them it was, then he is not defeated altogether. He can call on each of them for an explanation: see *Baker v Market Harborough Industrial Co-operative Society* [1953] 1 WLR 1472' ([1954] 2 QB at 82). (But cf *Hawkins v Dhawan and Mishiku* (1987).)

Roe was a case where the defendants gave evidence that the plaintiff's paralysis arose out of phenol solution seeping through invisible cracks in glass ampoules used for anaesthetics, and this did not arise through their negligence. The defendants therefore established the likely cause of the tragedy and rebutted the inference of negligence. It was held that they could not reasonably have been expected to have been aware of this sequence of events, given the state of knowledge obtaining at the time.

In *Cassidy v Ministry of Health* (1951) (p 272), Streatfield J had dismissed the case brought by the plaintiff on the basis that he had not proved negligence as the cause of his hand being rendered useless after an operation to relieve Duyputrens contracture. The Court of Appeal held that the maxim did apply and Denning LJ put the matter in this way:

> 'If the plaintiff had to prove that some particular doctor or nurse was negligent, he would not be able to do it. But he was not put to that impossible task. He says, "I went into the hospital to be cured of two stiff fingers. I have come out with four stiff fingers, and my hand is useless. That should not have happened if due care had been used. Explain it, if you can". I am quite clearly of the opinion that that raises a prima facie case against the hospital authorities: see per Goddard LJ in *Mahon v Osborne* [1939] 2 KB 14, 50. They have in no way explained how it could happen without negligence. They have busied themselves in saying that this or that member of staff was not negligent. But they have called not a single person to say that the injuries were consistent with due care on the part of all the members of their staff ... they

have not therefore displaced the prima facie case against them and are liable to damages to the plaintiff' ([1951] 2 KB at 365–6).

In *Clarke v Worboys* (1952) (p 279), a patient suffered a burn on her buttock following electric coagulation treatment which involved passing a current through her body via a pad. The plaintiff could not say precisely how the burn was caused. McNair J held that it might have been caused by a number of factors including the possible susceptibility of the plaintiff. The Court of Appeal reversed this decision, holding that the burning would not have occurred if reasonable care had been used and that the case was one of res ipsa loquitur. In *Brazier v Ministry of Defence* (1965) (p 259) McNair J did, however, hold that the doctrine applied in circumstances where a needle broke and lodged in the plaintiff's right buttock. The defendants rebutted the inference of negligence by adducing evidence, which was accepted, to the effect that the needle broke due to a latent defect in the shaft of the needle, and therefore they avoided liability (see also *Levenkind v Churchill-Davidson* (1983) (p 430)).

The application of the maxim will present few difficulties in relatively extreme and plain cases, where, for example, the operation has been performed on the wrong limb, or on the wrong side of the body or where a prescription has been administered in the wrong dosage or the wrong drugs have been used or where test results are ascribed to the wrong patient. However, these are precisely the cases where liability is normally admitted or there is little difficulty in establishing negligence in any event. In *Garner v Morrell* (1953) (p 346) the swallowing or inhalation of a throat pack during the course of dental surgery was held to call for an explanation from the defendants. In *G v North Tees Health Authority* (1989) (p 344), a child's swab became contaminated with another swab because the same slide had been used for both swabs and this led to an investigation seeking to explain how the six-year-old girl's vaginal swab had active male sperm on it. Not surprisingly, this case led to an admission of liability.

It is not, however, possible to be categorical about what may appear to be plain cases to the general public. The leaving of foreign objects in a patient's body is most likely to be found to be an act of negligence, but it cannot be stated in advance that the doctrine of res ipsa loquitur will always apply. In *Cooper v Nevill* (1961) (p 287), the Privy Council found that the trial judge was justified in finding that the leaving of an abdominal swab in a patient's body following a difficult emergency operation amounted to negligence. However, the court was of the view that it did not always follow that because such a mistake had been made that negligence had occurred. A mistake which would amount to negligence in a routine, so-called 'cold operation' might not amount to negligence in an emergency, so-called 'hot operation', where it may be no more than misadventure. The trial judge was also entitled to make a distinction between a restraining pack and a mopping pack, as these may indicate liability on different persons. Given the doctrine of vicarious liability as it now stands, such a distinction would be unlikely to alter the prospects of success of a plaintiff in such an action.

It appears reasonably well settled that in dentistry a fracturing of a jaw during certain operations does not give rise to an inference of negligence. In *Fish v Kapur* (1948) (p 332), a dentist left part of the root of a tooth in the jaw and also, by some unexplained means, fractured the jaw during extraction. The plaintiff relied on the doctrine of res ipsa loquitur, but Lynskey J held that the fact the fracture was caused in a process of extraction of the tooth was not of itself evidence of negligence. No doubt Mrs Fish's case was not helped by her own expert giving evidence that it was possible to fracture a jaw during an extraction without negligence. Similarly, in *Fletcher v Bench* (1973) (p 333) a dentist seeking to extract a molar broke a bone-burr leaving part of the burr inside the jaw. Ten days later the plaintiff's jaw fractured due to an infection that had arisen, and the burr was found at the very point of the fracture. The Court of Appeal held that the breaking of the drill and the fact that it was left there after the end of a difficult operation were not indicative of lack of care. In *Lock v Scantlebury* (1963) (p 432), the plaintiff suffered a dislocation to her jaw following the extraction of six teeth. This dislocation was not discovered by the defendant. Paull J held that the fact that the plaintiff's jaw had become dislocated during the extraction was not of itself proof of negligence. There was, however, held to be negligence in not subsequently discovering the dislocation.

The doctrine is frequently invoked in cases where patients suffer orthopaedic type injuries during the course of operations. In *Woodhouse v Yorkshire Regional Health Authority* (p 612), a plaintiff was operated on on two occasions and during the first operation her left ulnar nerve was damaged and during the second operation her right ulnar nerve was damaged. The judge was satisfied that the injuries ought not to have occurred if standard precautions were taken and accordingly inferred that they had not been. Conversely in *Moore v Worthing District Health Authority* (p 461) the plaintiff sued in respect of bilateral ulnar nerve lesions following a two hour operation. Both parties agreed that there was a risk of damage to the ulnar nerve and that the defendants had a duty to protect the ulnar nerve by wrapping it. The defendants adduced evidence that normal protection was afforded to the plaintiff and that the plaintiff's pre-existing polyneuropathy gave him a susceptibility to ulnar lesions. Accordingly, the defendants had shown a way in which the injury could have occurred without negligence.

A further example of ulnar nerve injury is to be found in the case of *Delaney v South Mead Health Authority* (p 307). Mrs Delaney underwent an operation for the removal of her gall bladder but subsequently developed pins and needles and clawing of the fingers in her left hand. She was diagnosed as suffering a lesion of the brachial plexus as well as ulnar nerve damage. Her case was essentially that the medical literature demonstrated that a brachial plexus lesion during surgery was preventable if proper care was taken and the likely explanation was an incorrect positioning of the arm during the operation. However, the judge accepted the evidence of the surgeon and anaesthetist that the arm was in the correct position throughout the operation and accordingly the presumption of res ipsa loquitur was dislodged. The Court of Appeal in *Delaney* indicated that it was doubtful whether the maxim was of much assistance in medical negligence cases when all the evidence had been adduced. In fact, the maxim only applies when the plaintiff is unable to explain how the injury occurred. If an explanation based upon facts is put forward it then becomes a matter of legal judgment as to whether the accident occurred in that way and if it did whether it amounted to negligence. In *O'Malley-Williams v Governors of National Hospital for Nervous Diseases* (p 484), the doctrine was held not to apply since the injury to the plaintiff in that case, namely partial paralysis to the right hand following an aortagram, was recognised as an inherent risk of the treatment.

In *Howard v Wessex Regional Health Authority* (p 391) a sixteen-year-old underwent a jaw operation following which she was rendered permanently tetraplegic. The plaintiff relied on the maxim res ipsa loquitur on the basis that the operation was routinely carried out with success and tetraplegia was not a known complication of it. However, the defendants dislodged the application of the maxim by adducing six witnesses to testify that nothing untoward had occurred during the operation which could have hyper-extended the neck to such a degree to cause insult to the spinal cord. Further the defence put forward an alternative non-negligent explanation namely that the paralysis was caused by emboli in some way entering the plaintiff's arterial system, a phenomenon known as fibro-cartilaginous embolism. The trial judge expressed the view that the maxim was inappropriate in the circumstances and could not apply if it was equally likely that her tetraplegia was caused by fibro-cartilaginous embolism as opposed to trauma during the surgery itself. The maxim was also said not to be applicable in the case of tetraplegia following severe hypoxia during birth in the case of *A v Bristol and West Hospital Authority* (p 217). The plaintiff's primary case was that the option to allow a vaginal delivery rather than a Caesarean section was negligent and alternatively that, having decided that a vaginal delivery was proper, they failed to have in position a plan to cope with complications likely to arise from the mother's previous history of dystocia during the birth of her second child. The defendant, however, adduced evidence that the obstetric plan was not negligent. Conversely in *Bull and Wakeham v Devon Health Authority*, where the defendants failed to provide an explanation for the inordinate delay in providing proper obstetric backup, negligence was established. Mustill LJ in *Bull* was of the view that the doctrine res ipsa loquitur did not assist, because all the facts were before the court and the case turned on the defendants' failure to provide proper obstetric cover.

Once the maxim is applicable, the rebuttal of the prima-facie case involves the defendant adducing an acceptable explanation. In *Saunders v Leeds Western Health Authority* (1985) (p 546), an infant plaintiff brought an action against the health authority and an anaesthetist, alleging negligent administration of anaesthetic during the course of a hip operation. After two hours, the plaintiff's heart stopped for approximately thirty to forty minutes. The plaintiff relied on the doctrine of res ipsa loquitur, and the defendants appeared to have conceded that the heart of a fit and healthy child did not stop under anaesthetics unless there was want of care. The defendants, however, sought to explain the cardiac arrest as being due to a paradoxical air embolism travelling from the operation site and blocking a coronary artery. This was not accepted as a plausible explanation, and the defendants were held to have failed to discharge the onus upon them.

A similar refusal by a trial judge to accept as reasonable the defendants' explanations of the medical mishap is to be found in the case of *Coyne v Wigan Health Authority* (p 292). Mrs Coyne was operated on to remove a swelling of the parotid gland and following the operation she became hypoxic and suffered serious brain damage. The defendants agreed that the doctrine res ipsa loquitur applied and they attempted to explain the cause of the hypoxia as due to a silent regurgitation of gastric content. The judge refused to accept this as satisfactory:

> 'Dr Greigg's (the defendants' doctor) report did not satisfactorily explain the apparent contradiction of his own conclusion. This is not surprising in view of the implausibility of the defendants' explanation. There is no instance recorded of silent aspiration leading to brain damage and only one such case was referred to in evidence ... If the patient was conscious or semi-conscious – I accept Professor Pain's evidence that silent regurgitation could not have occurred without laryngeal or broncho spasm being readily apparent' [1991] 2 Med LR 301 at 303).

CONCLUSION

In summary, for the doctrine to apply, the plaintiff's injury must give rise to a presumption of negligence, in that if due care was taken in the ordinary course of things such an injury ought not to have occurred. The plaintiff must also show that the thing likely to have caused the injury was under the control or management of the defendants. Further for the doctrine to apply, the plaintiff must not know how the injury did occur because if such facts as to the mechanics of the injury are adduced it then becomes a matter for the trial judge to ascertain whether the injury was caused by negligence. If the defendants do not call any evidence to rebut the inference of negligence, then the plaintiff will succeed. The defendants may, however, rebut the inference of negligence by adducing evidence which is reasonable and plausible that the injury could have occurred due to a non-tortious explanation. Finally the defendants may rebut the inference of negligence by adducing evidence that as a matter of fact all reasonable care was taken and no negligence occurred.

Section C

Common types of action

Chapter 8

Failures in diagnosis

Whether a practitioner has fallen below the standard of skill and care required by law will always depend upon the particular facts of each case and the precise circumstances which give rise to the allegations. Although it is possible to delineate the legal principles which operate to appraise the facts in question (eg the duty and standard of care, issues of causation and damage), it is not possible to formulate in the abstract what will or what will not constitute negligence. The complex variety of circumstances which entail the need for medical care or advice obviously gives rise to the possibility that the administering of that advice and care could be undertaken in a proper or an improper manner. There are, however, certain categories of malpractice actions which arise reasonably routinely from the literature and case law and which do raise particular issues. This and the following two chapters examine, by way of illustrations, the approach of the courts in dealing with typical categories of cases. The categories which are examined are neither intended to be exhaustive nor do they claim to be truly representative of the volume of actions brought. They do, however, indicate something of the flavour of the ad hoc and situational approach which characterises the law of medical malpractice.

Diagnosis is the basis of clinical judgment as it determines, firstly, whether there is a need to treat and, secondly, the mode of treatment required. To make a proper diagnosis, the practitioner must, if possible, take a full history, conduct a proper examination and, where appropriate, organise tests. If the practitioner does this, he is unlikely to be liable for misdiagnosis as the courts recognise that diseases and injuries can present in atypical ways, that practitioners are not infallible and that in some cases the state of medical science and art make diagnosis certain only with the benefit of hindsight. Alternatively a failure to take any or any proper history as occurred in *Chin Keow v Government of Malaysia* (p 276) and *Coles v Reading and District Hospital Management Committee* (p 283) is likely to result in a finding of negligence should damage occur.

A want of reasonable care has long been established as necessary to find against a doctor for misdiagnosis. In *Furstenau v Tomlinson* (1902) (p 343), a doctor diagnosed a skin infection as eczema and prescribed certain treatment which failed to alleviate the symptoms. The patient sought a second opinion and a correct diagnosis of scabies was made. The plaintiff sued the doctor for negligence. Walton J directed the jury that a mistake alone on Dr Tomlinson's part was not sufficient to enable the plaintiff to recover damages; he needed to show a want of ordinary amount of skill. Dr Tomlinson's defence was that the original mischief was eczema and that if there was any concurrent scabies it was so masked by the eczema that it was impossible to diagnose it at that time. The jury found for Dr Tomlinson.

In *Maynard v West Midlands Regional Health Authority* (1984) (p 456), the House of Lords had affirmed the *Bolam* medical standard of care in cases of misdiagnosis. Lord Scarman quoted with approval the Lord President in *Hunter v Hanley* 1955 SLT at 217 (p 396) to the effect that to establish medical negligence in misdiagnosis a plaintiff had to prove a failure such that no doctor acting with ordinary skill and care would commit. The decision in *Maynard* to use a particular diagnostic procedure could not amount to negligence, when a competent body of professional opinion would have used the same technique known as mediastinoscopy. In *Maynard* the plaintiff sued on the basis of a failure to diagnose tuberculosis which the treating physicians did think was likely. However they also thought the plaintiff might be suffering from Hodgkin's disease and accordingly underwent a diagnostic operation which, without negligence, resulted in damage to the laryngeal nerve. The House of Lords dismissed the plaintiff's appeal on the basis that a body of competent professional opinion was of the view that the diagnostic operation was reasonably undertaken, notwithstanding the fact that the plaintiff was more likely to have contracted tuberculosis.

Nevertheless some misdiagnoses are such that no average doctor using a proper degree of skill and care and taking a proper history and making a proper examination ought to make. Accordingly, missing obvious fractures or common diseases, or injuries, is likely to result in a finding of negligence particularly against the general practitioner or the casualty officer who tend to be in the 'front line' in these cases. According to Leahy-Taylor, *The Doctor and Negligence* (Pitman Medical, 1971) Chapter 4, the most common fracture missed in the five hundred cases looked at by the author in the Medical Protection Society files was the scaphoid and the most common dislocation missed was the hip, particularly when it presented with other major leg injuries. In *Hotson v East Berkshire Health Authority* (1987) (p 389), the defendants admitted liability in failing to diagnose a fracture of the left femoral epiphysis but the claim failed on the question of causation. Missing a diagnosis of a posterior dislocation of the right shoulder led to an admission of negligence in *Hughes v Hay* (1989) (p 392). In *Newton v Newton's Model Laundry Ltd* (1959) (p 480), the court found the defendants negligent for failing to conduct properly an examination which overlooked a fractured patella which was broken in eleven places. Similarly, in *Patterson v Rotherham Health Authority* (1987) (p 492), a failure to diagnose a fracture within a knee resulted in an admission of liability. Missing a hole in a skull of between one-quarter and a half of an inch led to a finding of negligence against the casualty officer who failed to take an x-ray or to discover the fractured site in *McCormack v Redpath Brown & Co* (1961) (p 445). In that case a worker had been hit on the head by a spanner dropped by a colleague, but the casualty officer was apparently overworked and assumed that he was dealing with just another cut head. Similarly, overlooking eighteen fractured ribs and a broken collar bone led to liability in *Wood v Thurston* (1951) (p 611). In *Wood*, the plaintiff presented in an intoxicated state saying that he had been pinned underneath a rear wheel of a lorry but assured the casualty officer he was all right and he wanted to go home.

Failures to diagnose Monteggia fractures which involve a fracture to the ulna together with dislocation of the head of the radius led to damages being awarded in the cases of *Champion v Grimsby Health Authority* (p 273) and *Prescott v Basildon Health Authority* (p 497). In *Clarke v City and Hackney Health Authority* (p 280) a similar but rarer fracture through the distal end of the shaft of the right radius and through the epiphysis at the lower end of the radius known as a Salter-Harris type IV fracture also went undiagnosed until approximately five years later when the plaintiff developed pain due to abnormal growth. The trial judge found that this was a negligent failure to diagnose coupled with a failing to be alert to the complications which might follow. (See also *Spinola v South Glamorgan Health Authority* (p 564).)

Failing to appreciate the significance of a poisoned finger and therefore to prescribe antibiotics led to a finding of negligence against a general practitioner in *Hucks v Cole* (1968) (p 392); and missing a chip fracture in *Saumarez v Medway and Gravesend Hospital Management Committee* (1953) (p 546) was deemed negligent in circumstances where the plaintiff, who was a violinist, was complaining of pain in the finger.

In *Harris v Bromley Health Authority* (p 370) a failure to diagnose a third degree tear following the birth of a child also led to damages being awarded. A rare example of the Court of Appeal overturning a trial judge's finding of no negligence is to be found in the case of *Connelly v Wigan Area Health Authority* (p 284). Mrs Connelly presented with recurrent symptoms of upper abdominal pain and vomiting and various diagnoses of peptic ulcer, pylorospasm, agitated depression and a hiatus hernia were made. In fact the plaintiff was suffering from gall bladder disease which in turn caused inflammation of the pancreas. Both the plaintiffs and the defendants' experts agreed at the trial that gall bladder disease should have been considered as a possible explanation for the patient's symptoms. The trial judge found that the reason for failing to consider that diagnosis was because of the way the plaintiff presented herself and the way she gave her history over the years to various doctors who attended her. The Court of Appeal did not accept that that was a reasonable inference to draw from the evidence, because detailed notes indicated what her symptoms were, and in those circumstances it was negligent to have failed to consider gall bladder disease as the cause of the plaintiff's problems.

In *Edler v Greenwich and Deptford Hospital Management Committee* (1953) (p 319), a casualty officer was found to have been negligent in failing to diagnose appendicitis in a young girl who died two days later. In *Burridge v Bournemouth and East Dorset Hospital Management Committee* (1965) (p 266), Cumming-Bruce J held that there had not been negligence in failing to diagnose appendicitis on 9 October 1961 as the condition at that time had probably subsided. The subsequent day there was a flare-up which was properly diagnosed although the registrar failed to act on the diagnosis quickly enough.

Diagnoses of ailments in babies and children give rise to particular difficulties. In *Riddett v D'Arcy* (1960) (p 523), a month-old baby who was icy cold and who had swelling round his eyes and exhibited a mauve type colour was diagnosed as having a cold rather than showing signs of heart failure due to staphylococcal pneumonia. The doctor was held negligent. In *Sa'd v Robinson and Dunlop; Sa'd v Ransley and Mid Surrey Health Authority* (1989) (p 541), Leggatt J found two general practitioners liable to an infant plaintiff for failing to diagnose significant damage to the oesophagus after the child had put her mouth to a spout of a hot teapot. Negligence was compounded in this case by failures in respect of a proper examination, timeous referral to hospital and failing to communicate adequate and full details to the hospital. Similarly a failure to diagnose a recurrence of septal haematoma in a three-year-old's nose led to damages being awarded in *Reay v South Tees Health Authority* (p 519). The child's fever in that case was misdiagnosed as being possibly due to measles. In *Thompson v South Tees Area Health Authority* (p 582) the failure to diagnose an intestinal obstruction due to intussusception led to damages of over £600,000 being awarded following the development of severe spastic quadriplegia.

Cursory examination resulted in liability against a general practitioner in *Patel v Adyha* (1985) (p 490), where a plaintiff suffered a collapse of her spine. The general practitioner failed to diagnose this condition and had never examined the plaintiff whilst undressed. Evidence was given that local stiffness or deformity would have been detectable with proper palpation or observation of the patient while she was bending.

In *Payne v St Helier Group Hospital Management Committee* (1952) (p 493), the patient was kicked in the abdomen by a horse. The casualty officer saw a bruise but concluded that there was no internal injury. Mr Payne was allowed to go home and subsequently he developed a fatal degree of peritonitis. The court found that the doctor should have re-checked his own diagnosis after further observation or should have obtained a second opinion (cf *Chapman v Rix* (1960) (p 274)). Accordingly, it may not be negligent to misdiagnose initially, but negligence may follow if a re-diagnosis should properly have been made following changes and developments in the patient's signs and symptoms. Similarly, negligence may be imposed where a general practitioner persists in a diagnosis of influenza, when persisting symptoms should have made him consider the possibility of a tropical disease as occurred in *Langley v Campbell* (p 425). A doctor lays himself open to allegations of negligence if he undertakes work outside his experience or speciality and fails to seek another opinion or to consider differential diagnoses.

Alternatively there are many cases which indicate the limits imposed on a practitioner by the manner in which a patient relates his symptoms or indeed by the manner in which the symptoms are presented through the patient. In *Crivon v Barnet Group Hospital Management Committee* (1958) (p 293), a pathologist who diagnosed cancer was not held negligent when it transpired that the growth was in fact non-malignant. Evidence was adduced and accepted that such an error could have been made even by the greatest expert in the field, and a wrong diagnosis did not mean a negligent diagnosis. In *Whiteford v Hunter* (1950) (p 603), a surgeon diagnosed, during the course of an operation on a prostate, an inoperable degree of cancerous growth. The plaintiff was informed of this terminal condition which in fact turned out to be benign. The doctor was criticised for not taking a biopsy or not using an instrument called a cystoscope. Medical witnesses gave evidence that to use the type of cystoscope typically available in the UK at that time and in the particular circumstances of the operation would not have been acting in accord with the general and approved practice. Similarly, no negligence was established in *Hulse v Wilson* (1953) (p 394) where a thirty-year-old man was diagnosed as suffering from a venereal disease when in fact he had cancer which necessitated the amputation of his penis. Finnemore J found the misdiagnosis had been made at a time when there was no reason to suspect the early stages of cancer, particularly in the light of this type of cancer being rare in a man of the plaintiff's age. In *Luke v South Glamorgan Area Health Authority* (p 437) negligence was not established in a failure to diagnose the development of a non-malignant tumour in the liver to a malignant tumour.

In *Warren v Greig; Warren v White* (1935) (p 599), the failure to diagnose leukaemia was not negligent. In *Sutton v Population Services Family Planning Programme Ltd* (1981) (p 570), negligence was established in a nurse's failure to take steps to diagnose a highly malignant form of cancer. In *Vaughan v Paddington and North Kensington Area Health Authority* (1987) (p 592), a false diagnosis of cancer which led to an unnecessary double mastectomy led to an admission of liability. Similarly, damages were awarded in the case of *Harling v Huddersfield Health Authority* where a false diagnosis of malignancy led to a left sided mastectomy.

In *Barker v Nugent* (1987) (p 237), a general practitioner was held not to have been negligent in a case where he failed to diagnose meningitis in a three week old baby. The court, which heard the action eleven years later, found that the child had not been sufficiently ill to warrant hospitalisation when the doctor examined it. The doctor was also held to have been entitled to bear in mind that the mother resided in a council home which had a nurse on its staff. In *Sadler v Henry* (1954) (p 542), a twenty-six-year-old woman died after suffering from localised meningitis which the GP had diagnosed as hysteria. Cassels J said that this was an error which others might well have made, and declined to find negligence. Similarly, in *Thornton v Nicol* (p 584) a doctor was acquitted of failing to diagnose periorbital cellulitis and thereby to send the child to hospital in a case where the infant plaintiff subsequently developed meningitis. The trial judge found that, at the time when the general practitioner examined the infant plaintiff, she was not so ill that no reasonable doctor could have failed to send her to hospital, and the diagnosis of conjunctivitis which he made was probably correct.

Where diagnostic tests would help a practitioner to make a correct diagnosis, a finding of liability is likely to be established where a faulty diagnosis is made and no such tests have been undertaken. In *Bagley v North Herts Health Authority,* an admission of liability was made following the failure to perform blood tests and an amniocentesis in circumstances where the plaintiff was pregnant and was known to suffer from a condition of blood incompatibility. In *Gardiner v Mounfield* (1990) (p 345) a finding of negligence was made for failing to diagnose a pregnancy in circumstances where the plaintiff presented as obese and also with a history of amenorrhoea. The court found that simple tests should have been undertaken, namely a Beta HCG test or, alternatively, urine tests at two weekly intervals which would have confirmed the pregnancy. (See also *Robinson v Post Office* (1974) (p 528), *Rance v Mid-Downs Health Authority* (1990) (p 517).)

Further illustrations of the court's refusal to find liability in cases include where a school doctor misjudged the severity of a child's hepatitis (*Holland v Devitt and Moore Nautical College Ltd* (1960) (p 385)); where a finger infection was overlooked because the patient presented with a sprain (*Hogg v Ealing, Hammersmith and Hounslow Area Health Authority* (1982) (p 383)); where a ruptured Achilles' tendon was diagnosed as a partially ruptured Achilles' tendon (*Rouse v Kensington and Chelsea and Westminster Area Health Authority* (1982) (p 535)); where a ship's doctor diagnosed a mild rheumatic complaint instead of acute rheumatoid arthritis (*Pudney v Union-Castle Mail SS Co Ltd* (1953) (p 498)). Neither did the striking temporal proof of error avail a widow in *Parkinson v West Cumberland Hospital Management Committee* (1955) (p 488). In this case a newly qualified doctor in his fourth day at hospital had spent nearly one hour investigating a patient's complaint of chest pain. The patient left the hospital with two tablets of codeine and was told to return later for x-rays. The patient died a quarter of an hour later from massive coronary thrombosis. Ashworth J found the examination had been careful, and there were signs and symptoms pointing away from the serious condition.

Finally, the courts have required proper and reasonable grounds for the certification of a person as insane or mentally ill so as to warrant forced committal to a mental institution. A number of cases illustrate the duty that a doctor owed to someone who was not his patient but who was brought to his notice, often by relatives with the intention of having the person committed under the various Lunacy Acts. In *Hall v Semple* (1862) (p 365) a local physician and surgeon signed a certificate under the current Lunacy Act after one of them had seen the patient in an excited and rude state. The defendant had been told a number of adverse things about the plaintiff by the plaintiff's wife. The jury found the doctor had signed the certificate without reasonable grounds and without proper examination and enquiry.

In *De Freville v Dill* (1927) (p 306), a matrimonial dispute resulted in a husband alleging that his wife, the plaintiff, was of unsound mind. The defendant signed the relevant certificate under the Lunacy Act 1890, and as a result a Justice of the Peace committed her to a mental hospital. The hospital released her the following day, finding no grounds for her detention, and the jury indicated negligence on the part of the doctor in failing to act with reasonable care, notwithstanding the fact that it was the plaintiff's husband and father-in-law who had employed the doctor.

A similar duty was found to have existed but not to have been breached in *Everett v Griffiths* (1920) (p 325), where a twenty-three-year-old represented himself in person in court with remarkable forensic ability to demonstrate that he was not insane contrary to the defendant's diagnosis. However, the certifying medical practitioner was found in the case to have acted with reasonable care and in good faith.

In *Harnett v Fisher* (1927) (p 369), a plaintiff was found to have been wrongfully confined in a lunatic asylum for nearly nine years because the certifying practitioner had acted negligently. A logical, but extremely harsh, application of the Limitation Act 1623 held he was time-barred in bringing his action. The Act allowed six years to bring an action, and because the plaintiff was not in fact insane he did not suffer from a disability so as to stop time running. Accordingly the six years had elapsed before he finally made his escape from the institution.

Leave to bring an action for wrongful certification under s 16(2) of the Mental Treatment Act 1930 was given in *Re Frost* (1936) (p 340), where the Court of Appeal upheld the view that to despatch a patient into an institution without medical examination and on the basis of behaviour contained in a short statement from the patient's doctor gave substantial grounds for indicating the doctor had acted without reasonable care. (For current cases see *Furber v Kratter* (1988) (p 341) and *Winch v Jones* (1985) (p 610) where leave was given to sue under s 139 of the Mental Health Act 1983; see also *Ralph v Riverside Health Authority* (p 517)); *James v London Borough of Havering* (p 401)).

Section 139(1) of the Mental Health Act 1983 stipulates that no person shall be liable in any civil or criminal proceedings in respect of any act purporting to be done under the mental health legislation unless the act was done in bad faith or without reasonable care. Further by s 139(2) of the Act civil proceedings may not be instituted in respect of such an act without leave of the High Court. The requirement for leave is imposed only upon those patients who are formally detained under the Act and does not apply to voluntary patients. By s 139(4) the requirement for leave does not apply to actions against the Secretary of State or against the Health Authority.

In *Walker v Semple* (p 596) an occupational health physician was asked by Liverpool City Council to prepare a report on the plaintiff, a council employee, concerning his fitness to continue working. Professor Semple diagnosed the plaintiff as suffering from schizophrenia and hypomania. On those grounds, he recommended that the plaintiff be medically retired. The plaintiff sued Professor Semple and adduced expert consultant psychiatric evidence that the plaintiff was suffering from depression and never had been suffering from schizophrenia or hypomania. The trial judge accepted that fact but went on to find that the defendants' error in diagnosis did not in fact amount to negligence because it was reached upon information which might well have misled the ordinary competent doctor. The Court of Appeal upheld this finding and also that the claim would have failed in any event on causation because the recommendation would still have been the same, namely the plaintiff was unfit to continue working because of his depression. (Cf *M (a minor) v Newham London Borough Council* (p 438).)

Chapter 9

Consenting, informing and advising

This chapter examines the case law that has arisen out of medical practitioners' failures to communicate adequately with their patients. These failures can arise where there has been no or no proper consultation or discussion before treatment, with the result that the patient as a matter of law may be said not to have consented to the treatment or to part of it. More typical cases involve allegations of failures by the medical practitioners to disclose to the patient the inherent risks in the proposed mode of treatment, so that although consent is given it is given without full knowledge of significant facts. Patients very frequently complain, following a detrimental outcome in treatment, that had they been given proper information, adequate advice and warnings they would not have agreed to a particular investigation or have consented to an operation or agreed to take the particular drugs or medicine in question.

These failures of communication stem from the imbalance of knowledge and power which is found at the base of the doctor/patient relationship. The courts, to a limited extent, have sought to redress this balance in two ways: firstly, by holding that any interference with a patient's body without his consent can amount to battery; secondly, by deeming a practitioner to be negligent if he falls below the standard of care in advising his patient. In general, except in cases involving a total absence of consent, the medical standard of care based on generally approved medical practice tends in the UK to prevail over any doctrine rooted in a patient's right to know. Precisely what information, risks and warnings a practitioner gives to a patient will primarily be determined by what a responsible body of medical practitioners would regard as appropriate. A failure to warn about a specific matter will not be regarded as negligent, unless it can be established that no responsible body of medical opinion would sanction the practitioner's failure to disclose the risk. English law has not embraced the transatlantic doctrine of informed consent, whereby a practitioner may be held to be negligent if the court finds that the reasonably prudent patient in the plaintiff's position would have been likely to attach importance to a risk or cluster of risks so that they were material to the plaintiff's decision to give an informed consent.

1. The absence of consent

Despite the absence of hostile intent, it is good law that if a practitioner performs an operation or other treatment on a patient without the patient's consent, an action will lie for battery or trespass to the person. The intentional interference with a patient without legal justification amounts to an actionable assault. Cardozo J put the matter succinctly in an American case when he said:

'Every human being of adult years and sound mind has a right to determine what shall be done with his own body: and a surgeon who performs an operation without his patient's consent commits an assault for which he is liable in damages. This is true except in cases of emergency where the patient is unconscious and where it is necessary to operate before consent can be obtained' (*Schloendorff v Society of the New York Hospital* 10 NE 92 (NY 1914)).

As has been indicated in Chapter 1, the legal justification for medical treatment on a person who is unconscious or who is mentally incompetent to give consent was determined by the House of Lords in *F v West Berkshire Health Authority* (1989) (p 327) as being based upon a doctrine of necessity whereby the practitioner acts in the best interests of the patient. Lord Donaldson MR in *Re T* (p 572) expressed the principles succinctly when he indicated:

'The law requires that an adult patient who is mentally and physically capable of exercising a choice *must* consent if medical treatment of him is to be lawful, although the consent need not be in writing and may sometimes be inferred from the patient's conduct in the context of the surrounding circumstances. Treating him without his consent or despite a refusal of consent will constitute the civil wrong of trespass to the person and may constitute a crime. If, however, the patient made no choice and when the need for treatment arises, is in no position to make one – eg the ... emergency situation with an unconscious patient – the practitioner can lawfully treat the patient in accordance with his clinical judgment of what is in the patient's best interest' ([1993] 3 Med LR p 307).

Therefore, if a doctor performs an operation which is of a non-emergency nature, and not one arising out of 'necessity', without the consent of the patient, the doctor is likely to be liable in trespass. This is true even if the doctor has acted in what he thinks was the best interest of the patient. In *Hamilton v Birmingham Regional Hospital Board* (1969) (p 367), a forty-year-old Catholic woman was sterilised without her consent after the birth of her third child which, like the others, was born by caesarean section. Mrs Hamilton had not been consulted about the operation at all, and the defendants admitted liability. Liability was also conceded in *Devi v West Midlands Regional Health Authority* (1981) (p 308), where, following an operation to repair the tear in Mrs Devi's uterus, the surgeon took the undiscussed and unagreed decision to sterilise her. Similarly, in *Cull v Butler* (1932) (p 296), Mrs Cull succeeded in an action for breach of contract and trespass to the person after a surgeon performed a hysterectomy on her, despite her specific refusal to consent to that operation, having consented to a curettage only. It appears that the patient's specific instructions had become detached from her notes (see also *Leigh v Gladstone* (1910) (p 429), *Latter v Braddell* (1881) (p 427), *Freeman v Home Office (No 2)* (1984) (p 339), *Mulloy v Hop Sang* (1935) (p 464), *Grayson-Crowe v Ministry of Defence* (p 359)).

In modern surgical operations, the consent from a patient which renders the medical bodily interference lawful is invariably written. In the National Health Service, a patient signs a consent form which contains a statement to the effect that the nature and purpose of the operation has been explained to him and consent is extended to alternative or further operations and anaesthetics that may be found necessary during the course of the operation. In such cases of written express consent, the extent of the consent will be subject to the construction of the actual words used and the actual operations undertaken. The consent cannot be construed as a carte blanche for the surgeon, as any additional and unintended surgical intervention must be deemed to have been necessary.

The effect of a written consent form was considered in the case of *Davis v Barking, Havering and Brentwood Health Authority* (1993) (p 302) where a plaintiff received a combination of a general anaesthetic and a caudal block in respect of an operation for marsupialisation of a Bartholin cyst. The plaintiff signed a consent form which contained the following:

> 'I Joan Davis of ... hereby consent to the submission of myself to undergo the operation of marsupialisation of a Bartholin cyst the nature and purpose of which have been explained to me by Dr Arathoom. I also consent to such further or alternative operative measures as may be found necessary during the course of the above-mentioned operation and to the administration of general, local or other anaesthetic for any of these purposes. No assurance has been given to me that the operation will be performed by any particular practitioner.'

During the course of the hearing the plaintiff's allegations of negligence were abandoned, but the case proceeded on the basis that she had not consented to a caudal block but had only consented to a general anaesthetic. The plaintiff had been left with continuing left leg problems which arose out of the administration of the block. The practitioner concerned gave evidence that he had not informed the plaintiff that he intended to give her a caudal block, because it was not his practice to do so when it was given in combination with a general anaesthetic of which the plaintiff was informed. On the evidence at the trial, the failure to tell Mrs Davis of the intention to give her a caudal block was found not to have been negligent because there was a recognised competent body of professional opinion who would also not have informed the patient. The trial judge was satisfied that the plaintiff had consented to the operation, the nature and effect of which had been explained to her in broad terms, and it was not therefore necessary or desirable to have so-called sectionalised consent whereby each stage in the operation needed specific consent:

> 'If one is to treat the administration of an injection for analgesic purposes while a patient is generally anaesthetised (for example the caudal block given to Mrs Davis), as something requiring separate consent why should separate consent not also be sought for an injection of for example morphine to provide analgesia when the patient begins to come round from the general anaesthetic ... Clearly if it is proposed that a patient should undergo two separate operations it is the duty of the doctors to give the patient appropriately full information about each of them. This is so whether they are to be performed on two occasions or one. Equally, clearly there is no obligation to explain every detail of what is proposed. That would be no more in the interests of the patient than to inform her of every risk, however remote. The extent of the particularity required, whether by way of detail or by way of explanation of risk, must be for the clinical judgment of the doctor, and in the event of a dispute about either the court will apply the *Bolam* test. Each case must depend on its own facts. Whether a particular aspect of what is proposed is a matter of detail or is in reality in a matter sufficiently separate to call for separate mention is a question of fact and degree. In my judgment, there is no realistic distinction between omitting to tell a patient that while she is under a general anaesthetic that a tube will be put in her trachea (which Mr Lewis accepts would not have vitiated consent) and omitting to tell her that while she is under a general anaesthetic a needle will be put into her caudal region to provide post-operative analgesia' (per McCullough J [1993] 4 Med LR 85 at p 90).

Consent may also be oral, or in certain circumstances, implied. In *Beatty v Cullingworth* (1896) (p 240), the plaintiff, a nurse, was diagnosed as having a diseased right ovary which required removal. She consented to this operation but did not agree to the removal of both ovaries should the need arise. The defendant surgeon said he could not promise in advance not to remove the left ovary because it would depend on what he found upon examination. The plaintiff told the surgeon as she came into the operating theatre that he should not remove either of the ovaries if he found both were diseased. The defendant replied that that should be left to him and he understood the plaintiff's wishes and would not do anything that he did not have to do. The plaintiff failed to reply to the surgeon's last statement. The surgeon removed the left ovary, as he determined it was necessary to save her life. The jury were instructed that the central issue was whether there had been tacit consent, and in finding for the doctor it appears they did construe such a position. (See also the Canadian case of *Ciarlariello et al v Schacter* (p 278) and *Mitchell v McDonald* (p 459)).

In *Breen v Baker* (1956) (p 259), a plaintiff signed a consent form containing the words: 'I agree to leave the nature and extent of the operation to be performed to the discretion of the surgeon'. Barry J construed these words as wide enough to extend consent from the intended dilatation and curettage to cover a total hysterectomy which was performed after fibrosis was found during the operation. (See also *O'Bonsawin v Paradis* (p 482).)

These cases indicate that where there is no consent and where consent cannot be reasonably implied or where the bounds of consent have been exceeded in a non-emergency situation, an action will lie in trespass to the person against the practitioner. Special considerations apply to consent in cases concerning minors, the mentally ill and those in a state of permanent unconsciousness; these specific cases are discussed in Chapter 1.

2. Knowledge of risks

Where the basis of a plaintiff's allegation is that inadequate information was given about the inherent risks of the treatment consented to, the courts have been quick to reject a cause of action in English law based on trespass. Consent is not vitiated by a failure to inform the patient fully of the details of the possible adverse consequences of the proposed operation so as to render the treatment an assault (*Chatterton v Gerson* (1981) (p 275), *Hills v Potter* (1983) (p 380), and *Sidaway v Board of Governors of the Bethlem Royal Hospital and the Maudsley Hospital* (1985) (p 554)). In such cases of alleged failure to disclose inherent risks, any cause of action that might exist has been held to lie in negligence.

It is clear law that part of a practitioner's duty of care is to give advice and information to a patient so that the patient understands the nature of the treatment proposed. The case law, however, illustrates the difficulty in determining just how much information a patient should receive: whether, for example, the curious should be told more than the uninquisitive, whether the doctor has a residual discretion to withhold or even distort information, and whether the standard of care in disclosure cases should be different in therapeutic and non-therapeutic circumstances.

In *Hatcher v Black* (1954) (p 372), the patient was not told that the partial thyroidectomy that she consented to carried a slight risk of permanent impairment in her voice. On the contrary, she was told that there was no risk. The operation left her with a paralysed vocal cord. Lord Denning summed up to the jury in the following way:

'What should a doctor tell a patient? The surgeon has admitted that on the evening before the operation he told the plaintiff that there was no risk to her voice when he knew that there was some slight risk; but that he did it for her own good because it was of vital importance that she should not worry ... he told a lie; but he did it because in the circumstances it was justifiable ... But the law does not condemn the doctor when he only does what a wise doctor so placed would do. And none of the doctors called as witnesses have suggested that the surgeon was wrong. All agreed that it was a matter for his own judgment. If they do not condemn him, why should you.'

The jury returned a verdict for the defendant.

The standard of care implicit in Lord Denning's words to the jury was the one adopted in *Bolam v Friern Hospital Management Committee* (1957) (p 250), where, inter alia, a failure to warn a plaintiff of a slight risk of a fracture occurring during the administration of an ECT was held not to have been negligent because it accorded with a practice adopted by a responsible body of medical opinion. This has come to be called the medical standard of care, and in disclosure cases the test is whether the quantity and quality of information disclosed to a patient is in accord with the practice adopted by either the profession as a whole or any responsible body of opinion within it. Accordingly, where information is generalised or where the risks are minimised or distorted, a defence will exist to an action for negligent disclosure if the practice accords with that of a respectable body of opinion within the profession.

In *Waters v Park* (1961) (p 599), a plaintiff was sterilised in a particular manner which was known to carry a slight risk of failure but which was adopted because of a heart condition from which she suffered. The surgeon's practice was to inform a patient in these circumstances of the failure risk, but he did not tell the plaintiff after the operation because he had no opportunity to do so in privacy on a crowded ward. The defendant gave the plaintiff an appointment, to come back in six weeks when he intended to tell her of the risk. The plaintiff never kept the appointment and she later conceived and required a further sterilisation. Her action failed on the basis that, notwithstanding it was this particular practitioner's practice and intent to disclose the risks to the plaintiff, there were two schools of thought about informing a patient, and in these circumstances the failure to tell the patient did not constitute negligence because there was a responsible body of opinion which would not have informed her in any event.

In *Wells v Surrey Area Health Authority* (1978) (p 600), a thirty-five-year-old Catholic mother, while exhausted during labour with her third child, was offered sterilisation and signed a consent form. She later sued in assault on the grounds that her consent was not valid, because she signed it when she did not realise the implication because of her particular condition. This cause of action failed on the basis that she did know what the complications of signing a consent form were. The hospital, however, were found negligent for failing to give her proper advice and counselling which was an important preliminary to sterilisation.

Bristow J considered in *Chatterton v Gerson* (1981) (p 275) the duty of care owed to a patient in respect of disclosing risks in a proposed treatment, and concurred with the reasoning in *Bolam* and *Hatcher* (above) that the doctor was required to explain what he intended to do, in the way a careful and responsible doctor in similar circumstances would have done. Miss Chatterton suffered from severe pain emanating from an operation scar and sought the defendant's help in alleviating it. She underwent a nerve block operation which failed to stop the pain, and contended she was not warned that this operation could result in numbness and muscle weakness. The first operation was unsuccessful, and a second operation was undertaken with the defendant merely informing the patient that she knew what to expect. This operation not only failed to alleviate the severe pain but also produced a loss of feeling in the right leg. Bristow J held that her claim in trespass failed because the doctor had explained in broad terms the nature of the operation, and her consent was therefore real. He also found that as a matter of fact the plaintiff had been given sufficient information in the circumstances and that the failure to warn about the loss of function in the leg was not unreasonable:

'In my judgment there is no obligation on the doctor to canvass with the patient anything other than the inherent implications of the particular operation he intends to carry out. He is certainly under no obligation to say that if he operates incompetently he will do damage. The fundamental assumption is that he knows his job and will do it properly. But he ought to warn of what may happen by misfortune however well the operation is done, if there is a real risk of misfortune inherent in the procedure, as there was in the surgery of the carotid artery in the Canadian case of *Reibl v Hughes* (1980) (p 521). In what he says, any good doctor has to take into account the personality of the patient, the likelihood of a misfortune, and what in the way of warning is for the particular patient's welfare. I am not satisfied that Dr Gerson fell short of his duty to tell the plaintiff of the implications of this operation, properly carried out ... there was no risk of significant damage to the motor nerves. There was no foreseeable risk that her leg and foot would be deprived of sensation or control, nor am I satisfied that anything done in the course of the second injection caused that result' ([1980] 3 WLR at 1014 c–h).

Similar principles were espoused in *Hills v Potter* (1984) (p 380). Mrs Hills sued for assault and battery and in negligence in respect of paralysis resulting from an operation designed to relieve neck deformity. She claimed that she had not been properly informed of the risks inherent in the operation and that such failure vitiated her consent or alternatively amounted to negligence. Specifically the plaintiff contended that she had not been told of any risk of the possibility of anaesthetic complications, death or paralysis. The defendant doctor, as in *Chatterton* (above), could not remember precisely the warning he gave but thought that it would have been his normal advice which varied according to the ability of the patient to understand it but would have included the risks of death, anaesthetic mishap or paralysis which was likely to be temporary or transient. The judge, Hirst J, found that the defendant had given a detailed explanation of the operation, its risks and complications and this was in full accord with accepted practice. The judge went on to affirm the view that the standard of care applicable to questions of treatment and diagnosis was also that applicable to questions of advice. He rejected the plaintiff's arguments that there should be a higher standard of care in disclosure cases, so that the practitioner had a duty to disclose sufficient information to found the basis of an informed consent as formulated in certain transatlantic cases. Hirst J said that the medical standard must always be one that is upheld by a substantial body of medical opinion which is both respectable, responsible and experienced in the particular field of medicine in issue. On the facts, he went on to indicate that the defendant's conduct would have in any event stood up to the much more rigorous so-called prudent patient test inherent in the doctrine of informed consent.

The House of Lords, in the leading case of *Sidaway v Board of Governors of the Bethlem Royal Hospital and the Maudsley Hospital* (1985) (p 554), further endorsed the approach in *Chatterton* and *Hills*, rejecting the applicability of the doctrine of informed consent. The doctrine, as established in the American case of *Canterbury v Spence* (1972) (p 269) and as discussed in the Canadian cases of *Reibl v Hughes* (1980) (p 521) and *Hopp v Lepp* (1980), postulates that the disclosure of risks should be made to any patient if the risk is material.

'A risk is thus material when a reasonable person, in what the physician knows or should know to be the patient's position would be likely to attach significance to the risk or cluster of risks in deciding whether or not to forgo the proposed therapy' (*Canterbury v Spence* (1972) 464 F 2d at 791).

What constitutes 'materiality' has been discussed in a number of Canadian cases and includes those risks that pose a real threat to life, health and well-being and even a small percentage chance may be determined as material. In *White v Turner* (1981) (p 602) the Ontario High Court, in considering material and special or unusual risks, was of the view that where an operation was elective as in the case of cosmetic surgery even minimal risks ought to be disclosed to patients. This approach, however, has been specifically rejected by the English Court.

In *Sidaway*, the plaintiff suffered from persistent pain in her arms, and during the course of spinal surgery to relieve nerve root pressure the spinal cord was damaged causing severe disablement. The trial judge, Skinner J, found that the surgeon, who had died before the trial, had not told the plaintiff of the risk of spinal cord damage although he had mentioned the possibility of disturbing a nerve root but not damage to the cord itself. Applying the *Bolam* test to the question of disclosure, the judge found that in failing to inform the plaintiff of the possibility of nerve cord damage the surgeon was acting in accord with a responsible body of competent neuro-surgeons who likewise never mentioned such risks so as to avoid frightening a patient. The risk of spinal cord damage was assessed at less than one per cent. The plaintiff's claim failed, and the Court of Appeal affirmed the trial judge's view that the law in relation to failures in diagnosis and treatment also applied to failures in the realm of advice. Lord Donaldson, the Master of the Rolls, reviewed the leading transatlantic cases giving rise to the prudent patient test in the doctrine of informed consent, but declined to incorporate those principles into English law:

'Once it is conceded, as of course it is, that a patient who is of sound mind, sufficient age and capable of exercising a choice is entitled to grant or to withhold consent to treatment as he sees fit, the relationship of doctor and patient must carry with it some duty to give information to the patient which will enable him, if he is minded, to reach a rational decision. The problem is how to define the duty and having defined it, how to determine whether the duty has been discharged ... what information should be disclosed and how and when it should be disclosed is very much a matter for professional judgment, to be exercised in the context of the doctor's relationship with a particular patient in particular circumstances. It is for this reason that I would reject the American formulation of the duty by reference to a "prudent patient" test'. ([1984] 2 WLR at 790–791).

The Master of the Rolls went on to indicate that the general duty of care included disclosing as well as withholding such information as was reasonable in all the circumstances to place the patient in a position to make a rational choice. The adoption of this so-called medical standard implicit in the *Bolam* test was not seen by the Master of the Rolls as abdicating responsibility to the medical profession. The practice held by the body of responsible practitioners had to be one that was rightly and properly held, and the court would not:

'... stand idly by if the profession by an excess of paternalism denies their patients real choice. In a word the law will not allow the medical profession to play God'. ([1984] 2 WLR at 791 g–h).

Lord Justice Browne-Wilkinson thought the American doctrine was rooted in a particular fiduciary relationship between doctor and patient in American law so that breach of relationship vitiated consent. He found no such justification for the doctrine in English law. He went on to formulate a proposition that a doctor was under a duty to disclose to the patient information relevant to the decision the patient would have to take, and this would include the benefits and risks but would be subject to the emotional state of the patient as well as, of course, the degree of risk concerned. There was also an explicit recognition of policy:

'It is inevitable that in considering this case one is acutely aware of the policy problem which it raises. In particular I have been very conscious of the need to ensure that the duty of care imposed by the law is not such as to inhibit the proper function of the medical profession in caring for the sick by exposing doctors to the threat of legal proceedings in which their actions will be judged by hindsight, not by reference to the standards of those skilled in the art, but by judge and jury. It is for this reason that I am not prepared to adopt the much stricter rules as to disclosure laid down in the transatlantic cases which involve an objective judgment both as to the materiality of the risk and the adequacy of the disclosure. It is common knowledge that such rules have led to a large number of claims against doctors based on failure to warn; in consequence, a number of states in the USA have introduced legislation to modify the doctrine of informed consent' ([1984] 2 WLR at 801 a–d).

The House of Lords in *Sidaway* (p 554) affirmed the Court of Appeal's reasoning that the *Bolam* test was applicable in deciding whether a practitioner was negligent in failing to disclose inherent risks in treatment. The House of Lords, by a majority for four to one, indicated that to prove negligence in such cases a plaintiff must show that a practitioner, in failing to warn, fell below the standards of practice regarded as proper by a competent body of professional opinion and accordingly the doctor was not under a duty to warn a patient of any material risk. Only Lord Scarman dissented and embraced a modified version of the doctrine of informed consent:

' ... I think that English law must recognise a duty of the doctor to warn his patient of risk inherent in the treatment which he is proposing; and especially so, if the treatment be surgery. The critical limitation is that this duty is confined to material risk. The test of materiality is whether in the circumstances of the particular case the court is satisfied that a reasonable person in the patient's position will be likely to attach significance to the risk. Even if the risk be material the doctor will not be liable if upon a reasonable assessment of his patient's condition, he takes the view that a warning would be detrimental to his patient's health' ([1985] AC at 889g–890a).

Even applying this test, Lord Scarman would not have allowed the plaintiff's appeal.

Lords Keith, Bridge and Templeman did indicate two glosses, however, on the *Bolam* test. First, their Lordships were of the view that there might be circumstances where treatment involved such a substantial risk of grave consequences that notwithstanding the view of the responsible body of medical opinion, a patient should be told of the risk, as no prudent medical man should refrain from telling the patient of that type of risk:

' ... I am of (the) opinion that the judge might in certain circumstances come to the conclusion that disclosure of a particular risk was so obviously necessary to an informed choice on the part of the patient that no reasonably prudent medical man would fail to make it. The kind of case I have in mind would be an operation involving a substantial risk of grave adverse consequences, as for example, the ten per cent risk of a stroke from the operation which was the subject of the Canadian case of *Reibl v Hughes*. In such a case, in the absence of some cogent clinical reason why the patient should not be informed, a doctor, recognising and respecting his patient's right of decision, could hardly fail to appreciate the necessity for an appropriate warning' (per Lord Bridge [1985] AC at 900 e–g).

Secondly, their Lordships indicated the position may be different if the patient specifically asked about risks:

'No doubt if the patient in fact manifested this attitude (of wishing to be informed of any risk) by means of questioning, the doctor would tell him whatever it was the patient wanted to know; but we are concerned here with voluntary unsought information about risks of the proposed treatment ... ' (per Lord Diplock [1985] AC at 895c).

Lord Bridge also indicated a similar view:

'I should perhaps add at this point, although the issue does not strictly arise in this appeal, that, when questioned specifically by a patient of apparently sound mind about risks involved in a particular treatment proposed, the doctor's duty must, in my opinion, be to answer both truthfully and as fully as the question requires' ([1985] AC at 898 b–c).

Thus in affirming the medical standard of care in disclosure cases, the House of Lords did manage to impose an outer limit on the practitioner's discretion and appear to have smoothed off some of the rougher edges of *Hatcher v Black* (1954) (p 372). It appears that it can no longer be part of the standard of care to lie to a patient in response to direct questioning.

A doubt, however, has been cast upon what appeared to be the clear indications by Lord Bridge and Lord Diplock in *Sidaway* concerning how a doctor should react to specific questioning by the Court of Appeal in *Blyth v Bloomsbury Health Authority* (p 250). Mrs Blyth sued for damages arising out of side effects she suffered from an injection of the contraceptive Depo-Provera. The plaintiff's case was that she was not warned about the side effects apart from irregular bleeding. The trial judge found for the plaintiff, but the Court of Appeal reversed the decision on the basis that the warning given was adequate. At her trial, the plaintiff had insisted that she had asked a series of specific questions. The Court of Appeal dealt with this question in the following way:

'The question of what a plaintiff should be told in answer to a general enquiry cannot be divorced from the *Bolam* test, any more than when no such enquiry is made. In both cases the answer must depend upon the circumstances, the nature of the enquiry, the nature of the information which is available, its reliability, relevance, the condition of the patient and so forth. Any medical evidence directed to what would be the proper answer in the light of responsible medical opinion and practice – that is to say the *Bolam* test – must in my view equally be placed in the balance in cases where the patient makes some enquiry in order to decide whether the response was negligent or not ... Indeed I am not convinced that the *Bolam* test is irrelevant even in relation to the question of what answers are properly to be given to specific enquiries, or that Lord Diplock or Lord Bridge intended to hold otherwise. It seems to me that there may always be grey areas, with difference of opinion, as to what are the proper answers to be given to any enquiry, even a specific one, in the particular circumstances of any case' ((1989) 5 PN 167 at 173 per Kerr LJ).

If this is indeed the law, it would appear that no patient has the absolute right for a comprehensive and truthful answer to a specific request in circumstances where a responsible body of medical opinion would properly contend the patient was unentitled to an honest reply. (Cf the Australian case of *Rogers v Whittaker* (p 532).)

An attempt to establish a different standard of care in cases concerning disclosure and advice in a non-therapeutic setting, as opposed to a therapeutic setting, was made in *Gold v Haringey Health Authority* (1987) (p 355). Mrs Gold was advised to undergo sterilisation after the birth of her third child. The operation was unsuccessful and she became pregnant again. She brought an action alleging, inter alia, a failure to warn her of the rate of unsuccessful sterilisations. She maintained that had she been informed of this failure rate her husband would have opted for a vasectomy instead. Schiemann J heard evidence that a substantial body of medical opinion at the time in question, 1979, would not have warned about the failure rate. If the *Bolam* test was applicable, therefore, the case would fail. The judge however drew a distinction between therapeutic and non-therapeutic settings and found the defendants liable. The Court of Appeal reversed the decision of the trial judge and applied the doctrine of law in *Sidaway* (above) to cover all aspects of the medical relationship, be this advice, diagnosis or treatment. Accordingly, advice in a contraceptive rather than a therapeutic context still fell to be considered within the *Bolam* medical standard of care.

The plaintiff also failed on appeal in *Gold* with respect to an argument accepted by the trial judge that the representation that the operation was irreversible amounted to a misrepresentation because the sterilisation failed. The Court of Appeal held that, as in *Eyre v Measday* (1986) (p 325), the word irreversible was referable to the fact that the operation was incapable of being reversed and not a representation that sterility would be guaranteed (cf *Worster v City and Hackney Health Authority* (1987) (p 612)). The Court of Appeal in *Gold* also distinguished *Thake v Maurice* (1986) (p 579) where a surgeon had been held negligent in not warning the patient about the risk of the failure rate in vasectomy. That case was unusual because expert evidence was not adduced by either side. Accordingly, to succeed in an action in negligence for a failure to warn or advise in respect of risks inherent in a proposed mode of treatment, a plaintiff must show either that no responsible body of competent practitioners in the specialism in issue would fail to disclose the risk or that the risk was so obviously necessary to an informed choice that no prudent practitioner ought to fail to disclose it. It would appear that, in rejecting the prudent patient test the House of Lords in *Sidaway* has given some authority to the prudent practitioner test.

Given this medical standard of care, it is perhaps not surprising that plaintiffs seldom succeed in such actions. In *Sankey v Kensington and Chelsea and Westminster Area Health Authority* (p 545), the plaintiff sued in respect of suffering a stroke following an arteriogram on the grounds that he had not been warned that the procedure carried such a risk. Evidence was accepted that the plaintiff was told that the risks in the operation were higher because of his blood pressure but the word stroke was not used. Expert opinion was accepted that the risk was under 2 per cent and was not substantially increased in the plaintiff's case and in those circumstances there was no need to mention the word stroke. Accordingly the plaintiff's claim failed.

In *Buckle v DeLaunay* (1970) (p 263), a doctor told a patient to whom he had prescribed parnate not to eat cheese or marmite. The plaintiff ate cheese and died. In an action brought by the deceased's husband, an allegation was made that the warning was not adequate because it failed to mention the danger of not complying with the doctor's instructions which could be fatal. The warning however was held to be adequate.

In *O'Malley-Williams v Governors of National Hospital for Nervous Diseases* (1975) (p 484), the plaintiff underwent an aortagram to assist in the diagnosis of loss of vision to the right eye. He was not told of any risk inherent in the procedure. During the course of administering the aortagram, damage was caused which resulted in partial paralysis of the right hand. Bridge J held, inter alia, that the failure to warn of a remote risk where the patient had not raised the question was not negligent. (See also *Moyes v Lothian Health Board* [1990] 1 Med LR 463 where risks in respect of an angiography were properly withheld, and *Heath v West Berkshire Health Authority* [1992] 3 Med LR 57 where a risk in respect of lingual nerve damage occurring during the extraction of a wisdom tooth did not at the time in question have to be disclosed). Plaintiffs may also have evidential difficulties when there is a factual issue as to whether a warning was given or not, particularly when the medical notes indicate that a warning was given (see *McLellan v Newcastle Health Authority* (p 448) and *McInnes v Bromley Health Authority* (p 446)).

A failure to advise on the risk of impotence involved in an ivalon sponge rectopexy operation did, however, lead to a finding of negligence in *Smith v Tunbridge Wells Health Authority* (p 562). Similarly, a failure to warn adequately on an array of risks arising out of brain surgery on a large arteriovascular malformation resulted in a plaintiff recovering damages for a left-sided hemiplegia (*McAllister v Lewisham and North Southwark Health Authority* (p 444).

3. Causation and negligent advice and omissions

If a plaintiff does establish that a practitioner has given inadequate advice or has omitted necessary information to a degree that was negligent, the plaintiff must thereafter persuade the court that had proper information or warnings been given the plaintiff would not have submitted to the therapy.

In *Smith v Barking, Havering and Brentwood Health Authority* (1989) (p 559), the plaintiff did establish a negligent failure to warn where a surgeon did not disclose that an operation to drain a cyst in the upper cervical canal carried with it an approximately twenty-five per cent risk of immediate tetraplegia. Without the operation the plaintiff might have been rendered tetraplegic in about one year, in any event. The operation did result in immediate and irreversible tetraplegia. Hutchison J held that a careful explanation was owed to the plaintiff before the operation, and the doctor had negligently failed to tell her, on the one hand, about the prospect of the twenty-five per cent risk and, on the other hand, the prospect of the risk if surgery was not undertaken. The plaintiff, however, failed to achieve substantial damages, for the judge further found that had proper disclosure been made the plaintiff would have been likely to have agreed to the operation in any event. She was awarded £3,000 for the shock and depression upon discovering without prior warning that she had been rendered tetraplegic. This case vividly illustrates the significance of the prudent practitioner test which the House of Lords in *Sidaway* (above) has imposed on the *Bolam* standard of care in disclosure cases. It also graphically illustrates the Pyrrhic nature of such a victory because, having cleared the hurdle of negligence, plaintiffs in this category of cases frequently fall at the hurdle of causation.

Similarly in *Goorkani v Tayside Health Board* (1991) (p 356), Mr Goorkani successfully established that there had been a negligent failure to warn him that a side effect of chlorambucil taken to prevent him from becoming progressively blind due to Behcet's disease could cause sterility which occurred in his case. The issue therefore became what would have happened had the plaintiff been properly informed of the risk of infertility:

'(Mr Goorkani) stated that if he had been told of the risk he would have discussed the matter with his wife or asked if his sperm could be kept. He further stated today, knowing that he has not gone blind in the interim, he would have chosen the risk of blindness to the risk of infertility. However, I consider that it is clear from the pursuer's evidence that this is being wise after the event and reviewing matters for the benefit of hindsight. In re-examination he was asked whether it would have made a difference if he had been told that if he did not take the drug he might go blind, but that if he took the drug he would be infertile and his reply was that he could not say what view he would have taken when he was younger ... Having regard to the whole evidence on this matter, I am not satisfied that the pursuer would have declined treatment by means of a drug or would have sought sperm banking' (per Lord Cameron [1991] 3 Med LR 33 at 38).

The plaintiff was therefore awarded restricted damages of £2,500 for the shock, anger, marital frustration and cultural shame arising out of the sudden shock of the discovery. (See also *Gregory and Gregory v Pembrokeshire Health Authority* (1989) (p 361).

Conversely in *Gowton v Wolverhampton Health Authority* (p 358) a negligent failure to advise Mr Gowton that he might become fertile again following a vasectomy notwithstanding negative results from a semen analysis, did result in damages being awarded when his wife subsequently became pregnant. The trial judge accepted on the balance of probabilities that Mrs Gowton would have continued to take the contraceptive pill had a proper warning been given. (See also *Smith v Tunbridge Wells Health Authority* (1994) (p 562) and *McAllister v Lewisham and North Southwark Health Authority* (p 444)). In *Sidaway v Bethlem Royal Hospital Governors* (1985) (p 554) the trial judge did accept that if the plaintiff had been told of the risk she would have declined the treatment. Generally speaking, however, particularly when plaintiffs are relatively ill and in pain or discomfort their cases tend to fail on this issue of causation (see *Hills v Potter* (p 380), *Chatterton v Gerson* (p 275)). For Canadian cases which have a seemingly high success rate see *Coughlin v Kuntz* (p 275), *Zimmer v Ringrose* (p 615). In the Australian case of *Rogers v Whittaker* (p 532) an ophthalmic surgeon was found negligent for failing to disclose a risk of 1 in 14,000 arising out of an operation on the plaintiff's right eye which could lead to blindness in the left eye (sympathetic ophthalmia). Mrs Whittaker made it plain she wished to know about possible complications in what was an elective operation, the right eye being injured almost 40 years previously. The court found the doctor had failed to answer her questions with proper care and skill and was also satisfied that if the risk had been disclosed the plaintiff would not have had the operation which left her blind.

4. Informing after the event

If a medical mishap does occur, the practitioner is most likely under a legal duty to explain to the patient what has occurred. Accordingly in *Gerber v Pines* (1934) (p 351), a doctor was found liable to a patient not because a needle broke during the course of an injection but because he failed timeously to inform the plaintiff that part of the needle had been left in her body. Du Parcq J found that there had been a breach of duty for not informing the plaintiff at once of what happened. Similarly, in *Cooper v Miron* (1927) (p 287) a dentist was found negligent for failing to inform a patient that part of one of her molars had broken off and disappeared down her throat.

A former Master of the Rolls, Sir John Donaldson, has also stipulated that it is part of a practitioner's duty to inform patients of what treatment they actually did receive, and in principle there appears to be nothing offensive to a patient seeking this information by an action for specific performance of such a duty to inform

(*Lee v South West Thames Regional Health Authority* (1985) (p 428), *Naylor v Preston Area Health Authority* (1987) (p 478). In *Naylor*, the Master of the Rolls expressed the following view:

> 'I personally think that in professional negligence cases, and in particular in medical negligence cases, there is a duty of candour resting upon the professional man. This is recognised by the legal professions in their ethical rules requiring their members to refer the client to other advisors, if it appears that the client has a valid claim for negligence. This also appears to be recognised by the Medical Defence Union, whose view is that "the patient is entitled to a prompt, sympathetic and above all truthful account of what has occurred": Journal of the Medical Defence Union, Spring 1987, p 23' ([1987] 1 WLR at 967 e–g).

A failure to inform a plaintiff that an abortion had failed led to liability and damages being awarded in *Scuriaga v Powell* (p 548). (See also the Canadian cases *Cryderman v Ringrose* and *Stamos v Davies* (p 564).)

Chapter 10

Substandard treatment

Most medical malpractice actions derive from accidents occasioned during the course of treatment or during after-care. In a review of five hundred cases contained within the Medical Protection Society files, Leahy-Taylor, in *The Doctor and Negligence* (Pitman Medical, 1971) ch 4, formed the view that the most common incidents concerning allegations of substandard treatment arose in cases involving retained swabs and other instruments after operations, burns, anaesthetic mishaps and cases where the wrong operation was performed. The vast bulk of such cases never get to trial. The following illustrative categories of substandard care are not intended to be exhaustive but they do reflect the type of case that has tended to be litigated in the past and accordingly demonstrate the approach of the courts in certain factual situations.

1. Surgical and allied mishaps

The House of Lords confirmed in *Whitehouse v Jordan* (1981) (p 604) that the *Bolam* test was applicable to errors in the course of treatment procedures including childbirth and surgery. It is axiomatic that not every mistake or error during the course of an operation or treatment programme will amount to negligence. If the practitioner can establish that he was acting within a mode of practice that was accepted as proper by a responsible body of practitioners and that he was using the requisite degree of skill and care during the administering of the treatment, he would not be liable for a mistake that occurred. In *Whitehouse*, the Court of Appeal reversed the decision of Bush J who found that Mr Jordan had delayed for too long before delivering a child by caesarean section and had pulled too hard and for too long with forceps. The House of Lords confirmed the Court of Appeal's ruling and in effect found that no error had been made by Mr Jordan, in the same way that no error had been made in the case of *Bolam*.

Where, however, errors have been found as facts, they quite frequently fall into a category of mistake which occurred notwithstanding the exercise of ordinary care and skill. In *Mose v North West Hertfordshire Health Authority* (1987) (p 463), a consultant orthopaedic surgeon operated to remove what was thought to be a cyst behind a child's right knee. The operation in fact revealed a tumour, and in removing the tumour three inches of the popliteal nerve was also removed, leading to a complete foot drop. The trial judge found that the surgeon had been negligent because he was not a person who was experienced in this type of work. Evidence was adduced that if an inexperienced surgeon discovered these circumstances the proper course would have been to have closed the wound and call a specialist surgeon to investigate. The Court of Appeal reversed this finding on the basis that the surgeon was in fact experienced in this type of work and was entitled to conduct the operation.

An issue as to the competence and experience of the surgeon arose in the case of *Burgess v Newcastle Health Authority* (1992) (p 264). A registrar undertook a bilateral shunt operation to relieve hydrocephalus which followed from an operation to remove a cyst in the patient's brain. The plaintiff suffered a right sided hemiplegia and alleged that the technique used to insert the catheter was not one that would be practised or approved by any responsible body of neurosurgeons and the stilette which was used to carry the catheter penetrated too deeply into the skull and ended in brain substance. The trial judge found that the doctor was competent to perform such an operation, the technique adopted of not moving the head during the operation was acceptable to a body of respected neurosurgeons and that the cannula did not penetrate too deeply. In those circumstances the bilateral shunt operation although imperfect was not due to any fault on the part of the registrar.

In *Ratty v Haringay Health Authority* (p 518), the Court of Appeal reversed a trial judge's finding of negligence in circumstances where a surgeon, having found a large mass in the pelvis whilst undertaking an operation, performed an abdomino-perineal resection in the belief that the patient had cancer. Subsequently it emerged that a hole had been caused in the bladder during the course of the operation, and a further operation was required to repair that hole. It was later revealed that the plaintiff in fact was suffering only from diverticulitis. The Court of Appeal found that the trial judge incorrectly found negligence because evidence from the defendants' consultants, whose standing and credibility was never in dispute, both considered that the surgeon had been right to perform the resection. The Court of Appeal did, however, concur with the trial judge's findings that there had been inadequate repair of the bladder and the plaintiff was awarded a sum of £5,000 in respect of damage arising out of that failure to properly repair. In *Yerex v Bloomsbury Health Authority* (1990) (p 614), the Court of Appeal upheld the trial judge's finding that the perforation of a bowel wall by a sigmoidoscope did not necessarily indicate negligence in a case where a 91-year-old plaintiff subsequently developed peritonitis and died.

In *White v Board of Governors of Westminster Hospital* (1961) (p 601), a surgeon who was operating on a child's squint inadvertently cut the retina while severing muscle and tendon attached by scar tissue. The eye shrank and had to be removed. The plaintiff was held to be a victim of mischance rather than of negligence. The scale of the operation was so fine that an error like this could occur notwithstanding that due skill, care and judgment had been exercised. In *O'Malley-Williams v Governors of National Hospital for Nervous Diseases* (1975) (p 484), an aortagram under a local anaesthetic proved difficult to administer. An attempt to pass the guide-wire through the femoral artery was abandoned and several attempts were required to pass it through the right axillary artery during which great pain was occasioned to the plaintiff. Bridge J held it was not negligent to continue to try to pass the wire because pain was not uncommon during this procedure under local anaesthetic. The plaintiff accordingly failed in his claim for damages arising out of partial paralysis of the right hand caused by nerve damage during the passing of the wire. In *Crawford v Board of Governors of Charing Cross Hospital* (1951) (p 293), no negligence was established against a doctor who had kept an arm extended at an angle of eighty degrees from the body during a transfusion. The result was a brachial palsy in the only good arm the plaintiff had. Knowledge that this was a dangerous method had only appeared in *The Lancet* six months previously.

A failure of aftercare was asserted in the case of *Hughes v Waltham Forest Health Authority* (1991) (p 393), in circumstances where a substantial leakage of bile occurred through a drain tube following the removal of the gall bladder. The trial judge found that the cause of this leakage was that a stone blocked the lower end of the common bile duct causing pressure to build up within the biliary tree and forcing bile out of the ligature tear of the cystic duct. This fistula in the cystic duct was not detected on ultrasound. However at the hospital a technique known as endoscopic retrograde cholangio-pancreatocogram (ERCP) was available but a decision was made not to use it. This technique would have allowed a viewing of the inside of the common bile duct. The trial judge was satisfied that it was negligent not to use the ERCP and it was further negligent to discharge the plaintiff before normal function had been demonstrated as indicated by other tests. The Court of Appeal once again reversed the trial judge's finding, on the basis that the decision not to refer for ERCP at the particular time was in accord with a practice accepted as proper and a similar line of reasoning was applied to the decision to allow the plaintiff to be discharged. The Court of Appeal also concluded that on the balance of probability the plaintiff's subsequent death less than two months later had not been caused by the failure to carry out the ERCP. (See also *De Freitas v O'Brien* (1993) (p 305).)

Conversely, in *Patten v Birmingham Regional Hospital Board* (1955) (p 492) a house surgeon who not only removed part of the wrong finger but also failed in time to stitch the fingers requiring treatment was found liable for the damage sustained to the hand. In *Cassidy v Ministry of Health* (1951) (p 272) a plaintiff, left with a virtually useless hand after an operation to relieve Dupuytrens contracture, established liability after the maxim res ipsa loquitur was held to apply. In *Saunders v Leeds Western Health Authority* (1984) (p 546), a four-year-old suffered a cardiac arrest while being operated upon. The doctrine res ipsa loquitur was held to apply, and the defendants failed to rebut the presumption of negligence. In *Croke v Wiseman* (1982) (p 294), the defendants admitted liability where an infant plaintiff suffered a cardio-respiratory failure while doctors were examining him. In *Wilsher v Essex Area Health Authority* (1988) (p 609) and in *Murray v Kensington and Chelsea and Westminster Area Health Authority* (1981) (p 406), negligence was established where babies were administered with excessive volumes of oxygen. In *Murray* no causation was established, and in *Wilsher* the House of Lords ordered a retrial on the question of causation. Negligence was also established in *Blackburn v Newcastle-upon-Tyne Health Authority* (1988) (p 249) when a plaintiff suffered severe brain damage after a tracheostomy tube became blocked with secretions. Either the medical or the nursing staff were negligent in failing to keep the tube clear.

In *Bovenzi v Kettering Health Authority* (1991) (p 256), a registrar was found to have been negligent when during the course of a D & C he gripped onto and pulled down on a piece of small bowel necessitating emergency resection. For this to happen, the forceps must have been clear of the wall of the uterus by approximately three inches. In *Winterbone v West Suffolk Health Authority* (p 608), the stitching of the bladder to the vaginal vault resulting in a fistula was found to have been caused by negligence. In *Munro v Oxford United Hospital* (p 465), the slipping of a gag during a tonsillectomy resulting in a plaintiff losing four teeth was found to be due to the negligence of the surgeon in preventing the gag from slipping. In *Ellinger v Riverside Health Authority* (1993) (p 320), negligence was conceded in a case where a plaintiff undergoing a minor operation for removal of a lump on her neck suffered a partial left accessory nerve lesion. (See also *Sandell v Worthing Health Authority* (p 544).)

The borderline between a negligent and a non-negligent mistake or error of judgment can be difficult to draw.. (See *Whitehouse v Jordan* (1981) (p 604) for the classic exposition of this distinction). Kilner-Brown J was faced with clear anguish in *Ashcroft v Mersey Regional Health Authority* (1983) (p 229) when he observed:

> 'This claim reveals a disgraceful state of affairs. Where an injury is caused which should never have been caused common sense and natural justice indicate that some degree of compensation ought to be paid by someone. As the law stands, in order to obtain compensation an injured person is compelled to allege negligence against a surgeon who may, as in this case, be a careful, dedicated person of the highest skill and reputation. If ever there was a case in which some reasonable compromise was called for, which would provide some amount of solace for the injured person, and avoid the pillorying of a distinguished surgeon, this was such a case' ([1983] 2 All ER 246 a–b).

The trial judge went on to find for the surgeon, after applying the *Bolam* test in respect of an operation to remove granulated tissue from an eardrum. This was a routine operation for the surgeon, which he had undertaken hundreds of times and had never caused the damage which was occasioned to the plaintiff, namely a severe paralysis of the facial nerve. The judge concluded:

> ' ... I am faced with the agonising question of deciding whether the probabilities are such that I am driven to say of Mr Siegler (the surgeon) that he has convinced himself that he did not use too much force when in fact he must have done so. It is not an easy problem and is a question of whether the proper inferences drawn from the primary facts are such that on this occasion Mr Siegler's belief in his carefulness is misplaced and that he did fall below the standard of care expected of him. In the end I have come to the conclusion that I cannot go so far.'

Leahy-Taylor (above) provides examples of much clearer cases which have led to settlement. These cases are derived from files and not from reported hearings. They include examples of a patient's healthy testicle being removed in a mistaken belief that it was part of a hernial mass, an amputation being necessary following the ligation of a femoral artery during an operation for a varicose vein, the snipping of a new born baby's finger whilst cutting the umbilical cord, fatal accidents resulting from a patient being given the wrong type of blood, and a death caused by the application of Nupercaine jelly into a patient's anus in the mistaken belief it was Lignocaine. (See also *Waghorn v Lewisham and North Southwark Area Health Authority* (1987) (p 594), *H v Ministry of Defence* (p 362), *Cavanagh v Bristol and Weston Health Authority* (p 273), *Doughty v North Staffordshire Health Authority* (p 311).

The increasing use of laparoscopic surgery (so-called key-hole surgery or minimally invasive surgery) has been described as the single biggest change in surgical practice this century. (See M Hobsley and J Scurr 'General Surgery' in Powers and Harris, ch 33, p 894). The technique used first by gynaecologists is now widely adopted by general surgeons, and as a result claims are being brought in respect of inadvertent damage caused by the instrument. Hobsley and Scurr expressed the following view:

> 'The majority of surgeons performing these procedures have had little experience in laparoscopic techniques. Some have attended courses; many have started the

procedure having read a single account. When a surgeon experiences a complication with laparoscopic surgery, it is important to establish, firstly, the experience of the surgeon, his familiarity with the technique, and in particular, the advice and information he gave to the patient before starting ... No competent and responsible surgeon will undertake these procedures without first establishing that they are safe, that he has sufficient experience to undertake them and that he has a full understanding and working knowledge of how to manage any complications which may arise. Any surgeon embarking upon these procedures without these qualifications would be considered negligent if complications arose' (Powers and Harris; p 894).

2. Needles and injections

Given the frequency of suturing and the routine use of injections in medical treatment, it is not surprising that mishaps occur which frequently give rise to allegations of negligence. The mere breaking of the needle of a hypodermic syringe is probably not indicative of negligence. In *Brazier v Ministry of Defence* (1965) (p 259), McNair J did, however, find that the breaking of a needle which remained lodged in the right buttock of the plaintiff required explanation. Mr Brazier alleged the one and a half inch fine needle broke because the ship's doctor treated it in a dagger-like fashion and stabbed him with it. This was rejected, and the defendant's explanation that a latent defect in the shaft of the needle caused the breaking was accepted.

In *Gerber v Pines* (1934) (p 351), a needle broke during an injection into the gluteus maximus muscle, and the defendant, a general practitioner, failed to inform the plaintiff. The broken part was removed five days later. The trial judge found no negligence in the administration of the injection but did find there had been a failure in disclosing to the plaintiff that part of a needle remained in her.

In *Corner v Murray* (1954) (p 289), a patient was left with most of the needle in situ after it broke while the doctor was extracting it. The trial judge accepted evidence that the breaking of a hypodermic needle was not an uncommon occurrence and could occur, as on this occasion, without any semblance of negligence.

Similarly, a schoolgirl failed in her action against a nurse, following the breaking of a number sixteen needle while injecting her thigh, which left approximately an inch of the needle in the patient. The trial judge dismissed the allegation that a longer and thicker needle should have been used as this would have caused more pain, and attributed the accident to an unexpected movement on the plaintiff's part as opposed to any act of pushing the needle in too far (*Marchant v East Ham Borough Council* (1955) (p 452)).

In *Hunter v Hanley* (1955) (p 396), an allegation that a needle used was too thin and fragile and that it had been withdrawn at a different angle from that at which it had been put in was rejected by the jury. (This matter was sent on appeal for retrial after a misdirection by the trial judge as to the standard of care).

Although it may not be negligent if the needle breaks whilst in use, failure to cope adequately with the consequences can of course give rise to liability. In *Henderson v Henderson* (1955) (p 376), a surgeon broke the needle whilst stitching a girl's throat after a tonsillectomy, leaving approximately one half of an inch in the throat. The surgeon made efforts with his finger and with a scalpel to find the fragment and made an incision when he thought he had located it. The search went on unsuccessfully for approximately one hour. The result was that the child suffered scarring of the throat. The needle was eventually extracted by an electro-magnet at another hospital. The trial judge found the surgeon negligent for persisting with the search.

Prospects of succeeding in such actions appear slightly better when it is proved that the injection was entered in the wrong place or was extravenous when intended to be intravenous. Liability was proved in *Caldeira v Gray* (1936) (p 269) where a quinine injection resulted in damage to the sciatic nerve causing immediate lameness. Liability was conceded in *Daly v Wolverhampton Health Authority* (1986) (p 298), where an injection caused a permanent neuroma after damaging a nerve or blood vessel.

McNair J in *Hayward v Curwen* (1964) (p 373) found neither negligence nor causation proved in a case where, following the injection of colchicine into the plaintiff's left arm, which caused no pain, the plaintiff developed median nerve palsy. The judge found that the correct vein had been chosen, that the manner of the injection was appropriate and it was not proved that any of the drug had been injected outside the vein.

In *Prout v Crowley* (1956) (p 498), an extravenous injection did occur after the needle came out of a vein, allowing a small quantity of ferrivenin to penetrate surrounding tissue and to cause an abscess. The trial judge held that this happened without negligence and that, when it did happen the doctor followed the correct procedure of applying a poultice as soon as he realised the mishap.

The Court of Appeal upheld an appeal in a similar set of circumstances in *Williams v North Liverpool Hospital Management Committee* (1959) (p 607). Here pentothal was inadvertently extravenously injected into what was described as an exceedingly fat arm in which the vein was difficult to find. The plaintiff sued in respect of the abscesses that resulted, and the trial judge found for her. The Court of Appeal reversed the decision, indicating that the doctor had taken all reasonable steps to ensure the needle was intravenous. The patient had not complained of pain and there was nothing to put him on notice that he had in fact missed the vein.

The Court of Appeal declined, however, to interfere with the trial judge's finding in *Walker v South Surrey District Health Authority* (1982) (p 596), where a nurse injected pethidine into the inside of a plaintiff's leg causing damage to a superficial nerve. The court determined that no careful nurse or doctor would have chosen such a site without compelling reasons. Puncturing the gall bladder while attempting a liver biopsy using a 6.7 inch needle was held to be negligent in *Carter v City and Hackney Health Authority* (1994) (p 270).

Injecting a patient at the wrong time may also give rise to liability, if there are contra-indications which normally would cause the skilful doctor to wait. In *King v King* (1987) (p 415), the plaintiff was administered the second of a combined vaccination against cholera and typhoid by his general practitioner at a time when he appeared excited and had a boil in front of his ear. Six hours later, he suffered a stroke rendering him hemiplegic. The trial judge's finding that the doctor had been negligent in injecting his patient at a time when he had a temperature was rejected by the Court of Appeal. There was no proof that the excited state indicated a raised temperature, nor did the boil constitute a contra-indication.

In *Hothi v Greenwich Health Authority* (1982) (p 389), no negligence was found where a patient was administered with an anti-convulsant drug after exhibiting signs of epilepsy. Unknown to the defendants, the plaintiff was suffering from a rare form of allergy to the drug which was deemed unforeseeable. In *Robinson v*

Post Office (1974) (p 528), a doctor was negligent in the timing of his anti-tetanus serum injections but no damage followed from his negligence.

Leahy-Taylor (above, ch 4) describes, inter alia, cases that reached negotiated settlements where an iron preparation was injected into the deltoid area of the arm against the manufacturer's recommendation that it should have been administered into the buttocks, and where a child who was vaccinated during a quiescent phase of eczema developed generalised vaccinia producing keloid scarring. (See also the Canadian cases of *Mitchell v McDonald* (1987) (p 459) and *Cardin v City of Montreal* ((1961) 29 DLR (2d) 492) where a doctor was found negligent for persisting in attempting to vaccinate a child, in the face of a mother's advice that she would return on another day when the child was calmer. See also *Tate v West Cornwall and Isles of Scilly Health Authority* (p 576), where liability was admitted following the injection of phenol into the sub-arachnoid space causing paraplegia.)

3. Drugs and anaesthetic accidents

The administration of an incorrect volume of the drug, including anaesthetics, will often give rise to liability. Frequently the mishap arises from a breakdown in communication between the practitioner who prescribed the drug and the practitioner who administered it. In *Collins v Hertfordshire County Council* (1947) (p 283), a junior house surgeon misheard a consultant's prescription and ordered from the pharmacist cocaine instead of procaine. As a result the patient was administered with a lethal dose. Hilbery J found the house surgeon, consultant and hospital liable. Similarly, where nurses misread a prescription and administered a lethal six ounces of paraldehyde instead of six drachms, they acted negligently (*Strangways-Lesmere v Clayton* (1936) (p 569)). A ward sister was also found negligent for allowing four extra injections of streptomycin over and above the thirty prescribed to a patient who as a consequence suffered permanent loss of balance (*Smith v Brighton and Lewes Hospital Management Committee* (1958) (p 559)).

In *Dwyer v Rodrick* (1983) (p 316), a general practitioner and a pharmacist were held negligent for diagnosing and dispensing a wholly inappropriate prescription of sixty Migril tablets, two to be taken every four hours as necessary, in respect of a patient suffering from migraine. The prescription was an obvious error and the pharmacist who dispensed the prescription failed to notice the error. The patient suffered gangrenous necrosis after taking thirty-six tablets in six days. Liability was apportioned 45% to the doctor and 55% to the chemist.

In *Prendergast v Sam and Dee Ltd* (1989) (p 497), the Court of Appeal upheld the trial judge's finding against a doctor and a chemist when a prescription of Amoxil was dispensed as Daonil. The pharmacist had made the error because the general practitioner's handwriting was poor enough to invite misreading. The trial judge held that the doctor's writing did amount to negligence because it reasonably permitted the misreading, but also the pharmacist was negligent in failing to comprehend the incompatibility of Daonil given the other items that were on the prescription. Liability was apportioned 25% to the doctor and 75% to the chemist.

In *Junor v McNicol* (1959) (p 407), a failure to ensure an infant patient was given a suitable amount of penicillin was described as a mistake. The doctor who dispensed the penicillin, however, was held not to be acting outside the instructions of the consultant surgeon and was not negligent. In *Vernon v Bloomsbury Health Authority* (1986) (p 593), Tucker J rejected the plaintiff's allegation that she had been given an excessive quantity of gentamicin for an overly long period and found that the doctor had acted in conformance with a proper mode of treatment. (See also *Ackers v Wigan Health Authority* (1986) (p 221), *Jacobs v Great Yarmouth and Waveney Health Authority* (1984) (p 399).) A massive overdose in the order of a factor of thirty of penicillin in *Kay's Tutor v Ayrshire and Arran Health Board* (1987) (p 410) led to an admission of negligence, but the infant plaintiff failed to prove that his profound deafness was due to the consequence of the toxic effect of the penicillin.

An over-hasty withdrawal from prescribed drugs gave rise to liability in *Hatwell v South West Metropolitan Regional Hospital Board* (1975) (p 372), where a plaintiff had Seconal and Valium immediately withdrawn by a psychiatrist upon admission to hospital. As a consequence the plaintiff suffered from violent tremors and had an epileptic fit during which she sustained a fractured jaw. Actions concerning side-effects caused by drugs are principally against the manufacturers of the drug companies (cf Opren, *Nash v Eli Lilly* (1993); Myodil, *Chrzanowska v Glaxo Laboratories* (1990) (p 278), Benzodiazepine (Valium), Ativan, Halcion, *AB v John Wyeth* (1992) (p 218)) but clearly failures to warn a patient adequately about the side-effects of drugs can give rise to liability on the part of the practitioner (cf *Goorkani v Tayside Health Board* (p 356)).

Anaesthetic accidents figure very largely in medical negligence cases due to the combination of powerful drugs and invasive equipment used during anaesthesia creating a very small margin for error which can result in severe brain damage or death. (See M Rosen and JN Horton, Chapter 32, Powers and Harris). Brain damage can occur following hypoxia, nerve injuries can be sustained due to poor positioning, awareness can occur due to a failure of anaesthetic and quite often damage is done to teeth whilst using the laryngoscope during intubation.

Where anaesthetic mishaps give rise to severe permanent brain damage they frequently raise the application of the maxim res ipsa loquitur. In *Coyne v Wigan Health Authority* (1991) (p 292) a plaintiff became severely hypoxic following extubation after an operation to remove a swelling from the parotid gland. The defendants conceded that the doctrine res ipsa loquitur applied, but sought to argue that the hypoxia was caused due to a silent regurgitation of gastric content. The judge rejected this explanation and found that the plaintiff's cyanosis occurred during extubation. (See also *Thomas v Wignall* (1987) (p 581) and *Saunders v Leeds Western Health Authority* (1984) (p 546).

In *Gray v Mid Herts Group Hospital Management Committee* (1974) (p 359), a young boy suffered extensive brain damage and eventual death following a cardiac arrest during the course of a routine operation. Waller J found that the anaesthetist was negligent in failing to monitor adequately the boy's pulse and breathing pattern. In *Voller v Portsmouth Corpn* (1947) (p 594), a plaintiff who contracted meningitis following a spinal injection established liability on the basis that there must have been some defect in the hospital's aseptic technique and that such an infection could not have arisen without negligence on the hospital's part (see also *Connolly v Camden and Islington Area Health Authority* (1981) (p 285), *Moser v Enfield and Haringey Area Health Authority* (1982) (p 463) and *Cunningham v Camberwell Health Authority* (1988) (p 296), *Corbett v Barking, Havering and Brentwood Health Authority* (p 288), *Routledge v McKenzie and Shires* (p 535), *Tombs v Merton and Sutton Area Health Authority, Ritchie v Chichester Health Authority* (p 525) and cases which result in criminal convictions for manslaughter: *R v Adomako* (p 499), *R v Sargeant* (p 513), *M v Prentice and Shulman*).

ANAESTHETIC AWARENESS

The courts in recent years have dealt with a number of claims arising out of so-called anaesthetic awareness, where patients are conscious during the course of an operation and so appreciate what is being done to them but are unable to communicate because of the paralysing effect of the anaesthetic agents they have received. Neuromuscular blocking drugs were not available before the early 1940s, and this probably explains the absence of claims concerning anaesthetic awareness before that time. In *Phelan v East Cumbria Health Authority* (p 494) liability was admitted where a plaintiff not only became conscious during the operation but felt pain during the drilling of his leg. Liability was also admitted in the case of *Davies v Mid Glamorgan Health Authority* (p 301).

Liability was established in *Kewley v Blackpool Wyre and Fylde Health Authority* (p 412) where a plaintiff regained consciousness during a caesarean section. The trial judge found that the practice of turning off a volatile anaesthetic agent isoflurane after the baby had been clamped or delivered was negligent. Liability was eventually admitted in the case of *Esson v Gloucester Health Authority (No 2)* (1994) (p 323) where a plaintiff became conscious during a laparotomy and experienced excruciating pain while being poked prodded and kneaded inside her abdomen.

In *Taylor v Worcester and District Health Authority* (1991) (p 578), McKinnon J found for the defendants in respect of an action brought for anaesthetic awareness during a caesarean section, on the grounds that the technique used was perfectly reasonable and had an incidence of awareness of less than 0.35%. There was no evidence to suggest that the technique had been carried out in other than a careful and competent manner, and the trial judge also was of the view that the plaintiff's claimed episode of awareness was in fact not one which took place during the operation but after reversal. Similarly in *Early v Newham Health Authority* (1994) (p 317) a failure to intubate at the first attempt led to a standard drill being carried out, which resulted in the plaintiff gaining consciousness at a time when her body was still paralysed due to suxamethonium. The trial judge found that it was not negligent to fail to intubate at the first attempt and the standard drill was a reasonable one to adopt, because although it ran the risk of a transient terror of the patient being conscious whilst still paralysed that was a better risk to run than one of hypoxia.

An earlier case of anaesthetic awareness occurred in *Ackers v Wigan Area Health Authority* (1986) (p 221), where a plaintiff received damages following a negligent failure to anaesthetise her during a caesarean section. Mrs Ackers was paralysed by a pre-operative relaxant, but was conscious and receptive to sensation during the one and a quarter hour operation during which she was not able to communicate her plight to the medical or nursing staff. In *Jacobs v Great Yarmouth and Waveney Health Authority* (1984) (p 399) a similar type of claim was not proved. Mrs Jacobs alleged a negligent administering of anaesthetic for an operation for a hysterectomy resulting in her being conscious but paralysed right up until the first incision. The Court of Appeal held that the trial judge was justified in concluding that the plaintiff had been mistaken and had transposed her pre-operative and post-operative states of consciousness.

CASES OF NO NEGLIGENCE

Not all mishaps will amount to negligence. In *Roe v Minister of Health* (1954) (p 531), the contamination of the anaesthetic was due to an unknown and unforeseen consequence of fractures in the glass ampoules which did not give rise to a foreseeable risk. In *Moore v Lewisham Group Hospital Management Committee* (1959) (p 460), a spinal anaesthetic was administered in circumstances where a body of medical opinion thought it should not be undertaken. However, evidence was received that an alternative body of medical opinion considered that it was a proper procedure. Barry J expressed sentiments which had been heard before and since:

> 'The courts could do no greater disservice to the community or the advancements of medical science than to place the hallmark of legality upon one form of treatment as opposed to another when there was difference of informed medical opinion as to their merits.'

In *Delaney v Southmead Health Authority* (1992) (p 307) the Court of Appeal rejected the argument that the doctrine res ipsa loquitur applied, in circumstances where a lesion to the brachial plexus was diagnosed following an operation of the removal of a gall bladder. The plaintiff contended that such an injury should not have occured if there had been proper positioning of the plaintiff's arm by the anaesthetist surgeon during the course of the operation. The Court of Appeal accepted the evidence of the surgeon and anaesthetist that in fact the arm was in the correct position throughout the operation and accordingly that they had exercised all reasonable care.

In *Davis v Barking, Havering and Brentwood Health Authority* (1993) (p 302) a plaintiff sued in respect of injury sustained during the administration of a caudal block following a general anaesthetic in respect of an operation for marsupialisation of a Bartholian cyst. During the course of the trial allegations of negligence were abandoned but it was contended that a separate consent would have been given both to the general and the local anaesthetic. The trial judge rejected such an assertion indicating that the consent form actually signed was appropriate to the circumstances of the operation and to insist upon separate consent forms being signed for separate modes of anaesthesia during the same operation was to encourage so called sectionalised consent and encourage actions to be brought in trespass which should in fact be brought in negligence.

4. Retained surgical products

The Medical Defence Union in a chapter headed 'Perennial Pitfalls' in their 1983 annual report indicated that some 203 cases were reported to it from all over the world in respect of a variety of retained foreign bodies left in patients which included 70 instruments, 54 swabs and 23 sutures (see Giesen 1988, p 139, n 79). Giesen provides interesting examples of tissues, swabs, sponges, packs, clamps, wires, tubes and forceps which illustrate the familiarity of this type of claim. It will be appreciated that once a plaintiff has proved that the retained body was left in as a result of the operation or treatment undertaken by the defendants, a good prospect of establishing liability arises. Accordingly most of these types of cases are settled (cf Leahy-Taylor (above) for such examples involving a swab left in after a caesarian operation, a drain tube left in after a mastectomy, and a Spencer Wells clip left in after an operation).

Reported cases frequently concern the separate liabilities of the surgeon and the nursing staff. This distinction took on great significance before the development of the doctrine of vicarious liability on the part of the hospital. In 1931 the Court of Appeal refused to interfere with the jury's finding of negligence against a surgeon following the leaving of a surgical pack measuring eight inches by ten inches in a patient's body after a gall-stone operation (*James v Dunlop* (1931) (p 401)). Five years later a doctor who inadvertently left a surgical gauze in a patient was found to be negligent in *Dryden v Surrey County Council* (1936) (p 314). In *Mahon v Osborne* (1939) (p 449), the Court of Appeal ordered a retrial where a judge directed the jury that a surgeon in all abdominal operations had the duty of searching to ensure that all swabs had been removed. The test was deemed to be whether the surgeon had exercised reasonable skill and care, and this was to be determined in the light of all the circumstances of the particular case. By a majority the court held that the maxim res ipsa loquitur applied.

In *Garner v Morrell* the Court of Appeal in 1963 upheld a finding of negligence in circumstances where during the course of an operation a throat pack which had been inserted into Mr Garner's mouth was swallowed or inhaled by him, and as a result he died of asphyxia. The defendants were held negligent on the basis that the throat pack was too short. In *Urry v Bierer* (1955) (p 591), a ten-inch surgical pack was left in a woman after a caesarian operation. The Court of Appeal rejected the surgeon's appeal which contended that he was entitled to rely on the nurse's count.

In 1961 the Privy Council in *Cooper v Nevill* (p 287) determined that the leaving of a swab inside a patient obviously amounted to a mistake but it did not necessarily amount to negligence. The medical and nursing staff might be, in certain circumstances, engaged in an emergency race against time. It might accordingly be negligence in certain circumstances to search for a swab that is known to be missing if the patient's life is in grave danger. However, in *Cooper* there was no evidence to indicate precisely what type of mistake had in fact occurred. The Privy Council found the trial judge was justified in finding that whether it was a mopping or restraining pack the surgical team had been negligent.

Similar considerations apply to other retained products. It is most likely that the maxim res ipsa loquitur will apply but it cannot be said in advance of the facts whether the defendants will be able to rebut the presumption of negligence. In *Morris v Winsbury-White* (1937) (p 462), the maxim was held not to apply as the hospital was deemed not to be vicariously liable for the surgeon, and on the particular facts of that case the tube that was left in the patient's body could have been left in by the operating surgeon or alternatively by nurses or other resident surgeons. In *Hocking v Bell* (1948) (p 381), a doctor was found negligent for allowing a two-inch part of a tube to break off and to remain in a patient's body. The defendants conceded negligence in *Pask v Bexley Health Authority* (1988) (p 489) following the discovery, one year after the patient's stomach had been pumped, of two and a half feet of plastic tubing in her body. (See also the Canadian case of *Anderson v Chasney* [1949] 4 DLR 71 where liability was established against a surgeon who left a sponge in a child's nostril causing suffocation in circumstances where it was not his practice to have tapes attached to the sponges or to have a nurse present to keep a count of the sponges.)

5. Childbirth, sterilisation and contraception

Given the volume of prospective mothers receiving medical care throughout their pregnancy and at childbirth, it is not surprising that allegations of negligence frequently arise. This is not only because of the inherent hazards of childbirth itself, but also because of the variety of risks that can arise throughout pregnancy and at labour with drugs affecting the mother and foetus, anaesthetic mishaps during labour, accidents in the use of forceps and accidents during caesarean sections. Data produced in 1991 (James *Risk Management in Obstetrics and Gynaecology,* Journal of Medical Defence Union 2) showed that a quarter of all claims dealt with by the Medical Defence Union arose from obstetrics and gynaecology and they accounted for approximately one third of the damages paid. Claims arising in obstetrics outnumber those in gynaecology by approximately two to one and four fifths of obstetric claims are brought on behalf of babies many alleging brain damage. In the remaining one fifth of cases, the claim is for maternal physical injury or death (Roger V Clements ('Obstetrics and Gynaecology' in Powers and Harris, ch 35).

The House of Lords in the leading cases of *Whitehouse v Jordan* (1981) (p 604) and *Sidaway v Board of Governors of the Bethlem Royal Hospital and the Maudsley Hospital* (1985) (p 554) has affirmed that the medical standard of care espoused in *Bolam* (1957) (p 250) applies to all aspects of diagnosis, treatment and advice in matters of pregnancy, childbirth, sterilisation and contraception.

A. CLAIMS ARISING OUT OF CHILDBIRTH

In *Kralj v McGrath* (1986) (p 420), liability was admitted in respect of treatment described as horrific and totally unacceptable during the course of the birth of twins. In *Mitchell v Hounslow and Spelthorne Health Authority* (1984) (p 458), spasticity caused by a failure to deal adequately with a prolapsed umbilical cord in a baby girl was found to amount to negligence. In *Bull and Wakeham v Devon Health Authority* (1989) (p 264) a difficult twin birth was not properly supervised with registrar or consultant back-up. As a result the second twin was born seriously disabled. The hospital was found negligent in failing to provide an adequate system of obstetric cover which had given rise to a real risk that proper care could not be given after the birth of the first twin (see also *Ritter v Godfrey* (1919) (p 524), *Wilsher v Essex Area Health Authority* (1988) (p 609), *Murray v Kensington and Chelsea and Westminster Area Health Authority* (1981) and *McKay v Essex Area Health Authority* (1982) (p 447)).

Some of the largest claims in medical negligence actions continue to be in respect of cerebral palsy creating as they frequently do a need for extensive care regimes. Damages of over £1,000,000 were awarded in the cases of *Almond v Leeds Western Health Authority* (p 226), *Cassel v Riverside Health Authority* and *Field v Herefordshire Health Authority* and *Faulkner v Wandsworth Health Authority*. These were cases where liability was not contested in respect of negligently managed births. Similarly, substantial damages were awarded in *Janardan v East Berkshire Health Authority* (p 402) (£708,500), *Willett v North Bedfordshire Health Authority* (£612,000) and *Lamey v Wirral Health Authority* (p 423) (£390,000), also cases where liability was admitted. In *Matthews v Waltham Forest Health Authority* (p 456) £650,000 was awarded as agreed damages when a plaintiff succeeded in establishing that his cerebral palsy was due to severe birth asphyxia as opposed to congenital abnormality. Also in *Flynn v Maidstone Health Authority* (p 334) liability was established in respect of a practitioner's failure to perform a caesarean section where a child suffered hypoxia following a vaginal delivery. Later damages were assessed at £552,000 (p 336).

Cases where liability was not established include *Hinfey v Salford Health Authority* (p 380), where the decision to allow vaginal delivery was held not to have been negligent and *A v Bristol and West Hospital Authority* (p 217), where the decision not to proceed to a caesarean section was once again upheld by the court as being in accord with the responsible body of medical opinion.

Cases where less catastrophic injury has been occasioned to a child during its birth include *Leckie v Brent and Harrow Area Health Authority* (1982) (p 428) where Mars-Jones J accepted that the maxim res ipsa loquitur applied in circumstances where a baby sustained a laceration to its face during the course of a caesarean section. The judge decided that such a cut could not have happened without negligence on the registrar's part. In *Giles v Pontefract Health Authority,* a plaintiff suffered damage to his brachial plexus causing under-development to his left shoulder as a result of a negligently handled birth.

Damages were awarded to a mother in respect of a severe depressive disorder in the case of *Kirby v Redbridge Health Authority* following the death of one of her twins arising out of a negligently handled birth. In *Lofthouse v North Tees Health Authority* (p 434) damages were awarded for negligent aftercare to a mother who was incorrectly stitched following the birth of her first child. In *Tredget and Tredget v Bexley Health Authority* (p 585), substantial damages were awarded both to a mother and a father for nervous shock arising out of the birth of their first son by caesarean section which was characterised by the judge as taking place in chaos or pandemonium. The child later died and £300,000 damages were agreed in a settlement following a finding of liability. In *Thomas v North West Surrey Health Authority* (p 580), liability was admitted in respect of very substantial brain damage suffered by a woman following a negligently handled abortion.

B. CLAIMS ARISING OUT OF FAILED STERILISATIONS AND ABORTIONS

Failed sterilisations and vasectomies have given rise to litigation which has raised significant issues concerning the standard of care, with respect to the degree of disclosure required, and also difficult questions on causation and on damages. According to Capstick *Patient Complaints and Litigation* (National Association of Public Health Authorities, 1985) p 68, by 1983 20% of married couples used sterilisation or vasectomy as a form of contraception. It is thought that the risks of re-canalisation of the fallopian tubes occur naturally in approximately one in 750 cases. Further risks may arise if the sterilisation technique was by way of clipping the fallopian tube, because occasionally the clip may be wrongly placed or may detach itself. The risk of re-canalisation is thought to be higher when the sterilisation is performed soon after delivery or abortion. Natural reversal following a vasectomy is thought to be in the region of about one in 5,000.

In *Emeh v Kensington and Chelsea and Westminster Area Health Authority* (1985) (p 321), a failed sterilisation was held to be due to negligence and breach of contract. The resultant birth of a congenitally deformed child was held to give rise to the right for damages for its so-called wrongful birth. The mother in this case refused to have an abortion, which was held by the trial judge to be a novus actus interveniens and a failure to mitigate her damages. The Court of Appeal reversed the trial judge's finding and said that it was not unreasonable for the plaintiff to decline to have an abortion. The Court of Appeal confirmed that it was not contrary to public policy to recover damages for the birth of a child whether healthy or abnormal.

This decision of the Court of Appeal in effect approved *Thake v Maurice* (1985) (p 579), where at first instance Pain J had found both breach of contract and negligence in respect of a failed vasectomy which resulted in the birth of a healthy child, and awarded damages for the upkeep of the child. The Court of Appeal heard the defendant's appeal in *Thake v Maurice* after *Emeh*. The finding of negligence in *Thake* was upheld although the Court of Appeal reversed Pain J on the question of breach of contract.

Emeh accordingly disapproved *Udale v Bloomsbury Health Authority* (1983) (p 589) where Jupp J had held it contrary to public policy to award damages for the birth of a healthy child. In *Udale*, the defendants admitted liability for failing to clip each fallopian tube in a laparoscopic sterilisation. Similarly, liability for failed sterilisations was admitted in the cases of *Benarr v Kettering Health Authority* (1988) (p 243), *Chaunt v Hertfordshire Area Health Authority* (1982) (p 276) and *Williams v Imrie* (1988) (p 606).

Conversely in *Palmer v Eadie* (1987) (p 487), a plaintiff did not prove negligence or breach of contract where a vasectomy failed. The urologist had given adequate warning of the failure risk and no breach of duty arose in the practitioner's failure to discuss with the patient the actual mode of operation undertaken. In *Gold v Haringey Health Authority* (1987) (p 355), the Court of Appeal reversed the decision of Schiemann J who had found negligence in failing to disclose the failure rate in sterilisation. The trial judge had been persuaded to make a distinction between therapeutic and non-therapeutic settings, and thought the *Bolam* test did not apply to non-therapeutic settings which would include the arena of contraceptive advice. The Court of Appeal, in applying *Sidaway v Board of Governors of Bethlem Royal Hospital and the Maudsley Hospital* (1985) (p 554), said that no distinction could be made and the medical standard applied in both settings.

In *Venner v North East Essex Area Health Authority* (1987) (p 592), a doctor who had not carried out a dilatation and curettage during a sterilisation, and therefore allowed an undiagnosed pregnancy to continue, was not found negligent. The trial judge found it was neither necessary nor desirable to have a dilatation and curettage as a matter of course, and the doctor was acting in accord with an accepted mode of practice.

In *Cronin v Islington Area Health Authority* (1987) (p 294), the plaintiff was sterilised following a caesarian delivery of her third child. The operation failed and she became pregnant again, and brought a case alleging negligence on the part of the consultant obstetrician who had not told her of the failure risks. Caulfield J dismissed the action, firstly on the basis that she had been warned. However, he also found that at this time in 1981 there was no duty to warn a patient that sterilisation might fail, since there was a substantial respectable body of medical opinion who would not have warned the patient in these circumstances. The judge went on to add that he did not accept the plaintiff's evidence that had she known about the failure risk she would have used contraception. She accordingly failed on the question of causation as well.

Similarly in *McLellan v Newcastle Health Authority* (p 448) the trial judge did not accept the evidence of the plaintiff that she had not been warned concerning the failure rate of a sterilisation effected by tubal ligation. (For other cases see Chapter 12, *Allen v Bloomsbury Health Authority* (p 225), *Britner v North West Regional Health Authority* (p 260), *Gardiner v Mounfield and Lincolnshire Health Authority* (p 345), *Salih v Enfield Health Authority* (p 542), *Gowton v Wolverhampton Health Authority* (p 358) and *Walkin v South Manchester Health Authority* (p 597).)

Unnecessary sterilisation led to liability in *Biles v Barking Health Authority* (1988) (page 162), as did sterilisation without consent in *Devi v West Midlands Regional Health Authority* (1981) (p 308).

6. Burns

A number of reported cases concern burns inadvertently occasioned to patients during the course of a variety of treatment requiring either the application of heat or of chemicals. Most are self-evidently negligent and raise the maxim res ipsa loquitur. In *Clarke v Worboys* (1952) (p 279), a patient undergoing electro-coagulation treatment suffered a severe burn on her buttock. The process involved passing a high frequency current via a pad. The Court of Appeal held that it was a case of res ipsa loquitur, and the presumption of negligence was not rebutted. In *Gold v Essex County Council* (1942) (p 354), a radiographer was found negligent in failing to protect a girl's face, causing disfiguring burns during treatment by Grenz rays for facial warts. Older cases are illustrated in *Ball v Caldwell* (1940) (p 236) (discolouration caused following irradiation on a breast lump); *Hall v Lees* (1904) (p 365) (burns by hot-water bottle); *Perionowsky v Freeman* (1866) (p 493) (scalded in a hip bath, no liability proved); *Smith v Pare* (1904) (p 461) (burns to the whole body following high frequency currents and x-rays); *Snell v Carter* (1941) (p 563) (burns which became gangrenous following oil and ray lamp treatment); and *Jones v Manchester Corpn* (1952) (p 406) (where before being administered a negligent lethal dose of pentothal, a patient suffered facial burns through contact with anaesthetics).

Leahy-Taylor (Chapter 4) describes further cases which have led to settlement, involving, inter alia, trichloroacetic acid instead of adrenalin being used to prevent nasal bleeding and causing burns; a heat candle being wrongly applied; diathermy electro-burns during a circumcision; and burns from suspension rods during a tonsillectomy. (See also *Medical Defence Union Annual Report 1990*, p 45, and *Grenvill v Waltham Forest Health Authority* (p 361).)

7. Dentists

The normal medical standard of care applies to dental practitioners, and there is no legal significance in treating them in a separate category to, say, doctors, pharmacists or nurses. Even before the espousal and refinement of the *Bolam* standard of care, it had been recognised that a dentist owed a patient the proper degree of skill and care of the averagely competent practitioner. In *Gordon v Goldberg* (1920) (p 357), the plaintiff sued a dentist on the grounds that two sets of artificial teeth which he had made for her did not fit and could not be adapted. Rowlatt J held that when people went to dentists they expected and contracted for skill and not for infallibility. In judging skill, account might be taken of the charges made, and the defendant in this case had charged very handsomely but the teeth he supplied were utterly unsatisfactory. Similarly in *Samuels v Davis* (p 544) a dentist who sued for his fees in respect of making a denture was unsuccessful on the ground that although no negligence had been established the denture was not fit for its purpose and as a matter of contract law no liability arose to pay for them.

Where a dentist works in conjunction with a doctor, the dentist is to some extent entitled to rely upon the doctor's diagnosis of the patient's general health. In

Warren v Grieg and *Warren v White* (1935) (p 599), a dentist was asked by a general practitioner to examine a patient who appeared to be suffering from pyorrhoea. Both dentist and doctor advised extraction of all the patient's twenty-eight teeth. The patient died within twenty four-hours following persistent bleeding. Post-mortem examination revealed that the patient in fact had had leukaemia. McKinnon J held that where a dentist worked jointly with a general practitioner, it was not part of a dentist's duty to discover the general health of the patient, and the dentist had not been negligent. In *Tanswell v Nelson* (1959) (p 575), a patient had ten teeth removed resulting in locking of the jaw. The dentist sent her to her general practitioner who diagnosed an abscess and treated her with antibiotics. In fact the plaintiff had suffered osteomyelitis which was not discovered until x-ray at a hospital. McNair J held that the dentist was entitled to rely on the doctor's opinion of the patient's response to the antibiotic treatment and the taking of x-rays.

Accidents during extraction which are in the nature of dislocations or the fracturing of a jaw appear rarely to give rise to the doctrine of res ipsa loquitur. In *Fish v Kapur* (1948) (p 332), the plaintiff relied on the maxim on the basis that part of the root of a tooth had been left in her jaw, and the jaw was fractured during extraction. Evidence was adduced that this could happen without negligence and the claim failed. In *Lock v Scantlebury* (1963) (p 432), no negligence was held to arise where a jaw was dislocated during extraction. However, failure to diagnose the fact on subsequent visits was held to be in breach of duty of care. In *O'Neill v Kelly* (1961) (p 484), a jaw bone was fractured during the use of a tool known as an elevator. However the trial judge rejected an inference that there must have been something wrong with the manner of the dentist's operation of the elevator and found as a fact that the fracture was due to a sudden jerk by the plaintiff. Similarly, in *Fletcher v Bench* (1973) (p 333), the Court of Appeal found no negligence arising out of a difficult extraction of an impacted tooth which resulted in part of a bone burr remaining in the patient's jaw after it had broken during drilling. The jaw later fractured after an infection set in, and did so at the point where the broken burr was eventually found. In *Bridges v Cornwall and Isles of Scilly Area Health Authority and Fisher* (p 260) liability was established in respect of damage caused to an artery during the performance of an operation known as condylotomy.

Damage can often occur to the lingual nerve during the extraction of wisdom teeth. In *Christie v Somerset Health Authority* (p 277) negligence was established in circumstances where direct trauma resulted through contact with the burr on a drill or alternatively when an elevator was removing a tooth. The defendant's contention that the nerve was damaged in the course of creating a flap notwithstanding careful and necessary stretching was rejected by the judge as being nothing more than a possibility. Similarly in *Heath v West Berkshire Health Authority* (p 375) negligence was established when the lingual nerve was damaged probably by the retractor being incorrectly positioned, incorrectly adjusted or alternatively arising out of misapplication of the drill itself. The trial judge found that at the date of the injury in 1986 there was still a respectable and responsible body of professional opinion that would not have warned of the small risk of unavoidable injury to the lingual nerve and that part of the plaintiff's claim failed. Liability was also established for lingual nerve damage in *Tomkins v Bexley Health Authority* (p 587) in which the judge was persuaded that the damage which occurred to the lingual plate and the lingual tissues, together with a 90 % severing of the nerve, indicated that the operator had been negligent. Conversely in

McAloon v Newcastle Health Authority (p 445) the trial judge was not persuaded that damage to the buccal as well as the lingual nerve was caused by negligence. The judge in fact found that both theories put forward by the plaintiff and the defendant were improbable and in those circumstances the plaintiff did not discharge the burden of proving her case.

A more clear-cut case where the maxim res ipsa loquitur arose is to be found in *Garner v Morrell and Another* (1953) (p 346), where the Court of Appeal held that the death of a patient from the swallowing or inhalation of a throat pack during the course of an extraction called for explanation by the defendants. If a mishap does occur during dental treatment the dentist, like other practitioners, is under a duty to inform the patient of the problem. In *Cooper v Miron* (1927) (p 287), the crown of a molar tooth broke off and disappeared during the course of extraction. After the effects of the anaesthetic had worn off, the plaintiff complained of breathing difficulties but was allowed to go home without being told about the loss of part of her tooth. She subsequently contracted septic pneumonia due to the lodging of the piece of tooth in the bronchus, and died approximately three months later. The dentist was found liable by a jury after it had been directed that it was part of the duty of a dentist when an accident of this kind occurred to inform the plaintiff about it.

In *Connor v Fison-Clarke* (1987) (p 286), a dentist was found negligent when extensive root therapy treatment and bridge work in the upper arch of the plaintiff's jaw caused malocclusion within the lower teeth. In *Foreman v Saroya* (p 336) liability was admitted where the plaintiff contracted hepatitis as a result of a reaction against halothane anaesthetic and where the defendant dentist ought to have known of the plaintiff's susceptibility to the anaesthetic as she had previously reacted to it.

8. Hospital administration and organisation

Actions frequently arise based upon failures to organise or to implement a proper system of institutional treatment and after-care. It is likely that a hospital owes a non-delegable duty of care directly to a patient irrespective of any vicarious liability (*Cassidy v Ministry of Health* (1951) (p 272)). In *Wilsher v Essex Area Health Authority* (1987) (p 609), the Court of Appeal expressed a view that a health authority which conducted a hospital so that it failed to provide doctors of sufficient skill and experience to give proper treatment could be directly liable in negligence to the patient (see Chapter 1). Part of this duty was held to be to provide a proper obstetric back-up cover to cope with difficult births (*Bull and Wakeham v Devon Health Authority* (1989) (p 264)).

Hospitals must also take steps to ensure their aseptic techniques are adequate so that equipment is properly sterile (*Voller v Portsmouth Corpn* (1947) (p 594)). Patients with or exposed to contagious diseases should be properly cared for and treated so that they do not spread infection to others (see *Heafield v Crane* (1937) (p 375) and *Marshall v County Council of the Parts of Lindsey, Lincolnshire* (1937) (p 454)). In *Vancouver General Hospital v McDaniel* (1935) (p 591), a patient died after she contracted smallpox because she had to share the same floor as smallpox victims in a hospital and because she also came into contact with nurses who were nursing the smallpox patients. The plaintiff herself had been admitted because she was suffering from diphtheria. The hospital avoided liability predominantly on the *Bolam* test, albeit twenty years earlier, by adducing evidence that their system of sterilisation rather than isolation was in accord with general and approved practice. (See also *Salisbury v Gould* (1904) (p 543).)

While in the care of a hospital, patients must be adequately supervised so that they do not come to foreseeable harm. Leaving a disabled child momentarily with a hot inhalant did not amount to negligence in *Cox v Carshalton Group Hospital Management Committee* (1955) (p 291), as on those particular facts the child had managed the inhaler previously. In *Gravestock v Lewisham Group Hospital Management Committee* (1955) (p 358), judged by the standards of a prudent parent or schoolmaster, a hospital was found not to be negligent for leaving a nine-year-old child momentarily alone with the result that the child took the opportunity of running down the ward and injured herself. However, leaving a seven-year-old in a ward by and open window through which he fell was found negligent in *Newnham v Rochester an Chatham Joint Hospital Board* (1936) (p 480). Liability was also established in *Smith v Lewisham Group Hospital Management Committee* (1955) (p 560), where an eighty-six year old lady who was placed on a four-wheel trolley without any protective railings fell off after the nurse attending her had left the cubicle to answer the telephone. (See also *Wilson v Tomlinson* (1956) (p 610).)

Particular problems arise concerning the degree of supervision required for patients who may harm themselves or injure others. The hospital wing of Winchester Prison was found not negligent in allowing a mentally defective inmate to attack a fellow patient in the hospital wing. The assailant had no previous record of such attacks and in the circumstances a failure to segregate was not deemed negligence (*Ellis v Home Office* (1953) (p 321)). In *Knight v Home Office* (1990) (p 419) no liability was established in respect of the suicide of a young man held on remand in Brixton Prison. The court determined that the standard of care in a prison hospital did not have to be as high as the standard of care in a psychiatric hospital outside prison, and in particular there was no negligence in failing to provide a patient-staff ratio as would be present in a psychiatric hospital. The court further held that there was no negligence in failing to provide 24-hour observation in the particular circumstances of the case, and supervision every 15 minutes by looking at the prisoner in his cell was sufficient. In *Holgate v Lancashire Mental Hospitals Board* (1937) (p 384), negligence was established in respect of a decision to allow an inmate detained at His Majesty's pleasure to have extended leave during which he attacked a member of the public. In *Drummond v Wonford House Hospital (Incorporated)* (1928) (p 314), a mental nursing home was found negligent for failing to watch adequately a patient with acute melancholia. The patient forced herself through a ten-inch square window and in doing so fractured her arm and jaw.

In *Thorne v Northern Group Hospital Management Committee* (1964) (p 584), the court recognised that the degree of care and supervision with respect to a suicidal patient was greater than that normally required. However a claim brought by the widow of a patient who committed suicide, after both the sister and the nurse had left the convalescent ward where the patient was being monitored, was dismissed. The judge thought it likely that the patient was waiting for such an opportunity to avoid her supervisors and take her own life. Conversely in *Selfe v Ilford and District Hospital Management Committee* (1970) (p 551), a seventeen-year-old suicide risk recovered damages in respect of serious injuries resulting to him after a failed suicide bid. He was left momentarily in a ward which had an open window by his bed and he jumped out of it. Hinchcliffe J held that in the particular circumstances there was a need for a continuous observation.

In *Size v Shenley Hospital Group Management Committee* (1970) (p 557), the Court of Appeal rejected a plaintiff's claim arising out of an attack perpetrated on him by an inmate of a mental hospital. The attacker, who shared a ward with the plaintiff but whose bed was near the nurse's desk, was, shortly before the attack, due to be taken to a secure ward following a hypomanic episode. He attacked just before the nurse could stop him, and it was held that in the circumstances the supervision had been adequate.

In *Hyde v Tameside Area Health Authority* (1981) (p 396), the Court of Appeal reversed a finding of negligent supervision in respect of the care afforded to a patient in a general hospital who attempted suicide after wrongly thinking he had terminal cancer. The Court of Appeal held that any failure to assess the true significance of the patient's mental distress was at best an error in clinical judgment that did not amount to negligence. In *Hyde,* the then Master of the Rolls Lord Denning expressed a view that he felt it unfitting that the personal representatives of a suicide should be able to claim damages in respect of his death.

In *Kirkham v Chief Constable of Greater Manchester Police,* that view was disapproved and the court held that such an action could not be defeated by the doctrine ex turpi causa non oritur actio, in that suicide was no longer such an affront to the public conscience that it should not give rise to a cause of action. Further, in cases where the deceased had impaired judgment due to for example clinical depression it could not be said that the doctrine of volenti non fit injuria applied (see also the Canadian case of *Jinks v Cardwell* (1987) (p 403)).

Failure to supervise staff, including medical staff, may also, in principle, give rise to negligence (*Wilsher v Essex Area Health Authority* (1987) (p 609)).

Failure to take x-rays or to administer tests, particularly simple tests such as blood and urine samples, constituted a significant background in the five hundred cases looked at by Leahy-Taylor (above). In *Braisher v Harefield and Northwood Hospital Group Management Committee* (1966) (p 258), the then Master of the Rolls, Lord Denning, indicated that it was not in every case where there had been a failure to take an x-ray that negligence would arise. The plaintiff in that case presented at casualty with a complaint that he had knocked his arm on some metal. A wound was stitched but no x-ray was taken. The arm continued to be painful until a piece of metal close to the surface was removed. The Master of the Rolls indicated that there was no liability arising in this case, because the plaintiff had not told the nurse or casualty officer what in fact happened, namely that a piece of metal had flown off a machine, but had told them he had knocked his arm on some metal.

In *Tanswell v Nelson* (1959) (p 575), both a doctor and a dentist were found not to be negligent in failing to have an x-ray taken on a jaw which would have revealed developing osteomyelitis. With regard to the doctor, McNair J said that the patient had presented with symptoms inconsistent with the osteomyelitis. Conversely, in *Kilburn v Swindon and District Hospital Management Committee* (1955) (p 414) a failure to x-ray a leg which had two fractures, and an arm which was also fractured, was held negligent (see also *McCormack v Redpath Brown & Co Ltd* (1961) (p 445) and *Elkan v Montgomery Smith* (1922) (p 320)).

Failure to carry out a blood test and amniocentesis in *Bagley v North Herts Health Authority* (1986) (p 234) and failure to establish a blood group in *Morgan v Gwent Health Authority* (1987) (p 461), led to admissions of liability on the part of the defendants. A system that resulted in a contamination of a child's vaginal swab with an adult's specimen carrying spermatozoa and which thereby resulted in an investigation concerning possible sexual abuse of the child was also undefended in *G v North Tees Health Authority* (1989) (p 344). In *Evason v Essex Health Authority* (1994) (p 324) a pathology report on the plaintiff's excised lymph node was confused with a sample taken from another patient and she was incorrectly told that she had cancer. The error was not discovered for 14 months during which time the plaintiff had six courses of chemotherapy, three laparotomies and the removal of her right ovary. The psychological effect on the plaintiff was profound. Eventually the defendants admitted liability in August of 1989 and damages were awarded in June 1990 of some £203,500. Conversely, in *Whichello v Medway and Gravesend Hospital Management Committee* (1954) (p 601), a failure to take a culture from a wound which was to be treated by surgery rather than through antibiotics was held not to have been negligent in the light of the then current medical opinion.

Neglecting to take a history or a proper history from a patient will normally result in a breach of duty (see *Chin Keow v Government of Malaysia* (1967) (p 276)). Equally, failure to allow a patient to explain her particular problems and predicaments led to a consultant physician being held liable in *Horner v Scarborough, Bridlington, Malton and Whitby Group Hospital Management Committee* (1966) (p 388) for an over-hasty diagnosis and for failing to take an x-ray.

Failing to communicate a case history or to ensure that proper notes and test results are available to other practitioners may also result in findings of negligence. In *Coles v Reading and District Hospital Management Committee* (1963) (p 283), a cottage hospital was found to have been negligent in failing to ensure that a patient attended a general hospital in circumstances where although he was told to go to such a hospital, he was suffering from shock at the time and simply thereafter attended his general practitioner. Conversely, in *Chapman v Rix* (1960) (p 274), a doctor working at a cottage hospital was not held negligent for failing to communicate the findings of his diagnosis to his patient's general practitioner. (See also *Bell v Secretary of State for Defence* (1986) (p 242).)

A casualty officer is under a general duty to a bona fide patient presenting in a hospital, and failure to examine such a patient can lead to liability (*Barnett v Chelsea and Kensington Hospital Management Committee* (1969) (p 238)). A casualty officer has some small discretion so that he may properly delegate trivial injuries to a nurse or may decline to see someone who has already contacted his general practitioner and is merely seeking a second opinion (*Barnett v Chelsea and Kensington Hospital Management Committee* [1969] 1 QB at 436g–437).

In *Bolitho v City and Hackney Health Authority* (p 251) the hospital admitted negligence in respect of a doctor's failure to attend to a two-year-old child. A ward sister thought the child's respiratory sounds were not good and bleeped a senior paediatric registrar. The registrar did not attend and asked a senior house officer to attend instead, but because the senior house officer's bleep was not working due to flat batteries she never got the message. The defendants, however, successfully defeated the claim on the basis that even if an attendance had been made the doctor would not have intubated the child as this would not have been her particular practice in those circumstances, and such a practice judged by the *Bolam* standard was accepted by the court as in accord with a responsible body of medical opinion.

9. General practitioners

A general practitioner has a duty to attend to a patient, which will include a person on his list as well as temporary residents. The doctor's terms and conditions, pursuant to his contract with the Family Health Services Authority (formerly the Family Practitioner Committee) also require the doctor, when requested, to attend to a person involved in an accident or an emergency in any place in his practice area (paragraph 4 of the 'Terms of Service for Doctors in the National Health Service' (General and Medical Services Regulations 1992, pp 40–41).

In *Barnes v Crabtree* (1955) (p 238), Barry J directed a jury that in the case of a real emergency a doctor under the National Health Service scheme had an obligation to treat any patient who was acutely ill. Whether this duty to attend includes a home visit will depend on all the circumstances of the case. In Barnes, the plaintiff, who had a history of arguments with her general practitioner, called at her doctor's surgery on Christmas Day saying she was ill. The general practitioner told her there was nothing wrong with her, did not examine her, and told her to get another doctor if she was not satisfied. The plaintiff refused to leave the premises, and eventually she was removed by the police. She sued the doctor for failing to attend to her, and the jury found that there was no case to answer. Barry J had directed the jury that the doctor's obligation was to render all proper and necessary treatment to the patient, and this did not mean he was required to make full clinical examination on each occasion. A general practitioner must make proper provision for adequate locum cover and ensure that the stand-in doctors are properly informed about his patients (see *Farquhar v Murray* (1901) (p 330) and *Ball v Howard* (1924) (p 236)).

The general practitioner should also have an adequate system of dealing with possible emergency cases if they come into the surgery, and this will extend to being vicariously liable for the acts of his receptionist for any negligent failure to communicate an emergency to him (*Lobley v Going* (1985) (p 431)). A general practitioner is also probably under a duty to take reasonable steps to ascertain a patient's new address in circumstances when he makes a call at the old address having been summoned by telephone and upon arrival at the address it is obvious that the patient has moved. In *Kavanagh v Abrahamson* (1964) (p 410), the doctor in these circumstances rang the door bell of the adjoining flats to see if he could ascertain the current address of his patient but met with no reply. The trial judge indicated that there was a measure of force in the criticism that the doctor might have done more but that of itself did not constitute negligence. In the same case the judge went on to find that the prescribing of compound codeine tablets without seeing the patient also did not, in the circumstances, amount to negligence.

Negligent prescription in *Dwyer v Rodrick* (1983) (p 316) led to liability against a general practitioner. The prescribing doctor was found liable for an obvious mistake, but one of his colleagues was found not liable for failing to notice the mistake during a home visit. The second doctor did not have the medical notes with him and had failed to see the prescription and had also failed to see the bottle of tablets on the table in the plaintiff's bedroom. In *Prendergast v Sam and Dee Ltd* (1989) (p 497), a general practitioner was found to be negligent with respect to his poor hand-writing which invited a misreading by the dispensing pharmacist, causing the plaintiff to suffer severe injuries because of the effects of the wrongly dispensed medicine.

In *Connolly v Rubra* (1937) (p 285), a general practitioner was held negligent for failing to take specimens of sputum and for failing to arrange for x-ray examination in respect of a patient who contracted undiagnosed tubercolosis from which he died.

Where a patient is under the care of a hospital, a general practitioner may, to a certain extent, rely on the diagnoses and advice given by the hospital doctors.

Accordingly, in *Edler v Greenwich and Deptford Hospital Management Committee* (1953) (p 319), an eleven-year-old girl who had suffered nausea and stomach pain was examined by a casualty officer. The hospital doctor said there was nothing wrong with the girl but if she got worse her father should bring her back to the hospital. In fact the girl's mother took the child to her general practitioner who was told what the hospital doctor had said and formed the view that the child probably had gastric trouble. The following day the child deteriorated and was rushed to hospital, but she died of a ruptured appendix. The trial judge held that the hospital doctor had been negligent but the general practitioner had not been negligent in relying upon the hospital's diagnosis.

However, there can be no abdication of the general practitioner's responsibility, and a failure to ascertain precisely what treatment a patient did receive in hospital may lead to negligence. In *Coles v Reading and District Hospital Management Committee* (1963) (p 283), a man sustained a severe crushing injury to his finger, and attended a cottage hospital where the wound was cleaned and he was told to go to the general hospital. Mr Coles did not go to the hospital but the following day saw his own general practitioner who failed to ascertain what had happened at the hospital but simply redressed the wound. Accordingly no anti-tetanus injection was given. Sachs J found the hospital negligent for failing to give the injection and for failing to make sure the plaintiff attended the general hospital, but also found the general practitioner negligent for failing to make proper enquiry.

A failure to refer a patient to hospital or to a specialist in time may result in negligence being established against a general practitioner. In *Lord v Spencer* (1994) (p 435) a general practitioner was found negligent in failing to refer a plaintiff who presented to him with a vitreous detachment on the 2 January which led on the 3 January to a retinal detachment. The trial judge was satisfied that had an immediate referral to hospital been made the retinal detachment would have been prevented and the plaintiff's sight preserved. (See also *Bova v Spring* (1994) (p 254). In *Marsden v Bateman* (p 453) a general practitioner and a midwife admitted negligence in failing to arrange for a prompt admission for an infant shortly after its birth, but the claim failed on the issue of causation as to whether the presenting condition of hypoglycaemia caused the baby's brain damage.

Conversely in *Stockdale v Nicolls* (1993) (p 567) a general practitioner was acquitted of a negligent failure to admit a child into hospital who developed septicaemia which led to permanent brain damage. It was also held that in the circumstances of that case it was not negligent to send an experienced practice nurse in response to the parents' first call. Similarly in *Thornton v Nicol* (p 584) a failure to diagnose periorbital cellulitis or to refer a ten-week-old child to hospital in time was not found to be negligent, in circumstances where it was reasonable to conclude that the child was suffering from conjunctivitis. (See also *Durrant v Burke* (1993) (p 315).)

Klein in *Complaints against Doctors* (Charles Knight, London 1973) has analysed Family Health Services Authority complaints made against general practitioners and demonstrates that a failure to visit or a delay in visiting, a failure to treat a patient in an emergency and a failure to provide deputising services are some of the most common causes of complaint (see Jarman, Chapter 23, Powers and Harris). Given the vast number of visits made by patients to general practitioners, medical negligence actions against GPs appear to be low. Jarman (above) has expressed the view that the reason for the relatively few cases of litigation against general practitioners is due to the Family Health Services Authority system of complaints which allows patients to ventilate grievances.

Further factors may include the personal relationship that frequently exists between a patient and the general practitioner. (Further cases involving general practitioners are discussed in Chapter 8 in those actions based on failures in diagnosis.)

10. Nurses

Like other health care professionals, nurses are under a duty to exercise reasonable care and skill in all of the disparate tasks they undertake. Historically, like other skilled personnel, nurses were considered to be independent contractors, and an employing hospital was not automatically vicariously liable for their torts. Today the employing hospital authorities are both vicariously liable for, and also provide an indemnity to, nurses in respect of actions based on a breach of their duty of care. Accordingly in a case like *Fussell v Beddard* (1942) (p 343) where a patient died after a nurse wrongly prepared a 1% anaesthetic solution instead of a 0.1% solution, the employing hospital would be vicariously liable for this act assuming negligence was established.

Where, however, a nursing agency supplies a nurse to an individual or to a hospital, the situation is less clear. The supplying agency is unlikely to be liable for the torts of the nurse during the course of her work. Much would depend upon the contractual terms, the representation made by the agency, and the steps taken by the agency to provide a competent nurse (see *Hall v Lees* (1904) (p 365)).

If the nurse was working within a hospital, whether within the National Health Service or a private hospital, it is likely that the hospital would be liable for the nurse's tortious acts. Such liability could be founded on the fact that, given the degree of control of the nurse's activities, she was in law a servant of the hospital or in any event was the hospital's agent. Alternatively, the hospital may be found to be under a non-delegable duty to provide nursing services to the patient. (See the discussion on vicarious liability in Chapter 1.)

Typical actions involving nurses concern allegations that a patient has not been properly supervised. In *Selfe v Ilford and District Hospital Management Committee* (1970) (p 551), liability was established in a case where three nurses, who had been allocated to a ward containing a seventeen year old suicide-risk patient, had failed to provide continuous observation. One nurse went to the kitchen, another to the lavatory and a third nurse was attending to a patient when the plaintiff climbed up on to the roof of the hospital and jumped off. The court held that in these particular circumstances there was a requirement for constant observation. Conversely, in *Thorne v Northern Group Hospital Management Committee* (1964) (p 584), no negligence was established in circumstances where there had been a temporary gap in supervising a patient who committed suicide during a momentary absence of the nursing staff.

In *Gravestock v Lewisham Group Hospital Management Committee* (1955) (p 358), a nursing orderly who had left a ward for a few moments to get the pudding course of a meal was found not to have been negligent in circumstances where a nine-year-old patient took the opportunity to run down the ward and to injure herself. In *Cox v Carshalton Group Hospital Management Committee* (1955) (p 291), McNair J found no negligence where a nurse had left a severely disabled thirteen-year-old girl alone for a few seconds with an inhaler which slipped and scalded her. In *James v Camberwell Health Authority* (p 400) the absence of a midwife for ten minutes during which the foetal heart rate suddenly dropped was held in the circumstances not to have been negligent. In *Gauntlett v Northampton*

Health Authority (1985) (p 349), allegations of inadequate supervision and inadequate note keeping were made against nursing staff in respect of a schizophrenic patient who set light to herself four days after telling her husband that she might do so. The husband passed on this information to a nurse who failed to record the fact in the nursing notes. Evidence was given at the trial that a note ought to have been made and the trial judge, Kilner Brown J, held that the omission amounted to a negligent oversight. The Court of Appeal, however, reversed his decision and found that there had been no negligence. The notes already contained references to the patient's preoccupation with thoughts of fire, and the omitted information was better judged as an indication of her abnormal mind rather than a warning of her impending suicide attempt. The Court of Appeal held that, judged by the standards of the reasonably competent and experienced nurse, the omission was not negligent

As with medical practitioners, many reported cases involving nurses feature allegations of substandard treatment and after-care. In *Powell v Streatham Manor Nursing Home* (1935) (p 496), the House of Lords restored the decision of the first instance judge, Horridge J, who found as a fact that a nurse had passed a rigid catheter vaginally and had caused a bladder perforation. In *Walker v South West Surrey District Health Authority* (1982) (p 596), the Court of Appeal declined to reverse the finding of Judge Vick that a midwife sister had injected, contrary to all good practice, pethidine into the inside of the plaintiff's right thigh. Negligence was also established in *Bayliss v Blagg* (1954) (p 240), where a matron had failed to notice a developing infection under a plaster cast which she had put on and which led to a child becoming severely disabled. In *Lowen v Hopper* (1950) (p 437), a failure to conduct a proper examination and to change a dressing led to a finding of negligence against a sister. In *Lovell v Southampton and South West Hampshire Health Authority* (p 436) damages on a conventional basis were agreed in the sum of £875,000 following a cardiac arrest to a three-year-old child who was recovering from a routine eye operation, in circumstances where the hospital staff knew she had a cold and a plug of phlegm entered her windpipe causing her to stop breathing. (See also *Sutton v Population Services Family Planning Programme Ltd* (1981) (p 570), *Parry v North West Surrey Health Authority* (p 488)).

Negligence was not established against nursing staff in *Pickering v Governors of the United Leeds Hospital* (1954) (p 494) where an elderly patient developed severe bed sores following an operation on a fractured femur. The nursing staff were held to have been acting in accordance with the surgeon's instructions, as he had forbidden the turning of the plaintiff during the early stages after her operation. (Similar accusations of bed sores were made in *Biss v Lambeth, Southwark and Lewisham Area Health Authority* (1978) (p 248) in a case which was struck out for want of prosecution). No liability was established in *Sullivan v Manchester Regional Hospital Board* (1957) (p 570) where a sister had failed to comprehend the significance of a patient's eye swelling following a nasal operation. The sister had attempted to reassure the patient and after four days asked a doctor to examine her.

Negligence in the dispensing of prescribed drugs was established in *Smith v Brighton and Lewes Hospital Management Committee* (1958) (p 559) where a sister had caused drugs to be administered beyond their prescribed course. The sister was criticised for failing to mark the intended termination of the treatment on the relevant notes. Nurses were also found negligent in the administration of a fatal dose of six ounces of paraldehyde instead of six drachms in *Strangways-Lesmere v Clayton* (1936) (p 569).

Where retained products are left in a patient following an operation, the nursing staff responsible for counting any of the products are likely to be liable for the oversight (see *Mahon v Osborne* (1939) (p 449), *James v Dunlop* (1931) (p 401), and *Urry v Bierer* (1955) (p 591)). The cases on retained surgical products indicate that a surgeon cannot simply rely on the nursing staff, but the corollary is that there is a high duty on the nurses in this context. Lord Justice Scott in *Mahon v Osborne* (above) said:

> 'The only matter on which I desire to say anything is on the relevance of the surgeon's duty with regard to the removal of packing swabs on any count by the nurses. His duty is undoubtedly to exercise care in the removal of the swabs, giving proper weight to the rare, but not impossible, risk of a swab having lost its Spencer-Wells clip. This risk, it is worth remembering, is one which depends not on the surgeon but on the nurses. It is their duty to see that each Spencer-Wells clip is in good order and that its safety catch is made well fast and the swab to which it is fastened is placed in the surgeon's hand. So, too, the check afforded by the count depends on the nurses. Those two risks are wholly external, both to the surgeon and to the patient. If an error has been committed, the surgeon cannot either control it or know it. Nonetheless, I do not doubt that over and above all the many signs of danger to the patient which are forcing themselves on his attention, the surgeon has to keep in his mind those two risks of error by the nurses. On the other hand, I do not think the surgeon should be deprived of all support from the count. In a difficult case, where he is anxious for the patient's sake to close the operation at the earliest possible moment, the fact that he is about to receive a check from the head sister, whom he knows to be careful, is one of the imponderable factors which he may properly have in mind, and indeed to have regard to it may sometimes save a patient's life' ([1939] 2 KB at 37).

Nurses can, of course, also be negligent in the routine quasi-domestic aspects of their job. In *Trew v Middlesex Hospital* (1953) (p 588), a nurse was found to be negligent in the manner in which she placed a tray of tea on a patient's lap. In *Pargeter v Kensington and Chelsea and Westminster Health Authority* (1979) (p 487) the simple act of giving a patient a cup of tea was held in principle to be negligent, if it was done without trial sips in circumstances where a patient was recovering from an operation. The trial judge, however, found that it was highly unlikely that the nurse did not give the patient trial sips of tea. Unfortunately the patient vomited the tea, because of the particular type of pre-operative drug he had been given, which resulted in his operative eye wound bursting.

11. Unregistered practitioners

Registered medical practitioners are qualified personnel pursuant to the provisions of the Medical Act 1983 in the case of doctors, and the Dentists Act 1984 in the case of dentists. A qualified practitioner will have his name on the register of either the General Medical Council or the General Dental Council, the regulatory bodies of the respective professions. Perhaps surprisingly, unqualified persons are not legally prevented from practising medicine, surgery or dentistry. Such practitioners, however, will commit an offence if they hold themselves out as being registered doctors (s 49 of the Medical Act 1983) or if they describe themselves as dentists, dental surgeons or dental practitioners (s 39 of the Dentists Act 1984).

The courts' attitude to non-qualified, non-registered practitioners has not only been to protect the public from the dangers of quacks but also to recognise the contribution of unorthodox and alternative modes of healing, particularly when controlled by organised and respected institutions. Generally speaking, if a person becomes a patient of an unqualified practitioner, the practitioner will owe a duty of care to the patient to exercise the degree of skill which he claims to have. (See the striking facts of the Irish case of *Brogan v Bennett* (1955) (p 262).)

In *R v Crick* (1859) (p 504), a herb doctor was found guilty of manslaughter following the death of the child to whom he had prescribed lobelia from which she died. Pollock CB indicated to the jury that whereas it was not a crime to administer medicine, it was criminal to administer it in a risky and careless manner and in this respect there was no difference between the most regular practitioner and the greatest of quacks. Six years later, in *Jones v Fay* (1865) (p 406), a plaintiff succeeded in an action for damages arising out of a prescription of pills given to him by the defendant chemist which resulted in mercury poisoning. The defendant had dissuaded the plaintiff from seeking medical advice, and Baron Pigott directed the jury that if a person acted as if he was a medical practitioner then he would be judged by those standards and not by the standards of the chemist and druggist which in fact he was (see also *Markham v Abrahams* (1911) (p 452)).

In *Snell v Carter* (1941) (p 563), a masseur and medical electrician was found negligent in respect of treatment he gave to a patient which caused burns that eventually became gangrenous and apparently resulted in the patient's death from toxaemia. Evidence was given that the treatment was inadvisable and useless and that anyone with any medical knowledge would have realised the danger. The county court judge, Judge Scobell Armstrong, found the defendant negligent but added his sympathies on the basis that he was a person competent to perform work under a doctor's recommendations in all normal cases, but this particular case had been unusual. This remark brought caustic comments from *The Lancet*:

> 'If comment can be added without disrespect to a careful and courteous tribunal, the decision and its rider exhibit the national compromise between two views of unqualified practice. One view resents any control of such practice, because unsupervised masseurs like the defendant may possess, or may at any moment discover, some therapeutic secret overlooked by orthodox medicine and because there is much more scientific truth in the world about us than is dreamt of in the registered medical practitioner's philosophy. The other view is that it is unfair to the public to leave electrical or radiological treatment so utterly uncontrolled that an unqualified man can cause fatal burns to a patient suffering from disseminated sclerosis. On this view the sympathy is even more needed by the public than by the unqualified man' ([1941] 2 *The Lancet* at 321).

(See also *Smith v Lowry* (1935) (p 560), where a blind osteopath and masseur was found negligent for fracturing a five-year old-child's leg during manipulation.) Similar judicial views were expressed by Atkinson J in *Sones v Foster* (1937) (p 563). Mr Sones was awarded damages arising out of the negligent treatment afforded to him by a naturopath, medical herbalist and health practitioner which resulted in an above-knee amputation. Evidence was adduced that had the plaintiff been given proper treatment he would have required a below-knee amputation. The defendant never held himself out to be a registered practitioner, and the trial judge stressed to the jury that alternative practitioners did render a great public service and the more reputable of them had formed themselves into associations. Atkinson J also emphasised that orthodox practice did not have the monopoly on healing power. No one was compelled to consult an unorthodox practitioner, but anyone who did could expect to receive the average skill, knowledge and efficiency of the particular area of expertise claimed. The jury held that Mr Foster had fallen below these standards. (See also *Turner v NS Hair Treatment Clinic* (p 588).)

Conversely, where an unqualified practitioner makes unwarranted representations about his ability to cure, the courts are likely to find him in strict breach of contract. In *Walton v Lief* (1933) (p 598) an osteopath and naturopath represented that he could cure the plaintiff of a severe skin disease. The jury found a breach of contract and awarded damages equal to the fees paid. In *Shallard v Arline* (1939) (p 553), the defendant was held liable for breach of contract and for fraudulent misrepresentation in respect of claims made that a facial rejuvenation programme was not only bound to work but was also harmless. The plaintiff in fact suffered severe burns which induced a mental breakdown. In *Hodson v Mellor* (1911) (p 382), the rather overblown representations made by an oculist were found to be in excess of the skill actually possessed. Mr Mellor claimed his system was based on irrefutable scientific principles which had long been justified by their outstanding success. His treatment of the plaintiff led to the worsening of her eye condition. Mr Mellor denied in evidence that his scientific experience had been gleaned from being a door-keeper at an eye hospital in Australia.

Section D:

Damages

Chapter 11

General principles

The normal outcome of a successful action for a plaintiff in a medical malpractice case is compensatory financial redress known in law as damages. The assessment of the amount of damages is based upon the principles and methods of calculation evolved in the laws of contract and tort with particular reference to personal injury litigation. This chapter seeks to summarise these principles and to illustrate their application in certain cases concerning medical negligence and breach of contract. Most medical malpractice cases concern personal injury and resultant consequential losses and expenses. The following chapter looks at those cases which arise from the so-called wrongful birth of a child and which principally accrue from failed sterilisations; these are not primarily based upon personal injury, but largely concern the financial consequences of raising an unplanned for child.

Once a litigant has proved a breach of duty and has shown that damage has resulted from that breach, the court will examine what monetary compensation should be awarded. Not every type of loss and expense will be recoverable. Just as a claim may fail on liability because the risk of the damage occurring was considered too remote, and was not therefore reasonably foreseeable, some types of damage are not recoverable because they are judicially determined as being too remotely connected to the negligent act. In the first concept of remoteness, concerned with questions of liability, there is no negligence or breach of contract because a practitioner should not reasonably be regarded as having to expect the unforeseeable. In the second usage, with respect to the quantum of damages, the courts have attempted to limit the consequences of a breach of duty to damage that is reasonably foreseeable as likely to flow from the negligence or breach of contract.

Whether a loss is considered as too remote is often inextricably connected with judicial reasoning that to recover certain types of losses would be offensive to public policy. For example, a married plaintiff who sustains a serious head injury as a result of negligence may develop personality changes or sexual dysfunctions which cause an irretrievable breakdown of his marital relations resulting in a divorce. In *Pritchard v JH Cobden Ltd* (1987), the court declined to allow a claim for the financial losses, such as maintaining two households, that followed divorce proceedings in a case where a 30-year-old husband suffered brain damage in a road accident (cf, however, *Jones v Jones* [1985] QB 704).

Again, in *Meah v McCreamer* (1985 and 1986) a man who suffered a head injury in a road traffic accident which caused a propensity to attack women, and who consequently raped several women and was imprisoned for life, recovered compensation for the loss of his liberty. His further claim, however, for compensation to reflect the amount of damages which he personally had to pay to the victims of his rapes, in separate actions brought against him, were held not to be recoverable, as being contrary to public policy and being too remote from the initial tortious act of the car collision. Woolf J held that the claim for indemnity in respect of the damages the plaintiff had to pay to his victims was essentially an indirect financial loss, and had the effect of imposing on the original tortfeasor liability in respect of injuries to persons owed no duty of care by the negligent car driver. To allow such a claim would be to impose a liability which was both indefinite in terms of the classes of person involved and, indeed, of an indefinite duration. It was also thought wholly inappropriate that criminal acts should be indemnified in such a manner.

A comparison of the two judgments of Woolf J in these separate actions is an instructive illustration of where a line has to be judicially drawn between what is recoverable, what is deemed too remote and what is deemed contrary to public policy (see *Meah v McCreamer (No 2)* ([1986] 2 All ER at 943)). In medical negligence cases, the courts drew this particular line when they struck out that part of a claim by an infant plaintiff who brought an action against doctors on the basis that, inter alia, she had been allowed to be born (see Chapter 4 and *McKay v Essex Area Health Authority* (1982) (p 447)). It is to be noted, however, that the courts recognise a claim in respect of raising a healthy or a non-healthy child who has been born due to breaches of duty concerning sterilisation, vasectomy, and abortion.

Once a type of damage is held not to be too remote or not contrary to public policy, the plaintiff is entitled to compensation notwithstanding that the type of damage occurred in an unforeseeable way. A burn injury which was a reasonably foreseeable consequence of the defendant's negligence in *Smith v Leech Brain & Co* (1962) led to the defendant being held liable for a cancer that developed as a result of the burn trauma. (See also *Hughes v Lord Advocate* (1963).) To this extent, a tortfeasor is required in law to take the victim as he is found. In *Hatwell v South-West Metropolitan Regional Hospital Board* (1976) (p 372), a plaintiff with clinical depression suffered a fractured jaw as a result of her medication being over-hastily withdrawn. The Court of Appeal confirmed that she was entitled to general damages for pain, suffering and loss of amenity which included her emotional distress and which should reflect the particular effect on the plaintiff's personality and constitutional predisposition. Similarly, in *Woodhouse v Yorkshire Regional Health Authority* (1984) (p 612), a plaintiff with a hysterical personality sustained contracture deformities to her fingers. She was awarded damages that compensated her for her hysterical reaction which, albeit unexpected, was recoverable at law. (See also the case of *Grieve v Salford Health Authority* (p 362).)

Such cases are to be distinguished from the case of *Page v Smith* ([1994] 4 All ER 522) where the Court of Appeal overturned an award of substantial damages in respect of a plaintiff succumbing to a recurrence of 'ME' (myalgic encephalomyelitis) on the basis that, inter alia, the injury was not reasonably foreseeable in the circumstances where the plaintiff had been in a road traffic accident but had sustained no physical injuries save for shock (this case is the subject of appeal to the House of Lords).

Once a plaintiff has established causation on the balance of probabilities, he does not have to show that one hundred per cent of his damages were caused by the negligent act. As indicated in Chapter 6, the approach of Pain J in *Clark v MacLennan* (1983) (p 279), and Simon Brown J in *Bagley v North Herts Health Authority* (1986) (p 234), was overruled by the House of Lords in *Hotson v East*

Berkshire Health Authority (1987) (p 389). Pain J had awarded sixty per cent of the full value of Mrs Clark's claim on the basis that, had she had the operation at the proper time, there was still a risk of approximately one-third that it would have failed. Similarly, Simon Brown J had reduced a plaintiff's damages by 5% in a case where a child was stillborn through the defendant's negligence. He accepted evidence that 5% of births resulted in stillbirths and accordingly reduced the damages by this amount. In *Hotson*, Lord Ackner specifically disapproved this approach:

'Once liability is established, on the balance of probabilities, the loss which the plaintiff has sustained is payable in full. It is not discounted by reducing his claim by the extent to which he has failed to prove his case with one hundred per cent certainty . . . . To do so would be to propound a wholly new doctrine which has no support in principle or authority and would give rise to many complications in the search for mathematical or statistical exactitude' ([1987] 3 WLR at 248 a–c).

A major exception to the principle that damages are not to be discounted by reducing a claim to the extent to which liability was not proved to 100% occurs in those cases of professional negligence against solicitors. Such actions typically arise in personal injury cases, where a plaintiff's solicitors have failed to issue or serve proceedings in time against the original tortfeasor and the claim becomes statute barred under the Limitation Act 1980, or in those cases where an action is struck out because of want of prosecution. In such cases, when a plaintiff subsequently sues his legal advisors, the court is required to calculate what the plaintiff's prospects of success were against the original tortfeasor.

For example, in *Gascoine v Ian Sheridan & Co and Latham*, a plaintiff originally sued in respect of irradiation cystitis and peritonitis arising out of alleged medical malpractice. The plaintiff's legal advisors failed to prosecute her claim and the defendant health authority had her action struck out, a decision confirmed on appeal (*Gascoine v Haringey Health Authority* (p 346)). The plaintiff then sued her solicitor and counsel who claimed that, although they had been negligent no damage arose because not only was the plaintiff's initial claim statute barred but also negligence by the hospital's practitioners could not have been established. The trial judge found that the plaintiff's first action against the hospital was not statute barred and in addition the plaintiff had a 60% chance of establishing negligence against the medical practitioners concerned. In those circumstances 60% of the full value of the plaintiff's claim was ordered to be paid by her legal advisors.

1. Heads of damage: general, special, provisional

The typical heads of damage in a medical malpractice case will accord with those in personal injury litigation which traditionally has separated so-called general from special damages. This distinction is analytically insignificant but is relevant for the purposes of pleading, procedure and the assessment of interest. Special damages are those losses and expenses that have actually been incurred and which can be calculated with reasonable precision at the date of the trial. They normally comprise specific losses of income, such as wages or profit, which arise as a result of the plaintiff being unable to work because of the injury, and also specific expenses that have been incurred because of the tort such as medical expenses, travel expenses, the costs of nursing care and attention, and damage to property or clothing. General damages are those which fall to be assessed and estimated, and accordingly involve a greater degree of judicial skill and discretion. General damages comprise the award made for the pain, suffering and loss of amenity occasioned by the breach of duty and also in respect of the future losses of income or profits and future expenses such as care and accommodation. The court, in assessing damages, must determine both past and present losses, some of which are entirely pecuniary and some of which are personal or non-pecuniary such as compensation for disfigurement and pain which has to be quantified in monetary terms.

The overriding principle is that a plaintiff should so far as is possible be put into a position he would have been in but for the injury done to him and thereby to compensate him for the harm done. This is normally done by the award of a once-and-for-all lump sum. In very limited circumstances, where new evidence comes to light, a party on appeal may be allowed to adduce new evidence if it is apparent that the plaintiff has been under-compensated. For example, in *Hughes v Hay* (1989) (p 392), the trial judge awarded a sum of £3,000 to cover the prospect of the plaintiff having difficulty in finding employment should he ever lose his job as a serving police officer. This award for disadvantage on the labour market was based on the assumption that he would be fit enough to carry on for a further ten years in the police force. The plaintiff appealed and sought leave to have the court consider new evidence that he was in fact subsequently retired after the trial from the police force on medical grounds, following a police medical examination three months later. The Court of Appeal allowed a retrial on the question of this discharge (see also *Reed v Oswal and Cleveland Area Health Authority* (1979) (p 521), *Mulholland v Mitchell* (1971)).

The courts will be slow to admit fresh evidence because they are governed by an overwhelming principle that there is an interest in litigation coming to an end. Accordingly, a case will only be reopened in exceptional circumstances on the basis of fresh evidence (see RSC Ord 59, r 10(2) and *Murphy v Stone-Wallwork (Charlton) Ltd* (1969), and *Jenkins v Richard Thomas & Baldwins Ltd* (1966)).

An important inroad into the principle that damages will be awarded on a once and for all basis has been made through the provisions of the Administration of Justice Act 1982, s 6, which has inserted s 32A into the Supreme Court Act 1981, thereby empowering the court to look again at a plaintiff's claim if a serious deterioration has occurred in a plaintiff's condition, as a result of an injury for which he has already received some compensation. The powers to award so-called provisional damages took effect from 1 July 1985 and are governed by specific rules of court (see RSC Ord 37 rr 7–10 and the Practice Direction [1985] 1 WLR 961). Before these provisions, a plaintiff who had a risk of, for example, contracting lung cancer or mesothelioma because of a previous exposure to asbestos and who at the date of trial was suffering from only a minor form of breathlessness would receive compensation for the breathlessness together with some, normally small, award for the risk of contracting cancer in the future. This situation created potential injustice both for the plaintiff and for the defendant. If the plaintiff did contract cancer, the award was too little to cope with the disaster and, similarly, if the serious condition did not occur insurers felt they had compensated for an eventuality which had not materialised. The power of the courts to award provisional damages removes this uncertainty by allowing a plaintiff: (i) to receive damages on the basis of the pain and suffering and loss of amenity that he has already incurred and that he will suffer because of the ordinary consequences of the injury; and (ii) to recover further damages at a later date if specific risks of further injury materialise.

The Act accordingly allows, upon the matter being pleaded and proved, for a further award to be made when a plaintiff suffers a serious disease or deterioration as a result of the original tort which gave rise to the cause of action. Before it makes an order that a right exists for a subsequent further award, the court must be satisfied at the first trial that the plaintiff might, at some indefinite time, suffer a serious disease or deterioration. The court is required to specify in the order what the deterioration or disease is, and to indicate within what period of time the second application for damages must be made (see *Patterson v Ministry of Defence* (1987)).

In *Hurditch v Sheffield Health Authority* (1989), the Court of Appeal held that a disagreement over medical evidence in respect of a worker's risk of contracting mesothelioma and lung cancer did not prevent a court entering judgment and making an award for provisional damages. In a case such as this the court held that the subsequent trial, should the plaintiff contract one of these diseases, could still hear evidence on causation and determine in the light of medical evidence whether the subsequent disease was attributable to the original asbestos exposure (see Purchas LJ, [1989] 2 WLR at 839 d–h). These provisions, flexible and helpful as they are, will not assist in those cases where the disability flowing from an injury which has been compensated by an award turns out to be worse than originally thought. The right to recover further damages arises only where nominated diseases or deteriorations have been stipulated in the order following a trial for provisional damages.

In practice, there has been a degree of judicial reluctance to award provisional damages except in very clear cases. In cases where there is a very small risk of a serious deterioration or a risk of contraction of a serious disease the court may exercise its discretion to make a final award (cf *Ivory v Martens, Butterworths Personal Injury Litigation Service* I (637) where the risk of a drain shunt in an infant plaintiff's head was said to be less than 2%). Further, if there is a certainty of a deterioration as opposed to a chance, then there is no scope for awarding provisional damages.

Again, in *Willson v Ministry of Defence* ([1991] 1 All ER 638) the court held that the requirement for a serious deterioration meant something beyond ordinary deterioration, such as routinely occurs in cases where an injured joint is likely to develop osteo-arthritis. Accordingly, in *Willson* it was held that even if the plaintiff did develop arthritis to the point at which he could no longer do his job, that was a consequence of the progression of the disease and was not to be equated with a serious deterioration, so an award for provisional damages was not made.

In *Middleton v Elliott Turbo Machinery Ltd* ((1990) Times, 29 October) the Court of Appeal held that a claim for provisional damages could not include a declaration to the effect that, if the plaintiff should die as a result of a serious deterioration, his dependants would be entitled to bring a claim under the Fatal Accidents Act 1976.

2. Structured settlements

The principle of the lump sum award, as opposed to periodic payments, has also been called into question by commentators, particularly with regard to cases where very large awards have been made to severely injured plaintiffs who require constant care, attention and rehabilitation. In *Lim Poh Choo v Camden and*

Islington Area Health Authority (1980) (p 430), Lord Scarman aired some of these concerns when he said:

> 'The course of this litigation illustrates with devastating clarity insuperable problems implicit in a system of compensation for personal injuries which . . . can yield only a lump sum . . . The award which covers past, present and future injury and loss must under our law be of a lump sum assessed at the conclusion of the legal process. The award is final, it is not susceptible to review as the future unfolds, substituting fact for estimation. Knowledge of the future being denied to mankind so much of the award as is attributed to future loss and suffering – in many cases the major part of the award – will almost surely be wrong. There is really only one certainty: the future will prove the award to be either too high or too low' ([1980] AC at 182h–183d).

Lord Scarman went on to indicate that attempting to deal with this problem in the way that Lord Denning, the then Master of the Rolls, indicated in the Court of Appeal in *Lim's* case, via interim payments, was inappropriate. Such a proposal raised issues of social, economic and financial policy which were not amenable to judicial reform, as they would almost certainly be controversial and could be resolved by legislation only. Problems of speculating what a plaintiff's life expectation would be, what the precise degree of disability will be, what particular level of care a plaintiff may require, the degree of rehabilitation which will be necessary, and any particular special resources and accommodation that a plaintiff may need led some insurance companies to investigate the concept of structured settlement.

This concept, developed in the United States of America and Canada, permits damages to be paid to a plaintiff through a mixture of a conventional lump sum together with annual payments for life or for a specified period. Legislation was not needed for structured settlements to become an important part of personal injury law. The impetus for this major development arose out of an agreement negotiated between the Association of British Insurers and the Inland Revenue in 1987, whereby a concession was made that payment by instalments of an antecedent debt in a form of an annuity could be treated as capital in the hands of the recipient and not income. Accordingly, it is now not uncommon for structured settlements to be undertaken by agreement between a plaintiff and the insurers of a defendant.

A structured settlement involves an agreement between the plaintiff and the defendant's insurers whereby the insurer agrees to become responsible for the defendant's debt namely the damages owed to the plaintiff by the defendant. The damages are usually calculated in the normal way but, instead of the plaintiff taking all of the lump sum, further agreement is reached whereby part of the total sum is given to the plaintiff immediately and the rest is used by the insurers to purchase annuities from a life insurance company. Such annuities when paid to the plaintiff do not attract taxation, because they are considered as instalments of a debt and therefore capital not income. The life insurer is required, however, as a matter of law to deduct tax from the payments it makes to the defendant's insurers but the defendant's insurers then gross up the net amount and pay that to the plaintiff. In turn, by agreement with the Inland Revenue, the defendant's insurers can recover the cost of grossing up as a deduction from its liability for corporation tax.

The great advantage for a severely injured plaintiff is the knowledge that damages should never run out, because the annuities will be agreed for life or for a period that on the medical evidence is likely to be for life. Further, the annuities can be retail price index-linked so that the effect of inflation will not whittle away the purchasing power of the periodic payment. Moreover the plaintiff may save very substantially in respect of tax because, although damages are not subject to taxation in personal injury actions (Income and Corporation Taxes Act 1988, s 329), income generated from damages invested as a capital sum is subject to income tax and in more serious cases can cause a 40% liability to taxation.

The defendant's insurers further derive benefits from a structured settlement because they require a discount on the structured sum before they are willing to enter into the agreement. Typical discounts tended to be in the range of 10%, although recently they have fallen to around $7^1/_2$%. (See Stephen Worthington, 'General Principles' Chapter 1 and Rodney Nelson Jones, 'Case Law' Chapter 2 in Goldrein and deHaas (eds), *Structured Settlements* (1993).)

Structured settlements have been agreed in many different types of actions arising out of road traffic accidents and industrial accidents and may include an agreement for the benefit of dependents in a fatal accident. Similarly, there need not be a finding of liability, but damages can be structured following agreement of a compromise offer between the parties. At present, there is no power for a court to impose a structured settlement, and the agreement can only be implemented by consent between the parties (see *Burke v Tower Hamlets Health Authority* (1989) (p 266), *Fournier v Canadian National Rly Co* (1927) and *Metcalfe v London Passenger Transport Board* (1938)).

In medical negligence cases, structured settlements have been made available notwithstanding the absence of liability insurers. Historically, until the implementation of the National Health Service and Community Care Act 1990, the health authorities were not permitted to insure against medical malpractice and claims were paid out of their own budgets and in some cases by funding from the Department of Health. Further, prior to 1 January 1990, damages were contributed to by the medical defence organisations in accordance with a sharing agreement concerning National Health Service hospital doctors set up in 1954 under Circular HM (54)32. The medical defence organisations did not pay corporation tax, so they had no incentive to enter into structured settlements. On 1 January 1990 the health authorities took over past and future claims arising out of medical malpractice in hospitals, and this provided an impetus for health authorities to consider structured settlements (see Richard Lewis, 'Health Authorities and the Payments of Damages by Means of a Pension', *Modern Law Review*, November 1993).

The first structure in a medical negligence action is the case of *Field v Herefordshire Health Authority* (p 331) in which the health authority pursued the normal route of purchasing annuities from life offices. The conventional award was agreed at £1,700,000, £550,000 of which was taken as a lump sum to deal with immediate and future expenditure principally of a capital nature involved in caring for a grievously injured child arising out of the negligent use of forceps at her birth. The structured sum produced an annuity of £59,000 per annum guaranteed for life or ten years together with two deferred annuities and a further lump sum being paid every five years. The saving to the Department of Health was estimated to be £200,000.

Subsequently the National Health Service Management Executive gave advice on 11 March 1992 to area health authority regional directors of finance that, instead of purchasing annuities from the life offices, a self-financed option would usually be best value for money. This method of self-funding allows payments to be made to the plaintiff directly from the health authority's own income. This has the advantage for the health authority of not having to pay out a large lump sum to a life office to purchase an annuity. It further has the benefit that, because health authorities and National Health Service trust hospitals do not pay tax, they are in a position to pay the plaintiff in full without deducting the tax which a life office must pay on a purchase life annuity.

An example of a self-funded structure is to be found in the case of *Lovell v Southampton and South West Hampshire Health Authority* (p 436). Victoria Lovell when she was three and three-quarter years old suffered irreversible brain damage following a cardiac arrest due to a plug of phlegm entering her windpipe whilst in the recovery room after an operation to correct a squint. Damages on a conventional basis were agreed in the sum of £875,000 of which the health authority agreed to structure £465,000 and provide periodic payments of £24,114.96 per annum increasing annually in line with the retail price index payable for life and for a guaranteed minimum period of ten years whether the child survived or not. The discount in that case was £47,000.

In *Flynn v Maidstone Health Authority (No 2)* (p 335) the health authority took no discount, in return for the plaintiff forgoing any minimum guarantee period of the annuity payments, which accordingly by agreement would cease on the plaintiff's death. A similar agreement had been reached in *O'Toole v Merseyside Regional Health Authority* (p 485) (see also *Tombs v Merton and Sutton Area Health Authority* for a further example of the structured settlement involving a hospital where a substantial discount of £100,000 was received). Increasingly, as the merits of structured settlements in hospital negligence cases are recognised on all sides, the trend has been for there to be no discount from the damages, provided that the plaintiff accepts that the periodic payments to him will cease on his death.

Lewis (above) has calculated that by August 1993, 25 structures were in place and many more were awaiting settlement and expressed the view that such agreements were likely to increase significantly in the future. However, it cannot be automatically assumed that a structured settlement will always be in the best interests of any particular plaintiff. In *Pimpalkhare v North West Hertfordshire Health Authority* (p 495), a plaintiff with quadriplegia following a negligently handled birth opted to accept a conventional sum of £1,270,000. That sum was approved and the matter was adjourned to consider a structured settlement in which the health authority sought a discount between £60,000 and £95,000 which left a contingency fund of £650,000 to purchase an annuity. The annuity produced would have been an index linked tax free income of £27,795. However, the plaintiff's solicitors' accountants using a model portfolio from the Public Trustee estimated that the plaintiff would be financially better off with a conventional award and that was approved by the judge. Practitioners accordingly not only have a duty to consider a structured settlement, but also to assess its financial benefits vis à vis other managed funds. The management of such funds may be undertaken in suitable cases by the court of protection, or by a trust.

3. Pain, suffering and loss of amenity

The award made in respect of the physical pain and suffering, and the effect on the lifestyle of the injured person necessarily focuses upon their particular consequences on that plaintiff. Accordingly, an award for the loss of a finger in an elderly person will be substantially lower than that for a young pianist whose promising career is blighted. So, for example, in *Nutbrown v Sheffield Health Authority* (p 481) a 72-year-old man who suffered severe brain damage following a prostatectomy and who was left with some insight into his disabilities was awarded £25,000. The trial judge came to the view that the appropriate sum to compensate such person for pain, suffering and loss of amenity, had he been aged 30 would have been £50,000 and he reduced the damages on the basis of the age of the plaintiff whose life expectancy was approximately ten years.

However, given that there is no obvious equation between physical injury and financial compensation, general damage awards tend to have a strong aspect of conventionality about them. In effect, awards under this head of damage are within a flexible judicial range which is influenced but not constrained by previous reported comparable cases. These cases do not have the authority of precedents but are persuasive. They are reported principally in: Kemp and Kemp, *The Quantum of Damages* Sweet & Maxwell, Volume 2 and 3, *Butterworths Personal Injury Litigation Service, Current Law Yearbook* (and monthly parts), and *Halsbury's Laws Monthly Review*. In addition, the Judicial Studies Board also publishes guidelines on general damages which are reproduced in Kemp and Kemp. In considering the level of damages in this respect, the judge is entitled to take a broad perspective of the effects of the injury including all aspects of past and future pain, discomfort, sickness, anxiety, loss of function, mental anguish, embarrassment, humiliation and, where appropriate, disfigurement. Loss of amenity may include the interference or cessation of leisure activities, sporting abilities, recreation and hobbies. If a particular career can no longer be followed then loss of enjoyment of work, if appropriate, may also sound in damages. Similarly, other losses such as the loss of enjoyment of family life, the loss of prospects of marriage, and losses through sexual malfunction will also be evaluated in money's worth.

If an injury or a disease is likely to shorten life, it is a matter statutorily singled out by the Administration of Justice Act 1982, s 1, for a judge to consider. Damages specifically for the acceleration of death as a separate head of damage, known as loss of expectation of life, were abolished by the Administration of Justice Act 1982 s 1, but the same section went on to enjoin the court in the following way:

'If the injured person's expectation of life has been reduced by the injuries, the court, in assessing damages in respect of pain and suffering caused by the injuries, shall take account of any suffering caused or likely to be caused to him by awareness that his expectation of life has been so reduced' (Administration of Justice Act 1982, s 1(1)(*b*)).

Awards for pain, suffering and loss of amenity necessarily involve a value judgment about the worth of the loss of an eye, a leg or the loss of one's reason, but they are in theory meant to be substantial compensation rather than a token solace and as such are to be based on objective assessments of loss. This principle was espoused in *H West & Son Ltd v Shephard* (1964) and confirmed by the House of Lords in *Lim Poh Choo v Camden and Islington Area Health Authority* (1980) (p 430). In *Lim*, a plaintiff sustained brain damage of such a degree that she was not aware of the catastrophe that had befallen her, but was nevertheless held to be entitled to receive full damages in respect of the deprivation of the ordinary amenities of life. The fact of her being unaware of the loss did not eliminate the actuality of the deprivation. Dr Lim suffered a cardiac arrest when aged 36 after a minor operation as a result of admitted negligence which left her a 'barely sentient human wreck'. She was awarded, inter alia, £20,000 for pain, suffering and loss of amenity at her trial in December 1977, on the basis that she had suffered a total loss, objectively appraised, of the amenities of life. The fact that Dr Lim was unaware of her predicament was not a relevant matter: nor was the court concerned with the question of how the plaintiff would use the award.

Awards for pain, suffering and loss of amenity in a so-called 'ordinary' case of tetraplegia or quadriplegia were given a guideline figure of £75,000 in *Housecroft v Burnett* (1986) for a plaintiff who was not in pain, was fully aware of the disability, had a life expectancy of twenty-five years or more and had retained facilities of speech, sight and hearing but obviously needed help with bodily functions. Miss Housecroft was aged 16 when she was rendered tetraplegic in a road traffic accident, and she was awarded £80,000 for pain, suffering and loss of amenity.

General damage awards are meant to keep up with inflation and any comparable case should be uplifted in accordance with the retail price index. The current maximum level of general damages (January 1995) is in the range of £130,000, as was awarded in the case of *Whiteside v Howes (Butterworths Personal Injury Litigation Service*, Bulletin No 25, November 1994), a case which concerned an 18-year-old injured in a road traffic accident who had suffered severe brain damage and was unable to stand or walk, cry, laugh or speak, was dependent on her mother for all domestic toilet activities but had a normal life expectancy and was fully conscious and aware of her predicament.

Medical negligence cases feature amongst the highest awards of damages, because many concern severe brain damage often involving children at birth with extensive expectations of life. In *Faulkner v Wandsworth Health Authority* (p 330) a 13-year-old was awarded in 1994, £125,000 general damages in respect of cerebral palsy following asphyxiation at his negligently handled birth. The plaintiff had a life expectancy of between thirty and forty years and a total award of £1,127,000 was made. In *Almond v Leeds Western Health Authority* (p 226), an award of £105,000 general damages was made in 1990 in respect of severe brain damage and dyskinetic cerebral palsy occasioned at birth with a total award of £1,156,000 being made. Similarly in *Willett v North Bedfordshire Health Authority* (1993) (p 606), £105,000 for general damages was awarded to a child with a life expectancy of 30 years who suffered from cerebral palsy and spastic quadriplegia. In *Janardan v East Berkshire Health Authority* (p 402) an award of £115,000 was made in respect of general damages following negligent obstetric management of a plaintiff who suffered severe cerebral palsy, had a life expectancy of 55, had virtually no power of speech and whose muscle tone was so grossly impaired that he could not sit independently let alone stand or walk. (See also *Lamey v Wirral Health Authority* (p 423), *Cassel v Riverside Health Authority* (p 271), *Nash v South Mead Health Authority* (p 476), *O'Donnell v South Bedfordshire Health Authority* (p 483)).

In *Aboul-Hosn v Trustees of the Italian Hospital* (1987) (p 220), a 19-year-old suffered irreversible brain damage reducing his mental age to two, as a result of negligent treatment following an operation to remove a cyst. The plaintiff was awarded £85,000 for pain, suffering and loss of amenity in circumstances where he could not walk except in a zombie-like fashion, his eyesight was severely impaired, he could not speak, he would never work or marry and he had some limited insight into his predicament. In *Thomas v Wignall* (1987) (p 581), a 16-year-old who suffered permanent brain damage after a negligently administered anaesthetic was awarded an agreed £60,000 damages in respect of pain, suffering and loss of amenity. The plaintiff was left in a position of severe intellectual impairment with mood swings that made her occasionally aggressive; she was barely able to communicate, required a wheelchair and was frequently incontinent.

In *Roberts v Johnstone* (1988) (p 527), an agreed figure of £75,000 was awarded to a plaintiff who was born with a severe haemolytic disease and suffered grievous disabilities including brain damage, due to the defendant's failure to give appropriate treatment to her mother during pregnancy. The infant plaintiff was hyperactive, incontinent, incapable of speech, was deaf, retarded and autistic.

Earlier cases include *Croke v Wiseman* (1982) (p 294) where an infant plaintiff who suffered brain damage following a cardiac arrest during treatment was awarded £35,000 in 1979 for severe quadriplegia. In *Connolly v Camden and Islington Area Health Authority* (1981) (p 285), an overdose of anaesthetic to a new-born baby rendered him epileptic, severely mentally disabled and unlikely to be able to walk properly. He was awarded £50,000 for pain, suffering and loss of amenity. In *Moser v Enfield and Haringey Area Health Authority* (1982) (p 463), a four-year-old suffered irreversible brain damage following a negligent anaes-thetic. The child had no insight into his condition of quadriplegia, was almost blind, was doubly incontinent and was unable to move. He had a life expectancy of approximately another twenty years. He was awarded £35,000.

In cases of less serious injuries, the judge will also be guided by comparable cases that may occur reasonably routinely in areas of non-medical personal injury. Many of these cases will present little difficulty in assessment. For example in *Mitchell v Liverpool Area Health Authority* (1985) (p 459), a one-month-old child who sustained circulation damage due to the defendant's negligence which resulted in an amputation of his arm below the elbow, was awarded £30,000 general damages for pain, suffering and loss of amenity. The Court of Appeal thought that this award was at the top of the range but declined to interfere with it. In *Hoffman v Sofaer* (1982) (p 382), a 47-year-old man was awarded £19,000 for a severely impaired wrist and hand, and a fused elbow, resulting from the negligent treatment of his general practitioner. In *Prescott v Basildon Health Authority* (p 497), failure to diagnose a Monteggia fracture led to an award of £15,000 general damages, in circumstances where a lorry driver was unable to continue driving a van beyond ten years because of deterioration in his right wrist. A similar failure to diagnose the condition in a six-and a half-year-old in *Champion v Grimsby Health Authority* (p 273) led to an award of £8,000 general damages. (See also *Mulla v Blackburn Hyndburn and Ribble Valley Health Authority* (p 464), *Reay v South Tees Health Authority* (p 519), *Connor v Fison-Clarke* (1987) (p 286), *McLoughlin v Greenwich and Bexley Area Health Authority* (1984) (p 449).)

Other cases encountered in the area of medical malpractice tend to be a little more removed from conventional personal injury, for instance the anaesthetic awareness claims. In *Ackers v Wigan Area Health Authority* (1986) (p 221), a plaintiff developed severe depression following a caesarean section for the delivery of her first child during which she was awake but unanaesthetised. She was unable to speak or inform the medical staff of her plight because she had been paralysed by a pre-operative relaxant drug. She was receptive to pain during the operation. She was awarded £12,000 general damages in June 1985. In 1991, £15,000 was awarded for general damages in respect of anaesthetic awareness in the case of *Patlan v East Cumbrian Health Authority*. Mr Patlan was awake during the course of an operation on his leg and felt the scalpel being applied and also his leg being drilled and described the pain like an electric shock. Mr Patlan tried to communicate to the practitioners by wiggling his toes, but he heard them say it was just reflexes. He also tried to stop breathing so as to alert the doctors but the ventilator started breathing for him. In *Esson v Gloucester Health Authority* (No 2) (p 323), £14,500 was awarded in general damages to Mrs Esson who was conscious during an exploratory laparotomy. She described her pain as excruciating and was aware of being poked, prodded and kneaded. She developed a post traumatic stress syndrome, some minimal symptoms persisting after five years. In *Davies v Mid Glamorgan Health Authority* (p 301) £3,000 was awarded for pain, suffering and loss of amenity in circumstances where a woman was conscious during an operation; she found this terrifying but did not experience actual pain. Finally in *Kewley v Blackpool Wyre and Fylde Health Authority* (p 412) £12,900 was awarded in general damages to a plaintiff who was awake during a caesarean section, was unable to communicate this fact to her doctors, and developed post traumatic stress disorder of moderate severity.

Psychiatric injury also featured prominently in the case of *Biles v Barking Health Authority* (1988) (p 246). Mrs Biles suffered clinical depression following a sterilisation which proved to be unnecessary. She had thereafter undertaken many steps in an attempt to conceive and had undergone several operations and tests which had caused pain and operation scarring. She had also developed severe sexual disfunction. She was awarded £45,000. In *G v North Tees Health Authority* (1989) (p 344), a mother and daughter were each awarded £5,000 general damages for pain, suffering and loss of amenity in circumstances where the infant plaintiff had been investigated for possible sexual abuse following the contamination of her vaginal swab with an adult's which had contained sperm. The child was examined and interviewed and as a result suffered nightmares and bedwetting. The mother had felt suicidal until the mistake was disclosed to her, and the affair had exacerbated her phobic anxiety state. (See also *Grieve v Salford Health Authority* (p 362), *Kerby v Redbridge Health Authority* (p 412).)

Gynaecological and obstetric injuries also figure frequently in medical negligent actions. In *Harris v Bromley Health Authority* (p 370) general damages of £28,000 were awarded in 1990 in respect of a failure to diagnose a third degree tear which damaged the plaintiff's anal sphincter. The plaintiff suffered with double incontinence and her sexual and social life was severely affected. In *Lofthouse v North Tees Health Authority* (p 434) the plaintiff's perineum was torn during the birth of her first child and was improperly stitched. The plaintiff needed four more operations to refashion the perineum and during two years was unable to have sexual intercourse. She was awarded £10,500 in 1992. In *Winterbone v West Suffolk Health Authority* (p 608) the plaintiff developed a fistula following the negligent stitching of her bladder to the vaginal vault during a hysterectomy and an operation to remove an ovarian cyst. The diagnosis was not made until two months after the operation and a further month passed before a successful repair was undertaken. The plaintiff was awarded £4,500 general damages in 1993. Similarly in *Marram v North Tees Health Authority* a plaintiff was awarded in 1992 £3,000 general damages for a vesico-vaginal fistula which was not closed until four and a half months later. In *Bovenzi v Kettering Health Authority* (p 256) £6,000 general damages was awarded in 1990 in respect of damage to the small bowel during a D & C operation requiring an emergency re-section, which left the plaintiff with bowel problems for six months and a six inch scar described as unsightly and ridged. In *Hill v Liverpool Health Authority* (p 379), a 43-year-old male suffered the removal of his left testicle following the negligent cutting off of the blood supply during the course of a vasectomy. He was awarded £22,500 in 1994 on the basis not only of his physical injury but his severe psychological reaction which caused impotency.

In *Morgan v Gwent Health Authority* (1987) (p 461), a plaintiff whose blood group was rhesus negative was negligently given a transfusion of rhesus positive blood which gave rise to potentially serious complications for any child that she might conceive. Only seventeen per cent of potential fathers would be compatible. The plaintiff received at first instance £8,000 which was increased to £20,000 by the Court of Appeal whose judges were persuaded that the breakdown of her engagement was due to the fact of the complications which would occur if her fiancé fathered her children.

The courts have also dealt with a number of cases where patients have been wrongly diagnosed as suffering from cancer. In *Vaughan v Paddington and North Kensington Area Health Authority* (1987) (p 592), a middle-aged woman with two adult children was told that she had contracted breast cancer and she agreed to a double mastectomy. She required a number of operations to fit and remove prostheses. In fact Mrs. Vaughan never did have cancer and she was awarded £25,000 for pain, suffering and loss of amenity which included pain and restriction in the back and arms caused by the operations, and for the fear that she was going to die, which she had had for approximately two and a half years. In *Harling v Huddersfield Health Authority* £36,400 general damages were awarded in 1992 to a 45-year-old plaintiff who underwent a mastectomy due to an incorrect diagnosis that the left breast was malignant. Subsequent operations to reconstruct the breast and to reduce the size of the right breast left bad disfigurement and the plaintiff suffered from depression, anxiety, frustration and embarrassment. In *Grayson-Crowe v Ministry of Defence* (p 359) £35,000 agreed general damages was paid in respect of an unwarranted hysterectomy on the basis of fibroids being cancerous. There was no evidence of malignancy in the pathology report, and the plaintiff became severely depressed and reclusive on account of her sterility. Similarly in *Evason v Essex Health Authority* (p 324) substantial damages amounting to £203,500, including general and special damages, was paid in respect of the confusion of tissue taken from the plaintiff's lymph node which resulted in her being wrongly diagnosed as suffering from cancer. Before the diagnosis was corrected the plaintiff underwent six courses of chemotherapy, three laparotomies and the removal of her right ovary. She underwent severe personality change and her career and marriage were destroyed and her physical and mental health were permanently impaired.

4. Loss of earnings and loss of earning capacity

A plaintiff, who, as a result of injuries, has been unable to work is entitled to recover as special damages the value of lost wages or profits up to the date of trial. These losses will be net of tax and National Insurance contributions. The loss of earnings may also include the monetary value of any benefits the plaintiff might have received, such as company cars and lost wage increases or lost prospects of promotion.

The loss of future earnings is considered as general damages, and the starting-point in its calculation is to consider the degree of disability. If a plaintiff is unable to work again he is entitled to his full losses until retirement age together with any pension loss. The annual amount of a loss is determined at the date of the trial and is based on the annual income the plaintiff would have received net of tax and National Insurance. This sum, called the multiplicand, is then multiplied by a figure based upon the period of years during which the inability to work will persist; this figure is called the multiplier. If for example, a plaintiff loses earnings over a period of forty years, that number will determine a maximum multiplier of approximately eighteen, which is considered appropriate by the court to account for the fact of accelerated receipt of the income.

The theory behind the use of the multiplier and multiplicand is to provide the plaintiff with a lump sum which when invested will produce an annual income commensurate with the loss incurred. The courts work on a notional rate of return on the capital sum invested of approximately 4.5% (see *Cookson v Knowles* (1978)). The multiplier may also be reduced to allow for other contingencies such as, for example, the unstable nature of the job or career the plaintiff was previously engaged in. The sum awarded is therefore meant to represent a capital amount which when invested will give an annual income equivalent to the plaintiff's lost income, so that the interest and capital combined are exhausted at the end of the period when the plaintiff would no longer have worked. The courts have eschewed a fine actuarial-based calculation and have used the mode of calculation based upon the multiplier and multiplicand, even where evidence indicates that in times of inflation it may undercompensate.

The courts have rejected the taking into account of the fact of inflation both in the calculation of loss of future earnings and loss of future pension rights (see *Lim Poh Choo v Camden and Islington Area Health Authority* (1980) (p 430), and *Auty v National Coal Board* (1985)). There is, however, mounting evidence that over the last twenty years the gross real return after taking inflation into account on risk-free investments was nearly always well under 4% per annum and probably nearer 2 to 2½%. This has resulted in increased pressure upon the courts to recognise the possibility that plaintiffs are systematically undercompensated in terms of the calculation of the future loss of earnings (see, for example, Kemp and Kemp, Chapter 8; *Actuarial Evidence in Related Calculations*, the report by the Working Party of Lawyers and Actuaries chaired by Sir Michael Ogden QC; *Structured Settlements and Interim and Provisional Damages* (Law Com No 125)).

A plaintiff with a reduced capacity to work will be awarded the difference between his pre-accident and post-accident working capacity, and will be under a duty to mitigate his loss by attempting to find suitable employment. In *Billingham v Hughes* (1949), the defendants were credited with an allowance representing the plaintiff's residual earning capacity as a radiologist in circumstances where his injury had meant that he could not pursue his career as a general practitioner.

A child injured at birth or at a very young age to a degree that the capacity to work is reduced or destroyed may claim for loss of earnings (see *Connolly v Camden and Islington Area Health Authority* (1981) (p 285)). In *Croke v Wiseman* (1982) (p 294), the multiplier/multiplicand approach was used by basing the annual prospective loss on the national average wage; this was held to be justified by the Court of Appeal given the quality of the infant plaintiff's background. In *Moser v Enfield and Haringey Area Health Authority* (1982) (p 463), a similar basis was used. In *Almond and Almond v Leeds Western Health Authority* (p 226) one and a half times the national average income was used as a multiplicand where evidence was accepted that the child in question would have been educated to a university or polytechnic level.

In *Cassel v Riverside Health Authority*, the infant plaintiff came from a family of successful lawyers and businessmen, and in view of that favourable background, the Court of Appeal upheld an award of £35,000 per annum net and refused to interfere with the multiplier of 10 where the child was 8 at the time of the trial and was likely to live until 65 or more. (See also *Janardian v East Berkshire Health Authority* (p 402).) Awards to infants for loss of future earnings are heavily discounted because of accelerated receipt, recognising that they are receiving at trial sums which they would not have earned until ten or more years later. So for example in *Moser* a multiplier of 5 was awarded where the period of acceleration was 7 years and the anticipated working life was 13. In *Almond*, where the acceleration was 12 years and the anticipated working life was 39 years, a multiplier of 10 was used.

Some serious injuries reduce the life expectancy of plaintiffs. The loss of earnings in those years known as the 'lost years' when the plaintiff will be deceased but would otherwise have been alive and working is recoverable. Since *Harris v Empress Motors Ltd* (1983), a plaintiff will normally be required to give credit for his living expenses, in calculating the 'lost years' claim for future loss of earnings. The reasoning is that the costs of maintaining himself will not be required in those notional lost years when the plaintiff will not be alive. For a couple with no dependent children, the credit given in this respect is normally approximately 50% of the net income. The percentage of living expenses to be deducted is lower if there are dependent children, approximately 30%, and higher if the plaintiff is unmarried. In the case of a very young child, the lost years claim is likely to be small, if awarded at all (cf *Croke v Wiseman* (1982) (p 294)).

The claim in respect of the lost years does not survive for the benefit of the estate of a plaintiff, having been specifically abolished by the provisions of the Administration of Justice Act 1982, s 4(2) for death occurring after 1 January 1983. Any dependants of a deceased may, however, claim in respect of the loss of their dependency pursuant to the provisions of the Fatal Accidents Act 1976. Certain categories of dependants are also entitled to a statutory award of £3,500 in respect of bereavement where a wrongful act caused death, prior to the 1 April 1991 and thereafter £7,500 (see Fatal Accidents Act 1976, s 1A, as amended by the Administration of Justice Act 1982, s 3(1), by which the Lord Chancellor has power to vary the statutory amount).

In cases where the lost earnings of a young woman are being assessed, it is probably not necessary to take into account the prospects of her marriage in determining a multiplier, particularly where no account for the plaintiff's loss of the prospect of marriage has been taken in the award for general damages for loss of amenity (see *Hughes v McKeown* (1985), *Housecroft v Burnett* (1986) and *Thomas v Wignall* (1987) (p 581)). In *Thomas v North West Surrey Health Authority* (p 580) a 27-year-old woman was awarded a multiplier of 13 in respect of loss of earnings in a case where life expectancy was normal but the plaintiff had no prospect of working, having sustained severe brain damage following an operation for an abortion.

An example of the court's approach in determining loss of future earnings can be found in *Aboul-Hosn v Trustees of the Italian Hospital* (1987) (p 220) where the court accepted that a young man with four 'A' levels and a place at university had a reasonable prospect of earning £18,000 per annum and applied a multiplier of 17, giving £306,000 loss of earnings. The plaintiff was also found to have lost reasonable prospects of having a company car, and £25,000 was added to the award in this respect. In *Nash v South Mead Health Authority* a 17-year-old was awarded at trial a future loss of earning capacity in the sum of £107,930.16. Mr Nash had suffered cerebral palsy due to a negligently handled birth and, although he had gross impairment of his physical function, his intellect was unaffected and he had passed eight GCSEs and was studying for two 'A' levels. The court held that he had a residual earning capacity in the sum of £5,640 per annum but had he not sustained his physical injuries he would have been capable of earning £14,635 per annum. He was accordingly awarded with a multiplier of 12, an annual partial loss of £8,995.

Often an injury results in a plaintiff being put at a disadvantage in relation to others in competing for jobs in the labour market. An injury may allow a plaintiff to continue working but may make him unsuitable for certain types of work and may, because of any continuing disability, make him less likely to get a job when competing with the fully able. The courts have recognised this as a basis for compensation, and an award is made in the circumstances for so-called disadvantage in the labour market and may be made whether a plaintiff is working or is unemployed at the date of the trial or indeed has not yet reached working age (see *Moeliker v A Reyrolle & Co Ltd* (1977), *Cooke v Consolidated Fisheries Ltd* (1977)). The award takes into account the fact that the disadvantage, that is being unemployed or underemployed for longer periods because of the disability, may not happen at all, and if it does happen may occur at an indeterminate date. The award is often based on the annual value of the plaintiff's wage and accordingly can be substantial if the risk of the plaintiff losing his job is very great (see *Foster v Tyne & Wear County Council* (1986)).

In *Mitchell v Liverpool Area Health Authority* (1985) (p 459), a one month old baby who suffered a below-elbow arm amputation was not awarded at first instance anything in respect of his claim for disadvantage on the labour market. The Court of Appeal held, however, that there was a realistic prospect that he would not earn as much as he would have if he had had no disability, and awarded £5,000 which reflected the heavy discounting required for accelerated receipt. Similarly, in *Giles v Pontefract Health Authority,* £20,000 was awarded in respect of future loss of earnings to a 9-year-old who suffered dystocia of his left shoulder at birth causing damage to the brachial plexus resulting in some paralysis. The child was obviously disadvantaged on the labour market, in that he could not lift heavy objects or perform some tasks which required the dexterity of both hands.

5. Expenses

Expenses incurred up to the date of trial are recoverable as special damages, thereafter as general damages. A plaintiff is entitled to recover all expenses reasonably incurred or which will be reasonably incurred and which foreseeably arise out of injury suffered. Such expenses can range from the travelling costs of relatives visiting a plaintiff while in hospital, medical fees, the cost of nursing care, the cost of domestic help, modifications to buildings, the extra costs of maintaining and running specially accommodated premises, appliances to aid the disabled, extra holiday costs incurred because of disablement, increased travelling and car costs, recompense for an inability to undertake household repairs, decorations or gardening, costs of physiotherapy and rehabilitation, to extra costs in respect of special clothing and bedding.

In the case of a patient who is unable to manage his own affairs, the costs of a trust fund or the Court of Protection fees are also recoverable (cf *Moser v Enfield and Haringey Area Health Authority* (1983) (p 463), where £9,300 was awarded in this respect, and *Aboul-Hosn v Trustees of the Italian Hospital* (1987) (p 220) where £34,500 was awarded for Court of Protection fees in a claim totalling £1,032,000). If the Court of Protection is to administer the fund, the precise amount of the award cannot be determined in advance of the total judgment sum as the fees are charged on a sliding scale according to the amount administered. (See rule 77 and the Appendix to the Court of Protection Rules 1984, SI 1984/2035, the *Supreme Court Practice* (Volume 2, 1988).) In *Cassel v Riverside Health Authority* both the costs of the Court of Protection and the costs of a professional receiver were allowed in the sums of £32,700 and £47,700 in a total award of over £1,000,000. The trial judge did not reduce this amount by ten per cent, notwithstanding that there had been agreement that liability would be entered for 90% of the value of the claim. The Court of Appeal held that the Court of Protection and the professional receiver's fees formed part of the damages, rather than part of the costs of the action, and as such they were subject to the agreed deduction of ten per cent.

Future expenses are normally calculated on a multiplicand and multiplier basis wherever possible, and the normal starting point is the expected longevity of the plaintiff. In cases where nursing and domestic care is required, the multiplier may be larger than that for a loss of earnings claim because in some cases the life expectancy of a plaintiff may not be reduced below the normal retirement age.

Medical expenses can be recovered, even if a plaintiff could have used the National Health Service, because of the specific provisions of the Law Reform (Personal Injuries) Act 1948 s 2(4). If, in fact, the National Health Service is used or is likely to be used in the future, the cost of private care is not recoverable. If a plaintiff has been in a National Health Service hospital, nursing home or other similar institution, he has to give credit for the savings in respect of his living expenses during that period of institutional care in respect of his award for loss of earnings (see the Administration of Justice Act 1982 s 5, which came into force on 1 January 1983).

If nursing and domestic care is rendered freely by a relative, the cost of giving that care is still recoverable notwithstanding that no money has changed hands (*Donnelly v Joyce* (1974)). The measure of nursing and other care gratuitously rendered may be the lost wages incurred by the carer if he/she had to give up a job to look after the disabled person (*Croke v Wiseman* (1982) (p 294)). In such a case where a job has been given up, the ceiling on the award is most likely to be the commercial rate which would be required to get a professional carer to do a similar job (see *Housecroft v Burnett* (1986)). Where the carer does not give up work, a claim still exists which will obviously depend on the level of care given; and again the ceiling on such an award is probably the going commercial rate (see *Cunningham v Harrison* (1973), *Aboul-Hosn v Trustees of the Italian Hospital* (1987) (p 220)).

In *Fish v Willcox and Gwent Health Authority* (p 332) the plaintiff gave birth to a child suffering from spina bifida in respect of which the defendants admitted liability. The plaintiff gave up her job of £4,000 per annum to look after her child, and the trial judge awarded £5,000 per annum in respect of the nursing care which she afforded to her child. The plaintiff appealed on the basis that she also should have been awarded her loss of earnings. The Court of Appeal held that this was not so, as it would amount to double recovery. The plaintiff was only able to do one job at a time, and she should not therefore be entitled to be paid for doing two jobs at once.

In cases where the carer does not give up work, it is usual for a deduction to be made from the commercial rate to take into account the fact that the carer does not pay tax and national insurance and no commission is payable to any nursing agency. In *Blackburn v Newcastle Area Health Authority* (1 August 1988, unreported) Owen J reduced the care claim by one-third to reflect these facts. In *Fairhurst v St Helens and Knowsley Health Authority* (p 329) the Crossroads rates of pay for a home help were used to evaluate care given by parents to a profoundly disabled girl. The deduction was limited to one quarter to reflect the fact that the parents' care involved special skills. (*See Butterworths Personal Injury Litigation Service* (Volume 1, paragraph 558), and also *Almond and Almond v Leeds Western Health Authority* (p 226) where 50% was conceded by counsel.)

Future care and attention can amount to a considerable award of damages in those cases where a plaintiff needs constant or near-constant attention. In *Cassel v Riverside Health Authority* (1992) the future care costs in respect of a child who would never live independently, marry or work were assessed at £508,564. In *Nash v South Mead Health Authority* £190,000 was awarded to a child who had dyskinetic athetoid cerebral palsy, and where much of the burden of looking after him fell on the parents and younger sister. In *Rialas v Mitchell* (1984), £143,552 was awarded for future nursing care and attention in respect of a seriously disabled child who was injured when he was six years old. The court held that it was not unreasonable for the child to be cared for at home, even though he could be cared for more cheaply in an institution. In *Aboul-Hosn v Trustees of Italian Hospital* (above), £76,650 was awarded for care up until the date of the trial, equivalent to four and three-quarter years at an annual value of £16,137. The cost of future care was divided into two periods. In the first period, where it was anticipated that the parents could cope with the help of a night auxiliary nurse, £234,102 was awarded. In the second period, where the plaintiff would be required to live in a home, a further £112,994 was awarded, plus £53,704 for costs of a rehabilitation programme and for assistance from physiotherapists, speech therapists and dietitians, making £400,800 for total costs of future care.

In cases where a large award is made for care, particularly with reference to institutional care, and also for loss of earnings, the courts have been careful to avoid duplication of awards in that an overlap may occur between the two heads of damage. If a plaintiff is in care in an institution, then notionally he does not require that part of his lost income which would be used for living expenses, because the plaintiff is catered for under the costs of institutional care (see *Lim Poh Choo v Camden and Islington Area Health Authority* (1980) (p 430)).

Just as inflation is ignored in the calculation of an award, so also is the possible effect of a higher rate of taxation being levied on the amount of interest generated by a large capital sum awarded. In *Hodgson v Trapp* (1988), the House of Lords overruled *Thomas v Wignall* (1987) (p 581) where the multiplier in respect of the loss of income and cost of future care was increased by one to reflect the higher risks of taxation that might accrue on the interest from the damages. The House of Lords took the view that it would only be in rare circumstances that an increase in the multiplier would in fact be justified (per Lord Oliver [1988] 3 WLR at 1299–1300).

Where a plaintiff is required to purchase special accommodation to enable him to manage his domestic life in a reasonable fashion, he is not entitled to the purchase costs of the property but only to the additional annual cost during his lifetime of providing that accommodation, which is currently valued at two per cent of the net capital cost per annum. In addition, any costs in converting the property, which do not amount to betterment, are recoverable (*Roberts v Johnstone* (1988) (p 527). In *Thompson v South Tees Area Health Authority* (1990) the need for a specially adapted bungalow was accepted by the court in the case of a severely disabled child. The parents had built a bungalow at a cost of £169,460 and two per cent of this cost was awarded for twelve and a half years, making a sum of £42,365, in circumstances where the life expectancy of the plaintiff was twenty to thirty years and she was aged nine at the date of the trial. In *Almond and Almond v Leeds Western Health Authority* (1990), £71,565 was awarded in respect of the need to move to and to convert special accommodation. In *Cassel v Riverside Health Authority,* (1992) £40,950 was awarded in respect of future accommodation. On appeal, the Court of Appeal found there was no expert evidence that a swimming pool was required for therapy as opposed to enjoyment, and that specific item was disallowed.

6. Deductions

The courts are required by statute to deduct certain statutory benefits paid to a victim who suffers a personal injury. Different statutory regimes apply to accidents occurring on or after 1 January 1989 and to those occurring before that date.

A. THE NEW REGIMES

The Social Security Act 1989 and the Social Security Administration Act 1992

Under these Acts, together with certain amendments in the Social Security Act 1990 and the Social Security (Recoupment) Regulations 1990, an entirely new system of deductions from personal injury damages has been set up. Under the scheme, practically all state benefits are deductible in full for a maximum period of five years and are deducted from the award and not simply from that part of the award which constituted loss of earnings. The scheme requires a defendant to pay to the Compensation Recovery Unit a sum equivalent to all the benefits that a plaintiff has received, as specified in a certificate of total benefit provided by the Compensation Recovery Unit. The period for which credit has to be given runs from the date of the injury or in the case of a disease, the date on which benefit is first claimed, to the date of payment of the damages. There is a maximum period of five years during which credit has to be given. The payments are made in total, notwithstanding that a plaintiff's damages might be reduced by contributory negligence or settlement reached in terms of less than a full value of the claim. Certain payments are exempt, the principal exceptions being those claims settled or judged to amount to £2,500 or less. These so-called small payments do not require any deductions at all. Further exemptions include payments under the Vaccine Damage Act 1979, awards made by the Criminal Injuries Compensation Board, payments made under the Fatal Accidents Act 1976 and periodic payments made under the terms of a structured settlement. In a structured settlement the total assessment of damages before any structuring is, however, subject to CRU deduction. The benefits which are to be deducted under the Social Security Administration Act 1992 include statutory sick pay, invalidity benefit, income support, family credit, reduced earnings allowance, retirement allowance, disability living allowance, sickness benefit, disablement benefit, unemployment benefit, attendance allowance, constant attendance allowance, severe disablement allowance, disability working allowance and mobility allowance. If a defendant fails to deduct the required amounts specified in the certificate of total benefit, he still remains liable to the Department of Social Security for such a sum. In calculating interest, the amount of the award is to be treated as reduced by the sum equal to the amount of the relevant payment specified in the certificate of total benefit (Social Security Act 1980, Sch 4, para 23 as amended by Social Security Act 1990, Sch 1, para 6).

Where a plaintiff is in receipt of state benefits before his injury and receives post-accident benefits he may be required to give credit for the post-accident benefits in the certificate of total benefit. This may be so even when the pre-accident benefits are no longer paid. To avoid this deduction from his general damages he should claim as an item of special damages those state benefits he would have received had his accident not occurred (*Hassall and Pether v Secretary of State for Social Security* [1995] 1 WLR 812, CA).

B. THE OLD REGIME

The Law Reform (Personal Injuries) Act 1948

This Act still remains relevant for injuries that occurred before 1 January 1989. The policy intention behind the Law Reform (Personal Injuries) Act 1948, s 2, was to prevent a plaintiff from so-called double recovery. The Act represents a political compromise and requires that one half of certain named benefits are to be deducted from the award for loss of earnings or disadvantage in the labour market for a period of five years from the date when the cause of action accrued. The named deductible benefits are sickness benefit, invalidity benefit, non-contributory invalidity pension and industrial disablement benefit which covers disablement gratuity and pension and hospital treatment allowance. The section also mentions injury benefit, which was abolished in April 1983. The argument that after the five year period has elapsed, the plaintiff should give credit for all of the benefits he continues to receive was roundly rejected in *Denman v Essex Area Health Authority* (1984) and *Jackman v Corbett* (1988) in favour of an alternative interpretation that the plaintiff should give no credit. A cause of action may be deemed to have accrued when damage which is more than negligible has occurred (*Cartledge v Jopling* (1963)). In some cases, therefore, it may be possible to argue where an injury or disease has been unattributed to the defendant's negligence or where there existed some small symptoms which were predominantly latent, that the five year period in question has run out before the benefits were paid. The benefits in question do fall to be deducted from an award for disadvantage in the labour market (see *Foster v Tyne and Wear County Council* (1986).

The prevailing judicial attitude has been towards deduction of other State benefits which are not stipulated within the 1948 Act. In *Hodgson v Trapp* (1988), the House of Lords unanimously held that both attendance and mobility allowances payable pursuant to the Social Security Act 1975, ss 35 and 37A fell to be deducted in full for the whole period they were likely to be awarded for (per Lord Bridge [1988] 3 WLR at 1285h–1286c). This reversed the Court of Appeal decision in *Bowker v Rose* (1978).

In the light of this mode of reasoning, full credit has to be given for certain benefits and receipts. These include statutory sick pay (*Palfrey v Greater London Council* (1985)); unemployment benefit (*Nabi v British Leyland (UK) Ltd* (1980), *Westwood v Secretary of State for Employment* (1985)); supplementary benefit and family income supplement (which on 4 April 1988 were renamed income support and family credit respectively) (*Lincoln v Hayman* (1982), *Gaskill v Preston* (1981)); reduced earning allowance (*Flanagan v Watts Blake Bearne & Co plc* [1992] PIQR P144).

Further, in *Hussain v New Taplow Paper Mill Ltd* (1988), a plaintiff, who was injured through the negligence of his employers, was required to give credit for the income he received while off sick which was paid to him under a scheme of permanent health insurance, the premium for which was paid by his employers and to which he did not contribute. The situation was held to be different in *Berriello v Felixstowe Dock and Railway Company* (1989) where an Italian seaman, who remained accountable for sums he had received to a fund administered by the Italian State, did not have to give credit for those sums because there was in fact no double recovery. In *Colledge v Bass Mitchells & Butlers Ltd* (1988), the Court of Appeal held that redundancy payments made to an injured workman, which arose because his injury made him more likely to be selected for redundancy, did fall to be deducted from a loss of earnings claim. If, however, on different facts a plaintiff would in any event have been likely to have been made redundant, the redundancy payments would not fall to be deducted as they would properly reflect the moneys paid for the previous service and loss of job.

There are two classes of receipts that may accrue to a plaintiff as a result of his injury and which are not required in law to be deducted from an award for damages. The first concerns insurance payments and pensions for which the plaintiff has contributed: (*Bradburn v Great Western Railway Company* (1874), *Parry v Cleaver* (1970), *Cunningham v Harrison* (1973), *Smoker v London Fire and Civil Defence Authority* ([1991] 2 AC 502)). The courts have considered as a matter of 'justice, reasonableness and public policy' (per Lord Reid in *Parry v Cleaver* ([1970] AC at 13)), that premiums previously paid by an injured person to protect him against a contingency such as an injury should not fall to the credit of the tortfeasor, arising as they do out of the prudence and income of the victims. A State retirement pension falls into this category, as does a contributory disability pension (see *Hewson v Downs* (1970)). Where, however, a plaintiff is claiming for loss of pension as a head of damage, he is required to give credit for any disability pension he receives, during the period for which he is claiming loss of the retirement pension (*Parry v Cleaver* (1970)).

The second class of exception is with respect to monies received through the benevolence of third parties motivated by sympathy for the misfortune of the plaintiff (see *Redpath v Belfast & Co Down Railway* (1947)).

In a Fatal Accidents Act 1976 claim, a widow was not required to give credit for her widow's pension which was paid to her on the death of her husband who was, at the time of death, in receipt of a retirement pension (*Pidduck v Eastern Scottish Omnibuses Ltd* (1989)). Section 4 of the Fatal Accidents Act 1976, as amended by s 3 of the Administration of Justice Act 1982, provides that:

> 'In assessing damages in respect of a person's death or an action under this Act, benefits which have accrued or will or may accrue to any person from his estate or otherwise as a result of his death shall be disregarded.'

Mrs Pidduck was not, on the wording of this Act, required to give any credit for the widow's pension she received because this arose on account of her husband's death. This was so notwithstanding the fact that she was entitled to, and did receive, a loss of dependency on her husband's own pension and was, accordingly, financially better off because of the death.

7. Interest

Interest is payable on the principle that a plaintiff is entitled to damages from the date when they accrued, and has therefore been kept out of money which is rightfully his, and which the defendants have continued to possess as an interest earning resource. A plaintiff is statutorily entitled to simple interest pursuant to the Supreme Court Act 1981, s 35A in cases where damages for personal injuries exceed £200 (see also County Courts Act 1984, s 69). No interest, however, can arise on future losses or expenses, as no loss has been incurred at the date of trial. Interest for continuing loss of earnings as special damages to the date of trial will run at one-half of the special account rate (formerly the short-term investment account rate) on the reasoning in *Jefford v Gee* (1970) that some of the loss had accrued immediately after the injury but some has accrued only immediately before the date of the trial, and one-half is a reasonable compromise. In those cases where the losses have accrued immediately after the accident, it is not offensive in principle to allow the full rate from the date at which the loss fully accrued. There is, however, some dispute on this issue because of conflicting opinion of the Court of Appeal expressed in *Dexter v Courtaulds* (1984) and in *Prokop v The Department of Health and Social Security* (1985). It is however desirable to plead the special circumstances if the full rate is being argued for, which in most cases would simply amount to the fact that the loss had accrued shortly after the tort.

In *Roberts v Johnstone* (1988) (p 527), the Court of Appeal held that nursing care expended before the trial was to be treated as special damage even where no-one had been employed but the adoptive mother had undertaken the caring role, and interest would therefore run at the higher rate. Interest runs at a lower rate in respect of general damages for pain, suffering and loss of amenity, currently at two per cent from the service of the writ (*Birkett v Hayes* (1982), *Wright v British Railways Board* (1983)). There would appear to be no good reason why the low rate of two per cent should apply to the conventional award for bereavement in a Fatal Accidents Act 1976 claim. General damages for pain, suffering and loss of amenity are to some extent inflation proofed because they rise more or less in line with the rate of inflation. However, conventional awards do not increase in the same manner and the amount for bereavement is statutorily fixed at £7,500. (Before it was abolished, the conventional award for the loss of expectation of life did attract the full rate of interest.) Full interest was awarded on bereavement damages in *Prior v Bernard Hastie & Co* (1987) and (*Sharman v Sheppard* [1989] CLY 1190).

Where there has been avoidable delay on the part of the plaintiff's advisers in prosecuting a claim the court may well abridge a claim for interest by reason of the delay. In *Nash v South Mead Health Authority* a 12-year delay in starting an action led to only seven years of interest being awarded in circumstances where a plaintiff injured at birth was 17 at the date of his trial. (See also *Spittle v Bunney* ([1988] 3 All ER 1031), *Cresswell v Eaton* ([1991] 1 All ER 484), *Corbett v Barking Havering and Brentwood Health Authority* (p 288).)

8. Aggravated and exemplary damages

As has been indicated, damages in tort are primarily compensatory and not punitive. There are, however, very limited exceptions in cases where the defendant has acted in such a high-handed manner that the court thinks it proper to make a punitive award. Such awards, known as exemplary damages, are normally constrained to situations where a government body or department has acted oppressively or where the defendant has sought to make a profit from the tort perpetrated on the plaintiff (see *Rookes v Barnard* (1964) and *Cassell & Co Ltd v Broome* (1972)). Similarly, an additional compensatory aspect to the award for damages may arise where the conduct of the defendant is so outrageous and perhaps motivated by spite and malice that the plaintiff's proper feelings of dignity and pride have been injured. These damages, known as aggravated damages, are more frequently awarded in defamation cases. See McGregor *Damages* (Sweet & Maxwell, 15th edn, 1988) p 1029, para 1623.

In medical mishap cases, the courts have indicated a reluctance to include an element of punitive damages in awards to plaintiffs. In *Kralj v McGrath* (1986) (p 420), Woolf J rejected the plaintiff's claim for aggravated damages arising out of an obstetric practice described as horrific and totally unacceptable:

> 'It is my view that it would be wholly inappropriate to introduce into claims of this sort, for breach of contract and negligence, the concept of aggravated damage ... it would be difficult to see why it could not even extend to cases where damages are brought for personal injuries in respect of driving. If the principle is right, a higher award of damages would be appropriate in a case of reckless driving which caused injury than would be appropriate in cases where careless driving caused identical injuries. Such a result seems to me to be wholly inconsistent with the general approach to damages in this area, which is to compensate the plaintiff for the loss that she has actually suffered, so far as it is possible to do so, by the award of monetary compensation and not to treat those damages as being a matter which reflects the degree of negligence or breach of duty of the defendant. I do, however, accept that the effect on a mother who during the course of her labour undergoes unnecessary suffering may be greater if this results not in the birth of a normal child but a child who is in the unfortunate condition that Daniel was here. It would be easier for a mother to forget or adjust to the consequences of that distressing experience if she has the comfort of a normal child. If instead of having the satisfaction in the birth of a normal child she has the distress of the knowledge that the child is disabled, subject to the disabilities that Daniel was, it would be more difficult for her to overcome the consequences and the unnecessary suffering may have a greater impact on her' ([1986] 1 All ER at 621 e–h).

Similarly, in *G v North Tees Health Authority* (1989) (p 344), no aggravated damages were awarded in the distressing circumstances where negligence led to the processing of a child as a possible victim of sexual abuse causing an aggravation of phobic anxiety in the child's mother and nightmares and enuresis in the child. In *Barbara v Home Office* (1984) (p 237) Leggatt J did make an award of £500 aggravated damages for the injury to the plaintiff's feelings in respect of a forcible injection by hospital officers on a prison inmate. However, the plaintiff's claim for exemplary damages was rejected on the basis that it did not follow that an act of mere negligence gave rise to such an award even if the victim regarded it as oppressive. (See also *H v Ministry of Defence* (p 362).)

Chapter 12

Claims for wrongful birth

1. Introduction

Where a woman conceives and gives birth to a child due to negligent advice or treatment concerning contraception, abortion, or sterilisation, questions arise as to what damages can be recovered in respect of the pain and suffering of childbirth, the loss of amenity to a mother in raising the unplanned child and the inevitable costs in raising and maintaining the child. Such claims have arisen out of a number of diverse circumstances, such as failing to diagnose and warn a woman that the child she was carrying might be affected by rubella (*Salih v Enfield Health Authority* (1991) (p 542), *McKay v Essex Area Health Authority* (p 447)), failing to give similar advice that an unborn child was at risk of a congenital deformity (*Fish v Willcox and Gwent Health Authority* (1994) (p 332)), failing to diagnose a pregnancy until an abortion under the Abortion Act 1967 was too late (*Gardiner v Mounfield and Lincolnshire Area Health Authority*), a failure to abort (*Scuriaga v Powell* (p 548), failed vasectomies (*Thake v Maurice* (p 579), *Gowton v Wolverhampton Health Authority* (p 358), *Benarr v Kettering Health Authority* (p 243) and failed sterilisation (*Udale v Grimsby Area Health Authority* (p 589), *Jones v Berkshire Area Health Authority* (p 405), *Allen v Bloomsbury Area Health Authority* (p 225), *McLellan v Newcastle Health Authority, Robinson v Salford Health Authority* (p 529) and *Walkin v South Manchester Health Authority* (p 597)).

Despite some initial hesitation by the courts in dealing with claims for wrongful birth it is now reasonably well established that the courts in principle will award damages in the following way:

(a) General damages for the mother in respect of the pain and suffering of childbirth, offset by the avoidance of the pain and suffering involved in a termination;

(b) General damages in respect of the lost amenity for a mother in raising a child who was born with disabilities. If the child is, however, normal the court will not be minded to award damages for loss of amenity on the basis that it is extinguished by the joy which raising a child brings;

(c) Special damages and future loss in respect of lost earnings incurred by the mother or carer who gives up work to look after the child;

(d) Special damages incurred in paying for the child's layette and other equipment;

(e) The cost of upkeep of the child, normally until 18 but possibly beyond. This would include maintenance and also any educational costs that might be incurred if the child would normally be educated privately. The costs might also include extending the home in certain circumstances.

2. The development of the courts' approach to wrongful birth

In *Scuriaga v Powell* (1980) (p 548), the plaintiff contracted with a doctor to conduct a lawful termination of her pregnancy. The termination was negligently carried out and a child was born. The trial judge awarded damages in respect of the plaintiff's loss of earnings and for the impairment of her marriage prospects, accepting the view that the recovery of such damages was not contrary to public policy. The trial judge also rejected a defence that any damage which the plaintiff had suffered was caused not by the breach of contract but by the plaintiff declining to undergo a second attempt to terminate her pregnancy. The Court of Appeal varied certain aspects of the award, but concurred in the view that the loss of future wages was recoverable. No claim was made in that case for the upkeep of the child.

Such a claim however was made and rejected by Jupp J in *Udale v Bloomsbury Area Health Authority* (1983) (p 589). The judge awarded £8,000 damages in total on the basis of the shock and anxiety that arose out of the unwanted pregnancy which had resulted from a negligent sterilisation. This sum included a claim in respect of the suffering caused by the pregnancy and birth itself, which was aggravated by the fear of having done the child inadvertent harm by taking drugs at a time when the mother was unaware she was pregnant. The judge rejected claims in respect of needing to extend the family accommodation to cater for the unplanned new arrival, for the baby's layette and for the cost of looking after the child up to the age of sixteen. Jupp J rejected these claims on the basis of public policy. The judge indicated that it would be highly undesirable that any child should learn that a court had publicly declared its life or birth to be a mistake and had awarded damages which could be conceived as proof of the child not being wanted. The judge also thought that, if such claims were allowed, it would create a subconscious pressure to encourage abortions by medical practitioners in order to avoid claims based on the cost of raising a child. The judge also inclined to the view that the birth of a child should be an occasion for rejoicing.

In *Thake v Maurice* (1985) (p 579), Pain J took a different view and made such an award in respect of the birth of a healthy child which had been born following a negligent vasectomy. The claim in this respect included the baby's layette (£717), the upkeep of the child till aged 17 (£5,960) and the mother's loss of earnings in that period. On a cross-appeal, the plaintiff further achieved general damages in the sum of £1,500 for the antenatal pain and suffering which Pain J had declined to award on the basis that the postnatal joy cancelled it out.

In *Emeh v Kensington and Chelsea and Westminster Area Health Authority* (1985) (p 321), the Court of Appeal preferred the view taken by Pain J to that taken by Jupp J and decided that it was not contrary to public policy to award damages for the wrongful birth of a child resulting in that case from a negligent sterilisation. Mrs Emeh, on appeal, received damages in respect of her own loss of earnings and the future costs of maintaining the child (£4,056 based on £507 per annum). She also received general damages for pain, suffering and loss of amenity in her own right for the normal birth and subsequent second sterilisation in the sum of £3,000. She further recovered the sum of £10,000 for her loss of amenity to cover the degree of future care that this child would need because it had been born with congenital deformities. The Court of Appeal in *Emeh* rejected the first instance reasoning of Park J who had determined that the plaintiff's failure to have an abortion when she found out that she was pregnant amounted to a novus actus interveniens or, alternatively, she had failed to mitigate her damages in not having the abortion. Purchas LJ, concurring with Lord Justices Slade and Waller, went on to analyse the public policy argument and saw it as misfounded:

'I see no reason for the court to introduce into the perfectly ordinary straightforward rules of recovery of damages, whether they are damages claimed for breach of contract or from tort, some qualification to reflect special social positions. If something has to be done in that respect, as Waller LJ cited from the speech of Lord Scarman in *McLoughlin v O'Brian* (1983), then that is a matter which falls more properly within the purview of Parliament' ([1985] QB at 1028 e–g).

The Court of Appeal in *Emeh* accordingly agreed with the reasoning of Pain J in *Thake v Maurice* (above) when he said:

'There remains some doubt whether the categories of public policy are now closed (see Cheshire and Fifoot *Law of Contract* (10th edn, 1981) p 318). However that may be, I take the view that a judge of first instance should hesitate long before attempting to ride this unruly horse in a new direction. In approaching this problem I firmly put sentiment on one side. A healthy baby is so lovely a creature that I can well understand the reaction of one who asks: how could its birth possibly give rise to an action for damages? But every baby has a belly to be filled and a body to be clothed. The law relating to damages is concerned with reparation in money terms and this is what is needed for the maintenance of a baby' ([1985] 2 WLR at 230 e–g).

3. The approach of the court after *Emeh*

Since the Court of Appeal's decision in *Emeh v Kensington and Chelsea and Westminster Area Health Authority* (above), the court has tended to treat wrongful birth cases in line with the normal principles applied to damages in personal injury cases.

In *Benarr v Kettering Health Authority* (1988) (p 243), Hodgson J awarded damages in respect of the educational costs (£19,534.32) of a child who was born as a result of a failed vasectomy. The judge said that the plaintiff was entitled to recover necessary expenses of which private educational fees were an example, in circumstances where the plaintiff educated his children privately. In *Williams v Imrie* (1988) (p 606), Hutchison J awarded a plaintiff the costs of maintaining a child who was born following a negligent sterilisation. These costs amounted to £6,065 from the end of the fourth year of the child's life to the age of 17. The costs before that amounted to £485 in the first year of the child's life and £676 up until the end of the fourth year. The plaintiff had to give credit for child benefit in this respect. The mother was awarded £4,000 for pain, suffering and loss of amenity which included the discomfort of the pregnancy, the worry that the child she was bearing might have been injured, and a further sterilisation which led to a four to five inch scar. The award also included the loss of the mother's earnings.

In *Allen v Bloomsbury Health Authority* (p 225) a total award of £87,450 was made to a plaintiff who gave birth to a healthy child who underwent a sterilisation while in fact she was pregnant. Brooke J awarded £1,250 general damages to the mother for discomfort and pain associated with the pregnancy and delivery, having offset against that the fact that the plaintiff avoided the pain and suffering associated with a termination. Brooke J would not have awarded any damages for loss of amenity in terms of the effort in bringing up a healthy child, because that would be generally offset by the joy of birth and the growth of a healthy child. In that case, the defendants had agreed £2,500 in respect of general damages before and after the birth so that sum was awarded. The judge then proceeded to award

£46,716 in respect of the loss of a mother's earnings, £556 in respect of cost of equipment, £2,850 for childminding costs and £2,818 in respect of a conversion of a garage into a fourth bedroom. The calculation of the cost of upkeep for the child was agreed for losses up to the trial date, in respect of which child benefit was deducted. For the future cost the figures provided by the National Foster Care Association were taken using a multiplier of eight, the child being six at the date of the hearing. This produced a sum of £27,152. As child benefit is not a relevant benefit within the meaning of the Social Security (Recoupment) Regulations, SI's 322/1990, 695/1991 and 2742/1991, it is arguable that in respect of any such claim arising after the 1 January 1989 credit need not be given for this benefit. (See the Social Security Administration Act 1992, Part 4 which now consolidates the Social Security Act 1989, s 22 and Sch 4, as amended by the Social Security Act 1990, s 7 and Sch 1.)

In *Robinson v Salford Health Authority* (p 529) the trial judge, in assessing the cost of the upkeep of an unplanned child, declined to use the National Foster Care Association figures on the basis that details of the family income and expenditure were available. £23,400 was assessed as the future cost of upkeep based on £50 per week using a multiplier of nine, the child being four at the date of the hearing. In *Fish v Wilcox and Gwent Health Authority* (1994) the plaintiff gave birth to a child with congenital deformities in circumstances where the defendants admitted they were negligent in failing to warn the plaintiff that she might carry such a child. The plaintiff gave up her job of £4,000 per annum to look after the child who needed constant attention. The trial judge awarded £5,000 per year for nursing care provided to the daughter, but awarded nothing in respect of loss of earnings. The Court of Appeal upheld this as a correct decision, on the basis that to give the mother the costs of care as well as the loss of earnings would amount to double recovery.

In *Salih*, the trial judge had awarded the plaintiff £68,000 total damages concerning the birth of a child suffering from rubella syndrome. The defendants admitted liability for failing to diagnose and warn the plaintiff that her child might have this condition. The plaintiff gave evidence at trial that she had intended to have four children but, because her third child was disabled by rubella syndrome, a decision was made not to have any further children and indeed a termination had subsequently taken place because of this. The Court of Appeal in a piece of remorseless logic held that because the couple had decided not to have a fourth child, they had to set off the saving of that expenditure, against the cost of maintaining their disabled child. Accordingly only those additional costs due to the child's condition were recoverable, rather than the basic cost of maintaining him.

In *Gardiner v Mounfield and Lincolnshire Area Health Authority,* a failure to diagnose a pregnancy until after an abortion could be lawfully carried out led to an award of £1,250 for pain, suffering and loss of amenity together with other damages making a total of £17,920. In *Rance v Mid-Downs Health Authority and Storr* (1990) (p 517) the plaintiff's claim failed on the grounds of public policy, in that her allegation of negligence was that if she had been told that her baby had a severe abnormality at 26 weeks she would have had an abortion up to 28 weeks. The trial judge found that because the child at that date would have been capable of being born alive, within the meaning of s 1 of the Infant Life (Preservation) Act 1929, any abortion under the Abortion Act 1967 would have been unlawful and accordingly the plaintiff's claim was not sustainable as a matter of public policy.

In *Walkin v South Manchester Health Authority* (1994) a plaintiff's claim was held to be statute barred in respect of an allegation concerning negligence over a failed sterilisation. The trial judge held that such a claim, including as it did the suffering of an unwanted birth, fell within s 11 of the Limitation Act 1980 in that the claim consisted of or included damages in respect of personal injuries to the plaintiff or any other person (Limitation Act 1980, s 11(1)). The judge further indicated that a failed vasectomy did not involve the suffering of an unwanted birth. In fact, all vasectomy cases featuring a claim for wrongful birth will always feature by definition an unnecessary birth. Practitioners should accordingly be cautious in relying on *Walkin* as authority for the proposition that a vasectomy claim concerning wrongful birth is not a claim within s 11 for the purposes of the Limitation Act 1980 but would fall within s 2, which would give a six year rather than a three year period of limitation. There are strong grounds for contending that a failed vasectomy action would be an action where the damages claimed by the plaintiff 'consist of or include damages in respect of personal injuries to the plaintiff or any other person' (s 11(1)). Clearly the mother giving birth could reasonably be described as an example of 'any other person' (cf the Court of Appeal's decision in *Walkin* (1995) Times, 3 July). For cases which support Potter J's judgment in *Walkin* see *Pattison v Hobbs* and *Naylor v Preston Area Health Authority* [1987] 1 WLR 958 (at 971).

Claims for wrongful birth are to be distinguished in principle from a claim for so-called wrongful life. No damages are recoverable, as a matter of public policy, for any action based upon damages premised upon a duty owed to a foetus of a right not to be born at all. (See *McKay v Essex Area Health Authority* (p 447) and chapter 4).)

4. Claims concerning the death of children at or near childbirth

Claims for so-called nervous shock may arise in circumstances where a mother loses a child due to negligence at the birth. In *Kralj v McGrath* (1986) (p 420) a mother was awarded £10,000 general damages in June 1985 for extreme pain she suffered in a birth described as horrific and totally unacceptable. As a result of the negligence, one of the plaintiff's twins died eight weeks later due to brain damage. The plaintiff was awarded damages for her own nervous shock and suffering but not for the grief and suffering of the child's death. She was further awarded £18,000 for future loss of earnings on the basis that she had become pregnant again, because it had always been her intention to have a family of three and had both twins survived a further pregnancy would not have been required given the couple already had a daughter.

In *Kerby v Redbridge Health Authority* (1993) a plaintiff also lost one of her twins after three days following a negligently handled birth and was awarded a total of £11,500. She was left with a scar as a result of the medical intervention required by the defendant's negligence, and she also suffered a moderately severe depressive disorder for six months. The trial judge awarded her £1,500 for the rigours of a further possible pregnancy. She was also awarded the statutory sum for bereavement under the Fatal Accidents Act 1976 in respect of the death of the child and in those circumstances the trial judge found she was not entitled to further general damages for the dashed hopes of bringing the pregnancy to a totally successful conclusion. She was further awarded funeral expenses and the sum of £750 for the dead child's estate in respect of general damages for his pain and suffering over the three days.

In *Grieve v Salford Health Authority* (p 362) £12,500 general damages were awarded in 1990 in respect of the delivery of a still born child which caused a severe reactive depression in the plaintiff who was a person prone to anxiety and depression. Finally in *Tredget and Tredget v Bexley Health Authority* (1994) (p 585), £300,000 damages in total were paid to a couple. Both suffered from post traumatic stress disorder, following a negligently handled birth at which the father was present, which led to the death of their son at the age of two days.

Section E

The practice of litigation

Chapter 13

Limitation and striking out for want of prosecution

The conduct of civil litigation is primarily determined by specific statutes such as the Supreme Court Act 1981 and the Limitation Act 1980 together with rules of court contained in the Rules of the Supreme Court 1965, and the County Court Rules 1981. Medical malpractice actions, like other civil prosecutions, are governed by these provisions and are rarely singled out for specific procedural determination, as for example in RSC Ord 25, r 8. Nevertheless, actions involving an alleged breach of a medical duty of care do routinely raise certain procedural difficulties which merit particular attention. This section looks at the courts' approach to civil litigation in four selected areas: those concerning limitation, the striking out of claims for want of prosecution, the mechanisms of pre-action discovery and the exchange of expert reports with specific reference to medical negligence litigation.

1. Limitation

A. THE PRIMARY LIMITATION PERIODS: LIMITATION ACT 1980, SS 2, 5 AND 11.

Since the Limitation Act 1623, the legislature has determined that it is in the interests of the public good that litigation should be brought within specified periods of time. The principle behind the implementation of a statutory defence that an action after a certain time will be barred has been that stale claims frequently cause injustice because the probative value of the evidence that is adduced is fundamentally flawed due to the passage of time. Particularly in those cases where oral evidence is required, the recollection of events fades after appreciable distances of time, witnesses may have died or disappeared, and accordingly the factual basis of the claim may be extremely difficult to evaluate and indeed to defend. To prevent potential defendants being exposed to indeterminate liability, specific periods for specific causes of action have been statutorily imposed: they are currently contained in the consolidating statute of the Limitation Act 1980.

Section 11 of the Limitation Act 1980 provides a three year primary limitation period in those actions for 'damages for negligence, nuisance or breach of duty' whether contractual, statutory or otherwise, and which 'consist of or include damages in respect of personal injuries to a plaintiff or any other person'. The three year period prescribed in this section runs from either the date when the cause of action accrued or from what is called the 'date of knowledge' of the injured person. Accordingly, for the overwhelming majority of cases which are brought alleging a breach of the medical duty of care (and which do involve personal injury), the primary period is three years. In actions based upon negligence, the accrual of a cause of action is when damage (which is more than negligible) has occurred (per Lord Reid in *Cartledge v Jopling* ([1963] AC at 771–2)). In most cases, damage will flow immediately from the negligent act, as for example in anaesthetic and surgical mishaps. In other cases, however, such as those involving a negligent prescription of a drug which causes a delayed form of harm, damage may occur years after its prescription and ingestion. There can accordingly be a significant time gap between the negligent act and the creation of damage that is more than negligible. In contract, however, a cause of action is deemed to accrue when a breach has occurred which, in the case of a doctor, would be when the doctor prescribed the drug in question to his private patient (see *Gibbs v Guild* (1881)). This distinction fortifies the benefit of suing in negligence or collaterally in both contract and negligence. However in cases of breaches of contract giving rise to a delayed manifestation of personal injury, a plaintiff would be able to rely upon the 'date of knowledge' defined in s 14 of the Act.

(i) 'Negligence, nuisance or breach of duty'

Prior to the House of Lords ruling in *Stubbings v Webb* ([1993] AC 498) the words negligence, nuisance or breach of duty had been construed as including those personal injuries that arose out of trespass to the person whether they were caused by an intentional or an unintentional assault (*Long v Hepworth* ([1968] 3 All ER 248), *Letang v Cooper* ([1965] 1 QB 232)). In *Stubbings v Webb,* the House of Lords held that in the case of deliberate assaults including rape and indecent assault any civil action brought by a victim falls outside the ambit of s 11 of the 1980 Act in that they do not constitute any 'breach of duty'. The effect of that judgment was to increase the primary limitation period to six years pursuant to s 2 of the Limitation Act 1980 as a non-personal injury action founded in tort. However, such claims could not be extended pursuant to the assaulted person's date of knowledge within the meaning of s 14; nor could the period of limitation be dispensed with under the provisions of s 33.

Those actions brought against medical practitioners based upon trespass to the person because of the absence of consent are likely, however, to be determined as falling within the provisions of s 11 of the Limitation Act 1980 on the basis that the medical assaults fall into the category of unintentional trespass to the person. In *Letang v Cooper,* the Court of Appeal held that where personal injury was inflicted unintentionally the only cause of action was in negligence. Clearly a cause of action other than negligence, namely trespass to the person, does exist in cases where there is no consent at all. Accordingly it is arguable that if a plaintiff sues both in negligence and for trespass to the person arising out of a medical malpractice, different periods of limitation would apply. To avoid this situation, the court is likely to find that the action founded on assault being an unintentional trespass to the person should probably be considered as a claim under s 11 of the Limitation Act 1980 (eg *Cull v Butler* (p 296), *Devi v West Midlands Regional Health Authority* (p 308), *Wilding v Lambeth Southwark Lewisham Health Authority*, Lexis 10 May 1982. See, however, *Dobbie v Medway Health Authority* (1994)).

(ii) 'Consists of or includes damages in respect of personal injuries to the plaintiff or any other person'

Not all medical malpractice actions consist of or include damages for personal injury. For example, in a case like *Whiteford v Hunter* (1950) (p 603), where a plaintiff had been wrongly informed that he had inoperable terminal cancer and as a result closed down his engineering practice, sold his house and went abroad, the claim would be for financial and consequential losses. This particular action, which in fact was brought in time and which failed to establish any breach of duty, illustrates a potential category of treatment-based cases which do not result in personal injury. Similarly, a negligent report on the health of a person which injuriously affects a plaintiff's prospects of getting or keeping a job or becoming insured would not involve any claim for personal injury (see eg *Dawson v Scott-Brown* (1988) (p 304)).

By the provisions of s 2 and s 5 of the Limitation Act 1980, six years is allowed to bring an action based on tort or simple contract not involving personal injury. In cases concerned with the wrongful birth of a child, a mother normally has a claim for general damages arising out of the discomfort and suffering from the unplanned pregnancy itself, and, frequently, from a subsequent sterilisation which should not have been necessary had a prior sterilisation been undertaken properly. For the most part, however, the larger claim lies in respect of the consequential expenses and losses that arise from the requirement to maintain the unplanned child. In *Pattison v Hobbs* ((1985) Times, 11 November) the Court of Appeal held that where the only claim arising out of a failed vasectomy was one for financial loss, then s 2 of the Limitation Act applied to impose a six year period of limitation rather than s 11. (See also *Naylor v Preston Area Health Authority* (p 478) where the then Master of the Rolls, Sir John Donaldson, indicated that a claim in respect of a failed vasectomy did not fall in within the definition of personal injuries.)

Where, however, a claim is brought in respect of the mother's personal injuries arising out of a birth, whether this is in respect of a failed vasectomy or a failed sterilisation, it is likely that s 11 will apply. In *Walkin v South Manchester Health Authority* (p 597), Potter J held that unlike a failed vasectomy a failed sterilisation involves the suffering of an unwanted birth and accordingly s 11 of the Limitation Act applies. The Court of Appeal upheld his reasoning (1995) Times, 3 July. In cases where a failed vasectomy includes a claim for the mother's pain and suffering arising out of the unplanned for birth (eg *Thake v Maurice* (p 579)) it is difficult to see why s 11 would not apply. The claim clearly includes a claim for personal injury, even if it does not consist of one, and moreover the mother on whose behalf the claim for personal injury is made is clearly 'any other person' within the meaning of s 11(1). (See also the Court of Appeal's determination in *Howe v David Brown Tractors (Retail) Ltd* ([1991] 4 All ER 30), *Paterson v Chadwick* (p 491), *Ackber v Green & Co* (1975).) The matter is not free from doubt because of the alternative argument that both claims are closely connected to the 'personal injury' of the wrongful birth (cf *Paterson v Chadwick* (1974) (p 491), *Ackbar v Green & Co* (1975)).

Personal injury is defined within s 38 of the Limitation Act 1980 as including any disease and any impairment of a person's physical or mental condition. Therefore any claim based on a psychological reaction to a medical breach of duty would be caught by the three year period.

B. DATE OF KNOWLEDGE: LIMITATION ACT 1980, S 11(4) AND S 14

Previously, strict periods of limitation found in earlier statutes worked patent injustice in those cases where the effect of the breach of duty was to cause a form of latent damage which only manifested itself in symptoms many years after the breach of duty. In extreme cases, a cause of action had expired before the injured person had any prospects of discovering the potential harm done to him. For example, s 2(1) of the Limitation Act 1939 allowed six years (for the most part) to bring an action in tort, whether it comprised a personal injury or not. In *Cartledge v Jopling* (1963), the plaintiff had in the course of his employment inhaled harmful dust which caused a form of injury which was undetectable by means of medical science until more than six years after the damage arose. Mr Cartledge was prevented from bringing an action, notwithstanding that his condition had substantially deteriorated, because of the strict interpretation of the limitation period:

'.... a cause of action accrues as soon as the wrongful act has caused specific injury beyond what can be regarded as negligible, even when that injury is unknown to and cannot be discerned by the sufferer; and that further injury arising from the same act at a later date does not give rise to a further cause of action .... it seems to be unreasonable and unjustifiable in principle that a cause of action should be held to accrue before it is possible to raise any action .... a cause of action ought not to be held to accrue until either the injured person has discovered the injury or it would be possible for him to discover it if he took such steps as was reasonable in the circumstances' (per Lord Reid ([1963] AC at 771–2)).

This situation was partially remedied by the enactment of the Limitation Act 1963 which permitted a plaintiff, with leave of the court, to bring a claim beyond the limitation period, if material facts concerning the cause of action were outside the actual or constructive knowledge of the plaintiff. The Limitation Act 1975 made a further modification to this principle of discovery by stipulating that it was not a material fact that a plaintiff, knowing the fact of his injury and its causation, did not know as a matter of law that he had a good cause of action.

These principles have now become consolidated within s 11(4) of the Limitation Act 1980, which allows time to run from the date of knowledge and within s 14 of the Act which defines the date of knowledge. Many of the leading cases on the proper construction of s 14 arise from medical malpractice actions or product liability cases against drug manufacturers, which frequently involve questions of determining when a plaintiff's symptoms are due to the medical mishap or the effect of the drug as opposed to the presenting symptoms and when the plaintiff knew or ought to have known that those symptoms were attributable to the acts or omissions of the defendant.

Section 14(1) provides:

'In s 11 and 12 of this Act reference to a person's date of knowledge are references to the date on which he first had knowledge of the following facts:

(a) that the injury in question was significant; and
(b) that the injury was attributable in whole or in part to the act or omission which is alleged to constitute negligence nuisance or breach of that duty; and
(c) the identity of the defendant, and
(d) if it is alleged that the act or omission was that of a person other than the defendant, the identity of that person and the additional facts supporting the bringing of an action against the defendant; and knowledge that any acts or omissions did or did not as a matter of law, involve negligence, nuisance or breach of duty is irrelevant.'

(i) ' .... the date at which he first had knowledge of the facts'.

The most authoritative statement on what constitutes knowledge within the meaning of s 14 is to be found in the product liability case of *Nash and others v Eli Lilly & Co and others* (p 466). These actions concerned preliminary trials on limitation in respect of claims arising out of the side effects of the drug Opren which included skin sensitivity, abnormal hair growth and liver and kidney failure. The drug was prescribed to relieve arthritic pain and was eventually withdrawn in the United Kingdom in August 1982 with extensive publicity. The Court of Appeal analysed in detail each individual plaintiff's case but, before doing so, laid down a number of principles governing the interpretation of both s 14 and s 33 of the 1980 Act.

Prior to this case, a distinction had been made between knowledge and belief derived from Lord Justice May's dictum in the case of *Davis v Ministry of Defence* (1985) that suspicion or belief or even reasonable belief on the part of a plaintiff did not constitute knowledge. This distinction was applied in *Wilkinson v Ancliff* (1986) and adopted in the case of *Stephen v Riverside Health Authority* (p 565). Mrs Stephen, who had worked as an unqualified radiographer, underwent a mammography in which the radiographer took ten films instead of four to six. She was told that she had received the dose of 34 roentgen to each breast and was informed that other than the erythema which had occurred in her upper chest for three months there was no danger from the effects of radiation. Nearly eleven years later on the 15 February 1988 the plaintiff issued a writ in respect of her increased risk of developing cancer which followed a view expressed by her medico-legal expert to her on the 20 February 1985. The trial judge found that in those circumstances although she had a suspicion or belief that she did have an increased risk of cancer, contrary to what experts had told her before the 20 February 1985, this did not amount to knowledge and in those circumstances the writ was issued within three years of her date of knowledge.

However, in *Nash v Eli Lilly* (above), the Court of Appeal expressed the view that it did not find any great deal of assistance in the distinction between knowledge and belief:

'In applying the section to the facts of these cases we shall proceed on the basis that knowledge is a condition of mind which imports a degree of certainty and that the degree of certainty which is appropriate for this purpose is that which, for the particular plaintiff, may reasonably be regarded as sufficient to justify embarking upon the preliminaries to the making of a claim for compensation such as the taking of legal and other advice' ([1993] 4 All ER 383 at 392 b–d).

Belief therefore may amount to or become knowledge, if it is firmly held enough to justify the taking of preliminary steps for instituting proceedings while obtaining advice about making a claim for compensation. In analysing whether a plaintiff does have this sufficiently firmly held belief or knowledge, consideration should be given to the intellectual capacity of the plaintiff to understand information and how information is evaluated by the plaintiff. The Court of Appeal also rejected the contention that time is suspended if an expert gives a report that, contrary to the plaintiff's belief, the injury is not attributable to the act or omission of the defendant. Alternatively, if a plaintiff whilst believing that an injury is attributable to the defendant's act or omission is also of the view that that belief requires confirmation from an expert, then knowledge will not arise until that confirmation is obtained. Time then will run against a plaintiff if he has a firm enough belief to warrant the taking of preliminary steps in instituting the proceedings. If those steps fail at first to confirm his belief because of negative expert opinion, but subsequently his belief is confirmed through a second or a third opinion, time will have run from the first date at which he had the belief irrespective of the earlier non-confirmation. If, however, the plaintiff has a suspended belief which he feels requires confirmation, time will not run until it is confirmed or alternatively if he had acted reasonably it would have been confirmed. These somewhat fine distinctions may well make it difficult in advance of the court's judgment for practitioners to give unambiguous advice as to precisely when a plaintiff has knowledge within the meaning of s 14 of the Act. (See also Nelson-Jones and Burton *Personal Injury Limitation Law*, ch 3.)

(ii) 'That the injury in question was significant (s14(1)(a))'

Time does not begin to run against a plaintiff until he has knowledge of four types of fact namely that his injury was significant, attributable to the act or omission of the defendant, whose identity he must know, or in certain circumstances the identity of a person who would be vicariously liable for the defendant. The first of these facts, significance, is defined by s 14(2):

> 'For the purposes of this section an injury is significant if the person whose date of knowledge is in question would reasonably have considered it sufficiently serious to justify his instituting proceedings for damages against a defendant who did not dispute liability and was able to satisfy a judgment.'

The effect of this section is to make most injuries significant, even relatively trivial ones, because the test implies that a defendant will be able to pay damages without liability being in issue. The only live issue within the sub-section is whether the plaintiff in question would *reasonably* have considered the injury worth prosecuting. In *Stephen v Riverside Area Health Authority* (p 565) the trial judge found that it was reasonable that a plaintiff did not sue in respect of the erythema and anxiety that she had, because she did not consider this sufficiently serious to warrant proceedings and knowledge that her injury was significant only came later when she knew that the overdose of radiation she had been subjected to could cause cancer.

In *Nash v Eli Lilly* (p 466) the Court of Appeal confirmed that the test of significance was partly subjective, namely whether the particular plaintiff in question could have considered the injuries sufficiently serious applying the test laid down by Lane LJ in *McCafferty v Metropolitan Police District Receiver* ([1977] 2 All ER at 775). In the Opren litigation, the court made a distinction between the normal or expected side effects of the drug and the injurious and unacceptable consequences which might not be immediately apparent to any particular plaintiff. Accordingly in *Hall v Eli Lilly* (p 366) the plaintiff realised that she had become 'a funny colour' but did not think that there was anything wrong with her, and both her general practitioner and his partner thought she was a healthy looking person and did not comment on her discolouration. It was not until June 1988 when she saw a hospital doctor that she was told she had photo-sensitivity and was advised to see a solicitor. The court held that her claim was not statute barred because she did not regard the injury as significant until June 1988 and her writ was issued on 15 September 1989.

The courts, however, have emphasised in a number of cases that significance is to be determined by looking at the first injury and not at any subsequent deterioration or any new manifestation arising out of the same accident. Accordingly, in *Miller v London Electrical Manufacturing Co Ltd* (1976), dermatitis contracted by a worker was held to be significant and started time running against him, notwithstanding that he later developed a much more serious form of eczema-based skin disease. Similarly in *Bristow v Grout* ((1986) Times 3 November) the court held that a facial injury sustained in a 1982 accident was held to be the significant injury and to cause time to run against a plaintiff, notwithstanding that in 1985 he developed a more serious hip injury.

In some medical negligence cases and in some disease cases, a plaintiff may not have knowledge that an injury is significant until informed of that fact by a medical practitioner. In *Driscoll-Varley v Parkside Health Authority* (p 313), the plaintiff was treated by a pin and traction in respect of a leg fracture in April 1984. The leg was subsequently fixed with a kunschner nail in May of 1984 and this was removed in July of 1985. The leg became hot, swollen and painful and blistered, and in September 1985 the plaintiff was advised that tests revealed that she had a piece of dead bone floating around causing infection. The court held that she knew her injury was significant in September 1985 when she was told about the infection.

(iii) Attribution

For time to run against a plaintiff, knowledge must be ascertained that the injury was attributable in whole or in part to the acts or omissions of the defendant. Attribution in this context means factual not legal causation, because s 14 specifically provides that knowledge that an act or omission 'did not as a matter of law involve negligence, nuisance or breach of duty is irrelevant'. In *Wilkinson v Ancliff plc Ltd* (1986) attribution was interpreted as meaning, not definitely caused by, but being capable of being attributed to. This accorded with an earlier interpretation found in *Davis v Ministry of Defence* (1985). This approach was reaffirmed in *Nash v Eli Lilly* (p 466) where attribution meant a real rather than a fanciful possibility of the injury being caused by the defendant's act or omission.

Many cases concerning attribution involve medical negligence actions. In *Davies v City and Hackney Health Authority* (p 302) a plaintiff who suffered from cerebral palsy was held not to have been aware of the act alleged to have caused his condition until he received a medical report some 23 years after his birth. This report from an expert alleged that an injection of Ovametrin into his mother while she was pregnant was responsible for his condition. In *Doughty v North Staffordshire Health Authority* (p 311), a plaintiff had 12 operations in an attempt to remove a birth mark on her face between 1957 and 1974. In 1974 she was told by her surgeon's successor that no improvement was possible, and he had doubted whether such a prolonged course of surgery should in any event have been embarked on. That information was held to provide the plaintiff with knowledge of attribution.

In *Driscoll-Varley v Parkside Health Authority*, a plaintiff was held to have knowledge of attribution that her leg injury was capable of being attributed to an act or omission alleged to constitute negligence on the 30 June 1988, notwithstanding that she sustained the presenting injury in the form of a fracture on the 18 April 1984. The plaintiff was treated by traction and then by a nail, and after the nail was removed on 28 July 1985 the leg became problematic. In September 1985 she was advised that there was a piece of dead bone floating around causing infection, and thereafter she had nine operations in an attempt to prevent her losing her leg. It was not until she received expert advice on 1 June 1988 that she knew the cause of her problem was that her leg had been removed from traction too early. The court held that she had knowledge of attribution on that date.

183

In *Hendy v Milton Keynes Health Authority* (p 377) time was held to run against a plaintiff in terms of attribution when she was told on 12 November 1985 that an operation that took place on 25 February 1985 had caused adhesions around the bladder and uterus, so that her right urethra had become caught up in the operation and injured. In *Khan v Ainslie* (p 413) attribution was established in February 1989 concerning an injury to a plaintiff's left eye, notwithstanding that a left iridectomy was performed in 1983 which left the plaintiff without sight. The plaintiff consulted solicitors in 1984 and received a negative expert report in 1985. Subsequently in February 1989 a second expert's opinion was received which said that the loss of sight was as a result of glaucoma and the delay in treatment. These cases illustrate that attribution may be delayed in cases where it is by no means clear whether the persisting problems of a plaintiff are extensions of the presenting condition or whether in fact there has been a medical mishap.

However, there have been a number of recent cases which emphasise that, even in medical negligence cases, knowledge of attribution need only be in relatively broad or general terms and the question of whether there has been negligence or not is as the section indicates an entirely irrelevant issue. In *Broadley v Guy Clapham & Co* (p 261), the Court of Appeal affirmed that knowledge of detailed acts or omissions, such as would be necessary to draft particulars of negligence, are not required. This is simply because knowledge that a cause of action in law exists is something specifically excluded by the section. In *Broadley,* the plaintiff underwent an operation in August 1980 to remove a foreign body from her knee. She developed nerve palsy creating a left foot drop, which was ascertained as having occurred in notes on 18 August 1980. In June 1983 she instructed solicitors and was seen in July by a surgeon who said the operation might have been performed negligently. The solicitors failed to prosecute a claim, and on 17 August 1990 she issued proceedings against her legal advisors. The plaintiff's ex-solicitors alleged that her claim against them was statute barred, and because of that the court needed to investigate whether the plaintiff's cause of action against her treating surgeon was in fact statute barred. The trial judge fixed the plaintiff with constructive knowledge of attribution before August 1981 on the basis that her foot drop had not got better as the surgeon said it would, and it would have been reasonable for the plaintiff to ask her GP or surgeon what had gone wrong. In the Court of Appeal, the plaintiff contended that her date of knowledge would be when she had knowledge of 'some act or omission which could adversely affect the safety of the operation or proper recovery from the operation, such as unreasonable interference with a nerve or failure reasonably to safeguard it from danger, or failure promptly to investigate and/or repair the nerve lesion in time' (p 12, A–B transcript).

Such a submission followed a similar and successful argument by the plaintiff in the case of *Bentley v Bristol and Western Health Authority* (p 244), a case where a sciatic nerve was damaged in a hip replacement operation. In *Bentley,* the trial judge found that time would run only from when the plaintiff knew that there had been a failure to carry out the operation safely and specifically that her injury might be due to excessive traction in the nerve. The Court of Appeal, however, rejected such analysis in *Broadley* and held that *Bentley* was wrongly decided. The court indicated that to require knowledge of such detail was in effect to require knowledge of all matters to establish negligence or breach of duty, and that was in stark contravention of the words of s 14(1) which stated that knowledge that the acts or omissions constituted negligence or breach of duty was irrelevant. The court held that knowledge for Mrs Bentley to establish attribution need only be:

'that her injury had been caused by damage to the nerve resulting from something which Mr Lowy (the treating surgeon) had done or not done in the course of the operation' (per LJ Hoffman at 4 E–G).

These arguments were endorsed by a differently constituted Court of Appeal in the case of *Dobbie v Medway Health Authority* (p 310), Mrs Dobbie was admitted for a biopsy on a lump in her left breast on 27 April 1973, and the surgeon considered that the lump was pre-cancerous and carried out a left mastectomy without microscopic examination of the lump and allegedly without her consent. On 14 May 1973 it was found that the lump was benign and she was told of this on 11 June 1973. The plaintiff was told that she was lucky that the lump was not cancerous. The plaintiff had a severe psychiatric reaction to losing her breast, and she took no steps to claim until she heard about a similar case reported in the newspaper and the local radio. At the trial on the limitation issue, Otton J found that time ran against the plaintiff when she was informed about the laboratory analysis of the lump and at that time her injury was capable of being attributed to the defendant's fault. The Court of Appeal dismissed the plaintiff's appeal, with the Master of Rolls Sir Thomas Bingham emphasising that attribution in such cases should be unproblematic:

'This test is not in my judgment hard to apply. It involves ascertaining the personal injury on which the claim is founded and asking when the claimant knew of it. In the case of insidious disease or a delayed result of a surgical mishap, this knowledge may come well after the suffering of the disease or the performance of the surgery. But more usually the claimant knows that he has suffered personal injury as soon or almost as soon as he does so ... Time starts to run against the claimant when he knows that the personal injury on which he founds his claim is capable of being attributed to something done or not done by the defendant whom he wishes to sue. This condition is not satisfied where a man knows that he has a disabling cough or shortness of breath but does not know that his injured condition is anything to do with his working conditions. It is satisfied when he knows that his injured condition is capable of being attributed to his working conditions, even though he has no inkling that his employer may have been at fault' ([1994] PIQR, Pt 5, p 353, at pp 357–8).

The Master of the Rolls went on to emphasise that knowledge of fault did not enter the equation:

'In some of the cases, judges have used language suggesting that knowledge of fault is needed to start time running. For instance in *Stephen v Riverside Health Authority* [1990] 1 Med LR 261 at p 261, Auld J said:

"The question that I have to answer is 'when did she first know that erythema moist spots, etc, were capable of being attributed to *excessive* exposure to radiation caused by an *improperly conducted* mammography' " (added emphasis).

In *Bentley v Bristol and Western Health Authority* ([1991] 2 Med LR 359 at p 364), which was disapproved in *Broadley v Guy Clapham*, Hirst J held that there had to be knowledge of some conduct or failure which could affect the safety of the operation. In *Nash v Eli Lilly & Co* ([1991] 2 Med LR 169) Hidden J described the act or omission complained of as:

"providing the plaintiff with a drug which was unsafe in that it caused persisting photo sensitivity and *failing to take reasonable and proper steps to protect the plaintiff* from such a conditional consequence" (added emphasis).

The situation is complicated when, as often happens, the plaintiff learns of the defendant's acts or omissions and of the criticism that it was negligent at the same time. But it is necessary to emphasise that knowledge of fault or negligence is not needed to start time running' (at p 359–360).

In *Dobbie* the court expressed the view that the plaintiff knew within a matter of hours that she had lost her breast and that of course was significant. She knew from the beginning, therefore, that her personal injury was capable of being attributed to an act or omission of the health authority. What she did not appreciate until later was that the health authority's act or omission was arguably negligent or blameworthy. That knowledge, however, did not stop time running against her. In less plain cases, such as the example given by the Master of the Rolls over the delayed result of a surgical mishap, attribution is likely to be later. However, a plaintiff, even in a medical negligence case, is increasingly likely to be fixed with attribution at an earlier rather than at a later date (see also the cases of *Atkinson v Oxfordshire Health Authority* (p 230) and *Colegrove v Smyth* (p 282).

(iv) Identity

The final fact a plaintiff must know, after significance and attribution are established, is the identity of the defendant and any other person who might be vicariously liable for the acts or omissions which caused the personal injury. In medical negligence and breach of contract cases this is most unlikely to cause many difficulties, given the vicarious liability of hospital authorities, their nursing and medical staff. Even in cases of private treatment where vicarious liability may be less clear, it is normally possible to determine the identity of potential defendants. Where a number of connected defendants are sued simultaneously and others, also connected, are sought to be added later, as may occur in a pharmaceutical product liability action, dicta in *Nash v Eli Lilly* indicate that the court might well fix a plaintiff with constructive knowledge in respect of the additional defendants on the basis that all identities of a group structure should be reasonably ascertainable. Conversely, however, in an action against drug manufacturers, where more than one unconnected company produced a drug, it may be very difficult to ascertain precisely which manufacturer was responsible for the actual drug ingested by any particular plaintiff, and this may well have the effect of delaying the running of time.

(v) Constructive knowledge

Section 14(3) provides:

> 'For the purposes of this section a person's knowledge includes knowledge which he might reasonably have been expected to acquire:
>
> (a) from facts observable or ascertainable by him; or
> (b) from facts ascertainable by him with the help of medical or other appropriate expert advice which it is reasonable for him to seek;
>
> but a person shall not be fixed under this sub-section of knowledge of a fact ascertainable only with the help of expert advice so long as he has taken all reasonable steps to obtain (and, where appropriate, to act on) that advice.'

The effect of this sub-section is to require a plaintiff to act reasonably in attempting to obtain information and, if he does not do so, to fix him with constructive knowledge on the assumption that if he had acted reasonably he would have obtained relevant knowledge and information. The court will therefore enquire into what, if any, steps the plaintiff did take which he reasonably ought to have taken by himself, or with the help of others to determine whether the injury was significant, attributable to the act or omission in question and caused by the particular defendants sued. What is reasonable will vary according to the subjective capabilities of the particular plaintiff in question. The test, however, is to a certain extent objective.

In *Davis v City and Hackney Health Authority* (1989) (p 302), a plaintiff who was born suffering from spasticity in June 1963 issued a writ on 1 April 1987. At the age of 17 he had asked his mother what had caused his disabilities, and she thought that his birth may have been mishandled but did not encourage him to claim damages. In September 1985, the plaintiff consulted solicitors and on or about 26 November 1986 an expert reported that the plaintiff's mother had been given an injection of ovametrin which caused the plaintiff's spasticity. The plaintiff was allowed to bring the action because the date of knowledge was determined by the court to be when he learned of the contents of the expert's report. The trial judge, Jowitt J indicated that in view of the plaintiff's disabilities, which included a serious speech defect, the delay in failing to take legal advice was not unreasonable. The judge said:

'The test is an objective one. The question is, looked at objectively, when might he, the plaintiff, reasonably have been expected to acquire those facts referred to in paragraph b of sub-section 3. In other words one applies an objective test, but it is an objective test applied to the kind of plaintiff I am here dealing with, with his disability, and looking at his age and his circumstances and the difficulties he has faced.'

In *Nash v Eli Lilly* (p 466), the court emphasised that in considering the particular plaintiff in question, his character and intelligence was a relevant factor. In the Opren litigation several plaintiffs were fixed with knowledge which they had been exposed to and which they were able to understand, coming from newspapers and television coverage, in respect of the drug's withdrawal and its possible side effects. Certain plaintiffs were also fixed with knowledge that they could have obtained from their doctors in circumstances where it was judged reasonable for a plaintiff to have sought such advice. In *Broadley v Guy Clapham & Co* (p 261), the Court of Appeal held that a plaintiff knew before August 1981, or could have known with the help of reasonably obtainable medical advice, that injury to her had been caused by damage to a nerve resulting from some act or omission during the operation in August 1980 to remove a foreign body from her left knee.

Conversely in *Colegrove v Smyth* (p 282) a plaintiff born with congenital dislocation of her hip in 1959 was not fixed with constructive knowledge in respect of an action started in November 1987. The plaintiff had been told by a doctor when she was eight or nine that if only she had been treated when she was younger she would not be having her problems. She did not discuss treatment with her mother until she was 25, and did not issue a writ until following a medical examination for a job in 1984. The trial judge was of the view that the plaintiff accepted her congenital dislocation of the hip as part of her life, and it was unrealistic to expect her to have questioned her mother or gone to solicitors earlier. Similarly in *Atkinson v Oxfordshire Health Authority,* a plaintiff was not fixed with constructive knowledge concerning an action started in 1989 in respect of an operation in 1967 when he was 17. Solicitors were instructed when the plaintiff was 21 but it was not until a fourth firm of solicitors obtained pre-trial disclosure revealing that respiratory problems in the operation had led to damage that knowledge of attribution was established. The court was satisfied that, looking at the plaintiff's conduct in obtaining advice over the years, he had not acted unreasonably. (See also *Khan v Ainslie* (p 413) and *Baig v City and Hackney Health Authority* (p 235).)

A plaintiff will not be prejudiced if he has been given wrong advice by his experts (*Marston v British Railways Board* (1976)). Such bad advice, however, will only stop the clock running if it concerns the factual basis of the claim. If a plaintiff receives bad legal advice to the effect that he has no cause of action in law, this would not prevent time running against him, because whether the plaintiff has a correct or an incorrect belief that he has a good cause of action or no cause of action at all is not a relevant consideration under the section. It might well, however, be the case that if the legal advice which is wrong concerns a failure to take certain steps to uncover material facts, the plaintiff will not be prejudiced by such bad advice because it is not essentially legal (*Central Asbestos Co Ltd v Dodd* (per Lord Salmon ([1973] AC at 556–6), *Fowell v National Coal Board* (1986), and *Farmer v National Coal Board* (1985)).

(vi) Fatal accidents

In fatal cases, the Limitation Act provides by s 12 a period of three years from the date of the deceased's death for the dependants to bring an action pursuant to the provisions of the Fatal Accidents Act 1976. Alternatively, the deceased's dependants have three years from the date of knowledge as defined in s 14 of the Act if this is later. Similarly, by s 11(5), the deceased's estate can bring an action three years after the death or three years from the date of the personal representative's date of knowledge. Claims brought by the estate in this respect would be limited to general damages for pain, suffering and loss of amenity before death and special damages that arose up to the date of death together with any funeral expenses. Claims under the Fatal Accidents Act 1976 would include loss of dependency. Section 13 provides the possibility of different periods applying to different dependents. In those cases where the cause of action is time barred, both the estate and the dependents may bring an application pursuant to the Limitation Act 1980, s 33, for an order that the time limits be applied. (For more detail, see Nelson-Jones and Burton *Personal Injury Limitation Law*, ch 6.)

(vii) Non-personal injury claims

In those small number of cases where the cause of action does not consist of or include any damages in respect of personal injuries, plaintiffs in medical malpractice actions may be able to rely on the provisions of the Latent Damage Act 1986. This Act has added s 14A to the Limitation Act 1980. Section 14A contains similar provisions to s 14 concerning the date of knowledge in non-personal injury actions based on tort. Such actions may now be brought six years from the date when the cause of action accrued or three years from the date of knowledge, subject to a stop gap period of fifteen years (s 14B).

(viii) Disability

If a plaintiff is under a disability when a cause of action accrues, time does not run pursuant to the provisions of the Limitation Act 1980, s 28, until the disability ceases. By s 28(6) any such action would be time barred three years after the disability ceased in cases concerning personal injury. A minor is considered to be under a disability until reaching the age of 18, pursuant to the Family Law Reform Act 1969, s 1(1). Accordingly, an infant plaintiff has until the age of 21 to issue a writ (an action is begun when the writ is issued, not when it is served, which can be up to four months later) in respect of any action consisting of or including a claim for personal injuries (*Tolley v Morris* (1979)).

An infant plaintiff is almost immune, therefore, from having his action struck out for want of prosecution, but there can be evidential difficulties both for plaintiffs as well as for defendants in leaving actions for many years until they are prosecuted. In *Bull and Wakeham v Devon Health Authority* (1989) (p 264), an action was commenced in 1979 by a mother for herself and for the benefit of her child in respect of the child's birth in 1970 which resulted in the child being rendered quadriplegic. The trial was heard eight years later by which time the consultant had died, and the mother's own claim for damages was dismissed as statute barred. The child, however, did in this case recover damages in respect of a negligent system of obstetric cover. The plaintiff in *Bull* was under a double disability because he was also incapable of managing his own affairs due to the brain damage he suffered at birth. In such circumstances, there is in effect no period of limitation.

A person is also under a disability if he is of unsound mind, by reason of mental disorder within the meaning of the Mental Health Act 1983, s 1(2), and is incapable of managing his own affairs. In *Blackburn v Newcastle Area Health Authority (No 2)* (1988) (p 249), a plaintiff required four firms of solicitors before he finally got his case on liability to trial in October 1987, following a cause of action accruing in October 1976 arising out of severe brain damage. Such plaintiffs are protected from time running against them and therefore also for an action being dismissed for want of prosecution. The court did take account of the delay by restricting interest to six years rather than eleven.

However, in *Hogg v Hamilton* ([1992] PIQR P387) (p 383), the Court of Appeal upheld the decision to strike out proceedings as an abuse of process, even though the plaintiff was a person to whom an extended and unexpired period of limitation was applicable. In *Hogg*, the plaintiff's fourth set of solicitors sought to add a health authority as a second defendant to a writ issued in 1989 brought against an anaesthetist, following permanent brain damage to a plaintiff which occurred in 1976. The first writ had been issued in 1978, and it was dismissed for want of prosecution in 1982 without apparently any mention being made of the plaintiff's disability. In *Headford v Bristol and District Health Authority* (p 374) an action was started 28 years after a medical mishap which occurred to a plaintiff at the age of ten months. The trial judge struck out the action as an abuse of process notwithstanding the fact that it was the first action brought. The decision was overturned on appeal. If a mental disability intervenes after the accrual of a cause of action, time continues to run (*Purnell v Roche* (1927)). However, in those cases where a plaintiff suffers from an intervening mental disability, there is specific power under s 33(3)(*d*) of the Limitation Act 1980 to consider this as a factor in determining whether the time limit should be overridden.

Although the definition of mental disorder within the Mental Health Act 1983, s 1(2) is broad (it includes mental illness, arrested or incomplete development of mind, psychopathic disorder and any other disorder or disability of mind), it did not avail the plaintiff in *Dawson v Scott-Brown* (1988) (p 304). In this action the plaintiff, an ex-Royal Navy seaman, alleged negligence against his surgeon-commander in respect of a report some thirteen years before he issued proceedings, which led to the plaintiff being discharged from the Navy in October 1974 on grounds of mental ill-health. The Master struck out the writ on the basis that the limitation defence was bound to succeed. The Court of Appeal concurred with this decision, indicating that being invalided out of the Navy did not make him unable to manage his own affairs pursuant to the provisions of the Limitation Act 1980, s 28 and he was therefore not under a disability as from the date of discharge. The plaintiff also argued that there had been concealment and, therefore, according to the provisions of the Limitation Act 1980, s 32(1)(*b*), time ran only when the concealment could with reasonable diligence have been discovered. The Court of Appeal said that, although the defendant had not disclosed his report to the plaintiff and had made it direct to the Navy, there was no question of the matter being deliberately concealed.

From 1 January 1989, an individual has the right to see any report prepared by a medical practitioner, which has been or is to be supplied for employment purposes or for insurance purposes, pursuant to the Access to Medical Reports Act 1988. Section 2 of the Act defines employment purposes as including a report by an existing or a potential employer. The Act requires the employer or insurer to seek the consent of the subject of the report before seeking such a report from a medical practitioner. The subject of the report, by s 4 has a right of access to the report before it is supplied and has a right to correct errors. Access to the report may be withheld if, in the opinion of the medical practitioner, allowing the subject to read the report would be 'likely to cause serious harm to the physical or mental health of the individual or others or would indicate the intentions of a practitioner in respect of the individual' (s 7(1)). A similar right on the part of the medical practitioner to withhold the report arises where the report would be likely to reveal information about another person or to reveal the identity of another person who has supplied information to the practitioner about the individual concerned. The county court has the jurisdiction to hear applications where the subject of the report claims a breach of the requirements of the Act.

C. THE DISCRETION TO ALLOW A TIME-BARRED ACTION TO PROCEED: LIMITATION ACT 1980, S 33

Since the provisions of s 1 of the 1975 Limitation Act, the court has had power to disapply a period of limitation and to allow a time-barred action to proceed. This inroad into the certainty of limitation law was a recognition that strict periods of limitation, even when they are accompanied by provisions concerning knowledge and discoverability of a cause of action, can still work injustice. A stark example is contained in the case of *Harnett v Fisher* (1927) (p 369) where a plaintiff who was negligently certified as of unsound mind and detained, pursuant to the powers of the Lunacy Act 1890, for nearly nine years in an institution was rendered remediless by the provisions of the Limitation Act 1623. Mr Harnett, a Kentish farmer, had taken a 'toxin given him by a quack' which caused transient insanity (see *Harnett v Bond* (1925) for the background facts). As a result of this he was originally properly detained, but thereafter wrongly redetained on the basis of the defendant simply watching him from the window when he was in the street. Mr Harnett brought his cause of action against the doctor in 1922 after making his escape from the institution some seven months earlier. A jury held that he had been wrongly detained for nine years, and awarded him substantial damages of £500. The House of Lords, however, confirmed the Court of Appeal's views that the action was time barred because, under the Limitation Act 1623, he had six years to bring the action and that time ran from 10 November 1912 when the negligent act and the damage, the loss of liberty, occurred. Since Mr Harnett was never insane, he could not rely on the disability provisions of s 7 of that Act. The plaintiff argued his own case with great skill and learning in the House of Lords, but their Lordships felt unable to accept his arguments that if he was treated in law as though he were mad then at least he should have the benefits of that detriment and the defendant should be estopped from saying his action was time barred when he never had an opportunity to consult his solicitors because of his incarceration. His case was dismissed with costs against him.

Section 2(D) of the 1939 Limitation Act was enacted because in many cases, plaintiffs were ignorant that as a matter of law they had a cause of action. This provision is now contained in s 33 of the Limitation Act 1980. Section 33 contains provisions for the court to set aside the time limit of three years from the date of the cause of the action or from the date of knowledge in those cases which consist of or include damages for personal injury, if it is satisfied that it is equitable to do so. (*Harnett's* case could not rely upon s 33 of the Limitation Act even today, because it did not consist of or include a claim for personal injury. However, it could rely on s 38(4) which conclusively presumes that a person is of unsound mind whilst detained under the Mental Health Act 1983.)

(i) Prejudice

Section 33 empowers the court with a wide discretion to disapply the time limits imposed in ss 11 and 12 concerning personal injury and death cases. The only major class of action excluded from s 33 are those cases where a second writ has been issued because the first writ was never served or renewed, or where the first action was struck out for want of prosecution or was otherwise discontinued (*Walkley v Precision Forgings Ltd* ([1979] 2 All ER 548)). Accordingly, if a solicitor fails to start an action and a time limit is passed, the court retains the discretion to grant a s 33 dispensation. If, however, a writ is issued but is not served, or if served the action is discontinued or struck out, no discretion exists. Lord Diplock in *Walkley* did indicate that there might be exceptional circumstances in which a court would allow a time-barred action to proceed where a writ had been issued but not served, but these are restricted to those circumstances where a plaintiff had been induced to discontinue an action by misrepresentation or by other improper conduct by the defendant and the defendant is effectively estopped from raising a Limitation Act defence. The reasoning behind the decision in *Walkley* is that the prejudice that arises in cases where a first writ has been issued is deemed not to flow from the provisions of the Limitation Act, but from the action or inaction of the plaintiff's legal advisers in failing to pursue an action rather than failing to start the action. For *Walkley* to be effective, the initial action must have been properly constituted. Accordingly a s 33 dispensation is available in those circumstances where an invalid writ which is a nullity has been issued, as for example against a company in compulsory liquidation without leave of the court (*Wilson v Banner Scaffolding Ltd* ((1982) Times, 22 June)). Section 33(1) requires the court to examine separately the respective prejudices that will occur to the plaintiff if the claim remains statute barred and to the defendant if it is allowed to proceed. In determining the type and amount of prejudice, the court is required by s 33(3) to look at all the circumstances of the case with particular reference to six specified factors. Following this investigation, the discretion is to be exercised if the court considers it equitable. The obvious prejudice to the plaintiff is being precluded from suing to obtain damages and in those circumstances it is always relevant for the court to consider, although not in great detail, the strength of the plaintiff's case on liability. If a plaintiff has such a weak case, limited only to a nuisance value, then little or no prejudice is likely to be

191

caused by refusing to allow the claim to proceed. A plaintiff's prejudice will therefore be at its highest when the defendant has no defence save for limitation and a plaintiff has no claim against, for example, his legal advisers for contributing or causing the delay.

The most significant recent judicial expression on prejudice is to be found in the case of *Hartley v Birmingham District Council* ([1992] 2 All ER 213). In *Hartley* Parker LJ became the first appellate judge to make some 'general observations' on the nature of s 33 prejudice, although like other appellate courts before him he refused to lay down guidelines. Lord Justice Parker thought that the prejudice referred to in s 33(1) was in fact likely to be equal and opposite, and the real focus of prejudice should be on evidential prejudice namely that which has affected the defendant's ability to defend the claim on its merits. Mrs Hartley's case was only a few hours statute barred, because the writ instead of being issued in the afternoon on 11 December was issued in the morning of the 12. Equally, however, the plaintiff had a cast iron case against her own solicitors. Lord Justice Parker, in allowing the plaintiff's appeal, indicated that the stronger the plaintiff's case the greater the prejudice will be if the claim is not allowed to proceed, and if it is allowed to proceed the defendant's prejudice will be at its highest precisely because it is a good claim on the merits. Alternatively, if the plaintiff has a weak case he is not prejudiced by not allowing the case to proceed because he is likely to lose, but if it was allowed to proceed the defendant would not be prejudiced given the prospects of defeating the claim. That analysis led the court to express a view that the prejudice resulting from the loss of the limitation defence would always or almost always be balanced by the prejudice of the plaintiff from the operation of the limitation provision. What was deemed to be important was the effect of the delay of the defendant's ability to defend. The court also expressed a view that, even when a plaintiff has a good case against a solicitor, there might still be prejudice in suing the solicitor because that solicitor may know a great deal about the plaintiff's claim, for example, on quantum. In *Nash v Eli Lilly* (p 466) a differently constituted Court of Appeal a year later said that Lord Parker's remarks were not of universal application. Prejudice could occur where there was disproportion between the level of costs the defendant would have to incur in defending a poor case and the likely level of damages a plaintiff might recover in any event. Such a situation, particularly, when a plaintiff was on legal aid, would make an action uneconomical to defend and this could constitute prejudice because a plaintiff might be in a position to extract a nuisance value settlement. Such an approach might well be applicable to high cost complex pharmaceutical or product liability actions (see the particular cases of Nash, Eaton, O'Hara and Jenkins in *Nash v Eli Lilly* (p 466) where a s 33 dispensation was refused partly on the weakness of the plaintiff's case which was based on the merits).

In *Donovan v Gwentoys Ltd* ([1990] 1 All ER 1018) prejudice that occurred before the expiry of the limitation period was held to be a relevant matter for the court to consider in granting a s 33 dispensation as it falls to be included under 'all the circumstances of the case'. In *Donovan,* the Court of Appeal held that the proper test was to examine the prejudice that had occurred after the expiry of the limitation period. The House of Lords reversed that construction and held that, in weighing prejudice to the defendant, it was always relevant to consider when the defendants first had notification of a claim. In *Hands v Colleridge-Smith and Horsburgh*, the Court of Appeal upheld a trial judge's refusal to grant a s 33 dispensation where a widow issued a writ on the 29 April 1985 in respect of the death of her husband on the 11 September 1981. The writ was in fact not served until 7 October 1988 and details of allegations against the practitioners were not supplied until April 1989, nearly seven and a half years after the death.

Economic prejudice arising out of alterations concerning the provision of responsibility for funding and paying damages in cases against hospitals is likely to be considered a relevant factor. Under the National Health Service and Community Care Act 1990, the district health authorities assumed responsibility for dealing with both new and existing claims arising out of the actions of hospital medical staff in the course of their employment, and the Medical Defence Societies which formerly indemnified doctors would subsequently only become involved when a practitioner was acting privately. (See Circulars HC (89) 34 and HC (FC) 89 22.) This arrangement was in force as of 1 January 1990. Accordingly it is arguable that where a defendant health authority becomes liable for such a claim because of delay by a plaintiff and had the plaintiff prosecuted an action timeously liability would have been the responsibility of the Medical Defence Societies, then prejudice has occurred. These arguments have been accepted in cases concerned with evaluating prejudice in striking out for want of prosecution (see *Ancliff v Gloucester Health Authority* (p 227) and *Gascoine v Haringey Health Authority* (p 346)).

In *Dobbie v Medway Health Authority* (p 310) not only was the plaintiff's claim held to be statute barred but a s 33 dispensation was refused, inter alia, on the grounds that the surgeon and hospital would be prejudiced by having the action hanging over them indefinitely (as in the case of *Biss v Lambeth, Southwark and Lewisham Health Authority (Teaching)* ([1978] 1 WLR 382)). The Court of Appeal upheld the trial judge's finding but Lord Justice Beldam did not think the Damoclean sword type of prejudice arose:

'I also agree that, in the circumstances of this case, the learned judge was right in the exercise of his discretion not to disapply the provisions of section 11 having regard to the level of time which had elapsed. However, I cannot agree with the judge that it was appropriate to take into account the factor which he took from the judgment of Lord Denning MR in *Biss v Lambeth, Southwark and Lewisham Health Authority (Teaching)* ([1978] 1 WLR 382) that there had been prejudice because the action had been hanging over the head of the attendant doctor for so many years. I do not see how such a consideration can apply to a doctor who does not know that any action is contemplated against him' ([1994] PIQR, Part 5 at 364–5).

In *Birnie v Oxfordshire Health Authority* (p 247) a s 33 dispensation was granted where the so-called Damoclean sword of prejudice hanging over an uninsured physician was not enough to prevent the plaintiff's claim being allowed to proceed, in circumstances where a writ had been issued three years outside his date of knowledge and nearly seven years since he was left paralysed below the waist following a barbotage.

(ii) Discretion

Section 33(3) stipulates six matters which the court ought to take into account in applying its discretion, and the case law that has arisen pursuant to this section is illustrative of how the court exercises its discretion. The six factors are exemplary only and are not exclusive and should not be looked at in isolation of each other. However, trial judges tend to look at each factor in turn. In *Nash v Eli Lilly and Co* (p 466) the Court of Appeal indicated that it would be very slow to interfere with the exercise of discretion under this section, but would do so where a judge either took into account factors which he should have ignored or ignored factors which he should have taken into account. Moreover, the court expressed the view that provided it was relevant the judge may take into account a factor not specifically listed in the sub-paragraphs of s 33(3), and alternatively if it was established that he failed to take into account any of the matters mentioned in s 33(3) which were relevant to the carrying out of the balancing exercise then his judgment would susceptible to attack.

(a) Section 33(3)(a): 'The length of, and reasons for, the delay on the part of the plaintiff'

Cases of lengthy delay of over 20 years have been allowed to proceed principally when they involve the contraction of insidious diseases, due to exposure to substances arising out of allegations of negligence concerning a system of work, rather than from a specific injury in a particular accident. In *Buck v English Electric Co Ltd* (1978), a pneumoconiosis case, the plaintiff was allowed to proceed sixteen years after the onset of her late husband's disease and twelve years since he knew that it was significant. The court was impressed by his attitude which was to continue working and to avoid what he thought was 'sponging' on his employers by bringing an action against them. Similarly, in *McCafferty v Metropolitan Police District Receiver* (1977), the plaintiff, who enjoyed his job, attempted to cope with his hearing difficulties by regarding them as a nuisance, and did not wish to sour relations with his employer. He was allowed to proceed with his action despite the fact that it was started in 1974 in respect of deafness and tinnitus that probably resulted from working conditions as far back as 1948 which had caused symptoms certainly since 1969.

What constitutes an acceptable period of delay and an acceptable reason for the delay will depend upon the particular facts of any one case. The courts will be looking for either a good or reasonable explanation for the delay or at least one that does not involve direct criticism of the plaintiff himself. Negative advice from a lawyer or delay caused by legal and other advisers is usually a basis for absolving a plaintiff of any personal criticism. In *Doughty v North Staffordshire Health Authority* (p 311) a delay of effectively nine years in a case relating to medical treatment received over a period of up to twenty-five years before proceedings occurred. The action was allowed to continue even though the treating surgeon was no longer able to testify because of his infirmity. The judge held that, notwithstanding the defendant's prejudice, since the medical records were still intact it was possible to have a fair trial. The judge accepted that the reasons for the delay were partly due to the discouraging expert opinion followed by negative legal advice, leading to a discharge of the plaintiff's legal aid certificate.

In *Hendy v Milton Keynes Health Authority* (p 378) a short period of a nine day delay which gave rise to no evidential prejudice was excused by the court in respect of a plaintiff's action for damages arising out of injury to her right urethra during a hysterectomy. In *Colegrove v Smyth* (p 282) Buckley J found that a claim initiated in November 1987 in respect of a failure to diagnose congenital dislocation of the hips at birth in February 1959 was not statute barred because of the plaintiff's date of knowledge. The plaintiff would have been able to sue in time until February 1980 because of her minority. The delay thereafter was due to her only realising that she might have a cause of action in December 1984. The trial judge indicated that he would have, if necessary, exercised the court's discretion under s 33 notwithstanding the fact that one of the defendants had died, another was 85 and two out of their three sets of medical records had been destroyed.

Conversely, as seen, in *Dobbie v Medway Health Authority* (p 310) a delay of 16 years from a date of actual knowledge in 1973 to the issue of a writ in 1989 was found to be inexcusable on the basis that the plaintiff should have taken advice and issued proceedings years before she did. This was so despite a psychiatric reaction to the loss of her breast which resulted in repeated overdoses and admissions to psychiatric hospitals. In *Nash v Eli Lilly* (p 466) several of the plaintiffs' claims involved delay because of a worry over what the legal action would cost (cf *Eaton, Boxal* and *O'Hara*) and such a reason appeared to find no sympathy with the court. In *Baig v City and Hackney Health Authority* (p 235) a plaintiff described as an educated and professional man sought to sue in May 1991 in respect of loss of hearing in his left ear following an operation in August 1983. The plaintiff pursued his case but received unfavourable reports. The trial judge found that a lot of the delay was largely unexplained and it had to be laid at the plaintiff's door. (See also *Hands v Colleridge-Smith and Horsburgh* (p 368), *Kidd v Grampian Health Board* (p 413).)

(b) Section 33(3)(b): 'The extent to which having regard to the delay the evidence adduced or likely to be adduced by the plaintiff or the defendant is or is likely to be less cogent than if the action had been brought within the time allowed by Section 11.'

The delay referred to in this sub-paragraph is delay since the expiry of the limitation period. However, since the case of *Donovan v Gwentoys* (above), the court may look at prejudice from the accrual of the plaintiff's cause of action under 'all the circumstances of a case' and all evidential prejudice is likely to be considered. In *Hartley v Birmingham District Council* (above) the Court of Appeal expressed the view that this factor is likely to be the most significant matter in the exercise of the court's discretion. The paramount consideration is to determine the effect, if any, on how the delay has weakened the defendant's ability to resist the claim on the merits. The mere fact of a very long delay will not necessarily be fatal to an application. If the case is one of a number which the defendants have previously defended or fully investigated and have taken proofs concerning the conditions of work or the system of work, then these matters would push the balance of advantage and disadvantage in the favour of the plaintiff (*Simpson v Norwest Holst Southern Ltd* (1980)). Where the incident was isolated, was not reported, or did not result in a proof from the witnesses or retention of evidence, then the defendant is likely to be severely prejudiced (see for example *Mahon v Concrete (Southern) Ltd* (1979), where the relevant x-rays had been destroyed).

In *Waghorn v Lewisham and North Southwark Area Health Authority* (1987) (p 594), the court exercised its discretion and disapplied the provisions of the Limitation Act 1980, s 11 in a case where a plaintiff knew a medical mishap had occurred in 1977 but did not serve a writ until 1985. The trial judge determined that the defendants had known about the plaintiff's complaints from 1978 and all the hospital records except for the nursing notes had been preserved. Although it was true that two further surgical procedures in 1980 and in 1983 had obscured what in fact had happened in 1977, the judge found that the evidence was only marginally less cogent and exercised his discretion in favour of the plaintiff.

Medical negligence actions, primarily based on the interpretation of expert evidence where clinical and nursing notes have been preserved, are accordingly more likely to be allowed to proceed than those which raise issues concerning consent and warning as to risks which largely hinge on all recollections. In *Baig v City and Hackney Health Authority* (p 235) the trial judge refused to allow the statute-barred action to proceed, inter alia, because that part of the plaintiff's action based upon a failure to warn and to discuss the merits and potential dangers of a stapedectomy performed 17 years prior to the issue of proceedings, meant that the practitioners concerned had no valuable recollection of what had been said at the time. Similarly in *Wilding v Lambeth, Southwark and Lewisham Area Health Authority* (Lexis 10 May 1982), a late amendment to an alleged lack of consent to a dental operation was refused, on the basis that the eight year delay prohibited any probative evidence being adduced based on the oral recollections of the practitioners concerned.

Conversely when all the notes are available and when there is little reliance on oral recollections, a court is more frequently sympathetic to a s 33 dispensation (see *Bentley v Bristol and Western Health Authority* (p 244), *Doughty v North Staffordshire Health Authority* (p 311), *Hendy v Milton Keynes Health Authority* (p 377) and *Kidd v Grampian Health Board* (p 413)). In *Kidd v Grampian Health Board* a plaintiff sued in respect of intra-muscular injections of paraldehyde given in October 1973, commencing her action in March 1989. The only issue in the case was whether such a form of injection was a recognised and acceptable form of treatment to control destructive behaviour. In those circumstances, because the delay had not seriously affected the evidence available, the claim was allowed to proceed. There are, however, examples of cases where the defendants have suffered significant evidential prejudice but the case has nevertheless been allowed to proceed. (See *Doughty v North Staffordshire Health Authority* where a surgeon had had a stroke and could not testify, and *Colegrove v Smyth* where the court said it would have exercised its discretion under s 33, if necessary, notwithstanding that one doctor had died, one was aged 85 and two out of three sets of medical records had been destroyed.)

(c) Section 33(3)(c): 'The conduct of the defendant after the cause of action arose including the extent (if any), to which he responded to requests reasonably made by the plaintiff for information or inspection for the purposes of ascertaining facts which were or might be relevant to the plaintiff's cause of action'

Health authorities may be held to account under this sub-paragraph, if they fail to give prompt and proper explanations of medical mishaps and if they have failed to provide information including clinical and nursing notes reasonably quickly. Obstructive behaviour on the part of the defendant personally, or the defendant's solicitors or insurers, may tip the balance in the plaintiff's favour (*Thompson v Brown Construction (Ebbw Vale) Ltd* (1981)). In *Mills v Dyer-Fare* (1987) Steyn J regarded a five-month delay in producing medical notes as a relevant factor in considering the exercise of his discretion under s 33. In *Atkinson v Oxfordshire Health Authority* (p 230) a plaintiff operated on in 1967 when aged 17 was found to have a date of knowledge within the three years prior to the issue of his writ on 6 July 1989. However, if the court had been required to exercise its discretion under s 33, it would have done so in the plaintiff's favour, because the large part of the delay was due to the defendants' own failure to tell the plaintiff's mother precisely what had happened during a second operation to evacuate a tumour on the right side of the brain. In *Scuriaga v Powell* (p 548) the court similarly found that if necessary it would have exercised its discretion in favour of the plaintiff. Miss Scuriaga's action was based on a failed abortion which resulted in the plaintiff giving birth to a live child. The defendant was found to have wrongly indicated to the plaintiff that the failure was due to a structural defect in her rather than in his own negligence. A six-month delay in producing notes due to a misunderstanding in *Baig v City and Hackney Health Authority* (p 235) was not, however, enough to sway the balance in the plaintiff's favour in an action concerning delay of over 17 years much of which was unexplained.

(d) Section 33(3)(d): 'The duration of any disability of a plaintiff arising after the date of the accrual of the cause of action'

Section 33(3)(*d*) specifically allows the court to consider the duration of any disability of the plaintiff arising after the date of the accrual of the cause of action. The disability can refer only to mental disability, as disability on account of minority cannot arise after the date of the accrual of the cause of action (cf *Dawson v Scott-Brown* (1988) (p 304), the Limitation Act 1980, s 38(2)). There are, however, dicta which have treated disability within s 33(3)(*d*) as physical disability arising out of the injury in question. (cf *Bater v Newbold* (Lexis 13 July 1991, CA)l, *Pilmore v Northern Trawlers Ltd* [1986] 1 Lloyd's Rep 552), and *Baig v City and Hackney Health Authority* ([1994]) 5 Med LR 1 at p 9)). Given the view expressed by Lord Diplock in *Thompson v Brown Construction (Ebbw Vale) Ltd* ([1981] 1 WLR 7440) that this paragraph was specifically designed to protect persons under a disability, namely a category that equity has always been zealous to protect, it is unlikely that such a wide interpretation of s 33(3)(*d*) is tenable. Little, however, turns on whether the sub-paragraph is to consider non-legal disability in the form of physical disability or infirmity, as those matters if excluded under this sub-paragraph are frequently taken into account in s 33(3)(*a*) where the court is investigating the reasons for the delay.

(e) Section 33(3)(e): 'The extent to which the plaintiff acted promptly and reasonably once he knew whether or not the act or omission of the defendant to which the injury was attributable, might be capable at that time of giving rise to an action for damages'

Section 33(3)(*e*) requires investigation into how the plaintiff acted once he knew that his injury was attributable to the acts of the defendants and gave rise to a cause of action. This date could well be later than the s 14 date of knowledge, because consideration can be given at this stage to the actual date when the plaintiff realised that the facts in question amounted to a cause of action in law. (See *Eastman v London Country Bus Services Ltd* ((1985) Times, 23 November)). Once a plaintiff has personal knowledge in respect of the cause of action upon which he sues, the court will enquire into how expeditiously the action was progressed before issue of the proceedings both in respect of the plaintiff's behaviour and the behaviour of his lawyers (*Thompson v Brown* (above)). In *Doughty v North Staffordshire Health Authority* (p 311) the court, however, was willing to excuse the tardiness of the plaintiff's advisers and exonerated the plaintiff of any personal blame in respect of failing to chivvy her lawyers, on the basis that she was busy looking after her handicapped daughter. Conversely in *Obembe v City and Hackney Health Authority* (p 485) parents sued in 1988 for alleged malpractice occurring at the birth of their son in 1979. They included a claim for damages in respect of themselves for psychiatric injury which was statute-barred and the court rejected the contention put forward that because they had 21 years to sue in respect of their son that was a reasonable excuse for not bringing their own action earlier.

(f)   Section 33(3)(f): 'The steps if any taken by the plaintiff to obtain medical legal or other advice and the nature of any such advice he may have received'

Finally, s 33(3)(f) investigates the steps, if any, taken by the plaintiff to obtain expert advice, and the nature of that advice he received. Accordingly, a plaintiff will be disadvantaged if he failed to take an opportunity of seeking advice which was readily available, as in the case of *Casey v J Murphy & Sons* (1979), where a worker who had contracted dermatitis could have obtained trade union backed legal services. The court is allowed at this stage to enquire into legal advice given, and legal professional privilege can be waived for this purpose so that, for example, negative advice given by counsel can be looked at (*Jones v GD Searle & Co Ltd* (1978), *Tatlock v GP Worsley & Co Ltd* (Lexis, 22 June 1989)). Negative legal advice is frequently a problem for plaintiffs in medical negligence actions, where there is often difficulty in obtaining favourable medical opinion on negligence and causation. A negative medical opinion will frequently lead to the discharge of a legal aid certificate.

In *Bentley v Bristol and Weston Health Authority* (p 244) the plaintiff received negative legal advice from two counsel based on negative medical opinion, but a third set of solicitors obtained a report from a well-known orthopaedic surgeon indicating that there had been undue traction during a process which damaged the sciatic nerve. The judge held that, if he had been required to exercise s 33, he would have done so in the plaintiff's favour because at all times the plaintiff personally was vigorously striving to carry her claim forward. (*Bentley* was overruled on the judge's finding in respect of the plaintiff's date of knowledge by *Broadley v Guy Clapham and Co* (p 261).) Similarly in *Waghorn v Lewisham and North Southwark Area Health Authority* a s 33 dispensation was granted in circumstances where a significant part of a plaintiff's delay was due to lack of supportive expert evidence.

(g)   Section 33(3): 'In acting under this section the court shall have regard to all the circumstances of the case ...'

The six factors identified in s 33(3), although addressed individually, will then be looked at in terms of the context of the case as a whole. 'All the circumstances of the case' may well include investigations into when the claim was first indicated to the defendants (*Donovan v Gwentoys Ltd* (above), *Hands v Colleridge-Smith and Horsburgh* (p 368)). Other factors which the court has been minded to consider concern whether a plaintiff has a claim over against legal advisers, whether a defendant is insured, whether a plaintiff is legally aided, the size of the plaintiff's claim on quantum and the strength of the plaintiff's case on liability.

In most medical malpractice actions, a degree of record keeping should preserve some cogent evidence. There may also be a recognition of the factual complexities that can arise in both formulating and appraising a claim. Again the court may allow some indulgence in respect of the natural reluctance of many patients to take issue with their doctors. Moreover, the often grave difficulty in obtaining proper expert evidence may help a plaintiff who finds himself statute barred. In *Birnie v Oxfordshire Health Authority* (1982) (p 247), a plaintiff who had become permanently paraplegic following treatment for pain relief in December 1972 issued a writ alleging negligence in August 1979. During this period of seven years, the plaintiff had become depressed and suicidal and had also contracted gangrene which resulted in an amputation. It was conceded that his claim was statute barred by approximately December 1976, but he relied on s 33 of the Limitation Act 1980. Glidewell J held that the delay before the plaintiff contacted his solicitors in 1977 was understandable because of the extreme difficulties the plaintiff had experienced, but that one year of the subsequent delay was inexcusable. The defendant was prejudiced because he was not insured and he had this action hanging over him. Alternatively, there were reasonably good notes available, and in balancing all the factors the judge allowed the action to proceed. In *Kidd v Grampian Health Board* (p 413) the court came to a view that it would generally be equitable to allow an action to proceed, if delay had not seriously affected the evidence available, and accordingly the claim was allowed to proceed. This illustrates an application of Lord Justice Parker's dicta in *Hartley v Birmingham City District Council* (above) to the effect that, if the delay has not seriously affected the evidence, the power to disapply would generally be exercised.

Conversely, in *Goodman v Fletcher* (1982) (p 356), the plaintiff's claim was struck out as statute barred, in circumstances where a writ was issued in March 1978 in respect of allegedly negligent treatment in July 1973. The plaintiff had learnt in approximately September 1974, and certainly by February 1975, that the diet prescribed for her by the defendant in respect of her allergies was inappropriate. Her claim was therefore prima facie statute barred. The Court of Appeal held that there had been great delay, and it would be impossible for the relevant doctor at trial in 1983 to have an accurate recollection of consultations which took place ten years earlier. The Court of Appeal considered this delay fatal to the exercise of discretion under s 33.

D. ABUSE OF PROCESS: LIMITATION AND DISABILITY

Section 38(2) of the Limitation Act 1980 states: 'for the purposes of this Act a person shall be treated as under a disability while he is an infant, or of unsound mind'

Unsoundness of mind is further defined in s 38(3) as having two requirements, namely the plaintiff is suffering from a mental disorder within the meaning of the Mental Health Act 1983, and is thereby incapable of managing and administering his property and affairs. Under s 28 of the Limitation Act 1980, limitation does not run for a minor or for a person of unsound mind until majority or until soundness of mind is restored. A plaintiff therefore who suffers from a disability has three years from the cessation of his minority or his disability to bring an action or if later, three years from his date of knowledge following the cessation of his minority or disability. The effect of this provision is that for a child who, for example, is permanently brain damaged at birth there is no limitation period during its lifetime.

The effect of this extended period of limitation was discussed in *Tolley v Morris* ([1979] 2 All ER 561) and in *Turner v WH Malcolm Ltd* (1992) Times, 24 August), cases which were concerned with striking out for want of prosecution. The court held that it was fruitless to strike out such actions, because fresh actions could be started which could not be struck out as an abuse of process save in exceptional circumstances. Such circumstances arose in *Janov v Morris* ([1981] 3 All ER 780) where a second writ started within the limitation period was struck out as an abuse of process because the first action had been struck out due to non-compliance with a peremptory order and, moreover, no explanation had been given as to why the order in the first action had not been complied with.

Medical practitioners and defendant health authorities can find themselves in a position of having to defend a claim against a person with a disability many years after the medical mishap without any limitation defence. Some protection was afforded to such defendants in *Hogg v Hamilton* (p 383) where the Court of Appeal held that proceedings could be struck out as an abuse of process of the court even though the plaintiff was a person to whom an extended and unexpired period of limitation was applicable. In *Hogg,* the plaintiff's fourth set of solicitors sought to add the health authority as a second defendant to a writ which had been issued in 1989, brought against an anaesthetist following permanent brain damage to the plaintiff which occurred in 1976. A first writ had been issued in 1978 which was dismissed for want of prosecution in 1982, without apparently the court being made aware of the plaintiff's disability. The particularly aggravating feature in *Hogg* was that the plaintiff's solicitors had indicated to the health authority when seeking documents that no proceedings were intended against them, and on that representation the health authority had disclosed privileged documents.

In *Bull v Devon Area Health Authority* (p 264), Lord Justice Slade emphasised that the Limitation Act allowed a person under a permanent disability to bring a claim at any time during his life and moreover the claim could be brought three years after his death. That action concerned a claim in respect of the birth of a twin which was tried some 17 years after the death. The Court of Appeal rejected submissions made by defence counsel that in such circumstances the court ought to be less ready to make inferences against the defendant due to the passage of time and of lost opportunity in defending the claim. The Court of Appeal expressed the view that a plaintiff in this position was not to be treated as prejudiced although, of course, the plaintiff may well have difficulties in proving his case after the passage of such a long period. Mustill LJ further emphasised the right of a disabled plaintiff to initiate an action at any time:

> 'Since this unfortunate plaintiff has been under a double disability for almost all of the time since the asserted cause of action arose, those who have the charge of his interests are entitled under statute to delay the institution of proceedings beyond the point of which the judge has rightly said, it would have been unfair to allow his mother to persist. Parliament must therefore have decided that the public interest in acquiring factual disputes to be litigated properly is outweighed, in such cases as this, by the public interest in giving the disadvantaged a long time in which to sue' ([1993] 4 Med LR 117 at 139).

In *Headford v Bristol and District Health Authority* (p 374) at first instance, an action started 28 years after a medical mishap that occurred to a plaintiff at the age of 10 months was struck out as being an abuse of process. This was so notwithstanding that it was the first action the plaintiff had brought and the plaintiff was under a permanent disability. The Court of Appeal, however, reversed this decision, reasserting the right of a person under a disability to bring an action pursuant to s 28 of the Limitation Act at any time during the disability and three years thereafter.

2. Dismissal for want of prosecution

Once an action is started by the issue of a writ, the court prescribes time limits for subsequent stages in the litigation, such as the service of the writ and statement of claim, the time for the defence and other pleadings to be completed, the period during which discovery and inspection of documents must take place, the date for a hearing for directions of the conduct of the action and, finally, for the setting down of the action for trial. The court has specific powers contained in RSC Ord 25, r 1(4) to dismiss an action for failure to take out a summons for directions within one month of when the pleadings are deemed to have closed. (In medical negligence actions, the automatic directions which apply to other personal injury actions pursuant to RSC Ord 25, r 8 do not apply.) The court has similar powers for failure to serve a statement of claim (RSC Ord 19, r 1), for default of discovery (RSC Ord 24, r 16(1)) and for default of setting down (RSC Ord 34, r 2).

In addition, the court retains an inherent power to dismiss an action for default in complying with the rules or in failing to prosecute the action. Disobeying a so-called peremptory order of the court, so that a party is held to have been guilty of intentional and contumelious conduct, may result in the action being struck out. More frequently, it is a dilatory conduct which results in applications to strike out for inordinate and inexcusable delay on the part of the plaintiff. Actions may be struck out if such improper delay gives rise to a substantial risk that it is not possible to have a fair trial of the issues, or is such that the defendants have suffered serious prejudice (*Birkett v James* (1978), *Allen v Sir Alfred McAlpine & Sons Ltd* (1968) and *Department of Transport v Chris Smaller (Transport) Ltd* (1989)).

(i) Delay

Delay which is deemed to be culpable in this context is that which has occurred after the limitation period has expired, and an action will not be dismissed for delay if there is still time to commence another action within the limitation period. The power to dismiss an action arises even in those cases where liability has been admitted and indeed a payment into court has been made, if the delay is such that it makes it difficult or impossible to have a fair trial on the quantum of damages (*Gloria v Sokoloff & Others* (1969), *Paxton v Alsopp* (1971)). Delay is considered to be inordinate, if it is materially longer than that which is normally regarded by the courts and legal practitioners as acceptable. Delay is usually inexcusable when it is caused by the plaintiff or the plaintiff's advisers, and the defendant has not caused or contributed to the delay (*Trill v Sacher* ([1993] 1 All ER 961)). Delay can occur when things are being done in a desultory fashion, and although the defendants must not contribute to the delay they are entitled to let 'sleeping dogs' lie (*Lev v Fagan* (1988), *Roebuck v Mungovin* ([1994] 1 All ER 568)). In *Roebuck* (above), the House of Lords held that if the defendant's conduct induced a plaintiff to further expense after a period of inordinate delay that would be a relevant factor in the exercise of a judge's discretion whether to strike the case out, but it did not constitute a procedural bar and the defendants were not estopped from relying upon such culpable delay.

(ii) Prejudice

Prejudice primarily connotes evidential difficulties occurring because of the delay, involving the loss of witnesses, the failing of recollections particularly in accident cases, and the loss of the pertinent detail to rebut allegations of negligence or breach of duty. Prejudice of a financial nature may arise, however, in those cases where it can be demonstrated and proved that the delay has caused an increase in the level of damages the plaintiff is likely to receive. In certain circumstances, because annual wage increases may be above the rate of inflation and because the multiplier does not diminish at the same rate as the years of delay in getting the case to trial, a plaintiff might be financially better off because he delayed (*Hayes v Bowman* (1988), *Newman v Hopkins* ((1988) Times, 28 December), *Doyle v Robinson* ((1993) Times, 22 September 1993)).

In assessing whether delay has caused serious prejudice, the court is entitled to look at the whole period of the delay from the cause of action. Whereas it is recognised that the delay in issuing within the limitation period is legitimate, the courts have stressed that if a plaintiff starts an action late in the day he must thereafter proceed with reasonable diligence. Moreover, the additional prejudice compared to that degree of prejudice which has already occurred before the issuing of the writ need not be great but only more than minimal (*Birkett v James* (1978), *Department of Transport v Chris Smaller (Transport) Ltd* (1989)). Further, in *Leniston v Phipps* (1988), Stuart-Smith LJ indicated that:

> 'Where prolonged culpable delay follows prolonged delay in the issue of or service of proceedings, the court may readily infer that memories and reliability of witnesses has further deteriorated in the period of culpable delay'. (See also *James Investments (Isle of Man) Ltd* and *Spartina Properties Ltd v Phillips Cutler Phillips Troy (A Firm)* (1987).)

In medical negligence cases, prejudice may also arise because the practitioners, or the hospitals where they practise, have the nuisance of an action hanging over them for many years. In *Biss v Lambeth, Southwark and Lewisham Area Health Authority (Teaching)* (1978) (p 248) Lord Denning indicated that businesses may be prejudiced by not being able to conduct their affairs with confidence because they have an action hanging over them, and similarly hospitals were after a time entitled to some peace of mind and entitled to close their files and tell their staff that they will no longer be needed to fight a very stale claim. In *Biss,* the plaintiff suffered from bed sores in 1965, allegedly from negligent nursing care, and was granted leave to start proceedings out of time in February 1975 under the provisions of the then Limitation Act 1963. Pleadings closed in July 1975 and in March 1977 the defendants sought to strike out the claim for want of prosecution. The Court of Appeal concurred with the Master who struck out the claim, finding there had been inordinate and inexcusable delay and serious prejudice. The prejudice in question was predominantly the Sword of Damocles hanging over the authority's head. In *Department of Transport v Chris Smaller (Transport) Ltd* (1989), the House of Lords expressed caution against allowing the mere fact of anxiety which accompanies all litigation to constitute serious prejudice. The eleven and a half years' delay in *Biss* was considered exceptional (per Lord Griffith ([1989] 2 WLR at 587h) and *Eagil Trust Co Ltd v Pigott Brown* ([1985] 3 All ER at 124)). See also *Gascoine v Haringey Health Authority* (p 346).

In *Joseph v Korn* (1984) (p 407), an action was brought by the mother of the deceased, alleging that the negligence of a general practitioner's receptionist led to the death of her son on 30 December 1971. The writ was issued on 23 December 1974, and the action was dismissed in March 1984 for want of prosecution. In dismissing the action, the Court of Appeal held that, notwithstanding the fact that there had been a full documented hearing shortly after the death instigated by the health authority, the claim 13 years later still involved disputed questions of fact.

In *Mansouri v Bloomsbury Health Authority* (1987) (p 451), the Court of Appeal upheld a dismissal of an action which was founded on a cause of action in June 1979 with a writ issued in June 1982. Counsel was asked to advise in March 1984 but was unable to do so, and a subsequent counsel, after requesting a further medical report, gave an opinion in May 1985. The matter was struck out in July 1985, a little over six years after the cause of action, on the grounds of inordinate delay. In *Rosen v Marston* (1984) (p 533), the plaintiff alleged negligent treatment in an operation for varicose veins in March 1977, and issued a writ in 1980. Approximately three years later, during which time nothing was done, an application was made to the defendants for the hospital notes, and they replied with an application to strike out. The Court of Appeal upheld the striking out on the basis of approximately two and a half years of unwarranted delay which caused prejudice to the defendant, because his recollection would be impaired and because he had suffered an unnecessary two years of anxiety and distress.

However, in *Westaway v South Glamorgan Health Authority* (1986) (p 600), although a delay was held to be inordinate and inexcusable, no prejudice was thought to have arisen in a case brought on the basis of a failure to diagnose a fracture which occurred in May 1976. The writ was issued in April 1979, the statement of claim served in June 1979, and a defence eventually filed in 1983 after the defendants had indicated an intention to settle. The plaintiff's solicitors failed to respond to a request for quantification of the claim, and the defendants issued in June 1985 a summons to dismiss the action. The Court of Appeal held that no prejudice had arisen because the substance of the claim was a failure to diagnose a fracture which must substantially be a matter of record.

Specific examples of health authorities being economically prejudiced are to be found in the cases of *Antcliffe v Gloucester Health Authority* (p 227) and *Gascoine v Haringey Health Authority* (p 346). Both these cases concerned prejudice that arose from changes in the payment of damages in medical negligence actions which occurred in the National Health Service taking effect on the 1 January 1990 in respect of so-called crown indemnity. Since that date, the hospital authorities became the payers of medical negligence damages rather than sharing the damages with the Medical Defence Associations in respect of National Health Service treatment in hospitals. Owing to delay by the plaintiffs in both the actions, the defendants were able to argue that they had incurred greater financial liability because they would have to satisfy the total judgments if the plaintiffs were successful. The court held that such a factor was a legitimate matter to take into account although in *Gascoine* it indicated that it might not be a determinative factor, because clearly the health authority did benefit to some degree in terms of the changes in its insurance arrangements for example by not having to contribute to the premiums paid by medical practitioners in their employment to the Defence Associations.

3. Automatic striking out in the county court

By the provisions of CCR Ord 17, r 11(9), a case may be automatically struck out if a request for a hearing date was not made within 15 months after the close of pleadings which are deemed to be 14 days after the delivery of a defence or 28 days where a counterclaim is served with the defence. Accordingly any medical negligence claim brought in the county court, unless directions are sought that the automatic directions do not apply, will be subject to this draconian measure. The court has held that in certain limited circumstances a case which is struck out may be reinstated (*Rastin v British Steel plc* ([1994] 1 WLR 732), *Hoskins v Wiggins Teape (UK) Ltd*). For a case to be reinstated, the plaintiff must show that apart from a failure to comply with the request for a hearing date the case has otherwise been prosecuted with at least reasonable diligence and the failure to comply with the rule was excusable. A plaintiff will be assisted in the first test, if he can show that an extension of time for the requisite period if sought in time would probably have been granted. A simple explanation that a plaintiff's adviser had forgotten to comply with a rule or had been ill for a short period of time or had been too busy or that a letter had been mislaid in the post is unlikely to assist him. If, however, the plaintiff can get across the threshold conditions the court will then consider whether it is proper to exercise its discretion to reinstate and at this stage will look at the interests of justice, the position of the parties and the balance of hardship. Any demonstration of significant prejudice by a defendant at this stage would normally be a conclusive reason for not exercising the discretion in the plaintiff's favour.

Further, if an action is started in the county court a plaintiff's legal adviser would be unwise to grant any general extension of time to serve a defence because a further form of automatic striking out can occur under Ord 9, r 10, where after one year no admission defence or counterclaim has been filed and the plaintiff has failed to enter judgment. It is likely that in these circumstances no enlargement of time is possible and no reinstatement can be made.

Chapter 14

Access to medical records and expert evidence

In medical negligence cases it is almost always necessary to obtain the medical records before commencing court action. A significant extension of a patient's right of access to medical records has been created, in respect of applications made after the 31 October 1991, by the Access to Health Records Act 1990. Prior to the coming into force of this Act patients had rights of access under the Supreme Court Act 1981, s 33, in respect of so-called 'pre-action discovery', rights under the Data Protection Act 1984 and under the Access to Medical Reports Act 1988. These different statutory rights continue to be of relevance although the Access to Health Records Act 1990 will become increasingly significant.

(i) The Access to Health Records Act 1990

This Act confers a statutory right of access to a patient's non-computerised health records. Such computerised records are still governed by the Data Protection Act 1994. By s 3 of the Access to Health Records Act 1990, an application for health records can be made by the patient or by others acting for him. These include a person authorised in writing on behalf of the patient, a person having parental responsibility for a patient who is a child, a person appointed to manage the affairs of the person under a disability and, in respect of deceased patients, the personal representative or any person who might have a claim arising out of the death. The holder of the record must allow inspection and supply a copy if asked within 40 days. If the record is not older than 40 days inspection and supply should be provided within 21 days. A health record as defined under s 1 consists of information, in a non-computerised form, relating to the physical or mental health of a patient made by or for a health professional in connection with the individual's care. Access is not to be given in respect of any record made before the 1 November 1991, unless the holder is of the opinion that the pre 1 November 1991 information is required to make the post 1 November 1991 information intelligible.

A health authority or the Family Health Services Authority should consult the relevant health professionals which include medical practitioners, dentists, opticians, pharmaceutical chemists, nurses, midwives, health visitors, clinical psychologists, child psychotherapists, speech therapists. The holder, however, need not give access in the case of a child where the application is made by the child or by a person authorised to make the application on the child's behalf unless the holder is satisfied that the child is capable of understanding the nature of the application (s 4). Where the parent or someone having parental responsibility for the child seeks access, access is not to be given unless the holder is satisfied that the child has consented to the application or that the child is incapable of understanding the nature of the application and giving access would be in the child's best interests (s 4(2)). A further restriction is imposed in respect of a deceased patient where an application is made by the personal representative or other person who might have a claim arising from the death. In such cases access should not be given if the record includes a note made at the deceased's request that he did not want access to be given in respect of such application.

Finally, under s 5(1), the holder need not give access where he is of the opinion that the information contained would be likely to cause serious harm to the physical or mental health of the patient or of any other individual. Further, disclosure need not be given when to do so could result in the identification of an individual who had provided information concerning the patient, unless that individual consents or that individual is a health professional who has been involved in the care of the patient (s 5(2)). If a patient is of the view that the records are inaccurate, he may apply to the holder to correct the record. The holder must correct the record or alternatively, if it is believed that the record is accurate, note in the record what the patient believes to be the inaccuracy.

The Act confers no civil action for damages that might arise out of inaccuracy in the records. By s 8(1) a patient may make an application to the High Court to obtain an order that the holder of the record complies with the requirements of the Act.

(ii) The Data Protection Act 1984

Where health records are computerised, the Data Protection Act 1984, s 21, gives a patient limited rights of access. Section 21(1) entitles an individual to be informed by a data user whether data held by him includes personal data of which the enquiring individual is the data subject. If the data user does have such information a copy must be provided to the data subject together with sufficient information to make it intelligible. However with respect to health records this right is limited by the Data Protection (Subject Access Modification) (Health) Order 1987, SI 1987/1903. By Regulation 4(2) of this Order the right of access to personal data relating to the physical or mental health of the subject which is held by a health professional is curtailed if:

(a) the information would be likely to cause serious harm to the physical or mental health of the data subject or
(b) the data disclosed would be likely to reveal the identity of another individual who has not consented to such disclosure either as
    (i) a person to whom the information or part of it relates or
    (ii) the source of the information or the information provided would enable the identity of the source to be deduced.

This restriction does not apply where the identity of any individual likely to be revealed is a health professional who has been involved in the care of the data subject (Regulation 4(3)). When the holder is not a health professional disclosure to the subject must not take place until the holder has consulted the health practitioners responsible for the clinical care of the subject and has ascertained whether or not the exemptions apply. Compensation is recoverable for damage or distress arising from the inaccuracy of the data, subject to the defence that the holder exercised reasonable care (s 22(1)).

(iii) Access to Medical Reports Act 1988

The Access to Medical Reports Act 1988 is restricted to those medical reports provided for the purposes of employment and insurance and, accordingly, will not generally result in the disclosure of any clinical or general practitioner's notes. The Act provides for the right of an individual to have access to a medical report from a practitioner who has been responsible for his clinical care in respect of any report written in the last six months for the benefit of an insurance company or an employer or prospective employer. The subject must give consent to a report being made and when consent is given the subject may stipulate that he is provided with a copy before a copy is supplied to the person commissioning the report. Section 7 provides an exception whereby there is no right of access when disclosure will be likely to cause serious harm to the physical or mental health of the individual or others, or would be likely to reveal information about another person or to reveal the identity of another person who has supplied information to the practitioner unless such a person consents or that person is a health professional involved in the care of the individual.

(iv) Pre-action discovery: Supreme Court Act 1981, s 33

Until the Access to Medical Records Act 1990 the procedure through which a plaintiff got access to his medical records was through pre-action discovery. The power of the court to make an order for pre-action discovery is contained within the provisions of the Supreme Court Act 1981, s 33 and RSC Ord 24, r 7A. (See also similar provisions in the County Courts Act 1984, ss 52–54 CCR Ord 13, r 7.) These provisions were, in the words of the Master of the Rolls, Sir John Donaldson, 'designed to facilitate settlements and to avoid fruitless actions' (*Lee v South West Thames Regional Health Authority* [1985] 1 WLR at 847c). The right exists for a person who is 'likely' to be a party in an action in which a claim for personal injuries is 'likely' to be made to obtain an order, before the action is commenced, against a person who is 'likely' to be another party and who is 'likely' to have documents in his possession, to peruse the documents if they are related to the issues arising out of the claim. In *Dunning v United Liverpool Hospitals' Board of Governors* (1973) (p 315), the likelihood of a plaintiff suing was construed as being in terms of a reasonable prospect; a mere speculative prospect would not be sufficient. In *Paterson v Chadwick* (1974) (p 491) a claim in respect of personal injuries was deemed in this context to include a claim against the plaintiff's solicitors for failing to sue in respect of an anaesthetic accident, and pre-action discovery was allowed against the hospital where the accident occurred. Similar powers are contained in the Supreme Court Act 1981, s 33 and RSC Ord 29, r 7A in any case (ie, not restricted to personal injury cases) for property to be inspected, photographed, preserved, or placed in the court's custody, and to have samples taken from, or experiments conducted on those pieces of property which may be the subject matter of proceedings. However, by s 35(4) of the Supreme Court Act 1981, these provisions only bind the Crown in actions for personal injuries or death. (See also County Courts Act 1984, ss 53–4.)

These provisions are most important in medical malpractice actions, because they allow a plaintiff to have access to medical and nursing notes and to all the relevant material such as x-rays, test results, reports, letters and so on that have been compiled during the course of treatment and are contained in the relevant records. They would also, in certain cases, afford an opportunity to inspect or test a particular machine. Such information may be vital to a potential litigant as it

207

forms the basis of the instructions to his legal and medical experts. In many cases, assessing the prospects of success is difficult or impossible without sight of such records. The recent tendency has been for hospital authorities, in particular, to release such information without the issuing of a summons, provided that the intended claim contains a proper level of detail (see the Department of Health and Social Security Circular HC (82) 16, for the official attitude regarding the disclosure of such information). Sometimes, however, it will not be possible to give any more than a brief outline of the circumstances of the mishap. Although the courts' approach is to avoid what they deemed to be fishing exercises, it has been recognised that at this early stage a plaintiff may not be able to condescend to details until after the information in question has been received, and that, of course, the prime object of this power is to assess a case before litigation (*Shaw v Vauxhall Motors Ltd* (1974)).

Section 33(2) of the Supreme Court Act 1981 and also s 52(2) of the County Courts Act 1984 enable the documents to be received by the applicant's legal advisers and any medical or other professional adviser, and may restrict disclosure to the prospective plaintiff on the basis that such disclosure might cause detriment to the patient's health and well-being. This wording reverses the decision in *McIvor v Southern Health and Social Services Board* (1978) and restores the decision in *Dunning v United Liverpool Hospitals' Board of Governors* (1973) (p 315). (Both these cases were concerned with earlier similar provisions contained in the Administration of Justice Act 1970, s 32(1).) There is, therefore, no power to restrict disclosure to a medical expert, and the previous attitude of health authorities seeking to impose such a condition in cases of voluntary disclosure has no foundation in law.

In *M v Plymouth Health Authority* (p 440), a plaintiff sought pre-action discovery in January 1990, and the defendant health authority supplied copies of the hospital records and subsequently made the original records available for inspection. The plaintiff's advisors, however, contended that they were entitled to a list of documents analogous to the normal rule of post-action discovery where a list of documents itemising every relevant document in the defendant's possession, custody or control is required. Brooke J held that the plaintiff's solicitors were not entitled to such a list and, given that the defendants had provided documents, neither were they entitled to require them to verify their pre-action discovery by affidavit (RSC Ord 24, r 7A). Brooke J, however, went on to give guidelines as to good practice indicating that defendant health authorities should supply all relevant documents, preferably with some kind of index system identifying where the relevant categories of documents are.

In *Stobart v Nottingham Health Authority* (p 567) applications were made in respect of three children who had died in different hospitals for pre-action discovery prior to the inquest. Rougier J ordered discovery on the basis that the proper conduct of the action included investigations at an early stage and, since the coroner was to determine the cause of death, that was a purpose within the reasons for granting pre-action discovery and was not a collateral purpose. Had the action involved deaths after 31 October 1991 the defendants would have had to have given access under the provisions of the Access to Health Records Act 1990.

In *Harris v Newcastle Health Authority* (1989) (p 370), the Court of Appeal determined that pre-trial disclosure of hospital records under the Supreme Court Act 1981, s 33(2) should normally be given when the conditions are satisfied, notwithstanding that there may be a strong defence of limitation. The case concerned a plaintiff who was born in October 1959 and was operated on in 1961 for a squint. The operation was unsuccessful, and four years later a further operation was performed but this did not wholly rectify the defect of the eyelid being closed and caused further pain. In February 1987 the plaintiff was encouraged to start an action, and she sought disclosure of the records. Both the district registrar and the judge refused the application on the grounds that the limitation defence was bound to succeed. The Court of Appeal, however, indicated that the application should in fact be granted because although there was a strong limitation defence the plaintiff's case was not clearly doomed to fail. Lord Justice Kerr said:

> 'If it is plain beyond doubt that a defence of limitation will be raised and will succeed then it seems to me that the court must be entitled to take that matter into account ... but I would accept in the normal run of cases even where a defence of limitation has a strong prospect of success, like here, it is very difficult for a court, on limited material, before pleadings and discovery, to conclude at that stage that the situation is such that the proposed action is bound to fail ... so in general I would accept the submission of counsel that issues relevant to limitation should not enter into consideration on applications for pre-trial discovery.'

In suitable cases, the professional adviser may include a so-called specialist scientific co-ordinator even if that person might be controversial. This was the situation in *Davies v Eli Lilly & Co* (1987) (p 300), where a journalist known to be critical of the drug industry was deemed a fit person to attempt to co-ordinate the massive documentation involved in a case where over a thousand plaintiffs were suing in respect of Benoxaprofen ('Opren'). This case concerned discovery after the issue of proceedings, but the principle is applicable to pre-commencement actions.

As a pre-commencement order against a potential defendant causes expense which may not be recoverable if an action is not initiated, RSC Ord 62, r 3(12) (CCR Ord 38, r 3) provides that defendants should normally have their costs unless the court thinks it inappropriate. In those cases where reasonable requests have been made by letter to health authorities who have refused or failed in a reasonable time to respond, the courts have denied the defendants their costs and on occasions given the plaintiff costs. Accordingly, in *Hall v Wandsworth Health Authority* (1985) (p 366), where there had been bad dilatory conduct, the applicant recovered her costs having written to the defendants and given them a six week period for the documents to be produced. Similarly, in *Jacob v Wessex Regional Health Authority* (1984)(p 399), the defendants had to pay the costs of an application where the plaintiff had pointed out that it would be a waste of public legal aid money if an application had to be made for the relevant documents. The application did become necessary – although the defendants conceded the notes, they wanted their costs, which in the event, the plaintiff was awarded.

If a prospective plaintiff wishes to have notes from someone who is not going to be a party, there is no power for a pre-commencement order to be made against a non-prospective third party. Once an action is started s 34 of the Supreme Court Act 1981, (County Courts Act 1984, s 53) empowers the court to order discovery of documents or inspection of property against a non-party in a personal injury action. In *Walker v Eli Lilly & Co* (1986) (p 595), Hirst J held that in circumstances where a plaintiff was suing a drug manufacturer, the plaintiff was entitled to his hospital notes and records kept by the health authority; and the judge indicated that health authorities and medical practitioners should readily respond to such requests from advisers of a plaintiff in cases where there is no particular consideration of confidentiality. (See also *O'Sullivan v Herdsmans* (1987).)

Rules of the Supreme Court Ord 24, r 7A(6) (CCR Ord 14, rr 4–5) preserve the right of a prospective defendant to claim privilege in respect of certain classes of documents held which the plaintiff may require. An example of such a document may be a report which was commissioned and compiled following a medical mishap. If the dominant purpose of this report was the anticipated legal action that would be brought by the victim, then such a document is privileged (*Waugh v British Railways Board* (1980)). The court will scrutinise such a claim for privilege and will not necessarily be content with what appears on the face of a document. Accordingly, in *Lask v Gloucester Health Authority* (1985) (p 427), a report which was made following an accident and in accord with the demands of a National Health circular with the purpose of preventing further accidents, but also to assist the defendants in anticipated litigation, was found not to be privileged. This was so despite affidavit evidence emphasising the significance of the documents in defending possible claims.

Privilege was, however, sustained in *Lee v South West Thames Regional Health Authority* (1985) (p 428). This case involved a child who sustained brain damage due to lack of oxygen following treatment he received after an accidental scalding injury at home. During the variety of treatments at different hospitals, the plaintiff was taken from a hospital within the jurisdiction of the Hillingdon Area Health Authority by an ambulance crew, for which the defendants were responsible. There was a possibility that something happened during the course of the ambulance journey, and the ambulance crew submitted a report to the Hillingdon Area Health Authority. The defendants disclosed the existence of the report but claimed privilege. Technically this privilege was not their own but that of Hillingdon Area Health Authority. The court, however, with 'undisguised reluctance' held that the two possible causes of action against the ambulance crew and against the hospital were not independent of each other and that Hillingdon Area Health Authority had not waived its own right of privilege, and the defendants could rightfully refuse to disclose the document. The Master of the Rolls, Sir John Donaldson, indicated in no uncertain terms that he thought there was something wrong if the plaintiff's mother could not get the document and begin to understand what had gone wrong and what had exactly caused the brain damage to her son. In this case, the Master of the Rolls thought that there might be an alternative route to obtaining the document. He indicated that *Sidaway v Board of Governors of Bethlem Royal Hospital and the Maudsley Hospital* (1985) (p 554) was authority for the proposition that medical practitioners owed patients a duty of care to inform them what treatment was going to be given them when they specifically asked. The Master of the Rolls, obiter, indicated that such a duty may exist when a patient asks what treatment he did in fact receive. It might, therefore, be possible to seek specific performance of a breach of an implied contractual term to inform. In *Naylor v Preston Area Health Authority* (1987) (p 478) the Master of the Rolls 'entirely repudiated' a view that such a cause of action would only arise in contractual cases but thought also it was a legal or equitable right arising in tort and therefore available to National Health Service patients.

In *Re HIV Haemophiliac Litigation* (p 394), the defendants refused to disclose categories of documents claiming that they were protected by public interest immunity. Such a claim can arise when the interests of confidentiality are determined by the court to outweigh the interest of justice in disclosure. (See

Campbell v Tameside Metropolitan Borough Council [1982] 2 All ER 791.) The Court of Appeal in the Haemophiliac case determined that the public interest in determining a fair trial of the allegations concerning failures by the Department of Health, the licensing authority under the Medicines Act 1968 and the Blood Products Laboratory outweighed the public interest in keeping the documents confidential. Conversely in *AB v the Scottish National Blood Transfusion Service,* (1990) the court declined to permit discovery of the name of a blood donor who had given blood infected with HIV virus as a result of which the plaintiff contracted the virus. The plaintiff wished to know the name of the donor so that he could sue him or her. (For a different approach taken by the Victoria Supreme Court in Australia, see *Australian Red Cross Society v BC* (p 232).)

A failure to give proper discovery by a defendant health authority may in certain circumstances result in a re-trial, as occurred in the case of *Cunningham v North Manchester Health Authority* (p 297). In *Cunningham,* the hospital authority told the plaintiff's advisers that the original x-rays had been destroyed and they had been replaced by miniaturised copies. In fact, at the trial it emerged that the defendant's experts had had access to the full size x-rays and arteriograms and obtained an evidential advantage by criticising the plaintiff's experts whose opinions were based on miniature copies. After the dismissal of the plaintiff's claim, the Court of Appeal allowed a re-trial following a fresh report from a consultant radiologist based on the evidence that emerged at the trial. The Court of Appeal commented that the authority had failed to a lamentable degree to comply with its duty to give proper discovery.

SUMMARY

Applications under the Supreme Court Act 1981, s 33 are likely to continue given that they have no exception in respect of non disclosure where serious harm to a patient is likely to arise or the confidentiality of an informant will be exposed. They are also necessary in cases seeking medical records dating before 31 October 1991. Conversely, the Access to Health Records Act 1990 will become increasingly important not least because it permits access to records held by persons not likely to become parties.

The disclosure of evidence: expert and lay witnesses

Given the central importance in medical malpractice actions of the medical expert's views whether a particular act or omission constituted a breach of duty, it is of crucial importance, particularly for plaintiffs, to know in advance of the trial what the defendant's experts are contending. Until the important case of *Naylor v Preston Area Health Authority* (1987) and the modification of RSC Ord 38, r 37 which took effect from October 1987, medical expert evidence on the question of liability was not normally disclosed between the parties. The Court of Appeal in *Naylor* unanimously determined that it was in the interests of refining the issues in dispute, saving costs and increasing the prospects of settlement to order simultaneous disclosure before trial of experts' reports (and the academic literature on which they relied) on the question of liability.

Many of the Court of Appeal's views in *Naylor* arose out of the difficulties that were experienced in *Wilsher v Essex Area Health Authority* (1987) (p 609). In *Wilsher,* the then normal course of events took place, and there was no exchange of experts' reports on liability before a trial. The Master of the Rolls in *Naylor* described the outcome of *Wilsher* as a 'total disaster'. Lord Justice Mustill eloquently expressed discontent:

> 'In the result the parties realised soon after the case began that they had misunderstood what the case was about. As was stated before us, it was fought 'in the dark'. It lasted four weeks instead of the allotted five days, which not only imposed great pressure of time on all concerned, but meant that the scheduling of the expert witnesses was put quite out of joint. The judge had nothing to read beforehand except some pleadings which told him nothing. The evidence of the plaintiff and the defendants' witnesses came forward in no sort of order, sometimes by instalments. Nearly 150 pages of medical literature was put in, without prior exchange, or any opportunity for proper scrutiny. All this could have been avoided if there had been adequate clarification of the issue before the trial ... I believe that practitioners do their clients and the interest of justice no service by continuing to pursue the policy of concealment ... to me it seems wrong that in this area of law, more than in any other, this kind of forensic blind man's bluff should continue to be the norm' ([1987] 2 WLR at 461).

The current RSC Ord 38, r 37 makes the disclosure of expert evidence reports the norm, in that unless the court considers there are special reasons for not doing so it will direct mutual disclosure which will normally be simultaneous. Some guidance was given by the Court of Appeal in *Naylor* as to what would constitute special reasons for not making the normal order for mutual disclosure. Sir Frederick Lawton expressed the following opinion:

> 'I have no hesitation at all in saying that in most actions for medical negligence there should be a direction for the substance of expert medical reports to be exchanged. In some cases, however, there may be good reasons why they should not be exchanged. The particulars of negligence may be so vague that it would be unfair to the defendants to expect their experts to deal with them until such time as the plaintiff had disclosed, either by further particulars or by his own experts' reports, exactly what his case was. In such a case a sequential direction for disclosure would be appropriate ... (in some cases) disclosure might enable the plaintiff, or his medical experts, to trim their evidence: but this is only likely to happen if there is a substantial dispute about primary facts or there is reason to think that the plaintiff's medical experts have mistakenly based their opinions on clinical findings which the defendants can prove, or think they can prove, were wrong. Another type of case is that in which the defendants are in possession of evidence, referred to in the expert medical reports, which goes to prove that the plaintiff is alleging that he is suffering from a non-existent disability or is exaggerating his symptoms or that his disability is due to an earlier trauma which he has not disclosed. The value of such evidence would be lost if the plaintiff became aware of it before trial. Since actions for medical negligence tend to raise difficult issues and vary greatly in complexity, I doubt whether directions for disclosure should ever be made automatically' ([1987] 1 WLR at 975h–976d).

Since these observations, a radical alteration in the Rules of the Supreme Court has occurred, allowing the court to order exchange of non-expert witnesses in all types of action in all the divisions of the High Court. Ord 38, r 2A(2) (CCR Ord 20, r 12A) allows the court at any stage, if it thinks fit for the purpose of disposing fairly and expeditiously of the case and to save costs, to direct that any party must serve on any other party, on such terms as the court thinks just, written statements of the oral evidence which the party intends to lead on any issues of fact to be decided at the trial. This significant incursion into the arena of open justice results in the precise nature of each side's case being known in medical malpractice actions before the trial begins. The rule is specifically designed to create a fair and expeditious hearing to eliminate the element of surprise and to procure proper settlements.

Order, 25 r 8(1)(*b*)(ii) provides that in personal injury actions written statements of witnesses should be served 14 weeks after the close of pleadings. These automatic directions do not apply to medical negligence cases (Ord 25, r 8(5)), but an order for exchange of witness statements is now routinely made on the summons for directions in a medical negligence case. Further, the Practice Direction from the Lord Chief Justice ([1995] 1 WLR 262) will result in the practice, already widespread, of trial judges ordering that the witness statement stands as evidence in chief pursuant to the provisions of Ord 38, r 2A(7)7(*a*). Accordingly, it will now be very rare indeed for a case to proceed to trial without an order for the simultaneous exchange of witness statements.

These provisions have probably reduced interlocutory hearings and, for example, have made it less necessary to apply for extensive interrogatories. No privilege can be claimed in respect of such a statement so as to prevent its disclosure. (Cf *Booth v Warrington Health Authority* (1992).) If, however, a party who has served a statement is not called as a witness to whom it relates, then no other party may put the statement of that witness in his evidence (Ord 38, r 2A(6)). The statement itself does not become evidence, until the maker is called and proves the document. There is, however, authority for the proposition that if in cross-examining a witness counsel puts to the witness an opposing witness statement, he thereby will allow his opponent to re-examine that witness on the whole of the witness statement (*Fairfield-Mabey Ltd v Shell UK Ltd* [1989] 1 All ER 576, *Youell v Bland Welch & Co* [1991] 1 WLR 122).

In *Easson v Gloucester Health Authority* (p 323) Morland J held that medical negligence cases do come within the requirements of Ord 18, r 12(1)(A) which require that a medical report is served with the plaintiff's statement of claim. The court held that it would only be in exceptional circumstances that it would be right to make an order dispensing with this requirement. The plaintiff had argued in *Easson* that to serve a medical report would have given the defendants an unfair advantage because frequently in medical negligence cases liability, causation and injury were inextricably connected. As a matter of practice, no advantage is necessarily obtained if the medical report restricts itself to condition and prognosis rather than addressing questions of negligence and causation. There is no need to serve a report on liability at this stage.

PART II

Medical negligence cases

*(an index of case subjects
follows at page 617)*

Re A

Consent: brain death: disconnection from ventilator

Johnson J. [1992] 3 Med LR 303

A was born on 24 April 1990. He was taken on 17 January 1992 from his home to a local hospital where no heartbeat could be detected. From there he was transferred to Guy's Hospital where signs of intentional injury to his head were found. He was placed on a ventilator. On the same day, an application was made to a Family Proceedings Court for an emergency protection order under the Children Act 1989, giving parental responsibility of A and his siblings to the local authority.

On 21 January a consultant paediatric neurologist at Guy's Hospital carried out tests on A. His pupils were fixed and dilated. On movement of the head, his eyes moved with his head. On his eye being touched with a piece of cotton wool, there was no response. On cold water being passed into his ear, there was no eye movement in response. On steps being taken, in effect, to cause him to 'gag', there was no reflex reaction. Nor was there reaction to pain being applied to his central nervous system. Finally, on his temporary removal from the ventilator to enable the carbon dioxide content of his body to increase, there was no respiratory response. The consultant was satisfied that A was brain stem dead.

On 22 January the parents applied to the Family Proceedings Court for a prohibited steps order. The order forbade, inter alia, the local authority to give consent to the switching off of the life support machine without the parents' consent which was not forthcoming. The nursing staff continued to feed A intravenously, but found it increasingly distressing to be caring for a child that they knew and believed to be dead.

Held: (i) A had been dead since 21 January.

(ii) it would be wholly contrary to his interests, such as they might now be, for his body to be subjected to continuing indignity.

(iii) as he was dead, it was not possible to exercise the inherent jurisdiction of the court over him as a child; nor was it possible to make him a ward of court.

(iv) however the court would make a declaration that A was dead for all medical and legal purposes and also make a declaration that, should the consultant or other medical consultant at Guy's Hospital consider it appropriate to disconnect A from the ventilator, in doing so they would not be acting contrary to law.

See p 12.

A v Bristol and West Hospital Authority

Brain damage: childbirth: res ipsa loquitur

Court of Appeal. CAT, 2 February 1994

The-27-year old mother of the plaintiff (A) had two previous children, both by vaginal deliveries which were uneventful save that there had been mild dystocia with the second. She was admitted to hospital for diabetes between 17 and 22 February 1989 when it was recognised that she was obese and that the foetus was macrosmic, the trunk being larger than the head. On 20 February an ultrasound scan showed its weight to be about 4 kilograms. Although the possible risk of shoulder dystocia was recognised, Dr Clarke (registrar) and Mr James (consultant) contemplated that the birth would be by vaginal delivery.

In the morning of 28 February Mrs A was admitted to hospital. At 5pm the labour was going well, and it was decided to proceed by vaginal delivery. At 5.55pm the baby's head was delivered, with midwives in attendance; Dr Clarke and the charge midwife were next door in the duty room. When at the next contraction around 5.57pm the midwives realised that the baby was not coming, they sent the message to Dr Clarke who entered the delivery room at 5.58pm.

He directed that Mrs A be put on lithotomy and asked for the anaesthetic registrar to be called. He tried to manipulate the baby between contractions, but was unable to do so. Mrs A was anaesthetised by 6.03pm. Dr Clarke did a further manipulation which was successful, and the baby was born at 6.04pm. Her heart was not beating and did not restart beating for a further 20 minutes. During that period of hypoxia, she sustained very severe brain damage and was left a tetraplegic.

The trial judge rejected the plaintiff's primary case that the option for a vaginal delivery rather than caesarian section was negligent. He held that, although there was a known risk of dystocia, it was comparatively small and, although greater in the case of diabetics, the expectation was that it could be handled. The plaintiff did not appeal against that finding.

Held: (i)   as to the submission that Dr Clarke did not get into the delivery room quickly enough and that he should have been there throughout, expert evidence amply supported the defendant's case that this was a clinical decision taken on the basis that they did not wish to have more people in the delivery room, because it was liable to distress the mother, and that it would make no significant difference whether Dr Clarke was in the room or immediately outside it two yards away.

     (ii)   the judge's conclusion that it was not negligent not to have administered the anaesthetic earlier could not be faulted.

   (iii)   in essence, the plaintiff's case was that, because the defendants decided to go for a vaginal delivery instead of a caesarian section, they ought to have had in position a plan to ensure that the baby was born in time to prevent hypoxia from the known risk of shoulder dystocia; because they failed, there must have been something wrong in the plan or its execution. That was in effect an attempt to pray in aid the maxim res ipsa loquitur, which had no application to this case.

   (iv)   there was a responsible body of medical evidence that supported what Dr Clarke had done. The defendants had not been negligent.

See pp 90, 126.

A B and Others v John Wyeth & Brother Ltd and Others

Drugs: group litigation: product liability

Court of Appeal. [1992] 1 WLR 168, [1992] 3 Med LR 190, [1992] PIQR P437

The plaintiffs (AB and others) brought a group action against the defendants, manufacturers of certain tranquillisers, alleging failure by the defendants to warn doctors that their drugs should only be used in limited circumstances due to the risk of patients becoming addicted to them. They claimed damages for the symptoms of tranquilliser dependency and for the suffering of withdrawing from the drugs.

In around 900 cases medical reports had been disclosed. Nearly all referred to the fact that a written statement had been received by the doctor from the plaintiffs' solicitors. The defendants contended that, when a medical report is served with the statement of claim in accordance with RSC Ord 18, r 12(1A), that report is a pleading and, in consequence, the reference in a report to written documents justified the defendants seeking disclosure of that document under RSC Ord 24, r 10. The plaintiffs disputed that the medical report should be regarded as a pleading, and relied on professional privilege for the statement.

Held: *(per Woolf LJ):*

'On a request made by the defendants on legal and medical advice each plaintiff should, in so far as this has not already been done, provide the details of the full relevant medical history of the plaintiff relied upon by the plaintiff's doctor for the purpose of preparing the report served with the statement of claim, in so far as that history is derived from a written document supplied to that doctor which has not already been disclosed. In addition, the identity and the author of that written document and its date should be disclosed. The identification of the document should not be treated as a waiver of any privilege that the plaintiff has in respect of that document.'

See pp 32, 122.

A B and Others v John Wyeth & Brother Ltd and Others (No 2)

Drugs: group litigation: product liability

Court of Appeal. [1993] 4 Med LR 1

About 17,000 claims arose out of the manufacture of benzodiazepine drugs: in particular, Valium, Ativan and Halcion. Mr Justice Ian Kennedy was appointed to monitor the resultant group litigation. He ordered that for claimants to be eligible to participate in it they must (a) have applied for legal aid by 24 September 1991 and (b) have served a writ and statement of claim (or in county court summons and particulars of claim) before 31 August 1992.

After 24 September 1991 over 500 further applications for legal aid in respect of Halcion had been received as a result of a series of events, including the settlement of a Halcion claim in the USA and the suspension of Halcion from use within the UK. On 6 May 1992 Mr Justice Ian Kennedy refused to extend the cut-off dates in favour of the Halcion claimants.

About forty claimants who had actions running in respect of Halcion appealed. Their concern was that a group of forty was unlikely to be large enough to select suitable lead cases. In addition they spoke for the 563 claimants who had not applied for legal aid before the cut-off date of 24 September 1991.

Held: the judge simply decided that these Halcion claimants who had not applied for legal aid by 24 September 1991 should not be entitled to join the existing group litigation; he did not preclude them from presenting their claims outside it. He did not act ultra vires; nor was there any basis upon which the court could or should interfere with the exercise of his discretion.

Per Balcombe LJ: 'Indeed I would go so far as to say that the judge was plainly right ... I am wholly unpersuaded, as was the judge, that the late addition of the Halcion claimants would do other than cause substantial further delay in the existing group action.'

Per Steyn LJ: 'I would add that in my view the Court of Appeal ought to be particularly reluctant in group actions to interfere with a trial judge's procedural directions. The judge invariably has a much better perspective of the interests of all the parties and of the needs of efficient case management than the Court of Appeal can ever achieve.'

See p 32.

AB v Scottish National Blood Transfusion Service

HIV: discovery: Scotland

Court of Session, Outer House. 1990 SCLR 263

The petitioner (known as AB) averred that he became infected with HIV virus as a result of blood transfusions administered to him in 1986 by the respondents, the Glasgow and West of Scotland Blood Transfusion Service. He applied under s 1 of the Administration of Justice (Scotland) Act 1972 for an order for disclosure to him and his legal advisers of the name and address of the person who donated the blood which was transfused. His sole purpose was to enable him to sue the donor, on the ground that he negligently failed to disclose his high HIV risk. He was also suing the respondents on the ground that their screening procedures were inadequate.

The Secretary of State for Scotland opposed the disclosure, on the ground that it would be injurious to the public interest. He concluded that any infringement of donor anonymity would put at risk a sufficient supply of blood to the health service nationally. His concern was that prospective donors would be discouraged from providing donations by fear of being sued.

Held: the validity of the Secretary of State's conclusion could not be investigated by the court, unless it appeared that the conclusion was patently unreasonable or had been expressed on an erroneous basis. Since that could not be said in the present case, the application must be refused.

Per Lord Morison: 'However, I entirely agree that it is offensive to any notion of justice that persons should be deprived of the ability to claim damages from those by whose negligence they have been injured. If public policy requires this, it seems to me that it would be reasonable for public policy to provide also some alternative means of compensation.'

See p 211.

Aboul-Hosn v Trustees of the Italian Hospital and Others

Damages: after-care: brain damage

Hirst J. (1987) 3 PMILL 54

On 30 September 1982, on the eve of his nineteenth birthday, the plaintiff (Samer Aboul-Hosn) underwent an operation at the National Hospital for Nervous Diseases for the removal of a colloid cyst from his brain. He had been transferred for the operation from the Italian Hospital to which he returned the next day. During the ensuing fortnight it was observed by computerised scanner that his ventricles were still abnormally enlarged due to a recurrence of hydrocephalus, ie raised intracranial fluid pressure. Between 15 and 17 October he suffered a progressive deterioration of this condition. It was correctly diagnosed but incorrectly treated.

The plaintiff sued the Italian Hospital and three doctors responsible for his treatment. He agreed not to pursue his claim against the Italian Hospital. The three doctors admitted liability.

Before the operation and its aftermath, the plaintiff was a bright and personable young man with four 'A' levels, a place at university and the prospect of a successful career. He suffered catastrophic and irreversible brain damage. His mental age had shrunk to that of a two year old. He could not speak, his eyesight was drastically impaired, and he walked in a zombie like fashion. He would never be able to work or marry. There was evidence that deep within him he had some insight into his appalling predicament.

Held: the plaintiff was awarded damages for:

Pain, suffering and loss of amenities	£ 85,000
Parents' past care and expenditure	£ 100,700
Future care in all its aspects	£ 400,800
Housing needs	£ 48,100
Future loss of earnings (including car)	£ 331,000
Court of Protection fees	£ 34,500
Agreed interest	£ 31,550
Total (rounded)	£1,032,000

See pp 154, 159, 160, 161.

Abrahams v Snowman

Operation: circumcision: penis

Ridley J (with special jury). [1910] 2 BMJ 1565

The plaintiff (Mr Abrahams) was the father of a young Jewish boy. Dr Snowman was a member of the Initiation Society, established for the purpose of carrying out the rite of circumcision among Jewish people. Mr Snadon performed the operation of circumcision on the plaintiff's son under Dr Snowman's supervision. The child was then taken to his mother. Later in the day the Society's nurse found that there was a great deal of haemorrhage. Dr Snowman was called for, but was not at home, so another doctor was called in to stop the bleeding.

The child gradually wasted and suffered from marasmus. The plaintiff sued Dr Snowman, alleging negligent performance of the operation. Evidence was given that the operation had been properly performed and that the marasmus was due to malnutrition.

Held: Ridley J described the case as grossly exaggerated, to say the least. He directed the members of the jury that if in their opinion the child's condition was brought about by reason of the negligent manner in which Dr Snowman performed or assisted at the operation, then their verdict should be for the plaintiff.

The jury returned a verdict for the defendant.

Ackers v Wigan Area Health Authority

Childbirth: caesarian: anaesthetic awareness: damages: post-traumatic stress disorder: depression

Russell J. [1986] CLY 1048, [1991] 2 Med LR 232

The plaintiff (Mrs Ackers) was aged 26 when her first child was delivered. A caesarian section operation was needed. Owing to the hospital's negligence, she was not anaesthetised but was paralysed by pre-operation muscle relaxant drugs. The surgeon and theatre staff were unaware of her plight. During the one and a quarter hour operation she was fully conscious, felt every sensation and was terrified and distressed by artificial ventilation of her lungs.

She developed a severe reactive depression. For the first three months after birth she had negative feelings towards her child. When she became pregnant again a further caesarian was necessary; for ten weeks she suffered terror and misery in fear of what lay ahead.

Thereafter she suffered continuing depression, mood changes, irritability, phobia of general anaesthetics and hospitals, and severe insomnia. She was also afraid of further pregnancy, which seriously impaired her sexual relationship with her husband. She was unable to face the required surgery for painful and embarrassing varicose veins and bladder cyst.

A course of abreactive therapy was planned. This would have involved her reliving her experiences and would have been very unpleasant. The prognosis was guardedly optimistic.

Held (June 1985):   the plaintiff was awarded £12,000 general damages for pain, suffering and loss of amenities. Other elements of her damages were £1,700 for the cost of future psychiatric treatment and agreed special damages of £75. Her total award was £13,775 plus interest.

See pp 122, 123, 155.

Airedale National Health Service Trust v Bland

PVS: consent: interests of patient: discontinuance of life-supporting treatment

House of Lords. [1993] AC 789, [1993] 1 All ER 821, [1993] 2 WLR 316, [1993] 4 Med LR 39, [1993] NLJR 199

In April 1989 Anthony Bland, then aged 17, went to Hillsborough football ground to support Liverpool. In the course of the disaster there, his lungs were crushed and punctured and the supply of oxygen to his brain was interrupted. As a result, he suffered catastrophic and irreversible damage to the higher centres of the brain. His condition was known as persistent vegetative state (PVS). All medical experts agreed that there was no prospect of recovery.

The plaintiff Airedale NHS Trust, the responsible health authority, sought declarations 'that, despite the inability of the defendant to consent thereto, the plaintiff and the responsible attending physicians—

(a)   may lawfully discontinue all life-sustaining treatment and medical supportive resources designed to keep the defendant alive in his existing persistent vegetative state including the termination of ventilation nutrition and hydration by artificial means; and

(b)   may lawfully discontinue and thereafter need not furnish medical treatment to the defendant except for the sole purpose of enabling him to end his life and die peacefully with the greatest dignity and the least of pain suffering and distress.'

The President of the Family Division of the High Court made these declarations, subject to a minor change of wording. The Official Solicitor appealed.

Held: (i)   there is no absolute obligation upon the doctor who has the patient in his care to prolong his life, regardless of the circumstances.

(ii)   the doctor's conduct in discontinuing life support can be categorised as an omission; he is simply allowing his patient to die.

(iii)   the question whether the patient should be kept on the life-support system indefinitely can only be answered by reference to the best interests of the patient, having regard to established medical practice.

(iv)   in a case such as the present, it is the futility of the treatment that justifies its termination. In these circumstances, a doctor is not required to continue life-prolonging treatment or care in the patient's best interests.

    (v) the doctor must act in accordance with a responsible and competent body of professional opinion. He will be doing so if he acts in accordance with the medical practice evolved by the Medical Ethics Committee of the BMA.

    (vi) for the time being, in cases of this kind, application should be made to the court to obtain its sanction for the course proposed. The matter will be kept under review by the President of the Family Division.

Per Lord Keith: 'Given that existence in the persistent vegetative state is not a benefit to the patient, it remains to consider whether the principle of the sanctity of life, which is the concern of the State, and the judiciary as one of the arms of the State, to maintain, requires this House to hold that the judgment of the Court of Appeal was incorrect. In my opinion it does not. The principle is not an absolute one. It does not compel a medical practitioner on pain of criminal sanctions to treat a patient, who will die if he does not, contrary to the express wishes of the patient. It does not authorise forcible feeding of prisoners on hunger strike. It does not compel the temporary keeping alive of patients who are terminally ill where to do so would merely prolong their suffering. On the other hand it forbids the taking of active measures to cut short the life of a terminally ill patient. In my judgment it does no violence to the principle to hold that it is lawful to cease to give medical treatment and care to a PVS patient who has been in that state for over three years, considering that to do so involves invasive manipulation of the patient's body to which he has not consented and which confers no benefit upon him.'

See pp 16, 57.

Akerele v R

Manslaughter: injections: drugs

Privy Council. [1943] AC 255, [1943] 1 All ER 367

Dr Akerele was a qualified medical practitioner in Nigeria. On 6 and 7 May 1941 he treated 57 children in Asaga. With a few exceptions, they were suffering from yaws. He injected nearly all of them with sobita which consisted of sodium bismuth tartrate. Ten of the children died.

Dr Akerele was charged with the manslaughter of one of them, Kalu Ibe. The trial judge found that he negligently prepared too strong a mixture of sobita. The boy had died from stomatis induced by bismuth poisoning. Dr Akerele was convicted and sentenced to imprisonment with hard labour.

Held: the single act of mixing too strong a solution in making up the preparation of sobita did not amount to criminal negligence. The negligence to be imputed depends on the probable, not the actual, result. The fatal consequences to the ten children did not convert carelessness into criminal negligence.

See p 58.

Ali v St Mary's Private Hospital and Another

Cardiac arrest: after-care: interrogatories

Court of Appeal. 21 October 1981

Mohammed Abdel Rahman Ali, an asthmatic, came to the UK from Khartoum to have a complicated tonsillectomy. On 13 September 1975 this was successfully carried out at

St Mary's Private Hospital. However, a few hours after returning to his bed, Mr Ali suffered a cardiac arrest and died.

The plaintiff (his widow) sued St Mary's Hospital and the anaesthetist, Dr Lahiri. Interrogatories were administered to Dr Lahiri. Sheldon J gave her leave to administer seven interrogatories to the hospital for answer by their matron.

Held: interrogatories will not be allowed unless they are necessary for fairly disposing of the action, and will not generally be allowed where the information can or will be proved by a witness at the trial so that the interrogatories will not save costs. On an undertaking from the defendants to call the nurses who attended the deceased during the last few hours of his life, the first interrogatory was deleted and the others were varied.

Per Stephenson LJ: 'In a case of this kind brought by the widow of a man who has died in hospital, there may be a good many things which the plaintiff cannot possibly know but which must be within the knowledge of the defendant hospital, and that is the kind of case, rather like an unwitnessed fatal accident or an accident in which the plaintiff is knocked unconscious, in which interrogatories as to the facts are ordered to enable the plaintiff to prove her case.'

Allan v Mount Sinai Hospital et al

Anaesthetics: consent: battery: injections: damages: foreseeability: Canada

Ontario High Court of Justice (Linden J). (1980) 109 DLR (3d) 634

In November 1972, the plaintiff (Venita Allan) entered the Mount Sinai Hospital in Toronto for a dilatation and curettage operation. When she first met Dr Hellman, the anaesthetist, in the hall outside the operating room, she said to him: 'Please don't touch my left arm. You'll have nothing but trouble there'. Dr Hellman's response was: 'We know what we are doing'.

The plaintiff was then wheeled into the operating room where Dr Hellman injected sodium pentothal and the other required anaesthetic chemicals into her left arm. He had no trouble in finding a vein. However a short time later he noticed that the needle had slipped out. This caused part of the solution to leak into the tissue of the arm interstitially, instead of entering the vein.

The normal consequence of injecting some sodium pentothal into the tissue of the arm, as a result of a needle slipping out of the vein, is that the patient has a sore arm for a day or two. Instead the plaintiff suffered a very severe reaction. She sued Dr Hellman for damages in battery and negligence. Her action against the hospital and other defendants did not proceed.

Held: (i) Dr Hellman exercised reasonable skill throughout. Needles can slip out without fault. He had not been negligent.

    (ii) the administration of an anaesthetic is a surgical operation which constitutes a battery, unless the patient consents to it. The plaintiff did not consent: she expressly instructed Dr Hellman not to start the anaesthetic in her left arm. He had committed a battery.

    (iii) because his responsibility was founded in battery, Dr Hellman was liable for all of the consequences flowing therefrom, be they foreseeable or unforeseeable. Even if nothing at all had gone wrong, he would have been required to pay nominal damages.

See p 7.

Allen v Bloomsbury Health Authority

Wrongful birth: damages: sterilisation (failed): pregnancy

Brooke J. [1993] 1 All ER 651, [1992] 3 Med LR 257, [1992] PIQR Q50

In June 1985 the plaintiff (Linda Allen) underwent an operation at Elizabeth Garrett Anderson Hospital for dilatation and curettage and sterilisation. When she attended a follow up out-patients' clinic there on 12 August 1985, she told a doctor that she had not had a period since before the operation and that her stomach and breasts felt swollen. The defendant health authority admitted negligence in that it was not ascertained at or shortly after that appointment that the plaintiff was by then about 12 weeks pregnant.

The plaintiff was worried that the four week old foetus might have suffered harm in the operation. However on 10 February 1986 she give birth to a baby daughter Faye, who proved healthy although she suffered temper tantrums, a slight speech defect and slight dyslexia. The plaintiff sued the health authority.

Held (January 1992): (i) a plaintiff mother is entitled to recover general damages (and any associated financial special damage) for the discomfort and pain associated with the continuation of the pregnancy and the delivery of her child, although she must set off against this claim a sum in respect of avoiding the pain and suffering and associated financial loss which would have resulted from the termination of the pregnancy under general anaesthetic. In the present case, for the period up to the birth, with the associated fear that Faye might be handicapped, after an offset for not having an abortion and any loss of earnings associated with that, the appropriate award was £1,250.

(ii) although the law recognises that if an unwanted child is born due to a doctor's negligence, a mother may suffer wear and tear and tiredness in bringing up a healthy child, the claim for general damages she might otherwise have had on this account is generally set off against and extinguished by the joy at the birth and growth of such a child. Nor under this principle should additional damages be awarded against the defendants because Faye had temper tantrums or defective speech or slight dyslexia. However the defendants had agreed a total of £2,500 for general damages before and after the birth, so that sum would be awarded.

(iii) the plaintiff mother is entitled to damages for her own financial loss due to losing earnings or incurring expenses because of her obligation towards the child. In this case, the plaintiff was entitled to £46,716 loss of earnings, £536 cost of equipment, £2,818 in respect of the conversion of the garage into a fourth bedroom and £2,850 child-minding costs.

(iv) the plaintiff mother is also entitled to damages for the financial loss she suffers because when the unwanted baby is born she has a growing child to feed, clothe, raise, educate and care for until the child becomes an adult. The defendants are liable to pay for all such expenses as may be reasonably incurred, having regard to all the circumstances of the case and to the child's position in life:

      (a)   the plaintiff was only entitled to recover the actual expenses she had incurred 'in maintaining' Faye up to the date of trial. Since she had been dependent on income support, this cost was modest. The parties agreed a total gross sum of £7,525 for five years and ten months up to the date of trial, based on a rate of £900 in the first year rising annually to £1,750 in the sixth year. Child benefit of £2,646 was then deducted, leaving a net sum of £4,879;

      (b)   for the cost of Faye's future maintenance, it was reasonable on the evidence in this case to take National Foster Care Association figures for the cost of maintaining Faye until she is 18. The average figure between the ages of 6 and 18 was £3,867 pa, from which £473 pa child benefit should be deducted, producing a multiplier of £3,394 pa. Applying a multiplier of eight produced £27,152 under this head.

    (v)   the total award to the plaintiff was therefore £87,450 plus interest.

See pp 128, 168, 170.

Allen v Norwich Health Authority

Split trial : costs : childbirth

W Crowther QC. QBD transcript, 13 January 1994

The plaintiff was a young child who was damaged at birth. The defendant health authority consented to separate trials on liability and quantum. Subsequently it admitted liability before experts' reports were due to be exchanged.

The plaintiff entered judgment and obtained an order that the plaintiff's costs of the action in respect of liability up to the date of the admission be taxed forthwith if not agreed and paid forthwith by the defendants. The defendants appealed.

Held: (i)   where a discrete part of a piece of litigation is finished, prima facie 'it would appear to the court when making an order for costs that the costs ought to be taxed at an earlier stage' pursuant to RSC Ord 62, r 8(2). In the absence of good reason, the plaintiff should not be out of his money for a substantial period.

      (ii) there was no reason to interfere with the decision that the costs up to the date of the admission be taxed/agreed and paid forthwith. It was entirely correct.

Almond and Almond v Leeds Western Health Authority

Childbirth: damages: substandard treatment: brain damage

Fennell J. [1990] 1 Med LR 370

On 13 January 1980 the plaintiff (Nicholas Almond) was born in Leeds Maternity Hospital. He sustained severe brain damage and suffers from dyskinetic cerebral palsy. The hospital authority admitted liability.

He had poor control and poor co-ordination of movement, combined with the presence of unhelpful and unwanted movements. This abnormality affected all the muscles of his body, including those used in speech, manipulation, standing and locomotion. He had dysarthria, a very major speech impediment. He was unable to undertake independently any of the ordinary activities of daily living. He could not stand without support nor walk. As a result, he could not look after himself in any significant way and needed considerable help in washing, dressing and undressing, and with his bodily functions and feeding. However, he had good higher centre neurological functions and his comprehension of language, general knowledge and academic attainments were normal, as was his sight and hearing. His physical handicap was permanent and his life expectancy was agreed at 61 years.

Held (April 1990):   (i) the right level award for an average case of tetraplegia then was £97,500. The plaintiff's very severely impaired powers of speech and his life expectancy justified an above average award of £105,000 of general damages for pain, suffering and loss of amenities.

(ii) his parents had given at least the care that two resident carers would have provided. The commercial cost of this would have been £145,400. It was reasonable to take his counsel's figure of £72,700 (half of commercial cost). From that must be deducted £23,610 for attendance and mobility allowance and invalid care allowance. Thus damages for past parental care were £49,090.

(iii) total damages for future nursing care were £505,000, subject to deduction of the relevant allowance.

(iv) on the basis that the plaintiff would live at home until he was 22, £10,000 should be awarded for future parental care by Mrs Almond but nothing by Mr Almond who was leaving the home to remarry.

(v) £71,565 was awarded for a move to and conversion of special accommodation.

(vi) the plaintiff would have been educated to university/polytechnic level and would have worked between the ages of 22 and 61 in a non-manual job paying 1.5 of the national average wage. Loss of his future earnings was assessed at £190,000 on a multiplicand of £19,000 and a multiplier of 10.

(vii) severe Disability Allowance did not fall to be deducted.

(viii) additional items produced a total award of £1,156,348.

See pp 126, 154, 158, 162, 163.

Antcliffe v Gloucester Health Authority

Surgeon: striking out: crown indemnity: kidney

Court of Appeal. [1992] 1 WLR 1044, [1993] 4 Med LR 14, 136 Sol Jo LB 146, [1993] PIQR P47, (1992) Times, 6 May

On 30 September 1981 the plaintiff (Mary Antcliffe) underwent at Gloucester Hospital an operation for removal of an infected kidney by a surgeon from the USA. On 14 December 1983 an English surgeon operated on her at the same hospital for a psoas abscess resulting from the first operation. She continued to suffer pain and discomfort until remedial surgery was performed in February 1984 at John Radcliffe Hospital in Oxford.

227

In April 1984 she instructed solicitors who obtained the hospital records. In January 1985 legal aid was granted. On 19 February 1986 her writ was issued. In April 1986 the writ and statement of claim were served. In July 1986 the defence was served together with a request for further and better particulars of the statement of claim. The requested particulars were served in September 1987. In February 1991 the plaintiff's solicitors wrote to the defendants requesting that the plaintiffs medical notes be forwarded to an orthopaedic expert. In March 1991 the defendants issued a summons to dismiss the action for want of prosecution.

Schiemann J upheld the refusal of the district judge to grant this. At the hearing of the defendants' appeal, it was accepted that time under the Limitation Act 1980 began to run in February 1983, that the plaintiff's delay had been inordinate and inexcusable and that the case should have been heard by 1989. The American surgeon could not be traced, but the English surgeon was still available. Had the case been concluded by December 1989, any damages and costs awarded to the plaintiff would have been paid by a medical defence organisation, whereas under new arrangements which took effect from 1 January 1990 they would be payable by the defendant health authority.

Held: (i)   if a defendant, by reason of a plaintiff's inordinate and inexcusable delay, has been brought into a position in which he is prejudiced in some feature of his business affairs or insurance arrangements the prejudice shall be taken into account.

        (ii)   the judge misdirected himself in refusing to do so. It is undesirable and unnecessary to limit the circumstances that may constitute prejudice for the purpose of supporting a striking out application based upon want of due prosecution of an action.

       (iii)   if the action had been brought to a reasonably expeditious conclusion in 1988 or 1989, an award of damages and costs in favour of the plaintiff would have been met from the funds of the relevant defence union. That constituted clear prejudice to the defendant caused by the plaintiff's delay.

       (iv)   in addition, some small benefit might properly be given to the difficulties of recollection that might afflict the English surgeon, and perhaps minuscule weight might be given to the fact that this case might cause some continuing anxiety to him.

       (v)   as a general proposition, inordinate and inexcusable delay on the part of a plaintiff which produces real prejudice to a defendant should ordinarily lead to the striking out of the action.

      (vi)   there was nothing in the circumstances of the present case to divert that ordinary result. The defendants' appeal would be allowed.

See pp 193, 203

Anwar v Wandsworth Health Authority

Cardiac arrest: damages: anaesthetics: after-care

Auld J. 31 January 1990

An asthmatic woman, aged 43, underwent an eye operation. She received negligent administration of anaesthetic followed by negligent treatment in the recovery stage. Consequently she suffered a cardiac arrest whilst recovering from the anaesthetic. She was rendered unconscious and remained so until her death three weeks later.

Held: an award of £900 general damages was made, not for pain and suffering but for the deprivation of the ordinary experience and amenities of life. Although the period of loss was short, the deprivation was great.

Appleby v Sleep

Pharmacist: prescription: contract

Court of Appeal. [1968] 2 All ER 265, [1968] 1 WLR 948

In April 1967 Mrs Magee took a National Health Service prescription to the Ferry Pharmacy in Hythe. This was owned by the defendant, Mr Ernest Sleep. She was handed a bottle of penidural syrup as prescribed for her child. A few days later she saw a lump in the medicine as it came out of the bottle and found this to be a piece of glass.

Mr Sleep was a registered pharmaceutical chemist who was engaged under a contract with the National Health Service Executive Council for Hampshire. They subsequently paid him for supplying the medicine. He was prosecuted under s 2 of the Food and Drugs Act 1955.

Held: Mr Sleep was not liable. There was no sale by him to the patient. His contract with the National Health Service Executive Council was a contract for services, not a contract of sale.

Per Lord Parker CJ: 'The first thing that is clear is that there will have been no sale by the chemist to the patient, the person presenting the prescription. Not only has that been so held, but it is clearly the case, because the patient is not paying for the medicine or drugs, and that is so even if there is a prescription charge.'

See p 26.

Ashcroft v Mersey Regional Health Authority

Aural: surgeon: operation

Kilner Brown J. [1983] 2 All ER 245

In January 1978 the plaintiff (Mrs Ashcroft) submitted herself to an operation on her left ear. It was performed by Mr Joseph Siegler, a surgeon of long experience and high reputation. The operation was for the removal of granulated tissue adhering to part of the ear drum, and is regarded as routine and perfectly safe. In this case, there was no bony covering to the facial nerve, the ear drum was close to the nerve and the granulations extended to the nerve. Mr Siegler got the forceps to bite on the facial nerve because he was searching for granulations which extended that far. The nerve was damaged and the plaintiff was left with a partial paralysis of the left side of the face.

The plaintiff's expert testified that the accident could only have happened due to negligence by Mr Siegler, and maintained that damage to the nerve was done by excessive force in the use of forceps. This was denied by Mr Siegler who was satisfied that he was using the forceps as he always did. He was supported by an eminent ear surgeon who also considered that he had not been negligent.

Held: it had not been proved that Mr Siegler fell below the standard of care expected of him. The plaintiff's case failed.

Per Kilner Brown J: 'The question for consideration is whether on a balance of probabilities it has been established that a professional man has failed to exercise the care required of a man possessing and professing special skill in circumstances which require the exercise of that special skill. If there is an added burden, such burden does not rest on the person alleging negligence; on the contrary, it could be said that the more skilled a person is, the more the care that is expected of him. It is preferable in my judgement to concentrate on and to apply the test which has long been established in the law and to avoid all commentary or gloss'.

See pp 44, 60, 118.

Ashton v Alexander and Trent Regional Health Authority

Error of judgment: dental: operation: fracture: jaw

Court of Appeal. 29 January 1988

In 1982 the plaintiff (Geoffrey Ashton) underwent an operation under general anaesthetic for removal of an unerupted molar tooth in his left lower jaw. This was carried out at Lincoln County Hospital by Mr Alexander who employed a hammer and chisel. The tooth was successfully elevated, but the plaintiff sustained a displaced fracture of the lower left jaw.

The plaintiff sued Mr Alexander and the hospital authority in the Lincoln County Court. Mr Alexander accepted in evidence that the likely cause was either excessive force on the chisel or insufficient removal of bone from the jaw causing fracture on elevation and that, if so, 'I would have fallen below my usual standard'. The Recorder found: 'the first defendant accepted fault on his part. I hold that he was negligent'.

Held: an error of judgment may, or may not, be negligent. The admission of a mistake does not equal an admission of negligence. The Recorder failed to apply the appropriate test of whether the error was one that would not have been made by a reasonably competent professional person professing to have the standard and type of skill that the defendant held himself out as having, and acting with ordinary care. Thus the defendants' appeal was allowed and a new trial ordered.

Atkinson v Oxfordshire Health Authority

Limitation: operation: deafness

S Tuckey QC. [1993] 4 Med LR 18

In 1967 the plaintiff (Keith Atkinson), then aged 17, was complaining of progressive deafness. The Radcliffe Infirmary confirmed that he suffered from bilateral acoustic neuromas. On 2 May 1967 the tumour on the left side of the head was removed. On 16 May 1967 he underwent a second operation to evacuate the tumour on the right side of the brain. Following this operation the plaintiff suffered numerous complications. He had great difficulty in communicating with people outside the family. He suffered from double vision, although his balance improved. Described by his mother as 'intelligent but unable to fight', he was entirely reliant on her.

When he was 21, solicitors were instructed. Attention focused on late referral to the Radcliffe and, after a medical expert reported that no one was to blame, negative legal advice was given. In 1972 Mrs Atkinson consulted a second firm of solicitors who gave negative advice, as did a third firm in 1980. Subsequently some concrete evidence emerged in the shape of a letter to the plaintiff's GP, a copy of which was also sent to the plaintiff, which referred to a pre-operative respiratory arrest. Mrs Atkinson then instructed a fourth firm of solicitors who obtained pre-trial disclosure revealing the respiratory problems in the operation and then favourable expert medical advice. The grounds of claim were that either the second operation was unnecessary or it was negligently performed and should have been stopped when it was seen that the plaintiff was suffering from distress.

The writ was issued on 6 July 1989. A preliminary trial on the limitation defence was held.

Held: (i) the plaintiff and his mother understandably felt that they had been up against a brick wall. Looking at their conduct in obtaining advice over the years, neither had acted unreasonably. The plaintiff was not to be fixed with relevant knowledge before 6 July 1986. His claim was not time-barred by s 11 of the Limitation Act 1980.

(ii) under s 33, were that relevant, the fact that if not allowed to proceed the plaintiff would be denied compensation for his serious condition was nearly balanced by the prejudice to the defendants of having to defend allegations of negligence so long ago when the anaesthetist had died and the surgeon had retired. However the balance just tipped in favour of the plaintiff, since to a large extent the delay was of the defendants' own making in that it would not have occurred if the plaintiff or his mother had been told at the time exactly what had happened during the operation. Had he needed it, discretion under s 33 would have been exercised to allow his action to proceed.

See pp 186, 196.

A-G of British Columbia v Astaforoff and Another

Canada: force feeding: prison inmate

British Columbia Court of Appeal. [1984] 4 WWR 385

In September 1981 Mrs Mary Astaforoff was convicted of arson and sentenced to three years imprisonment. She was a member of the Sons of Freedom Doukhobors religious sect. During her imprisonment she fasted intermittently, sometimes for long periods. A senior prison doctor examined her in 1983 and found her to be rational and of sound mind. She told him that she did not wish to be fed by force or to receive any medical treatment. She was in poor health, not only due to her current fast, but also by reason of previous fasting. He considered that she might die within days, or within a few weeks, unless provided with food.

The Attorney General of Canada sought a mandatory order directing the British Columbia Corrections Branch 'to provide such medical treatment as is deemed appropriate to preserve the life of the respondent Mary Astaforoff, although she does not consent to such treatment'.

Held: (i) the court had no power to make that kind of mandatory order. It could however make a declaratory order.

(ii) there was no statutory duty on the prison authority to feed a prisoner by force. It was not clear whether a common law duty existed.

(iii) there was not a clear case for making the declaration sought. The court should not do so.

Per Taggart JA: 'I should emphasize that we are here concerned solely with the existence of the duty contended for by the Attorney General of Canada. Put in the negative, we are not concerned with the power of the corrections authorities, or indeed of any other prison authorities, to forcibly feed prisoners under their care and control. I emphasize that because, in my view, there may arise circumstances which would entitle the corrections authorities, or other prison authorities, to plead, in answer to claims made by prisoners fed without their consent, the power to do so in the circumstances then present. So I emphasize again that we are not concerned with power, but rather with the existence of a duty.'

See p 47.

Australian Red Cross Society and Another v BC by her Litigation Guardian BD

HIV: discovery: interrogatories: Australia: blood transfusion

Victoria Supreme Court Appeal Division. [1992] 3 Med LR 273

The plaintiff (known as BC) was prematurely born at the Queen Victoria Medical Centre on 9 September 1984. She received 12 blood transfusions. By the age of six, she was suffering from AIDS and was not expected to live for more than two years.

She claimed that the blood which she received from 11 of the transfusions was not infected with HIV. The inference is that she was infected by the transfusion on 17 October 1984 from blood collected by the Red Cross two days before. The person who donated that blood, identified only as Donor 61, died on 1 September 1990.

The plaintiff's claim against the hospital that carried out the transfusions was compromised. She also sued the Red Cross as collector and supplier of the blood to the hospital. Her case was that the Red Cross negligently failed to take proper steps to screen, exclude or discourage donations of blood from donors belonging to groups, such as active homosexuals and users of intravenous drugs, that were known to be at high risk of carrying HIV infection.

On an interlocutory application, the issue was whether the Red Cross should be ordered to provide the plaintiff with the name, address, sex, age and occupation of Donor 61. She sought the information by answer to interrogatory and by inspection of discovered documents in unedited form which so far had been provided only in edited form.

Held: the judge was right to order this. He did not consider that the limited order would put at risk the public interest in the supply of blood. His decision that this factor did not outweigh the interests of the administration of justice was attended with no real doubt.

Re B (a minor) (wardship: sterilisation)

Consent:minor: wardship: sterilisation: psychiatric patient

House of Lords. [1988] AC 199, [1987] 2 All ER 206, [1987] 2 WLR 1213

B, a 17-year-old girl, was mentally retarded and epileptic. Her ability to understand speech was that of a six-year-old, and her ability to express herself that of a two-year-old. She lived under a care order at a residential institution for the mentally handicapped. She began to show signs of sexual awareness and drive, exemplified by provocative approaches to male staff and members and other residents and by touching herself in the genital area. She would be terrified, distressed and violent during normal labour, and if she underwent a caesarian section would be likely to pick at the operational wound and tear it open. She had an antipathy to small children. Any child born to her would have to be taken for fostering or adoption. She was unaware of sexual intercourse and its relationship to pregnancy. It was not feasible to discuss contraception with her. The only appropriate course offering complete protection was for her to undergo sterilisation by occluding the fallopian tubes. She did not have the mental capacity to consent to this.

Consequently the Sutherland Borough Council, in whose care she was, applied to make her a ward of court and for leave to be given for her to undergo a sterilisation operation. The Court of Appeal upheld the decision of Bush J to give leave for the operation to be carried out.

Held: in the exercise of wardship jurisdiction, the court's first and paramount consideration is the well being, welfare or interests of the ward herself. The necessity was to decide the right course in the best interests of the ward. The decision to grant leave for the sterilisation operation was correct.

See p 12, 13.

Re B (a minor) (wardship: medical treatment)

Consent: Downs Syndrome: minor: wardship

Court of Appeal. [1990] 3 All ER 927

B was born suffering from Down's Syndrome. She was also born with an intestinal blockage which would be fatal unless operated on. When her parents were informed of her condition, they took the view that it would be unkind to the baby to operate on her and that the best course was for her not to have the operation, in which case she would die within a few days.

The doctors contacted the local authority who made B a ward of court and applied to the judge for a direction that the operation be carried out. He declined on the basis that the parents' wishes ought to be respected. The local authority appealed.

Held: *(per Templeman LJ):*

'Counsel for the parents has submitted very movingly, if I may say so, that this is a case where nature has made its own arrangements to terminate a life which would not be fruitful and nature should not be interfered with. He has also submitted that in this kind of decision the views of responsible and caring parents, as these are, should be respected, and that their decision that it is better for the child to be allowed to die should be respected. Fortunately or unfortunately, in this particular case the decision no longer lies with the parents or with the doctors, but lies with the court. It is a decision which of course must be made in the light of the evidence and views expressed by the parents and the doctors, but at the end of the day it devolves on this court in this particular instance to decide whether the life of this child is demonstrably going to be so awful that in effect the child must be condemned to die, or whether the life of this child is still so imponderable that it would be wrong for her to be condemned to die. There may be cases, I know not, of severe proved damage where the future is so certain and where the life of the child is so bound to be full of pain and suffering that the court might be driven to a different conclusion, but in the present case the choice which lies before the court is this: whether to allow an operation to take place which may result in the child living for 20 or 30 years as a mongoloid or whether (and I think this must be brutally the result) to terminate the life of a mongoloid child because she also has an intestinal complaint. Faced with that choice I have no doubt that it is the duty of this court to decide that the child must live. The judge was most affected by the reasons given by the parents and came to the conclusion that their wishes ought to be respected. In my judgment he erred in that the duty of the court is to decide whether it is in the interests of the child that an operation should take place. The evidence in this case only goes to show that if the operation should take place and is successful then the child may live the normal span of a mongoloid child with the handicaps and defects and life of a mongol child, and it is not for this court to say that life of that description ought to be extinguished.

Accordingly, the appeal must be allowed and the local authority must be authorised themselves to authorise and direct the operation to be carried out on the little girl.'

B v Croydon Health Authority

Consent: force feeding: psychiatric patient

Court of Appeal. [1995] 1 All ER 683, [1995] 2 WLR 294, [1995] PIQR P145 (1994) Times, 1 December

Mrs B had been compulsorily detained in hospital under s 3 of the Mental Health Act 1983. She suffered from a psychopathic disorder which was incapable of treatment except by psychoanalytical psychotherapy. The hospital sought to feed her without her consent by naso-gastric tube. An application was made for an injunction to restrain the defendant hospital authority from doing so.

Section 63 of the 1983 Act provides: 'The consent of a patient shall not be required for any medical treatment given to him for the mental disorder from which he was suffering, not being treatment falling within s 57 or 58 above, if the treatment is given by or under the direction of the responsible medical officer'.

Section 145 (1) gives a wide definition to the term 'medical treatment' which includes 'nursing, care, habilation and rehabilitation under medical supervision'.

Held: (i)   if there had been no proposed treatment for Mrs B's psychopathic disorder, s 63 could not have been invoked to justify feeding her by naso-gastric tube.

(ii)   it did not, however, follow that every act which formed part of that treatment within the wide definition in s 145(1) must in itself be likely to alleviate or prevent a deterioration of that disorder.

(iii)   nursing and care concurrent with the core treatment, or, as a necessary prerequisite to such treatment, or to prevent the patient from causing harm to himself or to alleviate consequences of the disorder, were all capable of being ancillary to a treatment calculated to alleviate or prevent a deterioration of the psychopathic disorder.

(iv)   accordingly the tube feeding was lawful.

See p 47.

Bagley v North Herts Health Authority

Childbirth: hospital administration: damages: stillbirth: depression

Simon Brown J. [1986] NLJ Rep 1014

The plaintiff (Mrs Bagley) was a married woman who became pregnant. She suffered from a condition of blood incompatibility. This was known to the defendants' maternity hospital to which she was admitted to have the child. The hospital intended to perform a blood analysis followed by an amniocentesis which would probably have led to the induction of birth. The hospital failed to carry out that procedure, and after over ten hours' labour the plaintiff gave birth to a still-born child. The defendant (North Herts Health Authority) admitted liability.

The plaintiff suffered from severe depression, and her marriage was adversely affected. If the hospital had not been negligent, she would have had a 95% chance of giving birth to a normal child. The risk of mortality in any subsequent pregnancy was about 50%.

Held: the plaintiff was awarded general damages of £17,100 (£18,000 discounted by five per cent for the five per cent risk that she would have had a still-born child even if the hospital had not been negligent) to compensate her for:

(i)   her loss of the satisfaction of bringing her pregnancy, confinement and labour to a successful, indeed joyous, conclusion;

234

    (ii)   the loss associated with the physical loss of the child; the hospital's negligence frustrated her plans to enlarge her family, and her decision not to attempt a further pregnancy was reasonable;

    (iii) the illness brought on the plaintiff by her great misfortune; she had suffered a great deal over the four years to trial, and this suffering was likely to continue, although with psychiatric treatment it would diminish and possibly resolve.

Note: In *Hotson v East Berkshire Area Health Authority*, Lord Ackner stated that the discount of five per cent in this case was clearly wrong. The plaintiff had established causation on the balance of probabilities and should have been awarded the full £18,000.

See pp 77, 133, 146.

Baig v City and Hackney Health Authority

Deafness: limitation: operation

Rougier J. [1994] 5 Med LR 221

All his life the plaintiff (Mr Baig) suffered from chronic partial deafness. In August 1973 Mr McNab-Jones, an ear, nose and throat surgeon in the defendants' employment, performed on him a stapedectomy (the excision of a very small bone in the ear complex). Within a matter of weeks, the plaintiff noticed that all hearing in his left ear had been lost. In 1976, finding it impossible due to deafness to continue his work in a bank in England, he returned to his native Pakistan in order to start a business. By the end of 1977, he had abandoned any hope of improvement.

In 1984 he returned to England, and in March 1985 he wrote a long letter to the defendant hospital authority in which he asked for his medical records. In the second half of 1986 he consulted a specialist firm of solicitors. In March 1987 they received an equivocal expert's report. Further unfavourable reports were obtained from other specialists until in October 1989 a firmly optimistic report was received from a consultant otolaryngologist who opined that the cause of the additional handicap was that the operation had been done in the presence of manifest infection, instead of performing one operation to clear the infection and the second later to improve the hearing.

The plaintiff's writ against the hospital authority was finally issued in May 1991. There was a preliminary trial on the issue of whether his case was statute barred.

Held: (i)   knowledge in the Kantian sense of the relevant facts was not required. A sufficiently firm conviction would suffice, but that conviction must be right in the sense that it accorded with the way the case was ultimately advanced in reliance on specialist opinion.

     (ii) the knowledge must be, in any rate in general outline, just what it was that the defendant had failed to do which had caused the damage. Whether the plaintiff knew that this was negligent is irrelevant.

    (iii) the plaintiff must have had constructive knowledge back in the early 1980s. An operation which he had been assured was fairly certain of success had proved a disaster. He was an educated, professional man. At the very least, he was put on enquiry that something seemed to have gone very much amiss. It was unreasonable of him not to seek advice in the late 1970s.

    (iv) accordingly his case was prima facie statute barred.

     (v) it would not be equitable to allow the action to proceed under s 33 of the Limitation Act 1980 because:

(a) there was a largely unexplained delay which had to be laid at the plaintiff's door. This delay was inordinate;

(b) whilst the plaintiff's allegations of negligence in and about the performance of the operation could still be fairly tried, because copies of the medical records were still available, he also alleged a failure to warn or discuss the merits of the potential dangers of the operation. This was an issue which relied very heavily on personal recollection, and it was almost impossible that Mr McNab-Jones could have any valuable recollection of just what had been said;

(c) additionally, the defendants' insurance arrangements changed in 1990 with the result that they would now be liable to meet the plaintiff's claim in full;

(d) the chances of the plaintiff ultimately succeeding in this action were highly doubtful.

See pp 187, 195, 196, 197.

Ball v Caldwell

General practitioner: x-ray: burn: breast

Singleton J. [1940] 1 BMJ 750

In early 1933 the plaintiff (Miss Mabel Ball) injured her left breast. She consulted Dr Caldwell, a general practitioner, who gave her x-ray treatment. The condition cleared up until October 1934 when she consulted Dr Caldwell again. He found a hard lump and decided to irradiate it. He used an induction-coil apparatus with a coolidge tube working at 150 KV, giving one-third of a skin erythema dose. On 13 November he saw her again and gave her double the previous dose. He was in and out of the room during treatment, but never further away than the adjoining room.

The plaintiff suffered skin discolouration which made it impossible for her to wear low-cut dresses or a bathing costume. She sued Dr Caldwell. Expert evidence was given that her discolouration was due to a healed x-ray burn.

Held: the plaintiff's condition resulted from Dr Caldwell's negligence.

See p 129.

Ball v Howard

General practitioner: appendicitis

Bailache J. (1924) 1 Lancet 253

The plaintiff (Mr Ball) was operated on by Mr Howard for appendicitis. He requested that a specialist be called in, but Mr Howard said that this was not necessary. Initially the plaintiff made good progress after the operation, but then complications arose. A consulting surgeon was called in and performed another operation. The plaintiff made a good recovery from this.

He sued Mr Howard.

Held: Mr Howard was liable because he had committed two errors of judgement:

(i) in not attending at once to the plaintiff's call;

(ii) by going away without leaving proper instructions what to do.

See p 135.

236

Barbara v Home Office

Battery: injection: prison inmate: aggravated damages: exemplary damages: buttock

Leggatt J. (1984) 134 NLJ 888

The plaintiff (Mr Barbara) was arrested for an offence of possessing an offensive weapon. He was remanded in custody for a week at Brixton Prison so that a report on his mental condition could be prepared. Hospital officers there forcibly injected him in the buttock with a tranquillising drug called Largactil. He claimed damages for trespass to the person. The Home Office admitted liability.

Held: (i)   he was awarded £100 general damages for his physical injury and £500 by way of aggravated damages for injury to his feelings and dignity;

      (ii)   his claim for exemplary damages was rejected. Mere negligence should not be visited by an award of exemplary damages just because it resulted in a trespass which could, from the point of view of the person affected by it, be regarded as oppressive.

See pp 7, 167.

Barker v Nugent

Diagnosis: general practitioner: meningitis: duty of care

Rougier J. [1987] 3 MLJ 182

On 2 December 1975 the plaintiff child was delivered with the aid of forceps. On 10 December, when he weighed 2750g, he was discharged with his 17-year-old mother to a home run for unsupported mothers by the London Borough of Ealing. On 18 December she took the baby to Dr Nugent, a general practitioner, because of a bulging fontanelle, but when Dr Nugent saw him this had gone. On 23 December the baby weighed only 2450g. At about 6.00pm Dr Nugent conducted an apparently thorough examination and prescribed dicyclomine hydrochloride to stop vomiting after feeding. However the baby vomited up his evening and night feeds. Around 6.00am on 24 December the baby was awake with staring eyes. He uttered high-pitched cries and had convulsions.

The baby was taken to hospital where meningitis was diagnosed. This resulted in irreversible brain damage. Years later he sued Dr Nugent.

Held: the key issue was the baby's condition when Dr Nugent examined him on 23 December. The delay of over 11 years to trial gravely impaired the quality of evidence. It had not been established that Dr Nugent negligently failed to realise that the baby was sufficiently ill to merit immediate hospital admission. He was entitled to take account of the fact that the baby was in a council home with a nurse on its staff. The home had his telephone number and he lived nearby.

Judgment for the defendants.

See p 99.

Barnes v Crabtree

General practitioner: duty to treat: examination

Barry J (with jury). (1955) Times, 1–2 November

Around 2.20pm on Christmas Day 1952, the plaintiff (Miss Irene Barnes) called at the surgery of her general practitioner, Dr Crabtree. She had a history of quarrels with previous doctors and during visits to Dr Crabtree. When he opened his door, she said 'I am ill'. He told her that there was nothing wrong with her, and that if she was not satisfied she could get another doctor, and closed the door. Thereafter she peered through the window of his sitting-room and rang the bell again. He warned her that he would call the police. She responded by lying down in his porch. Dr Crabtree summoned the police who removed her. She sued him for failing to treat her.

Held: Barry J directed the jury that in a case of real emergency a doctor under the National Health Service scheme was under an obligation to treat any patient who was acutely ill. The doctor's obligation was to render all proper and necessary treatment to the patient. In a case of chronic illness, when he had been seeing the patient frequently, this did not mean that he was required to make a full clinical examination each time the plaintiff asked for it.

The jury found that Dr Crabtree had no case to answer.

See pp 45, 135.

Barnett v Chelsea and Kensington Hospital Management Committee

Casualty officer: duty to treat: causation: fatal

Nield J. [1969] 1 QB 428, [1968] 1 All ER 1068, [1968] 2 WLR 422

Around 8.00am on 1 January 1966, three night watchmen presented themselves at the casualty department of St Stephen's Hospital. They met the nurse on duty. One of them told her that they had been vomiting continuously since drinking tea at 5.00am. Another, Mr Barnett, did not speak but lay down, on armless chairs placed together, with his head resting on his hand. It was obvious that all three men were feeling ill. After several minutes the nurse agreed to telephone the casualty officer and told him, 'There are three men complaining of vomiting after drinking tea'. The doctor replied 'Well, I am vomiting myself and I have not been drinking. Tell them to go home and go to bed and call in their own doctors'. They drove away. Mr Barnett died a few hours later around 1.30pm.

It was found that the death was due to arsenical poisoning. There was no reasonable prospect of a suitable antidote being delivered before the death. The plaintiff's widow (Mrs Barnett) sued for damages.

Held: (i)   since the defendants provided and ran the casualty department to which the deceased presented himself with a complaint of illness or injury, they owed him a duty to exercise the skill and care to be expected of a nurse and casualty officer;

      (ii)   the defendants through their casualty officer were negligent and in breach of their duty, in that he did not see and examine the deceased and did not admit him to the wards and treat him;

    (iii)   but since the deceased would have died of the poisoning even if he had been treated with all care, the plaintiff had failed to establish, on the balance of probabilities, that the defendants' negligence caused his death.

Per Nield J: 'It is not, in my judgment, the case that a casualty officer must always see the caller at his department. Casualty departments are misused from time to time. If the receptionist, for example, discovers that the visitor is already attending his own doctor and merely wants a second opinion, or if the caller has a small cut which the nurse can perfectly well dress herself, then the casualty officer need not be called. However, apart from such things as this. . . the duty of a casualty officer is in general to see and examine all patients who come to the casualty department of the hospital.'

See pp 20, 44, 45, 68, 134.

Battersby v Tottman & State of South Australia

Australia: ophthalmic: psychiatric patient: risk disclosure: depression: drugs

Supreme Court of South Australia (1985) 37 SASR 524

The plaintiff (Mrs Battersby), who was born in 1931, suffered from severe depression. She had hallucinations and suicidal tendencies. Between 1966 and 1970 various forms of treatments were attempted at Hillcrest Hospital in Gilles Plains; these included two operations, a variety of drugs and electrical treatment. The most successful drug was Melleril. The recommended maximum dose was 800mg per day, since a dosage of Melleril at a higher rate causes a real risk of damage to the retina of the eye by producing retina pigmentation and ultimately blindness. Between November 1972 and November 1974 the plaintiff's dosage of Melleril as prescribed by Dr Tottman was 2400mg per day. He did not warn her of the risk to her eyes involved in the treatment. In November 1974 it was discovered that she had developed a retina pigmentation due to the excessive dosage which was hastily reduced until she was taken off the drug altogether in March 1975. Thereafter her mental condition improved. During the crucial period from 1972 to 1974 Dr Tottman did not arrange for her eyes to be periodically examined by an eye specialist.

The plaintiff sued Dr Tottman and the hospital authority on three main grounds. First, he should not have continued the high dosage Melleril treatment for such a long time when he knew of the danger to eyesight associated with it. Second, he failed to cancel or warn her about the danger of Melleril. Third, he did not arrange for her eyes to be monitored by an eye specialist. The trial judge found against her on all three grounds.

Held: (i) the plaintiff's plight was desperate. She was acutely depressed and dangerously suicidal. Other modes of treatment had failed. She faced the prospect of having to spend the remainder of her life closely confined in a mental institution with a constant risk of suicide. Dr Tottman's decision to take the risk of prolonged treatment by large doses of Melleril was considered a professional judgment and was supported by a body of medical evidence. The decision was not negligent.

(ii) the plaintiff's mental and emotional condition placed Dr Tottman in the position of having to make the decision for her. Mere knowledge of the risk of her vision would have been sufficient to give rise to a real risk of hysterical blindness. Moreover she was incapable by reason of her abnormal mental condition of using the information about the risks of Melleril as the basis for a calm or rational decision, and the result of refusal of treatment was likely to be indeterminate close confinement in a mental institution with a high risk of suicide. Accordingly Dr Tottman's decision not to acquaint her with the risk to her vision attendant upon the Melleril treatment was not negligent.

(iii) the trial judge was satisfied that Dr Tottman had applied his mind to the question of arranging regular examinations by an eye specialist and had decided that the risk involved in terms of the plaintiff's reaction was too great. This decision was not so erroneous as to be one which a competent and careful doctor could not reach in the circumstances.

The plaintiff's appeal was dismissed.

Bayliss v Blagg and Another

Diagnosis: nurse: infection: child patient

Stable J. [1954] 1 BMJ 709

In November 1949 the plaintiff (Christine Bayliss), a very young girl, became ill. In June 1950 she was taken to Gringley-on-the-Hill Children's Hospital and was put on to a frame to keep her left hip still. At the beginning of January 1952 the matron, Mrs Bertha Blagg, put her left leg into a plaster cast. Her father testified that she 'changed into an adult overnight'. When he suggested to Mrs Blagg that the plaster was too tight, she snubbed him by saying, 'This is not the first plaster I have put on'. On 15 January the plaintiff's toes turned blue.

When the plaster cast was removed on 16 January, there was swelling in the plaintiff's left calf and foot. The skin had an unhealthy look, and there was a grey pallor in the calf. The leg began to improve after the plaster was off, but at the end of January it became discoloured and the tissues of the calf started breaking down. The plaintiff became a cripple for life.

She sued Mrs Blagg and the hospital authority. Evidence was given at the trial that the leg became infected under the plaster.

Held: although the plaster had been put on with care and skill, there had subsequently been a high degree of negligence over a protracted period of time. The matron, Mrs Blagg, did not observe for herself or heed the warnings she received of the marked degree of deterioration practically from the moment the plaster was put on.

See p 138.

Beatty v Cullingworth

Consent: surgeon: operation: assault

Hawkins J (with jury). [1896] 2 BMJ 1525

In August 1892 the plaintiff (Alice Beatty), a hospital nurse, consulted Dr Cullingworth, senior obstetric physician at St Thomas' Hospital. He advised her that she had an inflamed cyst of the right ovary and that it was necessary to remove it. She consented to removal of the right ovary but told him that she could not agree to removal of the left ovary as well, since this would prevent her from having children. Dr Cullingworth doubted that removal of the left ovary would be necessary but added that it was impossible to be sure until the operation was proceeding and that he could not bind himself by any promise not to remove it. When the plaintiff entered the operating theatre she said 'Dr Cullingworth, if you find both ovaries diseased you must remove neither'. He replied 'You really must leave that to me, nurse. I know your wishes; you may be sure I shall not remove anything that I can

240

help'. She made no reply but got on to the operating table and submitted to the anaesthetic. During the operation he found that the left ovary was thick, opaque and diseased and deemed it necessary to remove it in order to save her life.

The plaintiff sued Dr Cullingworth for removing the left ovary wrongfully and without her consent, and for assault.

Held: Hawkins J directed the jury that if a medical man undertook an operation, it was a humane thing for him to do everything in his power to remove the mischief, provided that he had no definite instructions not to operate. The main question was whether the plaintiff had given a tacit consent.

The jury returned a verdict for the defendant.

See p 104.

Beausoleil v La Communauté des Soeurs de la Charité de la Providence et al

Canada: anaesthetics: consent: operation: trespass to person: spinal

Quebec Court of Queen's Bench, Appeal Side. (1963) 53 DLR (2d) 65

In 1955 the plaintiff (Louise Beausoleil) consulted Dr Cusson, an orthopaedic surgeon attached to the Hôpital du Sacré Coeur. She complained of backaches. He concluded that a disc operation was indicated, and she entered hospital. Well before the operation she told Dr Cusson that she wanted a general anaesthetic and not a spinal. He agreed to this and told her that he would so advise the anaesthetist.

On the fixed day, the plaintiff was given sedation and taken to the operating room where she told Dr Piuze, a staff anaesthetist, that she did not want a spinal. The chief anaesthetist, Dr Forest, then appeared some thirty minutes before the operation. The plaintiff repeated her wish for a general anaesthetic. He strenuously sought to convince her to accept a change to a spinal. According to her nurse: 'she did not want that type of anaesthetic, she refused and they continued to offer it to her; finally she became tired and said "you do as you wish" or something like that.' Shortly after, Dr Cusson came to the operating room. When he asked the anaesthetist to proceed with the giving of the general, he was told that the spinal had already been administered. The operation was then performed, and the plaintiff ended up paralysed from the waist down.

Held: (i) Dr Forest did not visit the plaintiff on the evening prior to the operation and he did not confer with Dr Cusson prior to administering the anaesthetic, as he ought to have done, because he came on the scene at the last minute.

(ii) although the plaintiff under sedation finally acquiesced in a spinal anaesthetic, Dr Forest had failed to obtain from her the valid consent to the change from general to spinal.

(iii) therefore he had violated the plaintiff's person and submitted her to a risk that she had refused to assume. He was responsible for the consequent damage.

(iv) the spinal anaesthetic caused the paralysis. The plaintiff was awarded $104,132 damages.

Per Casey J:

'when in cases in which there is no urgency the doctor for one reason or another is unwilling to render the services agreed upon by the patient the only course of action open to him is to withdraw. He may not overrule his patient and submit him to risks that he is unwilling and in fact has refused to accept. And if he does so and damages result he will be responsible without proof of negligence or want of skill. In these circumstances it is not a defence to say that the technique employed was above reproach or that what happened was a pure accident.'

See p 9.

Bell and Others v Gateshead Area Health Authority

Childbirth: damages: brain damage

Alliott J. (1986) Kemp & Kemp Vol 2: 1–518/1B

Kathryn Bell was born in 1978. Her skull was fractured during an induced birth. She suffered catastrophic brain damage. She was aged eight at the date of trial and had an expectation of life of thirty-two years. Her mental state was that of an infant of less than six months, and her physical skills those of one of less than twelve months. Her vision was minimal. She had moderate spasticity of her lower limbs. She could stand with help and walk a few steps with support. She could not care for herself and wore nappies. She could perceive sensations such as pain, heat or cold and could be comforted by being lifted or cuddled. Her disabilities were permanent. Her mother cared for her for almost the entire period before trial.

Held: the plaintiff was awarded (October 1986):

   (i)   general damages of £60,000 for pain, suffering and loss of amenities.

   (ii) £50,000 for past care and attention, reached by adding to her mother's lost earnings a sum of £80 per week and rounding down the resultant figure of £50,780.

   (iii) £20,000 for her own future loss of earnings (£4,000 × 5).

   (iv) £220,000 for future care and attention (multiplier 14).

Other heads of damages brought the total award up to £426,500.

Bell v Secretary of State for Defence

Communication: Crown Proceedings Act 1947: military hospital

Court of Appeal. [1986] QB 322, [1985] 3 All ER 661, [1986] 2 WLR 248

Trooper Wayne Bell, aged 20, was serving with the 15/19 King's Royal Hussars stationed in Germany. Between 6.10pm amd 6.40pm on 11 November 1978 he fell while engaged in some horseplay in barracks and received a blow to the head. At 7.30pm he was seen by an army doctor, Major Herbert, who recorded that he was suffering from the effects of drink and that he had a head injury. By 10.00pm, his condition was causing such concern that he was returned to the medical reception centre. When Major Herbert saw him again before midnight, he sent him to a German civilian hospital accompanied by a nursing sister who knew little, if anything, about his case. Trooper Bell died of his injuries.

The plaintiff (his father) sued on the grounds that his death was due to the negligence of army medical staff. He alleged, *inter alia*, that Major Herbert caused his son to be admitted to the German civilian hospital with an inaccurate and misleading case history and without any reference to the head injury. There was a trial on the preliminary issue on whether s 10 Crown Proceedings Act 1947 gave the defendant immunity.

Held: the plaintiff was entitled to allege that the death of Trooper Bell was due to a failure or omission to provide complete records to the civilian hospital. This failure or omission was suffered by him at the civilian hospital when he was no longer on Crown land. Therefore the defendant could not claim immunity under s 10 of the 1947 Act.

Note: The Crown Proceedings (Armed Forces) Act 1987 abolished the immunity under s 10 of the 1947 Act with effect from 15 May 1987, but does not operate retrospectively.

See p 134.

Benarr and Another v Kettering Health Authority

Vasectomy (failed): wrongful birth: damages: school fees

Hodgson J. [1988] NLJR 179

The plaintiffs (Mr and Mrs Benarr) decided that they did not want any more children. Consequently in June 1981 Mr Benarr had a vasectomy operation at one of the defendants' hospitals. The operation proved unsuccessful, for in October 1983 Mrs Benarr gave birth to a child, Catherine.

The plaintiffs sued the health authority. During the trial, the parties came to terms as to liability and most of the heads of damages. The issue of damages for Catherine's education remained outstanding.

Held: (i) if the victim of a negligent vasectomy is a father who in any event would have privately educated his children, he is entitled to be compensated for what in the circumstances of that family could properly be called necessary. Therefore Mr Benarr was entitled to be compensated for the future expense of Catherine's education.

(ii) on the basis of accountancy evidence that the average cost of this education in the 14 years between the ages of 4 and 17 inclusive was £2,441.79 per annum, with the lower fees falling in the earlier years, a multiplier of 8 was appropriate, so that the sum awarded for Catherine's future education was £19,534.32.

See pp 128, 168, 170.

Benson v Cambridge Regional Health Authority

Surgeon: operation: damages: face

Otton J. (11 November 1991, unreported)

The plaintiff, aged 19 months, underwent an operation to remove a persistent cyst (first branchial cleft anomaly) beneath the left ear. The surgeon damaged the right facial nerve, causing permanent partial paralysis on that side of the plaintiff's face.

As a result of the damage to the facial nerve, the plaintiff, aged ten at trial, had a disfigured face on the right side. This was scarcely noticeable when she was in repose, but became extremely evident when she smiled or cried. The disability was permanent. It was possible that the effect of the facial paralysis could worsen in future years; there was the chance of future surgery to compensate.

Held (November 1991): general damages of £35,000 were awarded for pain, suffering and loss of amenities.

243

Bentley v Bristol and Weston Health Authority

Limitation: operation: surgeon: hip: sciatic nerve: solicitors

Hirst J. [1991] 2 Med LR 359

On 15 June 1981 the plaintiff (Mrs Elsa Bentley) underwent an operation for replacement of her left hip. During the course of this her sciatic nerve sustained serious damage, noted by the surgeon on 16 June 1981. This was confirmed through an exploratory operation on 10 August 1981 and explained to the plaintiff shortly afterwards. She suffered severe pain combined with permanent loss of feeling and mobility in her left leg and foot.

In the autumn of 1981 she consulted a community health council. In April 1982 she instructed solicitor 1, but after a negative medical report and counsel's opinion her legal aid certificate was discharged. In February 1984 she instructed solicitor 2 who obtained a report from Mr RF Winkworth FRCS which was sent to the plaintiff on 16 September 1985. Although this report raised a number of possible causes of her injury including 'injudicious retraction', a second counsel gave pessimistic advice. In October 1986 she consulted AVMA who referred her to solicitor 3 who issued a writ on 12 September 1988. A subsequent expert's report stated that the surgeon was negligent in applying undue traction and taking inadequate steps to protect the sciatic nerve.

Held: the plaintiff's action was not statute barred because:

(i)*   the relevant act or omission was not the mere performance of the operation but the alleged excessive traction of the nerve and failure reasonably to safeguard it from damage. The broad knowledge that her injury was capable of being attributed to this was only acquired by the plaintiff at the earliest when she received Mr Winkworth's report on or shortly after 16 September 1985, within three years of issue of the writ.

(ii)   if necessary s 33 of the Limitation Act 1980 would have been applied in the plaintiff's favour, because otherwise she would suffer very severe prejudice and the defendants would not suffer material prejudice. Delays by her advisers should not count significantly against her, since she was vigorously striving at all times to carry her claim forward. All the hospital notes were available, including those of both the initial and subsequent exploratory operation, and there were before the court detailed witness statements from both surgeons.

*   overruled by Broadley v Guy Clapham & Co (p 261).

See p 184, 196, 198.

Berger v Eli Lilly & Co and Others

Drugs: limitation: Opren.

Court of Appeal. [1992] 3 Med LR 395

See *Nash v Eli Lilly & Co (n)* (p 466).

Bernier v Sisters of Service (St John's Hospital, Edson)

Burns: nurses: contributory negligence: causation: Canada

Alberta Supreme Court. [1948] 1 WWR 113

On 5 September 1946, the plaintiff (Mrs Evelyn Bernier) was admitted for an appendicectomy to St John's Hospital, Edson, in Canada. She did not mention that she had ever had frostbite in her feet or heels. At 10.18am on 6 September she was given a spinal anaesthetic. Her appendix was duly removed. At 11.05am she was returned to the surgical ward.

One nurse filled two hot-water bottles, one covered and one uncovered, testing the temperature by moving her hand in the running water from the tap. Another nurse placed the bottles inside the foot of the bed. At 11.30am both nurses left the ward without letting the sister know that there were hot-water bottles in the bed. Over the next twenty minutes the plaintiff started to moan and cry. Soon after midday, the bottles were removed.

By then the plaintiff had suffered third degree burns to both her heels. On 23 September she left St John's Hospital against her hospital doctor's advice. She sued the hospital authority which denied liability and alleged contributory negligence.

Held: (i) the hospital staff had been negligent in failing to test the hot-water bottles with a thermometer, in placing at least one of them in direct contact with the feet of an anaesthetised patient and in not having a nurse in almost constant attendance on a patient coming out of spinal anaesthesia;

(ii) the plaintiff was not guilty of contributory negligence. She had no reason to think that even if her feet had been frostbitten such a fact was a subject matter for disclosure on entering the hospital, or that her feet might be burned with a hot-water bottle. The allegation of failure on her part to communicate her pain was of little importance, since the damage was fully done by the time sensibility returned. Although she left the hospital on 23 September against medical advice and with the possibility of infection setting in, no such infection resulted from this.

See p 83.

Best v Wellcome Foundation Ltd and Others

Causation: general practitioner: Ireland: product liability: vaccine damage

Ireland Supreme Court. [1994] 5 Med LR 81

On 30 April 1968 the plaintiff (Kenneth Best) was born in Ireland. He suffered from eczema. On 17 September 1969 he received his first immunisation injection of DTP vaccine against diphtheria/whooping cough and tetanus at a dispensary supervised by Dr O'Keefe and controlled by the Southern Health Board. He received subsequent injections on 15 October 1969 and 19 November 1969. He suffered from encephalopathy, an acute brain disorder manifesting itself in epileptic seizures and gross mental retardation.

Records indicated that the batch of vaccine from which the first injection was taken was a batch BA3741 which was manufactured and tested by Wellcome in March 1968. This batch was tested by Wellcome in England in 1968. It passed the opacity test and the test for non-specific toxicity. However it showed a potency that was nearly eight times the minimum four iu per dose required by British Standards. Moreover it failed the mouse weight gain test: the mice subjected to it gained by the seventh day afterwards 0.56 of a gram in weight when they should have gained 3 grams. Nevertheless the batch of BA3741 was passed by Wellcome for release.

The plaintiff sued Wellcome Foundation Limited, Dr O'Keefe, the Southern Health Board and the Irish State. His parents testified at the trial that the first onset of the plaintiff's fits and convulsions occurred on the evening of 17 September 1969, the day on which he was first injected. His mother's evidence was that these turns continued daily from that time onwards on a number of occasions each day and that she complained to Dr O'Keefe about them two to three times a week. However he made no record of this in his diary until 7 January 1970. The trial judge held that Wellcome had been negligent but, relying on Dr O'Keefe's diary, found that the onset of the plaintiff's symptoms did not follow within a relatively short time of the first injection of the vaccine and that, therefore, his encepholapathy had not been caused by it. The plaintiff appealed on the issue of causation, and Wellcome applied to vary the finding of negligence.

Held: (i) (a) in 1968 Wellcome were the manufacturers of a vaccine which at that time a very considerable body of expert opinion held to contain the distinct possibility, however rare, of serious reaction in small children by way of brain or neurological damage. Therefore they owed a duty to exercise a high degree of care in regard to the testing before issue of such a vaccine where they knew, or must have known, that it would be injected into children at a very young age;

(b) merely to comply with mandatory or minimum requirements imposed by national health authorities in the area in which the vaccine was manufactured was not sufficient;

(c) having regard to the undoubted failure of the mouse weight gain test, the undoubted high figures for potency, and the persuasiveness of the evidence of those who supported a link between potency and toxicity, the trial judge was correct in concluding that Wellcome had been negligent in releasing batch BA3741.

(ii) having regard to the terms of the evidence given by the plaintiff's mother, the manner in which she dealt with cross examination concerning it, and the absence of a suggestion that she was attempting to mislead the court, the proper inference which the trial judge should have drawn was that the absence of entries of convulsions before 7 January 1970 in Dr O'Keefe's diaries, which were incomplete in other respects, was not sufficiently strong proof of the date of the first convulsion suffered by the plaintiff to displace the clear-cut evidence of his parents. The proper inference to be drawn from the evidence was that the plaintiff suffered a convulsion on the evening of the first injection on 17 September 1979. Accordingly the plaintiff was entitled to a judgment against Wellcome for their negligence in causing the personal injuries arising to him from the onset of the condition of encephalopathy.

(iii) since the effect of the DTP vaccine administered on 17 September 1969 was the cause of the plaintiff's condition, the dismissal of the actions against Dr O'Keefe, the Southern Health Board and the Irish State should stand.

Note: On the fourth day of a subsequent re-trial limited to quantum, settlement was reached and the plaintiff was awarded agreed damages of £2.75 million against Wellcome Foundation Ltd.

Cf *Loveday v Renton* (p 435).

See pp 40, 69.

Biles v Barking Health Authority

Sterilisation: damages: post-traumatic stress disorder: scarring

Webster J. [1988] CLY 1103

In 1973 the plaintiff, then aged 19, was sterilised. In 1979 she was told that this sterilisation had been unnecessary. Since then she had taken all steps to conceive, including four *in vitro* fertilisation attempts, and had to be assumed to be permanently sterile. Her treatment had included four full laparotomies, six laparoscopies, two painful hysterosalpingograms, many blood tests and injections. She had suffered a very painful ectopic pregnancy. There was a tender scar across her lower abdomen above the bikini line. Her sexual function was impaired, with dyspareunia and loss of libido, although a course of psycho-sexual therapy had led to a good prognosis on sexual function. Since 1980 she had suffered post-traumatic disorder causing clinical depression and anxiety.

Held: general damages (October 1987) for pain, suffering and loss of amenities were £45,000 in a total award of £52, 269.73.

Note: This case is sometimes entitled *Biles* v *North East Thames Health Authority*.

See p 156.

Birnie v Oxfordshire Health Authority and Another

Limitation: bedsores: gangrene: pain relief: amputation

Glidewell J. (1982) 2 Lancet 281

In December 1972 the plaintiff (Mr Birnie), who had severe pain in his side and legs, was admitted to a pain clinic under the care of Mr Lloyd, a specialist in pain relief. Mr Lloyd carried out barbotage on two occasions. After the second barbotage, on 19 December 1972, the plaintiff was permanently paralysed in his two lower limbs.

He became severely depressed and on 6 October 1973 he attempted suicide. He was in hospital between 6 October and 23 December 1973 during which period severe bedsores and gangrene developed.

The plaintiff needed further surgery, including a chordotomy in November 1974 and, due to gangrenous sores, the amputation of his right leg in July 1975. In 1977 he spent a week in a Scottish hospital where the doctor and nurses were critical of those who had allowed the bedsores to develop. In August 1977 he consulted solicitors. His depressive state continued until 1978.

The writ was issued in August 1979. It was accepted that the three year limitation periods covered by it expired not later than 19 December 1975 and 23 December 1976 respectively. The plaintiff relied on s 33 of the Limitation Act 1980.

Held: (i) in considering the delay, the plaintiff's state of health and state of mind had to be taken into account. For much of the time he was sunk in depression which produced inertia of will. The delay before he consulted solicitors was understandable. After he had consulted solicitors there had been a two year delay before the writ was issued, and ten to twelve months of this delay were without valid excuse;

(ii) so far as prejudice to the defendants was concerned, there was substantial documentation, although recollection was needed with regard to the barbotage and this was affected by the passage of time. Mr Lloyd was prejudiced in that he had the claim hanging over his head and was not insured. The nursing notes on the plaintiff's bedsores were available;

(iii) the prejudice to the plaintiff outweighed the prejudice to the defendants or the effect of delay on the cogency of evidence. The scale tipped in the plaintiff's favour even when the inexcusable delay by the solicitors was added. He was granted leave to proceed under s 33 of the Limitation Act 1980.

See pp 193, 198.

Biss v Lambeth, Southwark and Lewisham Area Health Authority (Teaching)

Dismissal for want of prosecution: bedsores: nurses

Court of Appeal. [1978] 2 All ER 125, [1978] 1 WLR 382

In March 1965 the plaintiff (Mrs Biss) contracted multiple sclerosis. She awoke at home to find that she could not move her legs. She was taken to Lewisham Hospital where she lay paralysed and helpless on her back. Bedsores developed and were very painful. She accused the nursing staff of negligence.

In 1966 she made an abortive attempt to claim damages, but her legal aid certificate was discharged after negative advice from Counsel. In 1973 she was encouraged through the Multiple Sclerosis Society to renew her claim. She obtained legal aid again.

In February 1975 she was granted leave to proceed under the Limitation Act 1963 and issued a writ alleging negligence by Lewisham Hospital. Pleadings were closed in July 1975. In November 1975 the hospital gave particulars of its defence and served on the plaintiff a request for further and better particulars. These were never supplied. Nine months later, in September 1976, she changed her solicitors. Subsequently she declined to travel to see her medical expert at Stoke Mandeville Hospital. The case was not set down for trial.

In March 1977 the defendants issued a summons to dismiss for want of prosecution. The Master granted it, but on appeal the judge (Sir Norman Richards) allowed the action to proceed.

Held: the defendants' appeal was allowed.

Per Lord Denning MR: 'Prejudice to a defendant by delay is not to be found solely in the death or disappearance of witnesses or their fading memories or in the loss or destruction of records. There is much prejudice to a defendant in having an action hanging over his head indefinitely, not knowing when it is going to be brought to trial. Like the prejudice to Damocles when the sword was suspended over his head at the banquet . . .

'Likewise the hospital here. There comes a time when it is entitled to have some peace of mind and to regard the incident as closed. It should not have to keep in touch with the nurses: saying "We may need you to give evidence"; or to say to the finance department: "We ought to keep some funds in reserve in case this claim is persisted in"; or to say to the keepers of records: "Keep these files in a safe place and don't destroy them as we may need them". It seems to me that in these cases this kind of prejudice is a very real prejudice to a defendant when the plaintiff is guilty of inordinate and inexcusable delay since the issue of the writ: and that it can properly be regarded as more than minimal. And when this prejudice is added to the great and prejudicial delay before writ (as the House of Lords says it may be: see *Birkett* v *James*) then there is sufficient ground on which to dismiss the action for want of prosecution.

'Applying this principle, I am clearly of opinion that this action should be dismissed for want of prosecution. It would be an intolerable injustice to the hospital–and to the nurses and staff–to have to fight it out twelve years after the incident–when they quite reasonably regarded it as closed eleven years ago. . .

'One word more. It is, I believe, accepted on all hands, that if the plaintiff is guilty of inordinate and inexcusable delay before issuing the writ, then it is his duty to proceed with it with expedition after the issue of the writ. He must comply with the Rules of Court and do everything that is reasonable to bring the case quickly for trial. Even a short delay after the writ may in many circumstances be regarded as inordinate and inexcusable: and give a basis for an application to dismiss for want of prosecution. So in the present case the delay of nine months was properly admitted to be inordinate and inexcusable.

"It is a serious prejudice to the hospital to have the action hanging over its head even for that time. On this simple ground I think this action should be dismissed for want of prosecution. I would allow the appeal, accordingly'.

See pp 138, 202.

Blackburn v Newcastle-upon-Tyne Health Authority

Brain damage: nurses: cardiac arrest

Lawton J. [1988] 4 PMILL 53

On 30 September 1976 the plaintiff (Keith Blackburn), then aged 34, entered the Newcastle General Hospital. He was suffering from pneumonia and pleurisy and was admitted to the Intensive Care Unit. From the start he had difficulty with his breathing. On 4 October a tracheostomy tube was inserted by means of a hole in his windpipe. On 5 and 6 October it was noted that large amounts of thick blood-stained sputum were being sucked out. The 6 October note read 'tracheostomy tube appears to be crusted, requiring a lot of humidification'. On 7 October the plaintiff's lips became blue, meaning that not enough oxygen was getting through. On 8 October he suffered a cardiac arrest. The registrar who was called to attend ordered the removal of the tracheal tube and noted 'Old tube blocked with blood-stained secretions'.

The plaintiff had suffered severe brain damage. He was left grossly disabled in thought, movement and speech, and with a childlike personality. He sued the hospital authority.

Held: the hospital staff had been negligent. By the evening of 7 October it should have been clear that not enough oxygen was getting to the plaintiff's brain. The tube had started to get crusted up on 7 October, but the crusting was not removed before 3.25pm on 8 October. The nursing and medical staff should have been alive to the danger of the tracheal tube becoming blocked. Someone had not sucked it out as regularly or frequently as (s)he should have done.

See p 117.

Blackburn v Newcastle Area Health Authority (No 2)

Brain damage: cardiac arrest: damages: Court of Protection: receiver: interest: solicitors

Owen J. QBD 1 August 1988

The plaintiff (Keith Blackburn) suffered severe brain damage in October 1976. He successively instructed three firms of solicitors who issued his writ in 1979 but failed to make substantial progress with his case. A fourth firm took over in 1986 and pursued the case to a trial on liability in October 1987. Lawton J found that the defendant health authority had been negligent.

At the subsequent hearing on quantum some heads of damages were agreed but there were areas of dispute over, *inter alia*, the Receiver's fees and interest.

Held: (i) as the defendants had caused the plaintiff's mental incapacity, they must compensate him for both the Court of Protection charges and the Receiver's fees. The family was entitled to appoint a solicitor as Receiver;

(ii) there had been gross delay. The case, if properly handled, should have come to trial in 1982. The period for interest on special damages should be abridged to six years from October 1976. General damages would attract interest from the date of service of the writ in 1981 to October 1984.

See pp 117, 189.

Blyth v Bloomsbury Health Authority

Contraceptive advice: risk disclosure: warning: rubella

Court of Appeal. [1993] 4 Med LR 151, [1987] 3 PMILL 10

In May 1978 the plaintiff (Mrs Blyth) was referred to University College Hospital for antenatal care. When she was admitted there in December 1978 for the birth of her baby, she received a vaccination against rubella and an injection of the contraceptive Depo-Provera. She suffered bleeding and menstrual irregularity due to the Depo-Provera.

Soon after the plaintiff received the rubella vaccine, Dr Burt, a member of the hospital staff, discussed Depo-Provera with her and told her of the side effect of irregular bleeding. Dr Burt did not tell her all the information available to the hospital which Dr Law had collated in her files. Medical experts testified that there was no need to do so.

The plaintiff sued the hospital authority and her general practitioner. The trial judge (Leonard J) found in her favour against the hospital authority.

Held: Dr Burt and the hospital were not negligent in failing to pass on more information. Irregular bleeding was the side effect that was known and recognized in 1978. The plaintiff was told about it. None of the expert witnesses suggested that the defendants were under any duty to provide her with the full picture of the information in Dr Law's files.

See p 110.

Bolam v Friern Hospital Management Committee

Psychiatrist: risk disclosure: fractures: ECT: depression: psychiatric patient: femur

McNair J (with jury). [1957] 2 All ER 118, [1957] 1 WLR 582

In August 1954 the plaintiff (John Bolam) was readmitted to Friern Hospital, a mental hospital. He was suffering from depression and on August 19 and 23 was treated for this condition by electro-convulsive therapy (ECT). ECT was carried out by placing electrodes on each side of the head and passing an electric current through the brain. If no relaxant drug is administered, one of the effects of ECT is to precipitate violent convulsive movements in the form of a fit in the patient, with muscular contractions and spasms attended by a very slight risk of bone fracture.

The defendants' doctors did not warn the plaintiff of the risks of the treatment. On August 23 the treatment was given to the plaintiff by Dr Allfrey who, in accordance with the hospital's normal practice, did not administer a relaxant drug or apply any form of manual restraint. The treatment was given to the plaintiff while he was lying on the couch. Dr Allfrey's precautions were to support his chin, to hold his shoulders and to place a gag in his mouth, while the nurses were present on either side of the couch to prevent him from falling off. He suffered bilateral fractures of the acetabula.

The plaintiff alleged that the defendants were negligent in:

(a)   failing to administer to him, before the current was passed through his brain, a suitable relaxant and/or drugs;

(b)   failing to provide sufficient manual control of his convulsive movements while undergoing the fit; and

(c)   failing to warn him of the risks he was running when he consented to the treatment.

Expert witnesses agreed that there was a large body of competent medical opinion that was opposed to the use of relaxant drugs and that it was also the view of some competent and respected doctors that the more restraint there was the more likelihood there was of fracture. The plaintiff's expert thought that a patient should be warned of the risk of fracture, but the defendants' doctors took the view that it was not desirable to warn a patient of the risk unless he asked about it.

Held: In directing the jury, McNair J stated:

'. . where you get a situation which involves the use of some special skill or competence, then the test as to whether there has been negligence or not is not the test of the man on the top of a Clapham omnibus, because he has not got this special skill. The test is the standard of the ordinary skilled man exercising and professing to have that special skill. A man need not possess the highest expert skill; it is a well established law that it is sufficient if he exercises the ordinary skill of an ordinary competent man exercising that particular art.

'A doctor is not guilty of negligence if he has acted in accordance with a practice accepted as proper by a responsible body of medical men skilled in that particular art. . . Putting it the other way round, a doctor is not negligent, if he is acting in accordance with such a practice, merely because there is a body of opinion that takes a contrary view'. . .

When dealing with warning about risks, McNair J added:

'Having considered the evidence on this point, you have to make up your minds whether it has been proved to your satisfaction that when the defendants adopted the practice they did (namely, the practice of saying very little and waiting for questions from the patient), they were falling below a proper standard of competent professional opinion on this question of whether or not it is right to warn. . .

'If you do come to the conclusion that proper practice requires some warning to be given, the second question which you have to decide is: if a warning had been given, would it have made any difference? The only man who can really tell you the answer to that question is the plaintiff, and he was never asked the question.'

The jury returned a verdict for the defendants.

See pp 14, 19, 44, 53, 57, 58, 106, 126.

Bolitho and Others v City and Hackney Health Authority

Cardiac arrest: causation: child patient: communication: registrar

Court of Appeal. [1993] 4 Med LR 381, [1993] PIQR P334

In December 1983 the first plaintiff (Patrick Bolitho), aged two, underwent at Brompton Hospital an operation to close a persistent ductus arteriosus. On 11 January 1984 he was admitted to St Bartholomew's Hospital and diagnosed as suffering from acute croup. At 12.40pm on 17 January 1984 the ward sister found that, although Patrick was still talking, his respiratory sounds were 'awful' and he was very white in colour. She bleeped Dr Horn, the paediatric senior registrar, who said that she would attend as soon as possible. Patrick improved but around 2pm, after a similar episode, the ward sister telephoned Dr Horn who had not yet arrived. Dr Horn attempted to ask Dr Rodgers, the senior house officer, to attend in her place. Dr Rodgers' bleep was not working, due to flat batteries, so she never got the message. At about 2.35pm Patrick collapsed because he was unable to breathe and suffered a cardiac arrest. In consequence, he sustained severe brain damage.

It was agreed that it was negligent of Dr Horn not to have attended Patrick when summoned by the ward sister. The hospital authority conceded that, if Patrick had been intubated at any time prior to the cardiac arrest at 2.35 pm, this would probably have averted his collapse and its serious consequences. The issue was what Dr Horn would have done had she attended and, in particular, whether she would have intubated Patrick and thereby averted his collapse. The plaintiffs' experts said that he should have been intubated immediately. The defendants' main expert, a consultant in paediatric respiratory medicine at Great Ormond Street Hospital, testified that he would have kept Patrick under observation but that he would certainly not have intubated him.

Held: (i) the judge was dealing with a breach of duty which consisted of an omission, and it was necessary for him to decide what course of events would have followed had the duty been discharged.

(ii) it was for the plaintiffs to prove that:

(a) either Dr Horn would have intubated, in which event they would have succeeded, whether or not all reasonably competent practitioners would have followed this course;

(b) or if (as she testified) she would not have done so, that her 'failure was contrary to accepted medical practice'.

(iii) even though he was dealing with causation, the judge was in these circumstances bound to rely on the evidence of the experts before him.

(iv) the expert evidence established that there was a responsible body of medical opinion against intubation on these facts, so there was no reason to disturb the judge's finding that causation had not been established.

See pp 57, 63, 73, 134.

Bonthrone v Millan and Others

Vaccine damage: causation: contra-indications: general practitioner: health visitor: Scotland

Scotland, Court of Session. (1985) 2 Lancet 1137

A boy was born on 4 October 1975. When he was examined six weeks later, he was found to be very large but normal. On 25 February 1976 he had his first DTP vaccine. A six month report by a health visitor showed him to be normal but overweight. On 4 May a second dose of DTP was given. On 10 May he had a spasm and, after further fits, was admitted to hospital. When discharged on 22 June, he had greatly deteriorated and his brain damage was severe.

The vaccine damage tribunal accepted that probably his brain damage was caused by pertussis vaccine, so £10,000 compensation was paid to his parents under the Vaccine Damage Payments Act 1979. The parents also sued for negligence, alleging that after the first vaccine the baby began to vomit regularly about half an hour or more after a feed and that he began to move his left arm in an unusual way. They blamed the general practitioner for administering the second vaccination without asking about symptoms which had emerged since the first, and the health visitor for not reporting the symptoms to the GP's group practice.

Held: (i) the defendants had not been negligent. The health visitor had neither seen nor been told by the mother of the regular vomiting or the arm movements. Nor was it established that the GP had failed to ask reasonable questions before the second vaccination;

     (ii)   it was not proved that the second vaccination was the cause of the spasms and brain damage.

Per Lord Jauncey: 'When about 50% of infantile spasms and other encephalopathic symptoms occurring at this age are cryptogenic, it seems to me difficult to say that these symptoms are more likely to be attributable to vaccine than any one of the unknown causes'.

See p 40.

Booth and Others v Warrington Health Authority

Discovery: witness statements: privilege: brain damage: nurses

Tucker J. [1992] 1 PIQR P137

The plaintiff (a baby girl) was born severely brain damaged. She and her parents sued the hospital authority for damages, alleging negligence in allowing delay to occur before the baby was delivered and in failing to monitor the foetal heart-rate. The authority denied negligence.

Student Midwife Mary Quigley and Sister Patricia Dolan were present and assisted in the delivery of the baby. They kept notes of the events occurring before, during and after it. After the litigation was commenced, they gave witness statements to the hospital authority and its solicitors. The authority's solicitors obtained an expert's report from a consultant obstetrician and gynaecologist. In the course of giving his opinion, he made a number of references to Sister Nolan and, in particular, to Student Midwife Quigley and referred to an explanation given by her 'in her report' (meaning in her statement).

The plaintiff applied for the defendants to produce for inspection, pursuant to RSC Ord 24, r 11, the two nurses' statements. Her counsel argued that through the expert's references the hospital authority had waived the privilege that attached to them.

Held: the mere fact that an expert witness in his own report refers to statements made by other witnesses does not, upon disclosure of the report at an interlocutory stage, constitute waiver of the privilege that otherwise attached to the statements. There has to be an unequivocal act to amount to waiver.

Note: Such witness statements would now be exchanged later in the litigation pursuant to RSC Ord 38, r 2A.

Bould v Wakefield Health Authority

Childbirth: damages: structured settlement: brain damage

HH Judge Herrod QC. Halsbury's Laws, 94/320

The male plaintiff suffered severe asphyxiation and brain damage at birth by reason of the defendants' negligent obstetric care. As a result he had severe cerebral palsy, moderately severe intellectual impairment and epilepsy. He was unable to walk any distance unaided and his speech was very indistinct. He required assistance with self care, would remain dependent on others and could not manage his own affairs. His life expectancy was 40–50 years. Liability was admitted.

It was agreed and approved that damages on a conventional basis were worth £950,000. £129,073 had already been paid out. £242,971 was required for immediate needs, including the purchase of a suitable home for the plaintiff and his mother and adaptations to his father's accommodation to enable visits. £69,706 plus £24,198 interest on moneys in court were to be invested in a contingency fund.

The proposals for the structure were that £33,250 be allowed as a discount to the defendants and that £475,000 be applied to fund annual payments by the defendants in a self-funded structure, starting at £21,500 per annum and rising in line with the retail price index. The plaintiff's accountants advised that the structured settlement would meet 57% of the plaintiff's needs over his projected life span, whereas conventional settlement would meet 37%. Jointly instructed accountants advised that, if conventionally invested, the sum required to match receipts from the structured settlement would be exhausted by age 45.

Held (October 1993):   the structured settlement was approved on the grounds that the plaintiff's needs in later life, when provision of care by his family would be more difficult, would be more adequately catered for through the structure.

Bova v Spring

Diagnosis: fatal: general practitioner: pneumonia

Sedley J. [1994] 5 Med LR 120

On Thursday 25 June 1987 Peter Bova, a 44-year-old nurse, first complained of being ill. He told his wife in the morning that he felt unwell and that it might be a cold or flu. He stayed in bed during the day and took paracetamol. In the evening, his wife thought that he looked shivery. He suffered from diarrhoea and vomiting during the night.

At 6.00am on Friday 26 June Mrs Bova telephoned the Burgess Hill Health Centre and asked for a visit. Dr Spring, a trainee general practitioner, arrived between 6.30am and 7.00am and spent fifteen to twenty minutes with Mr Bova in the bedroom. When he asked him what was the matter, Mr Bova replied that he had a pain in the right side of his chest and had had it for about a week since he lifted a lump of concrete. He said that he had taken paracetamol but that it had not helped the pain. He confirmed that he had had diarrhoea – about 12 motions over the last 24 hours – and had vomited once on the Thursday night.

Dr Spring then examined Mr Bova. He took his temperature by a strip thermometer which gave a reading of 36 to 37 degrees centigrade. He examined Mr Bova's throat and nose, finding confirmation of a cold in the congestion of the nose membranes. By palpation he obtained a systolic blood pressure reading of about 100 millimetres of mercury. He examined Mr Bova's chest and thought that the percussion note was normal and symmetrical. When palpating the chest wall, he elicited 'exquisite tenderness' over and below the right pectoral muscles. The only abnormality that he found in Mr Bova's abdomen was mild tenderness in the epigastrium and in the centre.

On completion of this examination, Dr Spring told Mr Bova that he thought that he had pulled a muscle in his chest and was suffering from viral enteritis. He prescribed codeine phosphate. He advised Mr Bova to drink as much fluid as possible and to avoid dairy products. He also stressed that a liniment, a hot water bottle or hot baths might help to alleviate the chest pain. When Mrs Bova asked him whether she should call the practice again if Mr Bova got any worse, Dr Spring replied 'by all means'.

When Mrs Bova returned from work on Friday 26 June, Mr Bova still looked as if he was in pain. His diarrhoea was not so bad overnight. When he went for a walk in the early afternoon of Saturday 27 June, he felt tired and walked so slowly that he could not get as far as he wanted. He was restless throughout Saturday night.

Between 6.30am and 6.45am on Sunday 28 June, Mrs Bova found diarrhoea and urine all over the floor and her husband unconscious, slumped over the bed and barely breathing. She telephoned urgently for a doctor. At 7.00am one came and immediately telephoned the hospital. The ambulance took nearly an hour to reach the house and, when it arrived, it appeared that the crew had no notion of the emergency to which they were coming. Mr Bova collapsed unconscious when they tried to lift him from the bed. He was pronounced dead shortly after reaching hospital.

The formal autopsy findings included a finding that the weight of the right lung was 1315 grams, as against 645 grams for the left lung. In an ordinary healthy man, the combined weight of the lungs should only be about 500 or 600 grams. There was a severe suppurative lobar pneumonia of the right upper lung with a fibrino-purulent exudate (ie pus) of the visceral pleura. The right middle and lower lobes on the left lung all showed congestion and severe pulmonary odema. The disease or condition directly leading to death was given as cardiac failure, due to severe hypokalaemia, due to gastroenteritis with severe diarrhoea and vomiting. The other significant condition contributing to the death was recorded as lobar pneumonia.

The plaintiff (Mrs Bova) sued Dr Spring for negligence.

Held: (i)   Mr Bova died as a result of acute pneumococcal pneumonia contracted on the Wednesday or Thursday, which both produced blood toxins precipitating violent diarrhoea and inflamed the lungs, in particular the right lung, to a point at which by early Friday morning he had a heavily infected right lung causing acute pleural chest pain. Undiagnosed and therefore untreated, the pneumonia proved fatal within little more than 48 hours.

(ii)   there is nothing inherently wrong with the use of a strip thermometer, but where the patient is visibly sick or not well perfused it may be inadequate.

(iii)   the systolic pulse reading of about 100 millimetres of mercury, like the temperature found, was not intrinsically worrying. It was in the context of the other possible findings that the temperature and blood pressure called for further investigation.

(iv)   the history obtained by Dr Spring of a muscle strain suffered a week earlier and getting worse was on the face of it contrary to the natural history of such strains, which are acute at first and then get better or, at worst, remain static for a time.

(v)   in these circumstances, it was incumbent on Dr Spring to be more circumspect than he was in eliminating other possible causes of the chest condition.

(vi)   Dr Spring was not guilty of elementary errors of examination, such as failing to elicit signs of consolidation of the lung. Nor, on the findings which he made, was he negligent in not referring Mr Bova to hospital.

(vii)   however he was negligent in failing to recognise the uncertainties attending his diagnosis. Had he done so, he would have had in mind the real possibility that, with an upper respiratory tract infection in the form of a cold, Mr Bova's chest might be pleural and a sign of pneumonia. The natural history of pneumonia, with its erratic but relatively rapid development of signs and symptoms, should have been present to his mind.

(viii)   had it been so, he should and would have arranged a follow up visit by himself or another member of the practice either for the late afternoon of the Friday or for the Saturday morning, in order to see whether the patient was any better and to test again for signs of lung infection. At the very least he should have told the plaintiff to telephone for a further domestic visit on the Saturday morning, if Mr Bova was not getting better in both his bowel and his chest condition.

(ix) had Dr Spring taken either of these courses, further examination would
probably by late afternoon on the Friday and certainly by the Saturday
morning have elicited the classic signs of pneumonia. This would have been
followed by prompt admission to hospital where x-ray examination would
have revealed the state of the lung, or by then both lungs, and more probably
than not medical intervention would have saved his life.

Per Sedley J: 'It is common ground that the minimum standard of care to be expected of
a trainee general practitioner is no lower than that to be expected of an experienced one....

There is no record of temperature, pulse rate, respiratory rate or blood pressure .... it is
somewhat surprising to learn, as I have done from the expert witnesses, that it is
considered acceptable in general practice not to record such data routinely, if only to
reassure other practitioners who may see that the patient has been properly monitored.
For the present, the harm done by the failure to make a record is exactly that which Dr
Spring now recognises in his own colleagues: the record is equally consistent with
normality or with a failure to do the tests....'

Bovenzi v Kettering Health Authority

D and C: operation: surgeon: pregnancy: damages

Nolan J. [1991] 2 Med LR 293

The plaintiff (Mrs Stephanie Bovenzi), aged 31, was admitted to hospital in Kettering for
the investigation and treatment of a partial miscarriage. She was in her twelfth week of
pregnancy. It was decided that an ERCP (evacuation of retained products of conception)
involving a D and C should be performed.

Mr Asaad, an acting registrar, performed the evacuation with a ten millimetre Karman
catheter. He then inserted polyp forceps to clear up any remaining products, starting with
the left wall of the uterus and working anti-clockwise. As he came to the posterior wall he
found some resistance and, assuming it to be a product, he gripped it and pulled it down so
that it was visible. To his horror, he found that it was not a product of conception but a
piece of small bowel.

An emergency re-section was carried out. There was a six to eight inch tear in the mesentery,
and eleven inches of the bowel were cut away. A one and a half centimetre tear made in
the posterior fundal region of the uterus required two stitches.

The plaintiff spent nine days in hospital. She was fed intravenously, and a drain was attached
to the top of her pubic region. She had problems with her bowels for six months, and had
no sexual relations with her husband until the summer of 1986. Otherwise, apart from the
scar, she made a quick and good recovery. The scar is six inches in length, and the drain
hole is still visible. A medical report in summer 1986 stated that the scar was unsightly and
ridged. A further report in November 1989 described it as sound and well healed, but it still
prevented the plaintiff from wearing a bikini.

The plaintiff sued the hospital authority. Experts on her behalf testified that, in order to pull
down the small bowel, the point of the forceps must have been pushed through the back of
the wall of the uterus (three inches beyond the wall). It was common ground that this would
have been negligent. It was agreed that small bowel damage was so rare as to be outside
the range of normal practice, although Mr Asaad had heard of one colleague in Egypt who
had pulled down the small bowel.

Held (October 1990)   (i)   the plaintiff's expert evidence was compelling. Moreover the extraordinary result supported the theory that it was caused by the defendant's negligence. The plaintiff was entitled to judgment.

(ii)   a suitable award of general damages for pain, suffering and loss of amenities was £6,000. Special damages had been agreed at £1,947.50.

See pp 117, 156.

Bowers v Harrow Health Authority

Brain damage: childbirth: limitation: post traumatic stress disorder: registrar: twins

Sir Michael Davis. [1995] 6 Med LR 16

The plaintiff (Mrs Wendy Bowers), then aged 28, became pregnant with twins. At 2.30am on 30 October 1984 she was admitted to Northwick Park Hospital. At 7.21am the first twin (Clare) was born by spontaneous delivery. Immediately afterwards Dr Brassil, the obstetric registrar, examined the plaintiff's abdomen and concluded that the second twin (Hayley) was presenting by the breech. When he performed a vaginal examination at 7.26am he felt, through the membrane, the left foot and also a hand. He artificially ruptured the membranes and applied traction by pulling on the left foot, but the baby did not descend through the cervix. Hayley's right hand, head and a loop of umbilical cord were also presenting, and he realised that at that stage the lie was transverse. He attempted to turn her head round by external podalic version 'to permit breech extraction', but he was unable to move the head or to change the lie. At 7.33am he decided that the baby would have to be delivered by caesarean section and contacted Mr Webb, the senior obstetric registrar, who arrived at 7.38am. At 7.40am it was found that Hayley's fetal heart beat had dropped to around 60 from a normal rate of about 140. At 7.45am Mr Webb performed a vaginal examination, found that a caesarean section was not required and that the head was in the occipital anterior position with a hand alongside it. He was able to effect a delivery with Wrigleys forceps.

Hayley was found to be hypoxic. She suffered from devastating brain damage, and no normal functions ever developed. Her parents cared for her until her death on 31 July 1991. The plaintiff suffered psychological trauma from the tragic outcome of the pregnancy, her anxiety over Hayley through her short life and her sorrow and distress at its inevitable outcome.

Immediately after the birth the plaintiff was seen by a paediatrician, Dr Briggs, who explained to her what had happened but without any hint of fault on the part of anyone, telling her that 'it was just one of those things'. After seeing a television programme in the summer of 1988, the plaintiff contacted AVMA who put her in touch with solicitors whom she saw in June 1989. They obtained a report from Professor Taylor in mid 1990, which described for the first time the nature of Dr Brassil's acts and omissions. On 27 June and 5 July 1991, Professor Trimble reported that the psychological trauma of and following the birth led to the development of the plaintiff's post traumatic stress disorder and that she had a recognisable psychiatric condition.

On 12 August 1992 the plaintiff sued on behalf of Hayley's estate and in respect of her own psychological injury. Subject to liability, the estate's damages were agreed at £141,392 and her own damages were agreed at £13,000. The defendant hospital authority contested the case on the grounds that Dr Brassil had not been negligent and that the plaintiff's own personal claim was statute-barred.

Held: (i) (a) what went wrong was that the supply of oxygen to Hayley was suddenly, dramatically and disastrously interfered with. This caused her brain damage.

(b) at the critical time, Dr Brassil thought that he had a longitudinal lie and treated it on that basis. The membranes were deliberately and artificially ruptured and traction applied with disastrous results. He ought to have realised that he had a transverse lie and acted conservatively.

(c) he was negligent and did not act in a manner acceptable to reasonable opinion. The presentation of the hand and the foot being felt together clearly established a transverse lie. There was no urgency, and Dr Brassil ought to have acted conservatively. Instead he precipitated a calamitous crisis.

(ii) (a) the plaintiff did not know of the acts and omissions of Dr Brassil until receiving Professor Taylor's report in mid 1990. She did not know that her own injury was capable of being attributed to the events surrounding Hayley's birth until after receipt of Dr Trimble's report in mid 1991. Therefore her court action had been commenced in time.

(b) had it been prima facie statute barred, it would nevertheless have been equitable to allow the case to proceed because the defendants in any event had to investigate and prepare to meet a case on liability due to the claim by the estate, the evidence had not been less cogent than if given five years ago since Dr Brassil would have been just as reliant on his notes and, apart from negligence which had been established in the estate's claim and the limitation point, the plaintiff's case was totally undisputed.

Boxall v Eli Lilly & Co and Others

Drugs: limitation: Opren

Court of Appeal. [1992] 3 Med LR 381

See *Nash v Eli Lilly & Co* (p 466).

Braisher v Harefield and Northwood Hospital Group Management Committee and Another

Diagnosis: casualty officer: x-ray: patient's history: arm

Court of Appeal. (1966) 2 Lancet 235

A piece of metal flew off a machine and entered the plaintiff's arm where it became embedded in fatty tissue. The plaintiff went to hospital where he told a nurse and the casualty officer that he had knocked his arm on some metal. The casualty officer examined the wound and inserted 17 stitches, but he did not see the foreign body. Nor was its presence detected when the stitches were taken out. No x-ray was taken.

The plaintiff's arm continued to cause him pain. Eventually the foreign body rose to the surface and was removed. He sued the hospital authority and the casualty officer. The trial judge found that they had not been negligent.

Held: as the plaintiff said that he had knocked his arm, there was no negligence in not taking x-rays. The appeal was dismissed.

Lord Denning MR observed that in some of the earlier cases doctors had been criticised for not having x-rays taken, with the result that they were sometimes taken unnecessarily. This case showed that the court did not always find that there had been negligence because a patient had not had an x-ray; it depended on the circumstances of each case.

See p 133.

Brazier v Ministry of Defence

Injection: res ipsa loquitur: needle breaking

McNair J. [1965] 1 Lloyd's Rep 26

In December 1956 the plaintiff (Reginald Brazier), a deep-sea diver, contracted an infected right hand while clearing up wrecks in the Suez Canal. He was treated in the sick bay of HMS Forth. When the sick bay attendant, Mr Bradbere, gave him by syringe an injection of procaine penicillin, the fine one and a half inch needle broke and lodged in the plaintiff's right buttock. In October 1960 it shifted to such a position in his groin that it caused him very severe pain and compelled him to give up his diving work.

The plaintiff sued the Ministry of Defence, alleging that Mr Bradbere held the syringe as if it were a dagger and plunged the needle into his buttock from a distance of twelve to eighteen inches, and that he failed to take proper care.

Held: (i)   there was no stabbing by Mr Bradbere with the syringe held in a closed fist; the insertion of the needle was done in the proper recognized manner.

(ii)   the evidence of the needle lodging in the plaintiff's right buttock required an explanation from the defendants as to how it could happen without negligence.

(iii)   they established that it probably happened due to a latent defect in the shaft of the needle, not by some misalignment of the cylinder and the needle at the moment of insertion or during the process of injection.

Judgment for the defendants.

See pp 88, 119.

Breen v Baker

Consent: hysterectomy: assault

Barry J. (1956) Times, 27 January

In November 1947 the plaintiff (Mrs Breen), who had had a fibroid in her uterus for years, suffered a heavy period and other symptoms. She consulted Miss Baker, a surgeon at Elizabeth Garrett Anderson Hospital. She signed a form consenting to an operation which stated, 'I agree to leave the nature and extent of the operation to be performed to the discretion of the surgeon'. On 11 December 1947, after a dilatation and curettage, Miss Baker performed on the plaintiff a total hysterectomy.

The plaintiff sued Miss Baker for assault, alleging that the hysterectomy was performed without her consent, and for negligence in deciding to carry it out.

Breen v Baker

Held: (i) the plaintiff's consent was not limited to curettage, so there was no assault;

(ii) as the defendant was justified in diagnosing fibrosis from the curettings; she was not negligent in deciding to remove the uterus.

Bridges v Cornwall and Isles of Scilly Area Health Authority and Fisher

Dental: operation: jaw: damages

HH Judge Hutchinson. [1992] CLY 1618

The plaintiff (Mrs Bridges) had been suffering from temporo-mandibular arthralgia (pain and stiffness in the jaw) for over a year. In January 1982, when she was aged about 58, Mr Fisher performed an operation known as a condylotomy to the left side of her jaw. This procedure included sawing through the jaw to free its movement. It achieved its intended effect, but there was a large amount of haemorrhaging.

After the operation the left side of the plaintiff's face felt heavy and distorted, with a sensation similar to that produced by an injection of local anaesthetic. This sensation was exacerbated by heat, cold and fatigue. She also suffered from an intermittent itching and prickling sensation. Touching the left side of her face caused an extremely unpleasant feeling, as a result of which she could not bear to be kissed. This led to sexual difficulties within her marriage and eventually a complete cessation of sexual relations. Her speech was affected when she was tired. She experienced pain when food or drink was placed in her mouth. She was unable to keep semi-liquid foods in her mouth so they occasionally fell out, causing her distress and embarrassment.

Held (June 1991): (i) Mr Fisher had performed the operation incompetently, causing damage to an artery, which in turn had caused the bleeding and led to nerve damage.

(ii) general damages of £16,000 were awarded for pain, suffering and loss of amenities.

Britner v North West Regional Health Authority

Sterilisation: peritonitis: damages

Steyn J. [1991] 6 PMILL 76

In July 1981 the plaintiff (Mrs Britner), then aged 27, underwent a routine sterilisation operation which was negligently performed. She contracted peritonitis and had suffered since with serious and chronic abdominal problems including adhesions to the intestinal tract. She had nine hospital admissions and five operations to relieve abdominal obstructions, in addition to a hysterectomy necessitated by the negligence. She also suffered symptoms of chronic pelvic inflammatory disease: lower abdominal pain, pain on defaecation, discomfort on intercourse and increased menstrual loss. The difficulty with intercourse caused great unhappiness, and after a few years intercourse ceased.

She suffered continuing pain in her lower abdomen, radiating into her back, and took daily analgesics. Every one to three months she suffered acute attacks of intestinal colic associated with vomiting, abdominal distension and severe pain. She was unable to return to work and was only able to do her housework between acute attacks. Her whole life had been affected – her married and social life, and her ability to work and care for her children. She still had grossly disfiguring scars from all the surgery. The prognosis was bad: she faced a future of continuing pain and acute attacks, with the possibility of symptoms worsening.

Held (March 1990):   (i)   general damages for pain, suffering and loss of amenities were set at £50,000.

                    (ii) £18,509 was awarded for her past loss of earnings, together with £57,000 for future loss of earnings.

                 (iii) £2,000 was awarded for her husband's loss of earnings occasioned by involvement in her care.

See p 128.

Broadley v Guy Clapham & Co

Limitation: operation: solicitor's: knee

Court of Appeal. [1993] 4 Med LR 328, (1993) Times, 6 July (1993) Independent, 9 September

On 13 August 1980 the plaintiff (Mrs Maureen Broadley) underwent an operation for the removal of a foreign body from her knee. The next day nerve palsy of the left lateral popliteal nerve was noted. She suffered left foot drop. Her post-operative treatment ceased in October 1980.

In June 1983, as a result of a conversation with nurses from a hostel near where she was working, she instructed the defendant solicitor. He arranged for her to be seen in July 1983 by an independent surgeon who told her that the operation might have been negligently conducted. No report was received from this surgeon, and no writ was ever issued by the defendant.

The plaintiff subsequently instructed new solicitors who issued her writ against her former solicitor on 17 August 1990. The defence pleaded limitation, ie, that her cause of action against the defendant occurred before 18 August 1984. Consequently a preliminary trial was ordered as to whether her date of knowledge against the surgeon and health authority under ss 11 and 14 of the Limitation Act 1980 was before 19 August 1981.

Turner J held that it was. The plaintiff appealed. It was argued that her date of knowledge was not reached until she knew of some act or omission, 'such as unreasonable interference with the nerve or failure reasonably to safeguard it from damage, or failure properly to investigate and/or repair the nerve lesion in time'.

Held: (i)   the use of the words 'unreasonable', 'reasonably' and 'properly' could only be justified if s 14(1)(*b*) required knowledge that the injury was attributable to negligence. However it was plain from the concluding words of s 14(1) that knowledge of negligence was irrelevant.

      (ii) it followed that the judge was wrong in *Bentley v Bristol and Weston Health Authority* to hold that knowledge must be proved of the mechanics of damage to a nerve.

     (iii) the plaintiff in this case knew before August 1981, or could have known with the help of reasonably obtainable medical advice, that her injury had been caused by damage to the nerve resulting from some act or omission of the surgeon during the operation. This was all the knowledge or imputed knowledge which she needed to have.

Broadley v Guy Clapham & Co

Per Balcombe LJ: 'In the course of his argument Mr Fenwick, Q.C. for the defendant, submitted that the knowledge of the plaintiff necessary for the purposes of s 14 could be considered under four heads:

(1) *Broad knowledge*

Carrying out the operation to her knee in such a way that something went wrong, namely that it caused foot drop (an injury to her foot).

The judge's findings of fact set out above establish that the plaintiff herself had this broad knowledge by February.

(2) *Specific knowledge*

Carrying out the operation in such a way as to damage a nerve thereby causing foot drop (an injury to her foot).

The judge's findings, which in my judgment are correct, establish that the plaintiff constructively had specific knowledge by 19 August 1981.

(3) *Qualitative knowledge*

Carrying out the operation in such a way as unreasonably to cause injury to a nerve (unreasonably to expose a nerve to a risk of injury).

(4) *Detailed knowledge*

(which I take it to be knowledge sufficiently detailed to enable the plaintiff's advisers to draft a statement of claim).

In my judgment qualitative or detailed knowledge goes beyond the standard necessary for the purposes of s 14 of the 1980 Act.

The judge came to the right answer for the right reasons. I would dismiss this appeal.'

Bentley v Bristol & Weston Health Authority (p 244) overruled.

See pp 184, 187, 198.

Brogan v Bennett

Alternative practitioner: representation: tuberculosis: Ireland

Irish Supreme Court. [1955] IR 119

From January to June 1950 Christopher Brogan was treated in County Longford Tuberculosis Hospital for tuberculosis of both lungs and made good progress towards an eventual recovery. Then there came into his hands a pamphlet entitled 'TB CONQUERED by Mr JH Bennett. . .of Kelly & Bennett, Divining Specialists, Longford'. His uncle and aunt visited Mr Bennett who produced a bullet on the end of a string, said he was going to 'x-ray' the patient, caused the pendulum to oscillate and pronounced the case to be a fairly bad one. He said that he could guarantee to cure Christopher Brogan and make him fit for work in three months' time. He told them his fees were £100 for a rich person and £20 for a poor person. After negotiations, he agreed to take £20 by instalments for the cure of Christopher Brogan.

Mr Bennett insisted that he leave hospital forthwith and return home. He prescribed medicine combined with what was in effect a starvation diet and said that the patient was to have no other food. He never made any detailed enquiry as to Mr Brogan's symptoms; nor did he ever visit him to ascertain his condition. Christopher Brogan left the hospital against his doctor's advice, underwent the rigorous diet and took the medicine which Mr Bennett supplied. His colour became darker, and his face became larger. In September Mr Bennett pronounced him cured. In fact Christopher Brogan was emaciated, and the condition of his lungs showed gross deterioration. On 15 October he died.

His father sued Mr Bennett. The trial judge found as facts that: at no time did the defendant hold himself out as having any professional or academic qualifications in medicine; he represented himself as having special skill and knowledge in the diagnosis, treatment and cure of tuberculosis; in fact the defendant possessed no special skill or knowledge in the diagnosis or treatment of tuberculosis; the death of Christopher Brogan was directly due to his acceptance of the ignorant advice given him by the defendant and to his adoption of the deleterious treatment prescribed by the defendant.

Held: if a person is induced to become a patient of an unqualified person on the recommendation that that person is skilled, the latter owes a duty to use care in exercising the skill and administering the treatment which he has offered. He is not expected to employ the degree of skill which would be expected from a qualified man. He is only liable for failure to employ such skill as he said he had. The defendant was liable because he failed to manifest the skill that he professed in the treatment of tuberculosis.

See pp 47,14.

Brown v Merton, Sutton and Wandsworth Area Health Authority (Teaching)

Childbirth: anaesthetics: quadriplegia: res ipsa loquitur: pleadings

Court of Appeal. (1982) 1 Lancet 159

In January 1979 the plaintiff (Mrs Carol Brown) went into St George's Hospital, Tooting, to be delivered of a child. In the course of preparation for giving birth, she underwent an epidural anaesthesia. She felt severe pain when receiving the second dose of epidural and developed quadriplegia.

The plaintiff sued the health authority and relied on the maxim *res ipsa loquitur*. In the defendants' Further and Better Particulars of the Defence, 'They admit that the maxim quoted is applicable. Enquiries are still being made in an endeavour to find out whether the onus of proof imposed by that maxim can be discharged by the defendants'.

Held: as the pleadings stood, there was no issue on liability; the only issue was as to damage. Therefore the correct order in respect of expert medical evidence was that the plaintiff and the defendants do mutually disclose their medical reports relating to the condition and prognosis of the plaintiff within a limited period, that such reports be agreed if possible, and that if those reports are not agreed the parties be at liberty to call medical witnesses limited to those whose reports have been so disclosed–limited to one witness by agreement.

Buckle v DeLaunay

General practitioner: prescription: warning: depression

Geoffrey Lane J. (1970) 2 Lancet 145

In 1963 and April 1966 Mrs Buckle attended her general practitioner, Dr DeLaunay, for nervous troubles and depression. On 20 June 1966 she was more distressed and felt that she was going to die, so he prescribed parnate, to be taken three times a day in doses of ten milligrammes. He gave her his usual verbal warning about cheese and parnate, saying: 'You must not eat cheese or marmite. That would be serious'. Mrs Buckle understood the warning. However she proceeded to eat some cheese.

On 24 June 1966 she died in hospital as a result of a massive cerebral haemorrhage which was caused by the ingestion of cheese on top of parnate. The plaintiff (her husband) sued Dr DeLaunay.

Held: the danger of parnate reacting unfavourably with cheese was well known, so it was Dr DeLaunay's duty to warn Mrs Buckle of the dangers of eating cheese and to see that she understood the warning. He was under no duty to mention any danger to her, let alone the danger of death. The warning was adequate. Dr DeLaunay had not been negligent.

See p 111.

Bull and Wakeham v Devon Health Authority

Childbirth: hospital administration: limitation: twins

Court of Appeal. [1993] 4 Med LR 117

In 1969 Mrs Pauline Bull, then 20, became pregnant. A twin pregnancy was diagnosed when she was admitted to hospital at 4.30pm on 21 March 1970. She was 33 weeks pregnant but her waters had broken 13 hours earlier. One twin was "vertex in brim" and the other was a breach presentation. She was seen by a senior house officer who was new to the job and by a registrar with five years' experience.

At about 7.30pm the first twin was born. The SHO asked for the registrar on call to be urgently summoned. Brisk vaginal bleeding indicated an emergency. The hospital's gynaecology department was over a mile away. When the registrar had not arrived after 25 minutes, the consultant was summoned. He came as quickly as he could, but an hour had by then elapsed since the birth of the first twin. The second twin was then delivered. He seemed hypoxic and pale. At 18 months, profound mental disability and spastic quadriplegia were diagnosed.

Mrs Bull commenced court action on 23 April 1979. It took another nine years for the case to come to trial. Memories had long faded, and the consultant had died. Her claim for her own damages was dismissed as statute-barred. The trial judge (Tucker J) found in favour of Stuart. The hospital authority appealed.

Held: the hospital's negligence had caused Stuart's brain damage. The system of obstetric cover had given rise to a real inherent risk that an obstetrician might not have attended reasonably promptly after the birth of the first twin. There had been no proved explanation for the inordinate delay.

See pp 24, 126, 131, 189, 200.

Burgess v Newcastle Health Authority

Operation: surgeon: head

Turner J. [1992] 3 Med LR 224

For some years before September 1981 the plaintiff (Anthony Burgess), then aged 60, had been suffering symptoms attributable to a hydrocephalus which in turn was caused by the presence of a benign colloidal cyst situated in the third ventricle. Accordingly on 9

September 1981 Mr Sengupta, the neurosurgeon, assisted by his registrar Dr Sastri, at the Newcastle General Hospital, performed a right frontal craniotomy for the microsurgical removal of the cyst. Although the operation was performed with the requisite degree of care and skill, it became apparent over the ensuing days that a degree of hydrocephalus persisted.

Consequently a 'bilateral shunt' operation was performed by Dr Sastri unsupervised, in an attempt to relieve the hydrocephalus. The catheter which he left in position in the Sylvian Fissure represented his third attempt to locate it in an appropriate site. The plaintiff suffered a right sided hemiplegia and aphasia from which he made only a partial recovery. He alleged that (a) the technique of cannulation of both lateral ventricles with the head turned to the left for the insertion into the right lateral ventricle was not one which would be practised or approved by any reasonable body of neurosurgeons and (b) the stilette which was used to carry the catheter forward on the left side was taken some 12 centimetres into the skull and ended in brain substance where its position was lateral to the frontal horn of the ventricle.

Held: (i) Dr Sastri was, unsupervised, competent to perform a bilateral shunt operation.

(ii) the plaintiff was positioned on the operating table with his head rotated to the left resting on a horse shoe collar. The midline of the head was horizontal.

(iii) Dr Sastri opened two burr holes either side of the midline in the positions shown life size in the occipital x-ray. These burr holes were not quite equidistant from the midline, and they were at differing heights above the external occipital protuberance. There is no significance in these (minor) deviations. They do not in themselves connote deficient procedure, nor make it more likely that the insertion of the cannula would enter the deeper structures of the brain. The track of the left catheter commenced at a higher point above the protuberance; the anterior point of termination was at approximately the same vertical level as that on the right. The tract was thus less likely to interfere with the vulnerable areas of the brain. The track was lateral to the intended line but, even so, did not trespass into areas of the brain that were of particular vulnerability.

(iv) the technique adopted by Dr Sastri of not moving the head during the operation was acceptable to a widely respected body of neurosurgeons.

(v) Dr Sastri did not insert or endeavour to insert the cannula on the left to a depth greater than seven centimetres. The track so made just impinged on the left Sylvian Fissure.

(vi) Dr Sastri inserted the catheter through the track so made.

(vii) Dr Sastri obtained a flow of CSF both when he passed the cannula and the catheter from the Sylvian Fissure. The tip of the catheter did not rest in brain substance. The fact that the catheter ended up in the Sylvian Fissure did not raise any suspicion let alone presumption of negligence against him.

(viii) the plaintiff's neurological deficits recorded in the hospital records resulted, on balance, from spasm of the middle cerebral artery located in the Sylvian Fissure when the advancing catheter made contact with it.

(ix) although the result of the bilateral shunt operation was not intended and was imperfect, that was not due to any relevant fault on the part of Dr Sastri.

Burke v Tower Hamlets Health Authority

Childbirth: caesarian: damages: structured settlement: brain damage

Drake J. (1989) Times 10 August

The plaintiff (Elaine Burke) sustained brain damage during a caesarian operation at the London Hospital. She applied for an order that her damages should take the form of periodical payments (ie a form of structured settlement). The defendant health authority objected.

Held: the court has no power to order periodical payments instead of a lump sum, except where both parties consent. The order could not be made in the face of the defendant's opposition.

See p 116, 151.

Burridge v Bournemouth and East Dorset Hospital Management Committee

Diagnosis: appendicitis: registrar: causation

Cumming-Bruce J. (1965) 1 Lancet 1065

At about 6.00am on 9 October 1961 the general practitioner to the plaintiff (Mr Burridge) sent for an ambulance and telephoned the hospital stating that it was an acute case of appendicitis. The plaintiff was put to bed in a ward. Soon afterwards his pain subsided. At 8.10am he was seen by the house surgeon who considered his symptoms and history insufficient to arouse suspicions of an inflamed appendix. He was examined during the day by the house surgeon again and twice by the surgical registrar.

At 10.00am on 10 October the plaintiff was examined by the surgical registrar. At 11.00am he was examined by the senior surgical registrar who at once diagnosed appendicitis and operated at 12.15pm, removing the gangrenous appendix.

The plaintiff sued the hospital authority, alleging that the delay in performing the appendicectomy permitted the appendix to rupture causing severe peritonitis.

Held: (i) it seemed probable that an acute obstruction of the appendix in the early hours of 9 October subsided but that the condition flared during the night of 9–10 October. There was no factor compelling a diagnosis of appendicitis while the plaintiff was in hospital on 9 October, and the hospital staff had not been negligent then;

    (ii) the surgical registrar negligently failed to take any steps after 10.00am on 10 October. However the resultant delay of one hour did not cause any part of the damage.

Judgment for the defendants.

See p 68, 97.

Burton v Islington Health Authority, Re de Martell v Merton and Sutton Health Authority

Childbirth: foetus' rights: Congenital Disabilities (Civil Liability) Act 1976: D and C

Court of Appeal. [1993] QB 204, [1992] 3 All ER 833, [1992] 3 WLR 637, [1993] 4 Med LR 8, [1992] PIQR P269, 136 Sol Jo LB 104

On 26 April 1967 Tina Burton was born with abnormalities. It was alleged that these were due to negligence by medical staff at the Whittington Hospital, London, in performing a dilation and curettage on her mother on 6 September 1966.

On 5 February 1967 Christopher de Martell was born at St Helier Hospital in Carshalton, suffering from severe physical disabilities. He alleged that these disabilities were caused by negligence on the part of the medical staff who attended his mother's confinement and his birth.

The defendant hospital authorities argued that the plaintiffs had no legal status at the times of the alleged negligence and, accordingly, no right to sue.

Held: (i)   the fact that the Congenital Disabilities (Civil Liability) Act 1976 deliberately refrained from legislating for cases arising before its enactment simply meant that these cases were to be left to the previous law.

        (ii)   the previous law was that, when a child not actually born at the time of a tort was subsequently born alive and viable, it was clothed with all the rights of action which it would have had if alive at the date of the tort.

Busuttill-Reynaud v Eli Lilly & Co and Others

Limitation: drugs: Opren

Court of Appeal. [1992] 3 Med LR 396

See *Nash v Eli Lilly & Co* O (p 466).

Re C (adult: refusal of treatment)

Consent: gangrene: injunction: prison inmate: amputation: schizophrenia

Thorpe J. [1994] 1 WLR 290, [1993] NLJR 1642, (1993) Times, 15 October, (1993) Independent, 15 October

The plaintiff (C) was 68 and of Jamaican origin. He came to England in 1956, his passage having been paid by the woman with whom he had lived since 1949. In 1961 she left him, and in 1962 he accosted her at work and after an altercation stabbed her. He was sentenced at the Old Bailey to seven years' imprisonment. While serving that sentence, he was diagnosed as mentally ill and transferred from Brixton to Broadmoor. On admission he was diagnosed as suffering from chronic paranoid schizophrenia. He mellowed over the years and was accommodated on an open ward of the parole house.

On 9 September 1993 the Broadmoor surgeon diagnosed gangrene in his right foot and transferred him to Heatherwood Hospital in Ascot. Mr Rutter, the consultant vascular

267

surgeon at Heatherwood, found a grossly infected leg with a necrotic ulcer covering the whole of the dorsum. He advised that the leg be amputated below the knee. C refused saying that he would rather die with two feet than live with one. Thereafter Mr Rutter negotiated more conservative treatment with C. On 22 September he obtained his consent to debridement of the dead tissue. The operation was performed on 23 September and was successful.

On 29 September C requested an undertaking that Heatherwood Hospital would not amputate his leg in any future circumstances, in recognition of his repeated refusals. This request was refused. C issued an originating summons seeking an injunction to prevent the hospital from amputating his right leg without his express written consent.

During his testimony, C expressed the grandiose delusion of an international career in medicine during the course of which he had never lost a patient. He expressed complete confidence in his ability to survive his present trials aided by God, the good doctors and the good nurses. He did not ascribe the condition of his foot to persecution by authority. He expressed his repeated objection to amputation and accepted the possibility of death as a consequence of retaining his limb. Mr Rutter testified that he would not amputate without C's consent, although he believed that the condition of the foot would once again threaten C's life.

Held: (i)   prima facie every adult has the right and capacity to decide whether or not he will accept medical treatment, even if a refusal may risk permanent injury to his health or even lead to premature death. A refusal can take the form of a declaration of intention never to consent in the future or never to consent in some future circumstances.

          (ii)   although C's general capacity was impaired by his schizophrenia, it had not been established that he did not sufficiently understand the nature, purpose and effects of the treatment he refused. Indeed, (a) he had understood and retained the relevant treatment information, (b) in his own way he believed it, and (c) in the same fashion he had arrived at a clear choice.

          (iii)   whilst the need for the injunction might be questioned after Mr Rutter's evidence, it would safeguard C against the possibility of Mr Rutter moving on. Further, an injunction binds a non-party with knowledge of its effect, so that its terms would protect C were he ever treated elsewhere.

C was granted the injunction that he sought.

See pp 9, 16, 47.

C and Another v S and Others

Abortion:- foetus' rights: father's status: parental objections

Court of Appeal. [1988] QB 135, [1987] 1 All ER 1230, [1987] 2 WLR 1108

In 1985 Mr C, a postgraduate student, met Miss S, a university student. In October 1986 their child was conceived. Miss S was X-rayed twice, on one occasion unshielded, before a scan showed in January 1987 that she was pregnant. In February her college doctor and a hospital consultant duly signed the certificate required under the Abortion Act 1967.

Mr C (the first plaintiff) applied on his own behalf and on behalf of the foetus named as 'a child *en ventre sa mère*' (the second plaintiff) for orders restraining Miss S from having the abortion or harming the foetus and the area health authority from carrying out the abortion or harming the foetus. Miss S was at least eighteen weeks' pregnant.

His case was that termination of the pregnancy at that stage would involve a criminal offence under s 1(1) of the Infant Life (Preservation) Act 1929, the provisions of which are unaffected by the Abortion Act 1967. The medical evidence was that a foetus of a gestational age between eighteen and twenty-one weeks could be said to demonstrate real and discernible signs of life but, if delivered then, would never be able to breathe.

Heilbron J dismissed the applications and held that a foetus cannot until birth be a party to court action. The first plaintiff appealed.

Held: the foetus was not 'a child capable of being born alive' within the meaning of s 1(1) of the 1929 Act. Accordingly the termination of the pregnancy would not constitute a criminal offence. The appeal was dismissed.

See p 55.

Caldeira v Gray

Injection: malaria: sciatic nerve: tropical disease: Trinidad

Privy Council. [1936] 1 All ER 540, (1936) Times, 15 February

In March 1930 the respondent (Frederick Gray) was being treated in Trinidad for malaria by the appellant (Dr Caldeira). Dr Caldeira gave him a quinine injection by inserting the needle of a hypodermic syringe into his right buttock. Immediately Mr Gray got off the operation bed, he walked with a dropped right foot and had to cling to Dr Caldeira for support. Mr Gray was permanently lamed. He sued Dr Caldeira on the ground that he had travelled beyond the safe area for injection and injured his sciatic nerve.

Held: the trial judge's finding of negligence was upheld.

See p 120.

Canterbury v Spence and Washington Hospital Center

Risk disclosure: informed consent: prudent patient test: causation: paraplegia: USA: spinal

US Court of Appeals, District of Columbia Circuit 464 F 2d 772 (1972).

In December 1958 the plaintiff (Jerry Canterbury), aged 19, began to experience severe pain between his shoulder blades. He was referred to Dr Spence, a neurosurgeon. In early February 1959 a myleogram was performed. Following this, Dr Spence told the plaintiff that he would have to undergo a laminectomy to correct what he suspected was a ruptured disc. The plaintiff neither objected to the proposed operation nor probed into its exact nature. When his widowed mother asked if the operation was serious, Dr Spence replied 'not any more than any other operation'. She signed a consent form. He did not tell either of them that there was a one per cent risk of paralysis inherent in the laminectomy operation.

Dr Spence performed the laminectomy on 11 February 1959 at the Washington Hospital Center. On 12 February the plaintiff fell from his hospital bed. A few hours after the fall, the lower half of his body was paralysed. He became permanently disabled.

The plaintiff sued Dr Spence and the hospital on the ground, *inter alia*, that Dr Spence negligently failed to disclose a risk of serious disability inherent in the operation. At the end of the plaintiff's case in chief, the trial judge directed that verdicts for the defendants be entered. The plaintiff appealed.

Held: (i)   every human being of adult years and sound mind has a right to determine what shall be done with his own body. True consent is the informed exercise of a choice. This requires a reasonable divulgence by physician to patient to make such a decision possible. The physician must warn of dangers lurking in the proposed treatment and impart information which the patient has every right to expect.

(ii) any definition of the scope of the duty to disclose in terms purely of medical professional standards is at odds with the patient's prerogative to decide on projected therapy himself. The law itself must set the standard for adequate disclosure.

(iii) the test for determining whether a particular peril must be divulged is its materiality to the patient's decision. A risk is material when a reasonable person, in what the physician knows or should know to be the patient's position, would be likely to attach significance to the risk or cluster of risks in deciding whether or not to forgo the proposed therapy. The main factors are the incidence of injury and the degree of harm threatened. A very small chance of death or serious disablement may well be significant.

(iv) the issue of causation should be resolved on an objective basis: in terms of what a prudent person in the patient's position would have decided, if adequately informed of all significant perils. The patient's testimony on this is relevant but should not dominate the findings.

(v) the jury should be the final arbiter of whether Dr Spence's non-disclosure was reasonable under the circumstances. A retrial was ordered.

See p 107.

Carter v City and Hackney Health Authority

Biopsy: gall bladder: laparotomy: liver

Mrs Justice Smith. (1994) AVMA Journal, Summer, p 6

In 1988 the plaintiff (Mr Carter) underwent a liver biopsy at St Bartholome's Hospital. This involved inserting a six to seven inch needle through his rib cage into the liver, in order to remove tissue for analysis. The doctor performing the procedure had had his arm in a sling for the previous few days due to a shoulder injury, although he was not wearing the sling on the day of the biopsy. He made three attempts to obtain liver tissue, adjusting the angle of the needle each time. Not only was he unsuccessful, but also he punctured the plaintiff's gall bladder. Subsequently there was an extensive leakage of bile which necessitated removal of the gall bladder by laparotomy three days later. The plaintiff was left with an eight inch scar along his abdomen and a predisposition to dyspepsia.

Held: (i) the argument that the doctor should not have carried out the procedure at all because of his injury was not accepted.

(ii) the needle had probably transversed the liver.

(iii) the doctor had negligently failed (a) to percuss the plaintiff properly and (b) to identify the middle area of the liver into which it would have been safe to insert the biopsy needle.

See p 120.

Cassel v Riverside Health Authority

Childbirth: Court of Protection: damages: receiver

Court of Appeal [1992] PIQR, Q168

The plaintiff (Hugo Cassel) was born in September 1982. Shortly before and after his birth he was severely asphyxiated. He suffered cerebral palsy, causing grave and irreparable brain damage. The defendant health authority submitted to judgment on liability for 90% of the value of his claim.

The plaintiff was mobile and of normal build. He could walk reasonably well, but could not run properly. He was clumsy and doubly incontinent. His mental age was that of a two or three year old. He would never be able to live independently, marry or work. There was a chance that his sleep patterns might improve in his teens. With optimum help he might, in time, be able to function as a four to five year old. He is likely to live until 65 or more.

In December 1990 Rose J awarded him a total of £1,191,990 including interest, broken down as follows:

SUMMARY OF AWARD

	Gross award	Net award (90%)	One-off costs	Not specifically allocated	Recurring costs Phase 1	Phase 2
	£	£	£		£ pa	£ pa
General damages	110,000>	99,000:		99,000		
Past care	95,751>	86,176:				
Future care	508,564>	457,708:			21,088	28,528
Future accommodation	45,500>	40,950:				
Future miscellaneous:						
– One-off appliances	2,702>	2,432:	2,432			
– Medical	5,000>	4,500:			250	250
– Extra purchases	13,014>	11,712:			651	651
– Educational toys	2,625>	2,362:			315	–
– Other	42,966>	8,670:			2,148	2,148
Future earnings	350,000>	315,000:		315,000		
	1,176,122>	1,058,510:				
Receiver		47,700:			2,650	2,650
Court of Protection		32,700:			1,817	1,817
Interest		53,080:	53,080			
					28,919	36,044
					x 7.5 =	x 10.5 =
TOTAL AWARD		1,191,990	182,638	414,000	216,892	378,460

The defendants appealed against (i) the award for loss of future earnings, (ii) the cost of building a swimming pool, (iii) the cost of sleeping attendance, and (iv) the failure to deduct 10% from the Court of Protection and receivers' costs.

Held: (i) in view of the plaintiff's very favourable family pattern, the judge was entitled to find that he might well have entered a profession or earned a similar income elsewhere at a net average of £35,000pa from the ages of 22 to 65. There was no justification for taking the national average earnings figures, even uplifted by 50%, as a basis of calculation. Since the multiplier allowing for accelerated receipt alone would have been 10.19, the judge's multiplier of 10 was high but not outside the acceptable range.

(ii) there was no expert evidence that the swimming pool was required for therapy rather than enjoyment. This item should be disallowed.

(iii) the uncertainty of the prognosis as to the chance of an improvement in the plaintiff's sleeping pattern did not justify a reduction in the cost of those employed to sleep at his house and look after him at night.

(iv) the fees of the Court of Protection and the professional receiver formed part of the damages, not of the costs of the action. As such, they were subject to the agreed deduction of 10%.

See pp 154, 162, 163.

Cassidy v Ministry of Health

Operation: surgeon: vicarious liability: res ipsa loquitur: hand

Court of Appeal. [1951] 2 KB 343, [1951] 1 All ER 574

The plaintiff (Michael Cassidy) was a 56-year-old labourer when in 1948 he found that the little finger and the ring finger of his left hand were becoming stiff and bent inwards. His panel doctor, Dr Flanagan, diagnosed Dupuytren's contracture and sent him to Walton Hospital. On 8 April 1948 he was operated on there by Dr Fahrni, a full-time assistant medical officer of the hospital. After the operation a nurse bandaged his hand and arm to a splint. The plaintiff complained of exceptional pain and was seen by Dr Ronaldson, a house surgeon, who instructed that morphia be administered. On 12 April Dr Fahrni examined the hand and decided to leave the splint and bandage as they were. Thereafter the plaintiff continued to complain of excessive pain, but Dr Fahrni told him he must put up with it. When the splint was finally removed a fortnight after the operation, it was found that the plaintiff had lost the use of all four fingers which had become stiff and bent into the hand.

The plaintiff sued the hospital authority. The trial judge (Streatfield J) dismissed his claim.

Held: the evidence showed a prima-facie case of negligence which had not been rebutted. The defendants were liable whichever of their employees had been negligent.

Per Denning LJ: 'When hospital authorities undertake to treat a patient and themselves select and appoint and employ the professional men and women who are to give the treatment, they are responsible for the negligence of those persons in failing to give proper treatment, no matter whether they are doctors, surgeons, nurses or anyone else.

'. . . I think it depends on this: Who employs the doctor or surgeon? Is it the patient or the hospital authorities? If the patient himself selects and employs the doctor and surgeon, as in *Hillyer's* case, the hospital authorities are, of course, not liable for his negligence, because he is not employed by them. Where, however, the doctor or surgeon, be he a consultant or not, is employed and paid, not by the patient, but by the hospital authorities, I am of opinion that the hospital authorities are liable for his negligence in treating the patient. . .

'If the patient had to prove that some particular doctor or nurse was negligent, he would not be able to do it, but he was not put to that impossible task. He says: "I went into the hospital to be cured of two stiff fingers. I have come out with four stiff fingers, and my hand is useless. That should not have happened if due care had been used. Explain it, if you can". I am quite clearly of the opinion that that raises a *prima-facie* case against the hospital authorities'.

See pp 19, 22, 23, 44, 87, 117, 131.

Cavanagh v Bristol and Weston Health Authority

After-care: ophthalmic: surgeon

Macpherson J. [1992] 3 Med LR 49

The plaintiff (Patrick Cavanagh) first noticed trouble in his right eye in October 1983 and was told this was due to a haemorrhage. In autumn 1984 scarring of the retina was seen after the haemorrhage cleared. In January 1985 at the Bristol Eye Hospital Mr Grey performed the operation of right vitrectomy and the removal of pre-retinal fibrous membranes. The plaintiff suffered a low grade post-operative infection. By May 1985 the right retina was totally detached and heavily infiltrated by inflammatory cells. On 3 May 1985 Mr Grey again admitted the plaintiff to the Bristol Hospital and performed upon the right eye a vitreous cavity aspiration, removal of membrane from the retinal surface and gas insufflation.

On 12 June 1985, when the plaintiff attended Mr Grey's retinal clinic for the last time, Mr Grey told him that his right eye would never see again, said that he would arrange a second opinion and that after that he would send for the plaintiff to see him again. Consequently on 15 July 1985 the plaintiff saw Mr Leaver at Moorfields Eye Hospital. Mr Leaver agreed with Mr Grey's conclusion and wrote on 18 July to Mr Grey to confirm this. The letter recommended continuation of steroid drops and indicated that there was still inflammation. However no follow-up appointment was arranged at the Bristol Eye Hospital. On 15 November, by when his right eye was unsightly and blind, the plaintiff began to lose sight in his left eye. Mr Audry at Oxford Eye Hospital promptly admitted him for enucleation (surgical removal of the right eye) on the basis that he was suffering from sympathetic ophthalmitis. Despite this, by early 1986 the plaintiff was blind in both eyes.

Held: (i)   after 12 June 1985 Mr Grey and all involved at the Bristol Eye Hospital failed to follow up the plaintiff after the second opinion came to them from Mr Leaver. If he had been examined again, even at monthly intervals after July, his deterioration would at once have been seen or at least he would have been properly alerted to the need to go to the hospital or to his doctor without waiting to be summoned should there be any deterioration or further problems. There had been a breach of the hospital authority's duty of care.

(ii)   but for this, by late October 1985 the plaintiff's right eye would have been enucleated. This would probably have prevented the onset of sympathetic ophthalmitis in the left eye.

Judgment was given for the plaintiff with damages to be assessed.

See p 118.

Champion v Grimsby Health Authority

Damages: diagnosis: fractures: arm

McCullough J. [1992] CLY 1680

In November 1978 the plaintiff (Elizabeth Champion), then six and a half years old, was injured in a PT lesson at school. She suffered a Monteggia fracture – a fracture of the left ulna, with dislocation of the head of the radius. The Grimsby District General Hospital treated the fracture of the ulna, but did not at the time diagnose the dislocation of the head of the radius. This diagnosis was only made in February 1980, too late for effective treatment. Had the dislocation been diagnosed immediately, there would have been a good chance that successful treatment would have given the plaintiff a completely healthy arm and elbow within the three months that it took for the fracture to heal.

After this period, the plaintiff did not initially suffer any particular symptoms and was able to live a normal life. In February 1980 a lump caused by dislocation was noticed. Even so, the plaintiff did not suffer any problems of pain and loss of function until after a period of rapid growth. By February 1985, at age 13, she was suffering symptoms of pain. These continued during adolescence until she became physically mature. Thereafter she continued to suffer some discomfort which sometimes became painful. The discomfort hindered her in certain activities, such as looking after her young baby. Whilst there was no risk of arthritis or further deterioration, there was also no chance of improvement.

Held (July 1992):　　(i)　£8,000 was awarded for pain, suffering and loss of amenities.

(ii)　a further £2,500 was awarded for future handicap on the labour market.

The total award was £10,500.

See pp 96, 155.

Chapman v Rix

Diagnosis: cottage hospital: general practitioner: communication: peritonitis: fatal

House of Lords. (1960) Times, 22 December

In October 1955 Edward Chapman, a butcher employed by Sainsbury's, was boning a piece of beef with a boning knife when the knife slipped and caused a wound in his abdomen. A telephone call for a doctor was made to Brentwood District Hospital, a general practitioners' (or 'cottage') hospital. Dr Rix received the call and promptly went to Sainsbury's shop. He felt around the wound and decided that it was glancing, forming the view that the knife had not penetrated the abdominal wall. At the hospital he conducted a further examination with a probe, told Mr Chapman that the wound was superficial and sent him home with emphatic instructions to see his own doctor, Dr Moore, that evening and to tell him what had happened and what had been done.

When Dr Moore called, Mr Chapman complained of stomach pains and nausea. Dr Moore did not know that Brentwood Hospital was a general practitioners' hospital and was under the impression that the diagnosis of a superficial wound had emanated from the casualty department of a fully staffed hospital. Consequently he thought Mr Chapman was suffering from a digestive disorder and prescribed liquid paraffin.

The next day Mr Chapman was worse. Dr Moore ordered him to be taken to Oldchurch Hospital where fulminating peritonitis was diagnosed. An operation was performed which revealed a half-inch wound of the small bowel. Unfortunately the diagnosis had come too late and Mr Chapman died on 23 October.

The plaintiff (his widow) claimed damages against Dr Rix. The trial judge (Barry J) found that Dr Rix's diagnosis was wrong but not negligent, as it was extremely difficult to ascertain the depth of an abdominal wound. Nor was Dr Rix negligent in not sending Mr Chapman to hospital, since close observation could be carried out at home by a nurse or a relation apprised of symptoms for which he or she must watch. However he considered that Dr Rix was negligent in not contacting Dr Moore to inform him of the exact nature of his findings.

Held:　　Dr Rix had given the patient emphatic instructions (which were carried out), an object of which must have been to guard, by observation, against the outside chance that penetration of the peritoneal cavity had occurred. If he had contacted Dr Moore direct, it was doubtful that he would have told him more than that after observation and probing he had concluded that there was no penetration. Dr Rix was not liable.

See pp 44, 98, 134.

Chatterton v Gerson and Another

Risk disclosure: consent: battery: causation: pain relief: anaesthetics

Bristow J. [1981] QB 432, [1981] 1 All ER 257, [1980] 3 WLR 1003

In February 1974 the plaintiff (Miss Elizabeth Chatterton) underwent, at the age of 55, a nylon darn repair operation for an inguinal hernia. Subsequently she suffered severe and chronic intractable pain around the post-operative scar in her right groin.

She was then referred to Dr Gerson, a consultant anaesthetist who ran a pain clinic at the Royal Sussex County Hospital. He advised an intrathecal phenol solution injection to block the pain. He told her that this would involve numbness over an area larger than the pain source itself, and might involve temporary loss of muscle power. The plaintiff consented, and Dr Gerson performed the operation in August 1974. After temporary relief the pain returned and she became numb down her right leg.

In February 1975 Dr Gerson put her name down for a repeat intrathecal block. He did not repeat his warning, simply telling her that the second operation would be a repeat of the first and she knew what to expect. In June 1975 the plaintiff had the second intrathecal phenol solution nerve block operation. Afterwards she continued to suffer acute pain in the scar area and could not tolerate clothing in contact with it. She also lost feeling in her right leg and could only move around with a stick.

She sued Dr Gerson and the East Sussex Health Authority for (i) battery, alleging that her consent to the operation was vitiated by lack of consent, and (ii) negligence, not in treatment, but in an alleged failure to give a reasonable explanation of the nature and implications of the operation.

Held: (i) (Battery) 'It is clear law that in any context in which consent of the injured party is a defence to what would otherwise be a crime or a civil wrong the consent must be real . . . In my judgment what the court has to do in each case is to look at all the circumstances and say "Was there a real consent?" I think that justice requires that in order to vitiate the reality of consent there must be a greater failure of communication between doctor and patient than that involved in a breach of duty if the claim is based on negligence. When the claim is based on negligence the plaintiff must prove not only the breach of duty to inform, but that had the duty not been broken she would not have chosen to have the operation. Where the claim is based on trespass to the person, once it is shown that the consent is unreal, then what the plaintiff would have decided if she had been given the information which would have prevented vitiation of the reality of her consent is irrelevant.

'In my judgment, once the plaintiff is informed in broad terms of the nature of the procedure which is intended, and gives her consent, that consent is real, and the cause of the action on which to base a claim for failure to go into risks and implications is negligence, not trespass. . . it would be very much against the interests of justice if actions which are really based on a failure by the doctor to perform his duty adequately to inform were pleaded in trespass.

'In this case in my judgment, even taking the plaintiff's evidence at its face value, she was under no illusion as to the general nature of what an intrathecal injection of phenol solution nerve block would be, and in the case of each injection her consent was not unreal';

(ii) (Negligence) the duty of the doctor is to explain what he intends to do, and its implications, in the way a careful and responsible doctor in similar circumstances would have done. Dr Gerson did not fall short of his duties in this respect. Moreover the plaintiff had not proved that, even if she had been further informed, she would have chosen not to have the operation since the whole picture was of a lady desperate for pain relief.

Her action failed both in battery and in negligence.

See pp 6, 8, 68, 105, 106, 113.

Chaunt v Hertfordshire Area Health Authority

Sterilisation (failed): registrar: abortion: hysterectomy: damages

Park J. (1982) 132 NLJ 1054

In February 1973 the plaintiff, who had a complicated gynaecological history, was admitted to hospital for a laparoscopic sterilisation. This operation was performed by a registrar on the misunderstanding that it was not a difficult case. In or about June 1974 she became pregnant. In August 1974 the pregnancy was terminated and a laparoscopic sterilisation was performed by a consultant in private practice. She experienced some pain for two to three days following the sterilisation. Later her periods became painful and their frequency increased. On finding also that fibroids were present in her uterus, her doctor and specialist advised vaginal hysterectomy.

The hysterectomy was performed in July 1975. Afterwards the plaintiff suffered intraperitoneal bleeding which the defendants failed to detect for five days. On 6 July a laparotomy was performed and two and a half litres of blood were sucked from her abdominal cavity. On 8 July she was transferred to Hammersmith Hospital where the diagnosis was 'post-operative bacteriods infection with septacaemia, general peritonitis, bronchopneumonia and pleurisy'.* She was on artificial respiration in intensive care and was finally discharged on 11 September 1975. In January 1977 she was readmitted to Hammersmith Hospital because of pelvic infection. She was treated with antibiotics but continued to have periodical bouts of pelvic infection thereafter.

Held (February 1982):   (i) general damages of £2,000 were awarded for the negligent sterilisation, for the unwanted pregnancy and the two further operations in August 1974. However no damages were awarded for the hastened hysterectomy, since the plaintiff would have needed this anyway at some stage.

(ii) general damages of £5,000 were awarded in respect of the negligent after-care following the hysterectomy for the septicaemia etc and bouts of pelvic infection.

*Note: This quotation is reproduced intact from the law report, although the authors are advised that the normal formulation would be 'post-operative bacterial infection with septicaemia'.

See p 128.

Chin Keow v Government of Malaysia and Another

Injection: penicillin: patient's history: standard of care: Malaysia

Privy Council. [1967] 1 WLR 813

In April 1960 Madam Chu Wai Lian, an amah employed at a social hygiene clinic in Kuala Lumpur, spoke to the staff nurse there about an ulcer on her right ankle and swollen glands in her thigh. The nurse took her to Dr Devadason, the medical officer in charge of the clinic. After he had examined her, she was given an injection of procaine penicillin from which she died within an hour. Her mother, the appellant, claimed damages.

In 1958 the deceased had been given a penicillin injection from which she suffered adverse reactions. This led to her outpatient card being endorsed with the warning 'allergic to penicillin'. Dr Devadason did not enquire into her medical history and ascertain this. He admitted that he knew of the possibility of a person developing hypersensitivity to pencillin after a previous injection and that he had been told by the nurse that the deceased had had a penicillin injection some years ago. He testified that he carried on because he had had no mishaps before.

Held: the test of negligence, as propounded in *Bolam* v *Friern Hospital Management Committee*, was based on the standard of the ordinary competent practitioner exercising ordinary professional skill. Consequently, evidence from witnesses of the highest professional standing or references to writings of distinguished medical authorities were not necessary. The evidence of medical witnesses at the trial made it clear that Dr Devadason was negligent in failing to make appropriate enquiry before causing the penicillin injection to be given.

See pp 60, 65, 95, 134.

Christie v Somerset Health Authority

Dental: house surgeon: operation: lingual nerve

Sir Michael Ogden QC. [1992] 3 Med LR 75

The plaintiff (Mr Christie) underwent an operation for removal of wisdom teeth at a hospital in Taunton. It was carried out by two young senior house officers. A flap on the buccal side of the left lower wisdom tooth was raised. An elevator (or retractor) was used to create the flap and was then kept in position between the burr on the drill and the nerve to act as a guard. The drill was used to remove some bone and to section the tooth into two, following which the tooth was elevated and removed. During the course of this operation, the plaintiff's lingual nerve was damaged. This resulted in almost complete loss of sense of taste, numbness of the tongue and other unpleasant consequences.

Some time after the operation, he travelled to see Mr Blackburn, an expert who explored the nerve and reported that the fascicles within it were disrupted. He saw two or three fascicles, instead of the four or five that there ought to have been.

The plaintiff sued the hospital authority who accepted that if either the burr came into contact with the nerve or the elevator was inserted in the wrong position and thereby crushed or ripped the nerve, then this was negligent. Their expert testified that the nerve was damaged, in the course of creating the flap, by careful and necessary stretching of the band of tissues in which the nerve was situated.

Held: (i)   the papers referred to in the defendants' expert's report related to tests on the nerves of rabbits and rats, involving application of considerable force. The evidence available to him amounted to nothing more than a possibility that such a theory was valid.

          (ii) a fascicle was severed. Direct trauma to the nerve occurred. It probably happened when the distolingual bone was being removed. It was unnecessary to determine whether the injury was caused by the retractor or the burr. Either explanation signified negligence.

The plaintiff was awarded agreed damages of £14,000.

Chrzanowska v Glaxo Laboratories Ltd

Group litigation: drugs: costs: product liability

Steyn J. [1990] 1 Med LR 385

The plaintiff (Barbara Chrzanowska) was injected with Myodil, an oil-based contrast medium, for the purpose of myelography. Subsequently she became severely disabled and was confined to a wheelchair. Her case was that this resulted from the oily nature of Myodil which remained in the body for many years and caused arachnoiditis.

She obtained legal aid and issued a writ against the manufacturers. It was anticipated that a large number of plaintiffs would follow suit and that, in due course, health authorities and individual doctors would be joined in the litigation.

The plaintiff applied for (i) the appointment of a single judge to hear all applications and the trial of the proposed actions and (ii) an order that any costs incurred or ordered to be paid by any plaintiff in the actions should be paid equally by all the plaintiffs.

Held: (i)   an assignment of a judge to hear group litigation in the Queen's Bench Division was a matter for the Lord Chief Justice. In the meantime, all applications in the Myodil litigation arising for hearing on the Northern Circuit were to be reserved for hearing before the two presiding judges on that Circuit.

(ii)   any costs ordered to be paid by or which fell to be borne by any plaintiff in the group litigation should, unless the court ordered otherwise, be paid or borne in equal proportion by each of the plaintiffs.

Per Steyn J: 'At present English law does not permit a class action in the sense in which that expression is used in the United States. Admittedly our law does recognise, by virtue of RSC Order 15, r 12, the notion of a representative action, the objective of which is one binding judgment on common questions, instead of a multiplicity of separate determinations. That procedure is no doubt capable of development, but its present limitations are such that it cannot be used where damages have to be separately assessed in respect of different cases. It seems that representative actions for damages are not permitted. In England the parties must use the ordinary procedures, devised for the trial of single actions, to cope with the exigencies of group litigation.'

See pp 32, 122.

Ciarlariello et al v Schacter et al

Battery: Canada: consent: injection: quadriplegia

Supreme Court of Canada. [1994] 5 Med LR 213

The plaintiff, a lady aged 49, underwent a cerebral angiogram following diagnosis of subarachnoid haemorrhage. The defendant neurosurgeon fully explained the diagnosis, the dangers inherent in the plaintiff's condition, the need for an angiogram and the risks involved. During the course of the angiogram the plaintiff insisted that the test was stopped. It resumed and, after ten to fifteen minutes, was completed. The plaintiff became quadriplegic due to the final injection.

Held: (i)   the action in battery failed, because the patient consented to the angiogram and its continuation.

(ii)   the action in negligence failed. Although a patient may consent to the renewal or continuation of a test, she must be informed of any material change in the circumstances which could alter her assessment of the costs or benefits of continuing the procedure. Here, there had been no material change in the circumstances and a valid consent was given to the continuation of the process.

See p 105.

Clark v MacLennan and Another

Operation: surgeon: departing from orthodox practice: standard of care

Peter Pain J. [1983] 1 All ER 416

On 11 June 1975 the plaintiff (Jacqueline Clark) gave birth to her first child at the John Radcliffe Hospital in Oxford. Within two days she was found to be suffering from stress incontinence. On 1 July Professor Turnbull and his senior registrar, Mr MacLennan, decided that an anterior colporrhaphy operation was desirable. Mr MacLennan performed this operation on 10 July, four weeks after the birth. A substantial haemorrhage occurred, and the repair initially effected by the operation later broke down. Despite two subsequent operations, the plaintiff's stress incontinence became permanent.

She sued Mr MacLennan and the Oxfordshire Area Health Authority. The complaint pursued at trial was that the operation was performed too soon. There was a general practice among gynaecologists that an anterior colporrhaphy should not be ordinarily performed until at least three months after birth, partly because time might heal and partly to reduce the risk of haemorrhage and breakdown of the operation.

Held: the departure from standard gynaecological practice was unjustified, and the defendants were in breach of their duty of care. Judgment for the plaintiff.

See pp 44, 65, 77, 146.

Clarke v Adams

Physiotherapist: burns: warning

Slade J. (1950) 94 Sol Jo 599

The plaintiff (Mr Clarke) was treated by Mr Adams, a physiotherapist, for a fibrositic condition of his left heel. Before applying the treatment, Mr Adams warned him: 'When I turn on the machine I want you to experience a comfortable warmth and nothing more; if you do, I want you to tell me.' As a result of the treatment, the plaintiff suffered injury by burning which led to his left leg being amputated below the knee.

Held: the apparatus was not defective but it was dangerous because burns caused by it could lead to serious consequences. There should have been a warning of danger, to the effect that the plaintiff's safety depended on his informing Mr Adams the moment he felt more than a comfortable warmth. Judgment for the plaintiff.

See pp 24, 44, 62.

Clarke and Another v Worboys and Others

Burns: cancer: mastectomy: res ipsa loquitur

Court of Appeal. (1952) Times, 18 March

In January 1947 the plaintiff (Mrs Helena Clarke) was found to be suffering from carcinoma of the breast. Consequently in February 1947 she underwent an operation at the Luton and

Dunstable Hospital for removal of her right breast. The operation was successful, but as extensive bleeding was expected electro-coagulation was applied. This involved the passing of a high-frequency alternating current through the patient's body via a pad placed on her right buttock. A severe burn was caused on this buttock, which caused permanent injury to the muscles.

The plaintiff sued the hospital authorities. Her case was that the hospital staff had not prepared the rod properly by moistening it in a saline solution before application. The trial judge (McNair J) dismissed the claim.

Held: this was a case of *res ipsa loquitur*. The accident was one of a kind which did not normally happen if reasonable care was used, and the evidence was that, if the apparatus was applied properly, burning was unknown. The hospital staff were negligent.

See pp 88, 129.

Clarke v City and Hackney Health Authority

Child patient: diagnosis: fracture: arm

Adrian Whitfield QC. (1994) AVMA Journal, Spring, 13

In 1978 the plaintiff (Darren Clarke), aged eight, jumped from a garage room and fell forwards onto his hands. He was taken to St Bartholomew's Hospital where the x-ray report recorded: 'There are fractures through the distal end of the shaft of the right radius and through the epiphysis at the lower end of the radius'. This was a description of classic Salter-Harris type IV fracture, the main risk being growth arrest. The doctors did not diagnose this. Their first course of action was to attempt an open reduction with 'talking anaesthesia', ie, they tried to pull the plaintiff's wrist back into shape without pain relief. Afterwards, the wrist was set in a Colles plaster and he was sent home. The wrist was still painful when the plaster was removed about six weeks later, but it seemed to get better with physiotherapy.

Because the bones had been set incorrectly, they could not grow in a normal fashion. About five years later another doctor noticed that the radius was not growing and that consequently the ulna was being pushed outwards at an incongruent angle. The only treatment was to cut the healthy bone down to the size of the damaged bone, which was done in a series of operations over the next two years. The plaintiff's right arm was left four and a half inches shorter from elbow to fingertip than his left arm. He was at increased risk of osteoarthritis and would probably need a fusion operation.

Held: (i) although this was a rare type of fracture, the hospital doctors were negligent in failing to diagnose it and in not being alert to the complications which might follow.

(ii) the plaintiff should have been anaesthetised and, under x-ray control, a closed reduction of the fracture should have been performed. This would probably have resulted in a normal wrist.

(iii) if a closed reduction proved impossible, the surgeons should have opened the wrist, reduced the fracture and held it in good position with Kirschner wires embedded into the plaster. Again, this would probably have resulted in a full recovery.

The plaintiff was awarded agreed damages of £45,000.

See p 97.

Clarke v Hurst and Others

Discontinuance of life-supporting treatment: South Africa: living will: persistent vegetative state

Thirion J.[1994] 5 Med LR 177

On July 30, 1988, while undergoing epidural treatment, Mr Clarke, then aged 63, went into cardiac arrest. Resuscitative measures were instituted, but he suffered serious and irreversible brain damage. As a result, he was in a persistent vegetative state with no prospect of any improvement in his condition and no possibility of recovery.

Mr Clarke had made a 'living will'. This directed that, if there was no reasonable expectation of his recovery from extreme physical or mental disability, he be allowed to die and not be kept alive by artificial means.

The applicant (his wife) applied to be appointed as his curatrix with powers to put an end to the artificial feeding regime in operation whereby he obtained the necessary sustenance for his bodily functions.

Held: the application would be granted because the feeding of the patient did not serve the purpose of supporting human life as it was commonly known and the applicant, if appointed as curatrix, would act reasonably and would be justified in discontinuing the artificial feeding and would therefore not be acting wrongfully if she were to do so.

Cockburn v Eli Lilly & Co and Others

Drugs: limitation: Opren

Hidden J. [1991] 1 Med LR 196

The plaintiff (Timothy Cockburn), a young man, was first prescribed Opren in March 1981 by his consultant. He continued to take it until it was withdrawn from the market in August 1982, but he could not remember seeing or hearing anything about its withdrawal. He suffered from photosensitivity in his eyes and skin from the summer of 1982 onwards. Neither his consultant nor his general practitioner told him that this was attributable to Opren.

His reading was limited to the sports and TV pages of the Sun and the Daily Mirror, so he did not read any newspaper articles about Opren. On 19 January 1988, because the racing had just finished on Channel 4, he found himself watching a programme about Opren called 'The Years Ahead'. Subsequently his mother wrote off for a facts sheet about it. On 2 March 1988 she and he wrote a joint letter to his general practitioner to verify that he had been on Opren.

In April 1988 he consulted solicitors. His writ was issued on 12 August 1988.

Held: (i) accepting his evidence, his actual knowledge of the relevant facts only started in January 1988 when he saw the television programme and was completed in April 1988 when he instructed solicitors (s 11(4)).

(ii) he was a young man of limited intelligence and interest, the width of whose life had been badly contracted by his general ill health since early childhood. He could not reasonably be expected to have acquired such knowledge at any earlier time (s 14(3)).

(iii) accordingly his claim was not statute barred (s 11(4)).

See *Cockburn v Eli Lilly & Co (No 2)* (p 282) and *Nash v Eli Lilly & Co* (I) (p 466).

Cockburn v Eli Lilly & Co and Others (No 2)

Drugs: Opren: costs

Court of Appeal. [1992] 3 Med LR 374

See *Nash v Eli Lilly & Co* (I) (p 466).

Colegrove v Smyth and Others

Diagnosis: limitation: hip

Buckley J. QBD transcript, 12 March 1992

In February 1959 the plaintiff (Kate Colegrove) was born with congenital dislocation of the hip (CDH). Although her mother noticed that from the time she started to get upright she walked oddly with a sailor-like roll, she said that the defendant doctors to whom she mentioned this brushed aside her concerns. Diagnosis of CDH occurred later at the Nuffield Hospital when the plaintiff was three and a half years old. When she was eight or nine years old, another doctor (Dr Summerville) said to her: 'If only this had been treated when you were younger, you would not have had to go through all this now.' She said that she did not discuss her treatment with her mother until she was 25. She was left with a far from normal hip which even in adult life required further serious operative treatment.

In December 1984, having applied for a position with the Oxford City Council, she attracted a medical examination. As a result of that, she instructed solicitors in January 1985. Her writ was issued in November 1987, claiming damages against the defendant doctors for negligently failing to diagnose CDH when she was around one year old. A preliminary trial of the limitation defence was ordered.

Held: (i) the omission of which the plaintiff must have had knowledge to set time running under the Limitation Act 1980 was the defendants' alleged failure to diagnose CDH, and the injury in question was the impairment of her condition that resulted from this.

(ii) Dr Summerville's statement to the plaintiff when she was a young child did not fix her with sufficient knowledge. It did not suggest that her condition was attributable to the doctors' acts or omissions. Nor did it give her knowledge of her earlier visits to the doctors.

(iii) there was no reason why the plaintiff should have ascertained the facts of the failure to diagnose earlier than December 1984. She accepted her CDH as part of her life. It was unrealistic to expect her to have questioned her mother or gone to solicitors earlier. Her court action was not statute barred.

(iv) even if it had been commenced out of time, the court's discretion under s 33 of the Limitation Act 1980 should be exercised in her favour. The defendants were prejudiced in that one had died and another was 85, and two out of their three sets of medical records had been destroyed. However that was just outweighed by the prejudice of shutting out what might be a valid claim in a very tragic case.

(v) the costs of the preliminary hearing would be reserved to the trial judge, to be decided by him after he had found whether the early conferences and meetings recorded by the plaintiff's mother took place as alleged.

See pp 186, 187, 194.

Coles v Reading and District Hospital Management Committee and Another

Cottage hospital: communication: warning: general practitioner: fatal: fingers

Sachs J. (1963) 107 Sol Jo 115, (1963) Times, 31 January

Mr Coles, aged 21, went to a cottage hospital after a lump of coal fell on his finger at work and severely crushed it. A nurse cleaned and covered his wound and told him to go to Battle Hospital for further treatment. He did not go, either because it was not clearly explained to him or because he was suffering from shock. Instead, the next day he saw his own doctor who did not ask what had happened at the hospital but simply redressed the wound. No anti-tetanus injection was given to him. He died of toxaemia due to tetanus infection. His father claimed damages.

Held: (i)   it was well known that, in cases such as this, failure to take anti-tetanus injection precautions could cause death. It was for the cottage hospital to give the anti-tetanus injection or to ensure that the patient got proper treatment. Mr Coles should have been given a document to take to Battle Hospital, stating what had been done and what should be done, with particular reference to anti-tetanus injections. Even if Mr Coles had realised that he had to go to Battle Hospital, but was not told of the importance of going or the danger in failing to do so, the hospital authorities would still have been negligent.

(ii)   Mr Coles' doctor probably assumed that the hospital had done everything necessary, but he should have made some enquiries. Even if the doctor had considered giving an anti-tetanus injection and decided that it was not necessary, he would have been neglecting elementary precautions. He too was negligent.

See pp 44, 95, 134, 136.

Collins v Hertfordshire County Council and Another

House surgeon: prescription: anaesthetics: hospital administration: pharmacist: consultant: vicarious liability

Hilbery J. [1947] KB 598, [1947] 1 All ER 633

In April 1945 James Collins had an extensive growth on his jaw which required a serious operation. This was performed at the Wellhouse Hospital in Barnet by Mr Hunt, a visiting surgeon employed part-time by the hospital. The hospital also employed as a full-time resident junior house surgeon Miss Knight, a final year student who had passed her examination in pharmacology but who was not then a qualified doctor.

The evening before the operation Miss Knight telephoned Mr Hunt to ascertain his orders. He ordered for Mr Collins one per cent procaine with 1-200,000th adrenalin. Miss Knight misheard procaine as cocaine. She went to the hospital pharmacist without any written order and told him to make up one per cent cocaine with the usual quantity of adrenalin. He dispensed to her one per cent cocaine with 1-20,000th adrenalin. Mr Hunt omitted to check that the solution was correct and so injected into Mr Collins a lethal dose which killed him. His widow claimed damages.

Held: (i)   the hospital authority was responsible for the hospital's dangerous and negligent system in the provision of drugs, whereby an unqualified person was able to obtain a dispensation for an extraordinary quantity of a dangerous drug without any prescription or order signed by a qualified person, and for the pharmacist's negligence in participating in this and failing to verify the order.

(ii) the hospital authority was also vicariously liable for Miss Knight's negligence as an employed resident junior house surgeon, but not for the negligence of Mr Hunt as visiting surgeon.

(iii) liability for the damages was apportioned equally between the hospital authority and Mr Hunt.

Note: It is submitted that, following the cases of *Cassidy* v *Minister of Health* and *Roe* v *Ministry of Health*, the hospital authority would now be held vicariously liable for Mr Hunt's negligence.

See pp 24, 44, 121.

Colston v Frape

Chiropodist: diagnosis: foot: advice

Barnstaple County Court. (1941) 1 Lancet 490

The plaintiff (Mrs Colston) visited Mr Frape, a chiropodist, for treatment for corns. She knew he was a chiropodist and not a surgeon. He advised her that her toes needed treatment. When she returned to him for this purpose, he took her foot in both hands and twisted and jerked it. She suffered pain and was unable to walk as well as before. The plaintiff sued Mr Frape for damages for negligence.

Held: Mr Frape had been negligently wrong, either in his diagnosis or in the action taken to remedy the trouble diagnosed; 'if he did not know, he ought to have advised Mrs Colston to see a doctor'.

Connelly v Wigan Area Health Authority

Diagnosis: gall bladder: pancreatitis

Court of Appeal. CAT, 15 March 1994

In 1967 the plaintiff (Mrs Dorothy Connelly), then aged 24, started to suffer from recurrent attacks of severe upper abdominal pain and vomiting. She was referred to various consultants, including Dr Perkins in 1969 and 1971 and Dr Lass in 1974. They variously diagnosed a peptic ulcer, a pylorospasm, agitated depression with some agoraphobic features, and a small hiatus hernia.

In June 1977 an ultrasound scan revealed multiple gallstones and a pseudo-cyst on the pancreas. In July 1977 her gall bladder was removed and the cyst was aspirated. It became apparent that throughout the years her condition had been caused by inflammation of the pancreas which itself was caused by a disease of the gall bladder.

Dr Lass had died before trial. Dr Perkins testified that 'the symptoms did not ring the bell for the complex of gall bladder disease', because the severity of the pain which he understood the plaintiff to be suffering was not sufficient. Both the plaintiff's expert and the defendants' expert agreed, as the judge found, that gall bladder disease should have been considered as a possible explanation for the symptoms and gall bladder x-rays should have been arranged to exclude or establish this.

However the judge concluded that 'the two consulting physicians, Dr Perkins and Dr Lass, have not been found to have been negligent. In my judgment they did, as it turns out, make a mistake in not considering gall bladder disease, but I am satisfied the reason for that is the way in which this plaintiff presented herself and gave her history over the years to the various doctors who attended her.'

Held: there was no evidence to justify that conclusion. The evidence of the description of symptoms was mostly clear in the very detailed notes. The totality of the evidence established that Dr Perkins and Dr Lass should have considered gall bladder disease as a possible cause of the plaintiff's symptoms and should have investigated by x-ray to ascertain whether it was the cause.

The plaintiff's appeal was allowed.

See p 970.

Connolly v Camden and Islington Area Health Authority

Anaesthetics: overdose: damages: brain damage

Comyn J. [1981] 3 All ER 250

In August 1976, when he was 17 days old, the plaintiff (Liam Connolly) was to undergo an operation at University College Hospital. He was given a serious overdose of anaesthetic.

He was reduced to being very severely mentally abnormal. He became subject to epilepsy. He was doubly incontinent. He could walk up to a maximum of one hundred yards, falling over frequently. He had a squint attributable to his brain damage. He was only capable of speaking a few words. He would never be able to work or marry and required constant care and supervision. He had feelings of affection and would become aware of his plight.

The plaintiff sued the hospital authority who admitted liability. When his case came to trial, he was aged four and three-quarters, and was expected to live to twenty-seven and a half.

Held: (i) general damages (April 1981) for pain, suffering and loss of amenities were assessed at £50,000.

(ii) the appropriate multiplier for cost of future care was 13¼.

(iii) on an agreed loss of earnings figure of £3,000 per annum, £7,500 was awarded for loss of the plaintiff's earnings during his shortened life span.

(iv) he was entitled to claim damages for loss of earnings during the lost years of his life, but on the material before the court this claim was assessed at nil.

The total award was £220,007.

See pp 122, 155, 158.

Connolly v Rubra

General practitioner: diagnosis: advice: tuberculosis: tests: second opinion: fatal

Court of Appeal. (1937) 1 Lancet 1005

In December 1930 Matthew Connolly suffered from an attack of coughing and called in Dr Rubra. He told him that his coughing was severe and accompanied by spasmodic attacks, that he had a raised temperature at night and spat blood which formed streaks in the sputum, that he had lost weight, and that in July 1929 he had had an attack of haemoptysis while bathing. He suffered from considerable bronchitis and when Dr Rubra was called in, was spitting so much blood that he kept a bowl by his bed. Dr Rubra treated him for bronchitis, but did not advise any special diet or treatment and did not have the sputum examined. Mr Connolly's condition got gradually worse in 1931 and by February 1932 he was seriously ill. Dr Rubra continued conservative treatment and dissuaded him from seeing a specialist. When Mr Connolly was finally examined by a specialist in March 1933, it was found that he had tuberculosis from which he died.

The plaintiff (his widow) sued Dr Rubra who died before trial. Expert witnesses agreed that when there was blood in the sputum, tuberculosis could not be eliminated without further investigation. The trial judge (Greaves-Lord J) found that Dr Rubra had been negligent.

Held: if a general practitioner has any doubt whether or not there are signs of tuberculosis, it is his obvious duty to make further examination. If he is not confident of his own judgement, he should call in an expert. To enable the expert's opinion to be of value, the doctor must take many specimens of the sputum, arrange an x-ray examination and continually watch the patient. Dr Rubra had done none of these things, so the trial judge's decision was justified.

See p 135.

Connor v Fison-Clarke

Dental: damages

Rose J. QBD 9 October 1987

The plaintiff went to Mr Fison-Clarke as her dentist between 1974 and 1980. In 1975 he carried out extensive root therapy treatment and bridgework in her upper arch.

From about mid-1981 the plaintiff began to suffer symptoms due to malocclusion: the poor fit of the bridge in relation to the trimmed crowns and the teeth of the lower jaw. The temporo-mandibular joints had become deranged. She suffered pain and tenderness over those joints, aching at the sides of the head, headaches and pain and tenderness in the neck. This pain and suffering lasted until mid-1984. From mid-1983 she also suffered some cosmetic impairment due to receding gums. She had to undergo remedial dentistry until the summer of 1985. The remedial treatment was more prolonged than should have been necessary due to the effects of years of malocclusion on the temporo-mandibular joints. She had continuing pain and discomfort in her right temporo-mandibular joint; it was possible that some of this might become permanent. She was aged 45 at trial.

Held: (i) Mr Fison-Clarke was negligent in respect of the fit of the bridge in relation to the trimmed crowns on which it rested and in relation to occlusion within the lower teeth;

(ii) general damages (October 1987) were assessed at £4,000 for pain, suffering and loss of amenities. The plaintiff was also awarded £5,337 agreed special damages in respect of the cost of remedial treatment and other expenses.

See pp 131, 155.

286

Cooper v Miron and Another

Dental: duty to inform of mishap: x-ray: causation: fatal: teeth: pneumonia

McCardie J (with special jury). [1927] 2 BMJ 40, (1927) 2 Lancet 35

In May 1925 Edith Cooper, aged 30, went to the National Dental Hospital to have three teeth extracted. The operation was undertaken under nitrous gas by Mr Davy, a third-year student, in the presence of Mr Miron, a registered dentist. During the operation, the crown of one molar broke off and disappeared down her throat. When she recovered from the anaesthetic, she complained to her sister of difficulty in breathing. However she was allowed to go home. No one at the hospital told her about the missing bit of tooth, and no arrangements were made for her further examination or treatment at the hospital. She contracted septic pneumonia, due to impaction of the piece of tooth in a bronchus, and died on 27 August.

The plaintiff (her mother) sued Mr Miron and the hospital superintendent.

Held: McCardie J directed the jury that one of the issues was whether Miss Cooper's life would have been saved if proper steps had been taken in time. Another was whether Mr Miron was guilty of negligence in not informing Miss Cooper or her friends what had taken place and in not taking steps to ascertain where the broken piece of tooth actually was. There seemed to be no doubt what was the duty of a dentist when an accident of this kind happened. He must tell the patient what had happened, and must take steps, by x-rays, to locate the foreign body and to have it removed if it was in a place of danger to the patient. Yet Miss Cooper left the hospital with no idea what had happened, and nothing was said about it to her sister who was with her.

The jury found that negligence had been proved against Mr Miron and that Miss Cooper's death resulted from this.

See p 45, 113, 131.

Cooper v Nevill and Another

Operation: surgeon: retained surgical product: res ipsa loquitur: Kenya

Privy Council. [1961] EA 63

Mr Nevill operated on the appellant (Mrs Rosetta Cooper) at a hospital managed by the Kenya European Hospital Association. He successfully performed a difficult emergency operation. However an abdominal swab was left in her body. Consequently she suffered for months much physical pain and acute mental distress and had to undergo another major operation.

Held: once it was undisputed that a swab had been left in the body, there must have been some mistake made by both Mr Nevill and the hospital authorities. Although there must have been some mistake, it did not necessarily follow that there was negligence. The whole team was engaged in a race against time. A mistake which would amount to negligence in a 'cold' operation might be no more than misadventure in a 'hot' one. But there was no evidence to suggest what kind of mistake this would be.

The trial judge was justified in finding: 'If the pack was a mopping pack, it was negligence on the part of the person who used it, whether it was Mr Nevill or his assistant, to lose control of it and leave it in the body. If it was a restraining pack, having regard to the small number used and their obvious position, the absence of movement and the lack of any particular need for haste at the conclusion of the operation, it was negligence on the part of Mr Nevill not to remove it, the responsibility being, as he admits, upon him to do so, and there being no justification for the departure from the normal routine'.

See pp 88, 125.

Corbett v Barking Havering and Brentwood Health Authority

Anaesthetics: damages: fatal: interest: solicitors

Court of Appeal. [1990] 1 Med LR 433

The plaintiff (Richard Corbett) was born by caesarean section on 27 October 1977. His mother, aged 29, died on 12 November 1977 as a result of complications of lung infection caused by mismanagement of anaesthetic procedures during the operation.

Between 1978 and 1981 the father instructed two firms of solicitors; his own claim was settled for £2,000 damages. In 1982 a third firm was instructed. In 1983 legal aid was granted for a claim on behalf of the plaintiff. In 1984 a writ was issued and served against one of the first two firms. In 1985 the plaintiff's writ against the defendant hospital authority was issued. In 1987 the case was set down for trial. The defendants admitted liability shortly before the hearing.

In June 1989 His Honour Judge Hayman awarded the plaintiff £32,000 (based on a multiplier of 12) for his dependency on his mother's lost services, a further £3,000 for the special value of the mother's services compared with those of a grandmother, and £15,110 interest for 7 of the 11 years from death to trial, a total of £50,110. The plaintiff appealed.

Held: (i)   while the correct approach was to calculate the multiplier from the date of death, account must be taken of the removal of many uncertainties (eg the plaintiff's survival to trial) and much of the acceleration of receipt during the 11 years that had elapsed. To award a future multiplier of only a half was bizarre. Taking into account a possibility that the plaintiff would have continued in education after the age of 18, an overall multiplier of 15 (11 to trial, 3 thereafter) should be substituted.

           (ii)   in view of the exceptional delay, and bearing in mind the fact of outstanding court action against one of the firms of solicitors, the judge's disallowance of 4 of the 11 years of interest should be upheld.

The judge's award was increased by £7,800 (3 x £2,600 pa).

See pp 122, 166.

Corder v Banks

Plastic surgeon: after-care: operation: communication: face

McNair J. (1960) Times, 9 April

In 1952 the plaintiff (then Miss Stella Corder) was a 29-year-old typist. She was distressed at what she regarded as a disfiguring condition below her eyes. Mr Banks, a plastic surgeon with rooms in Harley Street, agreed to operate on her under a local anaesthetic on the basis that she would be an out-patient. The operation was correctly performed.

It was clear that the first 48 hours after the operation were of crucial importance as during that period bleeding might occur and, if it was not attended to properly, irreversible damage might result. Consequently proper directions had to be given to an out-patient by the surgeon, as were given by Mr Banks, and the surgeon or a properly qualified substitute had to be available to deal with any untoward developments.

On the first day after the operation Miss Corder suffered substantial bleeding from the stitches. This continued intermittently for a day or so. She telephoned Mr Banks' consulting rooms but he never learned of her condition. Prudent surgical practice required that the bleeding be dealt with properly by a skilled surgeon. The plaintiff suffered definite and marked facial disfigurement.

Held: if a surgeon adopted a course of letting a patient go home and was relying on a telephone message from the patient to deal with an unexpected emergency that might arise, it was essential that the telephone should be adequately covered in the sense that messages would be received and transmitted to the surgeon. There was a failure by Mr Banks to keep his telephone adequately covered or a failure by those for whom he was responsible to inform him of the message. That failure amounted to professional negligence.

Corner v Murray

General practitioner: injection: needle breaking: res ipsa loquitur: back

HH Judge Tudor Rees. [1954] 2 BMJ 1555

In September 1951 the plaintiff (Arthur Corner) sustained a back injury at work. His general practitioner, Dr Murray, injected a local anaesthetic into the site of the injury. At the conclusion of the injection Dr Murray was about to withdraw the hypodermic needle from his body, when it broke off close to the mount. He was unable to extract the broken portion of needle and sent the plaintiff to the Central Middlesex Hospital. The piece of needle was removed there by operation the next day.

The plaintiff sued Dr Murray in the High Court, alleging that he had been negligent in administration of the injection. The case was transferred to the Brentford County Court. Expert evidence was given that the breaking of hypodermic needles was a not uncommon occurrence, the risk of which had to be accepted, and that this could occur without any negligence on the part of the doctor.

Held: there had been no negligence, or any semblance of negligence, on the part of Dr Murray. The plaintiff's case was dismissed.

See p 119.

Coughlin v Kuntz

Canada: diagnosis: exemplary damages: experimentation: informed consent: operation: surgeon: departure from orthodox practice

British Columbia Supreme Court, Cohen J. (1987) 42 CCLT 142

The defendant (Mr Kuntz), an orthopaedic surgeon, had spent an extraordinary amount of time and money on an examination of cervical disc disease. He had written an unpublished book, 'The Organs of Stress', in which he had defined as 'Kuntz's Syndrome' a previously undiagnosed syndrome of cervical disc degeneration. He had developed a technique for neck surgery which he called 'instant interbody fusion', using a homemade artificial spacer made of methyl methacrylate, and was the only orthopaedic surgeon who performed anterior cervical discectomy using this method.

In 1979 the British Columbia Medical Association wrote to the defendant, questioning the number of spinal procedures carried out by him. In 1980 the BCMA wrote to the BC College of Physicians and Surgeons with a request that the College investigate the defendant's skill and competence. In January 1982 the College requested the defendant to declare a moratorium on his neck procedure. He rejected this request, and in 1982 he was responsible for 51% of all cervical disc operations performed in British Columbia.

In July 1981 the plaintiff (Mr Coughlin) had been forced to jump off a runaway logging truck and sustained injury to his left shoulder. In January 1982 he consulted the defendant. After initially diagnosing a painful arc syndrome left shoulder, the defendant decided that the plaintiff's main problem was C5-C6 disc degeneration. Although the plaintiff had no symptoms in his neck, the defendant advised C5-6 anterior cervical discectomy and instant interbody fusion. In March 1982 Dr Noble, a WCB orthopaedic surgeon, diagnosed 'shoulder cuff damage to the left shoulder with impingement and pericapsulitis of the shoulder (frozen shoulder)' accompanied by 'degenerative changes in his neck for many years' and 'even now he has no restriction of cervical spine movement'.

Nevertheless in April 1982 the defendant proceeded with the operation he described as 'C5-6 anterior cervical discectomy and instant interbody fusion'. This involved the insertion of a methyl methacrylate spacer in the plaintiff's neck. Within a few weeks of the surgery, the spacer slipped and moved forward to jut into the plaintiff's oesophagus. This was physically irritating to him when he swallowed and caused him mental anguish. His left shoulder was still painful.

In May 1982 the defendant wrote 'with regard to his left shoulder, he has rotator cuff degeneration and stiffness and I would think he would be helped by left shoulder partial acromionectomy'. The plaintiff entered hospital for this in June, but had lost confidence in the defendant to such an extent that he fled the hospital at the eleventh hour rather than undergo another operation by him. Other surgeons performed two remedial operations, removing the artificial spacer and carrying out an anterior acriomioplasty on the plaintiff's left shoulder.

Held: (i)   by adopting a surgical procedure not used by other orthopaedic surgeons, and by continuing to use his unique procedure notwithstanding the request of his colleagues that he stop, the defendant placed himself in a precarious legal position.

(ii)   a careful orthopaedic surgeon would have operated on the plaintiff's shoulder first, and in any event would not have performed an anterior cervical discectomy on the plaintiff without first considering conservative treatment and confirming the diagnosis by the use of a diagnostic test, such as discography.

(iii)   the defendant's use of the methyl methacrylate spacer was experimental and unsupported by clinical study, and its insertion in the plaintiff's neck constituted negligence.

(iv)   the defendant was also negligent in failing in his duty to inform the plaintiff about the risks associated with his neck surgery including:

(a)   that the surgical procedure involving an artificial spacer invented by the defendant was unique to him;

(b)   the investigation by the BC College and its request for a moratorium on the procedure;

(c) the potential risks associated with the spacer's use, including migration and resorption of surrounding bone;

(d) the contrary opinion of Dr Noble;

(e) the option of conservative treatment.

(v) the defendant's behaviour towards his profession and the plaintiff was reprehensible. He was obsessed with his own unique theories. His conduct demonstrated a wanton disregard for the plaintiff's health and safety. $25,000 exemplary damages should be awarded, in addition to the compensatory damages.

Affirmed (1990) 2 WWR 737

See pp 65, 113.

Cox v Carshalton Group Hospital Management Committee

Child patient: nurse: supervision: burns: leg

Court of Appeal. (1955) Times, 29 March

The plaintiff (Valerie Cox), aged 13, was a child patient at Queen Mary's Hospital for Children, Carshalton. She suffered severely from poliomyelitis. She could not move her legs at all or sit up without being propped up, and could just move her arms a little. The method that the nurses devised for giving her an inhalant was to prop her up in bed with pillows, put a pillow on her lap, and a tray on the pillow, on which stood the bottle, which did not move at all easily. That method was tried successfully under supervision for two months, the child putting her hands on either side of the bottle.

In December 1952 the night nurse woke the child at 6.30am and gave her the inhaler. The nurse then had to go to the sluice about ten paces along the corridor. While she was out of the room, the inhalation bottle, filled with scalding liquid, fell on to the plaintiff's legs.

The plaintiff sued the hospital authority. The trial judge (McNair J) dismissed her claim.

Held: the positioning of the inhaler was carefully and properly done. The more difficult question was whether the little girl ought to have been left alone at all while taking the inhalant with the boiling water in it, helpless as she was. It might have been negligence in the early stages before it had been seen that she could manage the inhaler. But the trial judge was right in holding that when she had managed it quite well herself for a couple of months it could not be negligence on the part of the nurse, who had all the children under her care, to leave the room for a few seconds.

See pp 44, 132, 137.

Cox et al v Saskatoon

Canada: blood donor: operation: res ipsa loquitur: arm

Saskatchewan Kings Bench, Bigelow J. [1942] 1 DLR 74.

The father of the plaintiff (Mrs Cox) was a patient in the City Hospital, Saskatoon, and required a blood transfusion. She attended at the hospital for the purpose of providing the necessary blood. This operation was attempted by Dr Wright, an intern, assisted by two nurses. After he had worked on the plaintiff's right arm for thirty to forty-five minutes, an operation which usually took about ten minutes, the plaintiff suffered so much pain and her arm became so swollen and sore that Dr Wright decided to abandon the operation on the right arm without getting the desired quantity of blood. The operation was begun then on the left arm, but was soon abandoned without any damage to it. Dr Wright put an ordinary bandage on the left arm, and on the right arm he put glycerine and alcohol in addition to the bandage.

The plaintiff's right arm was badly damaged. Her condition was diagnosed as phlebitis, caused by lacerated tissue.

Held: (i)   the plaintiff had failed to prove any of her specific allegations of negligence.

(ii)   however, this was a case where the principle of res ipsa loquitur applied. The defendants had offered no satisfactory explanation as to how the damage could have occurred without negligence. The injury would not have happened, had they not been negligent. The plaintiff was entitled to recover damages.

Coyne v Wigan Health Authority

Anaesthetics: brain damage: res ipsa loquitur: head

Rose J. [1991] 2 Med LR 301

Shortly after 4 pm on 7 December 1981 the plaintiff (Mrs Jean Coyne), then aged 42, underwent at Leigh Infirmary an operation under general anaesthetic to remove a swelling from the parotid gland beyond the left parietal lobe. At 4.55pm she was taken to the recovery ward. Between 5.45pm and 5.50pm she was extubated. A staff nurse noted 'patient extubated at 5.45pm by Dr Novac. Breathing poor – patient became cyanosed and was re-intubated by Dr Novac at 6pm.' At 5.50pm Dr Novac (the anaesthetist) wanted to give the plaintiff a respiratory stimulant, Dopram, which was not immediately available. By reintubation at 6pm her pulse had risen to 150, according to the nurse's record, and her blood pressure had also risen markedly. This with cyanosis, a visible symptom, signified that she was suffering prolonged and significant hypoxia. She sustained brain damage with serious permanent consequences, including grand mal epileptic fits.

She sued the hospital authority which accepted that it was a case of res ipsa loquitur and endeavoured to explain that the hypoxia had occurred because of silent regurgitation of gastric content:

Held: (i)   the nurse's evidence was accepted in full. The defendants' experts should not have ignored his records entirely, since these referred to the occurrence and timing of cyanosis which was so crucial to the defendants' theory.

(ii)   the defence experts' conclusions were inconsistent. That was not surprising in view of the implausibility of their explanation. There was no recorded instance of silent aspiration leading to brain damage.

(iii)   the cyanosis occurred during the period of extubation. Res ipsa loquitur applied. The hospital authority was liable.

The plaintiff was awarded agreed damages of £150,000.

See pp 90, 122.

Crawford v Board of Governors of Charing Cross Hospital

Anaesthetics: blood transfusion: medical literature: arm

Court of Appeal. (1953) Times, 8 December

In 1950 the plaintiff (Robert Crawford) was admitted to Charing Cross Hospital for an operation to remove his bladder due to widespread growth of a tumour. He had only one effective arm (the left); the right had been useless to him since an attack of infantile paralysis long before.

The operation was performed in July 1950 and involved a transfusion of blood. The anaesthetist, Dr Clausen, kept the plaintiff's left arm extended at an angle of eighty degrees from the body so that the transfusion could be performed. Afterwards the plaintiff found that his left arm suffered a loss of power due to brachial palsy.

An article had appeared in The Lancet in January 1950 on the subject of the operation. Dr Clausen had not read this article. The trial judge (Gerrard J) in effect held that failure to keep himself familiar with the technical journals was negligence on his part. The testimony of the medical expert had shown no negligence by Dr Clausen.

Held: there was no evidence of negligence. It would be putting much too high a burden on a medical man to say that he must read every article in the medical press.

See pp 61, 65, 116.

Crivon v Barnet Group Hospital Management Committee and Others

Cancer: diagnosis: pathologist: standard of care: second opinion: x-rays: breast

Court of Appeal. (1958) Times, 19 November

In May 1950 the plaintiff (Mrs Myra Crivon) was operated on at the Wellhouse Hospital for the removal of a small lump in her breast. A specimen taken was submitted to the hospital's assistant pathologist, Dr Cogman, who reported that it looked as if she had cancer. The report was put in a paper clip above her bed in hospital. She saw it, looked up the meaning of 'carcinoma' and was very troubled.

On the basis of the report, Mrs Crivon eventually went to the Mount Vernon Hospital where she underwent deep x-ray therapy very intensively for a few weeks. It was then discovered that the original diagnosis of cancer was not agreed with by senior pathologists at the Wellhouse Hospital. Also the Mount Vernon pathologist reported that he did not think it was malignant cancer. The deep x-ray treatment was stopped. One of the sequels was that the condition of the skin had become marked and the surface destroyed. There were other potential hazards attendant on the therapy.

The trial judge (Hilbery J) dismissed the plaintiff's case.

The effective issue on her appeal was her allegation of negligent diagnosis. Professor Scarff, an eminent expert, had testified at trial that he would not even say that the diagnosis was wrong and that he might on that slide have come to the same conclusion himself.

Held: it was not negligent for a pathologist to appear to have come to a wrong decision which a great expert might himself have reached. A wrong diagnosis did not necessarily mean an unskilful or negligent diagnosis.

Once cancer was diagnosed, speed of treatment was essential. The mere fact that a second opinion was not taken and that there was no further check at Mount Vernon did not make out a case of negligence.

See pp 44, 98.

Croke v Wiseman

Cardio-respiratory arrest: brain damage: damages: child patient: quadriplegia

Court of Appeal. [1981] 3 All ER 852, [1982] 1 WLR 71

The plaintiff (James Croke) was born in March 1972. In December 1973 he became feverish with symptoms of croup and was taken to Northwick Park Hospital. While the doctors were examining him there, he suffered cardio-respiratory arrest. This resulted in brain damage giving rise to blindness, paralysis in all four limbs, double incontinence and inability to stand or speak. His mother gave up work as a teacher for several years in order to look after him. He was aged seven and a half at trial in November 1979, and was expected to live to forty. The hospital authority admitted negligence.

Held: (i)   the award by the trial judge (Michael Davies J) of £35,000 for general damages for pain, suffering and loss of amenities was correct.

(ii)   the judge was entitled to take into account the fact that Mrs Croke would lose pension rights as a teacher and to award the plaintiff £7,000 for that as part of the costs of future parental care.

(iii)   as the child's life expectancy was 32–33 years, the multiplier for the cost of future parental and nursing care should be reduced to 14 and the total award under this head to £119,000.

(iv)   the plaintiff should be awarded damages for his loss of earnings during the period that he will live but not during the lost years of his life. The judge was justified in assessing this at £5,000 per annum, the national average male adult wage.

(v)   The plaintiff's maximum working life from the ages of 18–40 would be 22 years, and, taking into account at least 11 years' accelerated receipt from the age of 7, the multiplier for future loss of earnings should be reduced to 5.

See pp 117, 155, 158, 159, 161.

Cronin v Islington Area Health Authority

Sterilisation (failed): risk disclosure: warning: causation

Caulfield J. (1987) 1 Lancet 638

In May 1981 the plaintiff (Mrs Cronin) discussed with her consultant obstetrician the possibility of sterilisation. She was pregnant with her third baby who was due for delivery by caesarean section. The consultant suggested sterilisation to be carried out at the same time as the caesarean delivery. She consented, and this was done. The plaintiff and her husband subsequently took no precautions against pregnancy. In 1983 she gave birth to another baby.

The plaintiff sued the hospital authority. She alleged that she was not warned of the possibility of sterilisation failure and that, had she been warned, while she would have undergone the operation she and her husband would have used birth control afterwards.

Held: her claim was dismissed because:

(i)   she had in fact been warned before the sterilisation operation of the risk of failure, both by the consultant and by the house officer who took her consent.

(ii) there was in 1981 no duty to warn a patient that sterilisation might fail, since at that time there was a substantial respectable body of medical opinion which would not have warned a patient in those circumstances.

(iii) the judge did not accept that the plaintiff, once sterilised, would have resorted to contraception.

See p 128.

Crossman v Stewart

Drugs: contributory negligence: face: ophthalmic: Canada

British Columbia Supreme Court. (1977) 5 CCLT 45

In January 1962, the plaintiff (Mrs Margaret Crossman) was referred to Dr Stewart, a dermatologist, in respect of a facial skin disorder. He diagnosed it as being discoid lupus erythematosus and prescribed a drug known as chloroquine or Aralen. The plaintiff continued to consult him until June 1962, and he gave her further prescriptions of the drug.

When her supply of the drug ran out, the plaintiff obtained a continued supply in an unorthodox manner. She was employed as a medical receptionist by another doctor and obtained the drug without a prescription from the salesman who supplied this doctor with his drug requirements. Dr Stewart did not know about this.

In December 1962, when attending a medical convention, Dr Stewart was alerted to the fact that in some cases patients who had consumed the drug over long periods had suffered irreversible damage to the retina of the eye, causing blindness or near-blindness. Consequently in January 1963, he called in the plaintiff and referred her to Dr Johnston, an eye specialist.

Dr Johnston's report in February 1963 contained the following passages: 'She gives a history of having had this medication for the past thirteen to fourteen months. . . slit lamp examination of the cornea revealed moderate central bilateral superficial keratopathy. . . Impression. Bilateral superficial keratopathy. . . which suggests a sequela of chloroquine therapy.'

The plaintiff was informed that the results of Dr Johnston's examination were negative. From March 1963 to March 1965 she continued to take the drug without Dr Stewart's knowledge. In March 1965 she consulted him again and continued on chloroquine therapy under prescription from him until September 1965.

In April 1966 signs of retinal damage were found. In 1968 it was determined that this was irreversible. By 1971 the plaintiff was nearly blind. She sued Dr Stewart.

Held: (i)   the standard of care, having regard to the inherent dangers involved in the use of the drug, must be very high. Dr Stewart had breached the high standard of care required through:

(a)   failure to peruse carefully the report of Dr Johnston, which stated that the plaintiff had been taking the drug for over a year.

    (b)   failure to discern from the presence of corneal changes that the probability of recent consumption of the drug existed.

   (ii) the plaintiff was guilty of contributory negligence in:

    (a)   obtaining prescription drugs from an unorthodox source;

    (b)   continuing to use drugs on a prolonged basis without obtaining 'prescription' renewals;

    (c)   continuing to use the drugs on a prolonged basis without consulting the prescribing physician.

   (iii) the plaintiff was two-thirds to blame and the defendant one-third to blame, so she was only entitled to recover one-third of the value of her claim.

See p 83.

Cull v Butler and Another

Hysterectomy: consent: breach of contract: trespass to person: hospital administration

Lord Chief Justice (with jury). [1932] 1 BMJ 1195

In 1929 the plaintiff (Mrs Ellen Cull), who was prone to epileptic fits, became pregnant. Two of her previous three pregnancies had failed. Not being well, she saw Mr Butler at the Royal Surrey County Hospital in Guildford. He advised removal of her uterus. After discussion with her doctor, Dr Cranstoun, it was decided that she should undergo instead the operation of curetting. Dr Cranstoun wrote to the hospital, stating that curetting was desired and that she refused the major operation. His letter reached the hospital office but became detached from other papers relating to the case. It remained unseen by Mr Butler who proceeded to perform a hysterectomy. The plaintiff sued Mr Butler and the hospital authority.

Held: the jury found that:

   (i) there was a negligent breach of contract on the part of the hospital authorities.

   (ii) there was a trespass on the part of Mr Butler, through the hospital authority's negligence.

See pp 7, 103, 178.

Cunningham v Camberwell Health Authority

Abortion: cardiac arrest: damages: quadriplegia: brain damage: Court of Protection

Court of Appeal. [1990] 2 Med LR 49

In January 1983 the plaintiff (Mrs Pearl Cunningham), then aged 39, was admitted to Dulwich Hospital for the termination of a pregnancy and sterilisation. An operation was carried out the next day to complete a spontaneous abortion. Immediately afterwards she had a cardiac arrest and a temporary failure of blood flow and oxygen supply to the brain.

The plaintiff suffered extensive brain damage. She had total loss of movement in her limbs. There was gross impairment of speech and communicative thought. She was unable to care for herself and required full-time care and supervision. She had a total loss of amenity, but was aware to some extent of her surroundings and still derived some pleasure from the company of her husband and three children. Her future life expectancy was fifteen years from trial.

She sued the hospital authority who admitted liability. Many heads of damages were agreed between counsel. Otton J awarded £655,126, including general damages of £75,000 and based on a multiple of eight.

Held: (i) general damages (July 1988) for pain, suffering and loss of amenities in an average case of tetraplegia such as this should be £90,000;

(ii) the appropriate multiplier for loss of future earnings and various future expenses was ten;

(iii) the damages would be reduced on account of attendance and mobility allowance received by the plaintiff.

See p 122.

Cunningham v North Manchester Health Authority

Diagnosis: discovery: fresh evidence: new trial: registrar: x-rays: amputation: leg

Court of Appeal. (1994) Independent, 15 February

On 22 October 1985 the plaintiff (Francis Cunningham) injured his left leg. X-rays were taken at the casualty department of the North Manchester General Hospital. The senior house officer showed the x-rays to the registrar who said there was a tibial plateau fracture and advised that a plaster of Paris cylinder should be fitted. When the plaintiff attended the fracture clinic on 23 October, he was examined by the same registrar who treated his case conservatively. He experienced increasing pain and was admitted as an emergency on 29 October. His leg was partially amputated in November 1985, and in April 1986 it was amputated below the knee.

He sued the hospital authority which informed his solicitors that the original x-rays had been destroyed and replaced by miniaturised copies. His medical experts, including a consultant radiologist who relied heavily on the miniaturised copies, considered that the plaintiff's popliteal artery was injured at the time of the initial injury and that this should have been detected clinically on 22 or 23 October 1985.

On the second day of the trial, counsel for the hospital authority informed the court that the original full size x-rays and arteriograms existed. Copies had always been available to the authority's experts who criticised the value of the miniature copies of the x-rays. Mr Justice Henry dismissed the plaintiff's claim.

The plaintiff appealed, applying for a new trial in reliance on a fresh report from his consultant radiologist, based not on the miniature copies which the photographic experts found to be very poor, but on the arteriograms disclosed at the trial.

Held: (i) this fresh evidence was of great importance. It could not have been available to the plaintiff at the trial. It should be admitted.

(ii) the judge had reached his decision on wrong radiological evidence due to the fault of the authority which had failed to a lamentable degree to comply with its duty to give proper discovery. In the special circumstances, a new trial would be ordered.

See p 211.

D v L

Quadriplegia: structured settlement: damages

FTSB, Winter 1994/95

The plaintiff (D) was rendered pentaplegic by medical negligence. Aged 20, he was totally dependent on a team of seven trained carers and a case manager. Interim payments were used to purchase and adapt a bungalow into a nursing home for him and to set up a 24 hour care regime. The continuing cost of care was £180,000 per annum. Medical experts estimated his life expectancy between 7 and 35 years, whilst the Life Office gave a rated age of 80.

The following settlement was agreed, on the basis that there would be no discount of the damages but no guaranteed minimum term:

Interim payments	£1,123,000
Compensation Recovery Unit recoupment	£13,000
Capital cost of structure	£1,165,000
Total	£2,300,000

The payments produced by the structure were as follows:

Type of annuity	Immediate
Initial net yield	15.5%
Initial annual sum	£180,000
Indexation	RPI
Equivalent gross yield after higher rate tax	25.8%
Payable for:	Life of plaintiff
Guarantee period	Nil

Daly v Wolverhampton Health Authority

Injection: scarring: damages: leg

Deputy Judge Patrick Bennett QC. [1986] CLY 1050

The plaintiff (Miss Daly) was aged 23 when she developed a permanent neuroma on her thigh due to damage to a nerve and/or blood vessel caused by an injection at one of the defendants' hospitals. Initially she suffered bruising and blistering and required daily dressings for over six weeks due to discharge from the wound. By the time of the hearing four years later, she still suffered an aching or burning sensation in her thigh after walking for more than half an hour or standing for any length of time; this was likely to resolve eventually. She was left with a permanent round scar on her thigh, which was 'visible, unsightly and nasty'; it embarrassed her and inhibited her from swimming or sunbathing.

Held (June 1986): general damages for pain, suffering and loss of amenities were assessed at £6,000.

See p 120.

Davidson v Connaught Laboratories et al

Canada: general practitioner: informed consent: injections: product liability: rabies: vaccine damage

Ontario Supreme Court, Linden J. (1980) 14 CCLT 251

On 17 August 1973 the plaintiff (Paul Davidson) and his brothers rolled a sick cow over on to its haunches. His sole contact with the cow was pushing its side. On 18 August, after the plaintiff had departed on holiday, it was discovered that the cow had rabies from which it died. When the plaintiff learned of this on 27 August, he telephoned Dr Hollows who advised him to take rabies vaccine and warned him about a 'flu-like reaction' from this. On 28 August the plaintiff telephoned Dr Kettyls, a virologist at the British Columbia Department of Health, who explained the dangers of the vaccine in detail, saying that it carried a risk of paralysis and even death with an incidence between 1 in 5,000 and 1 in 8,500.

The plaintiff collected a box of 14 vials of Semple rabies vaccine. The manufacturer's warning was that – 'injections of rabies vaccine ordinarily produce local areas of redness . . . the occurrence of encephalitis following the administration of rabies vaccine has been reported in many countries'. On the plaintiff's return home to Lindsay, Dr Hollows commenced the course of rabies vaccine injections which was continued by Dr Broadfoot.

In September 1973 the plaintiff contracted polyneuritis caused by the rabies vaccine. He sued Dr Hollows, Dr Broadfoot and the manufacturers. No evidence was given that the vaccine was defective.

Held: (i) the standard of care required of a doctor is to live up to the standard of reasonable care of other doctors of his type 'in the community or similar communities'.* Dr Hollows was not negligent in suggesting the injection of the rabies vaccine. Although the risk of rabies was slight, the consequences were potentially so severe. He did not depart from the standard of care in the Lindsay area when he failed to tell the plaintiff about the possible risk of paralysis and death; the risk of polyneuritis was so rare that a doctor need not necessarily tell a patient about it unless he asks. The same conclusions applied to Dr Broadfoot who was just carrying on from Dr Hollows. In any event, the plaintiff had already received detailed information of the risk from Dr Kettyls in British Columbia.

(ii) the written warning on the printed material placed in the boxes of vaccine given to the doctors was inadequate and unreasonable in the circumstances. The defendant manufacturer should have mentioned both myelitis and neuritis as possible side-effects of their drug. Both of these reactions were widely known and very serious indeed. However it would not have affected this case, since it was not the practice of Dr Hollows and Dr Broadfoot to discuss neurological side-effects with their patients and the plaintiff had received full information in British Columbia.

The plaintiff's claim was dismissed.

Per Linden J: 'A drug company cannot rely upon doctors to read all the scientific literature outlining the specific dangers involved in the many drugs they have to administer each day. They are busy people, administering to the needs of the injured and the sick. They have little time for deep research into the medical literature. They rely on the drug companies to supply them with the necessary data. With very little effort the defendant company could have included in the material that it gave to the doctors, who were administering the injections, all of the necessary facts. They did not. Even though these severe reactions were "extremely rare", I think it would have been advisable for the company to have presented the figures that were available, or at least to have referred the doctors to publications where those figures could be learned. Once they have the figures, then the doctors can properly assess the situation and decide whether they will recommend the vaccine or not, and how much information about the risks they should give to their patients. The doctors, however should have as full information as is reasonable in the circumstances.'

*The words in inverted commas constitute a controversial 'locality test' which is not recognised in English law.

See p 28.

Davies v Eli Lilly & Co and Others

Discovery: Group litigation: confidentiality: drugs: Opren

Court of Appeal. [1987] 1 All ER 801, [1987] 1 WLR 428

The plaintiff (Joy Davies) was one of over one thousand plaintiffs claiming damages for personal injuries due to Opren, the drug benoxaprofen. The first five defendants were the US manufacturers of the drug and their UK subsidiaries (the 'Lilly defendants'). The sixth and seventh defendants were the Committee on Safety of Medicines and the Department of Health and Social Security as the licensing authority under the Medicines Act 1968.

As the number and complexity of the documents to be produced on discovery necessitated special assistance, the plaintiff's solicitors engaged Mr Charles Medawar, a medical writer and journalist with a wide knowledge of medical and scientific specialities, to act as a specialist coordinator of the medical and scientific documents. The defendants objected to his being allowed to inspect their documents, on the grounds that he had published matter highly critical of the pharmaceutical industry in general and the Lilly defendants in particular.

Held: (i)   in relation to the requirement of RSC Ord 24, r 9 that a party allow 'the other party' to inspect the documents in his list, in the special circumstances of this extensive complex and important litigation, the previously recognized categories of agent should be extended to include someone doing the work described as being done by Mr Medawar.

      (ii)   on the additional evidence now available, Mr Medawar would not breach the duty of confidentiality and should be allowed to inspect the disclosable documents on giving to the court the following express undertakings:

        (a)   to preserve the confidentiality of the defendants' disclosed documents in terms which reflect what would otherwise be his implied obligation;

        (b)   not without the leave of the court or the consent of the defendants to publish or communicate anything (other than to the plaintiffs and their advisers) about the drug benoxaprofen as manufactured or marketed by the defendants under whatever name or about the role of the defendants in marketing or licensing it, subject, however, to a right to publish such matter in written form not less than twenty-eight days after giving the defendants a sight of the terms of the intended publication unless restrained by further order of the court. This undertaking should expire on 31 December 1992 unless earlier varied by the court.

See p 209.

Davies v Horton Road and Coney Hills Hospital Management Committee and Another

Risk disclosure: consent: assault: warning: fracture: ECT: back

Hallett J. [1954] 1 BMJ 883

In June 1951 the plaintiff (Charles Davies) suffered from insomnia and throat trouble. His general practitioner referred him to Dr Logan at the Gloucester Royal Hospital. Dr Logan advised five treatments of electro-convulsive therapy (ECT). He told the plaintiff that there was a possible risk of fractures or of dislocation of the jaw. He said that there was a risk, but it was a risk worth taking. During ECT the plaintiff received a crush fracture of his eighth dorsal vertebra.

He sued Dr Logan and the hospital authority for damages for assault and negligence, alleging that he had not been warned that the treatment might result in injury. Dr Logan testified as to his warning and said that relaxants had not then been introduced.

Held: (i) Dr Logan warned the plaintiff appropriately about the risks of the treatment. There had been no assault.

(ii) the treatment was administered carefully and efficiently in the usual and proper way. There had been no negligence.

Davies (Joseph Owen) v Eli Lilly & Co and Others

Group litigation: costs: drugs: Opren

Court of Appeal. [1987] 3 All ER 94, [1987] 1 WLR 1136

The plaintiff (Joseph Davies) was one of about 1,500 plaintiffs claiming damages for personal injuries due to taking Opren. About a thousand of the plaintiffs were legally aided. The plaintiff's action was selected for the purpose of giving directions applicable to all the actions. Hirst J ordered that any costs incurred by the plaintiff in a lead action should be borne proportionately by each of the plaintiffs in the other actions.

Held (RSC Ord 62, r 3(3)): the normal rule that costs should 'follow the event' did not preclude the order made. It meant that the costs discretion be exercised 'according to who wins' and did not prohibit an exercise of the discretion before the end of the case.

Per Sir John Donaldson MR: 'Put simply, but for present purposes wholly accurately, legal aid helps out those who lose cases, not those who win them. Legal aid makes "out and out" grants to those who lose cases. It only makes loans to those who win them'.

Davies v Mid-Glamorgan Health Authority

Anaesthetics: anaesthetic awareness: damages: operation

District Judge Reeves. Halsbury's Laws 94/2421

The plaintiff (Ms Davies), aged 65, entered hospital for a routine laparoscopy and biopsy of her vocal cords. She clearly warned hospital staff that she was allergic to the anaesthetic scoline. Nevertheless it was administered to her, and she suffered an allergic reaction to it.

As a result, she failed to breathe adequately after the operation and had to be admitted to the intensive care unit, where her trachea was re-entubed and her lung mechanically ventilated for six hours. She was unable to move, but was conscious and found the experience terrifying. She lost confidence in surgeons and anaesthetists in consequence.

Held (January 1994): although the plaintiff had not felt the pain of the surgeon's knife, such a terrifying experience should not be treated as a minor injury. General damages of £3,000 were awarded for pain, suffering and loss of amenities.

See p 123, 156.

Davis v Barking, Havering and Brentwood Health Authority

Anaesthetics: assault: consent

McCullough J. [1993] 4 Med LR 85

In December 1987 the plaintiff (Mrs Joan Davis) was to undergo an operation for marsupialisation of a Bartholin cyst at Harold Wood Hospital. Dr D'Souza, the anaesthetist, told her that he would give her a general anaesthetic but not that he would also give her a local anaesthetic in the form of a caudal block. She signed a form consenting 'to the administration of general, local or other anaesthetics'.

During the operation she was anaesthetised by a combination of a general anaesthetic and a caudal block. When she woke up afterwards, she found that her legs were numb and that she could not move them. Her right leg returned to normal, but trouble with her left leg persisted and she was left with a slight but significant disability. This was caused by administration of the caudal block.

She sued the hospital authority. Her allegations of negligence were withdrawn during the trial which proceeded to judgment on the issue of assault. Her case was that although she had consented to a general anaesthetic, she did not give her consent to a caudal block and was therefore assaulted when one was given.

Held: (i)   this would amount to a requirement of sectionalised consent, which would encourage the undesirable prospect of actions being brought in trespass rather than negligence.

           (ii)   where a claim is based on trespass to the person, the correct approach requires the court to ask: have the defendants shown that the plaintiff consented to a procedure the nature and effect of which had in broad terms been explained to her?

          (iii)   in this case, the answer was yes. The defendants were not liable.

Per McCullough J: 'If one is to treat the administration of an injection for analgesic purposes while the patient is generally anaesthetised (eg the caudal block given to Mrs Davis) as something requiring separate consent, why should separate consent not also be sought for an injection of, for example, morphine to provide analgesia when the patient begins to come round from the general anaesthetic?

If it is necessary to attach the patient to an electrocardiogram during surgery under general anaesthetic, ought not consent for that to be specifically sought lest, for example, the woman whose foot is to be operated upon may not have appreciated that while unconscious EC leads would be attached to her chest thus exposing her breasts?

And once this degree of sectionalisation is accepted, how long will it be before the court is invited to say that separate consent should be sought for separate steps in the surgical procedure itself?'

See pp 8, 104, 124.

Davis v City and Hackney Health Authority

Childbirth: limitation

Jowitt J. [1989] 5 PMILL 45, [1991] 2 Med LR 366

The plaintiff (Mr Davis) was born a spastic in June 1963. He could only move with considerable difficulty, and his speech was seriously affected. When he was about 17, he asked his mother what caused this. She replied that she thought his delivery might have been mishandled but discouraged him from claiming damages. In February 1983 he left his home to live with other disabled people. In August 1985 he met in a pub a law student who advised him that something could possibly be done in his case. In September 1985 he consulted solicitors. On 26 November 1986 they received a report from Professor Taylor.

The plaintiff's writ was issued on 1 April 1987. His case was that his mother was given an injection of Ovametrin which caused his spasticity. The defendant health authority pleaded limitation.

Held: (i)   the date of the plaintiff's knowledge for the purpose of s 11(4)(b) of the Limitation Act 1980 was 26 November 1986 or a few days after that when the contents of Professor Taylor's report were communicated to him.

       (ii)   in view of his disability, the plaintiff had not been delaying unreasonably in failing to take legal advice earlier than he did. Consequently he should not be fixed with any earlier date of knowledge under s 14(3). His claim was not statute-barred.

Per Jowitt J: 'I turn now to s 14(3). The test is an objective one. The question is, looked at objectively, when might he, the plaintiff, reasonably have been expected to acquire those facts referred to in paragraph (b) of subsection (3). In other words one applies an objective test, but it is an objective test applied to the kind of plaintiff I am here dealing with, with his disability, and looking at his age and his circumstances and the difficulties he has faced'.

See pp 183, 187.

Davis v London County Council

Nurses: anaesthetics: burns: vicarious liability: face

Lush J (with jury). (1914) 30 TLR 275

In October 1912 the plaintiff (Miss Davis) became a pupil in the 'babies class' at Barnsbury Park elementary school. In November the doctor told her mother that an operation was necessary for the removal of her adenoids and tonsils. On the teacher's advice the child was sent to the Islington Medical Treatment Centre, and a fee of one shilling was paid to London County Council. The operation took place on 13 December. When the child was brought back to her mother, her face was swathed in bandages and her lips blistered. The nurse who brought her back told Mrs Davis that some of the anaesthetic had been spilled and had burned the child's cheek. The operation had been performed by one doctor at the centre, with a second doctor acting as anaesthetist.

The Islington Medical Treatment Centre was conducted by a number of Islington doctors under an agreement as to the treatment of schoolchildren with the London County Council, who paid contributions varying with the amount of work done to the children. The doctors provided the premises and had the power to refuse cases. The plaintiff sued the London County Council. It was admitted that anaesthetic had been spilled, but negligence was denied.

Held: (i)   the jury found that the anaesthetist had not been guilty of negligence.

       (ii)   Lush J stated that a contrary verdict would have imposed no liability on the London County Council, as it had discharged its duty to the plaintiff when it engaged competent professional men to perform the operation.

See p 21.

Dawson v Scott-Brown

Medical report: limitation: striking out

Court of Appeal. CAT, 18 October 1988

The plaintiff (Richard Dawson) was an able-seaman in the Royal Navy. Surgeon-Commander Scott-Brown reported on his medical condition. His reports led to the plaintiff being discharged from the Royal Navy on the grounds of mental ill-health in October 1974.

In July 1987 the plaintiff issued a writ, alleging negligence in relation to Surgeon-Commander Scott-Brown's reports and treatment. The Master struck out his Statement of Claim and dismissed the action.

Held: (i)   the fact that the plaintiff was invalided out of the Navy on the ground of mental ill-health did not mean that he was incapable of managing his affairs, so the extension of time in s 28(1) of the Limitation Act 1980 did not apply.

       (ii)   the Surgeon-Commander took no steps to conceal what he was reporting. While he did not disclose the reports to the plaintiff, this was because it was to the Navy that the reports were made. Thus the plaintiff could not rely on s 32(1)(b) of the Limitation Act 1980.

      (iii)   the Master was entitled to conclude that, since the limitation defence was almost inevitably bound to succeed, the action was an abuse of the process of the court and should be dismissed.

See pp 179, 189, 197.

Day v Eli Lilly & Co and Others

Drugs: limitation: Opren

Court of Appeal. [1992] 3 Med LR 382.

See *Nash v Eli Lilly & Co* (D) (p 471).

De Coste v South Tyneside Health Authority

Casualty officer: causation: damages: testicle

HH Judge Stephenson. [1992] 8 PMILL 19

When aged 21, the plaintiff (Kevin de Coste) lost his right testicle due to a casualty officer's failure to consider testicular torsion. The defendant hospital authority admitted negligence. A dispute on causation (whether the testicle would probably have been saved otherwise) was resolved in the plaintiff's favour.

In addition to the loss itself, he had suffered some psycho-sexual trauma, a degree of embarrassment and a problem with premature ejaculation. By trial seven years later, he was married and able to enjoy sexual relations with his wife. He had no significant continuing problems. A full recovery was anticipated.

Held (January 1992):   general damages of £7,500 were awarded for pain, suffering and loss of amenities.

De Freitas v O'Brien and Another

Operation: surgeon: spinal

Court of Appeal. [1993] 4 Med LR 281, (1995) Times, 16 February

The plaintiff (Mrs de Freitas) suffered intermittently severe low back pain since July 1986. This deteriorated in the summer of 1988. On 15 July 1988 the first defendant (Mr O'Brien), an orthopaedic surgeon who specialised in spinal surgery, operated on her at the London Clinic and found an annular tear in the L4/5 disc. Soon after her discharge on 7 August, the plaintiff began to develop further severe pain and swelling in the small of her back. The first defendant readmitted her to the London Clinic and kept her under observation for ten days. He found that she had restricted leg raising, a wasted right buttock and pain which was unresponsive to physiotherapy and analgesics. Moreover the plaintiff was complaining about an altered pattern of pain, radiating from the small of her back down through her right buttock and thigh to her knee. The London Clinic did not have facilities for a CT scan or an MRI at that time. His clinical assessment was that she was suffering from a nerve root compression probably caused by something he had done at the first operation. A myleography failed to confirm this, but it confirmed his suspicion that the first operation had disturbed the geography of the lumbar spine, tilting it to the right and backwards, giving rise to a realistic prospect of nerve root compression inter alia in those parts distal to the central spinal canal not covered by the myelogram. Consequently he decided to operate again on 26 August 1988. The plaintiff continued thereafter to suffer considerable pain which was partly relieved by an epidural injection from a physician on 6 September.

On 9 September the operation wound drained 70mls of purulent material; wound swabs taken that day grew enterococci and E coli. Following treatment it seemed by 14 September that the wound was under control, but late that evening there occurred a sudden outpouring of cerebral spinal fluid (CSF) from the operation wound in her back, indicating that the wall of the dural sac had been breached. She was referred to the second defendant (Mr Campbell-Connolly) who first saw her on 19 September. He took the view that it would be courting disaster to operate to close the leak from the dura: the risk was that this would shut in any residual infection and enforce the chances that the CSF would become infected. It was better, in his view, to let the CSF continue to drain out. The plaintiff remained under his care at the London Clinic until she was moved on 30 September. The second defendant did nothing except to watch and monitor her condition carefully.

On 3 October at the National Hospital for Nervous Diseases in Maida Vale a senior registrar operated to close the fistula through which the CSF had leaked, and a lumbar drain was inserted. This was replaced by a lumbar peritoneal shunt on 10 October. Although the immediate problem of the CSF had been corrected, by November 1988 the plaintiff was suffering from chronic arachnoiditis. Her condition was unlikely to improve.

She sued the first defendant; eventually, her case against him was simply that his decision to operate on 26 August was negligent. Her experts testified that as, neither the first defendant's examinations nor the myelography of the plaintiff disclosed neurological signs of compression, it probably was not present and he should not have operated on 26 August without clear evidence of an identified lesion. The first defendant's experts, who were spinal surgeons, endorsed his logic in thinking that the pain might have been due to a nerve root compression brought about by the altered alignment of the vertebrae at the L4/5 level, that a possible unresolved nerve root compression was potentially too damaging to leave, and so he had no alternative but to explore it by an operation. She joined the second defendant; her case against him was that his selected option of wait and see exposed, for an unnecessarily prolonged period, the nerve roots in the dura to the debris of the cavity wound infection. It was conceded in evidence that there were other consultants and neurosurgeons who would have come to the same view as him.

The trial judge found that there is a separate specialism of surgeons comprising both orthopaedic and neurosurgeons engaged wholly or mainly in spinal surgery. In their hands, the dangers of an exploratory operation are minimal. There is in principle nothing unreasonable in their carrying out such an operation. He dismissed the claim, relying on the principle that a doctor was not guilty of negligence 'if he has acted in accordance with a practice accepted as proper by a responsible body of medical men . . .' (*Bolam v Friern Hospital Management Committee*, p 250)

The plaintiff submitted that the Bolam test was not designed to enable small numbers of medical practitioners, intent on carrying out otherwise unjustified exploratory surgery, to assert that their practice is reasonable because it is accepted by more than one doctor. She relied upon the principle that 'the court must be satisfied that the standard .... accords with that upheld by a substantial body of medical opinion . . .' (*Hills v Potter*, p 380).

Held: (i)   the judge had not fallen into error by not considering whether the body of surgeons had to be substantial. It was sufficient if he was satisfied that there was a responsible body of opinion.

(ii)   the issue could not be determined by counting heads. It was open to the judge to find the fact that a small number of specialists constituted a responsible body and that that body would have considered the surgeon's position justified.

(iii)   the plaintiff had failed to discharge the burden of proof that the defendants had been negligent.

See pp 64, 117.

De Freville v Dill

Negligent certification: psychiatric patient: duty of care: causation

McCardie J. (1927) 96 LJKB 1056

In 1917 the plaintiff (Muriel de Freville) married the son of a Gloucestershire vicar. The marriage became unhappy. In June 1926 she visited the vicarage where her husband and small son were staying. Her husband put her out of the house, so she re-entered by the servants' entrance. She was detained in the servants' hall while someone telephoned to summon Dr Dill, a Stroud doctor who was medical attendant to the vicar and his wife. When Dr Dill arrived, he spent a few hours with the plaintiff and telephoned the relieving officer who brought a certificate appropriate to the Lunacy Act 1890. Dr Dill completed and signed it, stating that the plaintiff 'was a person of unsound mind and a proper person to be taken charge of and detained under care and treatment'.

Consequently the plaintiff was taken to a Justice of the Peace who, without examining her or calling in another doctor, made a reception order. She was driven to Gloucester Mental Hospital where she spent the night. The next day the hospital decided no ground existed for her detention. She was discharged and sued Dr Dill for negligent certification.

Held: (i)   the jury found that Dr Dill had not acted with reasonable care.

(ii)   McCardie J held that Dr Dill owed the plaintiff the duty of reasonable care, even though he was never employed by her and had acted on behalf of her husband or father-in-law.

(iii)   McCardie J further held that, notwithstanding the Justice's omissions, Dr Dill's certificate was the cause of the plaintiff's detention.

See pp 80, 100.

de Martell v Merton and Sutton Health Authority

Childbirth: foetus' rights: Congenital Disabilities (Civil Liability) Act 1976

Court of Appeal. [1993] QB 204, [1992] 3 All ER 833, [1992] 3 WLR 637, [1993] 4 Med LR 8, [1992] PIQR P269, 136 Sol Jo LB 104.

See *Burton v Islington Health Authority* (p 267) and also p 55.

Delaney v Southmead Health Authority

Anaesthetist: operation: res ipsa loquitur: gall bladder

Court of Appeal. CAT 9 June 1992.

In June 1985 the plaintiff (Stephanie Delaney), aged 28, underwent an operation for a cholecystectomy. The general anaesthetic was administered by Dr Hall. The removal of the gall bladder was entirely successful. However three or four days after the operation the plaintiff was complaining of pins and needles in her left hand and clawing of the third and fourth fingers. A lesion of the brachial plexus was diagnosed; the ulnar nerve had been damaged.

Although the plaintiff had fractured her left clavicle in 1975, the trial judge found that there was no significant narrowing of the thoracic outlet and that Dr Hall had not been negligent in using her left arm to administer the anaesthetic. The plaintiff accepted these findings on appeal and alleged that her left arm was hyper-abducted, ie placed away from the side of her body more than 90°, certainly over 60°, and externally rotated, that is to say the hand being turned in the upwards position, thereby imposing excessive strain and stretch on the nerve. It was common ground that it was proper practice and not negligent for the arm to be abducted to a position of 45° and the hand held in the pronated position, that is to say with the palm downwards. The judge accepted the evidence of both Dr Hall, the anaesthetist, and Mr Thomson, the consultant surgeon supervising the operation, that that was the position in which the arm was throughout the operation.

The plaintiff's counsel relied on articles in the medical press in which the brachial plexus lesion during surgery is described as preventable if proper care is taken and argued that the articles showed that there were only two possible explanations of the injury: first, a narrowing of the thoracic outlet, which the judge had negatived, and second, a hyper-abduction and external rotation of the arm. He submitted that the maxim res ipsa loquitur applied.

Held: (i) if the human body was a machine which operated in accordance with the immutable laws of mechanics and with arithmetical precision, such an argument might be unanswerable. But even at post mortem, not everything is known about an individual human being. The judge was entitled to conclude that it was impossible to explain how the lesion had occurred.

(ii) it is doubtful whether the maxim res ipsa loquitur is of much assistance in a medical negligence case, at any rate when all the evidence has been adduced. Even if applied, it could be rebutted by the defendants giving an explanation of what happened which is inconsistent with negligence (not the limb on which they relied here) or by showing that the defendants had exercised all reasonable care.

(iii) the judge was entitled to accept Dr Hall's evidence about the position of the plaintiff's arm during the operation. There was no ground for holding that Dr Hall was negligent.

See pp 89, 124.

Department of Health and Social Security v Kinnear and Others

Vaccine damage: striking out: advice: group litigation

Stuart-Smith J. (1984) 134 NLJ 886, Times, 7 July, (1984)

Section 26 of the National Health Service Act 1946 had given the DHSS and local health authorities a discretion whether arrangements should be made to immunise people against diseases other than smallpox and diphtheria. Pursuant to this, acting in good faith, the DHSS had adopted a policy of promoting immunisation against whooping cough.

Victims of the whooping cough vaccine, who had suffered injury as a result of a reaction to inoculation, sued the DHSS, the manufacturers of the vaccine and the relevant regional health authorities. Their Statements of Claim were partly based on the department's formulation and promotion of its policy. They also alleged that the DHSS had given negligent or misleading advice to local health authorities concerning the circumstances in which such inoculations should be performed and the criteria to be applied in deciding whether an individual should be inoculated.

The DHSS applied under RSC Ord 18, r 19 to have the Statements of Claim in six actions struck out on the basis that they disclosed no reasonable cause of action.

Held: the policy could not give rise to a cause of action. It was within the limits of the DHSS' discretion and the result of its bona fide exercise. Even allegations of negligence against DHSS employees – eg in failing to submit relevant reports to those taking the policy decisions – could not found a cause of action against the department.

However, steps of an 'operational' rather than a 'policy' nature were action-able if taken negligently. It was arguable that allegations about negligent and misleading advice by the DHSS as to the manner and circumstances in which immunisations were to be performed were in the 'operational' category. Therefore these allegations would not be struck out.

See pp 38, 47.

Devi v West Midlands Regional Health Authority

Operation: surgeon: sterilisation: battery: consent: damages

Court of Appeal. [1981] CA Transcript 491

In June 1975 the plaintiff (Sheela Devi), a 29-year-old Sikh, underwent at the defendant's hospital in Walsall an abdominal operation to repair perforation in her uterus. The surgeon performing the operation decided then and there to perform a sterilisation operation as the abdomen was opened, since he thought this to be in the plaintiff's interest. In fact, there had been no discussion with her as to whether a sterilisation should be contemplated. The defendants admitted liability for sterilising her without her consent.

The sterilisation caused her considerable shock and upset. It also prevented her from having two more children to add to the four she already had. In May 1980 the trial judge (Kilner Brown J) awarded her £4,000 general damages to cover these aspects.

The plaintiff had been emotionally upset since the operation. She suffered from total loss of libido, and had ceased to have sexual intercourse with her husband except on rare occasions. He had since died. She showed marked signs of hysteria, and a diagnosis of hysterical hypochondriasis was made. There was also an element of exaggeration. Improvement was expected. The trial judge awarded £2,750 under this head.

Held: there were no grounds for interfering with either the judge's assessments or
with his total award of £6,750 general damages for pain, suffering and loss
of amenities.

See pp 7, 103, 129.

Devon County Council v S

*Blood transfusion: Jehovah's witness: child patient: consent: interests of patient:
parental objections*

Thorpe J. [1993] 11 BMLR 105

S was four and a half years old. He suffered from T-cell leukaemia with a high risk of death.
Intensive chemotherapy would give him a 50% chance of cure. It involved the transfusion
of blood or blood products. There was no other treatment that held any prospect of cure.
S's parents, who were dedicated Jehovah's witnesses, objected to any blood transfusion.

The plaintiff local authority issued an originating summons, invoking the inherent
jurisdiction under s 100 of the Children Act 1989 and applying for an order permitting blood
transfusion. The parents responded by seeking prohibited steps orders under the Act.

Held: the welfare of the child was the paramount consideration. The religious
convictions of the parents could not be allowed to deny their son a 50% chance
of survival and to condemn him to inevitable and early death. The relief sought
by the originating summons was overwhelmingly established and should be
granted.

See p 12.

Distillers Co (Bio-chemicals) Ltd v Laura Anne Thompson

Drugs: warning: jurisdiction: thalidomide: Australia

Privy Council. [1971] AC 458, [1971] 1 All ER 694, [1971] 2 WLR 441

In August 1961, when Laura Thompson's mother was pregnant, her doctor in New South
Wales prescribed for her Distaval, the principal ingredient of which was thalidomide. She
obtained it from a chemist in New South Wales and took it. There were no warnings of
danger on the printed matter supplied with the drug. In April 1962 Laura Thompson (the
plaintiff) was born without arms and with defective eyesight.

Distillers, an English company incorporated in Great Britain, obtained the substance
thalidomide in bulk from its German manufacturers and used it to manufacture the drug
Distaval. They sold it to an Australian company which marketed it in New South Wales.
The plaintiff sued both Distillers and the Australian company in the Supreme Court of New
South Wales.

Held: (on appeal by Distillers): the alleged negligence of failure to give a warning
that Distaval could be dangerous if taken in the first three months of pregnancy
occurred in New South Wales and injured the plaintiff there. Consequently
her cause of action arose in the New South Wales jurisdiction and she could
sue Distillers there.

See pp 32, 52.

Dobbie v Medway Health Authority

Limitation: mastectomy: operation: surgeon: breast

Court of Appeal. [1994] 5 Med LR 160, [1994] NLJR 828, (1994) Times, 18 May.

On 26 April 1973 the plaintiff (Margaret Dobbie) was admitted to Sheppey General Hospital for a biopsy on a lump in her left breast. On 27 April, while she was under anaesthetic, the surgeon considered (without microscopic examination) that the lump was pre-cancerous and carried out a left mastectomy, allegedly without her consent. On 14 May laboratory analysis revealed that the lump was 'fibro-adenosis with cyst formation', benign and not cancerous. She was told of this on 11 June 1973.

The effect of losing her breast was devastating. The next few years of her life were marked by repeated overdoses and admissions to psychiatric hospitals. She took no steps to claim until in May 1988 her daughter told her about a similar case reported on local radio. The plaintiff contacted AVMA and instructed solicitors who started court action on 5 May 1989.

At the preliminary trial of the limitation defence, it was submitted on her behalf that until 1988, when she had first known that excision of the lump for microscopic examination could and should have preceded removal of the breast, she had lacked the requisite knowledge to set time running against her under s 11 of the Limitation Act 1980, since she lacked knowledge that something had happened which was not an ordinary result of surgery; and that there had to be knowledge that something had gone wrong.

Held: (i)   the plaintiff knew from the beginning that her personal injury was the direct result of the surgeon's act or omission. What she did not appreciate until later was that this was arguably negligent or blameworthy. Her lack of that knowledge did not stop time beginning to run. The judge was right to hold that her claim was statute-barred.

        (ii)   she was a grievously injured woman who had suffered much and whose claim, if allowed to proceed, might be very strong. But the delay, after the date of actual knowledge in 1973, was very long indeed. It would be unfair to require the hospital authority to face the claim arising out of events that occurred so long ago. The judge's refusal to exercise his discretion under s 33 of the 1980 Act in her favour should be upheld.

See pp 178, 185, 193, 195.

Doe v United States of America

AIDS: blood transfusion: causation: child patient: foreseeability: surgeon: USA: tonsillectomy

United States District Court (Rhode Island). [1990] 2 Med LR 131.

On 21 April, 1983, the plaintiff, then five years old, underwent a tonsillectomy performed at Newport Naval Hospital by Dr Richard Busch, a naval surgeon. At the conclusion of surgery Dr Busch placed stitches at the inferior poles of both tonsils using 0 chromic material.

He was discharged on 22 April but was brought back to the hospital's emergency department on 26 April after vomiting blood and blood clots. Dr Busch carried out electrocauterization under local anaesthetic, the plaintiff having to be physically restrained. The plaintiff was given a half unit (125 cc) blood transfusion and admitted to hospital. Haemorrhaging began again a few hours later and he was taken to the operating theatre where additional 0 chromic sutures were applied. He received two units of blood while in the operating room and two further units that night.

On 4 May he was discharged, but that evening he suffered the most severe episode of bleeding and was returned to the hospital. Dr Busch advised the mother that a carotid ligation might be necessary. She expressed a total lack of faith in the doctor and asked him to do only what was necessary to control the bleeding until her son could be transferred to another hospital. Dr Busch sutured the area again, this time using non-soluble silk material. Two more units of blood were administered.

The next day the plaintiff was transferred to Boston Children's Hospital where he was attended by Dr Ellen Friedman, a paediatric otolaryngologist. She observed extensive tissue necrosis in an area extending well beyond the tonsillar fossa. She suctioned away the old blood clots to inspect the area. When she did so the plaintiff began haemorrhaging profusely. The bleeding did not stop until Dr Friedman completed a seven hour carotid artery ligation operation. The plaintiff's blood loss was estimated at 600 cc, between one third and half of his total blood volume. During the procedure and his post-operative recovery he received 47 units of blood at the hospital.

He was discharged about a month later. In April 1987 he was diagnosed as HIV positive. His condition deteriorated and, in March 1989, he was diagnosed as having developed AIDS.

The plaintiff brought an action in the United States District Court for the District of Rhode Island, contending that his condition resulted from Dr Busch's negligence.

Held: (i) Dr Busch had been negligent in dealing with the plaintiff's episodes of post-operative bleeding.

(ii) the plaintiff had established causation in that:

(a) but for Dr Busch's actions and the delay in performing a carotid artery ligation, he would have required no more than two units of blood rather than the 54 units actually received;

(b) statistical evidence showed that the HIV contaminated blood most likely came from the additional units that had to be administered at the children's hospital due to Dr Busch's negligence.

(iii) by the end of 1982 blood transfusions were generally recognised as a possible mode of transmitting AIDS, even though the exact method of transmitting was still unknown. Consequently, at the time of the plaintiff's tonsillectomy, blood transfusions presented a clearly foreseeable risk that the patient could contract AIDS, and it had been recognised for many years that transfusions could transmit other life-threatening diseases.

The plaintiff was awarded damages which included US$800,000 for pain and suffering.

Doughty v North Staffordshire Health Authority

Limitation: operation: scarring: surgeon: face: plastic surgery

Henry J. [1992] 3 Med LR 81

On 20 April 1957 the plaintiff (Mrs Doughty) was born with an extensive birth mark, known as a port wine stain, on the right side of her face. A plastic surgeon, Mr Growcott, operated twice on her when she was five. Thereafter there was no turning back. She had had 12 operations by the time of his retirement in 1974. His successor then advised that no significant improvement was possible and questioned whether it had been right to embark on the long course of surgery. Her face had been significantly scarred by the operations, and some of the port wine stain remained.

In 1976 she consulted solicitors who obtained a limited legal aid certificate. In 1978, after a discouraging expert's opinion, counsel advised that there was no case and the certificate was discharged. In 1982 she gave birth to a severely handicapped daughter and became preoccupied with looking after her. In 1985 she was put in touch with AVMA. Around this time she was divorcing her husband who had blamed her for their daughter's genetic disorder and walked out on her. AVMA referred her to a solicitor who contacted her in April 1986. He let the case go to sleep until he issued a writ on 2 December 1987. After an expert's report, there was a conference with counsel in March 1989. The statement of claim was not served until February 1990. The defence pleaded limitation.

Held: (i)   the plaintiff knew when she saw her surgeon's successor in 1974 that her injury was significant and that it was attributable to the course of surgery: Therefore her case was prima facie statute barred by s 11 of the Limitation Act 1980.

     (ii)   (a)   the length of the delay was considerable. The reasons were discouraging professional advice, compounded by the limitations on the legal aid certificate;

           (b)   the reality of the delay was a trial in 1991 rather than 1980. The most serious effect on evidence was that the surgeon had a stroke in 1989 that left him unable to testify. This distinctly reduced the cogency of the defendants' evidence, but the basic medical records were still available;

           (c)   the plaintiff's present solicitors did not act promptly, but in view of all her other problems the plaintiff could not be blamed for any failure to chivvy or activate them;

           (d)   the course of treatment had blighted the plaintiff's childhood and affected her whole life. She was not to blame for the delay. Although there was prejudice to the defendants, as a fair trial was still possible it was equitable under s 33 to disapply s 11 of the Limitation Act 1980.

The defendants were found negligent, and the plaintiff was awarded £30,000.

See pp 118, 183, 194, 196, 197.

Dransfield v Rotherham and Mexborough Hospital Management Committee and Another

Fracture: operation: arm

Court of Appeal. CAT, 19 February 1976

The plaintiff (Colin Dransfield) suffered a fracture of his left humerus in 1922 or 1923. Metal plates were inserted to hold it in position and metal bands were put round the broken bone. Around 1960, suppurations from the arm developed. The plaintiff's general practitioner referred him to Rotherham Hospital. He was seen there by Dr Murray who recommended an operation to remove the metal objects. Dr Murray performed this in April 1968. During the course of the operation, damage was caused to the radial nerve in the plaintiff's left arm and he suffered from a dropped left wrist.

The plaintiff sued Dr Murray and the hospital authority. His expert asserted that the radial nerve should have been exposed at the start of the operation. The defence expert and Dr Murray testified that the radial nerve was embedded in thick fibrous growth that had built up over the bone and that the proposed course would have been more dangerous than the one adopted.

Held: the trial judge (Pain J) was entitled to prefer the evidence of the defendants and to hold that Dr Murray did not fall in any way below the duty of a competent doctor in the circumstances. The fact that surgical operations involve risks and that in the course of an operation one of the risks materialises does not mean that those conducting the operation have been at fault. There was no possible ground for suggesting that the judge was wrong in holding that the defendants were not negligent.

Driscoll-Varley v Parkside Health Authority

Limitation: surgeon: leg: consultant

Hidden J. [1991] 2 Med LR 346

On 18 April 1984 the plaintiff (Ann Driscoll-Varley) was assaulted by her then husband who kicked her and caused her to fall downstairs. She was taken straight to St Mary's Hospital in Paddington where she was treated by traction, with a pin through her right heel, until 30 April. On 1 May the pin was removed and plaster encased round her leg. On 2 May a supervised attempt at walking showed this to be unsuccessful. On 3 May her leg was fixed by the insertion of a nail. The wound improved, and by spring 1985 she was able to walk normally.

After the Kunschner nail was removed on 28 July 1985, her leg became hot, swollen, painful and blistered. In September 1985 Mr Johnson, the new consultant, advised that a sinogram be carried out and then informed her that he felt that there was a piece of dead bone floating around, causing infection. She had great faith in Mr Johnson who performed nine operations on her over the next twelve months up to September 1986 in an effort to obtain satisfactory union. She was also terrified of losing her leg.

In August 1986 she instructed solicitors who issued a writ in April 1987. She instructed them not to serve it, for fear of alienating Mr Johnson who continued to treat her. In June 1987 he referred her to another specialist who fixed her right tibia using a Gross-Kempf nail with two cross screws and discharged her from his care in November 1987. She instructed new solicitors who received expert advice on 30 June 1988 that the cause of her problem was that her leg had been removed from traction too early. They obtained an ex parte order extending the validity of the writ and served it in July 1988. In early May 1989 the defendants on appeal obtained an order setting aside the renewal and service.

On 4 May 1989 a fresh writ was issued. After close of pleadings, a preliminary trial of the limitation defence was ordered.

Held: (i) the plaintiff knew that her injury was significant by September 1985 when the sinogram showed that her leg had not correctly set and that there was dead bone.

(ii) it was only on 30 June 1988 that the plaintiff learned that her injury, in the sense of failure of the damaged leg to respond to treatment in a normal and satisfactory manner, was capable of being attributed to the act or omission alleged to constitute negligence, namely prematurely taking her off traction and mobilising her limb.

(iii) the burden of establishing any earlier date of constructive knowledge under s 14(3) of the Limitation Act 1980 was upon the defendants.

(iv) it was perfectly reasonable for the plaintiff, with her burning desire to keep her leg and her firm faith that the best way to do so was to continue with treatment by Mr Johnson, to act as she did. The defendants had not discharged the burden of fixing her with any earlier constructive knowledge.

(v) accordingly the action was not statute barred under s 11 of the Limitation Act 1980.

See p 183.

Drummond and Another v Wonford House Hospital (Incorporated)

Psychiatric patient: supervision: breach of contract

Avory J (with jury). [1928] 1 BMJ 287, (1928) 1 Lancet 411

After the birth of her third child, the plaintiff (Mrs Drummond) had become obsessed with the idea that she had committed an unspeakable crime and had expressed intense dislike for her husband and children. On the advice of Dr Grant Wilson, she was removed to a mental nursing home in Exeter. Dr Grant Wilson told Dr Morton, medical superintendent of the home, of the suicidal tendencies exhibited by her. He said that she was extremely restless and agitated, and that she had delusions of persecutions and all the symptoms of acute puerperal melancholia. He suggested that she should enter the hospital as a voluntary patient but that if Dr Morton thought that was not safe he would certify her as a lunatic.

The plaintiff was watched unceasingly until her second night. Dr Morton then withdrew the night nurse and substituted visits every half hour. In the absence of a nurse, the plaintiff broke the glass of a window and forced herself through an aperture measuring less than ten inches square and through the bars guarding the window. She struck an iron balustrade and fractured her arm and jaw.

When the plaintiff recovered her mental balance, she and her husband sued the proprietors of the nursing home for negligence and breach of contract.

Held: Avory J directed the members of the jury that the defendants owed a duty to take reasonable care and to exhibit reasonable skill in the treatment of all patients admitted to their institution. They had to ascertain whether the defendants had been guilty of negligence and whether Dr Morton, knowing what he did, was right in withdrawing the night nurse on the second night.

The jury returned a verdict for the plaintiffs.

See p 132.

Dryden v Surrey County Council and Another

Operation: retained surgical product: nurses

Finlay J. [1936] 2 All ER 535

Dr Stewart performed a minor operation on the plaintiff (Mrs Dryden) at the defendant's hospital at Epsom. She remained in hospital for a week. Two days later she was examined by Dr Keble, her general practitioner, who extracted from her body a black evil-smelling sausage of surgical gauze. This was plugging that Dr Stewart left in her after the operation. She contracted pyelitis and cystitis.

The plaintiff alleged negligence against Dr Stewart and the hospital nurses. She claimed, *inter alia*, that she had a swelling which could be detected by anyone swabbing, that she had a profuse and foul-smelling discharge and that she was sent home without her temperature being taken. Both the hospital anaesthetist and Dr Stewart saw her several times after the operation. They saw nothing wrong, and she made no complaint to them. Dr Keble did not detect the discharge until he extracted the gauze.

Held: (i)   Dr Stewart had negligently left the gauze in the plaintiff's body.

(ii)   the nurses were not negligent. They had no reason to know that the gauze had been left in, so they were under no duty to remove it. As the plaintiff's temperature had pursued a normal course, it was unnecessary for them to take it again on the morning on which she left the hospital.

See p 125.

Dunning v United Liverpool Hospital's Board of Governors

Discovery

Court of Appeal. [1973] 2 All ER 454, [1973] 1 WLR 586

In April 1963 the applicant (Mrs Florence Dunning) developed a cough and was admitted to the Royal Infirmary at Liverpool for further investigations. She became gravely ill in hospital and her personality changed. The doctors were at first uncertain of the diagnosis and treated her with different drugs. When she left hospital after 17 weeks, her walking and memory were impaired and she was a different woman altogether.

In 1969 she was granted legal aid limited to getting a medical opinion. The hospital refused to disclose her clinical notes to her medical expert unless it was assured that no action would be brought against it. The assurance was not given, so the clinical notes were not produced. Her expert reported that his assessment had been considerably hampered by their absence.

The applicant issued an originating summons under s 31 of the Administration of Justice Act 1970. By it she asked for an order that the hospital should disclose the medical records and case notes that it had about her treatment.

Held: they should be produced to the plaintiff's medical adviser or such medical consultant as he should advise.

Per Lord Denning MR: 'I think that we should construe "likely to be made" as meaning "may" or "may well be made" dependent on the outcome of the discovery. One of the objects of the section is to enable a plaintiff to find out–before he starts proceedings–whether he has a good cause of action or not. The object would be defeated if he had to show–in advance–that he had already got a good cause of action before he saw the documents.'

Per James LJ: 'In order to take advantage of the section, the applicant for relief must disclose the nature of the claim he intends to make and show not only the intention of making it but also that there is a reasonable basis for making it. Ill-founded, irresponsible and speculative allegations or allegations based merely on hope would not provide a reasonable basis for an intended claim in subsequent proceedings.'

See pp 207, 208.

Durrant v Burke

Brain damage: general practitioner: child patient

HH Judge Fallon. [1993] 4 Med LR 258

On Sunday 6 December 1981 the plaintiff (Marlo Durrant), then seven months old, became ill and began to vomit. A doctor from a deputising service attended, diagnosed gastroenteritis and prescribed a medicine.

The plaintiff was no better on 7 December. At 4pm his mother telephoned the defendant (Dr Burke) who examined him on a home visit around 7pm. Marlo appeared slightly lethargic, but his general condition seemed good; he was suffering from both diarrhoea and vomiting; he exhibited no symptoms of deterioration. Dr Burke confirmed the diagnosis of gastroenteritis and prescribed merbentyl, an anti-colic medicine. He stressed to the mother that it was crucial to keep the level of fluids up and that the child should have sips of fluid as often as possible. He told her to telephone if Marlo was not better in the morning and to telephone in any event if he deteriorated.

Later on 7 December and also on 8 December, Marlo's mother tried to give him clear fluids as instructed but he vomited these up. Her main worry was not the fluid intake, but the fact that the child was not eating. She found that he would take cereal, and so she gave him cereal without any significant fluid intake. Giving the cereal stopped him from vomiting.

On 9 December at about 11am she telephoned the surgery and said that Marlo was still not eating, but that the diarrhoea and the vomiting had improved although he was still not well. When Dr Burke visited at 2pm, he found that the child was severely dehydrated and arranged for his immediate admission to the Children's Hospital in Bristol. Marlo was found to be suffering from hypernatraemic dehydration. He suffered brain damage.

Held: (i) the defendant had given the plaintiff's mother adequate and proper instructions on 7 December. She was intelligent and the home atmosphere was good, so he was under no additional duty to check on the child the next morning in the absence of any contact from her.

(ii) unfortunately it was the mother's understandable concern with the baby not eating, which led her to feed him cereal, that was the cause of the trouble. Had she merely done what the doctor told her to do, namely to give a little fluid often, then the condition of hypernatraemic dehydration would probably not have developed as it did.

(iii) the defendant had not been negligent. The claim must fail.

See p 136.

Dwyer v Rodrick and Others

General practitioner: prescription: pharmacist: gangrene: apportionment of liability: toes: neck

Court of Appeal. (1983) 127 Sol Jo 805

The plaintiff (Mrs Joan Dwyer) suffered persistent pain in her neck. On 20 November 1973 Dr Rodrick diagnosed migraine and prescribed sixty Migril tablets, two to be taken every four hours as necessary. This prescription was a patent mistake. It was taken on the same day to the shop of Cross Chemists (Banbury) Ltd where a qualified pharmacist dispensed the tablets without noticing the error. On 23 November Dr Jackson, Dr Rodrick's partner, visited the plaintiff at her home. He did not have her clinical notes with him, so he did not know she had been prescribed Migril. He did not discover this on his visit and prescribed Stemetil for her complaint of vomiting. When Dr Jackson visited her again on 26 November he discovered that she had taken thirty-six Migril tablets in six days. She suffered gangrenous necrosis and loss of part of each toe, peripheral nerve damage and other serious injuries.

The trial judge (Stuart-Smith J) held all three defendants liable in negligence and apportioned liability at 45% to Dr Rodrick, 15% to Dr Jackson and 40% to Cross Chemists. Dr Jackson appealed.

Held: Dr Jackson did not see the Migril bottle. He was not negligent in not finding out on 23 November that the plaintiff was taking Migril.

Note: It had been agreed between counsel that, if Dr Jackson's appeal should succeed, Cross Chemists would accept the extra 15% liability. Thus the final apportionment was 45% to Dr Rodrick and 55% to Cross Chemists.

See pp 121, 135.

Re E (a minor)

Blood transfusion: consent: minor: parental objections:

Ward J. [1994] 5 Med LR 73

E was a 15-year-old who had religious objections, supported by his parents, to being given a life saving blood transfusion.

Held: he had not reached the required degree of understanding for his refusal of consent to be effective. In any event, the court was empowered to override his refusal.

See *Re R (a minor) (wardship: medical treatment)* [1991] 4 All ER 177 (pp 515–516).

See p 10.

Re E (a minor) (medical treatment)

Consent: hysterectomy: interests of patient: sterilisation

Sir Stephen Brown. [1991] 2 FLR 585, 7 BMLR 117, (1991) Times, 22 February

E was a 17-year-old mentally handicapped girl. She suffered from extremely heavy and erratic menstrual periods which she could not understand. After trying various medical methods, the gynaecologists advised hysterectomy for therapeutic reasons. The purpose of the operation was to relieve E's extremely distressing symptoms. Its object was not sterilisation which would be the incidental result. Her parents consented to the operation.

Held: there was a clear distinction between an operation to be performed for a genuine therapeutic reason and one purely to achieve sterilisation. In a case falling within the therapeutic category, such as this, the parents could give a valid consent and a declaration by the High Court was not necessary.

See pp 11, 13.

Early v Newham Health Authority

Anaesthetics: anaesthetic awareness: appendicitis: operation: senior house officer

Patrick Bennett QC. [1994] 5 Med LR 214

In January 1990 the plaintiff (Sarah Early), then aged 13, was admitted to the Newham General Hospital with an acutely inflamed appendix. In the afternoon, she was taken to the operating theatre to have an appendectomy. The anaesthetist was a senior house officer, Dr Ugalde. He administered an intravenous injection of thiopentone, 100 micrograms of fentanyl and 100 milligrams of a drug called suxamethonium. The effect of the latter drug was to paralyse the plaintiff, thereby rendering it necessary for Dr Ugalde to insert into her lungs an endotracheal tube via the oesophagus, in order to enable oxygen to reach the lungs and the plaintiff to breathe. Dr Ugalde examined the plaintiff's vocal cords and could see part of them with the laryngoscope. He asked the ODA for a tube. He saw three quarters of the cords, but then when he tried to intubate he could not see them. He tried once for a distance of about 10–15 inches and then stopped. He then followed the defendant's drill to be carried out in the case of a failed intubation.

'Where the intubation fails, cricoid pressure should be maintained, ventilate with oxygen, do not give a second dose of suxamethonium, do not persist with repeated attempts at intubation, turn patient on side, call for help. If the procedure is not for a life-threatening condition, continue oxygenation, allow the patient to wake up.'

The effect of the thiopentone, the anaesthetic which put the plaintiff to sleep, wore off before the effect of the suxamethonium. Consequently the plaintiff regained consciousness at a time when her body was still partly paralysed. This caused her panic and great distress until she had recovered all her physical functions.

She sued the hospital authority. Witnesses gave evidence that the defendant's drill which Dr Ugalde followed was used in a number of well known London hospitals as well as in Sweden and Holland.

Held: (i) Dr Ugalde was not negligent in failing successfully to intubate the first time. This was one of those recognised occasions when even experienced anaesthetists may have unexpected difficulty in intubating a patient. It did not result from any lack of care, skill or competence on the part of Dr Ugalde.

(ii) the drill was not such that no reasonably competent authority would have adopted it. On the contrary, it showed that the defendant hospital authority had applied its mind to the problem of failed intubation and come up with a reasonable solution. A risk of a transient terror was run, but at the same time the risk of far greater injury by hypoxia was avoided.

The plaintiff's claim was dismissed.

See p 123.

Eaton v Eli Lilly & Co and Others

Limitation: drugs: Opren

Court of Appeal. [1992] 3 Med LR 383

See *Nash v Eli Lilly & Co* (E) (p 471).

Edgar v Lamont

Duty of care: breach of contract: substandard treatment: fingers: Scotland: amputation

Scotland, Court of Session. 1914 SC 277

In June 1913 Mrs Jessie Edgar cut her finger. Dr Lamont was sent for. She was under his care for the next fortnight. She suffered great pain and finally had to have the finger amputated.

She sued Dr Lamont, alleging that this was due to his improper treatment. He argued that it was a claim for breach of contract and that his contract was with her husband who had agreed to pay for his services.

Held: Mrs Edgar was entitled to sue. A doctor owes a duty to the patient, whoever has called him in and whoever is liable for his bill, and it is for breach of that duty that he is liable.

See pp 18, 44.

Edler v Greenwich and Deptford Hospital Management Committee and Another

Diagnosis: appendicitis: casualty officer: general practitioner: causation: advice: child patient: peritonitis: fatal

Finnemore J. (1953) Times, 7 March

Iris Edler, aged 11, became ill with abdominal pains and vomiting on Saturday 7 July 1951. She was ill throughout the night. On Sunday 8 July the plaintiff (her father) took her to the Miller Hospital in Greenwich where she was examined by Dr Hewlett-Clarke, the casualty officer, who was told about the pains and vomiting. When asked where the pain was, she put her hand over the middle of her stomach and moved it to and fro. She winced every time that her abdomen was touched on examination. The doctor then carried out a rectal examination and said afterwards that there was nothing wrong with the girl but if she got worse that day her father should bring her back to the hospital.

She remained ill. On 9 July her mother went to see the family's panel doctor, Dr Mehta, who, on being told what the hospital doctor had said, thought it was probably gastric trouble. On 10 July she got worse and Dr Mehta arranged her immediate admission to hospital where under operation there was found an advanced state of peritonitis and a ruptured and gangrenous appendix. The child died. Her father sued the hospital management committee and Dr Mehta.

Held: (i)   Dr Hewlett-Clarke was negligent in failing to diagnose appendicitis. It was no defence to say that he told the father to bring the child back if she got worse, because the father was sent away with the idea that nothing was wrong. Everything that ensued was due to the faulty diagnosis.

   (ii)   as Dr Mehta was told that the hospital had said that there was nothing wrong, it was impossible to say that he was negligent. There was nothing that provided an excuse for Dr Hewlett-Clarke's negligence or a break in the chain of causation.

See pp 80, 97, 136.

Edwards v Mallan

Dental: representation: breach of contract: teeth

Court of Appeal. [1908] 1 KB 1002

The plaintiff sued in the High Court, alleging as follows in her Statement of Claim:

'1. The plaintiff has suffered damage from the negligence and unskilfulness of the defendant as a surgeon dentist employed for reward by the plaintiff to extract one of her teeth.

2. The plaintiff in February 1907 was suffering from toothache, and went to the defendant to have a tooth extracted by the defendant's "painless process", and on February 18 the defendant or his operator or other representative agent did extract the said tooth, but so unskilfully that broken portions of the said tooth were left in the jaw, whereby illness, pain and suffering were caused to the plaintiff.'

Held: there was no allegation of a breach of contract to use a painless process. The action was simply an action based on unskilful dentistry. Thus it was an action in tort, not contract (and so could be remitted to the county court under s 66 of the County Courts Act 1888 (since repealed) if the plaintiff had no visible means of paying the defendant's costs.

See p 44.

Elkan v Montgomery Smith

Diagnosis: fracture: x-ray: causation: ankle

McCardie J. (1922) 1 Lancet 548

The plaintiff (Mrs Elkan) injured her ankle in a fall. She consulted Dr Montgomery Smith. No x-ray was taken for a considerable time. She continued to place weight on her ankle. When an x-ray was finally taken, it showed that there had been a fracture of the lower end of the fibula, and of the lower end of the shaft of the tibia with partial dislocation backwards of the foot near the ankle-joint.

The plaintiff became lame and sued Dr Montgomery Smith, alleging that he had opposed x-ray examination and that his treatment had made her worse.

Held: (i) Dr Montgomery Smith had in fact recommended the employment of x-rays, and had diagnosed and treated the case with proper care.

(ii) the plaintiff's lameness was due not to the treatment but to her own conduct in over-working the ankle.

Judgment for the defendant.

See p 133.

Ellinger v Riverside Health Authority

Damages: operation: neck

Adrian Whitfield QC. (1993) AVMA Journal, January, p 16

In 1987 the plaintiff (Mrs Ellinger) underwent a minor operation under local anaesthetic for removal of a lump on her neck. Owing to negligent performance of this, she suffered a partial left accessory nerve lesion. In consequence her left trapezius muscle was wasted, which caused significant limitation of movement in her left shoulder and difficulty in lifting any weight with her left arm. She suffered acute pain in her left shoulder and neck. She was right handed. The pain reduced in intensity after two years.

By trial, when she was 33 years old, she had a moderate ache present every day together with periods of more acute pain upon any activity involving the use of her left shoulder. She was left with a cosmetic disability consisting of (a) an asymmetry of the shoulders due to the muscle wasting on the left and (b) a six centimetre scar on the left side of her neck which was the result of two operations carried out under general anaesthetic in 1988 and 1989 in unsuccessful attempts to repair the accessory nerve. There was no prospect of improvement in her condition.

She had been married for only five months before the operation; the injury had caused intimate activity with her husband to be painful ever since. She had been keen and active in a variety of sports. Now she could only play tennis with discomfort, some movements in swimming were painful, cycling would only be possible with a specially adapted 'recumbent bicycle', and skiing caused pain in her shoulder.

She continued to be able to work as a management consultant, albeit with some aching of her left shoulder. However she was unable to perform many of the tasks, particularly the lifting and carrying, involved in caring for her baby who was born in 1991. Consequently she had to employ a nanny. Her husband's salary was insufficient to cover this. Therefore she returned to work after her maternity leave in order to pay for the nanny. Otherwise she would have stayed at home to look after the child and the second baby she was likely to have in 1993. The nanny would still be required, together with a home help to undertake the heavy housework which the plaintiff could not manage.

Held: (i) general damages of £30,000 were awarded for pain, suffering and loss of amenities. This included £5,000 for the loss of amenity involved in being forced to remain in a demanding job for 16 months and in thereby being deprived of the day to day enjoyment of bringing up her baby during this period.

(ii) special damages were agreed at £1,980. No award was made in respect of the cost of the nanny up to the date of trial, on the grounds that the plaintiff paid for this out of earnings which she would not have received but for the defendants' negligence.

(iii) £115,410 was awarded for the future cost of the nanny and home help.

The total award was £147,390 plus £2,415 interest.

See p 118.

Ellis v Home Office

Duty of care: prison inmate: supervision: segregation: psychiatric patient

Court of Appeal. [1953] 2 QB 135, [1953] 2 All ER 149, [1953] 3 WLR 105

In July 1949 the plaintiff (Mr Ellis) was in Winchester prison awaiting trial. Under suspicion of illness, he was in the hospital wing. One morning the only prison officer in attendance left the wing for a period. While he was away, a prisoner named Hamill went into the plaintiff's cell and hit him violently on the head at least twice with some implement. Hamill was convicted of unlawfully wounding the plaintiff.

In April 1949 Dr Fenton, the prison medical officer, had learned that Hamill might well be mentally defective. He kept him in the hospital wing for observation. However, when Dr Fenton examined Hamill he did not think that he was likely to commit an act of violence. Hamill did not have a previous record of such acts.

The plaintiff sued the Home Office for failing to segregate Hamill and failing to safeguard the plaintiff against him. The trial judge (Devlin J) dismissed the claim.

Held: the mere fact that Hamill was mentally defective did not make him likely to commit an act of violence. Dr Fenton had no reason to anticipate this. The plaintiff's case failed.

See pp 50, 132.

Emeh v Kensington and Chelsea and Westminster Area Health Authority and Others

Sterilisation (failed): wrongful birth: novus actus interveniens: damages: public policy abortion

Court of Appeal. [1985] 1 QB 1012, [1984] 3 All ER 1044, [1985] 2 WLR 233

In May 1976 the plaintiff (Kathleen Emeh), a married woman who already had three healthy children, underwent an abortion and sterilisation operation at St Stephen's Hospital. In January 1977 she learned that she was 18–20 weeks pregnant. She decided against another abortion. When her baby Elizabeth was born, it was found to be congenitally abnormal. The trial judge (Park J) held that the sterilisation operation had been performed negligently and in breach of contract.

Held: (i)   the plaintiff's refusal to undergo an abortion was not so unreasonable as to eclipse the surgeon's negligence. Save in the most exceptional circumstances, the court should not declare it unreasonable for a woman to decline to have an abortion in a case when there is no evidence that there were any medical or psychiatric grounds for terminating the particular pregnancy. Consequently the defendants' plea of *novus actus interveniens* failed, as did their argument that the plaintiff had failed to take reasonable steps to minimise the damage.

    (ii)   it is not contrary to public policy to recover damages for the birth of a child, whether healthy or abnormal.

    (iii)   the plaintiff was awarded.

      (a)   £3,000 for pain and suffering up to trial in December 1982;

      (b)   £10,000 for future pain, suffering and loss of amenity, including the extra care to be given to the child over the years;

      (c)   £7,000 for the plaintiff's loss of future earnings;

      (d)   £1,736 for the cost of maintaining the child up to trial;

      (e)   £507 per annum with a multiplier of 8 for the future cost of maintaining her;

      (f)   the cost of a second sterilisation operation;

      (g)   the cost of a layette (£248).

See pp 55, 80, 127, 169.

Enright v Eli Lilly & Co

Brain damage: product liability: public policy: USA: pregnancy

New York Court of Appeals. (1991) MLJ 126.

The plaintiff was a nine-year-old girl with cerebral palsy. Her grandmother had taken diethylstilboestrol (DES) during pregnancy in 1959. Her mother, born in 1960, had deformities in her reproductive system. It was alleged that these had led to the plaintiff's premature birth and neurological injuries.

She was one of about one hundred 'DES granddaughters' suing for damages in various US states. DES had been marketed for about thirty years in the belief that it reduced the risk of miscarriage. In 1971 it was banned by the US Food and Drug Administration because of evidence of an abnormal incidence of vaginal and cervical cancer in the daughters of women who had taken DES during pregnancy.

Held: there was no right to pursue a third generation DES injury claim.

Per Chief Judge Sol Wachtler: 'For all we know, the rippling effects of DES exposure may extend for generations. It is our duty to confine liability within manageable limits. Limiting liability to those who ingested the drug or were damaged in utero serves this purpose.'

See pp 32, 55.

Esson v Gloucester Health Authority

Anaesthetic awareness: medical report: pleadings

Morland J. (1994) AVMA Journal, Spring, p 8

In December 1988 the plaintiff (Sandra Esson) underwent exploratory abdominal surgery at Gloucester Royal Hospital. She alleged that the anaesthetist was negligent, with the result that during two stages of the operation she recovered consciousness and that in consequence she suffered acute pain and severe psychiatric injury.

Medical records were disclosed to the plaintiff's solicitors in October 1989. Her writ against the defendant hospital authority was issued in July 1990 and served in November 1990. Her statement of claim was served in January 1991, unaccompanied by any medical report. On the defendant's application, the district judge ordered that she serve a medical report as to condition and prognosis within 28 days and that the time for service of the defence be extended to 28 days thereafter.

At the hearing of the plaintiff's appeal, her counsel argued that medical negligence cases were a very special kind of personal injury action, that in medical negligence liability causation and injury were intertwined issues, and that the plaintiff serving a medical report with the statement of claim would give the defendants an unfair advantage.

Held: (i) the fact that an action is one for medical negligence does not result in any fetter on the court's discretion under RSC Ord 18, r 12(1A) and (B). At most, it is a circumstance to which the court will have regard in exercising its discretion.

(ii) in the majority of negligence cases, there should be strict compliance with the rules. Only in exceptional cases would it be right to make an order dispensing with the requirements of Ord 18, r 12(1A).

(iii) the present case was no exception, specially in view of the sluggish progress of the claim.

(iv) accordingly it was ordered that 'the plaintiff do within 28 days serve a medical report' and 'the defence to be served within 28 days of service of the plaintiff's medical report.'

See p 213.

Esson v Gloucester Health Authority (No 2)

Anaesthetic awareness: damages: operation: laparotomy

HH Judge Owen. Halsburys Laws 94/1854

In December 1988, the plaintiff (Sandra Esson), aged 43, developed severe abdominal pain associated with vomiting and was admitted to Gloucester Royal Hospital. She underwent an exploratory laparotomy under general anaesthetic. She was conscious during the operation, but was paralysed by the action of muscle relaxant and thus unable to communicate her condition to theatre staff. She had a feeling of being poked, prodded and kneaded inside her abdomen. The pain was excruciating.

She recalled hearing muffled voices in the operating theatre. An expert's report supported her contention that the drug doses were inadequate to provide the general anaesthetic required. Eventually the defendant hospital authority admitted liability.

After the experience, the plaintiff withdrew from contact with people and continued to have troubling and intrusive thoughts about the operation. She also experienced feelings of insecurity, reflected in variable anxiety and depressive symptoms. She still had some residual symptoms of this post-traumatic stress syndrome two years later, but they were not so severe as to warrant psychiatric intervention. She suffered some minimal remnants of post-traumatic stress disorder after five years.

Held (July 1993): general damages of £14,500 were awarded for pain, suffering and loss of amenities.

See pp 123, 156, 213.

Evason v Essex Health Authority

Cancer: costs: diagnosis: damages

Welster J. [1994] 10 PMILL 5

In September 1983 the plaintiff (Mrs Sandra Evason) underwent surgery in which a lymph node was removed from her left groin. Owing to an error in the hospital laboratory, a diagnosis of cancer was made: the pathology report stated that the lymph node was affected by secondary carcinoma and that a breast primary was likely. In fact she did not have cancer: the tissue taken from the lymph node was confused with a sample taken from another patient. The error was not discovered for 14 months. During this period the plaintiff was treated for cancer and underwent six courses of chemotherapy, three laparotomies and the removal of her right ovary. The effect upon her personality of living for 14 months under a sentence of death was traumatic; by the end, her career and marriage had been destroyed and her physical and mental health were permanently impaired.

In early 1985 she consulted her first solicitors. In June 1987 the defendant hospital authority offered £10,000 general damages. In August 1987 the plaintiff changed her solicitors. In August 1989 liability was admitted. In May 1990 the defendants paid £135,200 in court. In June 1990 Mr Justice Jupp awarded a total of £203,500 damages.

Owing to her serious degree of psychological disturbance, the plaintiff required much more attention and reassurance than average from her solicitors. This was reflected in the claim in her bill of costs for 85 hours of partner's attendance, including telephone calls. Although it was not suggested that any of these hours had been invented, the district judge on taxation allowed only 25 hours.

Held: (i) the district judge should have taken the plaintiff as he found her after the hospital's error. He should have taken into account, for the purposes of taxation, her special and unusual needs for personal attendance. In failing to do so in practice, he erred in principle.

(ii) only 17¾ hours of the partner's attendances should be disallowed. Four of these were the result of inevitable duplication which must have occurred as a result of the change of solicitors.

(iii) the district judge was right to allow an uplift of 75% for care and conduct.

See pp 134, 157

Everard v Hopkins

Breach of contract: duty of care

Coke CJ (with J). (1615) 2 Bulst 332

In December 1611 the servant of the plaintiff (Mr Everard) was hurt by a cartwheel. The plaintiff agreed with Mr Hopkins, a common surgeon, that Mr Hopkins would undertake the cure for a fee of five marks. The treatment caused the servant more pain and left him lame and unable to work.

The plaintiff sued Mr Hopkins, alleging that he had been negligent and had applied unwholesome medicines to the servant's wounds.

Held: the pleading was neither good nor formal. In view of the nature of the contract, the plaintiff ought to have pleaded that he had paid the money. The servant could not base an action upon the plaintiff's contract with Mr Hopkins, but he could bring a case for the negligent application of unwholesome medicines.

The court was inclined to be of opinion for the plaintiff, but as the pleading was defective no judgment was given. The case was adjourned and then settled.

Everett v Griffiths and Another

Psychiatric patient: negligent certification

Court of Appeal. [1920] 3 KB 163

In early 1919 the plaintiff (Mr Everett), then aged 23, was residing with his parents in Islington. On 21 March, following a complaint by his mother, he was removed to Islington workhouse and detained in the observation ward. On 24 March Dr Anklesaria, the medical officer of the workhouse, who had examined and visited the plaintiff several times and had watched him through the peep-hole, certified him to be insane and a proper person to be detained. Pursuant to the Lunacy Act 1890, the plaintiff was sent on 27 March to Colney Hatch mental asylum where he remained until his escape on 9 April.

He was subsequently accepted to be sane and represented himself in court with remarkable forensic ability. However the Lord Chief Justice entered judgment for the defendants.

Held: Dr Anklesaria was under a duty to the plaintiff to act with good faith and reasonable care. His good faith was accepted, and there was no evidence that he was negligent.

See p 47, 100.

Eyre v Measday

Sterilisation (failed): breach of contract: risk disclosure

Court of Appeal. [1986] 1 All ER 488

In 1978 the plaintiff (Mrs Mary Eyre), then aged 35, consulted Mr Measday, a gynae-cological surgeon. it was agreed that he should carry out a sterilisation by laparoscopy. She was to undergo this on a budget scheme as a private patient who made a modest payment. Mr Measday performed the operation completely. However in April 1979 the plaintiff discovered that she was pregnant, and in October 1979 she gave birth to a fine healthy boy.

Mr Measday did not mention that there was a chance of 2–6 in 1,000 that pregnancy might occur following the operation. He emphasised the irreversibility of the procedure. The plaintiff sued him for braach of contract or warranty to render her irreversibly sterile. The trial judge (French J) found in favour of Mr Measday.

Held: (i) the contract was a contract to perform a laparoscopic sterilisation rather than to render her abolutely sterile. The reference to irreversibility simply meant that the operative procedure was incapable of being reversed; it was not a guarantee that the operation was bound to sterilise the appellant.

(ii) in the absence of any express warranty, the court should be slow to imply against a medical man an unqualified warranty as to the results of an intended operation. It is most unlikely that a responsible medical man would intend to give a warranty of this nature, as distinct from an undertaking that he would perform the operation with reasonable care and skill.

See pp 27, 111.

F v F

Consent: hysterectomy: interests of patient: sterilisation

Sir Stephen Brown. (1991) Times, 29 April

F, aged 29, had been severely mentally handicapped from birth and spent most of her day in a wheelchair. She was cared for at home by her parents. She suffered from heavy painful menstrual periods with which she could not cope. Her general practitioner and two consultant gynaecologists advised hysterectomy. The object of the operation was to relieve the distressing medical symptoms. Sterilisation would be the incidental result.

F's mother applied for a declaration from the High Court that the hysterectomy would not be unlawful.

Held: a declaration by the High Court was not necessary, when two gynaecologists advised that the operation was in the best interests of the patient for therapeutic reasons.

See p 15.

F v W

Childbirth: quadriplegia: structured settlement

FTSB, Autumn 1994

The plaintiff (F), aged 8, suffered spastic quadriplegia due to negligent procedures during his birth. Medical evidence suggested that he 'could live well into his fourth, fifth or sixth decade'.

The following settlement was agreed:

Interim payments	£30,000
Accommodation costs	£168,659
Capital cost of structure	£500,000
Cash to be paid forthwith	£184,042
Other damages	£51,341
Total	£934,042

No discount was sought by the defendant hospital authority. The structured sum of £500,000 was applied to buy three annuities.

(i) Type of Annuity	Immediate
Initial net yield	4.3%
Initial annual sum	£10,000
Indexation	RPI
Equivalent gross yield after higher rate tax	7.2%
Payable for:	Life of plaintiff
Guarantee period	16 years
(ii) Type of Annuity	Deferred
Deferred period	10 years
Initial annual sum (in today's terms)	£13,103
Indexation	RPI
Payable for	Life of plaintiff
Guarantee period	6 years
(iii) Type of Annuity	Step
Lump Sum payment every:	5 years
Initial lump sum (in today's terms)	£10,000
Indexation	RPI
Payable for:	Life of plaintiff
Guarantee period	3 payments

F v West Berkshire Health Authority and Another

Psychiatric patient: consent: sterilisation: trespass to person: interests of patient: standard of care

House of Lords. [1989] 2 All ER 545

F, aged 36, suffered from serious mental disability. She had the verbal capacity of a child of two and the general mental capacity of a child of four. Since 1967 she had been a voluntary in-patient at a mental hospital. She formed a sexual relationship with a male patient there. From a psychiatric point of view, it would have been disastrous for her to conceive a child. There was a serious objection to each of the ordinary methods of contraception.

F's mother, acting as her next friend, sought against the health authority a declaration that the absence of consent would not make sterilisation of F an unlawful act. The trial judge (Scott Baker J) granted the declaration. The Court of Appeal dismissed the Official Solicitor's appeal.

Held: (i) no court has jurisdiction to give or withhold consent to such an operation in the case of an adult.

(ii) however the court has jurisdiction to declare the lawfulness of such a proposed operation. Although such a declaration is not necessary, in practice the court's jurisdiction should be invoked.

(iii) the application should be by way of originating summons issuing out of the Family Division of the High Court. The applicants should normally be those responsible for the care of the patient or those intending to carry out the proposed operation. The patient must always be a party and must normally be a respondent. Subject to the judge's discretion, the hearing will be in chambers but the decision and reasons will be given in open court.

(iv) to be lawful, in the absence of consent, the operation or other treatment concerned must be in the best interests of the patient, either to save the

327

patient's life or to ensure improvement or prevent deterioration in her physical or mental health. In making such decisions, the doctor must act in accordance with a responsible and competent body of professional opinion.

(v)   the judge had been right to grant the declaration sought.

Per Lord Brandon: 'At common law a doctor cannot lawfully operate on adult patients of sound mind, or give them any other treatment involving the application of physical force however small (which I shall refer to as "other treatment"), without their consent. If a doctor were to operate on such patients, or give them other treatment, without their consent, he would commit the actionable tort of trespass to the person. There are, however, cases where adult patients cannot give or refuse their consent to an operation or other treatment. One case is where, as a result of an accident or otherwise, an adult patient is unconscious and an operation or other treatment cannot be safely delayed until he or she recovers consciousness. Another case is where a patient, though adult, cannot by reason of mental disability understand the nature or purpose of an operation or other treatment. The common law would be seriously defective if it failed to provide a solution to the problem created by such inability to consent. In my opinion, however, the common law does not fail. In my opinion, the solution to the problem which the common law provides is that a doctor can lawfully operate on, or give other treatment to, adult patients who are incapable, for one reason or another, of consenting to his doing so, provided that the operation or other treatment concerned is in the best interests of such patients. The operation or other treatment will be in their best interests if, but only if, it is carried out in order to either save their lives or to ensure improvement or prevent deterioration in their physical or mental health. . .

'With respect to the Court of Appeal, I do not agree that the *Bolam* test is inapplicable to cases of performing operations on, or giving other treatments to, adults incompetent to give consent. In order that the performance of such operations on, and the giving of such other treatment to, such adults should be lawful, they must be in their best interests. If doctors were to be required, in deciding whether an operation or other treatment was in the best interests of adults incompetent to give consent, to apply some test more stringent than the *Bolam* tests, the result would be that such adults would, in some circumstances at least, be deprived of the benefit of medical treatment which adults competent to give consent would enjoy. In my opinion it would be wrong for the law, in its concern to protect such adults, to produce such a result.'

Per Lord Goff: 'I feel bound to express my opinion that, in principle, the lawfulness of the doctor's action is, at least in its origin, to be found in the principle of necessity. This can perhaps be seen most clearly in cases where there is no continuing relationship between doctor and patient. The doctor in the house who volunteers to assist a lady in the audience who, overcome by the drama or by the heat in the theatre, has fainted away is impelled to act by no greater duty than that imposed by his own Hippocratic oath. Furthermore, intervention can be justified in the case of a non-professional, as well as a professional, man or woman who has no pre-existing relationship with the assisted person, as in the case of a stranger who rushes to assist an injured man after an accident. In my opinion, it is the necessity itself which provides the justification for the intervention.

'I have said that the doctor has to act in the best interests of the assisted person. In the case of routine treatment of mentally disordered persons, there should be little difficulty in applying this principle. In the case of more serious treatment, I recognize that its application may create problems for the medical profession; however, in making decisions about treatment, the doctor must act in accordance with a responsible and competent body of relevant professional opinion, in the principles set down in *Bolam* v *Friern Hospital Management Committee*.'

See pp 7, 16, 57, 103.

Fairhurst v St Helens and Knowsley Health Authority

Brain damage: child patient: damages: interest

HH Judge David Clark. [1995] PIQR Q1

The plaintiff (Deborah Fairhurst) was born on 26 February 1970. She suffered bilirubin encephalopathy, a serious brain injury, when she was a new born baby. The hospital authority conceded negligence.

The plaintiff was retarded and functioned at a mental age of no more than four. She was profoundly deaf. Her level of understanding was rudimentary. She had difficult behavioural traits. She also suffered from recurrent epileptic fits. She was expected to live to the age of 50, 25 years from the date of trial.

She attended a local school until 1976. Then she attended the Royal School for the Deaf in Manchester as a weekly boarder until March 1993. Thereafter she attended on a weekly basis at a private residential home for profoundly deaf people with psychological difficulties. The home was expensive with a high staff to resident ratio.

Held (August 1994):

(i) the award for the plaintiff's care to date had to compensate her parents for their care over the first 24 years of her life, over and above the care which they would have devoted to her had she been uninjured. Her mother had no firm plans for returning to work after her birth. The hours of care basis of valuation was preferable to the loss of earnings basis. The Crossroads rates of pay for home help should be taken, but the deduction therefrom should be only one quarter rather than one third because caring for the plaintiff involved special skills over and above those normally possessed by Crossroads' assistants or nursing auxiliaries. There should be no uplift for the fact that parental care was given at weekends. The total award under this head should be £66,570 subject to deduction of agreed benefits of £31,389, producing a net award of £35,181.

(ii) the figure for past loss of earnings had been agreed at £50,000. Pursuant to s 5 of the Administration of Justice Act 1982, the figure of £12,000 should be deducted as the sum agreed between the parties to represent the saving arising from the plaintiff's maintenance at public expense.

(iii) so far as interest on special damages was concerned, even though the plaintiff's parents and their advisers were not at fault in respect of the delay in bringing the case, this delay had increased in real terms the capital value of the claim due to the application of the principle that multipliers for future loss run from the date of trial. Accordingly it was appropriate to halve the amount of interest which would otherwise have been awarded.

(iv) the proper multipliers for the future were 14 for care, even though a strict application of the 4% discount table would have produced a figure closer to 15, and 12 for future earnings.

(v) on the authority of *Lim v Camden and Islington Health Authority* (p 430), it was necessary to assess the deductions from the award for future care to represent the saved living expenses arising from the plaintiff being maintained at the private residential home. The appropriate deduction was £100 per week in respect of the period when the plaintiff would be staying there full time and £80 per week for the period when she would be home at weekends.

(vi) agreed general damages of £110,000 for pain, suffering and loss of amenities, and other items brought the total award inclusive of interest up to £847,639.

Note: On interest, see *Nash v Southmead Health Authority* (p 476).

See p 162.

Farquhar v Murray

Diagnosis: general practitioner: communication: locum: fingers: Scotland: amputation

Scotland, Second Division. 1901 SLT 45, (1901) 3 F 859, 38 SLR 642

Mr Farquhar, an Edinburgh grocer, alleged that on 9 April 1900 a finger of his right hand was scratched by a rusty nail. The finger having swollen, he consulted Dr Murray, his regular medical attendant. Dr Murray pronounced the finger to be affected with erysipelas. He prescribed a medicine to be taken and an ointment to be applied; he also told Mr Farquhar to poultice the finger with linseed and oatmeal. He called again on 10 April and directed Mr Farquhar to continue the poulticing and to use the medicines until he called again the next day.

Dr Murray never came. On 25 April Mrs Farquhar wrote to him. This led to a visit on 26 April from Dr Mackenzie who stated that Dr Murray was away on holiday, that he was looking after his practice in his absence and that Dr Murray had not left any message about the case. When Dr Mackenzie examined the finger, he said that it had been too long poulticed and wrote out a prescription. Eventually the finger had to be amputated.

Mr Farquhar sued Dr Murray, averring that 'the defender carelessly and grossly neglected his duty to the pursuer as his patient by failing to visit him as he had promised to do after giving directions for the treatment of his finger. The defender further absented himself suddenly from home without any communication to the pursuer of his intention to do so, and without making any arrangement for medical attendance on the pursuer during his absence. There was thus, on the part of the defender, a culpable want of attention and care, and a gross neglect of his professional duty'. The Lord Ordinary dismissed the action as irrelevant.

Held: the case was relevant and fit to be tried.

See p 135.

Faulkner v Wandsworth Health Authority

Brain damage: childbirth: damages

HH Judge Hordern QC. (1994) AVMA Journal, Spring, p 2

Around 2.15pm on 25 May 1979 the mother of the plaintiff (Paul Faulkner) was admitted to St George's Hospital. Syntocinon was commenced in order to augment labour. At 10.20pm, the CTG began to show decelerations in the fetal heart rate indicative of fetal hypoxia. An epidural was administered to her, following which the CTG showed bradycardia in the fetal heart rate lasting for about seven minutes and dropping to as low as 60–70 bpm. The CTG continued to exhibit variable deep decelerations. It was decided to continue with a normal delivery after which syntocinon was recommended. Between 1.40am and 3.00am on 26 May 1979, the CTG exhibited severe decelerations in the fetal heart rate, some of which lasted for between one and three minutes. Between 3.00am and 4.08am, the trace exhibited severe long decelerations in the fetal heart rate when on occasions it was as low as 60 bpm. The plaintiff was born at 4.08am in an asphyxiated condition.

Aged 13 at trial, he suffered from cerebral palsy of the spastic athetoid type. He had no voluntary movement of his limbs. Nor could he speak intelligibly, except for occasional one syllable words. However his eyesight and hearing were unimpaired, and generally his health was good. He had some control of his head, so he was able to control his wheelchair and use communication aids. He clearly had an insight into his own condition. Life expectancy was assessed at between 30 and 40 years.

Held: general damages for pain, suffering and loss of amenities were assessed at £125,000 out of a total award of £1,177,077 plus interest.

See p 154.

Fell v Eli Lilly & Co and Others

Limitation: drugs: Opren

Court of Appeal. [1992] 3 Med LR 398

See *Nash v Eli Lilly & Co* (Q) (p 476).

Field v Herefordshire Health Authority

Childbirth: damages: structured settlement

Phillips J. [1991] 7 PMILL 72

The plaintiff (Rebecca Field) was born in November 1984. Forceps were negligently used during the delivery. There was no sign of spontaneous breathing at the birth. She had to be supported by artifical respiration. She remained extensively paralysed and received continuous artificial respiration via a tracheostomy. She could only speak a few words to her parents who had provided her with constant care. Life expectancy was extremely uncertain. She would probably live into her twenties and possibly into her thirties.

The Health Authority admitted liability. The level of conventional damages was agreed at £1,700,000. When the case came to court on 4 June 1991, it was adjourned for a structure to be considered.

It was agreed that a lump sum of £550,000 be paid. The original cost of the structured programme was £1,042,000, but subsequently a lower quote enabled this to be reduced. The saving to the Department of Health on behalf of the Treasury exceeded £100,000 in any event. After allowing for the advantage to them of paying around £1,600,000 almost five months later than otherwise, their total saving approximated to £200,000.

The structured sum purchased the following payments to Rebecca:

(a)   an immediate amount of £59,000 pa, payable monthly, increasing every year at the rate of 5% pa compound, and guaranteed for her life or ten years, whichever be the longer;

(b)   a deferred amount of £15,315 pa, starting in five years' time, payable monthly, increasing at 5% pa compound, and guaranteed for her life or ten years from the first payment, whichever was the longer;

(c)   a deferred amount of £32,578 pa, starting in ten years' time, payable monthly, increasing at 5% pa compound, and guaranteed for whichever proved to be longer of her life or five years from the first payment;

(d)   a lump sum payable at the end of every five years, based on the sum of £50,000, to be increased in line with the retail price index, only to be paid while she was alive.

Phillips J approved the settlement on 31 October 1991.

See p 151.

Fish v Kapur and Another

Dental: fracture: res ipsa loquitur: jaw

Lynskey J. [1948] 2 All ER 176

In May 1946 a wisdom tooth was troubling the plaintiff (Mrs Fish). She went to the premises occupied by Mr SK Kapur and asked him to remove the tooth. She saw a nurse who took her into the surgery and placed her in the dentist's chair. The defendant dentist, Mr IK Kapur, came in and she was given an anaesthetic. In the extraction, he left part of the root of the tooth in the jaw. Also, by some means unexplained, the jaw was fractured.

The plaintiff called at trial Dr Devas, a doctor of medicine, who said in evidence that it is possible to fracture a jaw during extraction without any negligence. Her other expert, Mr Siggers, a dental surgeon, testified that when one is extracting teeth, fractures may occur without fault on the part of the dentist and equally one may leave in the root of the tooth without any blame attaching to him. The defendant did not give evidence. The plaintiff relied on the doctrine of res ipsa loquitur.

Held: the fact that the fracture was caused in the process of extraction of the tooth was not in itself any evidence of negligence. There was nothing left on which a finding of negligence could be based. The plaintiff's case must fail.

See pp 44, 88, 130.

Fish v Wilcox and Gwent Health Authority

Damages: wrongful birth: spina bifida

Court of Appeal. [1994] 5 Med LR 230, 13 BMLR 134

In 1977 the plaintiff (Mrs Linda Fish) suffered a miscarriage. The foetus was found to be anencephalic (ie, without a brain) and suffered from exomphalus (ie, its abdominal contents were protruding through the umbilical cord). This meant that any future pregnancies might be attended by risks of congenital deformity. The defendants failed to tell her about these abnormalities.

In 1979 the plaintiff gave birth to a boy, Anthony, who was perfectly normal. However in 1985 she gave birth to a girl, Cally, who suffered from spina bifida. She sued on the grounds that she should have been told about the abnormalities of the foetus in 1977, so that those in charge of her ante-natal care in 1985 would have subjected her to tests and scans which would have revealed the congenital deformity in the foetus and she would have been able to have an abortion. The defendants admitted liability.

The plaintiff gave up her job, for which she was paid £4,000 pa net, in order to look after Cally who needed constant attention. In 1991 she was diagnosed as suffering from multiple sclerosis and would not be able to look after Cally without considerable help.

In April 1992 Mr Justice Swinton Thomas awarded the plaintiff £234,387 damages and interest. This included £34,167, assessed at £5,000 pa, for the nursing care provided by her to Cally up to the date of judgment. The plaintiff appealed on the basis that in addition he should have awarded her loss of earnings which had been arithmetically agreed at £20,000.

Held: this would be wrong; it would amount to double recovery. The plaintiff could not recover both her loss of earnings and damages for her services in looking after Cally.

Per Stuart-Smith LJ: 'If the plaintiff had had to give up highly paid work in order to look after her daughter, then no doubt she would have recovered that figure by way of loss of earnings rather than the figure which the judge in fact assessed, subject, as O'Connor LJ said in the Housecroft case, to the ceiling, being the cost of providing professional care. It may be that if the plaintiff's earnings had been slightly in excess of the cost of providing professional care, it would nevertheless have been reasonable for her to give up that employment to look after her child, and in those circumstances it seems to me that the court would properly award her the full loss of earnings. But that was not this case, and the judge properly, as it seems to me, awarded an additional element for the additional burden of looking after Cally as opposed to the work which the plaintiff had previously done. But the essence, in my judgment, of the case is that the plaintiff is not entitled to make a profit out of it. As I have indicated, she cannot do two jobs at once and she is not entitled to be paid for doing two jobs at once.'

See pp 161, 168.

Fletcher v Bench

Dental: fracture: infection: x-ray: res ipsa loquitur: jaw

Court of Appeal. [1973] 4 BMJ 118

On 12 September 1968 the plaintiff visited his dentist at his Twickenham surgery. The dentist set to work to remove the plaintiff's lower third right molar under local anaesthetic. The tooth was impacted and did not respond to forceps. The dentist used a bone-burr. While he was drilling the bone, the bone-burr broke leaving a bit of it inside the jaw. Ultimately with another burr the dentist removed the bone around the tooth and got it out with forceps. He was unable to find the bit of broken burr.

On 13 September the plaintiff visited the dentist in much pain; he was suffering from swelling and stiffness of the jaw. Away on holiday the plaintiff twice saw another dentist who found that the socket was infected, dressed it and alleviated the pain. On 22 September the plaintiff's jaw fractured due to the infection. When he visited his dentist again on 23 September, the socket was badly infected. An x-ray showed that the broken bit of burr was stuck at the very point of fracture. On 26 September the tip of the bone-burr was finally removed.

The plaintiff sued his dentist. The trial judge dismissed the claim.

Held: the breaking of the drill and the fact that it was left there at the end of a difficult operation were not indicative of a lack of care. After 13 September, the plaintiff did not see his dentist again until 23 September by which date the fracture had already occurred. The defendant was not liable.

See p 89, 130.

Fletcher v Sheffield Health Authority

Infection: limitation: preliminary trial: operation: leg

Court of Appeal. [1994] 5 Med LR 156

The plaintiff (Ms Fletcher) was born on 18 March 1959, jaundiced and with rhesus incompatibility. Thus she needed an exchange transfusion. Following this an infection set in, which was treated with penicillin, but which proved to be penicillin resistant. Swabs from septic spots were taken. The results would have been known by 23 March, and that finding should have been dealt with urgently. The plaintiff's case was that, negligently, these results were not passed to the paediatrician caring for her until four days later, but by then it was too late to prevent the onset of osteomyelitis. She developed septic arthritis, which led to considerable destruction of her femur and her hip was dislocated.

Despite a series of operations, the left leg did not grow so well as the right. The plaintiff further contended that the defendants were negligent in the performance of a leg lengthening series of operations carried out on her in 1975–76.

By her 18th birthday in 1977, she suspected that the 1975–76 leg lengthening procedure had not been performed competently. However her case in respect of the alleged 1959 negligence was that the significance of the delay in passing the lab analysis to the doctors responsible for the treatment was not appreciated until it emerged in conference with counsel on 28 November 1991.

The plaintiff had issued her writ in respect of the second alleged negligence in July 1989, amending it in November 1989 to add the claim of negligence at birth. The defendants applied for an order that the limitation issue be tried first. Their case on this was that the plaintiff should at least have investigated the 1975–76 treatment and procedures earlier and, had she done so, this would have led her back to the 1959 records, so she would have been fixed at an early stage with constructive knowledge of both the incidents of negligence. They also denied causation.

Held: (i)   the first limitation issue would therefore be on the question of constructive knowledge, bringing with it the necessity for calling expert medical opinion on each side. The focus would be on when the plaintiff should have had knowledge of the 1975–76 negligence, and whether that knowledge would have led her to discovery of the negligence alleged at birth.

      (ii)   in so far as this was decided in the defendant's favour, the second issue would be the exercise of the court's discretion to disapply the primary limitation period. It would investigate the evidence carefully, in order to assess the effect of additional delay since March 1980 on its cogency, and would assess the strength of the plaintiff's case. Such an exercise would be likely to range over a large part of the evidence, both factual and expert, that would be heard in the trial on liability itself.

     (iii)   accordingly the judge's assessment that the limitation issues could not be separated from the issues of negligence and causation could not be faulted; and the conclusion that the limitation issues should not be tried as a preliminary issue was one to which he was entitled to come.

Flynn v Maidstone Health Authority

Brain damage: caesarian: cardio-respiratory arrest: childbirth

Tuckey J. QBD transcript, 26 October 1992

In 1971 Mrs Shirley Wallace had given birth to a healthy boy after a long and difficult induced labour, culminating in a suction and forceps delivery. In 1988 she became pregnant with the plaintiff (Victoria Flynn). Unbeknown to anyone before birth, the baby was suffering from intra uterine growth retardation. The last few days of the pregnancy were full of problems.

At 2.16am on 3 November 1988 Mrs Wallace, then aged 39, was admitted to the labour ward of Maidstone General Hospital with a history of regular contractions since midnight. She was about eight days over term. Noting her desire for a normal delivery, the senior house officer monitored her condition until the consultant Mr Pentecost came on to the ward at 8am. Mr Pentecost saw Mrs Wallace at 8.05am and decided to administer syntocinon to induce the birth. This was started at 9.15am, and the dose was increased by degrees. There were decelerations recovering fairly well. By 10.30am contractions were one every five minutes.

At 11.50am a vaginal examination was performed to assess progress and to rupture the membranes. Upon rupture, thick and fresh meconium stained liquor drained. By this time, the cervix had dilated to five centimetres. The trace showed numerous repetitive dips, some of which were late, no accelerations and reduced base line variation. The midwife contacted a GP trainee who saw Mrs Wallace at 12.10pm. In view of the meconium stained liquor and persistent decelerations, she requested Mr Pentecost by 12.15 to visit and reassess the situation. When he arrived at 12.45, he decided to let the labour proceed.

It proceeded with disastrous consequences. At 13.05 a further vaginal examination found that the cervix was nine centimetres dilated. At 13.20 the foetal heart was down to 60 beats a minute: an obvious emergency. Oxygen was administered, and the GP trainee was contacted. At 13.25 it was recorded that the foetal heart continued to decelerate. Further vaginal examination showed that the cervix was fully dilated. When Mr Pentecost returned at 13.40, he delivered the foetus with forceps.

Soon after birth, the plaintiff's condition deteriorated and she suffered two episodes of cardiorespiratory arrest. The arrests, in turn, had probably been caused by meconium aspiration syndrome as a result of fetal distress in the second stage of labour after 13.15.

Held: (i) none of the experts disputed passages in Mr Gibb's book that thick and fresh meconium indicates a situation of high risk and great concern and that, where in addition the CTG trace is abnormal, 'delivery should be expedited unless it is expected without delay.'

(ii) Mrs Wallace's age, the fact that the delivery was after term, her anxiety, her antenatal history and the risk of UGR meant that Mr Pentecost's decision after rupture of the membranes at 11.50 to allow labour to proceed exposed the baby to unacceptable risk. As the cervix was only five centimetres dilated at 11.50, early vaginal delivery could not have been expected.

(iii) Mr Pentecost should have decided between 12.15 and 12.45 to perform a caesarean section. His decision to allow the labour to continue was negligent.

(iv) such a caesarean section would have been performed by 13.15 and would probably have prevented the plaintiff's hypoxia and consequent brain damage. The defendant hospital authority was liable for this.

See p 126.

Flynn v Maidstone Health Authority (No 2)

Brain damage: childbirth: damages: structured settlement: cardiac arrest

Otton J. 28 July 1994

In November 1988 the plaintiff (Victoria Flynn) was born at Maidstone General Hospital. She became severely ill with respiratory problems which resulted in a cardiac arrest.

Following this, she suffered multiple convulsions and became severely handicapped by cerebral palsy. Her life expectancy was assessed at 20 years.

Damages on the conventional basis were assessed at £552,500. An interim payment of £50,000 had been made. The plaintiff's parents were paid £35,000 in respect of the special damages claim. £117,500 of the damages went into a contingency fund. The balance of £350,000 was applied to purchase an RPI linked annuity of £27,154 pa.

Interim payment	£50,000
Payment to parents	£35,000
Contingency fund	£117,500
Structured sum	£350,000
Discount	Nil
Total	£552,500

A distinctive feature of the settlement was that no discount was given to the defendant hospital authority for participating in the structure, in return for which it was agreed that there would be no minimum guarantee period for the annuity payments which would cease on the plaintiff's death.

When approving the structured settlement, Mr Justice Otton commented that he 'had never seen one quite so good.'

See pp 126, 152.

Foreman v Saroya

Anaesthetics: dental: damages: hepatitis

Master Foster. [1992] CLY 1739

The plaintiff (Ms Foreman), aged 41 at trial, contracted hepatitis as a result of a reaction against halothane anaesthetic administered by her dentist (Mr Saroya). He ought to have known of her susceptibility to this anaesthetic, as he had previously administered it to her with an adverse reaction. His negligence was not in dispute.

Soon after the administration of the anaesthetic, the plaintiff suffered severe abdominal pains and began to vomit. For the next two weeks, she experienced lethargy and loss of appetite. She was admitted to hospital for a week. Thereafter she was advised to refrain from any physical exertion, including sexual intercourse, for six weeks. During this period, she was unable to carry out her usual household chores, easily became tired and did not work. Subsequently she had to abstain from alcohol for six months. Though told that she was lucky to be alive, she made a complete recovery.

Held (January 1992): the plaintiff was awarded £2,250 general damages for pain, suffering and loss of amenities.

See p 131.

Forster v Eli Lilly & Co and Others

Drugs: limitation: Opren

Court of Appeal. [1992] 3 Med LR 386

See *Nash v Eli Lilly & Co* (H) (p 473).

Fowler and Another v South-West Metropolitan Regional Hospital Board and Another

Fracture: penicillin: gangrene: arm

Pilcher J. [1955] 2 BMJ 387

In February 1952 the plaintiff (Mrs Irene Fowler) fell in her garden. She sustained a fracture of both bones in the right forearm, and there was a small punctured wound caused by the bones. She was taken to the Yeatman Hospital, Sherborne, where she was treated by Dr McIntosh. The fracture was reduced. An unpadded plaster cast was applied to the plaintiff's arm, but she was not given any penicillin injections. Her arm became infected with gas gangrene and had to be amputated.

The plaintiff and her husband sued Dr McIntosh and the health authority.

Held: the defendants were liable in negligence. It was impossible to absolve Dr McIntosh from some responsibility for his failure to treat the plaintiff with a course of penicillin injections. Good practice demanded that a fracture of that kind should not be enclosed at once in an unpadded cast. The fitting of a close and unpadded plaster immediately after the reduction of the fracture interfered with the circulation, creating a condition in which the preventive and curative effects of free circulation provided by nature were removed.

Fox v Riverside Health Trust

Anorexia nervosa: declaration: force feeding: psychiatric patient: declaration

Court of Appeal. (1993) Times, 28 October

Carolyn Fox was detained in hospital for treatment under s 3 of the Mental Health Act 1983. She suffered from anorexia nervosa. The hospital doctor was desperately anxious about her condition.

The hospital informed her solicitors that it was intended to apply for an order for force feeding. Her solicitors had no legal aid and were unable to attend at the hearing. Stuart-White J heard the medical evidence ex parte and accepted that force feeding was necessary to save life. He granted an interim declaratory order stating that Ms Fox could be force fed either by spoon with restraint or if considered to be necessary by nasal tube with sedation.

Held: interim declaratory relief was unknown to English law. There was no jurisdiction to grant an interim declaratory order.

Fredette v Wiebe

Abortion: Canada: contributory negligence: general practitioner: tests: wrongful birth

British Columbia Supreme Court, Taylor J. (1986) 29 DLR (4th) 534.

The plaintiff (Beverley Fredette), was a single 17-year-old high school student who had become pregnant the previous month during a reunion with her then boyfriend. She went to see the defendant (Dr Ellen Wiebe), a Vancouver general practitioner, with a view to getting an abortion. On 22 December 1978, when the plaintiff was five weeks pregnant, the defendant competently attempted abortion by a suction and curettage procedure.

She told the plaintiff to make an appointment to have a post operative examination in one to two weeks' time. Such a check-up was one of two safeguards relied on to identify cases in which the procedure might have failed. The second was the routine laboratory examination of tissue removed by the operation. The first safeguard failed because the plaintiff never returned for her check-up. The second failed because the defendant never examined the laboratory report on the tissue that she had removed. There was no fetal tissue in this at all: a clear warning that the procedure had probably failed.

In mid-March 1979 the plaintiff discovered, in her 17th or 18th week of pregnancy, that the abortion had failed. She decided to have the baby, even before she learned that she was carrying twins. After they were born in July 1979, she sued for damages.

Held: (i)   the defendant was negligent in failing to ensure that she examined the pathology report. Had she done so, the operation could have been repeated during the ninth week of pregnancy when the plaintiff would probably have consented to it.

      (ii)   the plaintiff was guilty of contributory negligence, assessed at 50%, in failing to arrange the post-operative check-up. Had she done so, she would have learned at an early stage that she was still pregnant.

     (iii)   the plaintiff's refusal to undergo an abortion 18 weeks into her pregnancy was foreseeable and a reasonable response to its developing state. She had not unreasonably failed to mitigate her loss.

Per Taylor J: 'By the time she discovered that the abortion had failed Beverley was close to the half-way point in her pregnancy. It might be said that morally – and perhaps logically, too – termination of pregnancy would amount to the same thing then as at the five-week stage when she had her original operation. But the law must be concerned rather with the way in which a normal, reasonable woman would be likely to view that matter – with how a woman's mind is likely to work in fact rather than with how someone might say it ought to work.

I find that the plaintiff was unwilling to consider the possibility of abortion at that point. I accept Dr Sutter's evidence that she decided on having the baby, as she then believed, even before she underwent ultrasound examination and discovered – that is to say, actually saw – that she was carrying twins. From that point on she was determined to have and keep these children.

If Beverley had inquired into the possibilities of abortion at that stage she would have learned that it was by then too late to repeat the procedure which she had undergone three months earlier. She would have found out that an abortion performed after 16 weeks of pregnancy must be done by a more radical process, a procedure involving the induction of premature labour with the patient fully conscious. I accept the medical evidence that this procedure tends, both physically and psychologically, to be a far more distressing experience for the patient.

I do not accept the defendant's contention that it would be reasonable to expect that a woman who was willing to undergo an abortion at five weeks would still be willing to have an abortion three months later.

I find the defendant's contention that Beverley ought to have offered the twins for adoption at birth is open to similar objection.

I must do the best I can, in deciding the probable reaction of the ordinary reasonable woman; by relying on what I believe to be reasonable inferences from the evidence I have concluded that the advance of pregnancy may be expected to be accompanied by progressive development in the expectant mother of a need to bear the child – the need to have, to know and to raise the child – which may not necessarily have been felt at all earlier in the pregnancy.

I think it is for this reason wrong to say of a woman who seeks an abortion in the early stage of pregnancy and at a later stage decided to bear and keep her child that she has simply 'changed her mind'. It will certainly be true that her mind has changed. That change is likely to a large extent to be caused, I think, by a process linked to the physical advance in her pregnancy.'

See p 83.

Freeman v Home Office (No 2)

Prison inmate: consent: injection: trespass to person

Court of Appeal. [1984] QB 524, [1984] 1 All ER 1036, [1984] 2 WLR 130

The plaintiff (David Freeman) was serving a life sentence at Wakefield Prison. He behaved in a disruptive way, suffered from bouts of depression and attempted suicide on a number of occasions. In August 1972 Dr Xavier, a prison medical officer, prescribed Stelazine to be taken orally. The plaintiff refused to take it. Between September and December 1972 he received injections of Serenace and Modecate prescribed by Dr Xavier. He alleged that these injections were administered against his will and by force and sued for trespass to the person.

Held: where in a prison setting a doctor has the power to influence a prisoner's situation and prospects, a court must be alive to the risk that what may appear to be a real consent may not in fact be so. Essentially the matter is one of fact. The trial judge (McCowan J) rejected the plaintiff's evidence and justifiably found that he had consented.

See pp 9, 103.

Frenchay Healthcare NHS Trust v S

Consent: interests of patient: discontinuance of life supporting treatment: PVS

Court of Appeal. [1994] 2 All ER 403, [1994] 1 WLR 601, (1994) Times, 19 January

In June 1991, S, who had hitherto been a fit, energetic and sane young man, took a large overdose of drugs with the result that he suffered acute and extreme brain damage. He was taken to a hospital in a state of deep unconsciousness. In October 1991 he was transferred to a rehabilitation unit in the Bristol area. The consultant there concluded that he was in a persistent vegetative state (PVS). This opinion was shared by a professor of neurology and by a consultant neuropsychiatrist who both saw S from time to time.

The treatment which S underwent at the rehabilitation unit involved an intensive nursing regime with attention of one sort or another every two hours: toilet, bathing, relieving his bladder, emptying his bowels, turning him, and so on. Until June 1993 he was fed through a nasogastric tube as the only practicable way of feeding him. That became unsatisfactory because as a result of restlessness following each feed S repeatedly pulled on the tube and there was some evidence of bleeding in the stomach, probably caused by the tube itself. Accordingly the nasogastric tube was removed and a consultant surgeon performed an operation to insert a gastrostomy tube through the stomach wall and into the stomach to permit him to be fed in that way.

On 10 January 1994 it was found that the gastrostomy tube had been removed from S's body, probably as a result of his own movement, pulling it out of the stomach. In the absence of a tube, it was impossible to feed S at all. His consultant considered that re-siting the gastrostomy tube so as to resume feeding would not serve any ulterior purpose and would be against S's best interests. He accepted that not re-siting the tube would cause death within a limited period, but added that there was no reason to expect lack of food or fluid to cause suffering or ill effect. S's mother strongly favoured this latter course; his father was equivocal.

On 12 January the plaintiffs (Frenchay Healthcare NHS Trust) applied to the Bristol District Registry of the High Court for a declaration that, despite the inability of the defendant patient, S, to consent, the plaintiffs and their physicians (a) might lawfully refrain from renewing and/or might lawfully discontinue all life-saving treatment and medical support measures designed to keep the defendant alive in his existing persistent vegetative state including the termination of ventilation, nutrition and hydration by artificial means; (b) might lawfully discontinue and thereafter need not furnish medical treatment to him except for the sole purpose of enabling him to end his life and die peacefully with the greatest dignity and the least of pain suffering and distress; (c) that if death should occur following such discontinuance or termination the cause of death should be attributed to the natural and other causes of S's persistent vegetative state; and (d) that such discontinuance or termination and any other things done or omitted to be done in good faith in accordance with the order should not give rise to and should be without any civil or criminal liability therefor on the part of the plaintiffs or any participant whether physician, hospital or others.

On 13 January 1994 Swinton Thomas J granted the declaration as sought. The Official Solicitor immediately appealed on S's behalf. The appeal came before the Court of Appeal on 14 January.

Held: (i)   the safeguard of an application to the court had been satisfied. However it was inevitable that emergencies must occur in which application to the court is not possible, even though this case was not one of them.

          (ii)   there will be other situations, such as the present, in which although it is possible to come to court, it is not possible to present the application in a leisurely way. The facts must be considered very critically, but it would be wrong to allow the appeal simply on the basis that there had not been time for as full an exploration as might otherwise be desirable.

          (iii)   although there were suggestions in the medical reports of what might be interpreted as volitional behaviour by S, there was very little doubt in the evidence, specially from the doctors who knew him best, that S was in a persistent vegetative state, that there was no prospect of recovery, and that he had no cognitive function worth the name.

          (iv)   the fundamental question was what was in the best interests of the patient. The court must reserve the ultimate power and duty to review the doctor's opinion in the light of all the facts. In this case, there was no reason to dissent from the answer which the consultant had given and the course proposed by the plaintiff hospital trust.

The declaration was upheld.

See *Airdale NHS Trust v Bland* (p 222) and see p 17.

Re Frost

Psychiatric patient: negligent certification: duty of care: leave to sue: false imprisonment

Court of Appeal. [1936] 2 All ER 182

Robert Frost was a pauper aged 75. On Saturday 24 August 1935 he buried his wife. Afterwards he was in a very excitable condition and drank heavily. On the request of Mr

Frost's daughter, Dr Dean wrote: 'Please receive into hospital Robert John Frost of 11 Warriker Street, aged about 75 years. He requires hospital treatment. Requires to be kept under observation.'

On 25 August after receiving this letter by hand, an official at the Anlaby Road Institution, Kingston-upon-Hull, dispatched an ambulance with a driver and an attendant to Mr Frost's home. Without his consent they took him away to the institution. Dr Todd, the senior medical officer, issued a certificate for his detention, although he had not personally examined him. He was kept in a mental ward for four days.

Mr Frost was subsequently examined by two independent doctors who found no sign of mental incapacity. He applied under s 16(2) of the Mental Treatment Act 1930 for leave to bring court action against the Kingston-upon-Hull Corporation for false imprisonment and wrongful detention. Goddard J granted this application.

Held: there was sufficient evidence to justify the judge in concluding that through their acting only upon Dr Dean's letter and failing to get any medical man or expert to examine Mr Frost before they took him to the mental ward, there were substantial grounds for the contention that the appellants acted without reasonable care.

See p 100.

Furber v Kratter and Others

Psychiatric patient: leave to sue: substandard treatment: false imprisonment

Henry J. (1988) Times, 21 July

The plaintiff was a mental patient detained under a hospital order at Moss Side Special Hospital. After a violent and unprovoked attack on a ward sister, she was placed under a 'seclusion' regime for 16 days. That meant that she was locked alone in a side room off the ward. The room was furnished simply with a mattress. She was naked during the 16 days.

She applied under s 139 of the Mental Health Act 1983 for leave to sue the three hospital staff responsible for negligence and false imprisonment. She alleged that during the 16 days she had been denied nursing care, clothing, reading and writing materials. She further alleged that the regime of seclusion was imposed not as a treatment but as a punishment in order to humiliate her.

Held: (i)   she was entitled to sue in negligence, because if her allegations of wrongful imposition of the regime were substantiated it was eminently arguable that general damages for discomfort, suffering and loss of amenities could be recoverable.

       (ii)   she was entitled to sue for false imprisonment, even though she was already detained under a hospital order by sentence of the court, because it was possible for a regime to be so intolerable and prejudicial that it would render unlawful an imprisonment which had been lawful.

See p 100.

Furniss v Fitchett

New Zealand: confidentiality: general practitioner: novus actus interveniens: medical report: paranoia

Supreme Court, Wellington. [1958] NZLR 396

Dr Fitchett was the regular doctor of both the plaintiff (Mrs Furniss) and her husband. She entertained (unfounded) suspicions that her husband was doping her and that he was insane. These led to domestic discord which affected his health. A separation had been discussed. Dr Fitchett had declined a request from the husband's solicitor to arrange for the plaintiff to be certified for committal to a mental institution.

On 21 May 1956 the husband, in a distraught state, consulted Dr Fitchett and said: 'You must do something for me, doctor – give me a report for my lawyer.' After deep thought, the defendant then wrote out, signed and gave to the husband a document which was worded as follows:

'Mrs Phyllis CL Furniss   21.5.56
32 Mornington Road

The above has been attending me for some time and during this period I have observed several things:

(1) Deluded that her husband is doping her.
(2) Accuses her husband of cruelty and even occasional violence.
(3) Considers her husband to be insane and states that it is a family failing.

On the basis of above I consider she exhibits symptoms of paranoia and should be given treatment for same if possible. An examination by a psychiatrist would be needed to fully diagnose her case and its requirements.

Yours faithfully
A J Fitchett.'

Later, the plaintiff took proceedings against her husband for separation and maintenance orders. During the Magistrates' Court hearing of her application, in the course of cross-examination her husband's solicitor produced the above document to her. She suffered shock and subsequently sued the defendant for libel, which she abandoned in view of the defence of justification, and for negligence.

Held: (i) the defendant should have been aware that the certificate, which he handed to the plaintiff's husband to be given to her solicitor, without marking it as confidential or otherwise restricting its use, would be likely to come to her knowledge and, on doing so, be likely to injure her health.

(ii) he owed her a duty at common law to ensure that this should not happen. Since he took no precautions to prevent it, the jury was entitled to find that he had been negligent.

(iii) the alleged novus actus interveniens – the showing of the certificate to the plaintiff by her husband's solicitor – was the very thing which the law required the defendant to take care to avoid. The resultant damage was not too remote, even though its immediate cause was the act of the solicitor and not of the defendant.

The jury's award to the plaintiff of £250 damages was upheld.

Furstenau v Tomlinson

Diagnosis: error of judgment: mistake: skin complaint

Walton J (with special jury). [1902] 2 BMJ 496

The plaintiff (Mr Furstenau) was suffering from a skin infection. Dr Tomlinson diagnosed this as eczema. In spite of the remedies supplied and prescribed, the plaintiff's condition got worse and he finally sought a second opinion. The doctor whom he then consulted diagnosed scabies. The plaintiff's wife was also found to be suffering from this.

The plaintiff sued Dr Tomlinson, alleging negligence and ignorance. The defence was that the original mischief was eczema, and that if there were any concurrent scabies the latter was so masked by the former that it was impossible for anyone to diagnose it at that time.

Held: Walton J directed the jury that a mistake alone on Dr Tomlinson's part was not sufficient to enable the plaintiff to recover damages; negligence and the want of an ordinary amount of skill had to be proved before the jury could find for the plaintiff.

The jury returned a verdict for the defendant.

See p 95.

Fussell v Beddard

Anaesthetic: nurses: overdose: duty of care: vicarious liability

Lewis J. [1942] 2 BMJ 411

Mrs Fussell had to undergo an operation for removal of gall-stones. The surgeon and the anaesthetist, Mr Beddard, decided that anaesthesia should be induced by an epidural nerve block with decicaine. Mr Beddard told a sister that decicaine would be used and instructed her to prepare a solution of 0.1% She was highly qualified and had been in charge of the theatre for six years. Believing that she was carrying out his instructions, she prepared a solution of 1%. Mrs Fussell died of the overdose.

The plaintiff (her widower) sued Mr Beddard.

Held: the anaesthetist did not owe a duty to do more than state clearly to a responsible and efficient sister the anaesthetic he required. Mr Beddard had not been negligent.

Note: It is submitted that, following the cases of *Cassidy* v *Ministry of Health* and *Roe* v *Minister of Health*, on the same facts today a patient suing a health authority which is vicariously liable for any negligence on the part of the anaesthetist or the sister might reasonably expect to succeed.

See p 137.

Re G

PVS: consent: interest of patient: discontinuance of life-supporting treatment

Sir Stephen Brown. (1995) 2 Medical Law Monitor 4

After a motor cycle accident in 1991, G had been in a persistent vegetative state. The hospital applied for a declaration entitling it to withhold artificial feeding. G's wife, in

Re G

conjunction with his physicians and the Official Solicitor, supported this application. G's mother opposed it, however, on the basis that the sanctity of life required artificial feeding to be continued.

Held: it was in G's best interest to be allowed to die. Although the views of an opposing relative were important, they could not be determinative.

Re GF

Consent: hysterectomy: interests of patient: sterilisation

Sir Stephen Brown. [1992] 1 FLR 293 [1993] 4 Med LR 77

G had been seriously disabled from birth. Although she was 29 years of age, she had the mental age of a five year old. She had no sense of balance and was confined to a wheelchair. She lived with her parents. For many years she had suffered from excessively heavy periods. She was unable to take care of her own menstrual hygiene or basic sanitary care. She dreaded having her periods and was embarrassed and humiliated by the experience.

At the instance of her general practitioner, she consulted a consultant gynaecologist who discussed the case with a consultant obstetrician and gynaecologist. Her condition could not be satisfactorily relieved by hormone treatment. All doctors considered that the only practicable option was a hysterectomy with ovarian conservation. The object of this operation would be therapeutic, although its incidental effect would be sterilisation.

GF's mother issued a summons seeking a declaration that the operation might lawfully be carried out. The Official Solicitor represented GF's interests.

Held: (i) no application for leave to perform a hysterectomy is necessary, even though the incidental effect is sterilisation, where two medical practitioners are satisfied that the operation is:

    (a) necessary for therapeutic purposes;

    (b) in the best interests of the patient;

    (c) and that there is no practicable less intrusive means of treating the condition.

    (ii) as their conditions were satisfied in the present case, the declaration sought was unnecessary. If necessary, it would have been granted. The operation should be carried out to safeguard GF's health.

See p 15.

G v North Tees Health Authority

Hospital administration: tests: post-traumatic stress disorder: sexual abuse: damages: aggravated damages: child patient: skin complaint

Eastham J. [1989] FCR 53

A six year old girl was being treated by a hospital for a skin complaint. When she attended on 6 February 1986, her mother reported to the doctor that the child was suffering from a vaginal discharge. A vaginal swab was taken. It was reported to have active male sperm on it, indicating sexual intercourse. The child was admitted to hospital and subjected to a very painful internal examination, since it was thought that she might have been sexually abused for about two years. She also underwent a series of interviews by police officers and social workers.

On 10 February it was discovered that a mistake had been made. The practice at the hospital was to use one slide for two swabs. The slide upon which the child's swab was put was also used for a swab for an older person who had obviously had sexual intercourse. The mother was promptly informed of the error. She and her daughter sued the health authority who admitted liability.

The mother, a single parent, was extremely upset and depressed. Her family reacted badly, and she felt suicidal until the mistake was discovered. She suffered an exacerbation of a phobic anxiety state. She improved after counselling. The prognosis was promising.

The child suffered nightmares and enuresis. She became preoccupied with sexual assaults and her genital organs, and developed a fear of doctors and dread of the police. She responded well to counselling. However future gynaecological examinations might make her anxious.

Held: the case could adequately be dealt with by compensatory damages without awarding aggravated damages. The mother and child were awarded general damages of £5,000 each (December 1987).

See pp 50, 88, 134, 156, 167.

Gale v Cowie

Psychiatrist: injection: drugs: medical literature: state of knowledge: depression: anxiety

Lawton J. (1965) 2 Lancet 1341

In December 1960 the plaintiff (Mr Gale) consulted Dr Cowie, a psychiatrist. The plaintiff complained of anxiety and depression for which another doctor had prescribed him Amytal and Nardil. Dr Cowie agreed to treat him, telling him not to take the pills before he came for treatment. On 27 January 1961, in the course of treatment, Dr Cowie injected him with Methedrine. The plaintiff felt greatly distressed, thought that he was about to die and lost consciousness. His depression was aggravated.

The plaintiff sued Dr Cowie. Evidence was given that, at the time of the injection, no medical writer had drawn attention to the risks of injecting Methedrine into a patient who had taken Nardil. The danger was first described in 1962.

Held: in view of the absence of published warning, at the time of the injection, about the dangers of the combination of Methedrine and Nardil, Dr Cowie should not be blamed for not appreciating that the combination would bring about the unfortunate consequences that followed. He had not been negligent.

See p 61.

Gardiner v Mounfield and Lincolnshire Area Health Authority

Damages: diagnosis: wrongful birth: pregnancy

Scott Baker J. [1990] 1 Med LR 205

On 6 March 1984 the plaintiff (Ms Gardiner) attended a consultation with the first defendant (Mr Mounfield) at the County Hospital at Louth. Her general practitioner's referral letter stated that 'this obese, overweight, young lady gave a history of amenorrhoea and scanty menstruation in the previous two months.' She had stopped taking the pill about two months before the consultation, and was concerned that she might be pregnant. She told Mr Mounfield that she thought she felt movements in her abdomen and complained of tenderness to the breasts. He discussed the history with her and carried out an examination which included an internal examination and an examination of her breasts. He was convinced that her problems were related to her being excessively overweight. He firmly advised her that he did not think that she was pregnant, that she should continue to take the pill and that she should endeavour to lose weight.

In mid-September 1984 the plaintiff found that she was pregnant. She did not want to have a child, but it was too late for an abortion. Her baby was born on 3 November. It was a normal delivery, and there were no complications. Had the plaintiff been informed early enough that she was pregnant, she would have had a termination under general anaesthetic. She sued Mr Mounfield and the hospital authority.

Held: (i)   the evidence supported the case that this was a full term child. Thus the plaintiff was pregnant at the time of the consultation.

      (ii) the possibility of pregnancy should reasonably have been detected by Mr Mounfield because of the plaintiff's breast symptoms, the fact that she was concerned that she might be pregnant and the date of her last period sometime in January.

     (iii) there were two courses that were reasonably open to him: either to arrange a Beta HCG test, which would have resolved conclusively whether she was pregnant, or to arrange for urine tests at two weekly intervals.

     (iv) instead he mistakenly dismissed from his mind the possibility that she was pregnant, because she was overweight and he could see no clinical signs of pregnancy. This error constituted negligence.

     (v)   the plaintiff was awarded general damages of £1,250 for pain, suffering and loss of amenities out of total damages of £17,920 plus £1,735 interest.

See pp 99, 128.

Garner v Morrell and Another

Dental: operation: retained surgical product: res ipsa loquitur: fatal

Court of Appeal. (1953) Times, 31 October

In April 1948 Charles Garner attended the surgery of the defendants, Arnold Morrell and William Morrell, for the purpose of having teeth extracted. One defendant performed the operation of extraction, and the other administered the anaesthetic. During the course of the operation, a throat pack which had been inserted in Mr Garner's mouth was swallowed or inhaled by him. In consequence he died of asphyxia. His widow claimed damages.

Held: there was ample evidence to support the finding of the trial judge (Sellers J) that the throat pack was too short. The occurrence of the accident called for an explanation from the defendants, and the explanation offered by them had largely broken down. The accident could and should have been avoided; and the fact that a similar accident had never happened before was against the defendants.

See pp 88, 131.

Gascoine v Haringey Health Authority and Others

Cancer: hysterectomy: radiotherapy: striking out: peritonitis

Court of Appeal. [1992] PIQR P 416 [1992] 3 Med LR 291, (1992) Times, July 30

In 1978 the plaintiff (Ms Gascoine) underwent a hysterectomy. A few days later, a pathological examination of her uterus showed an infiltrating squamous cell carcinoma.

Consequently, she was given a course of external radiotherapy. In February 1980 it was found that, due to this treatment, she had developed general peritonitis. After a series of operations, it was also discovered that she had suffered irradiation necrosis of the small bowel. Her case was that the decision to carry out external radiotherapy was negligent and unnecessary.

Her writ was issued on 1 September 1983. No statement of claim was ever served. In January 1990 the NHS instituted new arrangements which increased the liability of health authorities to pay damages as against individual doctors. In May 1991 the master struck out the plaintiff's claim on the grounds of want of prosecution and failure to serve a statement of claim. Tudor Evans J on appeal upheld this order. The plaintiff appealed.

Held: (i) the judge's finding that there were periods of inordinate and inexcusable delay totalling at least three years between 1985 and 1989 must be viewed in the context of the overall delay from 1978 onwards. This was important, because the court has to balance prejudice to the plaintiff against the legitimate interest of the defendants.

    (ii) (a) although medical records remained, the judge was properly entitled when assessing prejudice to take into account the effect of the passage of time upon the witnesses' recollection.

    (b) he was also entitled to have regard to the 'Sword of Damocles' effect of an action of this sort hanging over the heads of professional medical men, particularly when still in practice, who naturally would like to have the matter resolved as soon as possible.

    (c) the court was also entitled to take into account the change in financial arrangements introduced within the health service.

    (iii) when the delay was considered in the context of the matters relied upon collectively as establishing prejudice, that prejudice was sufficient to warrant the dismissal of the action. The plaintiff's appeal would therefore be dismissed.

Per Woolf LJ: 'The approach which I have just indicated, as I see it, is entirely in accord with the judgement of Lord Denning and Geoffrey Lane LJ in *Biss v Lambeth, Southwark & Lewisham Health Authority* [1978] 1 WLR 382. Mr Francis, in addition to referring to that case, referred to the speech of Lord Griffiths in the later case of *Department of Transport v Chris Smaller (Transport Ltd* [1989] AC 1197. Mr Francis submits that if one looks at what Lord Griffiths had to say, caution has to be exercised in taking into account this factor. In the course of his speech Lord Griffiths repeated a note of caution which he expressed in the Court of Appeal in *Eagil Trust Co Ltd v Pigott Brown* [1985] 3 All ER 119 at 124. In that case he had said: 'Any action is bound to cause anxiety, but it would as a general rule be an exceptional case where that sort of anxiety alone would found a sufficient ground for striking out in the absence of any particular prejudice.' The case of *Biss* is an example of such an exceptional case, the action hanging over the doctors for eleven and a half years, with professional reputations at stake. As I read Lord Griffiths' speech in the *Department of Transport v Chris Smaller* he is not seeking to water down what was said in the earlier *Biss* case. He was distinguishing between the ordinary incidence of anxiety, which is the inevitable consequence of any action, with the sort of situation which was being considered by this court in *Biss* and which is being considered by the court in this case. The court, in adopting an approach to which I have made reference, is not adopting any special standard in respect of medical men, it is merely recognising the fact that certain allegations are bound to cause more anxiety than others, and an allegation of medical negligence is a serious allegation, for the reasons which I have sought to explain. In this case, I regard the fact that this action has been hanging on in the way that it has as a matter which would inevitably cause prejudice to the individual doctors concerned and, that being so, it was a matter which it was appropriate for the judge to take into account . . .

I accept that it would be wrong for the court to exclude from its consideration the fact that the Health Service has decided to adopt this new arrangement presumably because it is thought that the arrangement is beneficial to the proper workings of the Health Service. Nonetheless in those cases which, as a result of inordinate and inexcusable delay, straddle the period when they should have been dealt with under the former arrangements if the action had proceeded, but would now have to be dealt with under the new arrangements, it does seem to me that it can be said that there is some element of prejudice which results from delay. Putting it at its lowest the individual defendant district health authority will be put to administrative disadvantage in consequence of the delay. It will be saddled with a judgment, if it were to be found liable, which could result in greater financial prejudice to it than it would if it had been dealt with under the former arrangements. Therefore the fact of the changed arrangements is a matter with which the court can have regard. However, in having regard to it, the court should not, in my judgment, regard it as a matter of such significance that it would in itself justify an action being struck out. The prejudice is something to be taken in account together with other prejudice, if it exists, as justifying the view that in all the circumstances the appropriate conclusion is that an action should be struck out.'

See pp 147, 193, 202, 203.

Gascoine v Ian Sheridan & Co and Latham

Cancer: causation: limitation: peritonitis: counsel: solicitors

Mitchell J. [1994] 5 Med LR 437

After an abnormal cervical smear the plaintiff (Mrs Joan Gascoine), aged 46, was examined in February 1978 by Mr Clements, a consultant gynaecologist at the North Middlesex Hospital. He reported that appearances suggested dysplasia or carcinoma in situ and proposed a vaginal hysterectomy which he performed on 6 April 1978. The resultant histological report dated 14 April stated: 'Uterus. . . . there is an erosion surrounding the external os with a radius of 1.0 to 1.3 cm (Blocks 2-5 cervix: 6.7 body). Histology: the 'erosion' described above is in fact an infiltrating squamous carcinoma. It is invading the cervix for a depth of 2mm. Excision appears to be completed. The endometrium is proliferative and shows no significant abnormality'.

Mr Clements wrote to Dr Matthews, the consultant radiotherapist at the North Middlesex Hospital, who saw the plaintiff and advised Mr Clements that she should be treated with a course of external pelvic radiation. That course began on 8 May 1978 and was completed on 20 June 1978.

On 30 June 1978 irradiation cystitis was diagnosed. In February 1980 the plaintiff was found to be suffering from peritonitis. In August 1981 investigation revealed further conditions attributable to the radiotherapy. These necessitated an ileostomy.

In June 1983 the plaintiff consulted the defendant solicitors, Ian Sheridan & Co. Her writ was issued in September 1983 and served on the hospital authority in August 1984. The second defendant, Peter Latham, was the plaintiff's counsel. In May 1991 her action was struck out for want of prosecution, a decision that was confirmed on appeal.

The plaintiff therefore sued the defendant solicitors and counsel who admitted that they had been negligent but contended that her original case would not have succeeded because:

(i) it was statute barred and;
(ii) negligence by the hospital authority could not have been established.

Held: (i) the act which was alleged to constitute the negligence to which the plaintiffs injury was attributable was not the manner of administering the external pelvic radiation but rather the decision to treat her with it. The plaintiff remained unaware of the possibility that her injuries were 'attributable' to the decision to administer external pelvic radiotherapy until long after the issue of the writ in September 1983. Her case was not statute barred. Mrs Gascoine could not be criticised in any aspect of her conduct prior to this point.

(ii) Mr Clements and Dr Matthews did not give appropriate attention to the problem presented by the plaintiff's condition. Each fell below the standard of a competent practitioner professing skill in the field of his or her speciality. Each had a duty to take expert advice. Had they done so, there was some prospect in 1978 of them having been advised that the mainstream of current thinking was against proceeding to treat by radical irradiation. If the plaintiff could establish that:

(a) the risk to the plaintiff of lymph node metastasis was significantly lower than the risks attaching to external irradiation of the whole pelvis and

(b) in 1978 any practitioner of reasonable competence would so have regarded the risk,

then to have proceeded in those circumstances to treat with external pelvic irradiation was negligent. The plaintiff had a 60% chance of establishing this.

(iii) as the defendant lawyers had admitted negligence, judgment should be given against them in favour of the plaintiff who was therefore entitled to 60% of the full value of her claim.

Note: See *Gascoine v Haringey Health Authority* (p 346) and p 76.

Gauntlett v Northampton Health Authority

Psychiatric patient: supervision: nurses: schizophrenia: causation

Court of Appeal. CAT, 12 December 1985

In September 1979 the plaintiff (Mrs Pamela Gauntlett), then aged 24, suffered the latest in a series of mental breakdowns. On 14 September she took an overdose of tranquillising tablets and was admitted to Northampton General Hospital. She expressed bizarre and florid delusions about Jesus Christ having a stake driven through his heart, vampires, snakes etc and said that she would have to die.

On 15 September she was transferred to St Crispin's Hospital, a mental hospital, where a diagnosis of schizophrenia was made. When her husband left her after a visit on 16 September, she handed him a box of matches, saying 'You had better take these because I may set fire to myself'. He told a nurse who did not record it.

On 20 September the plaintiff went to the washroom and toilet by herself. She there set fire with a box of matches to the tee-shirt which she was wearing, burning herself badly and leaving severe and unsightly scarring.

She sued the health authority for inadequate supervision. The trial judge (Kilner Brown J) found in her favour.

Held: (i) the trial judge did not ask himself the key question: 'should a reasonably competent and experienced nurse have foreseen that if she omitted to make a note of this incident, there was a risk that the patient might not be closely supervised and might, if she got the opportunity, set her clothes on fire?' or 'is this an omission which no reasonably competent and skilled nurse would make in the circumstances of this case?' His finding of negligence could not be justified.

(ii) causation had not been established. It had not been shown that a note of the matches incident would probably have resulted in the plaintiff being accompanied by a nurse to the washroom on every occasion, and so prevented her from setting light to her clothes.

See p 44, 69, 138.

General Medical Council v Dr R

Anaesthetics: consent: dental: assault

General Medical Council. (1995) 310 BMJ 43

The complainant, a 22-year-old woman, attended her local dental surgery for extraction of two wisdom teeth and two other teeth. She knew that she was to have a general anaesthetic and gave her consent, both verbally and by implication. She signed a form which stated: 'I would like the dentist named overleaf to examine me under the NHS and give me every necessary care and treatment which I am willing to undergo within any arrangements.' There was no consent form specifically for the anaesthetic. During the procedure, whilst the complainant was still unconscious, the respondent (Dr R), a consultant anaesthetist, loosened her clothing and inserted in the immediate post operative period a diclofenac suppository for pain relief. He had not discussed this with the complainant beforehand. In accordance with his usual practice, however, he told her about it while she was in the recovery room.

Unfortunately he had inadvertently inserted the suppository into her vagina. The resulting symptoms led her to suspect that she might have been raped. She reported the matter to the police who arrested the respondent and the dentist but decided not to charge them. Nevertheless a report was sent to the GMC who brought charges under a disciplinary procedure.

On the respondent's behalf, evidence was called from several senior anaesthetists who confirmed that the practice in many hospitals was not to obtain specific consent in advance for the use of diclofenac suppositories. It was said that these were no different from any other form of post operative pain relief, including intramuscular injections which might be given in the buttock and therefore might also entail disturbing or removing clothing on the lower part of the body.

The GMC called evidence from other anaesthetists who testified that in their hospitals specific consent was always taken for the use of diclofenac suppositories. The GMC's experts drew a distinction between suppositories and intramuscular injections and, in particular, drew a distinction between a general dental surgery and a hospital. They said that the expectations and perceptions of a patient who arrived fully clothed in a general dental surgery were completely different from those of a patient who attended even a day case unit. The very presence of lower underwear emphasised that a patient did not anticipate treatment to the lower part of the body.

Held: (i) the following charges were found proved against the respondent:

1. Prior to administering the general anaesthetic and when it was so required, you

   (a) did not explain to the patient what form the general anaesthetic would take or ensure that this was explained to her;

   (b) did not ensure that the patient was told that a [diclofenac] suppository would or might be inserted into her as a form of pain relief;

    (c)   did not obtain from the patient valid informed consent to the insertion into her of a [diclofenac] suppository.

  2. (a) Whilst the patient was under the general anaesthetic you inserted a [diclofenac] suppository into her vagina;

    (b) in carrying out this procedure you inserted the said substance without [the patient's] prior valid informed consent and thus assaulted her.'

  (ii) the respondent was found guilty of serious professional misconduct and admonished.

Note: Cf *Davis v Barking, Havering and Brentwood Health Authority* (p 302).

Gerber v Pines

Injection: general practitioner: needle breaking: duty to inform of mishap: rheumatism

Du Parcq J. (1935) 79 Sol Jo 13

The plaintiff (Mrs Rebecca Gerber) was undergoing a course of injections for her rheumatism by Dr Pine at his surgery. Six had been given successfully when on 11 August, while he was injecting into the muscle known as the gluteus maximus, the needle broke. He was unable to get it out of the plaintiff's body and did not initially tell her that it was there. On 16 August it was removed by operation. The plaintiff sued Dr Pines who testified that the breaking of the needle was due to a sudden muscular spasm.

Held: no negligence in the performance of the injection was proved against Dr Pines, and there was apparently nothing wrong with the needle. However, as a general rule, a patient in whose body a doctor found that he had left some foreign substance was entitled to be told at once. There was a breach of duty and negligence on the doctor's part in not at once informing either the patient or her husband on the day of the accident.

See pp 45, 113, 119.

Gerdes-Hardy v Wessex Regional Health Authority

Costs: general practitioner: pleadings: leg: amputation

Court of Appeal. [1994] PIQR P368

On 21 July 1987 the plaintiff (Mrs Gerdes-Hardy), a 52-year-old night porter, dropped a chair onto her right foot. That morning she attended the casualty department at the first defendants' Andover Ward Memorial Hospital. Unknown to her, she was already suffering from ischaemic vascular disease. On 27 July 1987 she was examined by her general practitioner, the second defendant Dr Allan. On 29 July she was admitted as an emergency at the Royal County Hampshire Hospital. On 31 July she underwent a below the knee amputation of the right leg, and on 5 August 1987 a further above the knee amputation.

Initially she sued the first defendants for alleged negligence at the Andover War Memorial Hospital, together with the second defendant. In their defences, neither defendant blamed the other. Subsequently, the second defendant in an amended defence blamed the first defendant for alleged negligence by staff at the Royal County Hampshire Hospital. The plaintiff adopted these allegations and reamended the statement of claim.

During the course of the trial, the second defendant conceded that he was negligent in his examination of the plaintiff on 27 July 1987 and judgment was entered against him. The trial judge found that there was no negligence by either the Andover War Memorial Hospital or the Royal County Hampshire Hospital and gave judgment for the first defendants against the plaintiff. The trial judge ordered the second defendant to pay the costs of the plaintiff and the first defendants in all matters save the Andover War Memorial allegations. So far as they were concerned, he ordered the first defendants' costs to be paid by the plaintiff. She appealed against that order for costs.

Held: (i)   where a plaintiff succeeds against only one of two defendants against whom she has sought to exploit separate causes of action, if that defendant has not blamed the other, the normal order for costs in most actions will be that the plaintiff pays the cost of the successful defendant. But the decision as to costs is discretionary, and there may be circumstances in which the court will order that the unsuccessful defendant pays the costs of the successful defendant, even though the unsuccessful defendant has not sought to blame his co-defendant.

        (ii) if it was not reasonable to join the successful defendant, that will militate in favour of the plaintiff herself having to pay the successful defendants' costs. In this case, however, it was reasonable for the plaintiff, on the strong advice from initial medical reports she had, that the Royal Andover Hospital could be considered to be negligent, to sue the first defendants in respect of that alleged negligence.

        (iii) if the plaintiff had initiated proceedings by suing only the second defendant, he would then have made the allegations which he did make about her treatment of the Royal County Hampshire Hospital, which would have resulted in the plaintiff being properly advised to join the first defendants as a further defendant in the action. Thus the same two defendants would have become parties to the action at the behest of the second defendant.

        (iv) all therefore that could be laid at the door of the plaintiff was that she made additional allegations against the first defendants, namely the Andover War Memorial Hospital allegations, which in the event did not succeed. Those additional allegations, reasonably made on advice, should not result in an order for costs adverse to her.

        (v) the second defendant should pay the costs of both the plaintiff and the first defendant, without any exception, to be taxed on the standard basis if not agreed.

Giles v Pontefract Health Authority

Childbirth: damages: shoulder

Dyson J. [1994] 7 CL 119

The plaintiff, aged nine at trial, suffered at birth dystocia of his left shoulder with consequent damage to the brachial plexus, resulting in a Duchenne Erb plexus paralysis. The musculature of the left shoulder and left side of the chest was less well developed than that of the right. The left scapula was two to three centimetres higher than the right. The left arm was thinner and less developed and could not be elevated or abducted beyond 135°. Although there was good elbow movement, there was limited pronation and supination of the arm. Hand and finger movements were good, but getting his left hand into the correct position to perform complex movements was difficult and often impossible. He tended to pass objects from his left into his right hand, in order to manage them better, and had difficulty holding and using a fork with his left hand. When he was running, his left arm took on an abnormal posture with the elbow flexed, the arm internally rotated and the forearm pronated. There was no sensory loss.

The plaintiff coped well with all the aspects of daily life, eg fastening small buttons, appropriate to a boy of this age. There was some teasing at school due to the disability. The injury was cosmetically significant, and there would be no improvement. He would never be able to lift heavy objects bimanually or to perform deft bimanual tasks rapidly. Some sporting and social activities would not be open to him. Although he was of normal intelligence, an employment consultant testified that he would be restricted to the lower paid end of the clerical and administrative labour market.

Held (June 1993):   (i)   general damages for pain suffering and loss of amenities were assessed at £25,000.

(ii)   in addition, £20,000 was awarded for loss of future earnings, based on a multiplier of 10 and a multiplicand of £2,000.

Gillick v West Norfolk and Wisbech Area Health Authority and Another

Consent: minors: contraceptive advice: parental objections

House of Lords. [1986] AC 112, [1985] 3 All ER 402, [1985] 3 WLR 830

The Department of Health and Social Security issued a circular to area health authorities. This contained advice that a doctor consulted at a family planning clinic by a girl under 16 would not be acting unlawfully if he prescribed contraceptives for the girl, so long as in doing so he was acting in good faith to protect her against the harmful effects of sexual intercourse. It further advised that in exceptional cases the doctor could prescribe contraceptives without consulting the girl's parents or obtaining their consent, if in the doctor's clinical judgement it was desirable to prescribe contraceptives.

The plaintiff (Mrs Victoria Gillick), who had five daughters under the age of 16, brought an action seeking (i) against the DHSS and the area health authority a declaration that the advice contained in their circular was unlawful, and (ii) against the area health authority a declaration that a doctor employed by it could not give contraceptive advice or treatment to any of her children aged under sixteen without the plaintiff's consent. The Court of Appeal granted the declaration sought.

Held: the declarations had been wrongly granted. A girl under 16 did not, merely by reason of her age, lack legal capacity to consent to contraceptive advice and treatment by a doctor. A doctor had a discretion to give such advice or treatment without her parent's consent, provided that the girl was old enough to have sufficient understanding and intelligence to enable her to understand fully what was being proposed.

Per Lord Fraser of Tullybelton: 'It seems to me verging on the absurd to suggest that a girl or boy aged 15 could not effectively consent, for example, to have a medical examination of some trivial injury to his body or even to have a broken arm set. Of course the consent of the parents should normally be asked, but they may not be immediately available. Provided the patient, whether a boy or a girl, is capable of understanding what is proposed, and of expressing his or her own wishes, I see no good reason for holding that he or she lacks the capacity to express them validly and effectively and to authorise the medical man to make the examination or give the treatment which he advises.'

Gillick v West Norfolk and Wisbech Area Health Authority and Another

Per Lord Scarman: 'Parental right yields to the child's right to make his own decisions when he reaches a sufficient understanding and intelligence to be capable of making up his own mind on the matter requiring decision. . . . In the light of the foregoing I would hold that as a matter of law the parental right to determine whether or not their minor child below the age of 16 will have medical treatment terminates if and when the child achieves a sufficient understanding and intelligence to enable him or her to understand fully what is proposed. It will be a question of fact whether a child seeking advice has sufficient understanding of what is involved to give a valid consent in law. Until the child achieves the capacity to consent, the parental right to make the decision continues save only in exceptional circumstances. Emergency, parental neglect, abandonment of the child or inability to find the parent are examples of exceptional situations justifying the doctor proceeding to treat the child without parental knowledge and consent; but there will arise, no doubt, other exceptional situations in which it will be reasonable for the doctor to proceed without the parent's consent.'

Per Lord Templeman: 'I accept also that a doctor may lawfully carry out some forms of treatment with the consent of an infant patient and against the opposition of a parent based on religious or any other grounds. The effect of the consent of the infant depends on the nature of the treatment and the age and understanding of the infant. For example, a doctor with the consent of an intelligent boy or girl of fifteen could in my opinion safely remove tonsils or a troublesome appendix.'

See p 9, 52.

Gladwell v Steggall

Alternative practitioner: duty of care: knee

Vaughan J. (1839) 5 Bing N Cas 733

The plaintiff was a ten year old girl. While working in the fields with her father in the 1830s, she complained of a pain in the knee and went home. Her mother sent for the defendant who, though a clergyman, practised also as a medical man. He attended the plaintiff, with disastrous consequences for her.

Held: having accepted employment by the plaintiff as a surgeon, the defendant negligently carried out his duties as such. Judgment for the plaintiff.

See pp 18, 44.

Gold and Others v Essex County Council

Radiographic: burns: substandard treatment: vicarious liability: child patient: face

Court of Appeal. [1942] 2 KB 293, [1942] 2 All ER 237

In June and July 1940 the plaintiff (Ruth Gold), then aged five, was taken by her mother to Oldchurch Hospital for treatment for warts on her face. The visiting dermatologist, Dr Burrows, ordered treatment by Grenz rays. This was given by Mr Mead, a qualified radiographer who was employed by the hospital as a technical assistant. While the plaintiff was undergoing treatment, her face was covered with a lead-lined rubber cloth which protected all but the affected part of her face. This happened on some five occasions.

354

As the warts did not yield to this treatment, Dr Burrows prescribed applications of double the strength. On 11 July 1940 the plaintiff's mother took her again for treatment. Mr Mead was in a hurry. Instead of getting the lead-lined cloth, he covered the child's face with only a piece of ordinary lint. Her face was severely burnt, and she suffered permanent disfigurement. The trial judge (Tucker J) found that Mr Mead was negligent.

Held: as the radiographer, Mr Mead, was employed by the defendant hospital authority under a contract of service, the authority was liable for his negligence. This was so even though his work was of a skilful or technical nature. In this legal context, he was in exactly the same position as a nurse.

See pp 21–22, 44, 129.

Gold v Haringey Health Authority

Sterilisation (failed): risk disclosure: warning: contraceptive advice

Court of Appeal. [1988] QB 481, [1987] 2 All ER 888, [1987] 3 WLR 649, [1988] 1 FLR 55

In 1979 the plaintiff (Mrs Phyllis Gold) was pregnant with her third child. She and her husband were discussing his having a vasectomy. Miss Witt, a consultant at the North Middlesex Hospital, suggested that she be sterilised. None of the hospital doctors mentioned the failure rate of the operation which was about six per thousand if carried out immediately after childbirth. On 19 August 1979 the plaintiff gave birth to a daughter, Nicola. On 20 August Dr Arzanghi performed the sterilisation operation at North Middlesex Hospital. The operation did not succeed, for in October 1982 the plaintiff gave birth to her fourth child, Darren.

Her claim that the operation was carried out negligently was rejected by the trial judge (Schiemann J). She also alleged negligence in failing to disclose that the operation had a failure rate, saying that if she had known this she would not have had the operation and her husband would have been vasectomised instead. The unanimous medical evidence was that a substantial body of doctors would not have given any warning about the failure rate in 1979. However the judge found that the *Bolam* test applied only to advice given in a therapeutic context and not to advice given in a contraceptive context. He found that the defendants had been negligent in not warning the plaintiff that the operation might not succeed.

Held: there was no reason to distinguish between advice given in a therapeutic context and advice given in a non-therapeutic context. The *Bolam* test applied to contraceptive advice as well as to therapeutic advice. As there was a body of responsible medical opinion which would not have given any warning as to the failure of female sterilisation, the defendants were not liable.

See pp 110, 128.

Goode v Nash

General practitioner: duty of care: gratuitous services: ophthalmic: burns: Australia

Supreme Court (South Australia). (1979) 21 SASR 419

On 25 May 1974 the Lions Clubs of Southern Districts were conducting glaucoma screenings at the Willunga District Hall. Mr WP Nash, aged 24, presented himself for testing. The tests were free and Mr Goode, an experienced general practitioner, was giving his services free of charge. Dr Goode placed a hot tonometer upon Mr Nash's left eye.

Mr Nash suffered a burn which left him with scarring of the cornea and reduced vision. He sued Dr Goode.

Held: Dr Goode must have been negligent. It may be that he left the tonometer in the sterilising flame for longer than usual, or that he allowed less time than usual for it to cool, or perhaps there was a combination of both. Although he was engaged in a valuable community service, entirely on a voluntary basis, he was liable to pay damages.

See pp 18, 46.

Goodman v Fletcher and Others

Limitation: advice: striking out

Court of Appeal. 4 October 1982

The plaintiff (Miss Goodman) suffered from a number of allergies. In June and July 1973 she consulted Dr Buisseret who advised her to go on a gluten-free diet. In September 1974 she learned that he had recommended this on an empirical basis, that is, he wanted to see what was going to happen. In February 1975 she was discharged from the Peace Memorial Hospital with a dietary recommendation that included gluten.

In March 1978 she issued a writ against Dr Buisseret (among others). In April 1981 she served an inadequate Statement of Claim. A substitute Statement of Claim was served in November 1981, alleging that Dr Buisseret's advice was negligent and wrong. In April 1982 her case was struck out as statute-barred.

Held: (i)   the plaintiff probably knew in September 1974 that Dr Buisseret's diagnosis and advice were in error, and she certainly knew it by February 1975. Thus her case was prima facie statute barred by s 11 of the Limitation Act 1980.

(ii)   the delays had been great, and it would be impossible for Dr Buisseret at a trial in 1983 to have an accurate recollection of the consultations ten years earlier in 1973. The delay was fatal to any exercise of discretion under s 33 of the 1980 Act.

See p 199.

Goorkani v Tayside Health Board

Causation: damages: ophthalmic: risk disclosure: Scotland

Court of Session, Outer House. [1991] 3 Med LR 33

In 1978 the pursuer (Mr Goorkani) was diagnosed as suffering from Behcet's disease. One of the effects of the disease was to cause eye damage leading to blindness. By 1981 he had lost almost all the effective sight in his right eye. In about August 1981 he reported as an out-patient to Ninewells Hospital with a complaint of inflammation to the left eye. On 2 October he was admitted to the Eye Ward there, complaining of further deterioration in the sight of his left eye. Initial treatment to reduce the inflammation in that eye was unsuccessful. On 8 October 1981 Dr Frew, consultant physician, prescribed the drug Chlorambucil as an immuno-suppressant. This continued to be prescribed for Mr Goorkani at the dosage of 5mg daily until the end of May 1983. It successfully reduced symptoms in his left eye, whereas otherwise he would have lost the sight in it and have been rendered blind.

However the Chlorambucil also caused him to become irreversibly infertile. Dr Frew was aware of the risk of this, but never advised Mr Goorkani of it. Nor was he offered sperm banking. When Mr Goorkani, who was of Iranian origin, and his wife learned of his infertility in 1984, they were shocked and angry. He felt so ashamed that he was unable to tell his father and stated that he did not feel like a man any more. Their plans to have further children were frustrated. Mr Goorkani sued the hospital authority.

Held (January 1990):

(i) Dr Frew, who knew of the risk of infertility and accepted that he should have warned Mr Goorkani of it, had negligently failed to do so.

(ii) since sperm banking did not become available as a regular service at Nine Wells Hospital until 1987, Dr Frew had not been negligent in making no offer of sperm banking in 1981.

(iii) Mr Goorkani would in late 1981 or early 1982 have been prepared to accept the risk of infertility, in return for the chance of saving his sight by continuing to take Chlorambucil. Accordingly he was not entitled to damages for the infertility itself.

(iv) the loss, injury and damage sustained as a consequence of the failure to warn him of the risk of infertility was restricted to the degree of distress and anxiety which arose from his discovery of this. A reasonable award for the loss of self-esteem, the shock and anger at the discovery of his infertility, together with the frustration and disruption which ignorance and the sudden shock of discovery it brought to the marital relationship, was £2,500.

See pp 68, 112.

Gordon v Goldberg

Dental: alternative practitioner: breach of contract: teeth

Rowlatt J. (1920) 2 Lancet 964

In the absence of her usual dentist, who was serving in the army, the plaintiff (Mrs Gordon), aged nearly eighty, consulted Mr Goldberg who practised dentistry but was not upon the Dental Register. She had been attracted by his advertisement describing himself as 'DDS American Dentistry'. He made her two sets of artificial teeth for which she paid him sums of £31 15s and £40. Neither fitted her, and she suffered great pain.

The plaintiff sued Mr Goldberg. Expert evidence was given that the teeth did not fit, that they were wanting in articulation between the upper and lower jaws, and that it was impossible to adapt them.

Held: Mr Goldberg was liable. When people went to dentists they expected and contracted for skill, not for infallibility. In judging skill, account might be taken of the charges made. Mr Goldberg had charged very handsomely, but the teeth that he supplied were utterly unsatisfactory.

See pp 30, 129.

Gowton and Another v Wolverhampton Health Authority

Causation: damages: risk disclosure: vasectomy: contraceptive advice

Gage J. [1994] 5 Med LR 432

In early 1986 the plaintiffs (Mr and Mrs Gowton) found that she was pregnant with their fourth child. On 7 July 1986 they saw Mr Marcheck, a registrar at New Cross Hospital at Wolverhampton. On the same day, each signed a consent to a vasectomy on Mr Gowton. On 8 August the vasectomy was carried out. On 25 September a semen test carried out on a specimen supplied by Mr Gowton proved negative. On 20 November the second semen test proved negative. On 26 November 1986 Mr Marcheck wrote to Mr Gowton that: 'Your recent semen analysis is clear. You may now discontinue contraceptive precautions'. In the latter part of January 1988 Mrs Gowton discovered she was pregnant with their child, Jade, who was born on 30 August 1988.

The plaintiffs sued the hospital authority on the grounds that Mr Marcheck had failed to warn them of the possibility of Mr Gowton becoming fertile again after negative results from the semen analysis.

Mr Marcheck testified that it was his invariable practice to give such a warning; he accepted that not to do so before the operation would be to fall below acceptable standards.

Held: (i)   whilst there must have been some conversation at the pre-operative interview about the need to wait for two semen tests to see if the operation had been successful or completed, Mr Marcheck negligently failed to make it clear that after two tests there remained a risk of a late reversal of the vasectomy.

      (ii)   had she known of the risk of reversal, it was probable that Mrs Gowton would have continued to take the contraceptive pill. Had a proper warning been given, it was very improbable that she would have become pregnant.

      (iii)   the plaintiffs' counsel had submitted that the appropriate figure for general damages for the pain and suffering and loss of amenities associated with the birth was £2,500. That figure was below what could have been expected for the discomforts and strains of pregnancy followed by the pangs of labour. However since the plaintiffs contended for this, that was what would be awarded.

See pp 113, 128, 168.

Gravestock and Another v Lewisham Group Hospital Management Committee

Supervision: child patient: nurses

Streatfield J. (1955) Times, 27 May

Pauline Gravestock (the plaintiff) was a nine year old patient in Lewisham Hospital. On 13 August 1952 the orderly left the ward for a few minutes in order to get the pudding course of a meal. Contrary to the rules, the plaintiff ran down the the ward and, swinging on the swing doors, tripped on the stud and was seriously injured.

Held: on the purely disciplinary side, the duty of a hospital was no higher than that of a school. The duty of the defendant should not be measured by any more severe standard than that of a schoolmaster, which was that of an ordinary prudent parent. Measured by the scales of the prudent parent, the defendants had provided adequate supervision.

See pp 44, 132, 137.

Gray v Mid Herts Group Hospital Management Committee

Anaesthetics: cardiac arrest: child patient: damages: fatal: brain damage: hernia: paraplegia

Waller J. (1974) 118 Sol Jo 501

Edward Gray was born in September 1968. In October 1969 he entered St Alban's City Hospital for an inguinal hernia operation. He was given 5 mg of Omnopon as a premedication. Difficulty in breathing was the first untoward sign to be observed. He had a cardiac arrest due to anoxia.

Edward had suffered widespread brain damage in the operation. He became blind and deaf, showing a typical picture of spastic paraplegia. From time to time he had fits, and he was doubly incontinent. He sometimes had periods of crying which could not be stopped. While he was not aware of his surroundings, he had a slight reaction to familiar and friendly touch. He died due to his brain damage in July 1972. His father sued the hospital authority.

Held: (i) careful monitoring would have given warning in time to avoid the consequences that followed. The anaesthetist was not keeping a good look-out on the chest and re-breathing bag, and he was not continually monitoring the pulse. The hospital authority was liable for the anaesthetist's negligence;

(ii) taking into account the child's very young age, his comparatively long two and three-quarter year period of survival, and his slight reaction to touch, general damages were assessed (March 1974) at £5,000 for his loss of amenities. A further £500 was awarded for loss of expectation of life.

See p 122.

Grayson-Crowe v Ministry of Defence

Damages: Germany: hysterectomy: military hospital: trespass to person: D and C: depression

Potts J. [1992] CLY 1663

In January 1987 the plaintiff (Miss Grayson-Crowe), then aged 30, was employed as a bar and club assistant by NAAFI in Germany. She was referred to a British Army obstetrician and gynaecologist with a history of irregular periods, prolonged bleeding and a palpable mass in the right iliac fossa. Fibroids were suspected. She was admitted to the British Military Hospital in Hanover for a D and C and laparotomy.

During the operation, the surgeon noted that the plaintiff's uterus was healthy with a large posterior-wall fibroid the size of a fetal head, and other multiple sub-serous anterior-wall and lateral-wall fibroids. The tubes and ovaries were normal. The surgeon proceeded forthwith to carry out a hysterectomy, leaving the plaintiff's fallopian tubes and ovaries intact.

The plaintiff first discovered that a hysterectomy had taken place, after overhearing nurses on her ward discussing her condition. The surgeon then told her that he had carried it out because he had found fibroids within her uterus which could have become cancerous. Two months later, she was informed that a pathology report showed that she had multiple fibroids but no evidence of malignancy.

As she began to realise that the operation had not been necessary, she became withdrawn, introverted and depressed. She could not reconcile herself to the fact that she could not have children. She became reclusive. She avoided former friends with children. She married in 1988, but the marriage had not been a success. Sexual relations with her husband were painful and irregular. By February 1991 she was suffering from severe symptoms of depressive illness, including anhedonia, sleep disturbance, loss of appetite and social phobias. She gave up work. Eventually her general practitioner referred her for psychotherapy.

She sued, alleging negligent failures in diagnosis and treatment and also removal of her uterus without her consent. The defendants admitted liability, but disputed items of special damages such as the cost of psychotherapy and loss of earnings.

Held (June 1992):   (i)   the plaintiff was suffering from a depressive illness due to the defendants' negligence. She was awarded the full cost of psychotherapy and associated travelling expenses for 18 months, and loss of earnings from March 1991 until trial and thereafter until the conclusion of the psychotherapy.

(ii)   together with an agreed figure of £35,000 for general damages for pain, suffering and loss of amenity including interest, and agreed miscellaneous expenses including £500 for hormone replacement therapy, the total award including interest was £67,210.

See pp 103, 157.

Greensides v Bath Hair and Beauty Clinic

Alternative practitioner: cosmetic: damages: scarring: warning

Rutherford DJ. *Halsbury's Laws Annual Abridgment* 1993, para 934

The plaintiff (Miss Greensides), aged 23, had small red 'thread veins' on both legs at knee and thigh level. The defendants offered treatment of the veins by means of electrolysis. They did not warn her of the possibility of failure or scarring. Once a fortnight she received up to 20 treatments: a needle applied to the skin vertically which penetrated then caused acute discomfort when it was activated by the therapist operating a foot switch. Multiple punctures were made during each session, and occasionally there was bleeding. At least 30 needle pricks were received in a 20 minute session.

The plaintiff subsequently developed thick scars at a few of the treated areas. These were at first purplish red and itchy, and slowly became pale, flatter and more comfortable. She was left with white shiny scarred areas that could be seen quite easily at a distance of normal conversation. The scars were no longer itchy or tender. They did not restrict the movement of the legs. They were unlikely to tan in sunlight, so might be more obvious in summer. Cosmetic camouflage was impracticable. The scars were not amenable to surgery. No improvement was expected.

In addition, the plaintiff suffered a psychological reaction. She was disappointed in the failure of the procedure, and was unwilling to tell her boyfriend what had occurred. She wore trousers rather than skirts, and was self-conscious on the beach. She was not absent from work as a result of the injuries.

Held (October 1993):   (i)   general damages of £3,750 were awarded for pain, suffering and loss of amenities.

(ii)   special damages of £621 and interest of £158 brought the total award up to £4,529.

Gregory and Gregory v Pembrokeshire Health Authority

Pregnancy: tests: communication: causation: Down's syndrome

Court of Appeal. [1989] Med LR 81

In autumn 1979 the plaintiff (Mrs Jacqueline Gregory), then aged 28, was pregnant with her second child. Her own first child was normal, but when in her forties her mother had produced a mongol. On 19 November Dr Davies performed an amniocentesis test at Withybush Hospital and sent the sample to a laboratory at Cardiff. On 7 December the laboratory informed the hospital that the sample had not produced sufficient cultures to make testing possible. By then the plaintiff was 21 weeks and 2 days into her pregnancy. The hospital staff omitted to tell her that the test had failed until she saw Dr Davies in February 1980. When her baby was born in April, he turned out to be a mongol (a Down's Syndrome baby).

Mr & Mrs Gregory sued the hospital authority. The trial judge (Rougier J) found that (i) the failure of the hospital staff to inform the plaintiff at the earliest practicable moment that the amniocentesis test had failed to produce a result was a breach of their duty of care to her, but (ii) if timeously informed she would have accepted the advice that Dr Davies would have given not to proceed with a repeat test, since any abortion resulting from this would have had to be carried out more than twenty-four weeks into her pregnancy. Accordingly, he dismissed her claim.

Held: this was *par excellence* a case in which the judge's impression of the plaintiff and Dr Davies was of the utmost importance, since he had to evaluate the likely impact of Dr Davies' advice on her. There were no grounds for interfering with the judge's findings.

See pp 68, 113.

Grenville v Waltham Forest Health Authority

Limitation: operation: burns: buttock

Court of Appeal. CAT, 18 November 1992.

On 4 May 1988 the plaintiff (Anne Grenville) underwent a sterilisation operation at a hospital operated by the defendants. Within the next two days, she noticed a burn on her right buttock. She consulted her general practitioner about it on 14 May and saw a doctor at the hospital about it on 16 June. Her solicitors sent a letter before action on 21 June 1988. Legal aid was granted. From October 1988 they tried to find a medical expert to report, but due to practical difficulties the plaintiff was not seen by one until March 1991.

On 2 May 1991 a clerk from the plaintiff's solicitors attended Bow County Court with particulars of claim and asked that a summons be issued as a matter of urgency. The court failed to issue the summons until 9 May. The defence pleaded limitation. The plaintiff's application under s 33 of the Limitation Act 1980 for the limitation period under s 11 to be disapplied was dismissed by the district judge whose decision was upheld on appeal by Mr Assistant Recorder Roberts. The plaintiff appealed and was allowed to adduce fresh affidavit evidence.

Held: (i)   the most striking feature of the case was that the limitation period expired at a time when the plaintiff's solicitors had sought to issue process.

   (ii)   the consequence might well be that an action by the plaintiff against her solicitors for negligence might fail, in which event she would have no redress.

   (iii)   it was pertinent that the plaintiff's solicitors were not, as the assistant recorder believed on the information before him, inactive between October 1988 and March 1991.

    (iv) the assistant recorder did not appear to have taken into account the degree of prejudice, albeit small, which would necessarily accrue to the plaintiff if she had to sue her solicitors in negligence.

    (v) the assistant recorder, having regard to events at Bow County Court and to the history of the case, did not appropriately assess the prospects of success against the plaintiff's solicitors in an action for negligence.

The plaintiff's appeal was allowed.

See p 129.

Grieve v Salford Health Authority

Childbirth: damages: stillbirth

Rose J. [1991] 2 Med LR 295, [1990] 6 PMILL 54

On 21 September 1986 the plaintiff (Jacqueline Grieve), then aged about 21, was in labour at the Hope Hospital. This labour was unnecessarily prolonged and painful due to delay in making an aborted attempt at forceps delivery and consequent lateness of a caesarean section being performed. Eventually the child was delivered stillborn. The hospital authority admitted liability.

Even prior to the stillbirth, the plaintiff was a vulnerable personality who intermittently suffered from anxiety and depression and had been treated for a nervous condition after a road traffic accident in 1985. She had been obsessed with having a baby and had purchased an astounding profusion of toys in readiness for the birth.

The stillbirth was particularly damaging to the plaintiff because its fundamental cause was mismanagement of the final stages of labour and she was given a variety of inconsistent explanations. It caused damage to her vulnerable personality and some of the symptoms of sleeplessness and loss of appetite characterised as reactive depression. She found it difficult to love anyone else thereafter, and this clouded her relationship with her mother. She had been set back in starting a family. She was expected to recover by about four years after the stillbirth.

Held (March 1990):   (i) she was awarded £12,500 general damages for pain, suffering and loss of amenities in respect of the initial prolongation of labour, degree of additional pain, loss of the child, loss of the satisfaction of bringing the pregnancy to a successful conclusion, and four years of psychological damage.

    (ii) in addition, special damages of £1,250 were awarded in respect of layette.

The total award was £13,750 plus £921 interest.

See pp 146, 156, 178.

H v Ministry of Defence

Jury trial: penisectomy

Court of Appeal. [1991] 2 All ER 834

The plaintiff (H) was a 27-year-old regular soldier when he consulted the Army Medical Service about curvature of his penis which was diagnosed as Peyronies disease. He underwent a special test which involved injecting the penis with a saline solution. Shortly afterwards, a blister developed at the site of the injection and he fell ill. Tests revealed that the penis had become infected. He agreed to undergo an operation for a skin graft at the site of the blister. While he was anaesthetised, it became clear that not only was it impossible to do the skin graft, but that there was no alternative to amputating the major part of the penis. Whatever the general nature of the consent to the operation that he gave, he went into the theatre expecting to undergo a skin graft but on recovering from the anaesthetic found that he had undergone penisectomy.

The plaintiff suffered great psychological trauma. He attempted to commit suicide. He could not continue as a soldier. He suffered personality changes. He developed a phobia of coming into contact with women. He lived in social seclusion.

He sued the defendants who admitted liability. He applied for a trial before a judge with a jury.

Held: (i) pursuant to s 69 of the Supreme Court Act 1981 and the case of *Ward v James* [1965] 1 All ER 563, trial by jury is normally inappropriate for any personal injury action in so far as the jury is required to assess compensatory damages, because the assessment of such damages must be based upon or have regard to conventional scales of damages.

(ii) therefore trial in this case should be by a judge alone.

Per Lord Donaldson MR: 'Although Mr Jay in the court below was unable to suggest a case where trial by jury of a personal injuries claim would be appropriate and this undoubtedly contributed to the judge's decision, we think that there might well be such a case, albeit not one in which only compensatory damages are being sought. If, for example, personal injuries resulted from conduct on the part of those who were deliberately abusing their authority, there might well be a claim for exemplary damages and this could place the case in an exceptional category which, since it is not expressly contemplated by s 69, would fall within the general judicial discretion with its bias against a trial by jury, but yet is not dissimilar to a claim for malicious prosecution or false imprisonment in respect of which there is a legislative intention that there shall be a jury trial, unless there are contraindications'.

See pp 118, 167.

H v Y

Damages: structured settlement

FTSB, Winter 1994/95

The plaintiff (H) was severely handicapped following negligent surgery. She will be dependent on others for the rest of her life. When she was nine years of age, medical experts assessed her life expectancy to be a further 50 years.

The following settlement was agreed.

Interim payments	£80,000
Capital cost of structure	£578,500
Contingency Fund	£130,000
Total	£788,500

In exchange for a minimum guarantee period of five years, to apply to the immediate annuity only, no discount was sought by the defendants.

The payments produced by the structure were as follows:

Type of annuity	Immediate
Initial net yield	5.1%
Initial annual sum	£21,500
Equivalent gross yield after higher rate tax	8.5%
Indexation	RPI
Payable for:	Life of plaintiff
Guarantee period	Nil

Plus,

Type of annuity	Deferred
Deferred period	11 years
Initial annual sum (in today's terms)	£18,000
Indexation	RPI
Payable for:	Life of plaintiff
Guarantee period	Nil

Plus,

Type of annuity	Step
Lump sum payment every:	5 years
Initial lump sum (in today's terms)	£33,711
Indexation	RPI
Payable for:	Life of plaintiff
Guarantee period	1 payment.

Haines v Bellissimo et al

Psychiatric patient: suicide risk: diagnosis: Canada: psychologist: schizophrenia: fatal

Ontario High Court of Justice (Griffiths J). (1977) 82 DLR (3d) 215

Robert Haines was born in 1931. He first suffered from schizophrenia in 1954. In November 1971 he commenced treatment at the McMaster University Medical Centre where a diagnosis of chronic residual schizophrenia was made. Dr Bellissimo, a psychologist with a doctorate in clinical pyschology, was designated as his therapist. In 1974 Mr Haines' mental health deteriorated: he suffered from hypomania and depression and became socially disruptive.

On 28 June 1974 Mrs Haines, his wife, discovered in the garage of their house a shotgun which he had purchased on 24 June. She told Dr Bellissimo who saw Mr Haines. Mr Haines assured him that he had no immediate plan for suicide. After Dr Bellissimo had threatened to call the police, Mr Haines finally handed over the gun to him. Weighing all factors, such as that there had been no recent stressful situations and no immediate suicide plans, Dr Bellissimo decided not to hospitalize him.

On 29 June Mr Haines secretly bought another shotgun. On 1 July he entered the garage and shot himself to death. The plaintiff (Mrs Haines) sued Dr Bellissimo and the medical centre for failing to prevent his suicide.

Held: the duty and standard of care imposed on a psychiatrist, or a clinical psychologist applying therapy in a specialised capacity in a hospital environment, is the same required of physicians in all fields of medicine and surgery. If the patient's mental condition and actions were such that a reasonably prudent psychiatrist or psychologist would under the circumstances have anticipated a suicide attempt, then the concept of reasonable care in treatment requires the therapist to take all reasonable steps, including hospitalization of the patient if necessary, to prevent or reduce the risk of self-destruction. Dr Bellissimo's opinion on 28 June that there was no immediate risk of suicide was reasonable. He had not been negligent in deciding not to hospitalize Mr Haines.

Judgment for the defendants.

Hall and Wife v Lees and Others

Nurses: burns: vicarious liability

Court of Appeal. [1904] 2 KB 602

The plaintiff (Mrs Hall) needed a serious operation. Her surgeon asked the Oldham Nursing Association for two nurses to attend on her during the operation. After the operation, while the plaintiff was still under anaesthetic, a very highly heated hot-water bottle came into immediate contact with her body, instead of being shielded by a blanket as it should have been. She was severely burnt. One or both of the nurses had been negligent.

The object of Oldham Nursing Association was 'to supply aid and instruction in skilled nursing by nurses located in Oldham'. The Association's rules provided, inter alia, that 'when at a case the nurse shall not absent herself from duty without permission from the patient's friends' and that 'only such cases shall be undertaken as are attended by a medical man, whose instructions the nurses must implicitly follow'. A printed form was sent with each nurse, including a report on her 'to be filled in by employer'.

Held: the Association never undertook to nurse the female plaintiff, but only to supply duly qualified nurses for that purpose. The nurses were not the servants of the Association for the purpose of nursing the patient, and the Association was not liable for their negligence.

See pp 129, 137.

Hall v Semple

Psychiatric patient: negligent certification: duty of care

Crompton J (with jury). (1862) 3 F & F 337

The plaintiff (Richard Hall) was a respectable tradesman aged 56. His marriage had proved very unhappy, and there were bitter dissensions and disturbances between him and his wife. Since 1856 she had been making efforts to get him certified as a lunatic. On 28 July 1862 she consulted Dr Semple, a local physician. She told him that the plaintiff slept with a drawn sword by his bedside and had threatened to stab her and, further, that he laboured under the delusions that she was ruining him and improperly associating with other men. Dr Semple saw the plaintiff at his shop the same day, found him excited and rude, and left after ten minutes. On 29 July Dr Semple discussed the plaintiff with Mr Guy, a surgeon whom Mrs Hall had been consulting, and without further examination or enquiry, they signed certificates under the Lunacy Acts that the plaintiff was of unsound mind. The next night he was seized and forcibly carried to an asylum.

Soon after his release in mid-August, the plaintiff sued Dr Semple. Evidence was given at the hearing that the sword was only an old theatrical sword which hung up in his bedroom where Mrs Hall did not sleep anyway, and that she had in fact been pawning items and running into debt. The plaintiff denied accusing her of adultery.

Held: Crompton J directed the jury that a man may hate and detest his wife very much and yet not be a madman. The question was whether Dr Semple acted negligently in signing the certificate without reasonable grounds and without proper examination and enquiries.

The jury returned a verdict for the plaintiff.

See p 100.

Hall and Others v Eli Lilly & Co and Others

Drugs: Opren: limitation

Hidden J. [1992] 3 Med LR 233

One of the plaintiffs (Mrs Elizabeth Hall) was prescribed Opren from 6 November 1980 to 5 August 1982. She heard on television in August 1982 that anyone taking Opren should stop and returned her pills to the chemist. She did not have any discoloration then. In each year thereafter her skin became what she called 'a funny colour' and looked as if she had been abroad and picked up a tan. A naive, not to say, simple lady, she 'did not think there were nowt wrong with me'. Her general practitioner regarded her as a very healthy-looking person. His partner, who saw her from time to time, did not comment on her discoloration.

In June 1988 she saw a hospital doctor called Mr Patrick who picked up her photosensitivity and, when she mentioned Opren, advised her to see a solicitor. She duly did so, and her writ was issued on 15 September 1989. There was a preliminary trial on the limitation issue.

Held: her claim was not statute-barred because:

    (i)   she did not regard the injury as significant and capable of being attributed to Opren until June 1988 when she first saw Mr Patrick. She did not have actual knowledge until then.

    (ii) the defendants had not established any constructive knowledge. Just as she drew no connection between Opren and the changing colour of her skin, neither did her general practitioner nor his partner.

Note: This case did not go to appeal. Those that did are reported under *Nash v Eli Lilly & Co.*

See p 182.

Hall and Others v Wandsworth Health Authority

Childbirth: anaesthetics: discovery: costs

Tudor Price J. [1985] 1 PMILL 7, 129 Sol Jo 188, (1985) Times, 16 February

In December 1982 Mrs Patricia Hall gave birth to twin daughters in St George's Hospital. During labour she was given an epidural injection on two occasions. Since then she had recurring episodes of paralysis and other disabilities. She contemplated court proceedings.

On 1 June 1984 her solicitors wrote a full letter before action to the hospital administrator, requesting production to them of the hospital notes and other records. They gave proper undertakings of confidentiality. They stated that if they had not, within 6 weeks of the date of the letter, been notified of consent to disclose the documents, and within a further 14 days received the documents, they would commence proceedings.

They received no disclosure, so on 4 October 1984 they issued an originating summons pursuant to s 331(2) of the Supreme Court Act 1981. On 5 November, Master Creightmore ordered disclosure within 28 days. Only in February 1985 were copies of case notes finally disclosed.

Held: it was clear from the wording of RSC Ord 62, r 3(12) that normally the defendant to such an application will have his costs paid by the plaintiff. In a small number of cases, the conduct of the defendant will justify the court in ordering him to pay his own costs. Mrs Hall's case was a worse example of dilatory conduct by the defendants. The six weeks suggested by her solicitors were a reasonable period. There was no reasonable excuse for failure to disclose the record to them before the hearing by the Master. The defendants should pay her costs of this hearing.

Note: In two associated cases, in which the defendant's delays were less pronounced, the Master's decision not to make any order as to costs was upheld.

See p 209.

Halushka v University of Saskatchewan et al

Consent: test subject: anaesthetics: assault: cardiac arrest: risk disclosure: Canada: experimentation

Saskatchewan Court of Appeal. (1965) 53 DLR (2d) 436

In August 1961 the plaintiff (Walter Halushka), a student at the University of Saskatchewan, was told that he could earn fifty dollars by being the subject of a test at the University Hospital. He reported to the anaesthesia department where Professor Wyant told him that a new drug was to be tried out, that electrodes would be attached to his arms, legs and head, and that it was a perfectly safe test. Professor Wyant also told him that an incision would be made in his left arm and that a catheter would be inserted into his vein. The plaintiff agreed to undergo the test and signed a form of consent.

On 23 August he underwent the test which involved a new anaesthetic agent known commercially as Fluoromar. The described procedure was followed except that the catheter, after being inserted into his left arm, was advanced towards his heart. At 11.32am the anaesthetic agent started to be administered to him. At 12.25pm he suffered a complete cardiac arrest and was unconscious for four days. As a result of the experiment, Professor Wyant concluded that as an anaesthetic agent Fluoromar had too narrow a margin of safety and it was withdrawn from clinical use in the University Hospital.

The plaintiff sued Professor Wyant and the university for assault and negligence. Professor Wyant had not informed him that the new drug was in fact an anaesthetic of which he had no previous knowledge, nor that there was a risk involved with the use of an anaesthetic, nor that as far as he knew no test using Fluoromar had been conducted before.

Held: the duty imposed upon those engaged in medical research to those who offer themselves as subjects for experimentation is at least as great, if not greater than, the duty owed by the ordinary physician or surgeon to his patient. There can be no exceptions to the ordinary requirements of disclosure in the case of research as there may well be in ordinary medical practice. The researcher does not have to balance the probable effect of lack of treatment itself. The example of risks being properly hidden from a patient when it is important that he should not worry can have no application in the field of research. The subject of medical experimentation is entitled to a full and frank disclosure of all the facts, probabilities and opinions which a reasonable man might be expected to consider before giving his consent. There was ample evidence on which the jury was entitled to find that the plaintiff had given no effectual consent. The defendants were liable in trespass.

See pp 50, 65.

Hamilton v Birmingham Regional Hospital Board and Another

Sterilisation: consent: damages

Cusack J. [1969] 2 BMJ 456

The plaintiff (Mrs Katie Hamilton) was 40 years old and the mother of three sons aged 11, 8 and 2. All her children had been delivered by caesarian section. On the occasion of the delivery of her third child in June 1966, she was sterilised without her consent. She had never been asked whether she wanted to be sterilised. Liability was admitted by the hospital authority and by Dr Keates who performed the operation.

The plaintiff, a Roman Catholic, said that if she had been advised that having further children might be dangerous to her health or life she still would have declined sterilisation, preferring to put her own life at risk. The sterilisation had deprived her of the chance of having more children and of deciding whether to do so.

Held (April 1969):   general damages of £750 were awarded.

See pp 7, 103.

Hancke v Hooper

Surgeon: vicarious liability: standard of care

Tindal CJ (with jury). (1835) 7 C & P 81

In June 1834 the plaintiff (Mr Hancke), who was a whitesmith, went into the shop of Mr Hooper, who was a surgeon in the London Road, and asked to be bled. Two of Mr Hooper's apprentices were in the shop, and he himself was engaged in an adjoining back parlour. The plaintiff told the young men that he had a disease in his head, for which he had been bled before, and found relief from it. Upon this, he was bled by the senior apprentice in the presence of the other. The bleeding took place in the basilic vein, where it appeared from an old cicatrix that the plaintiff had been bled before. During the operation the apprentices observed the blood to flow more freely than usual, so they called for Mr Hooper who came in and told them when to stop and himself tied up the plaintiff's arm.

The plaintiff suffered considerable swelling and discolouration of the arm and was confined to bed for a month. Surgeons testified that all the appearances were consistent with proper performance of the operation.

Held: Tindal CJ directed the jury: 'The defendant is responsible for the act of his apprentice; therefore the question is whether you think the injury which the plaintiff has sustained is attributable to a want of proper skill on the part of the young man, or to some accident. A surgeon does not become an actual insurer; he is only bound to display sufficient skill and knowledge of his profession.'

The jury returned a verdict for the defendant.

See p 58.

Hands v Coleridge-Smith and Horsburgh

Fatal: limitation

Court of Appeal. CAT 14 May 1992.

On 1 September 1981 Ronald Hands, who was suffering from a severe pain in the stomach, was admitted to hospital. On 11 September 1981 he died.

On 29 April 1985 the plaintiff (his widow) issued a writ against the health authority. She never served it. On 4 October 1988 she applied to amend the writ by adding the present defendants. On 7 October 1988 the amended writ was served on them. This was the first notification of her claim. In December 1988 she obtained a favourable experts' report. In April 1989 she supplied details of the alleged negligence.

She applied under s 33 of the Limitation Act 1980 for the time limit in s 11 to be disapplied. Mr J Crowley QC, sitting as a deputy High Court judge, upheld the master's refusal to grant this. The plaintiff applied for leave to appeal.

Held: (i) as the defendants were totally unaware that they might have to meet a claim until October 1988, and as they had no details of the alleged negligence until April 1989, some seven and a half years after dealing with the case, the judge was almost bound to reach the conclusion which he did.

          (ii) the truth was that the plaintiff had left it too late to bring these defendants into the proceedings, and the reason for that, no doubt, was because the earlier medical opinion was unfavourable.

The plaintiff's application was dismissed.

See pp 195, 198.

Harnett v Fisher

Psychiatric patient: negligent certification: limitation

House of Lords. [1927] AC 573

The appellant (Mr Harnett) was a Kentish farmer. On 10 November 1912 Dr Fisher, a country doctor, was asked by another doctor to examine him. From a window he watched the appellant for a short time in the street and took note of his demeanour. Subsequently he made an attempt to get into conversation with him. As a result he signed a certificate in the form required by the Lunacy Act 1890, in which he pronounced the appellant to be of unsound mind. On the petition of the appellant's brother, a Justice of the Peace made a reception order on the same day. The appellant was confined in a lunatic asylum and licensed houses for lunatics until he escaped on 15 October 1921. On 31 May 1922 he started court action against Dr Fisher.

Held: the appellant was not of unsound mind, and Dr Fisher had acted negligently. However, the appellant was debarred from recovering damages by the Limitation Act 1623, since the six years limitation period ran from the date of his detention on 10 November 1912. As he was never insane, time was not prevented from running by reason of disability.

See pp 100, 190.

Harrington v Essex Area Health Authority

Operation: after-care: burden of proof

Beldam J. (1984) Times, 14 November

Complications occurred after an operation to the plaintiff. He alleged that the defendants were negligent in their treatment of him.

Held: as it was impossible to select between two possible explanations for these complications, the plaintiff had failed to discharge the burden of proof. The defendants were not liable.

Harris v Bromley Health Authority

Childbirth: damages: sphincter

Ognall J. Unreported

In 1982, when the plaintiff (Mrs Harris) was aged 35, a third degree tear occurred during the birth of her third child. This damaged her anal sphincter. The defendants failed to diagnose the injury for a week, after which it was stitched.

Owing to the delay in surgical repair, combined with the fact that the plaintiff could not face the prospect of further surgery, there was little improvement. She had to have her fourth child by caesarean section, due to the risk of further injury. She suffered incontinence of both faeces and flatus and had to wear pads constantly. She suffered an urgency of defaecation and associated difficulty with hygiene. The flatulence was exacerbated by another condition which necessitated a high fibre diet. Her personal dignity was greatly affected. The injury also caused sexual difficulties. The plaintiff's condition inhibited her social life, gave her a constant sense of anxiety and would impair her chances of finding suitable employment after her children were older. The condition was permanent and might deteriorate in later life.

Held (November 1990): general damages of £28,000 were awarded for pain, suffering and loss of amenities. In addition, there was agreed future financial loss of £3,234. The total award was £31,234.

See pp 97, 156.

Harris v Newcastle Health Authority

Operation: discovery: limitation: ophthalmic

Court of Appeal. [1989] 2 All ER 273, [1989] 1 WLR 96

The plaintiff (Veronica Harris) was born in October 1959. She suffered from a squint in her left eye. Around April 1961 her parents consulted Mr Lake who conducted an operation either at the Fleming Memorial Hospital or at the Royal Victoria Infirmary. The result was that her eyelid became nearly closed.

In 1965 Mr Howard was consulted. He performed a further operation. This resulted in some cosmetic improvement, with the eyelid opening more. However she since suffered pain which became progressively worse.

In February 1987 a nurse suggested to the plaintiff that the problem was not of natural origin. Indeed, the plaintiff had always connected it with the operation which she had had as a small child. She consulted solicitors who applied for pre-trial disclosure of the hospital records under s 33(2) of the Supreme Court Act 1981. The district registrar and the judge (Staughton J) refused on the ground that there was no point in ordering pre-trial discovery when a limitation defence was virtually bound to succeed.

Held: the plaintiff's counsel had stated that proceedings were likely to be instituted, so the jurisdictional requirements of s 33(2) were satisfied. Although there was a strong limitation defence, the plaintiff's case was not clearly doomed to failure. The application for pre-trial discovery should be granted.

Per Kerr LJ: 'If it is plain beyond doubt that a defence of limitation will be raised and will succeed, then it seems to me that the court must be entitled to take that matter into account. . . But I would accept that in the normal run of cases, even where a defence of limitation has a strong prospect of success, like here, it is very difficult for a court, on limited material, before pleadings and discovery, to conclude at that stage that the situation is such that the proposed action is bound to fail and therefore frivolous, vexatious or otherwise ill-founded. So in general I would accept the submission of counsel that issues relevant to limitation should not enter into consideration on applications for pre-trial discovery'.

See p 208.

Harrow v Islington Health Authority

Operation: surgeon: striking out: spinal: paraplegia

Court of Appeal. CAT 12 June 1990

On 5 March 1980 the plaintiff (Mrs Ann Harrow) underwent an operation by Mr Lowy at the Royal Northern Hospital for a prolapsed intervertebral disc. Her case was that she suffered an injury in the course of the operation, as a result of which she became paralysed from the waist down.

She consulted solicitors in April 1981. Her writ was issued in February 1983 and served almost a year later. The statement of claim was served in May 1986. The defence was served in October 1986. Further and better particulars of the defence were served in May 1987. Discovery was completed in September 1987. The summons for directions was issued in December 1988. The defendants served a summons to dismiss her claim for want of prosecution in January 1989.

Held: (i)   the difficulties, such as they were, in replacing the plaintiff's expert neurological surgeon who had dropped out of the case, could not begin to justify the delay between October 1986 and December 1988. This delay was inordinate and inexcusable.

(ii)   what would have to be investigated at the trial was why Mr Lowy made the decisions that he did: eg how much bone he needed to remove, how much force he needed to use, and so on. Ten years after the operation, he no longer had any independent recollection of the detail of such matters. A fair trial was no longer possible.

(iii)   accordingly the judge had been right to dismiss the case for want of prosecution.

Hartley and Another v Jackson and Lewin

Fracture: x-ray: leg

Horridge J (with special jury). (1933) 1 Lancet 1148, [1933] 1 BMJ 942

On 30 July 1931 the plaintiff, aged 17, sustained a compound fracture of the femur in a traffic accident. On 3 August he was admitted to the defendants' nursing home. The fracture was reduced there. On 7 August the plaintiff's injured leg slipped off the foot of the bed, due to its not having been properly fixed, and was twisted. On 20 August his father removed him from the home. On 21 August his family doctor advised him that the result of the reduction operation was very bad and that, unless something was done, the plaintiff would become a cripple for life.

The plaintiff and his father sued the nursing home's owners who were a Kings Lynn surgeon and his partner. Expert evidence was given that the fracture had never been properly set, that an x-ray should have been taken to see the effect of the correction and that traction should have been applied to keep the bones in position.

Held: Horridge J directed the jury that the law applicable to the case was simple. A man who professed to be a consulting surgeon must use due care and skill. It would not follow that he did not use due care and skill merely because some other surgeon would have given different treatment. The surgeon gave no guarantee that his treatment would succeed; he was not negligent merely because it did not succeed. Nor was he negligent because he adopted a method which others would not have adopted, provided that his method was not in itself negligent and improper.

The jury found that the defendants had been negligent, both in relation to the incident on 7 August and otherwise.

Hatcher v Black and Others

Operation: risk disclosure: thyroidectomy

Denning LJ (with jury). (1954) Times, 2 July

In November 1951 the plaintiff (Mrs Celia Hatcher) had been suffering from goitre. She was referred to St Bartholomew's Hospital where she saw Dr Black. He diagnosed a toxic goitre and discussed with her the possible alternatives, an operation in hospital or medical treatment with drugs. He pointed out that it would take a long time by drugs and did not tell her that there was a slight risk to her voice involved in the operation. Mr Tuckwell performed on her a partial thyroidectomy at the hospital. Her left vocal cord was paralysed, and she alleged that the operation had permanently damaged her voice.

Held: Lord Justice Denning directed the jury:

(i) that it was for them to say whether Dr Black had told her that there was no risk whatsoever, or he may have prevaricated to put her off, as many a good doctor would rather than worry her. Even if he told her, that was not necessarily a matter for censure; the law did not condemn a doctor when he only did what a wise doctor so placed would do.

(ii) all the doctors testifying had said that damage to the laryngeal nerve was a well-known hazard in such an operation, notwithstanding all care, and there was no suggestion that Mr Tuckwell had done anything that he ought not to have done.

The jury returned a verdict for the defendants.

See pp 59, 105, 110.

Hatwell v South-West Metropolitan Regional Hospital Board

Epilepsy: psychiatrist: drugs: psychiatric patient: fracture: jaw: depression

Court of Appeal. 5 November 1976

In 1969 the plaintiff (Miss Ruth Hatwell) was suffering from severe endogenous depression. She had been taking drugs known as Seconal and Valium, prescribed by her general practitioner. On 23 December 1969 she was admitted to Belmont Hospital and seen by a psychiatrist, Dr Markus. He ordered the withdrawal of all drugs from her forthwith.

On 24 December the plaintiff suffered from violent tremors. In the afternoon she had an isolated attack of grand mal epilepsy, with the result that she fell and fractured her jaw. She suffered substantial pain and emotional distress. She was left with deviation of her jaw two units to the left on opening. There was also an area of anaesthesia below the malar prominence of her left cheek.

The trial judge (Norman Richards J) held that Dr Markus' medical treatment had been negligent in that, having regard to the nature and extent of the drugs prescribed by the general practitioner, if there was to be a withdrawal of drugs it should not have been so immediate and so complete. He awarded her general damages (December 1975) of £600 for pain, suffering and loss of amenities.

Held: the general damages should be increased to £1,000. The damages payable should be referable to the plaintiff's actual personality, even if, as a result of that personality, the damages were greater than they would have been for someone in a less vulnerable condition. The defendants had to take the plaintiff as they found her.

See pp 122, 146.

Hay v Grampian Health Board

Brain damage: psychiatric patient: Scotland: supervision: suicide risk: nurse

Court of Session, Outer House (Lord Johnston). (1995) HCRR, March p 2

In Spring 1987, when she had been a patient at the defendants' hospital, G had attempted suicide by hanging. On 10 April 1989 she was admitted to the same hospital as a voluntary patient suffering from a depressive illness. At about 9.25pm she went from the ward to the toilet area. A few minutes later, she was found hanging by a scarf from a shower tap within the bathroom area that adjoined the toilets. She survived and now suffers from irreversible brain damage.

Expert evidence at trial made it clear that a nurse always had to know where a suicidal patient was and that, although it would have been perfectly acceptable under the close observation regime to leave the patient in the toilet cubicle, the nurse had to be aware that she was there and not in the bathroom.

Held: (i)   G was displaying suicide ideation. Accordingly there was a real risk of her attempting suicide. That had to be taken into account as an essential part of the maintenance of the patient's regime.

(ii)   the fact that she went directly to the bathroom established that the regime imposed for her by the hospital management had broken down to a material extent, leading to her suicide attempt.

(iii)   the defendants had been negligent in allowing this to happen and were liable.

Hayward v Curwen

Injection: drugs: causation: gout: consultant

McNair J. (1964) Times, 29 January

The plaintiff (Tom Hayward) had for some years been a sufferer from disabling attacks of gout. He had been under the care of Dr Wilson, a consultant specialist in physical medicine, who had prescribed colchicine at first orally and later by intravenous injection. On 19 August 1959, Dr Wilson being ill, Dr Curwen visited the plaintiff at his home and injected the drug intravenously into his left arm. The plaintiff told Dr Curwen at the time that this caused him no pain or discomfort. However he later developed median nerve palsy.

Held: (i)   Dr Curwen had not been shown to be negligent in the choice of vein in which to inject; nor was he negligent in asking the plaintiff to grip his own left arm in order to distend the vein. Dr Curwen's belief that if any of the drug injected intravenously had been accidently injected into the tissues outside the vein the patient would have experienced pain was reasonable.

           (ii)   with regard to causation, it had not been shown that the median nerve palsy was due to colchicine injected accidently outside the vein, rather than to the growth of a haematoma.

See pp 69, 120.

Headford v Bristol and District Health Authority

Anaesthetics: operation: res ipsa loquitur: striking out: cardiac arrest

Court of Appeal. [1995] 6 Med LR 1, (1994) Times, 30 November

The plaintiff (Mr Headford) was born on 31 October 1963. During an operation at the Bristol Royal Hospital for Sick Children on 1 September 1964, he developed respiratory difficulties which led to hypoxia and cardiac arrest. This resulted in permanent brain damage.

His parents immediately believed that something had gone wrong with the operation. They alleged that the day afterwards a doctor and two nurses advised them that they had run short of oxygen, and that they were promised that there would be an enquiry but never told of the result. However only in 1980 did they start to consider the possibility of a claim.

During the 28 years after the operation, the anaesthetist and the theatre sister died, as did the consultant neurologist and consultant paediatrician in whose care the plaintiff was. No anaesthetic record had been maintained. There had been extensive developments in the administration of anaesthetics since 1964. However the surgeon was still alive, and it was his post-operation note that formed the basis of the plaintiff's case.

His writ was issued on 13 July 1992 through his father and next friend. The statement of claim alleged that the administration of the anaesthetic had been negligent and relied on the maxim res ipsa loquitur. After close of pleadings and exchange of experts' reports and witness statements, the defendants applied to strike out the statement of claim on the ground that it was an abuse of the process of the court.

Held: (i)   s 28 of the Limitation Act 1980, unlike s 28(4), contained no longstep or cut-off point. In permitting an action to be started within six years of the end of a disability, Parliament expressly contemplated that in the case of minors an action may not be started until 24 years after the conduct of which complaint is made. Absent a longstep, there was nothing inherently objectionable in 28 years or any other particular period.

           (ii)   although s 28 is permissive, it confers a right in general to bring proceedings in negligence at any time during the period of continuing disability. The issue of a properly pleaded first writ, within the time limit pleaded by Parliament, is unlikely to be capable of being categorised as an abuse of process.

           (iii)   the delay did not not need explanation, since the writ was issued within the time allowed by Parliament. Prejudice arising to the defendants was immaterial.

           (iv)   the plaintiff's action must be allowed to proceed.

See pp 189, 200.

Heafield v Crane and Another

Hospital administration: duty of care: infection: warning: segregation: fever

Singleton J. (1937) Times, 31 July

The plaintiff (Mrs Marjorie Heafield) entered the Ashby-de-la-Zouche Cottage Hospital to have a baby. One of the hospital rules was that no infectious case should be kept at the hospital. After the birth of her child, she was removed from the maternity ward to a general ward. A woman there was found later to be suffering from puerperal fever. The plaintiff caught it from her. She became crippled in the hips, and one of her shoulders and a wrist were also affected. She sued Mr Crane, the hospital chairman, in his representative capacity and also Dr Hart who had attended her in the hospital.

Held: (i) the hospital authorities ought to have known that the hospital was dangerous, but no warning was given to the plaintiff. They failed in their duty to her when they placed her in a ward where there was a deeply suspicious case;

(ii) Dr Hart had in the hospital a patient who was a gravely suspicious case. He ought to have isolated that patient to prevent the infection spreading. When he found that the plaintiff had been put in the same ward as that patient, it was his duty to have her removed and do everything to prevent her becoming infected. He also had neglected his duty towards her.

See pp 24, 131.

Heath v West Berkshire Health Authority

Damages: dental: lingual nerve: operation: risk disclosure

Mantell J. [1992] 3 Med LR 57

In July 1986 the plaintiff (Mrs Hayes) went into the Royal Berkshire Hospital to have three wisdom teeth removed. She was not told that the removal of wisdom teeth carried with it a small percentage risk of unavoidable injury to the lingual nerve.

The teeth were removed under local anaesthetic and sedation by Miss Patel who was assisted throughout by a student. It was necessary to insert a retractor between the periosteum and the bone, so as to ease the lingual nerve away from the bone which was to be removed by the drill, and also to interpose the retractor or its blade between the nerve and the business end of the drill, in order to act as a shield. During the course of the removal of the lower third molar, some injury was caused to the lingual nerve. This was probably caused by the direct application of the burr of the drill.

The plaintiff was left with a permanent partial loss of taste. The left half of her tongue was unaffected. The right half was generally anaesthetised and unable to pick up sensations of taste, but she continually experienced in it a sensation of 'pins and needles' and intermittently a sharp 'shooting' pain of moderate severity. Moreover if she put her tongue in a certain position, or if pressure was applied to certain parts of her mouth and tongue, she might also suffer pain.

Held: (i) in 1986 there was a respectable and responsible body of professional opinion who would not have warned in the circumstances of this case. Therefore the absence of warning was not negligent.

(ii) the injury to the lingual nerve was the result of some lack of care and skill on the part of Miss Patel and/or her student assistant. It was probably caused by the retractor being incorrectly positioned in front of the nerve or incorrectly adjusted to the drill in front of the nerve or through some inadvertent mis-application of the drill itself.

(iii) general damages for pain suffering and loss of amenities were assessed at £12,000. Special damages were agreed at £65.

Judgment was given in favour of the plaintiff for £12,065.

Hegarty v Tottenham Hospital Management Committee and Others

Nurses: causation: pneumonia: fatal

Court of Appeal. 20 February 1976

On 1 April 1969 Patrick Hegarty, a 30-year-old labourer, contracted measles. On 5 April he was admitted to St Ann's Hospital, Tottenham. On 9 April polyneuritis was diagnosed. It was feared that he might develop pneumonia. By 13 April he was having difficulty with his breathing and was placed in a Kelleher rotating alligator tank respirator (or iron-lung). Thick white secretions were removed from his throat. Apart from short periods of removal for x-ray, he remained in the iron lung until he died on 17 April. Broncho-pneumonia was found on autopsy.

His widow sued the hospital authority and three of the doctors. The trial judge (Swanwick J) found that the doctors were negligent in failing to operate the iron lung in such a manner as to prevent the inhalation and pooling of secretions; and that the pooling of these secretions caused the broncho-pneumonia which killed the patient.

Held: (i) as the supposed failure was never part of the plaintiff's substantive case, as it was never put to the main doctor concerned, and as it cast more than a suspicion of negligence upon the nursing staff against whom the plaintiff made no allegations at all, the conclusion of negligence could not be allowed to stand.

(ii) the plaintiff had not established that the pooling of the secretions was the cause of the broncho-pneumonia. The most that could be said was that such pooling might perhaps have occurred and might perhaps have precipitated the broncho-pneumonia.

See p 69.

Henderson v Henderson

Surgeon: tonsillectomy: needle breaking: departing from orthodox practice: child patient: Scotland

Lord Guthrie (Scottish Court of Session). [1955] 1 BMJ 672

In March 1951 Marion Henderson underwent an operation for the removal of her tonsils and adenoids. This was performed by Mr Henderson, a surgeon, at Maryfield Hospital, Dundee. Severe bleeding occurred at the end of the operation, and Mr Henderson took measures to control this by stitching. While he was doing so, the needle broke, and two-thirds of it, about half an inch in length, remained in the child's throat. A stitch was inserted with a fresh needle, and the bleeding was brought under control.

At that point the bulb in the headlamp used by Mr Henderson failed, plunging the theatre into almost total darkness. Replacement of the bulb took only a few seconds, and continuous anaesthesia by gas was administered while the broken needle was sought. Mr Henderson probed the child's soft palate with his finger and the blunt end of forceps. After about fifteen minutes he thought he felt the needle and made an incision with a scalpel. The needle was not found and a stitch was inserted in the incision. The search lasted unsuccessfully for an hour.

Next day the missing part of the needle was removed at another hospital by an electro-magnet. The child had received severe scarring of her throat during the earlier efforts to find it. She sued Mr Henderson.

Held: although normally meticulous, Mr Henderson had negligently departed from proper surgical procedure in the circumstances. It should have occurred to him that prolonged probing and stretching of the fibres would have serious and possibly permanent consequences. Had he exercised the care and skill reasonably to be expected of a surgeon, after a few minutes he would have desisted from his blind search.

See p 119.

Hendy v Milton Keynes Health Authority

Hysterectomy: limitation: operation: ureter

Blofield J. [1992] 3 Med LR 114; [1992] PIQR, P 281, (1991) Times, 8 March

On 25 February 1985 the plaintiff (Mrs Hendy) underwent a hysterectomy and a bilateral salpingo-oophorectomy performed by Dr Dua. Afterwards she felt very low, became incontinent and suffered from diarrhoea. On 26 March 1985 a further operation was performed by Mr Walker and her health improved.

On 12 November 1985, in the course of a follow-up, she saw Dr Didier who told her that in the operation performed by Dr Dua there had been adhesions around the bladder and uterus with the result that her right ureter had become caught up in the operation and injured. Owing to her imperfect recovery from the operation combined with concern over her daughter's marital problems and the death of her pet dog, it was not until September 1986 that she went to a Citizens' Advice Bureau.

They referred her to solicitors who obtained medical records and in 1987 instructed Dr Huntingford who finally reported in July 1988. He criticised Dr Dua's use of sutures and concluded that if the adhesions of the bladder to the uterus were such as to increase the risk of damage to the ureter, Dr Dua should have positively identified the ureter to avoid damage and/or he should have asked for his supervisor's assistance.

On 21 November 1988 the writ was issued. A preliminary trial on limitation was ordered.

Held: (i)   (a)   the plaintiff could be held to have sufficient knowledge within s 14 of the Limitation Act 1980 if she appreciated that her problem was capable of being attributed to the first operation, even when the particular facts of what specifically went wrong were not known to her. She received sufficient information from Dr Didier who was giving an expert opinion;

          (b)   accordingly the three year limitation period expired on 12 November 1988 and her case was prima facie statute barred.

      (ii)   (a)   the length of the delay was only nine days;

          (b)   all the witnesses and all the notes were available;

          (c)   taking into account the other concerns, the plaintiff acted reasonably and promptly once she knew that she might have a claim. Her solicitors as her agents could have acted more promptly, but that was not a major factor;

(d) some small criticism could be levelled at her solicitors, but she did not have a cast iron case against them;

(e) she would be substantially prejudiced if unable to bring the action. The defendants accepted that there was no prejudice to them. It was right to exercise the discretion on the plaintiff's behalf.

See pp 184, 196.

Hendy v Milton Keynes Health Authority (No 2)

Error of judgment: hysterectomy: surgeon: registrar: ureter

Jowitt J. [1992] 3 Med LR 119

In February 1985 the plaintiff (Mrs Hendy) underwent an operation for an abdominal hysterectomy at the Milton Keynes General Hospital. It was performed by Dr Dua, a gynaecological registrar. In the course of ligating the uterine pedicle he unintentionally passed a suture around the plaintiff's right ureter, with the result that it was occluded. In consequence, urine was no longer able to drain from the right kidney into the bladder. Pressure therefore built up in the occluded ureter between the suture and the right kidney, and the ureter burst so that urine from the breach in the ureter began to leak into the abdominal cavity and out through the vagina.

In March 1985, at the same hospital, the pelvic cavity was opened up again, and the damaged ureter was repaired and implanted into the wall of the bladder by Mr Walker with Dr Dua in attendance.

Held: (i) the incidence of non-culpable ureteric damage in normal cases was exceedingly rare. Such cases could only be the result of a correspondingly rare closeness of the ureter to the uterus.

(ii) the remedial operation did not disclose any evidence that the ureter was unusually close to the mid-line. The damaged ureter in its undisturbed position lay within the normal parameters.

(iii) the explanation of what went wrong was that Dr Dua did not sufficiently push the plaintiff's bladder down at the sides.

(iv) it was accepted that, in the absence of pathology or other abnormality, the competent surgeon should make a sound visual assessment of the position of the bladder which would reliably tell him whether the ureters were in a position of safety.

(v) accordingly, in deciding that the bladder was in an acceptable position, Dr Dua had made a misjudgment that amounted to negligence.

See pp 184, 194.

Herskovits v Group Health Co-operative of Puget Sound

Cancer: diagnosis: causation: damages: USA: loss of chance

Supreme Court of Washington. 664 P 2d 474 (Wash. 1983)

In early 1974 Leslie Herskovits attended the Group Health Cooperative with complaints of pain and coughing. Chest x-rays revealed infiltrate in the left lung. Rales were present. The chest pain and coughing became persistent and chronic by December 1974. He was treated with cough medicine.

In June 1975 Mr Herskovits visited Dr Ostrow for a second medical opinion. Within three weeks, Dr Ostrow's evaluation and direction to Group Health led to the diagnosis of cancer. In July 1975 his diseased lung was removed, but no radiation or chemotherapy was instituted. In March 1977 Mr Herskovits died at the age of 60.

The plaintiff (his widow) sued the hospital authority, alleging failure to make an early diagnosis of the lung cancer. The trial court granted the defendant's motion for summary judgment for dismissal, on the basis that Mr Herskovits probably would have died from lung cancer even if the diagnosis had been made earlier.

Counsel agreed that for the purpose of the appeal the court was to assume that the failure to diagnose cancer in December 1974 and the consequent six month delay reduced Mr Herskovits' chances of survival from 39% to 25%. It was undisputed that he had less than a 50% chance of survival at all relevant times.

Held: (i)   a 14% reduction, from 39% to 25%, in the deceased's chances of survival, was sufficient evidence of causation to allow the jury to consider the possibility that the delay in diagnosing the cancer was the proximate cause of death.

        (ii)   this reduced chance of survival did not necessitate total recovery for all damages caused by the death; rather, damages should be awarded based only on damages caused directly by premature death, such as lost earnings and additional medical expenses etc.

Per Dole J: 'To decide otherwise would be a blanket release from liability for doctors and hospitals any time there was less than a 50% chance of survival, regardless of how flagrant the negligence'.

See p 77.

Higgins v Eli Lilly & Co and Others

Drugs: limitation: Opren

Court of Appeal. [1992] 3 Med LR 385

See *Nash v Eli Lilly & Co* (G) (p 472).

Hill v Liverpool Health Authority

Damages: operation: testicle

Smith J. [1994] 3 CL 139

In July 1985 the plaintiff (Mr Hill), aged 43 at trial, underwent a vasectomy. As a result of complications, he underwent a further operation in February 1987. During this the surgeon negligently cut off the blood supply to his left testicle.

In consequence, this testicle became devitalised. The problem was not immediately recognised. For six weeks he had an open wound on the side of his scrotum which was painful, foul-smelling and discharging dead tissue. During this period, he underwent an operation under general anaesthetic during which the wound was cleared. The discharge and pain continued, and he underwent a further operation for removal of the left testicle. Thereafter he made a satisfactory physical recovery and returned to work ten weeks after the negligently performed operation.

He was left with the cosmetic defect of having only one testicle. His unwillingness to have a prosthesis fitted was reasonable. He no longer swam with his children, due to embarrassment in the changing rooms. He suffered a severe psychological reaction, feeling incomplete as a man and sexually inadequate. He gradually became impotent. His marriage came under strain and he became irritable, sarcastic and hurtful to his wife. Probably his marriage would survive and in time he would become less unhappy, but it was only possible that he would recover the ability to have sexual intercourse.

Held (December 1993):   general damages of £22,500 were awarded for his pain, suffering and loss of amenities.

See p 156.

Hills v Potter and Another

Surgeon: risk disclosure: battery: consent: neck: quadriplegia

Hirst J. [1983] 3 All ER 716, [1984] 1 WLR 641n

In January 1974 the plaintiff (Mrs Sylvia Hills) underwent at the Radcliffe Infirmary an operation performed by Mr Potter for spasmodic torticollis, a deformity of the neck. As a result of the operation she was paralysed from the neck downwards. No negligence in performance of the operation was alleged.

Mr Potter had seen the plaintiff in September 1973 and explained what the operation involved. He said that any major operation, such as this one, carried certain risks but they should not be exaggerated. There was always a small risk of the patient dying or something going wrong with the anaesthetics and a risk of paralysis or at least weakness to the arms and legs, which might only be temporary or transient.

The plaintiff sued Mr Potter and the hospital authority for:

(a) negligently failing to provide her with all appropriate information as to the risk; and

(b) assault and battery on the basis that her consent was not real. None of the three surgical experts said that they would have given more detail than Mr Potter.

Held: as Mr Potter's practice accorded with that upheld by a substantial body of respectable and responsible medical opinion, he was not negligent. The plaintiff's undoubted consent to the operation that was in fact performed negatived any possibility of liability for assault and battery.

See pp 6, 105, 107.

Hinfey v Salford Health Authority

Brain damage: breech delivery: childbirth: senior house officer

Christopher Holland QC. [1993] 4 Med LR 143

On 26 March 1975 Mrs Eileen Hinfey, aged 29 and thought to be 38 weeks pregnant, was seen in an ante-natal clinic at Hope Hospital. Dr Rahman, a registrar, elicited by clinical examination that her baby was in a breech presentation. The radiologist reported 'Abdomen:

single apparently normal foetus, breech presentation. Maturity judging from the knees approximately 36 weeks, but this does appear to be a big baby. I take it the mother is not diabetic. Pelvimetry: slightly asymmetrical maternal pelvis.' Mrs Hinfey's pelvis was a normal size.

In the morning of 14 April 1975 she was admitted to Hope Hospital. Between 1.15pm and 5.50pm the contractions were rated initially as fairly strong, one in three to four minutes, but they got no stronger and the last entries for this period were: 'contractions one in five'. At 3.35pm 'thick meconium draining' was noted. At 5.50pm she was seen by the registrar, Dr Wake, who allowed the labour to proceed and ordered a Syntocinon drip to be put up. Between 6.15pm and 9.15pm Syntocinon was administered at an increasing rate, the contractions increased in strength and frequency, and the foetal heart rate (while remaining regular) increased to the upper end of normal range. Thereafter the labour proceeded, monitored by midwives. The note for 11pm was: 'breech visible, urge to push'. The note for midnight was: 'breech visible. Dr Nuttall informed.'

Early on 15 April 1975 Dr Nuttall, a senior house officer, undertook an assisted breech delivery. When the plaintiff (Sinead Hinfey) was born at 12.32am, she weighed 8 pounds and 7 ounces. Her condition was parlous. She had suffered cerebral palsy due to hypoxia. Although resuscitation saved her from death, she was permanently brain damaged.

In 1989 she claimed damages through her mother as next friend. She alleged that a caesarean section should have been performed and that the delivery should not have been conducted by a relatively inexperienced senior house officer. The case was heard in December 1991, 16¾ years after her birth.

Held: (i)   a decision in favour of caesarean section should have reflected an accumulating combination of factors: (a) a breech presentation; (b) the size of the baby; (c) the fact that Mrs Hinfey was primigravida; (d) the fact that Mrs Hinfey was of short stature; (e) the fact that her pelvis was not large and was said to be slightly asymmetrical; (f) the fact that the baby was post-mature; (g) the fact of the passage of meconium; (h) the failure to make progress in the early stages, or between 11pm and midnight; (i) the signs of developing foetal distress. The obstetric team was good, committed and skilled. Setting aside the size of the baby, the team did not so depart from the standards of proper care in its continuing evaluation of such factors that its sustained decision to allow Mrs Hinfey to proceed to vaginal delivery was negligent.

        (ii)   at 8lbs 7oz (3.85 kilograms) Sinead was a big baby. Since her skeletal size was normal, the inference was that she was well fleshed. However she was in the bracket of normal, albeit at the upper end. Clinical assessment (ultrasound not being available in 1975) would not have shown that Sinead was too large for safe vaginal delivery; until a baby's weight reaches 10 lbs, a clinician cannot be confident that it will be significantly big. In summary, it could not be found that Sinead's size could and should have been clinically assessed so that in conjunction with the other available signs caesarean section should have been directed.

        (iii)   whilst Dr Nuttall was relatively inexperienced, there was no hint that anyone at the time was dissatisfied with his selection or his performance. There was no evidence to condemn his assumption of the task, still less to find a causative link between such assumption and Sinead's condition.

The plaintiff's claim was dismissed. See p 126.

Hocking v Bell

Operation: after-care: retained surgical product: causation: thyroidectomy

Privy Council. [1948] WN 21

In March 1938 Dr Bell performed a thyroidectomy on the plaintiff (Mrs Stella Hocking). Her case was that a few days later, when Dr Bell undertook the removal of a rubber drainage tube from her wound, he negligently left in situ a portion of its inner end, which broke off, and never got it out. She alleged that the foreign body, enclosed in a suppurating cavity, brought about violent and painful attacks of tetany and that in October 1939, during a particularly severe tetanic spasm, a portion of tube was carried into her mouth due to the bursting out from her left tonsil of the abscess surrounding the foreign body. Dr Bell denied that this was possible.

Held: it could not be said that no reasonable jury could have reached the jury's verdict, namely that Dr Bell had negligently injured the plaintiff by leaving in the site of the operation a portion of rubber tube somewhat less than two inches long. There was no adequate ground for ordering a new trial, and the verdict should be restored.

See p 125.

Hodson v Mellor

Alternative practitioner: representations: standard of care: ophthalmic

Manchester County Court. [1911] 1 BMJ 1489

In 1908 the plaintiff (William Hodson) had a cataract in his right eye. It had not developed to the stage when an operation could be performed. He obtained through a newspaper advertisement a booklet which stated: 'Mr William Mellor, the famous eye specialist, rightly claims to have been the recipient of more unsolicited praise from people he has cured than any man in the country . . . The "William Mellor" system of eye treatment is based on irrefutable scientific principles which have long been justified by their outstanding success'.

The plaintiff saw Mr Mellor who examined his eye, and said he could cure it without an operation and guaranteed that he would do so. Over two years Mr Mellor gave him drops for the eye and some medicines and pills. The drops inflamed the eye which became worse.

The plaintiff sued Mr Mellor for negligence and breach of contract. Mr Mellor testified that he had practised as an oculist in Manchester for 16 or 17 years. He admitted that he had been in Perth, Australia, but denied that he had ever been a door-keeper at the eye hospital there or that his sole scientific experience had been gained in that capacity.

Held: this was a case in which a person held himself out to possess skill which he did not possess and, by means of very optimistic advertisements, he persuaded people to come and consult him. The judge found for the plaintiff.

See pp 30, 141.

Hoffman v Sofaer

General practitioner: damages: arm

Talbot J. [1982] 1 WLR 1350

In August 1976 the plaintiff (Mr Hoffman), an American then aged 47, was visiting London. He was right handed and had pain in the right arm which he attributed to lifting heavy luggage. He consulted Dr Sofaer, a general practitioner, who diagnosed tennis elbow. Dr Sofaer administered lignocaine, hydrocortisone and hyaluronidase by injection. He later admitted liability for negligent treatment.

The plaintiff experienced further pain in his elbow and became feverish. An abscess formed in the region of his right elbow, which necessitated multiple incisions under general anaesthesia. In September 1976 he returned to the United States. His right upper arm was wasted, and an operation was performed to save it. X-rays taken in October 1977 showed absence of the radial head and solid fusion of the right elbow at an angle of 75° of flexion. Owing to the condition of his arm, in January 1978 he suffered a fall which resulted in a transverse undisplaced supracondylar fracture of the right humerus. He was left with an arthrodesed elbow and severe impairment of wrist and hand function. He was greatly limited in do-it-yourself tasks and his work. He had difficulty in writing and could no longer pursue his hobby of photography.

Held: (i)   general damages for pain, suffering and loss of amenities were assessed at £19,000 (May 1981);

           (ii)   judgment for all the plaintiff's other damages—eg loss of earnings, medical expenses, loss of holiday, cost of employing others to perform his former work in the home—was given in U.S. dollars, as that was the currency in which his losses were suffered.

See p 155.

Hogg v Ealing, Hammersmith and Hounslow Area Health Authority and Another

Cottage hospital: diagnosis: nurses: patient's history: fingers

Forbes J. [1982] 4 MLJ 174

On 3 October 1975 the plaintiff, then aged 11, cut his left hand on some glass, and a splinter entered his palm below the ring finger. His mother removed the splinter and disinfected the hand. On 9 October he fell on his left hand, bending back the ring and middle fingers. By 10 October the ring finger was swollen. He was seen by a nurse at the casualty department of a cottage hospital. An x-ray revealed no bony injury; lead lotion was applied, and he was told to return next day if necessary. As the swelling was worse, his mother took him back to the cottage hospital in the afternoon where an orthopaedic surgeon, who was holding a clinic there, saw him for three to four minutes and diagnosed a soft tissue injury to the proximal interphalangeal joint.

Two days later the plaintiff's hand was very swollen and he was admitted to another hospital as an in-patient. He was left with a permanently flexed ring finger which did not respond to physiotherapy. He sued alleging a negligent failure to diagnose and treat the infection at the cottage hospital.

Held: neither the nurse nor the surgeon was told of the earlier injury on 3 October. Consequently there were no grounds for suspecting an infection in the hand when they saw the plaintiff. They had not been negligent.

See p 99.

Hogg v Hamilton and Another

Brain damage: operation: striking out: solicitors

Court of Appeal. [1992] PIQR P387.

On 29 June 1976 the plaintiff (Michael Hogg, suing by his father and next friend) underwent a vagotomy and gastroenterostomy at a hospital operated by Northumberland Health

Authority. The anaesthetist was Dr Hamilton. Afterwards, as a result of hypoxia and cardiac arrest which occurred when he was in a recovery room, he suffered permanent brain damage and remained under a serious disability.

In December 1978 his first solicitors issued a writ against the health authority. Second solicitors who took over the case were unable to obtain supporting medical evidence. In January 1982, at a hearing in which no mention was made of the plaintiff's disability, his action was dismissed for want of prosecution.

Later in 1982, Dr Hamilton retired. Knowing that the claim had been struck out, he destroyed his anaesthetic record cards. Similarly, by 1985 the health authority's solicitors destroyed their files. So did Dr Hamilton's defence union.

From 1982 to 1986, a third firm of solicitors was investigating a possible professional negligence claim against the second firm. In 1987 a fourth firm wrote for the hospital records to the health authority which initially declined to disclose them. On 4 December 1987 the fourth firm wrote a further letter, explaining that the records were required with a view to issuing proceedings against the second firm and ending 'we would again stress that there is no intention to attempt to resurrect the proceedings against your health authority'. In reliance on this, the authority sent them not only the full medical records but also privileged witness statements.

After obtaining reports, the fourth firm issued a writ against Dr Hamilton alone on 13 March 1989. In November 1990, when his application to strike out this action was dismissed, leave was given to the plaintiff to join the health authority as second defendants. The amended statement of claim was served in January 1991.

The health authority's application to strike out the action was refused by the district judge. Brooke J allowed the appeals of both defendants. The plaintiff appealed.

Held: (i) proceedings can be struck out as being an abuse of the process of the court, even though the plaintiff is a person to whom an extended and unexpired limitation period is applicable.

(ii) the judge was fully entitled to conclude that the commencement of the second action, in the context of prejudice which had undoubtedly been suffered by the defendants and the assurance that had been given to the authority, was an abuse of the process which entitled him to strike out the action against both defendants.

See pp 189, 200.

Holgate and Another v Lancashire Mental Hospitals Board, Gill and Robertson

Prison inmate: duty of care: supervision

Lewis J (with jury). [1937] 4 All ER 19

John Lawson had very early in life shown criminal tendencies. After convictions for wilful damage, indecent assault, housebreaking and theft, he was sent to a reformatory school. He was then tried and acquitted for attempted rape. Within two months he was charged with robbery with violence and two cases of indecent assault. In February 1927 he was ordered to be detained during His Majesty's pleasure and was sent to the Calderstone Institution.

An application was made for him to go out on licence to the house of his brother who would have taken a holiday and been at home to look after him. This application was refused. When it was later repeated and granted, no enquiries were made of the brother nor undertakings sought from him. In June 1936, during his leave, Lawson visited the house of the plaintiffs (Mr and Mrs Holgate) where Mrs Holgate was alone. She gave him food and began to mend a garment at his request, when he struck her on the head and hand with a piece of wood, causing severe injury.

The plaintiffs sued Lancashire Mental Hospitals Board, Dr Gill (the superintendent) who had agreed to Lawson's initial leave, and Dr Robertson (the acting superintendent) who had granted an extension of it.

Held: Lewis J directed the jury that they should not find negligence if the defendants were only guilty of an error of judgement. The question was whether, bearing in mind the care and control of mental defectives which they must exercise, the defendants failed to take reasonable care.

The jury found that all three defendants were negligent.

See pp 19, 50, 132.

Holland v Devitt and Moore Nautical College Ltd and Another

School doctor: diagnosis: vicarious liability: medical literature: fatal: hepatitis

Streatfield J. (1960) Times, 4 March

Peter Holland had suffered from mild attacks of epilepsy since the age of three. In May 1954, when he was a 15-year-old pupil at the Devitt and Moore Nautical College, he was stricken with infective hepatitis. Dr Thomas, the school medical officer, concluded that it was a mild case. He put the boy on a full fat-free diet and glucose and kept him in bed. Peter told him that he felt perfectly well: there was no nausea, no vomiting and his appetite was normal. He showed continued improvement, even after being allowed to get up in his room, although without completely recovering. Dr Thomas allowed him to go home for the school half-term holiday on 5 June, partly because he feared that the emotional disturbance of refusing this might adversely affect the epilepsy. The day after his return to school, Peter had a relapse. His disease progressed, and in 1957 he died of cirrhosis of the liver. His father sued the college and Dr Thomas.

According to its prospectus, the college held itself out as providing medical attention including treatment in the sick-bay. Dr Thomas had to visit the college on Tuesdays and Fridays and attend the boys in the sick-bay when sent for.

Held: (i) the college had undertaken to provide treatment in the sick-bay, and that could not be read as limited to treatment by the sister. Therefore if Dr Thomas was negligent, the college would be vicariously liable.

(ii) all the doctors had agreed that the general practitioner in charge of the case was in the best position to judge, and that statements in textbooks were no substitute for his judgement. Not only was there no negligence, but also no mistake was made in the first stage. It was the cruellest misfortune that, in spite of all indications to the contrary, the disease had turned out to be more severe than thought.

See pp 65, 99.

Hollis v Dow Corning Corp et al

Breast: Canada: product liability: res ipsa loquitur: risk disclosure: warning

British Columbia Court of Appeal. *Halsbury's Laws Annual Abridgment* 1993, para 1768 94/369, (1993) 103 DLR (4th) 520

In July 1983 the plaintiff (Miss Hollis), aged 23, met Dr Birch, a plastic surgeon, to discuss the possibility of surgery to correct abnormalities of her breasts. She decided to undergo surgery which would include the implantation of breast prostheses in both breasts.

In October 1983 Dr Birch operated and inserted an implant in each of the plaintiff's breasts. The implants were 'gel-filled, low profile round' sylastic implants manufactured by the first defendants (Dow Corning Corporation).

By the spring of 1984, the abnormality in the breasts had returned. As a result, Dr Birch operated on her again. During the course of this operation, the plastic surgeon assisting Dr Birch stretched the areolae of the plaintiff's breasts, which involved the application of 'light pressure' to them.

In January 1985 the plaintiff noticed a lump in her right breast and experienced pain in it. In March 1985 another plastic surgeon, Dr Quayle, operated to remove the implants. He discovered that the left implant was intact, but the right implant had ruptured. The silicone gel from the right implant was lying in the breast cavity, which was red and swollen.

An article published by Dow in 1976 included the following: 'Be certain that the patient understands that following implantation, abnormal squeezing or trauma to the breasts could conceivably rupture the implant.' The 1979 product insert included the following reference to the possibility of implant rupture: 'If the implant should accidentally rupture during insertion or be nicked with a sharp instrument or suture needle during closure, remove the implant and replace.' From 1975 to 1984 Dow received reports of between 77 to 81 ruptures of implants of the kind received by the plaintiff. In 1985, for the first time, their literature contained full and detailed warnings.

Dr Birch testified that in 1983 he warned between 20% and 30% of his patients of the possibility of implant rupture.

Held: (i) since there was more than one possible cause of the rupture, it was not appropriate for the trial judge to have recourse to res ipsa loquitur to draw an inference of negligence against Dow. The evidence did not support his conclusion that the rupture of the implant had been caused by negligent manufacture on the part of Dow.

(ii) Dow had relevant information at its disposal, with respect to the risk of rupture, which it did not make available to the medical community. Although 77–81 ruptures over a nine year period was statistically low, the consequence of a failure adequately to warn of the extent of that risk was significant in terms of potential harm to the plaintiff. Dow was not required to issue a warning each time a rupture occurred, but it would not be expecting too much to expect Dow to issue updated information in this regard to the medical community on a yearly basis, or sooner if the circumstances warranted it. A manufacturer should not be too coy about revealing the risks associated with its product and then expect to avoid liability by placing the full burden of those risks on either the medical community or the patient. Dow had negligently failed to give due warning of the risk of rupture.

(iii) the evidence disclosed that plastic surgeons were aware of the possibility of rupture in 1983, although its incidence was thought to be rare. Dr Birch acknowledged that he was aware of this possibility in 1983 and he thought it significant enough to warn 20% to 30% of his patients. The effect of his not warning the plaintiff was to preclude her from making an informed choice as to whether to proceed with the implant surgery despite the risk of rupture. Dr Birch should have warned her about this and was negligent in having failed to do so.

Holmes v Leeds Health Authority

Dental: damages: scarring

District Judge Greenwood. [1992] CLY 1616

The plaintiff (Mrs Holmes), aged 29, underwent an operation under general anaesthetic for removal of some teeth. During this she suffered a burn or wound to her upper lip from a high-speed dental drill burr-shank.

When she recovered from the anaesthetic, the burn/wound was very sore and raw. She was advised to smear Vaseline on the area until the wound healed, which occurred after three weeks.

It left a scar one centimetre wide and one and a half centimetres high on the left side of her upper lip. It was thin and white and did not cross or distort the vermilion border. It could not be significantly improved by surgery. The plaintiff was embarrassed by the scar, which was visible at conversational distances, and felt that other people noticed it. She no longer used her own sun-bed, because a suntan made the scar more noticeable. It sometimes tingled, especially in cold weather.

Held (February 1992):   the plaintiff was awarded general damages of £1,100 for pain, suffering and loss of amenities.

Hooper v Young

Damages: hysterectomy: kidney: psychiatric injury: ureter: depression

Sir Michael Davies. *Halsbury's Laws Annual Abridgment* 1994, para 975

In July 1990 the plaintiff (Ms Hooper), who had a history of pre-menstrual syndrome, underwent a routine hysterectomy. After the operation, she developed severe back pain and vomiting. There was also a constriction of the left ureter, with hydronephrosis of the left kidney, probably caused by a stitch too close to the left ureter.

A repair operation and re-implantation were performed eight days after the original operation. She was discharged 12 days later, but was re-admitted with left loin pain and vomiting one month after the second operation. A nephrostomy was performed, and she was discharged after a further ten days. She was again re-admitted the following day with suspected kidney infection, and spent a further eight days in hospital.

She suffered refractory depression, and was unable to travel to work and consequently was made redundant. She was able to find local employment. The prognosis was that her depression would improve with physiotherapy.

Held (November 1994):   (i)   she was awarded general damages of £17,500 for pain, suffering and loss of amenities.

(ii)   additional heads of £27,167 special damages, £42,000 for loss of future earnings and handicap on the labour market, £2,537 for the cost of future therapy and £6,820 interest resulted in a total award of £96,024 damages and interest.

Hopley v British Transport Commission and Others

Anaesthetics: operation: state of knowledge: medical literature: hospital administration: fatal

Pilcher J. (1960) 2 Lancet 1452

In January 1954 Mr Hopley was knocked down by a lorry and seriously injured. He was admitted to hospital and needed an operation. He was anaesthetised with an explosive mixture of oxygen, nitrous oxide and cyclopropane. While he was on the operating table, it became necessary to deepen anaesthesia, and the anaesthetist decided to change from an open to a closed circuit. For this purpose he had to remove the terminal metal cylinder of the breathing tube from a metal orifice on the anaesthetics trolley. As he did so a spark, caused by a static electrical charge on the apparatus, ignited the anaesthetic and an explosion took place. As a result Mr Hopley, whose lungs had been full of the gas, died about one and a half hours later.

The plaintiff (his widow) sued the lorry driver's employers, the anaesthetist and the hospital authority. Evidence was given that in 1947 an authoritative textbook on anaesthesia, dealing with the risk of sparks, recommended that the relative humidity of an operating theatre should not be less than 60% when explosive anaesthetics were being used. When the explosion occurred, however, the humidity in the theatre was 25% or less. This was due to a minor failure of the air conditioning plant two days before the operation, which could easily have been put right.

Held: (i)   the anaesthetist was entitled to assume that the humidity was correct; his first duty was to a patient who was in a bad state. It would be wrong to convict him of negligence.

(ii)   the hospital authority was liable for failing to maintain the correct humidity.

See p 61.

Horner v Scarborough, Bridlington, Malton and Whitby Group Hospital Management Committee

Consultant: substandard treatment: patient's history: diagnosis: physiotherapist: femur

Edmund Davies J. (1966) 2 Lancet 47

On 6 March, 1961 the plaintiff, then aged 76, found that she could not move her left leg and had pain from the hip downwards. She had had osteoarthritis of the knee joints for many years but had led a fairly active life. After visits on 7 and 14 March, her general practitioner referred her on a non-urgent basis to the temporary consultant physician at the local hospital's rheumatism clinic. He mentioned that she had asked for a wheelchair.

When the consultant saw her on 24 March, he gave her a gruff reception, would not let her explain about her leg and said 'You must get up and walk. You cannot have a chair' (a wheelchair on the NHS). Although she demonstrated her inability to walk, he did not examine her knee. He wrote to her general practitioner, referring to her 'unwillingness' to move, and stating that the provision of a wheelchair would 'complete her downfall'. He sent her to the physiotherapy department for walking exercises and short-wave diathermy.

She attended five times between 7 and 17 April. She was supported in walking by two physiotherapists. They stated that it was difficult to say whether she was limping and that she complained of pain. The walking exercises were not continued after the second visit, but the diathermy was persisted in until the physiotherapists referred her back to the clinic.

The plaintiff was then seen by a different consultant who, after an x-ray, diagnosed a displaced fracture of the neck of the femur. After an unsuccessful attempt at pinning, an arthroplasty was performed on 2 May. She sued the hospital authority, the temporary consultant and the physiotherapists.

Held: (i)   the temporary consultant had jumped too hastily to the conclusion that the plaintiff was unwilling, rather than unable, to do what was asked of her on 24 March. She was complaining of such pain and presented such signs as should have led to a thorough examination by the temporary consultant and an x-ray forthwith. The hospital authority was liable for his negligence;

(ii) the physiotherapists were governed and influenced by the view of the plaintiff's condition implicit in the consultant's instructions. They should not have detected that something was radically wrong. They had not been negligent.

See p 134.

Hothi v Greenwich Health Authority and Another

Consultant: prescription: tests: foreseeability: epilepsy

Croom-Johnson J. (1982) 2 Lancet 1474

At 10.00pm on 28 June 1976 the plaintiff (Mr Hothi), then aged 24, was admitted to hospital with a severe head injury. He was deeply unconscious. A brain scan was ordered. On 29 June Mr Neil-Dwyer, consultant neurosurgeon, took control of the case. At 12.30pm slight twitching and chewing of the jaw on the right side were observed. Mr Neil-Dwyer believed that there were signs of focal epilepsy and that there was a need to reduce oedema in the brain. Phenobarbitone was given three times a day, and later a decompression operation was performed. The plaintiff continued to take phenobarbitone until his discharge on 26 July when he was provided with a supply for two further weeks.

After he went home, the plaintiff developed a severe rash on the trunk. He suffered persistent symptoms of Stevens-Johnson syndrome. He sued the health authority and Mr Neil-Dwyer, contending that phenobarbitone should not have been prescribed and/or that sensitivity tests should have been carried out beforehand.

Held: the defendants were not liable. Where there was epilepsy, it was correct to prescribe an anticonvulsant. Phenobarbitone was a proper drug for the purpose and had been prescribed in the correct quantity. The plaintiff's adverse reaction to it was not foreseeable. The chance of Stevens-Johnson syndrome was so remote that no doctor could be negligent because there was a very slight risk that some hypersensitive person might have an adverse reaction.

See pp 79,120.

Hotson v East Berkshire Health Authority

Diagnosis: loss of chance: fracture: causation: damages: femur

House of Lords. [1987] AC 750, [1987] 2 All ER 909, [1987] 3 WLR 232

On 26 April 1977 the plaintiff (Stephen Hotson), then aged 13, was playing in the school lunch hour. He climbed a tree to which a rope was attached, lost his hold on the rope and fell some twelve feet to the ground. Within hours he was taken to St Luke's Hospital, Maidenhead. The hospital staff examined him but failed to diagnose he had sustained an acute traumatic fracture of the left femoral epiphysis. He was sent home and for five days was in severe pain. On 1 May 1977, when he returned to the hospital, x-rays of his hip disclosed the correct diagnosis. He suffered an avascular necrosis of the epiphysis, causing disability of the hip joint with a virtual certainty of future osteoarthritis. He sued the health authority who admitted negligence in failing to diagnose the injury on 26 April 1977.

The trial judge (Simon Brown J) made the following findings of fact:

'(1) Even had the health authority correctly diagnosed and treated the plaintiff on 26 April there is a high probability, which I assess as a seventy-five per cent risk, that the plaintiff's injury would have followed the same course as it in fact has, that is, he would have developed avascular necrosis of the whole femoral head with all the same adverse consequences as have already ensued and with all the same adverse future prospects.

'(2) That seventy-five per cent risk was translated by the health authority's admitted breach of duty into an inevitability. Putting it the other way, their delay in diagnosis denied the plaintiff the twenty-five per cent chance that, given immediate treatment, avascular necrosis would not have developed.

'(3) Had avascular necrosis not developed, the plaintiff would have made a very nearly full recovery.

'(4) The reason why the delay sealed the plaintiff's fate was because it allowed the pressure caused by haemarthrosis – the bleeding of ruptured blood vessels into the joint – to compress and thus block the intact but distorted remaining vessels with the result that even had the fall left intact sufficient vessels to keep the epiphysis alive (which, as finding (1) makes plain, I think possible but improbable) such vessels would have become occluded and ineffective for this purpose'.

On the basis of these findings, he awarded the plaintiff £150 for his pain and suffering from 26 April to 1 May plus 25% of the £46,000 damages attributable to the avascular necrosis as compensation for loss of the 25% chance of a recovery. The Court of Appeal dismissed the defendant's appeal against this latter element.

Held: in determining what happened in the past, the court decides on the balance of probabilities. Anything that is more probable than not is treated as a certainty. Unless the plaintiff proved on a balance of probabilities that the delayed treatment was at least a material contributory cause of the avascular necrosis, he failed on the issue of causation and no question of quantification could arise. The judge's findings of fact were that on a balance of probabilities the injury caused by the plaintiff's fall left insufficient blood vessels intact to keep the epiphysis alive. This amounted to a finding of fact that the fall was the sole cause of the avascular necrosis. The appeal was allowed on the ground that the plaintiff failed to establish that the health authority's negligence caused his avascular necrosis and its consequences.

Per Lord Ackner: 'Once liability is established, on the balance of probabilities, the loss which the plaintiff has sustained is payable in full. It is not discounted by reducing his claim by the extent to which he has failed to prove his case with one hundred per cent certainty. The decision of Simon Brown J in the subsequent case of *Bagley* v *North Herts Health Authority*, reported only in [1986] NLJ Rep 1014, in which he discounted an award for a stillbirth, because there was a five per cent risk that the plaintiff would have had a stillborn child even if the hospital had not been negligent, was clearly wrong. In that case, the plaintiff had established on a balance of probabilities, indeed with near certainty, that the hospital's negligence had caused the stillbirth. Causation was thus fully established. Such a finding does not permit any discounting. To do so would be to propound a wholly new doctrine which has no support in principle or authority and would give rise to many complications in the search for mathematical or statistical exactitude.

'Of course, where the cause of action has been established, the assessment of that part of the plaintiff's loss where the future is uncertain involves the evaluation of that uncertainty. In *Bagley*, if the child had, by reason of the hospital's breach of duty, been born with brain injury, which could lead in later life to epilepsy, then it would have been a classic case for the evaluation, inter alia, of the chance of epilepsy occurring and discounting, to the extent that the chance of that happening fell below 100 per cent, what would have been the sum of damages appropriate if epilepsy was a certain consequence.'

See pp 26, 29, 65, 74, 75, 96, 147.

Howard v Wessex Regional Health Authority

Operation: res ipsa loquitur: surgeon: tetraplegia: spinal

Morland J. [1994] 5 Med LR 57

In November 1982 at Poole General Hospital the plaintiff (Michelle Howard), then aged 16, underwent a sagittal split osteostomy to remedy a deficiency in the growth of her lower jaw. The operation succeeded in achieving this but, some 12–18 hours after its completion, she suffered a paralysis from C6 downwards. This rendered her permanently tetraplegic.

She sued the hospital authority. She did not allege any particular surgical error. The case was brought upon the basis that before the operation began she was a fit and healthy girl. The operation is carried out successfully worldwide, and tetraplegia due to damage to the spinal cord is not a known complication of it. However if those taking part in the surgical procedures hyper-extended and applied shearing stress to her neck, injury to the spinal cord could result. It was admitted on her behalf that that was the only possible explanation for the catastrophe. She relied upon the maxim res ipsa loquitur.

Six witnesses in the theatre during the operation testified that nothing untoward occurred during it and that there was nothing that could conceivably be a traumatic incident involving the plaintiff's neck. The consultant surgeon stated: 'I guarantee that nothing out of the ordinary occurred . . . nothing compromised the plaintiff by way of positional movement'. Other witnesses observed 'it was a textbook operation' and 'the operation went perfectly'.

The case for the defence was that there was no evidence of hyper-extension or of the use of excessive or shearing force in carrying out the surgery. Moreover their positive case was that there was a non-negligent explanation. This was that emboli located themselves in the arteries and/or veins supplying the cervical cord causing ischaemia to the spinal cord and a 'fat cord' developed at the level of C6 resulting in the tetraplegia. It was suggested that these emboli came from a fragment of a spinal disc which became detached and in some way entered the plaintiff's arterial venous system and translocated to the area of C6. This phenomenon is known as fibro-cartilaginous embolism (FCE). It is exceedingly rare; only 29 cases have been recorded world wide.

Held: (i)   the application of the maxim res ipsa loquitur was inappropriate. The issue was whether the plaintiff established on the balance of probabilities that her tetraplegia was the result of traumatic injury negligently inflicted upon her cervical spine during surgery. If it was equally likely that her tetraplegia was caused by FCE, her case must fail.

  (ii)   although the plaintiff's spinal pain and tenderness after the operation were consistent with trauma, this trauma would have had to have been gross involving not only hyper-extension but a shearing force as well. A trauma or series of traumas of sufficient intensity could not have occurred without being observed by those in theatre. However all those involved were not only honest but also extremely conscientious. If anything untoward had occurred in theatre, they would have said so in evidence.

  (iii)   whilst the lordosis observable in the post-operative x-rays was consistent with trauma, it was equally consistent with muscle guarding to prevent pain resulting from muscle tenderness from the neck being held in extension during surgery.

  (iv)   although it was possible to interpret the myelogram as showing detachment of the posterior longitudinal ligament, it was more likely to be an artefact.

  (v)   it had not been established that the plaintiff's tetraplegia was caused by negligence during surgery. The more probable cause was FCE.

See pp 69, 89.

Hucks v Cole and Another

General practitioner: diagnosis: communication: penicillin

Court of Appeal. [1993] 4 Med LR 393, [1968] 118 NLJ 469, (1968) 12 Sol Jo 483, (1968) Times, 9 May

The plaintiff (Mrs Hucks) was under the care of Dr Cole, a general practitioner with a diploma in obstretics, during and after her confinement. On 4 October 1963 her ring finger became swollen and a sore developed on it with several yellow spots. Dr Cole told her it was nothing to worry about and did not inform the maternity hospital where, on 10 October, she gave birth. On 11 October the hospital, alarmed by the condition of her finger and the fact that one of her toes was similarly affected, isolated her from other patients. On 12 October a bacteriological test was taken and an antibiotic, tetracycline, administered to her. The bacteriological report indicated that she was suffering from fulminating septicaemia. On 16 October the five day course of tetracycline ended. However, although her lesions had not fully healed, Dr Cole did not then begin a course of penicillin treatment or prescribe antibiotics for her. The plaintiff's voice was permanently impaired.

Held: Dr Cole was to be judged as a general practitioner with a diploma in obstetrics. He had allowed the plaintiff to enter hospital with a septic finger and had not notified the hospital of her condition. He failed at the appropriate time to put her on to penicillin or more antibiotics. He had been negligent.

Per Lord Denning MR: 'A doctor is not to be held negligent simply because something has gone wrong. He is not liable for mischance or misadventure; or for an error in judgement. He is not liable for taking one choice out of two or favouring one school rather than another. He is only liable when he falls below the standard of a reasonably competent practitioner in his field. . . .'

Sachs LJ, concurring, said that when the evidence showed that a lacuna in professional practice existed by which risks of grave danger were knowingly taken, then however small the risks, the courts must anxiously examine that lacuna, particularly if the risks could be easily and inexpensively avoided.

See pp 59, 62, 97.

Hughes v Hay and Another

Consultant: diagnosis: damages: fresh evidence: shoulder

Court of Appeal. CAT, 13 April 1989

In April 1982 the plaintiff (Barry Hughes), then a serving police officer, was involved in a road traffic collision in which he fell from his motor cycle and injured his right shoulder. About three weeks later his general practitioner referred him to Mr Hay, a consultant orthopaedic surgeon. Mr Hay did not diagnose the true nature of the injury which was a posterior dislocation of the right shoulder joint. In consequence the plaintiff was left with a substantial disability instead of a minor one.

The plaintiff sued the other motor cycle rider and Mr Hay. Liability was admitted. In May 1988 the trial judge (Hugh Carlisle QC) awarded damages which included £3,000 in respect of the future disadvantages of the plaintiff on the open labour market, on the assumption that he would be able to serve out his remaining ten years in the police force. In June the plaintiff appealed. In September 1988, following a medical examination, he was discharged from the police on medical grounds.

Held: this was a classic case for the exercise of the Court of Appeal's discretion in favour of the plaintiff. Justice would not be done unless the additional development of his discharge from the police force became the subject matter of a retrial.

See pp 45, 96, 148.

Hughes v Waltham Forest Health Authority

Fatal: surgeon: causation: pancreatitis: gall bladder

Court of Appeal. [1991] 2 Med LR 155

On 4 January 1984 William Hughes, a 38-year-old TV sound engineer, was admitted to Whipps Cross Hospital, complaining of acute biliary colic. An ultra-scan confirmed the presence of multiple small stones in a distended gall bladder. After he had suffered a further attack of acute cholecystitis, on 19 January Mr Bursle (an experienced surgical registrar) performed the operation of cholecystectomy for removal of the gall bladder.

On 21 January Mr Hughes developed substantial leakage of bile through the drain tube inserted at the operation. It was obvious that there was a fistula, probably in the cystic duct. An ultrasound scan failed to show up the lower end of the common bile duct. Endoscopic retrograde cholangiopancreatography (ERCP) was available at the Middlesex Hospital for viewing the inside of the common bile duct. Mr Bursle spoke to the senior registrar there who opined that the fistula was likely to close without ERCP intervention and agreed to allowing Mr Hughes' condition further time to settle before embarking on this.

On 28 January Mr Wellwood, a consultant surgeon specialising in gastroenterology and oncology, and Mr Bursle withdrew the drain tube a short distance. On 29 January the flow of bile reduced dramatically, and by 31 January it had virtually ceased. On 3 February the drain was removed altogether. On 6 February Mr Hughes, who wanted to return home, was allowed to do so as he lived nearby and was on the telephone.

By 11 February Mr Hughes' condition had deteriorated again. When Mr Wellwood and Mr Bursle saw him on 13 February, he was suffering from abdominal distension and looked unwell and had some fever. They operated that evening and removed nine litres of bile-stained fluid; a special examination by x-ray (a cholangiogram) disclosed a blockage of the common bile duct close to its junction with the duodenum. Mr Wellwood performed an operation to remove the obstruction which was a gall stone. This operation involved a transduodenal sphincteroplasty which involved a risk of subsequent pancreatitis.

After the operation Mr Hughes' condition appeared to improve for a few days, but by 20 February it was clear that further complications had occurred. A third operation revealed that an abscess of the pancreas had formed. He eventually died on 20 March of acute necrotising pancreatitis.

The plaintiff (his widow) sued the hospital authority. Gatehouse J found at the trial that the fistula had reopened at some stage between 31 January and 13 February, because the stone had again blocked the lower end of the common bile duct and the pressure build-up within the biliary tree had again forced bile out of the ligature tear in the cystic duct. He held that Mr Wellwood and Mr Bursle had been negligent in two respects:

(i)   they should have sent Mr Hughes for the proposed ERCP examination at latest during the week beginning 31 January;
(ii) they were at fault in discharging Mr Hughes on 6 February before the result of the tests showed that his function had returned to normal.

The defendant hospital authority appealed.

Held: (i) the decision not to refer the deceased for ERCP at that stage was endorsed as being in accordance with a practice accepted as proper within the profession by an eminent surgeon practising in the same field. There was evidence that the specialist unit which would have conducted the ERCP examination also considered the decision a proper one. The fact that two other distinguished surgeons were critical of the decision, or that the decision ultimately turned out to be mistaken, did not establish that Mr Wellwood and Mr Bursle had been negligent.

(ii) a similar line of reasoning applied to the decision to allow the deceased to be discharged home on 6 February. The judge did not ask himself whether this represented a clinical judgment which no competent surgeon exercising reasonable care and skill in his speciality could have made. Had he done so, he could only have concluded that Mr Wellwood and Mr Bursle were not negligent.

(iii) in any event, it could not be concluded on the balance of probability that either the failure to carry out ERCP examination or the discharge of the deceased from hospital on 6 February was an effective cause of his death.

The defendants' appeal was allowed.

See pp 64, 69, 117.

Hulse v Wilson and Others

Cancer: diagnosis: consultant: causation: penisectomy

Finnemore J. [1953] 2 BMJ 890

In 1948 the plaintiff (Daniel Hulse), then aged about 30, underwent tests for venereal disease in Birmingham Hospital. He was also seen by Dr Wilson at West Bromwich Hospital. The pain increased, and in January 1949 the plaintiff was admitted to West Bromwich Hospital where they still thought that he was suffering from venereal disease. Mr Kirkham performed a minor operation, which disclosed an ulcer, and sent the plaintiff home three days later. In March he saw another surgeon who diagnosed cancer. In July his penis was amputated.

The plaintiff sued the hospital doctors and the hospital authority for negligently diagnosing venereal disease instead of cancer.

Held: (i) there was no reason for Dr Wilson to suspect cancer in the early stages, and at that time there was no reason for the case to be treated as urgent.

(ii) Mr Kirkham did not delay too long in satisfying himself that venereal disease was not the cause, since such a cancer was extremely rare, especially in a young man.

(iii) even if Mr Kirkham had immediately diagnosed cancer, it was not proved that the amputation could have been avoided.

Judgment for the defendants.

See pp 69, 98.

Re: HIV Haemophiliac Litigation

Discovery: HIV: public policy: group litigation

Court of Appeal [1990] NLJR 1349

The 962 plaintiffs were haemophiliacs or the wives and children of haemophiliacs who were infected with HIV and had or would develop AIDS, as a result of treatment with Factor 8 concentrate imported from the USA which was infected with the HIV virus.

They brought an action against 220 defendants, including the Department of Health. Their case against the Department was that it was in breach of its statutory duty under the National Health Service Act 1977 and was negligent in failing to achieve self sufficiency in blood products for England and Wales.

The Department claimed that no cause of action lay for breach of statutory duty or negligence. It resisted disclosure of 600 documents relating to the policy of self sufficiency in blood products, claiming public interest immunity.

Held: (i) the plaintiffs had at least a strongly arguable case that a claim for damages could lie for negligent acts or omissions in the performance of functions under the National Health Service Act 1977.

(ii) the balancing exercise between the public interest immunity and the public interest in a fair trial of the claim made by a large body of grievously injured plaintiffs, came down decisively in favour of the plaintiffs.

(iii) the plaintiffs needed documents revealing the process by which policy decisions were arrived at for the proper presentation of their case. It was necessary that both sides should know the actual grounds for decisions which led to the continued use of infected blood products.

(iv) Similarly a case was made out for production of documents on the role, resources and planning of the Blood Products Laboratory and the National Blood Transfusion Service, warnings to blood donors, screening of donors, heat treatment and steps to minimise the risk of hepatitis infection, whether and how to adopt self sufficiency in blood products.

See pp 25, 34, 37, 48, 210.

Hunt v East Dorset Health Authority

Counsel: costs: legal aid

Hobhouse J. [1992] 2 All ER 39

The plaintiff (Robyn Hunt) sued the defendants for damages for medical negligence. Her case, which was relatively complex, was worth about £400,000. The trial resulted in judgment for the defendants.

The plaintiff was legally aided. Without obtaining legal aid authority to do so, her solicitors had instructed Leading Counsel who represented her before and at the trial. His fees of £14,425, plus VAT, were disallowed on taxation, although the taxing master accepted that it would otherwise have been a suitable case for Leading Counsel.

The relevant regulations at the time were the Legal Aid Regulations 1980. Regulation 60(1) stated that, unless authority is given in the certificate or in some other specified way 'a Queen's Counsel or more than one counsel shall not be instructed'. Reg 64(4) provided that 'where costs are incurred in instructing a Queen's Counsel or more than one counsel . . .', in the absence of the appropriate certificate or other authority 'no payment in respect of these costs shall be allowed on any taxation, unless it is also allowed on a party and party taxation'.

Held: the regulations were express and mandatory. The matter was governed by actual authority. It was not a question of discretion for the taxing master who, in the absence of legal aid authority, had been right to disallow Leading Counsel's fees.

Per curiam: 'Further, there is a provision which is a safeguard for any counsel who may be instructed. In reg 60(2) it is required that every set of papers delivered to counsel shall include the relevant certificate. It is incumbent on counsel to check whether the appropriate certificate and authority exists: if the regulations are being complied with he will be supplied with that document together with his instructions. If he does not find that document with the instructions that are tendered to him then it is incumbent upon him, if he seeks to look to the legal aid fund thereafter for remuneration, to see that the appropriate authority and certificate is obtained and supplied to him. If he does not take the simple and elementary course that is expressly spelt out in the regulations, then he may find that he is acting without remuneration: the situation is in his hands and it is for him to require it to be remedied if anything has been overlooked.'

Note: The corresponding regulations now are Regs 59(1) and 63(3) of the Civil Legal Aid (General) Regulations 1989.

Hunter v Hanley

Injections: needle breaking: diagnosis: bronchitis: Scotland: buttock

Scotland, First Division. 1955 SC 200, 1955 SLT 213

Mrs Hunter suffered from chronic bronchitis for which Dr Hanley was treating her by a course of 12 injections of procaine penicillin into her buttocks with a size 16 needle. In November 1951, during the twelfth injection, the needle broke as Dr Hanley was withdrawing it and the end remained embedded in Mrs Hunter's body.

She sued Dr Hanley for his alleged failure to use a suitable hypodermic needle. The trial judge directed the jury that 'gross negligence' must be proved. The jury returned a verdict for Dr Hanley.

Held: the direction was inaccurate, so the jury's verdict could not stand. A new trial was ordered.

Per the Lord President (Clyde): 'In the realm of diagnosis and treatment there is ample scope for genuine difference of opinion and one man clearly is not negligent merely because his conclusion differs from that of other professional men, nor because he has displayed less skill and knowledge than others would have shown. The true test in establishing negligence in diagnosis or treatment on the part of a doctor is whether he has been proved to be guilty of such failure as no doctor of ordinary skill would be guilty of if acting with ordinary care. The standard seems to be the same in England'.

See pp 58, 64, 96, 119.

Hyde v Tameside Area Health Authority

Standard of care: diagnosis: foreseeability: public policy: supervision: suicide risk: depression: quadriplegia

Court of Appeal. (1981) Times, 16 April

On 7 February 1972 the plaintiff (Mr Hyde) tried to kill himself. He was in a ward on the third floor of the general hospital at Ashton-under-Lyne. In the middle of the night he got out of bed, smashed the window and jumped out on to the roadway. He survived but had total paralysis of the arms, body and legs, and loss of bladder and bowel control.

When admitted on 26 January, the plaintiff was suffering from a very painful right shoulder. On 31 January he was treated with cervical traction, but the pain was so severe it had to be discontinued. During a blizzard on 1 February he got out of bed, put on a pullover and slippers and attempted to discharge himself. Hospital notes for 2 February showed that he was then more composed. Another patient testified that from 1 to 4 February the plaintiff got terribly depressed and was crying. Thereafter he was seriously ill in body. It subsequently emerged that he thought (wrongly) that he had cancer and was going to die.

It was alleged that if the plaintiff had been treated carefully, the nurses and doctors would have noticed his depression and called in a psychiatrist who through treatment might have prevented the suicide attempt. The trial judge (Lincoln J) found liability against the health authority and awarded the plaintiff £200,000 damages.

Held: the nurses and doctors had treated the plaintiff with the utmost care and competence. Even if this finding was wrong, in failing to assess the true significance of his mental distress, they had only made an error of clinical judgement which was not such an error as to amount to negligence. Moreover the plaintiff's suicide attempt was too remote a consequence of an error to be the subject of damages.

Lord Denning MR expressed the view that the policy of the law should be to discourage actions in respect of suicides and attempted suicides. Lord Justice Watkins and Lord Justice O'Connor concurred in allowing the appeal on the ground that the evidence did not establish any breach of duty by the hospital.

See pp 44, 79, 133.

Ingless v Intransit (t/a Woodlands Medical Group (UK))

Damages: scarring: tattoos

Deputy District Judge Millard. [1992] CLY 1729

The plaintiff (Mr Ingless), aged 43 at hearing, underwent laser treatment at the defendants' clinic, in order to remove two tattoos on his lower left forearm. The treatment was negligently conducted.

In consequence, despite three further treatments by the defendants over a two year period, the plaintiff was left with two ugly patches of scarring. Two or three further operations would be needed to reduce the scarring to a less obtrusive level. After each treatment he was unable to take part in hobbies of riding, rugby and swimming for between four and six weeks.

By the hearing, five and a half years after the initial treatment, he had been unable to afford remedial surgery and was conscious of the scarring when swimming. There was no continuing pain or inconvenience, but the scarring would be permanent without further surgery.

Held (May 1992):   (i)   general damages of £2,500 were awarded for pain, suffering and loss of amenity.

                         (ii)   special damages were £1,007, and £1,000 was awarded for further medical treatment.

Iqbal v Irfan

Child patient: circumcision: damages: operation: penis

District Judge Palmer. [1994] 9 CL 163

Dr Irfan performed a circumcision on the plaintiff, a seven-month-old boy. He used a plastibel which was too large, or failed to apply it far enough towards the base of the shaft of the penis, with the result that the foreskin was left substantially intact. The plaintiff was left with phimosis and a pinhole meatus in the foreskin through which the urethra and glans could not be seen. He was examined twice under anaesthetic. A repeat circumcision was successfully performed six months after the first operation. There were no long term sequelae.

Held (June 1994):   general damages of £2,000 were awarded for pain, suffering and loss of amenities.

Re J* (a minor) (medical treatment)

Anorexia nervosa: consent: interests of patient

Court of Appeal. [1992] 4 All ER 627, [1992] 3 Med LR 317

J was born in March 1976. Her father died of a brain tumour in 1981, and her mother died of cancer in 1984. She was taken into care. She was bullied by the older child of her first foster family. In 1989 her second foster mother had to undergo surgery for breast cancer. This was followed in February 1990 by the death of J's grandfather to whom she was greatly attached.

In June 1990 she started to suffer from anorexia nervosa. In January 1991 she was admitted to a specialist residential unit where she began injuring herself by picking her skin, a symptomatic consequence of suffering from anorexia nervosa. By August 1991 her condition had deteriorated to the point at which for a short time she had to be fed by nasogastric tube and have her arms encased in plaster.

In January 1992 the local authority was granted leave under s 100(3) of the Children Act 1989 to apply for the exercise by the court of its inherent jurisdiction. In March 1992, J reached the age of 16. Thorpe J authorised the removal of J to, and her treatment at, a London hospital which specialised in the treatment of eating disorders. J wanted to stay where she was, and was adamant that she would not consent to further use of a nasogastric tube.

On 30 June 1992, the second day of the appeal hearing, the Court of Appeal was informed that J had not taken solid food since 21 June and that her weight had dropped from 39kg on 16 June to 35kg on 30 June. This was a weight of five stone, seven pounds for a girl five feet and seven inches tall. The agreed medical opinion was that, should she continue in this way, within a week her capacity to have children in later life would be seriously at risk and a little later her life itself might be in danger.

Consequently the Court of Appeal made an emergency order enabling J to be taken to and treated at a specialist hospital in London, notwithstanding the lack of consent on her behalf, and continued with the hearing of legal argument.

Held: (i)   section 8 of the Family Law Reform Act 1969 gives minors aged 16 and 17 a right to consent to surgical, medical or dental treatment. However that does not imply a corresponding right to refuse such treatment.

(ii)   no minor of whatever age has power by refusing consent to treatment to override a consent to treatment by someone who has parental responsibility for the minor and a fortiori a consent by the court. Nevertheless such refusal is a very important consideration, its importance increasing with the age and maturity of the minor.

(iii)   the inherent powers of the court under its parens patriae jurisdiction are theoretically limitless, and certainly extend beyond the policies of a natural parent. Thus it has power to override the refusal of a minor, by authorising the doctors to treat the minor in accordance with their clinical judgment, subject to any restrictions which the court may impose.

(iv)   the paramount consideration of the court is the well being, welfare or interests of the minor. If this is threatened by a serious and imminent risk that the child will suffer grave and irreversible mental or physical harm, the court when called upon has a duty to intervene.

(v)   it is a peculiarity of anorexia nervosa that the disease itself creates a wish not to be cured, or only to be cured if and when the patient decides to cure herself, which may well be too late.

(vi)   accordingly the judge's decision to authorise removal to and treatment at a specialist hospital was correct.

Per Lord Donaldson M.R: 'good parenting involves giving minors as much rope as they can handle without an unacceptable risk that they will hang themselves.'

*Reported in All ER as *Re W*. See p 11.

Jacob v Wessex Regional Health Authority

Discovery: legal aid: costs

Master Turner. [1984] CLY 2618

The plaintiff asked for disclosure of various hospital documents. There ensued comprehensive correspondence from the plaintiff's solicitors as to the relevant authorities and the reasonableness of the request. They pointed out that, as the plaintiff was legally aided, an application would result in unnecessary public expense. The health authority refused the disclosure.

Consequently the plaintiff applied for specific discovery pursuant to s 33 of the Supreme Court Act 1981 and RSC Ord 24, r 7A. Before the hearing of the application, the health authority agreed to disclose the hospital documents but claimed its costs pursuant to RSC Ord 62, r 3 (12).

Held: the circumstances were appropriate for the court to 'otherwise direct'. The health authority should pay the plaintiff's costs of the application in any event.

See p 209.

Jacobs v Great Yarmouth and Waveney Health Authority

Anaesthetics: injection: causation: hysterectomy: anaesthetic awareness

Court of Appeal. 29 March 1984. (1984) 1 Lancet 1249

In July 1976 the plaintiff (Mrs Shelagh Jacobs) underwent an operation for hysterectomy at Lowestoft Hospital. Dr King-Davies, the anaesthetist, administered 3.5ml of althesin to her, a small woman weighing 7 stone 5 lb. She alleged that he negligently missed the vein so that, although she was paralysed by a subsequent injection of pavulon, she remained conscious and aware of the operative procedures right up to the minute of the first surgical incision for the operation itself.

Held: the trial judge (Forbes J) was justified in concluding that the plaintiff's allegation was mistaken, and that the more probable explanation of her experience was that as she regained consciousness of the operation, not realising that it had already taken place, she became aware of a number of incidents and had transposed them in her mind to the period before the operation.

See pp 122, 123.

Jago v Torbay Health Authority

Physiotherapist: spinal: back

Court of Appeal. Lexis, 23 May 1994

In July 1985, after an operation on his left knee, the plaintiff (Mr Jago) attended Paignton for physiotherapy. He was offered physiotherapy on his back. He alleged that a male physiotherapist carried out some forceful treatment on him which placed great strain on his back and that, during the course of this treatment, he felt something go wrong with the lower part of his spine on the right hand side and that he was in such extreme pain that he cried. His case was that he had suffered severe continuing back pain ever since combined with post traumatic stress disorder and depression. The defendant hospital authority denied that the plaintiff had suffered a click in his back during the specified treatment or that he complained of specific pain during it.

Two photographs tendered in evidence at the trial showed the plaintiff standing up and cutting a hedge, looking perfectly fit, and standing at the top of a four step ladder leaning over to cut the top part of the hedge. Neighbours testified that within the two years before the hearing he had been seen on a ladder, painting the top storey of his three storey house, and that he had been seen cleaning his car, standing up.

Held: once the trial judge had accepted the evidence of the photographs and the neighbours, she was entitled to form (as she did) a strong adverse view as to the alleged state of health of the plaintiff and his credibility. Faced with the conflict of primary evidence, she was entitled to prefer that of the defence and to dismiss the plaintiff's claim.

James v Camberwell Health Authority

Brain damage: childbirth: nurse

HH Judge Fawcus. [1994] 5 Med LR 253

The first child of the mother of the plaintiff (Hannah James) had been born by caesarean section in December 1983. Mrs James went into spontaneous labour on 4 April 1985 at term plus eleven days and was admitted to King's College Hospital at about 9.45pm. The CTG trace showed a sudden drop in fetal heart rate at 1.55am on 5 April 1985. This was probably the commencement of severe and prolonged bradycardia. However there was an error in the machine's clock reading system which meant that the crisis commenced at 2.20am (according to the plaintiff) or 2.30am (according to the defendant hospital authority). There had been nothing on the trace earlier to indicate any cause for concern. No midwife was present in the room until Sister Midwife Brown returned at 2.40am. Thereafter prompt action was taken which resulted in the plaintiff's birth at 3.04am. It transpired that she was suffering from cerebral palsy brought on by hypoxia caused by severe prolonged fetal bradycardia.

Held: (i) the fault in the machine's clock reading system was 35 minutes, not 25 minutes, so the crisis in fact commenced at 2.30am.

(ii) Sister Midwife Brown's absence from the room between 2.30am and 2.40am was not such as to justify the assertion that her actions fell below the standards that the public is reasonably entitled to accept. From the point of view of forestalling any risk that might arise from trial of labour, her continued presence was not medically essential.

(iii) five minutes was a reasonable time within which the drop within the fetal heart rate should have been observed.

(iv) even if Sister Midwife Brown's absence from the room between 2.30am and 2.40am had given rise to a finding of a lack of reasonable care, the plaintiff would have been unable to prove that the saving of at most ten minutes would have materially lessened the plaintiff's disability.

The plaintiff's claim was dismissed. See p 137.

James v Dunlop

Surgeon: retained surgical product: nurses: res ipsa loquitur: fatal

Court of Appeal. [1931] 1 BMJ 730

On 11 December 1928 Dr Dunlop operated on Mr James and removed some gall-stones. Mr James remained ill, and on 20 March 1929 a second operation was performed by Dr Burrell. He discovered a surgical pack in Mr James' body. Having been left there in the first operation, it set up a fistula from which he died on 27 March.

The plaintiff (his widow) sued Mr Dunlop. The evidence at trial was that between three and five packs had been inserted and that the pack which had been left was eight inches by ten inches. Dr Dunlop said that he asked 'Are all the swabs out?' and heard a female voice answer 'Yes', but he was not sure to whom the voice belonged. The jury found negligence proved.

Held: the fact that counting might be exercised by some other people did not absolve the doctor from the necessity of making some reasonable search before he put any question to the nurse with regard to the count. Any jury who had felt the towelling pack and seen the size of it would conclude that it was careless not to have taken it out. Moreover they had not been satisfied on the evidence that a suitable assurance had been given.

Dr Dunlop's appeal was dismissed.

See pp 125, 139.

James v London Borough of Havering and Dr Pruss

Leave to sue: false imprisonment

Court of Appeal. CAT 12 February 1992

The applicant (Jennifer James) was living at home in Upminster with her mother and stepfather. At 10.45 pm on 7 October 1986 the police telephoned Mrs Apps, a social worker, and informed her that the applicant had struck her stepfather on the head with an ornament, knocking him out. When Mrs Apps arrived she found the house in disarray, with glass all over the place. The mother explained that the applicant had walked through the glass doors in the kitchen to reach her stepfather. Mrs Apps went upstairs and spoke to the applicant who was in bed and wrapped up like a ball with blankets over her head. When Dr Pruss arrived, he questioned the applicant who did not appear to understand what was going on around her. Dr Pruss and Mrs Apps considered that the applicant (and her mother) appeared to be mentally ill. They considered that there was a sufficient emergency present for them to make an order removing her to hospital.

The applicant applied under s 139 of the Mental Health Act 1983 for leave to sue the proposed defendants for false imprisonment.

Held: it was virtually unarguable to allege that Dr Pruss and Mrs Apps acted without reasonable care. There was no dispute that there had been a disturbance, that the ornament had been thrown and had struck the stepfather, and that the house was in disarray with the glass doors broken. Acting in an emergency, there were ample grounds for the doctor and social worker to take the course that they did.

The applicant's application for leave to appeal was refused.

See p 100.

Janardan v East Berkshire Health Authority

Brain damage: childbirth: damages

McCullough J. [1990] 2 Med LR 1

In April 1985 Mrs Janardan went into the Wexham Park Hospital where her plaintiff son (Rajiv Janardan) was born. The hospital was negligent in its obstetric management and in the delivery. In consequence, both mother and child were injured. Mrs Janardan's claim was settled for £25,000.

Owing to asphyxia at birth, the plaintiff suffered choreic and athetotic cerebral palsy. By the age of five, he could see and hear normally, and his intelligence and other mental faculties were normal, but he had virtually no power of speech. His other chief disability was in his motor control: his ability to control his muscles was so grossly impaired that he could not sit independently, let alone stand or walk. He could not chew properly and had difficulty in swallowing, so he tended to choke. He was afflicted by involuntary movements that were almost constant and affected his head, trunk and all four limbs. He could not dress, feed, wash or bath himself or get to the toilet. He vomited frequently. His bladder and bowel movements were not totally controlled.

His palsy would never recover, although there might be limited changes in the pattern of his motor disorder. He would always need help with dressing, feeding, washing and other bodily functions. He would probably need a wheelchair when older. His speech might improve, but would at best be very slow and difficult to understand. He was of above average intelligence and might be able to pass A levels, but his earning power would at best be minimal. His life expectancy was about to the age of 55.

Held (May 1990):   (i)   the plaintiff's condition merited an award for pain and suffering and loss of amenity somewhat higher than the £100,000 which would be given to the average tetraplegic, especially as he was injured at birth. General damages of £115,000 would be awarded under this head.

(ii)   the overall award consisted of the following heads:

Pain and suffering	£115,000
Special damages (agreed)	£33,000
Future medical and therapeutic needs (agreed)	£53,000
Future care and attendance	£280,000
Loss of earning capacity	£75,000
Costs associated with the home (agreed)	£62,500
Computer aids, appliances and misc (agreed)	£75,000
Transport and travel (agreed)	15,000
Total	£708,500
Interest	£14,619

See pp 126, 154, 159.

Jefferson v Griffin Spalding County Hospital Authority

USA: caesarian: consent: childbirth

Supreme Court of Georgia. 274 SE 2d 457 (Ga 1981).

Mrs Jessie Mae Jefferson was in the 39th week of pregnancy and due to begin labour at any moment. In the past few weeks, she had presented herself to Griffin Spalding County

Hospital for pre-natal care. The examining physician found that she had a complete placenta previa; that the placenta was between the baby and the birth canal; that it was virtually impossible that this condition would correct itself prior to delivery; that it was a 99% certainty that the child could not survive natural childbirth (vaginal delivery); that the chances of the mother surviving vaginal delivery were no better than 50%; and that a delivery by caesarean section prior to labour beginning would have an almost 100% chance of preserving the life of the child, along with that of the mother.

On the basis of religious beliefs, Mrs Jefferson informed the hospital that she did not need surgical removal of the child and that she would not submit to it. Further, she refused to take any transfusion of blood. The hospital authority petitioned the court.

Held: (i)   a viable unborn child has the right under the US Constitution to the protection of the State.

(ii)   the intrusion into the life of the mother was outweighed by the duty of the State to protect a living, unborn being from death.

(iii)   the court ruled that:

'Jessie Mae Jefferson is hereby ordered to submit to a sonogram (ultrasound) at the Griffin Spalding County Hospital or some other place which may be chosen by her where such procedure can be given. Should said sonogram indicate to the attending physician that the complete placenta privia is still blocking the child's passage into this world, Jessie Mae Jefferson, is ordered to submit to a caesarean section and related procedures considered necessary by the attending physician to sustain the life of this child.'

See pp 8, 13.

Jenkins v Eli Lilly & Co and Others

Drugs: limitation: Opren

Court of Appeal. [1992] 3 Med LR 388.

See Nash v Eli Lilly & Co (J) (p 473).

Jinks v Cardwell et al

Canada: fatal: post-traumatic stress disorder: psychiatric patient: supervision: schizophrenia

Ontario Supreme Court (High Court of Justice). (1987) 39 CCLT 168

From 1969 Gordon Jinks was periodically admitted to hospital for acute attacks of reactive schizophrenia. The last was in September 1983 at Wellard County General Psychiatric Hospital, during which he had hypotensive attacks in reaction to his drug treatments. On 19 September he had a restless night. At 4am he was given 50mg Largactil 'to reduce agitation' with no effect. At 5.45am he was banging his head into the bolster of the bed. At 7.10am he was seen wandering around. At 7.25am someone was detected in the bathroom near his room. The assistance alarm in the bathroom had not been working for some time. The viewing mirror in the nurses' station did not give a view of it. It was locked from the inside. When the door was finally unlocked, Mr Jinks was found lying on his side in a bathtub with the water running. He could not be revived. His left upper arm, left forehead and the left side of his nose were scalded by hot water. He had died of asphyxia due to drowning.

The plaintiff (his widow) was asked to come to the hospital. Dr Abraham said to her 'I have something sad to tell you. Your husband passed away. He drowned. He committed suicide in the bath tub.' The plaintiff was shocked and responded 'no – he wouldn't do that, he loved life.'

Held: (i) the probable cause of death was accidental drowning due to hypotensive reaction to the drugs he was receiving.

(ii) in view of the severe disturbance of mind from which the patient was suffering that morning, his known reaction to the drugs he had been administered, and the unsafe nature of the bathroom, a reasonable person could foresee that he was likely to come to harm. The hospital negligently failed to protect him.

(iii) it is likely that Dr Abraham told the plaintiff that her husband committed suicide because this would look better for the hospital. He had no valid reason to suggest this. At best he was negligent, at worst he was callous and unfeeling. In either event, it was a tortious act which caused her physical and emotional distress.

See p 133.

Johnstone v Bloomsbury Health Authority

Breach of contract: declaration: senior house officer

Court of Appeal. [1991] 2 All ER 293, [1991] 2 Med LR 38

The plaintiff (Dr Christopher Johnstone) was employed by the defendants as a senior house officer in the obstetric department of University College Hospital in London. Paragraph 4(b) of his contract of employment provided that he was required to work a basic 40 hours per week and, in addition, he was required to be available on call for a further 48 hours on average: a total average of 88 hours per week.

The plaintiff alleged in his statement of claim that the defendants required him to work intolerable hours with such deprivation of sleep as to damage his health and put at risk the safety of his patients. He alleged that he had been required to work very long hours, in some weeks exceeding 100, with inadequate periods of sleep, that over one weekend he worked a 32 hour shift with only 30 minutes' sleep, and that on another weekend he was on call for 49 continuous hours (during which period he was 'bleeped' more than 60 times) and was able to sleep for a total of seven hours. He further alleged that in consequence he suffered from stress and depression, was lethargic and that his appetite and ability to sleep were diminished; he had been physically sick on occasions and had felt desperate and suicidal.

He sought damages and

(a) a declaration that the plaintiff could not lawfully have been required to work under his contract of employment for a continuous period of more than 24 hours without a break of not less than 8 hours.

(b) a declaration that the plaintiff could not lawfully have been required by the defendants to work under his contract of employment for so many hours in excess of his standard working week as would foreseeably injure his health, notwithstanding that in consequence the total number of such excess hours worked by him might have amounted on average to fewer than 48 per week.'

The defendants conceded that there was an arguable case both for a declaration and damages in respect of the requirement to work in excess of 24 hours without a break of eight hours. However they applied for the prayer for declaration (b) to be struck out, on the grounds that the requirement to work up to 88 hours a week on average was based on the express terms of the contract.

Held: while paragraph 4(b) of the contract of employment gave the defendants the discretionary power to require the plaintiff to work up to 88 hours a week on average, that power had to be exercised in the light of their duty to take reasonable care for his safety, ie their duty to take reasonable care not to injure their employee's health. Accordingly the prayer in the writ and statement of claim should not be struck out.

Per Stuart-Smith LJ: 'Mr Beloff's suggested solution was that if a potential house officer thought that he could not perform the hours required, he should not take the job. Although the principle that if you cannot stand the heat in the kitchen you should get out, or not go in, may often be a sound one, it would have serious implications if applied in these circumstances. Any doctor who wishes to practice has to serve at least one year as a house officer in a hospital; the NHS are effectively a monopoly employer. Is the aspiring doctor who has spent many years in training to this point to abandon his chosen profession because the employer may exercise its power to call upon him to work so many hours that his health is undermined? I fail to see why he should not approach the matter on the basis that the employer will only exercise that power consistently with its duty to have proper regard to his health and safety. The fact that one doctor may have less stamina and physical strength than another does not mean that he is any less competent at his profession.

See p 45.

Jones v Berkshire Area Health Authority

Registrar: sterilisation (failed): wrongful birth: damages

Ognall J. QBD 2 July 1986

In 1977, the plaintiff (Mrs Jones), then aged 26, agreed to surgical sterilisation. Mr Woofson, a surgical registrar, performed the operation. In summer 1978, the plaintiff started to feel generally unwell, tired, dizzy and occasionally afflicted by 'blackouts'. Her girth increased and she missed her periods. She feared that she was suffering from cancer, perhaps of the womb. When she consulted her general practitioner in August 1978, he told her that she was 28 weeks pregnant. In January 1979, she gave birth by caesarian section to a healthy baby girl.

The plaintiff sued the hospital authority on the basis that at no time was she advised that, despite the sterilisation operation, there was a small risk that she might conceive and that, had she known this, when she became unwell she would have suspected pregnancy, consulted her general practitioner and had an abortion. The trial judge accepted her evidence and found that the health authority was liable.

Held: general damages (July 1986) for pain, suffering and loss of amenities were assessed at £2,750 to cover the plaintiff's fear that she had cancer and the need for a caesarian operation. The total award was £32,963.

See p 168.

Jones v Fay

Pharmacist: prescription: advice: standard of care: bronchitis

Pigott B (with jury). (1865) 4 F & F 525

The plaintiff (Mr Jones) was a painter. In May 1864 he went to the shop of Mr Fay, a chemist and druggist, and complained of pain in the stomach, called painter's colic. Mr Fay prescribed and dispensed a preparation of bluepill. The plaintiff collected these pills on several further occasions. Whenever he asked if he should have medical advice, Mr Fay dissuaded him from it and said that he would set him right. The plaintiff suffered severe salivation and subsequently contracted bronchitis and dropsy, aggravated by the weakness caused by the salivation.

He sued Mr Fay. Evidence was given that the bluepill contained a large proportion of mercury. Mr Fay claimed that he had administered rhubarb pills, not bluepill.

Held: Pigott B directed the jury that if a person acts as medical practitioner, he is liable although he is only a chemist. The question was whether the pills that Mr Fay gave the plaintiff were bluepill, for it was admitted that such treatment would have been improper in a case of colic.

The jury returned a verdict for the plaintiff.

See p 140.

Jones v Manchester Corpn and Others

Anaesthetics: burns: overdose: hospital administration: casualty officer: supervision: apportionment of liability: fatal

Court of Appeal. [1952] 2 QB 852, [1952] 2 All ER 125

In January 1950, William Jones was burnt about the face at work. He was taken to Ancoats Hospital where he was seen by two young doctors. Dr Sejrup, a house surgeon who had qualified in 1947, was acting as casualty officer. Dr Wilkes, who had obtained her degrees in 1949, was acting as anaesthetist that day, but she had no special qualifications as such and not much experience. The two young doctors decided to clean up Mr Jones' face under an anaesthetic. Dr Wilkes first applied nitrous oxide gas with oxygen by means of a mask over his face, thereby rendering him unconscious. When it was realised that the mask would be in the way, it was decided to switch to pentothal. Dr Wilkes injected the ordinary dose given to a person who has not had any anaesthetic (ten cubic centimetres). She allowed only ten seconds between the first five cubic centimetres and the second five, whereas she knew she ought to have allowed 30 seconds. By the time she had finished, Mr Jones was dead.

The trial judge (Oliver J) awarded the plaintiff widow damages against Mr Jones' employers, Manchester Corporation, in respect of the burns to his face. He held that Dr Wilkes and the hospital authority were liable in respect of his death.

Held: (i) the death was caused through negligence in the administration of the anaesthetic.

(ii) the employer cannot have an indemnity, if he himself has contributed to the damage or bears some part of the responsibility. It would be extremely unjust if hospital authorities, by getting inexperienced doctors to perform their duties for them, without adequate supervision, should be able to throw all responsibility on to those doctors as if they were fully experienced practitioners. The hospital board was not entitled to an indemnity against Dr Wilkes.

(iii)   Dr Wilkes was not entitled to a complete indemnity from the hospital board, since it was admitted that she was negligent to a degree that was inexcusable even in an inexperienced person.

(iv)   the proportion of responsibility for the damage should be 20% to Dr Wilkes and 80% to the hospital board.

See pp 24, 44, 60, 62, 129.

Joseph v Korn and Another

General practitioner: vicarious liability: receptionist: dismissal for want of prosecution: fatal

Court of Appeal. CAT, 31 July 1984

The son of the plaintiff (Mrs Joseph) died of gastro-enteritis on 30 December 1971. She alleged that this was due to negligence by the child's general practitioner and his receptionist. Following a complaint, there was a full hearing by the appropriate health authority committee in 1972. The plaintiff's writ was issued on 23 December 1974. In March 1984 her action was dismissed for want of prosecution.

Held: there had been inordinate delay which was at least partly the plaintiff's fault. The delay had prejudiced a fair trial of the action, which would have to take place at least thirteen years after the event. Although there a full transcript of the enquiry evidence, there were still disputed questions of fact.

The plaintiff was refused leave to appeal.

See p 202.

Junor v McNicol and Others

Diagnosis: consultant: house surgeon: penicillin: fracture: amputation: Scotland: gangrene: child patient

House of Lords. (1959) Times, 26 March

On 2 July 1953 James Junor, then aged six, fell from a gate and fractured his left forearm, sustaining also a small wound on his inner forearm. After treatment locally, his mother took him to the Raigmore Hospital where he was seen by Dr McNicol, a house surgeon, and Mr Murray, a consultant in orthopaedic surgery. Mr Murray's diagnosis was a greenstick fracture of both bones of the forearm 'potentially compound' by which he meant that it was possible that the small wound communicated with the fracture. He instructed reduction of the fracture and a dry dressing on the wound, but said nothing to Dr McNicol about penicillin. She interpreted his instructions as meaning that the fracture was to be treated as a simple fracture. When the boy was in the theatre, she administered half a million units of penicillin and gave him anti-tetanus serum. She authorised his discharge on 3 July.

James' condition deteriorated on 5 July. He was hurried back to hospital and his arm was amputated in the shoulder joint, as gangrene had set in with such severity as to threaten his life. His father sued Dr McNicol and the hospital authority.

Held: there was no doubt that a mistake had been made in letting the boy out of hospital and he had not been given adequate treatment with penicillin. Dr

McNicol's primary duty was to carry out the consultant's instructions unless they were manifestly wrong. In view of the opinion which the consultant had conveyed with regard to the wound, this was not a case in which she should have disregarded what she believed her instructions to be. Dr McNicol had not been negligent.

See p 60, 121.

Re KB (adult) (mental patient: medical treatment)

Anorexia nervosa: consent: force feeding: psychiatric patient: declaration

Ewbank J. (1994) 19 BMLR 144

K had suffered from anorexia nervosa since the age of 14. In September 1993, when she was 18 years old, she was detained in a general hospital under s 3 of the Mental Health Act 1983. She thought that she was fat and that she needed to reduce her weight. However her weight should have been about 53kg (about 8 stone), but had fallen to 38kg. She was given naso-gastric feeding, because she had refused to eat normally.

This force feeding required a second medical opinion. The Mental Health Commission, realising that, in relation to this patient, naso-gastric feeding was hardly the administration of medicine, told one of the doctors to stop signing the requisite form. This led the health authority to apply for a declaration of the lawfulness of feeding by naso-gastric tube without the consent of the patient.

Dr C, the consultant psychiatrist in charge of K's case, testified that anorexia nervosa was an eating disorder with deranged thought processes and that she regarded K as suffering from very severe mental illness. She said that K did not have the capacity finally to understand and make decisions. With one exception, she had taken nothing in the way of food or drink for the last few days before the application. Dr S said that she might live for another 14 to 21 days, if she continued to refuse food, and then she would die. She considered that K did not understand the true situation.

It was agreed that feeding by naso-gastric tube constituted medical treatment. The health authority submitted that the feeding by tube was given to K for the mental disorder from which she was suffering. On behalf of K it was argued that the feeding was for physical symptoms, not for mental illness.

Held: (i) the mental disorder (anorexia nervosa) from which K suffered was an eating disorder. Relieving symptoms is just as much a part of treatment as relieving the underlying cause. If the symptoms are exacerbated by the patient's refusal to eat and drink, the mental disorder becomes progressively more and more difficult to treat, so the treatment by naso-gastric tube is an integral part of treating the mental disorder itself. This treatment is necessary to make psychiatric treatment of the underlying cause possible at all. Accordingly feeding by naso-gastric tube in circumstances of this type of case is treatment envisaged under s 63 of the Mental Health Act 1983.

(ii) K suffered from a severe mental illness. The treatment which she was refusing was related to the mental illness, not to some unconnected physical condition. Dr C's evidence established that K did not have the capacity to refuse her consent to this treatment.

(iii) a declaration was granted that the detention of the defendant pursuant to s 3 of the Mental Health Act 1983 permitted the plaintiff under the provisions of s 63 of that Act by its servants or agents to treat the defendant by administering food or fluids including feeding by naso-gastric tube so long as she remained a patient under s 3.

Note: See *B v Croydon Health Authority* (p 234) and *Re T* (p 572).

Karp v Cooley and Liotta

Heart transplant: surgeon: operation: informed consent: fraud: experimentation: causation: USA

US Court of Appeals, Fifth Circuit. 493 F 2d 408 (1974)

In March 1969, Haskell Karp was admitted to St Luke's Episcopal Hospital in Houston, after a long and difficult ten-year history of cardiac problems. Tests showed that he had triple vessel disease where all three coronary arteries were occluded. Electrocardiograms showed evidence of extensive scarring and damage, and chest x-rays showed enormous cardiac enlargement. His pacemaker was about to fail.

Soon after Mr Karp's admission, Dr Denton Cooley recommended a heart transplant. Mr Karp rejected this, preferring 'some alternative procedure'. A wedge excision was considered but not performed. In late March Dr Cooley began to discuss with Mr Karp another alternative, involving the temporary implant of the first totally mechanical heart, to which after at least two discussions Mr Karp signed the following consent on 3 April:

'. . . In the event cardiac function cannot be restored by excision of destroyed heart muscle and plastic reconstruction of the ventricle and death seems imminent, I authorise Dr Cooley and his staff to remove my diseased heart and insert a mechanical cardiac substitute. I understand that this mechanical device will not be permanent and ultimately will require replacement by a heart transplant. I realise that this device has been tested in the laboratory but has not been used to sustain a human being and that no assurance of success can be made. . . '.

Dr Cooley told Mr Karp that the chances of the wedge excision procedure failing were 30% and that the mechanical heart had kept a calf alive for more than 40 hours. He did not discuss with Mr Karp the number of animals in which the device had been tested.

When Mr Karp entered the operating room on 4 April he was near death, 'mottled and blue'. The operation began with Dr Cooley as chief surgeon and Dr Liotta as first assistant. Dr Cooley performed a wedge excision but, due to extensive scarring of the heart, there was not enough healthy muscle remaining to form an efficient pump to support Mr Karp's life. Consequently, his heart was removed and the mechanical device was inserted. He responded well and remained alive.

Subsequently a donor was found. The heart transplant operation was performed on 7 April, about 64 hours after the mechanical device had been implanted in Mr Karp. He died on 8 April, some 32 hours after the transplant surgery.

The plaintiff (his widow) sued Dr Cooley and Dr Liotta on the grounds of fraud, lack of informed consent, negligent surgery and negligent experimentation. The district court directed verdict and entered judgment for the defendants. The plaintiff appealed.

Held: (i) the plaintiff's reliance on what she was and was not told was misplaced. Consent of the wife for the husband's operation has no significance under Texan law unless she is legally authorised to give such consent. The relationship of husband and wife does not itself create such a legal authorisation.

(ii) what was significant was what Mr Karp was told. The consent form was consistent with Dr Cooley's testimony. Each step of the three-step operation was specifically set out in the consent form signed by Mr Karp. Moreover, as death was imminent after the wedge excision procedure, there was no causal relationship between the harm and the alleged lack of informed consent to the mechanical heart.

(iii)   there was no evidence of fraud; the district court had been right to direct a verdict for the defendants on the fraud counts.

(iv)   a specialist like Dr Cooley is bound to exercise the degree of skill and knowledge that is ordinarily possessed by similar specialists. Since the expert testimony provided no evidence of negligent surgical acts or omissions by the defendants, a directed verdict for both defendants was proper.

(v)   an action for experimentation must be measured by traditional malpractice evidentiary standards based on how a reasonably careful and prudent physician would have acted under the same or similar circumstances. The record contained no evidence that Mr Karp's treatment was other than therapeutic. A directed verdict for the defendant was warranted.

Kavanagh v Abrahamson

General practitioner: duty of care: prescription: examination: causation: bronchitis: fatal

Fenton Atkinson J. (1964) 108 Sol Jo 320

Mr and Mrs Kavanagh (the plaintiff) had been National Health patients of Dr Abrahamson for some years. They moved without notifying him. A few months later the plaintiff called at his surgery and told him that her husband did not feel well and might have caught influenza. He gave her a prescription for compound codeine tablets with instructions.

The next day the plaintiff called again at the surgery and asked him to visit Mr Kavanagh who had got worse. Later that day Dr Abrahamson visited the address on his records but obtained no reply to repeated ringing of the doorbell. He realised that the Kavanaghs must have moved and rang the doorbell of an adjoining flat. As there was no answer, he left to pay other urgent visits.

Two days later the plaintiff called at the surgery. Dr Abrahamson visited Mr Kavanagh who turned out to have bronchitis and died in hospital two days later.

Held: (i)   there was a measure of force in the criticism that Dr Abrahamson might have done more than he did after calling and finding that the Kavanaghs had moved. However that was not, in itself, a negligent failure.

(ii)   no doubt it was unusual to prescribe without seeing the patient, but so prescribing compound codeine tablets was not negligence in the absence of evidence that they made any difference.

See p 135.

Kay's Tutor v Ayrshire and Arran Health Board

Injection: overdose: causation: penicillin: meningitis: child patient: deafness: Scotland

House of Lords. [1987] 2 All ER 417

On 28 November 1975 Andrew Kay, then aged two and a half, was admitted to Seafield Children's Hospital in Ayr. Tests led to a diagnosis on 29 November of pneumococcal meningitis. The consultant paediatrician in charge of the case, Dr McCure, instructed that 10,000 units of penicillin be injected intrathecally. The injection was carried out shortly after noon by Dr Adam-Strump, a senior house officer. By mistake he injected 300,000 units of penicillin. The massive overdose rapidly produced toxic effects. The child went into convulsions and later developed a degree of hemiparesis. Dr Adam-Strump realised his mistake immediately and remedial measures were urgently instituted. These were successful in saving Andrew's life, and by 1 December the immediate ill effects of the overdose appeared to have been surmounted. He was discharged from hospital on 24 December. His parents before then had begun to suspect that he had been suffering from deafness. This proved to be the case. He suffered profound bilateral deafness.

His father sued on his behalf the hospital authority who admitted liability for Dr Adam-Strump's negligence. The authority contended that the consequences of his negligence were limited to the convulsions and hemiparesis and denied that the overdose had caused the deafness. Expert evidence was given at the hearing that, whereas deafness was a common sequel of meningitis, in no recorded case had an overdose of penicillin caused deafness.

Held: this was not a case of two competing causes of damage. The medical evidence simply failed to prove any causal link between the penicillin overdose and the deafness. The weight of the evidence was that the deafness was caused by meningitis. The father's appeal was dismissed.

See pp 36, 69, 72, 122.

Kenyon v Bell

Diagnosis: hospital doctor: causation: loss of chance: child patient: ophthalmic: Scotland

Scotland, Court of Session. 1953 SC 125

On 15 March 1951 Mr Kenyon found his sixteen month old daughter Emily lying on the kitchen floor of his house in Dundee. Her head was resting upon a broken cup, and the lower lid of her left eye was cut and bleeding profusely. She was taken by two neighbours to the Dundee Royal Infirmary where she was seen by Dr Bell, the resident medical officer there. One of the neighbours informed him of the circumstances, and Dr Bell instructed a nurse to put drops into the child's eye and to apply a powder. No other treatment was ordered. He informed the neighbour that it was not necessary to consult the family doctor or to return to the infirmary.

The child's eye began to water around the end of June 1951. She was taken to her family doctor who at once ordered her removal to Dundee Royal Infirmary. It was found that there was severe internal haemorrhage in the left eye, which had a detached retina and a bulged iris. The eye was removed on 10 July 1951.

Mr Kenyon sued Dr Bell on the basis that as a result of his alleged negligence the child lost her eye or alternatively lost a material chance that her eye would be saved.

Held: (i)   the loss of a chance of saving the eye was not of itself a matter which would warrant a recovery of damages.

(ii)   if, however, the chance of saving the eye by proper treatment was so material that the natural and reasonable inference was that its loss was due to the absence of such treatment, this would entitle the case to succeed.

Note: This reasoning was followed by the House of Lords in *Hotson v East Berkshire Health Authority*.

See p 74, 77.

411

Kerby v Redbridge Health Authority

Childbirth: damages: fatal: depression: twins: scarring

Ognall J. [1993] 4 Med LR 178, [1994] PIQR QI

In June 1988 the plaintiff (Mrs Mary Kerby), then aged 38, was admitted to one of the defendants' hospitals. She gave birth to twins by caesarian section. One of these, John, lived for three days, heavily sedated and on a life support machine, before dying due to hypoxia. The defendants admitted liability.

The plaintiff suffered a moderately severe depressive disorder for six months. Diminishing sequelae remained thereafter. The constant reminder of what might have been in the presence of Robert, the surviving and healthy twin, militated against her total recovery. The surgical intervention necessitated by the defendants' negligence left a permanent bikini scar which was modestly troublesome around the time of menstruation.

Held (February 1992):
(i) the plaintiff was awarded £10,000 for her own pain and suffering plus £1,500 for the rigours of a possible further pregnancy, a total of £11,500 general damages for pain, suffering and loss of amenity.

(ii) she was not entitled to further general damages for dashed hopes – the loss of the satisfaction of bringing the pregnancy to a totally successful conclusion – since these were incorporated in the fixed sum of £3,500 for bereavement damages.*

(iii) funeral expenses agreed in the sum of £857 brought the total award to the plaintiff for herself to £15,857.

(iv) in addition, she was awarded on behalf of John's estate £750 general damages for his pain and suffering.

The total award was £16,607 plus interest.

Bagley v North Hertfordshire Health Authority (p 234) not followed.

See pp 156, 172.

Kewley v Blackpool Wyre and Fylde Health Authority

Anaesthetic awareness: damages: operation: caesarian: post-traumatic stress disorder

HH Judge Morison. *Halsbury's Laws Annual Abridgment* 1994, para 973, (1994) AVMA Medical and Legal Journal, Spring, p 7

The plaintiff (Ms Kewley), aged 27, underwent an elective caesarean section due to disproportion. She recalled losing consciousness and shortly thereafter regaining it and feeling an intense burning pain across her abdomen, accompanied by slight tugging sensations. She was paralysed by the action of muscle relaxant drugs, and thus unable to communicate her condition to the theatre staff. She was unable to breathe, see or hear anything and felt that she was going to die. Subsequently she suffered from a post-traumatic stress disorder of moderate severity, which manifested itself in nightmares, lack of confidence, claustrophobia and increased psycho-physiological arousal.

The plaintiff alleged that the amount of isoflurane (volatile anaesthetic agent) administered had been inadequate and had on occasions been turned off. The defendants denied liability and argued that, in the absence of specific recall of incidents, what the plaintiff suffered was 'dreaming' and that her memories related to the post-operative period.

Held: (i) whilst the amount of isoflurane was barely acceptable, the anaesthetist's practice had been to switch off the isoflurane after the baby had been clamped or delivered, which significantly increased the risk of awareness and fell below the proper professional standards expected of a consultant anaesthetist at the time.

(ii) the plaintiff was awarded £12,900 general damages, £675 interest and £600 special damages for a course of psychotherapy counselling.

See p 123.

Khan v Ainslie and Others

Limitation: ophthalmic

Waterhouse J. [1993] 4 Med LR 319

On 13 June 1983 the plaintiff (Mr Khan) was examined by the first defendant, an ophthalmic medical practitioner. She inserted mydriatic drops in his left eye. He felt considerable pain in it and reported to the other effective defendant, a locum general practitioner, who gave him painkillers. Another doctor subsequently referred him to the local hospital where on 27 June 1983 a left iridectomy operation was performed. It proved to be unsuccessful, and the plaintiff was left without sight in his left eye.

In December 1983 he complained to the Family Practitioner Committee that the drops had caused his injury. In January 1984 he consulted solicitors who in January 1985 received a negative expert report that praised the first defendant. After his solicitors' supplementary questions were answered by the expert, his legal aid certificate was discharged in March 1985.

At the end of 1987, the plaintiff saw a television programme featuring AVMA. He contacted them and they referred him to new solicitors who issued a protective writ on 30 November 1988. In February 1989 they obtained an expert opinion that the plaintiff had lost the sight of his left eye totally 'as the result of closed angle glaucoma and of the delay in its treatment'. In June 1989 they received a further favourable report from a professor in general practice.

The writ was subsequently served. A preliminary trial was ordered.

Held: (i) it was only when the first favourable expert's report was received in February 1989 that the plaintiff first had knowledge that the injury to his left eye was attributable to the defendants' acts or omissions (delay, not drops) that were alleged to constitute negligence.

(ii) there was no unreasonable failure by the plaintiff's first solicitors to follow up the first expert's negative report. Having regard to the general tenor of this report, there was no reason to infer that this expert would have reported favourably if different questions had been put to him. The plaintiff should not be fixed with constructive knowledge in early 1985.

(iii) accordingly his action had been commenced in time.

See pp 184, 187.

Kidd v Grampian Health Board

Injections: limitation: Scotland

Lord Morton of Shuna. [1994] 5 Med LR 251

In April 1973 the pursuer (Elizabeth Kidd), then aged 16, was admitted to the Royal Cornhill hospital in Aberdeen because the children's home in which she was living had difficulty in coping with her disruptive behaviour. She was admitted under the Mental Health (Scotland) Act 1960 and, apart from a short period after she absconded in July, remained in the hospital until October 1973. While in hospital, she was given intra-muscular injections of paraldehyde to control her behaviour.

Some months after the birth of her youngest child in March 1983, she began to have serious pain in her buttocks radiating into her legs. In December 1984 she saw a general practitioner who arranged an x-ray which reported '. . . there are several calcific densities in the soft tissues consistent with previous injection sites'. In March 1986 she consulted a solicitor.

In March 1989 court action was commenced on her behalf. At the preliminary trial on the issue of limitation, it emerged that there was no dispute about either the dates or the quantities of the paraldehyde injections. The only disputes on the merits of the case were whether intra-muscular injections of paraldehyde were in 1973 a recognised and acceptable form of treatment to control disruptive behaviour and whether the pursuer's present condition was caused by the 1973 injections. Counsel for the hospital authority accepted that they would not have difficulty in obtaining and leading evidence as to the relevant medical practice in 1973, and he did not suggest any way in which the authority would be evidentially prejudiced in meeting the pursuer's case.

Held: (i)   the courts should generally find it equitable to allow an action to proceed, if the delay had not seriously affected the evidence available for the defenders.

(ii)   as it was clear that in the present case that the delay had not seriously affected the evidence that would be required to decide the issues in dispute, it would be equitable to exercise the court's discretion to allow the action to proceed if it was time barred.

(iii)   accordingly, it was unnecessary to decide whether the pursuer's claim was in fact prima facie statute barred.

See pp 196, 199.

Kilburn v Swindon and District Hospital Management Committee

Diagnosis: casualty officer: x-ray: examination: fractures: damages: knee: wrist

Pilcher J. [1955] 2 BMJ 145

The plaintiff (Frederick Kilburn) fell from his scooter. He was a 'mountain of a man' weighing 22 stone. He arrived at Savernake Hospital, near Marlborough, in a very dirty state, wearing half a dozen coats and jumpers and not having shaved for a week. Mr Wheeler, the acting casualty officer, concluded that he had been shaken up. Sticking plaster was put on his knees, and he was given a cup of tea and sent on his way.

Two and a half hours later, the plaintiff was admitted to the Royal Berkshire Hospital, Reading, where he was x-rayed, and it was discovered that he had sustained two fractures in his left knee and a fracture of the right wrist. He sued the Savernake Hospital Authority.

Held: (i)   Mr Wheeler's examination was not a proper one, and could not be expected to discover what was wrong. The hospital authority was liable for his negligence.

(ii)   the damages would necessarily be small (£20), because the treatment which the plaintiff ought to have received at Savernake Hospital he did in fact receive about three hours later at the Reading Hospital.

See p 133.

King v King

General practitioner: injection: contra-indications: tropical disease

Court of Appeal. 9 April 1987. (1987) 1 Lancet 991

In 1980 the plaintiff (Jeffrey King), a generally fit man aged 22, was planning a holiday in Morocco. The travel agents recommended that he should be inoculated against typhoid and cholera. On 8 May Dr King, his general practitioner, gave him an injection of a combined vaccination against cholera and typhoid. When the plaintiff attended for the second injection on 29 May, he was excited and had a small boil in front of his right ear. Six hours after the second injection, he suffered a stroke which left him with marked right-sided hemiplegia.

He sued Dr King. The trial judge (Rose J) found that it was negligent of Dr King to have given him the second injection because there were indications that should have caused him to postpone it, namely a temperature and the boil. Dr King appealed.

Held: the fact that the plaintiff was excited (shortly before his holiday) did not justify the judge's inference that he was probably suffering from a raised temperature. There was no evidence that the presence of a boil alone led to an increased risk of a stroke. Dr King had not been negligent.

See p 120.

Kinnear and Others v Falconfilms NV and Others (Hospital Ruber Internacional and Another, third parties)

Fatal: jurisdiction: third party proceedings: Spain

Phillips J. [1994] 3 All ER 42

On 19 September 1988 the actor Roy Kinnear was making a film near Toledo in Spain, when he was thrown from a horse and sustained severe injuries to the pelvic girdle. He was taken to the hospital Ruber Internacional where he died some 24 hours later.

On 20 September 1988 the Spanish police commenced legal proceedings in relation to the death. The first stage of the proceedings consisted of an investigation of the material facts, but the proceedings could potentially have led to criminal charges and a civil claim. On 26 September 1988 the first plaintiff (Mrs Kinnear), the actor's widow, became a party to these proceedings. At the end of the investigative stage, no criminal charges were brought and no claim for compensation was advanced.

On 23 August 1991 the plaintiffs (the administrators of Roy Kinnear's estate, and Roy Kinnear Enterprises Ltd) issued a writ commencing proceedings in England against the defendants (Falconfilms NV and the producer and director of the film). The plaintiffs alleged that both Mr Kinnear's accident and his death were caused by the defendants' breach of contract and negligence. The defendants denied this in their defence and alleged that the Hospital Ruber Internacional and Dr Juan Andrades, who practised there as an orthopaedic surgeon, were guilty of medical malpractice in treating Mr Kinnear and that this was the sole cause of his death.

In July 1992 the defendants obtained leave to issue a third party notice against Dr Andrades and the hospital (the third parties). In October 1992 the defendants served the notice on the third parties in Spain. In June 1993 the third parties applied to set aside the third party proceedings. In October 1993 the plaintiffs issued a summons to join the third parties as fourth and fifth defendants. In November 1993 the third parties commenced proceedings in the plaintiffs in Spain, claiming inter alia a declaration that they had no liability to them.

Article 6(2) of the Brussels Convention 1968 scheduled to the Civil Jurisdiction Judgments Act 1982 provides that: 'a person domiciled in a Contracting State may also be sued . . . (2) as a third party in an action on a warranty or guarantee or in any other third party proceedings, in the court seised of the original proceedings, unless these were instituted solely with the object of removing him from the jurisdiction of the court which would be competent in this case . . .'

Article 21 of the Convention provides: 'where proceedings involving the same cause of action and between the same parties are brought in the courts of different Contracting States, any court other than the court first seised shall of its own motion stay its proceedings until such time as the jurisdiction of the court first seised is established. Where the jurisdiction of the court first seised is established, any court other than the court first seised shall decline jurisdiction in favour of that court.'

Held: (i)   where domestic procedure permits a third party to be joined in proceedings, this is likely to be on grounds which justify overriding the basic right of the third party to be sued separately in the country of its domicile. Those grounds are almost certain to be some form of nexus between the plaintiff's claim against the defendant and the defendant's claim against the third party. In this case, the nexus between the plaintiff's claim arising out of the fall from the horse and the defendant's claim against the third party based upon the treatment in hospital was likely to be sufficient to justify the special jurisdiction granted by Article 6(2).

(ii)   where one tortfeasor wishes to reduce his liability to reflect the fact that another tortfeasor shares responsibility for the plaintiff's damages, it may be impossible to do this unless all the relevant parties are brought before the same tribunal. That was the practical reality in the present case and, so far as the defendants were concerned, only the English jurisdiction offered that possibility. That abundantly justified the application of Article 6(2).

(iii)   the courts discretion to grant or refuse leave to issue the third party notice should be exercised in favour of the defendants. Admittedly the English jurisdiction was not a convenient one in which to determine the issue of whether there was medical malpractice in Madrid. What was more important was that the issue would in any event be raised in the English proceedings and there was no alternative forum available to the defendants in which to seek contribution from the third parties.

(iv)   Article 21 did not debar the third party proceedings in England. Mrs Kinnear never reached the stage of initiating a claim for compensation in the Spanish proceedings. Moreover investigative proceedings in Spain were not 'between the same parties' as the third party proceedings in England. Even if the third parties were party to the Spanish proceedings, the defendants plainly were not. Accordingly Article 21 posed no bar to the court's jurisdiction over the third party proceedings.

(v)   the problem with the plaintiff's application to join the two third parties as fourth and fifth defendants was that the third parties had met this application by a pre-emptive strike. The proceedings that they commenced in Spain in November 1993 were 'between the same parties' as the proceedings that the plaintiff sought to commence by adding them as additional defendants. By the strategy of commencing proceedings for a negative declaration in Spain, the third parties had successfully precluded the English court under Article 21 from asserting jurisdiction over the claim that the plaintiff sought to bring against them.

(vi)   so far as the plaintiffs were concerned, the appropriate order was that they have leave to amend their pleadings to add the third parties as additional defendants, but that after the third parties had been served the proceedings against them should be stayed, pending the resolution of any issues raised in relation to Spanish jurisdiction.

Kinnear and Others v Falconfilms NV and Others (No 2), (Hospital Ruber Internacional and Another, third parties)

Blood transfusion: causation: diagnosis: fatal: novus actus interveniens: Spain: third party proceedings: apportionment of liability

Hidden J. 21 December 1994

Roy Kinnear had been engaged by the defendants to play the part of Planchet in a film to be called 'The Return of the Musketeers'. On 19 September 1988 a sequence which was being filmed required him to ride a horse very fast across the Alcantara Bridge near Toledo. At the end of the bridge when horse and rider had to make a turn to the left on the road immediately away from the bridge, the horse slipped, stumbled and threw Mr Kinnear to the ground. He sustained injuries which necessitated his transfer to a hospital in Toledo. The defendants arranged for him to be transferred by ambulance on the same afternoon to the Hospital Ruber Internacional in Madrid (the first third party) where his care was assumed by Dr Ayala (the second third party).

At the time of the transfer from Toledo to Madrid, Roy Kinnear was suffering from a major injury, namely a two and an eighth inch split in the symphysis pubis and a similar opening of the right sacroiliac joint together with associated disruption and tearing of blood vessels. During the night he was in extreme pain and was sick many times. No doctor visited him that night. Around 4.45am he was given an injection for his sickness but, after a lull, he was sick again. He was extremely thirsty and looked pale. He complained that his legs were numb and that he had pins and needles. His normal blood pressure was around 120.

When Dr Ayala* arrived at the hospital around 7.30am, he examined Mr Kinnear and took a blood sample at about 8.20am. He found his blood pressure to be 80 over 50 millilitres of mercury. He called for a urologist because the blood pressure had dropped and he suspected internal bleeding. The results of the blood tests, which were received by 8.30am, showed that the haematocrit was 35.9% and the haemoglobin 12.3grams. Dr Ayala calculated that Mr Kinnear had lost 750 centilitres of blood which was 15%; he considered that it was a 30% loss that would need transfusion. He thought that the results were low but not dangerously so. Between 10.00am and 12 noon the urologist Dr Guil examined Mr Kinnear, prescribed fluid therapy and requested an ultrasound examination of the kidneys and bladder. The ultrasound did not give a clear picture, so a further blood test was performed. In the afternoon, purely for the purpose of having a CAT scan, Mr Kinnear was taken to another hospital, the Clinica Ruber, where he died.

Held: (i) Mr Kinnear was in a state of hypovolaemic shock on the morning of 20 September 1988 by 6.40am when Dr Ayala was telephoned.

(ii) the symptoms of hypovolaemic shock are well-known to the medical profession both in England and in Spain. The learning on shock and its treatment is international.

(iii) Dr Ayala should have diagnosed that morning that Mr Kinnear was exhibiting clinical signs accepted both in this country and in Spain of hypovolaemic shock and that he needed immediate treatment for that condition.

(iv) the cause of that shock was the blood loss which Mr Kinnear had suffered in and subsequent to the riding accident, as a result of the defendants' negligence on the previous day.

(v) Dr Ayala knew or should have known on the morning in question that Mr Kinnear had lost and might be continuing to lose a significant volume of blood. An acute blood loss of 15% required transfusion. Haemoglobin and haematocrit values could only be used in the presence of full circulating volume.

417

(vi)   it was accepted medical practice both in England and in Spain that such a loss of blood and such a state of shock must be the subject of immediate treatment by the infusion of sufficient liquids to restore the blood volume and treat the shock. The existing drip was clearly insufficient for this.

(vii)   the failure at any time that morning of Dr Ayala or of anyone else from the Ruber to address his mind to this problem and to order such treatment was clearly negligent, as was the failure of the Ruber to offer any such treatment.

(viii)   this negligence was an immediate causative factor in Mr Kinnear's death. Had he been given that treatment at any time on the morning of 20 September 1988, he would not have died.

(ix)   the extent of the third parties' responsibility, far from being insignificant, was greater than that of the defendants. The amount of the contribution recoverable from them was 60% of the £650,000 payable by the defendants to the plaintiff under the terms of the consent judgment.

(x)   the third parties' negligence did not amount to novus actus interveniens. The possibility of a misdiagnosis or of negligent treatment was foreseeable, all the more so since Mr Kinnear was consigned to a Madrid hospital which had little or no experience of patients who had very recently suffered trauma.

(xi)   the defendants' negligence in relation to the riding accident was assessed at 30% of the whole.

(xii)   the defendants' negligence in transferring Mr Kinnear from an efficient public hospital with all facilities in Toledo to the Ruber in Madrid which they knew or ought to have known had disadvantages of little or no experience in accepting patients with recent trauma straight off the streets, of not having an intensivist on duty throughout the day, of not having the ability in its ordinary rooms to monitor vital signs sufficiently often, and also of not having been given a notice by the defendants of the decision to send Mr Kinnear there, amounted to a degree of negligence assessed at 10%.

*Dr Ayala is the same person as Dr Andrades in *Kinnear (No 1)*.

Kirby v Eli Lilly & Co and Others

Drugs: limitation: Opren

Court of Appeal. [1992] 3 Med LR 394

See Nash v Eli Lilly & Co (M) (p 475).

Kitchen v McMullen

Canada: informed consent: hepatitis: blood transfusion

New Brunswick Court of Appeal. [1990] 1 Med LR 352, 62 DLR (4th) 481

On 20 August 1982 the plaintiff (Gerald Kitchen), aged 38, had a molar tooth extracted. The dentist sutured the tooth socket. On 24 August a stitch became loose, and blood began to ooze from the socket. The plaintiff attended the emergency department of the Dr Everett Chalmers Hospital. Tests established that his blood-clotting factor was low.

On 25 August Dr McMullen (an internist) diagnosed the plaintiff as suffering from mild haemophilia A. He administered cryoprecipitate, a concentrated replacement blood product. On 26 August, at the suggestion of the hospital laboratory, he replaced this with Hemofil, another concentrated factor VIII replacement blood product, which was packaged with express warning of the risk that it might cause hepatitis. Dr McMullen did not explain this risk to the plaintiff who received transfusions of Hemofil on 26 and 27 August.

Approximately one week later the plaintiff experienced nausea, abdominal pain and extreme fatigue. He was diagnosed as having post transfusion non-A, non-B hepatitis. He suffered from its effects for about one and a half years.

He sued Dr McMullen for not having informed him of the risk. The medical evidence was that he required an infusion of blood factors to stop the delayed bleeding, and that the risk of contracting hepatitis in consequence was exceedingly small. No other viable means of treatment was established.

Held: (i)   the risk of transmitting hepatitis was an 'unusual or special risk' which was known to occur occasionally. Dr McMullen was under a duty to disclose this risk to the plaintiff. His admitted omission to do so was a breach of this duty.

           (ii)   in weighing the risk inherent in the treatment against the potential consequences of leaving the condition untreated, a reasonable person in the plaintiff's position who was informed of the 'unusual' risk of hepatitis would have consented to the infusion of Hemofil to stop the bleeding in his mouth.

The plaintiff's appeal was dismissed.

Knight v Home Office

Fatal: prison inmate: suicide risk: supervision

Pill J. [1990] 3 All ER 237

On 17 September 1981 Paul Worrell, aged 21, attacked a man in a public house. On 18 September he was remanded in custody to Brixton Prison. On 23 September he attacked another prisoner. On 10 October he assaulted a prison officer. On 16 October he attempted to stab himself in the eye with a plastic fork. On 9 November he cut his face with a razor blade. On 4 December a sheet was found tied in a noose around the window bars in his cell. On 7 December he was noisy and very disturbed and banged and kicked his cell door.

On 22 December he pleaded guilty at the Inner London Crown Court to wounding with intent to cause grievous bodily harm. The medical experts agreed that he was suffering from mental illness. The court made an order under s 60 of the Mental Health Act 1959 for his admission within 28 days and his detention in Bethlem Royal Hospital.

Owing to his suicidal tendencies, he was kept in Brixton Prison under Special Watch B which provided for him to be located in a cell on the observation landing and observed at not less than 15 minute intervals. He was not put under Special Watch A which required continuous observation. Since he was violent, it was not appropriate to keep him in a ward with other prisoners.

At about 8.15am on 12 January 1982 the two patrolling officers heard another prisoner shout that a man was hanging in his cell. They went there and found Mr Worrell hanging by the neck. A sheet and towel had been tied together, one end placed round his neck and the other round a window bar in the cell; there was a chair under the window. Unsuccessful efforts were made to revive Mr Worrell whose condition had not given cause for concern within 15 minutes of the other prisoner's shout.

The plaintiffs (his personal representatives) claimed damages on behalf of his estate and his infant son.

Held: (i)   the law does not require the standard of care in a prison hospital to be as high as the standard of care in a psychiatric hospital outside prison. A psychiatric hospital's main purpose is to treat. The prison's central function is to detain. Whilst the prison authorities have a duty to protect a mentally ill patient against himself, including the possibility of suicide, the duty is tailored to the function to be performed. There was no negligence in the failure to provide the patient/staff ratio present at a psychiatric hospital.

      (ii)   nor was there negligence in the defendants' failure to transfer the prisoner to a psychiatric hospital. This would have occurred on 15 January. There was nothing which the prison authority could do to expedite it.

      (iii)   the prison doctors were not negligent in failing to keep Mr Worrell on Special Watch A during the weeks after 4 December. He was placed on medical observation to stabilise his condition. The hospital order was a source of contentment to him. The experience of 24 hour observation, described as dehumanising, would have made treatment more difficult on transfer to Bethlem Royal Hospital. The doctors consciously exercised a clinical judgment.

      (iv)   the presence and accessibility of the bars did not involve a breach of duty by the defendants. Even if it did, a different window design would probably not have prevented the death.

The plaintiffs' claim was dismissed.

See pp 24, 25, 61, 132.

Kralj and Another v McGrath and Another

Childbirth: substandard treatment: damages: aggravated damages: post-traumatic stress disorder: twins: fatal

Woolf J. [1986] 1 All ER 54

The plaintiffs (Sally and Peter Kralj) had their first daughter in 1977. They had planned a family of three. In 1979 Mrs Kralj became pregnant again. It was arranged that her confinement would take place on a private basis at St Theresa's Hospital in Wimbledon under Mr McGrath, a consultant obstetrician. Tests showed that Mrs Kralj was expecting twins, one of which was in the transverse position. She was admitted to St Theresa's on 19 March 1980. After 8.00pm Mr McGrath set up a drip of Syntocinon to accelerate labour, and at 10.05pm the first twin, Thomas, was born. No anaesthetist was present.

After a slight lull, the contractions started again. Mr McGrath told Mrs Kralj to push, and the next thing she experienced was dreadful pain. She realised that Mr McGrath had put his arm inside her, entering by the vagina. She tried to stop him but hospital staff were holding her down. This lasted for 40 minutes. She was then taken down to the operating theatre, and the second twin Daniel was delivered by caesarian section. He was born in an extremely debilitated state and died eight weeks later due to brain damage.

Mrs Kralj suffered vaginal bleeding for three months. She also had the caesarian scar. She suffered pain, as a result of which it was about two years before she could enjoy sexual intercourse. She suffered nervous shock as a result of seeing and being told what had happened to Daniel and grief due to his death.

Mr Kralj sued Mr McGrath and St Theresa's Hospital on behalf of Daniel's estate. Mrs Kralj sued for her injuries and financial loss. The claims were brought in tort and in contract.

Liability was admitted by both defendants. The treatment was described at the hearing as horrific and totally unacceptable.

Held: (i)   it would be wholly inappropriate to introduce into claims of this sort the concept of aggravated damages. This would be inconsistent with the general compensatory approach to damages in this area.

(ii)   Mrs Kralj was entitled to be compensated for the shock she suffered as a result of being told of what had happened to Daniel and of seeing him during her visits, but damages for her grief and suffering at his death were not payable.

(iii) so far as her distress at Daniel's disabilities and grief over his death worsened the consequences of her own injuries, the court could take this into account.

(iv)   she was awarded (June 1985) £10,000 general damages for her pain, suffering and loss of amenities.

(v)   the expected additional pregnancy to have the third child and the attendant financial losses were reasonably foreseeable and not too remote. She was awarded £18,000 for future loss of earnings on an agreed multiplicand of £5,360 per annum.

See pp 126, 167, 172.

Krujelis v Esdale et al

Canada: after care: anaesthetics: cardio-respiratory arrest: fatal: nurse: child patient

British Columbia Supreme Court, Gould J. (1971) 25 DLR (3d) 557

In July 1987 Ivars Krujelis, aged 10, entered St Paul's Hospital in Vancouver for plastic surgery, under general anaesthetic, to correct over-prominent ears. The surgery was performed without complication. Dr Esdale was the anaesthetist. At nearly 9.45am Ivars was brought into the Post-anaesthetic Recovery Room (PAR). There were six other patients in it. Three of the five nurses had just gone for their coffee break. Neither of the remaining nurses checked or observed him. When the other three returned around 10.10am, one of them examined Ivars, who looked cyanotic, and found no vital signs. An alarm bell was sounded, but it was too late. Ivars had suffered respiratory failure followed by cardiac arrest in the PAR. Irreparable brain damage had occurred, and in February 1991 he died without having regained consciousness.

His personal representatives pursued proceedings against, inter alios, Dr Esdale and the hospital proprietor. A cardiologist practising at the defendant hospital testified that, in an anaesthetised patient stricken by respiratory failure followed by cardiac arrest, an observer would notice his blue colour (cyanosis) and that he was not breathing, or was struggling to get air. If some air was getting through, there would be a wheezing sound. A nurse in a PAR Room should be able to observe such a critical condition from 25ft away and, if prompt remedial action were not taken, permanent brain damage would occur within three to four minutes.

Held: (i)   Dr Esdale was not liable. He had no control or jurisdiction over the PAR and no vestige of reasonable anticipation that Ivars would receive anything but the best of care in it.

(ii)   Ivars' tragic injury was the result of inadequate observation of him. That inadequacy arose from the absence of three of the five nurses on duty, on coffee break, during what was ordinarily the busiest time of day for the PAR Room. Consequently negligence attached to the hospital, by the omissions of its PAR staff.

Re L (a minor)

Re L (a minor)

Abortion: consent: interest of patient: parental objection

Hollis J. [1992] 3 Med LR 78

L was an illegitimate girl who lived with her natural grandparents. When 12 years old, she became pregnant by a 16 year old boy. She was made a ward of court. Then the local authority applied by originating summons for an order giving leave to have her pregnancy terminated. The application was supported by L, the boy and her grandparents. L's mother opposed it on the grounds that 'I don't believe in abortion. It is not right to take the baby's life'.

After seeing L, Dr Brice of the British Pregnancy Advisory Service deposed that 'she was a small girl, overpowered by her mother and grandmother. She had a small pelvis and I understand L was more than 12 weeks' pregnant. There was considerable risk of trauma to the uterus and risk of haemorrhage. L's grandmother was surprised to hear of the risks, particularly the physical risks if L's pregnancy continued. After examination I advised that L's best interest was to have the pregnancy terminated.' The other medical evidence was conflicting.

Held: (i)   The welfare of the child (L) was the paramount consideration. Her wishes were important but not decisive. Her mother's wishes were also important but could be overridden.

      (ii)   If the mother's view was allowed to prevail, L would be forced to continue with the pregnancy against her own expressed wishes. That would cause mental turmoil. She might reject the baby. She might have to face the trauma of considering what should happen to it. She might have to leave school for a long period.

     (iii)   It was in the best interests of the ward (L) to have the pregnancy terminated. A continuation of the pregnancy would involve greater risk to the ward's physical and mental health than if the pregnancy were terminated.

See p 12.

La Fleur v Cornelis

Canada: causation: contract: plastic surgery: operation: informed consent: nasal: scarring

Barry J. (1979) 28 NBR (2d) 569

In March 1976 the plaintiff (Debra La Fleur), aged 25, consulted the defendant (Dr Cornelis), a specialist in cosmetic surgery, about her desire to have the size of her nose reduced. The interview lasted ten minutes, and there was no talk of risk. She told the defendant what she wanted, namely a smaller nose, and he agreed to provide her with it. He said 'no problem, you will be very happy'. She decided to proceed and paid $600 for the operation, known as rhinoplasty.

During this operation, the defendant elevated the skin and flesh on the dorsum or bone and cartilage running under the skin from the tip of the plaintiff's nose upwards, and removed pieces of bone and cartilage. He then placed the flesh and skin back in place, using sutures inside the nose. One suture was placed through the nose from side to side, and the ends were tied in a knot over the nose about one centimetre up from the tip. Gauze was placed under the nylon 50 suture between the suture and the flesh of the nose. This nylon caused a scar or indentation on the plaintiff's nose.

Held: (i) the operation was negligently performed, because the method used lacked protection for the nose. The scar would not have been made, if the defendant had adequately protected the surface of the nose under the suture with lead or a firm covering.

(ii) the plaintiff was a healthy young woman submitting herself for elective surgery and paying a fee of $600. There was a high duty on the defendant to explain the risk of a ten per cent chance of a scar. Even if he had done so, however, the plaintiff would still have proceeded with the operation.

(iii) the defendant entered into a contract to provide the plaintiff with a smaller nose. He made an express agreement, without explaining the risk, and failed to carry out his part of the contract. He breached the contract, leaving her with a scarred nose and a minimal deformity, and was liable for this breach.

Lamey v Wirral Health Authority

Brain damage: childbirth: damages

Moreland J. [1993] CLY 1437

The plaintiff suffered anoxic brain damage at her birth in March 1982. Although aged eleven by trial, she had the abilities of a six-year-old. She was mentally handicapped, and her mental ability was unlikely ever to develop beyond that of a child of ten or eleven. Her only residual physical disability was clumsiness, although there was also permanent asymmetry of the mouth and a slight speech defect. She was uninhibited and hyperactive. It was unsafe for her to go out unsupervised, which would probably operate as a further constraint on her ability to mature and develop. She would never be able to live independently and she was not expected to be able to undertake any paid work. Possessed of some insight into her disabilities, she became frustrated, had temper tantrums and appeared to realise that children of her own age did not play with her. Her mental disability largely deprived her of a meaningful life. She was expected to survive until the age of 52.

Held: (i) general damages for pain, suffering and loss of amenities were assessed at £80,000.

(ii) £50,000 was awarded for care at trial, and £250,465 for future care (based on a multiplier of 18).

(iii) £58,800 was awarded for loss of future earnings (based on a multiplicand of £8,400 and a multiplier of 7).

(iv) sundry special damages were £7,416; sundry future expenses were £23,720; the award for Court of Protection fees was £12,110.

(v) deduction of £92,472 for DSS benefits reduced the total award to £390,039 plus interest.

See pp 126, 154.

Landall v Dennis Faulkner & Alsop and Others

Counsel: immunity from suit: medical report: solicitor: striking out

Holland J. [1994] 5 Med LR 268

In December 1981 the plaintiff (David Landall), then a serving soldier, sustained a back injury in a road accident that was caused by the negligence of William Clarke. He instructed the first defendants (Dennis Faulkner & Alsop, solicitors) to prosecute his claim for damages against Mr Clarke. They instructed the second defendant (Simon Maskrey of Counsel) and the third defendant (Mr J Scott-Ferguson, a consultant orthopaedic surgeon). On 28 November 1986 the first defendants delivered their brief to the second defendant. On 10 February 1987 the third defendant reported that he had spoken to Mr Clarke's medical expert and they were agreed that the correct medical operation for the relief of the plaintiff's symptoms would be spinal fusion, and with this there would be a very good chance of relief of all his symptoms. Pursuant to this, on 16 February 1987 the plaintiff's claim was settled at the doors of court on the advice of the first and second defendants for £41,000 damages plus costs. In August 1987 the operation for spinal fusion was carried out, but it was not a success and the plaintiff alleged that it led to a deterioration of his symptoms.

He sued all three defendants for professional negligence. They applied to strike out his pleadings pursuant to RSC Ord 18, r 19.

Held: (i)   it was common ground that it was a matter of public policy that there is immunity for suit for a witness with respect to evidence given in the course of court proceedings. It was further common ground that this immunity extends to cover a proof or a report prepared for trial by a witness.

(ii)   the plaintiff's attempt to argue that the third defendant was not only an expert for the purposes of the litigation but was also a medical advisor to the plaintiff, so that he was providing advice as to the potential efficacy of a spinal operation for the guidance of a plaintiff as a patient, failed. It was clear that the third defendant's report of 10 February 1987 constituted '. . . pre-trial work.. . . so intimately connected with the conduct of the case in court that it could fairly be said to be a preliminary decision affecting the way that the case was to be conducted when it came to a hearing'. Immunity for suit extended to it.

(iii)   immunity for suit also covered the second defendant's advice to the plaintiff to settle his claim for £41,000. Indeed it was difficult to conceive of an activity so intimately connected with court proceedings as advising at the court door. Two aspects of public policy were pertinent. First, any litigation as to a court door settlement necessarily requires a court to balance that settlement with what might have been obtained by litigation before a known (and not a notional) court of comparable jurisdiction – the risk of bringing the administration of justice into disrepute was obvious. Second, in his conduct at the court door, the barrister has a duty not just to his client but also to the court.

(iv)   although from July 1985 the original statement of claim against Mr Clarke could as a matter of law been amended so as to sue for provisional damages, the prospective operation for spinal fusion was discussed on the basis of its chances of success, never on the basis that it might result in a deterioration of the plaintiff's condition. Accordingly the allegation that the second defendant negligently failed to advise amending the pleading so as to claim for provisional damages was frivolous and vexatious.

(v)   it would be difficult to mount any case against the second defendant until after receipt of the third defendant's report of 10 February 1987. Even if that were not so, any act or omission on the part of the second defendant after delivery of his brief on 28 November 1986 was so intimately connected with the hearing on 16 February 1987 as to be subject to immunity from suit.

(vi)   the allegations of negligence against the first defendants in relation to the legal advice on settlement were the same as those alleged against the second defendant. The first defendants had no separate identity in relation to the advice. To allow the plaintiff's claim to proceed against them would result in a blatant outflanking of the second defendant's immunity. The plaintiff's claim against the first defendant was also vexatious and an abuse of process.

(vii)   The claims against all three defendants were struck out.

Note: Section 62(I) of the Courts and Legal Services Act 1990 now provides:

'A person:

(a)   who is not a barrister; but
(b)   who lawfully provides any legal services in relation to any proceedings,
       shall have the same immunity from liability for negligence in respect of his acts or
       omissions as he would have if he were a barrister lawfully providing those services'.

See pp 46, 49.

Landau v Werner

Psychiatrist: departing from orthodox practice: anxiety

Court of Appeal. (1961) 105 Sol Jo 1008

In March 1949 Dr Landau, a psychiatrist, undertook the treatment of the plaintiff (Miss Werner), a middle-aged spinster in an anxiety state. Psychotherapeutic consultations took place twice a week in his consulting rooms. By the end of July the plaintiff felt much better. However, she had fallen deeply in love with Dr Landau and told him that for that reason she had decided not to continue with the treatment. He thought she was not yet well. Between August 1949 and March 1950 he took her out to tea and dinner in restaurants and visited her once in her bedsitting room; they also discussed spending a holiday together. By March 1950 the plaintiff's condition had deteriorated. Dr Landau resumed formal treatment but finally abandoned it as of no avail.

The plaintiff sued Dr Landau. The trial judge (Barry J) found that he had been negligent.

Held: the real question was whether the social meetings, and discussion about a holiday together, were bad and negligent practice in the sphere in which the doctor worked. The medical evidence was all one way in condemning social contacts, and the doctor had failed to convince the trial judge that his departure from standard practice was justified. The judge had reasonably decided that his unwise treatment had led to the grave deterioration in the plaintiff's health. It was negligent and in breach of the doctor's duty to his patient.

Per Sellers LJ: 'A doctor's duty is to exercise ordinary skill and care according to the ordinary and reasonable standards of those who practise in the same field of medicine. The standard for the specialist is the standard of the specialists.'

See pp 44, 65.

Langley v Campbell

General practitioner: diagnosis: loss of chance: tropical disease: malaria

Cusack J. (1975) Times, 6 November

Mr Langley had been sent by his employers to Uganda and returned on 1 July 1970. On the evening of 9 July he felt unwell with fever, headache and alternate sweating and shivering. Dr Campbell, his general practitioner, called the next day. He was told that Mr Langley had just returned from Uganda and that he had suffered malaria during the war. Dr Campbell diagnosed influenza and prescribed accordingly. He called again on 11, 13 and 15 July. Mr Langley continued to deteriorate, so his family called in another doctor

425

who had him transferred immediately to hospital where two Asian doctors immediately diagnosed malaria. He died on 18 July.

The plaintiff (his widow) sued for damages. The medical evidence was that if malaria had been diagnosed by 13 July, or even 15 July, and treatment put in hand, there would have been a good chance of recovery.

Held: if a general practitioner knew that a patient he thought had influenza had just come back from the tropics and was not getting better, he should have considered that it might be a tropical disease of some kind. Dr Campbell had fallen short of the standard of care to be observed by a general practitioner in his position and was negligent.

See pp 60, 98.

Lanphier and Wife v Phipos

Fracture: diagnosis: wrist

Tindal CJ (with jury). (1838) 8 C & P 475

In September 1835 the plaintiff (Mrs Lanphier) was walking in a field when she came across a cow and, in her alarm, tripped and fell on her right wrist. She called in Mr Phipos, a surgeon and apothecary, who said that he thought the small bone of the arm was broken. He put splints on and bound her arm from the elbow to the wrist, leaving the hand hanging down. The swelling and inflammation of the arm spread over the next seven weeks, but Mr Phipos continued to say that it was going very well.

Another surgeon, Mr Vandenburgh, was called in. He found that there was a fracture of the small bone of her arm and a partial dislocation of the third bone of the palm of her hand. He put on longer splints which supported the hand and sent some lotion which reduced the swelling and inflammation. However the plaintiff had so lost the use of it that she could not use a knife or fork, or dress or undress herself with it. She sued Mr Phipos.

Held: Tindal CJ directed the jury: 'Every person who enters into a learned profession undertakes to bring to the exercise of it a reasonable degree of care and skill. He does not undertake, if he is an attorney, that at all events you shall gain your case, nor does a surgeon undertake that he will perform a cure; nor does he undertake to use the highest possible degree of skill. There may be persons who have higher education and greater advantages than he has, but he undertakes to bring a fair, reasonable, and competent degree of skill, and you will say whether, in this case, the injury was occasioned by the want of such skill in the defendant. The question is, whether this injury must be referred to the want of a proper degree of skill and care in the defendant or not.'

The jury returned a verdict for the plaintiff.

See p 58.

Lask v Gloucester Health Authority

Discovery: privilege

Court of Appeal. (1985) Times, 13 December

The plaintiff (Mrs Margaret Lask) sued for disclosure of a confidential accident report. National Health Service circulars required this to be completed by health authorities, both for the use of solicitors if litigation arose in respect of the accident, and also to enable action to be taken to avoid a repetition of the accident. The form itself referred only to the former purpose.

Held: the dominant purpose of its preparation had not been for submission to solicitors in anticipation of litigation. Therefore the report was not subject to legal professional privilege and should be disclosed to the plaintiff.

See p 210.

Latter v Braddell and Others

Consent: examination: assault

Court of Appeal. (1881) 50 LJQB 448

The plaintiff was a domestic servant of Captain and Mrs Braddell. Mrs Braddell requested Dr Sutcliffe to examine the plaintiff, in order to ascertain whether she was pregnant. The plaintiff objected, but undressed on Dr Sutcliffe's orders and submitted to an examination. Dr Sutcliffe used no violence or threats. He merely examined her and ascertained that she was not pregnant. Captain and Mrs Braddell were not present.

The plaintiff sued all three of them for assault. At the trial the judge directed a verdict for Captain and Mrs Braddell, and the jury found for Dr Sutcliffe.

Held: (i) to make out an assault by Dr Sutcliffe, the plaintiff had to show that he used violence or the threat of it. There was no evidence of this, and the jury were entitled to find that she submitted.

(ii) there was no evidence that Captian and Mrs Braddell authorised Dr Sutcliffe to examine the plaintiff without her submission.

The plaintiff's appeal was dismissed.

See p 103.

Leckie v Brent and Harrow Area Health Authority

Childbirth: registrar: caesarian: res ipsa loquitur

Mars-Jones J. (1982) 1 Lancet 634

When the infant plaintiff's mother was admitted to hospital, difficulty with the birth was expected due to a posterior lie and an undescended head. After an unsuccessful trial of labour, signs of foetal distress were observed and a caesarean section was required for urgent delivery. The operation was performed by a registrar. When he made the incision, the baby sustained on her left cheek a cut of 1.5 cm which penetrated full-thickness skin. The wound was sutured after she was handed to the paediatrician.

She sued the hospital authority, alleging that the registrar had been negligent and relying on the maxim *res ipsa loquitur*. Expert evidence was given that such a cut was extremely rare. Also the defendants' expert admitted that a cut of 2 mm should not occur.

Held: the hospital authority was liable. The cut could not have happened without negligence on the registrar's part.

See p 127.

Lee v South West Thames Regional Health Authority

Discovery: disclosure of report: privilege: duty of care: right to know treatment received: child patient: burns: brain damage

Court of Appeal. [1985] 2 All ER 385, [1985] 1 WLR 845

In April 1983 the plaintiff (Marlon Lee), then aged one, was severely scalded by boiling water in a domestic accident. He was taken to University College Hospital (North East Thames RHA). On the same day the hospital sent him to the burns unit at Mount Vernon Hospital (Hillingdon AHA). Next day he developed respiratory problems. He was put on a respirator and sent back to University College Hospital still on a respirator in an ambulance of the London Ambulance Service (South West Thames RHA). When he was weaned from the respirator about three days later, he was found to have very severe brain damage, probably due to lack of oxygen.

Marlon's mother, acting as his next friend, applied for pre-action discovery under RSC Ord 24, r 7A against all three health authorities. South West Thames claimed legal privilege in respect of a memorandum prepared by the ambulance crew. The hospital records had suggested that there was a problem in the ambulance transfer. Mount Vernon Hospital had asked the London Ambulance Service for the report with a view to obtaining legal advice on the hospital's liability to Marlon. Thus South West Thames primarily were advancing Hillingdon's claim to privilege.

Held: the cause of action asserted against South West Thames was not a wholly independent cause of action, but arose out of the same incident as that which rendered Hillingdon a likely defendant. The principle is that a defendant or potential defendant shall be free to seek evidence without being obliged to disclose the result of his researches to his opponent. Hillingdon had not waived its rights to privilege. Disclosure could not be ordered.

Per Sir John Donaldson MR: 'We reach this conclusion with undisguised reluctance, because we think that there is something seriously wrong with the law if Marlon's mother cannot find out what exactly caused this brain damage.

'A doctor is under a duty to answer his patient's questions as to the treatment proposed. We see no reason why this should not be a similar duty in relation to hospital staff. This duty is subject to the exercise of clinical judgement as to the terms in which the information is given and the extent to which, in the patient's interests, information should be withheld. Why, we ask ourselves, is the position any different if the patient asks what treatment he has in fact had? . . .

'If the duty is the same, then if the patient is refused information to which he is entitled, it must be for consideration whether he could not bring an action for breach of contract claiming specific performance of the duty to inform. In other words, whether the patient could not bring an action for discovery, albeit on a novel basis'.

See pp 30, 45, 114, 210.

Leigh v Gladstone and Others

Prison inmate: force feeding: assault

Lord Alverstone CJ (with jury). (1910) 26 TLR 139

On 22 September 1908 the plaintiff (Mrs Marie Leigh), a suffragette, was convicted on charges of resisting the police and disturbing a meeting held by Mr Asquith and was sentenced to four months' imprisonment with hard labour. She was sent to Winson-Green Prison where she declined food. Between 25 September and 30 October Dr Helby, the prison medical officer, subjected her to forcible feeding, sometimes through the mouth and sometimes through the nose.

The plaintiff claimed damages for assault and an injunction against Mr Gladstone (the Home Secretary), Dr Helby and the prison governor. Dr Helby testified that on 25 September she was looking ill, her pulse was high, her breath was unpleasant, and that he considered it dangerous to allow her to starve any further.

Held: Lord Alverstone CJ directed the jury that it was the duty of the prison officials to preserve the health of the prisoners, and *a fortiori* to preserve their lives. If they forcibly fed the plaintiff when it was not necessary, the defendants ought to pay damages. The medical evidence was that at the time she was first fed it had become dangerous to allow her to abstain from food any longer.

The jury returned a verdict for the defendants.

See p 103.

Lepine v University Hospital Board; Lepine v Monckton

Epilepsy: supervision: Canada

Alberta Supreme Court. (1965) 54 DLR (2d) 340

The plaintiff (Mr Lepine) had suffered from epilepsy for ten years. This took two forms: grand mal seizures, and automatism. On 17 July 1961 he had a seizure at a hotel, headed for a fire escape and was stopped. He was strapped to a stretcher and taken to the University Hospital where he was put in the ward for Dr Monckton's patients on the fourth floor. During the next week he had approximately 28 epileptic seizures of which 17 were automatisms.

In the early morning of 24 July the plaintiff became difficult, noisy and psychotic. At 9.50 am he was found wandering outside the hospital and told the police: 'The nuts in the hospital have a bomb.' While he was being returned to the hospital he bolted, knocked over a little girl and hit a sergeant. He told the police to go ahead and shoot him, he had nothing left. When they got him back to the ward, the orderly left to get a nurse and doctor.

The plaintiff, who had been sitting beside a window, went to the bathroom. Just as he returned, Dr Monckton came in and spoke to him. The plaintiff, with his head down, walked to the chair which was near the window, stepped up on it and jumped through the glass and fell to the pavement four storeys below, where he suffered very serious injuries.

He sued Dr Monckton and the hospital authority. The trial judge found that the hospital was negligent but not Dr Monckton.

Held: (i) the hospital negligently failed to provide constant supervision which would have prevented the plaintiff's final jump and his escape which led to it;

(ii) Dr Monckton, who was the only one with the training and experience to assess the level of supervision necessary for the plaintiff's safety, shared in the hospital's negligence and was jointly liable.

Levenkind v Churchill-Davidson

Operation: surgeon: res ipsa loquitur: causation: shoulder

Kenneth Jones J. (1983) 1 Lancet 1452

The plaintiff (Malcolm Levenkind), aged nineteen, had recurrent dislocations of his right shoulder. On 16 July 1976 Mr Churchill-Davidson, an orthopaedic surgeon, performed a Putti-Platt repair. The musculocutaneous nerve was damaged during the operation. The plaintiff lost the use of the muscles in the right upper arm, and the biceps became wasted and functionless.

He sued Mr Churchill-Davidson for negligence and relied on the maxim *res ipsa loquitur*.

Held: the defendant, an experienced surgeon, did not expose the musculocutaneous nerve. On the balance of probabilities, the injury was caused by traction. Traction with no more than normal force could have caused the lesion, and that would not have involved negligence. Mr Churchill-Davidson was not liable.

See p 88.

Lim Poh Choo v Camden and Islington Area Health Authority

Operation: cardiac arrest: damages: brain damage

House of Lords. [1980] AC 174, [1979] 2 All ER 910, [1979] 3 WLR 44

In February 1973 the plaintiff (Dr Lim Poh Choo) was a 36-year-old senior psychiatric registrar. She was admitted to the Elizabeth Garrett Anderson Hospital for a dilatation and curettage operation. When she was in the recovery room after the operation, she suffered a cardiac arrest. The health authority admitted liability.

The plaintiff, who was described as a remarkably intelligent doctor, had a future career in psychiatry ahead of her. Following the operation, she suffered from extensive and irremediable brain damage. This left her only intermittently, and then barely, sentient. She was totally dependent on others.

Held: (i)   compensation should as nearly as possible put the party who has suffered in the same position as he would have been if he had not sustained the wrong. An attack on the total of damages awarded as being excessive, merely by reason of its size, must fail. It is necessary to show that one or more of the component items of the award are wrong.

(ii)   the fact of unconsciousness does not eliminate the actuality of the deprivation of the ordinary experiences and amenities of life; and it is of no concern to the court to consider any question as to the use that will thereafter be made of the money awarded. As the plaintiff's loss of the amenities of her good and useful life was total, the trial judge's award in December 1977 of £20,000 general damages for pain, suffering and loss of amenities was suitably substantial and not excessive.

(iii)   the plaintiff was entitled to an award for loss of earnings, since a genuine deprivation (be it pecuniary or non-pecuniary in character) is a proper subject of compensation. This is subject to a deduction in respect of the expenses of earning the income that has been lost.

(iv)   the correct approach for taking account of the plaintiff's living expenses was to deduct the 'domestic element' from the cost of care. Damages for the cost of future care must be assessed on the basis that capital as well as income is to be used in meeting the expenditure.

(v)   only in exceptional cases will the risk of future inflation be brought into account in the assessment of damages for future loss. It is pure speculation whether inflation will continue at present, or higher, rates, or even disappear. Inflation is best left to be dealt with by investment policy.

(vi)   after discounting for accelerated payment, the contingency that the plaintiff may not live out her full expectation of life, and the availability of capital as well as income to meet the cost of care, the multiplier of the trial judge (Bristow J) of 18 for the cost of future care was reduced to 12 from the date of the House of Lords judgment in June 1979.

(vii)   as it was necessary to fix the multiplier for loss of future earnings by reference to pre-accident rather than post-accident expectation of life, the trial judge's multiplier of 14 should not be varied.

(viii) after taking into account fresh evidence of the cost of future care, the House of Lords reduced the trial judge's total award to £229,298.64 plus interest.

See pp 150, 153, 158, 162.

Littrell v United States of America

Jurisdiction: military hospital: USA

Court of Appeal. (1993) Independent, 2 December, [1994] PIQR P141

The plaintiff (Ricardo Littrell) was a staff sergeant in the US Air Force stationed in the United Kingdom. In December 1987 he suffered an asthma attack at home and was taken for treatment to the US Military Hospital at the US base at Lakenheath in Suffolk. The treatment involved the administration of an intravenous drip, by reason of which he claimed that he lost the use of his right arm.

He returned to live in the USA and received a disability pension from the US Government. His claim for compensation in the USA was barred by the doctrine that the US Government was not liable for injuries to servicemen sustained on active duty as a result of the negligence of others in the armed forces.

Consequently he issued a writ in England instead, naming the United States as first defendant.

Held: the UK High Court must decline jurisdiction, since the defendant was immune from suit. The activity in question was the medical treatment by the US Government, in one of its base hospitals, of a member of its forces, in the context of its maintenance of those forces in the UK. The acts complained of were jure imperii (the exercise of sovereign, immune authority).

Lobley v Going and Others

General practitioner: vicarious liability: receptionist: standard of care: epiglottitis

Court of Appeal. CAT, 9 December 1985

At about 9.00am on 2 January 1979 the plaintiff (Simon Lobley), aged 22 months, started to suffer with a sore throat. Around 11.00am his father rang the surgery of the family's general practitioners, Dr Going and Dr Nunn, and it was suggested that the child be brought to the early evening surgery. They arrived around 5.00pm. The surgery was busy. Mr

Lobley, who had left Simon sitting down with his wife, told the receptionist, Mrs Porter, his name and that he had rung earlier about his son. Mr Lobley said 'He has got worse; he is having a bit of difficulty in breathing'. Mrs Porter asked him to take a seat. Mr Lobley added 'We would like to get in as soon as possible because of his breathing', to which Mrs Porter replied 'OK, I'll see what I can do'. They sat for a quarter of an hour whereupon Mr Lobley successfully insisted that Simon be seen immediately.

When Dr Going saw the child, he consulted Dr Nunn and telephoned for an ambulance. Simon suffered a hypoxic interlude on the way to hospital. His condition was promptly diagnosed there as epiglottitis. The consultant paediatrician and his registrar attempted to insert a tube into the child's lungs. While they were doing this, he had a cardiac arrest. He suffered irreparable brain damage with very serious disabilities.

The trial judge (Kenneth Jones J) dismissed his claim for negligence against Dr Going, Dr Nunn and the hospital authority. He appealed solely on the basis that Dr Going and Dr Nunn were vicariously liable for the negligence of their receptionist, Mrs Porter.

Held: if it is brought to a receptionist's attention that a small child has been brought to a surgery in an ill condition, with respiratory difficulties about which the parents are genuinely concerned, it is her duty to inform a doctor immediately, and if she fails to do so she is guilty of negligence. However it is not enough for the parent to indicate a measure of concern about the child and then expect the receptionist to embark on enquiries as to the exact basis of such concern. It had not been clearly communicated to Mrs Porter that she was being called upon to deal with an emergency. The trial judge was justified in concluding that she had not been negligent.

See pp 21, 135.

Lock v Scantlebury and Another

Dental: anaesthetics: diagnosis: after-care: res ipsa loquitur: jaw

Paull J. (1963) Times, 25 July

On 14 November 1960 the plaintiff (Miss Betty Lock) was seen by Mr Dawson, a dentist admitted about two years previously who was employed by Mr Scantlebury as his assistant. Mr Dawson extracted six teeth from her upper jaw and two from the lower while Mr Scantlebury administered the anaesthetic.

After the extraction, the plaintiff visited a doctor who gave her pain-killing tablets. On 4 December she visited Mr Dawson and complained that she could not speak properly or eat, and said that she was sure there was something wrong with her face. He examined her and told her that she was getting along nicely and told her to visit him again later. When she did so, after more pain-killers from her doctor, Mr Dawson again did not discover any dislocation and was prepared to do a filling. She turned round and walked out.

Eventually it was discovered that her jaw was dislocated. In June 1961, at Mount Vernon Hospital the dislocation was got back into place manually. She sued Mr Scantlebury and Mr Dawson.

Held: the plaintiff's jaw had become dislocated during the extraction, which of itself was not proof of negligence. However there had been negligence in failing, either on that day or on two subsequent visits, to discover that the dislocation had taken place.

See pp 89, 130.

Locke v Camberwell Health Authority

Costs: discovery: fresh evidence: arm: counsel: solicitors

Court of Appeal. [1991] 2 Med LR 249

The plaintiff (Ms Locke) suffered from angina. In September 1981 Dr Gishen commenced cardiac catheterisation procedure on her at King's College Hospital. After unsuccessful attempts via the femoral arteries in the right and left legs, a further attempt was made via the right brachial artery. The artery went into spasm, there was clotting, the blood flow ceased and the procedure was terminated prematurely. Surgery was performed some thirty minutes later by Dr Bentley, but was only partially successful. The plaintiff was left with continuing disability in her right arm.

She instructed Mr Davies, a solicitor, to make a claim. He obtained legal aid and instructed Dr Sutton, a highly qualified cardiologist, to whom the defendants disclosed hospital records. In 1984 Dr Sutton raised three matters, in particular that there was no record of the anti-coagulant heparin having been administered during the catheterisation procedure. High Court action was pursued. In a second report in 1985, Dr Sutton noted that the defence pleaded Dr Gishen had administered 3,000 units of heparin but again commented on the absence of any note to that effect in the hospital records. In 1986 the defendants served their list of documents and disclosed copies. At counsel's request, Dr Sutton confirmed in 1987 that they contained nothing that he had not already seen.

In October 1987 junior counsel succinctly advised for the purposes of the legal aid certificate that the plaintiff had a good arguable case. In 1988 leading counsel was instructed and advised in February 1989 that the claim should not be pursued on the grounds that, despite the absence of any corroborative note, if Dr Gishen stated on oath that he had used heparin the judge would probably believe him. When Mr Davies sought to discontinue the plaintiff's case, the defendants applied for an order that he personally pay their costs.

At the end of the first day of the hearing of their application, their counsel produced a document which he described as 'the crown jewel in the case': a Cardiac Catheterisation Procedure Record (CCPR) which mentioned 'Hep 3000 units'. Assuming that this had been in the records throughout, the judge ordered that Mr Davies personally pay the defendants' costs from 1 November 1987 (after receipt of counsel's October 1987 opinion).

Subsequently affidavits were sworn by both the plaintiff's counsel, Mr Davies and Dr Sutton, the effect of which was to make it highly improbable that the CCPR was ever disclosed to the plaintiff's advisers, medical or legal, until it was produced in court. They applied for the affidavits to be admitted as fresh evidence on appeal. The defendants opposed this, but their counsel conceded that the CCPR had probably never been disclosed either to Dr Sutton or in the copy documents supplied in August 1986.

Held: (i)   the affidavits should be admitted as fresh evidence. They were credible and shot away the foundation on which the judge's decision was based. In view of the way in which the CCPR was suddenly produced at the hearing, such affidavit evidence could not have been available beforehand with the exercise of reasonable diligence.

           (ii)   the brevity of counsel's October 1987 opinion was understandable, since he had advised on at least seven prior occasions and the purpose of this opinion was simply to have the limitation on the legal aid certificate removed. Moreover counsel had already checked with Dr Sutton that the documents disclosed by the defendants in 1986 did not contain anything new.

           (iii)   Mr Davies' conduct could not be fairly criticised. He had acted promptly throughout and followed to the letter the advice that he sought and received from counsel. It was unfortunate that the 'crown jewel' document was not revealed to the plaintiff's advisers earlier. His appeal must be allowed.

Per Taylor LJ:

'(1) In general, a solicitor is entitled to rely upon the advice of counsel properly instructed.

(2) For a solicitor without specialist experience in a particular field to rely on counsel's advice is to make normal and proper use of the Bar.

(3) However, he must not do so blindly but must exercise his own independent judgment. If he reasonably thinks counsel's advice is obviously or glaringly wrong, it is his duty to reject it.

(4) Although a solicitor should not assist a litigant where prosecution of a claim amounts to an abuse of process, it is not his duty to attempt to assess the result of a conflict of evidence or to impose a pre-trial screen on a litigant's claim.

(5) The jurisdiction to order costs against a solicitor personally is one which falls to be exercised with care and discretion and only in clear cases.'

Lockley v National Blood Transfusion Service

Costs: legal aid

Court of Appeal. [1992] 1 WLR 492

The plaintiff (Marie Lockley), who was legally aided, sued the defendants for damages for negligence. Her statement of claim was served on 17 October 1989. On 8 November 1989 the defendant applied for an extension of time for service of the defence. The application was heard on 16 November 1989. The district registrar extended the time for service until 30 November 1989 and ordered: 'the costs of and incidental to this application by the defendants, not to be enforced without the leave of the court save as to set-off as against damages and/or costs'.

The plaintiff appealed on the grounds that an order for costs against a legally aided party 'by way of set-off as against damages and/or costs' was barred by the relevant provisions of the Legal Aid Act 1988 and the regulations made thereunder.

Held: a direction for the set-off of costs against damages or costs to which a legally aided person becomes entitled in the action is permissible. The set-off is the same as that available to or against parties who are not legally aided.

The plaintiff's appeal was dismissed.

Lofthouse v North Tees Health Authority

Childbirth: damages: registrar: perineum

HH Judge Ebsworth. [1992] CLY 1664

The plaintiff (Mrs Lofthouse), was aged 24 when admitted to the defendants' hospital for the birth of her first child in April 1988. Her perineum was torn in the process. A registrar stitched it too tightly.

Sexual intercourse was impossible because of the pain and restriction of the size of the introitus. Four more operations were needed to refashion the perineum, with success finally achieved in May 1990. In the intervening two years, the plaintiff had suffered pain and unhappiness which affected her marriage. Her ability to cope had diminished, and she required counselling.

Held (April 1992):   general damages of £10,500 were awarded for:

    (i)   the initial operation having been carried out wrongly;

    (ii)   the further four operations, which had involved admissions to hospital resulting in discomfort and distress with recovery periods of up to six weeks;

    (iii)   inability to have sexual intercourse for two years, in the context of a previously happy marriage, and the effect which that had upon her;

    (iv)   the subsequent fear of vaginal childbirth.

See pp 127, 156.

Lord v Spencer

Causation: damages: general practitioner: ophthalmic

HH Judge Colyer. (1994) AVMA Journal, Spring, p 10.

On the afternoon of 2 January 1987 the plaintiff (Ms Lord), aged 64, consulted her general practitioner, Dr Spencer. Three days before, she had noticed a sudden change of vision in her right eye. It had became misty and was like looking through a watery curtain. He did not refer her to hospital. The retina detached on the afternoon of 3 January. The plaintiff attended hospital on 4 January, and retinal surgery was performed the next day. Unfortunately, through no fault of the hospital, the complication of proliferative vitreo-retinopathy set in. The plaintiff lost the sight of the right eye.

By trial it was accepted that: on 2 January the plaintiff had a vitreous detachment, the precursor of a retinal detachment; Dr Spencer should have referred her to hospital; she would have attended hospital on the evening of 2 January; and laser treatment would have been carried out on the morning of 3 January.

Held: (i)   the laser treatment would probably have prevented the retinal detachment and hence saved the sight in the plaintiff's right eye.

    (ii)   she was awarded £20,000 general damages for pain, suffering and loss of amenities.

See p 136.

Loveday v Renton and Another

Vaccine damage: contra-indications: causation: product liability

Stuart-Smith LJ. [1990] 1 Med LR 117, (1988) Times, 31 March

In 1970 and 1971, when she was a baby, the plaintiff (Susan Loveday) was treated with whooping-cough vaccine by Dr Renton. She suffered permanent brain damage.

She sued Dr Renton on the basis that the vaccine was administered in disregard of one or more of the contra-indications. She put forward four suggested biological mechanisms to explain the alleged link between the vaccine and her brain damage, one of which was febrile convulsions.

The most important epidemiological evidence was derived from the National Childhood Encephalopathy Study. This supported the theory that diphtheria tetanus pertussis (DTP) vaccine sometimes caused febrile convulsions.

Held: all four suggested biological mechanisms were improbable. The study did not provide evidence that febrile convulsions following the DTP vaccine caused permanent brain damage.

The plaintiff had failed to show on the balance of probabilities that pertussis vaccine could cause permanent brain damage in young children. It was possible that it did; the contrary could not be proved. But in the result the plaintiff's claim failed.

(Obiter): even if the preliminary issue of causation had been resolved in her favour, any plaintiff would face insuperable difficulties in proving negligence on the part of the doctor or nurse who administered the vaccine.

See pp 36, 38, 69, 78.

Lovell v Southampton and South West Hampshire Health Authority

Brain damage: cardiac arrest: damages: structured settlement: child patient

Otton J. 27 November 1992

In June 1984, when the plaintiff (Victoria Lovell) was three and a quarter years old, she was admitted to Southampton Eye Hospital to undergo a routine operation to correct a squint. Hospital staff were aware that she had been suffering from a cold. Whilst she was in the recovery room after the operation, a plug of phlegm entered her windpipe and she stopped breathing. Cardiac arrest occurred, and Victoria suffered severe irreversible brain damage.

Damages on the conventional basis were agreed shortly before trial at £875,000. Mr Justice Otton approved this on 30 March 1992 and adjourned the case to allow investigation of a structured settlement. Negotiations were protracted, as the defendant Health Authority was directed by HM Treasury and the Department of Health to put forward a self structure.

£287,000 was paid as interim payments and other lump sums. A further £76,000 plus £37,306 interest since 30 March was payable immediately of which £50,000 was paid into the Court of Protection as a contingency fund and £63,306 was paid to the Receiver. The structured sum is £465,000 from which the Health Authority was to make periodic payments. Their discount was £47,000.

Lump sums	£363,000
Interest from 30 March 1992	£37,306
Structured sum	£465,000
Health Authority discount	£47,000
Total (including interest)	£912,006

Under the structure, the Health Authority was to pay £24,114.96 pa, increasing annually in line with the retail price index, payable for life subject to a guaranteed minimum period of ten years whether Victoria survives or not. These payments are guaranteed by the Department of Health, in the event of the Health Authority ceasing to exist. Indeed, the payments to be made by the Health Authority are being provided by the Department of Health.

The case came again before Mr Justice Otton when he approved the structured settlement and the arrangements relating to it.

See pp 138, 152.

Lowen v Hopper and Another

Nurses: res ipsa loquitur: blood donor: causation

Hilbery J (with jury). [1950] 1 BMJ 792

The plaintiff (Mrs Ivy Lowen) gave blood eight times without ill effect at the Rochford Municipal Hospital. Dr Hopper, the hospital medical officer, took her blood on the ninth occasion. The plaintiff reported to the sister after the operation that she was losing an undue quantity of blood. However the sister did not examine her thoroughly or replace the sodden dressing. The plaintiff's right arm became septic and she was left with a long permanent scar.

She sued Dr Hopper and the hospital authority. Dr Hopper was dismissed from the case for lack of evidence of negligence.

Held: Hilbery J directed the jury that the mere fact that the plaintiff's arm became septic after the operation did not of itself establish negligence. If they believed that there had been a want of reasonable skill and care, they would have to decide whether that was the cause of the arm becoming septic. There was some evidence from which they might infer that germs had entered the plaintiff's system from blood-soaked dressing.

The jury found that the hospital had been negligent.

See p 138.

Luke v South Glamorgan Area Health Authority

After-care: cancer: diagnosis: liver: surgeon

Hollings J. QBD transcript, 11 January 1990

On 1 November 1978 Royston Luke, aged 34, was admitted to Cardiff Royal Infirmary as an emergency, suffering from right hypochondrial pain radiating into the back. He was transferred to the University of Wales where an initial diagnosis of gallstones was made. He returned to the same hospital under the care of their general surgeon Mr Wade. An ultrasound scan on 29 November indicated the presence of gallstones. However when a laparotomy was performed on 30 November it was found that the gall bladder was normal, so the ultrasound scan must have given a false reading or been falsely read.

However the liver was abnormal: it was adherent to the diaphragm, bled easily and on excision biopsy discharged some necrotic material. A specimen was sent for histology to Dr Leopold, a histopathologist, who reported on 11 December 1978: 'The necrotic lesion is a tumour, or possibly a hamartoma of liver cell derivation . . . There is an area of scarring, and also fragments which are necrotic. I believe this to be benign, but caution is always needed because of the extraordinary psychological* innocence of some hamartoma. The liver biopsy shows mild, non-specific, partial inflammation, the cause undisclosed.' His conclusion was 'liver adenoma with mild hepatitis.'

Although noting the caution, Mr Wade did not resect the tumour because he thought that the risk was too high compared to the benefit. Three alpha-fetoprotein tests over several days gave normal readings of 11, 11 and 10. Mr Luke was discharged from being an in-patient on 8 December 1978. A report was sent to his general practitioner. The clinical follow-up showed that liver function tests returned to normal on 5 January 1979, the full blood count was normal, the ESR became normal, there was a steady increase in weight, and pain when present was on the left side which is not associated with the liver.

In January 1984 Mr Luke went to his general practitioner, complaining of severe right hypochondrial pain. By March 1984 ultrasound revealed a large hepatic lesion and the alpha-fetoprotein level was grossly elevated. He eventually died at the age of 40 from a large hepatoma on 30 October 1984. The plaintiff (his widow) sued for damages.

Held: (i) it is probable that the tumour in 1978 was an adenoma which converted later into a hepatoma. Mr Wade was not at fault in not guarding against this possibility, in the light of professional knowledge in 1978.

(ii) Mr Wade was right, in the light of medical knowledge and practice in 1978, not to resect the tumour. There was only a remote possibility of the adenoma being a hepatoma – that is, malignant – and the alpha-fetoprotein test was normal. The operation had a mortality risk of 5–10%. If the tumour proved to be malignant when resected, there was a risk that the operation might release malignant cells into the body and so accelerate death.

(iii) ultrasound was in an early stage in 1978, and Mr Wade knew that it had already given false results. In 1978 it was not common clinical practice to monitor for tumours with ultrasound. Mr Wade was conforming to what was then considered usual and prudent practice by not using it for follow-up purposes.

(iv) even if ultrasound and alpha-fetoprotein tests had been performed until 1981, it is not probable that they would have shown the conversion of the adenoma into a hepatoma in view of the unusual length of time between the detection of the adenoma in December 1978 and the onset of symptoms of haematoma in December 1983.

(v) There had not been any negligence. The plaintiff's claim must be dismissed.

* the word 'psychological' is difficult to understand in this context and may indicate a typing error in the transcript.

See p 98.

M (a minor) and Another v Newham London Borough Council and Others

Causation: duty of care: minor: sexual abuse: psychiatrist

House of Lords. (1995) Times, 30 June

The first plaintiff (M) was born in January 1983 when the second plaintiff (her mother) was 17. In 1987 doctors were concerned that the cause of M's urinary infection might be sexual abuse. An appointment was made by the local authority for the child to be examined by a psychiatrist employed by the local health authority to ascertain whether she had been sexually abused and, if so, the identity of the abuser. On 13 November 1987, M was interviewed by the psychiatrist in the presence of the social worker. The interview was recorded on videotape with the mother absent. During the session the social worker left the room and asked the mother for the names of her father, husband and boyfriend, which she gave.

It was pleaded that the psychiatrist had concluded that M had been sexually abused by the mother's boyfriend, the father of another of her children (but not M) who lived with her at the time. In fact, M did not identify him as the abuser but a cousin with the same first name as him, who had previously lived at her mother's address. M said that the abuser had left the mother's home and was not her mother's boyfriend. At the end of the interview, M's mother was told by the psychiatrist and the social worker that her boyfriend had sexually abused M. The child subsequently told her mother that he had not. When her mother tried to tell the social worker of this denial, he and the psychiatrist wrongly took this as an attempt to persuade the child to retract her allegation.

On the same day, on the local authority's application, a place of safety order was made by the Newham Justices. On 24 November 1987, a Family Division judge adjourned the local authority's application that M be made a ward of court but ordered that the local authority be granted care and control, that the child should not return home and that the mother's access be limited. M was placed with foster parents. During the course of the wardship proceedings, her mother saw the transcript of the interview on 13 November. She informed the local authority of the mistake that had been made. The local authority reported this to the judge who on 21 November 1988 ordered that M be rehabilitated with her mother, after one year's enforced separation.

M and her mother sued the local authority, the local health authority and the consultant psychiatrist employed by the health authority. They claimed that as a result of the separation each suffered a positive psychiatric disorder diagnosed as anxiety neurosis. They pleaded negligence and breach of ss 1 and 18 of the Child Care Act 1980. The claims were struck out as disclosing no reasonable cause of action.

Held: (i)   Where Parliament had conferred a statutory discretion on a public authority, nothing which the authority did within the ambit of the discretion could be actionable at common law. It was not just and reasonable to superimpose a common law duty of care on a local authority in relation to performance of its statutory duties to protect children.

(ii)   although the psychiatrist must have appreciated that there might have been court proceedings in which she would have been a witness. She and the health authority could rely on witness immunity as an answer to the claim against them.

(iii)   M was not the patient of the psychiatrist whose duty of care was owed to the local authority who engaged her to perform the task of eliciting the facts about sexual abuse. The psychiatrist did not owe M a duty of care in relation to the advice which the psychiatrist gave to the local authority, as it was never intended that the psychiatrist should give that advice to M.

(iv)   nor did the psychiatrist owe a duty of care to the mother. She was not the subject of a diagnostic interview by the psychiatrist.

(v)   the claims by both M and her mother were rightly struck out.

See pp 43, 44, 46, 48, 50, 101.

M v E

Brain damage: childbirth: structured settlement: damages

FTSB, Spring 1994

Owing to negligent procedures at birth, the plaintiff (M) suffered severe cerebral palsy. When she was ten years old, medical reports suggested that a 'minimum life expectancy of 40 years would be a reasonable estimate'.

The following settlement was agreed:

Capital cost of structure	£746,500
Court of Protection Fund	£213,500
Other damages	£75,000
Total	£1,035,000

M v E

The payments produced by the structure were as follows:

(i)   An initial yield of 4.4%, producing a sum of £15,000 pa in the first year, increasing each year in line with the retail price index, and payable for life.

(ii)   In ten years (when the plaintiff would be 20 years of age), the further sum of £25,000 pa, increased in line with the RPI and payable for life.

The structure was approved.

M v L

Brain damage: childbirth: structured settlement: damages

FTSB, Autumn 1994

The plaintiff (M) suffered brain damage at birth that resulted in cerebral palsy. When he was aged ten, medical experts estimated his life expectancy at a further 15 to 25 years.

The following settlement was agreed:

Interim payments	£27,750
Accommodation costs	£175,000
Capital cost of structure	£242,000
Court of Protection Fund	£75,000
Discount	£18,000
Total	£537,750

The payments produced by the structured settlement were as follows:

Type of annuity	Immediate
Initial net yield	6.9%
Initial annual sum	£18,700
Indexation	RPI
Equivalent gross yield after basic rate tax	9.2%
Payable for	Life of plaintiff
Guarantee period	5 years

M v Plymouth Health Authority

Discovery: costs: ophthalmic

Brooke J. [1993] 4 Med LR 108, [1993] PIQR P223

The plaintiff (M) was born in 1978. There was concern about her eyesight in May 1988. Her optician referred her to specialists at a local hospital. She was discharged as giving rise to no particular problem in July 1988. Worries arose again in March 1989 when it was said that she was bumping into things and that her eyesight had deteriorated. She saw a neurologist and went into hospital for testing. In April 1989 a diagnosis was made of a thalamic tumour extending towards the optic chiasma.

She sought legal advice on a claim against those responsible for her care in 1988 for failing to avoid the tumour reaching the size it had reached in April 1989. Her solicitors sought in January 1990 pre-action discovery against the defendant hospital authority whose solicitors supplied copies of the hospital records in April 1990. They subsequently made the original records available for inspection, but refused to supply an itemised list.

440

Held: (i) section 33(2) of the Supreme Court Act 1981 provides for pre-action discovery. It was not disputed that disclosure of the hospital records was appropriate in this case.

(ii) RSC Ord 24, r 7A empowered the court to order that the pre-action discovery be verified by an affidavit from the party providing it. In this case, what the defendants had provided in April 1990 was ample so they should not be obliged to swear an affidavit. Had one been necessary, the deponent should have been at liberty to use the customary form of words and then exhibit to that affidavit, copies of the 150 or so documents all paginated so there could be no dispute as to what had been produced.

(iii) There is no reference to a list in either the Act or the Rules. The plaintiff's solicitor was not entitled to the itemised list that he sought.

(iv) The legally aided plaintiff should be ordered as was standard to pay the defendants' costs of the application, not to be enforced without leave of the court, but it was not appropriate to add that these defendants' costs be set off against any damages and costs that might subsequently be awarded to the plaintiff.

Per Brooke J: 'I was told by Mr Michael Brooke who appears on behalf of the health authority that, whatever may have been the practice in the early years following the introduction of the new legislative arrangements, nowadays health authorities are willing to submit voluntarily to applications for pre-action discovery provided that they are satisfied that the appropriate criteria have been met. They will first as a matter of courtesy, I was told, clear the matter with any consultants or other professional men or women who may have had the care of the plaintiff and whose notes were to be disclosed.

It is, in my judgment, desirable so far as possible for this process to be conducted quickly, relatively cheaply and efficiently. Obsessive attention to detail is likely to lead to unwarrantable delay and expense. A procedure which involves the health authority bringing its documents into one place and having them copied and paged, and then disclosing them in a way in which what is disclosed is accompanied by some sort of list identifying where the different categories of documents are located, is a form of procedure which should be aimed at so far as possible.

The solicitors' clerk who had the conduct of this matter for the plaintiff had had unhappy experiences in other cases which had led him to require of health authorities against whom clients of his firm were bringing cases to produce in the first instance an itemised list of every conceivable document under the sun which they might have in their possession. This is in my judgment very far removed from what is necessary or desirable, especially as it is likely to be the wish of the clients of his firm that the matter is pursued with reasonable expedition.

If the original documents, which as I have said are likely to be working documents, are copied in this way, then on any application to inspect them they are likely to be in the same order. Both sides' solicitors will have a paged bundle (when I say paged I mean a bundle which starts at page 1 rather than at page 117) and if any dispute arises as to whether a document was disclosed at an early voluntary stage they will be able to refer straight to the paged bundle and see whether or not the document was indeed disclosed. It was quite obvious that one of the concerns of the plaintiff's solicitor in this case was that there might be a dispute as to whether a document was or was not disclosed if one did not have an itemised list of every single document which in due course could be checked if a dispute arose.

The procedure I have described is, in my judgment, an appropriate course for a defendant health authority to take. Of course, if it wishes to take a different course it is always at liberty to do so and different health authorities and their solicitors will have different practices.

The purpose of this exercise is to enable the plaintiff's advisers to receive copies of the relevant documents reasonably quickly from the health authority so that they can refer them both to an expert and, if necessary, to counsel to advise if there is a prima facie case of liability on which an action should be brought, or if there appears to be no liability at all. I was helpfully reminded by Miss Tracy Forster, who appears for the plaintiff, that on a number of occasions this kind of pre-action discovery leads to no action at all being brought, and this also shows how desirable it is to limit pre-action expenditure of time and money.

At the next stage, and this happens in every type of civil litigation – it is not confined to medical negligence litigation – if it appears to the plaintiff's advisers that any documents or categories of documents appear to be missing from what have been disclosed, then it is appropriate for them to make specific requests for those documents or categories of documents, or they may wish to have better copies of what was disclosed. It may also be that the experts they have retained may indicate an additional line of inquiry which may lead to the health authority then seeking documents from some other unit in its area, perhaps relating to the patient's previous medical history. This is a typical course of events in the context of discovery, whether it is pre-action or post-action.

If, in due course, the plaintiff's solicitors wish to inspect the originals then the closer the paged bundle they have already received of copy documents is to the order in which the originals are held, the easier it will be for them to conduct inspection.

It may then be that the situation is reached when on good grounds the plaintiff's advisers may feel that there has been inadequate disclosure and that it is necessary to pin the defendant health authority down on affidavit by obtaining an order. In my judgment, the approach of the plaintiff's solicitors in this case was to move far too fast to what may be necessary in the final resort, instead of going through the kind of procedure which was being suggested at all material times by the defendant's solicitors, which appears to me to have been practical, sensible and economic . . .

I accept the submission made by counsel for the defendants that if an affidavit was required then a convenient way in which the affidavit might be prepared would be for the appropriate representative of the health authority to make his affidavit in the customary form, exhibiting to it paged copies of all the relevant documents so that there could be no doubt as to what was being produced.

Of course, if one is dealing with a case where pre-action discovery may be by the filing cabinet rather than by the file, it may be inappropriate to follow this course, but even more so it would be inappropriate to require the defendant health authority to list every document item by individual item if the scope for potential discovery is likely to be on that kind of grand scale.

In this judgment I have sought to set out general principles. It may well be that there are local variations depending on local practices. However, if, on the one hand, there is a suggestion that the Act and the rules can only be complied with by an itemised list of every single item and on the other hand, a suggestion that the Act and the rules can be complied with by the copying of all the relevant documents, preferably with some kind of index system identifying where relevant categories of documents are, then I have no hesitation in forming the view that all that is necessary is the second of these alternatives.'

See p 208.

M v W

Brain damage: childbirth: damages: structured settlement

FTSB, Spring 1994

The plaintiff (M) suffered brain damage due to allegedly negligent procedures at birth. The defendants did not admit liability. When he was eight years of age, medical experts assessed his life expectancy to be a further 20 to 40 years.

The following settlement was agreed:

Capital cost of structure	£450,000
Discount	£35,000
Court of Protection Fund	£245,000
Other damages	£45,000
Total	£775,000

The payments produced by the structure were as follows:

Type of annuity	Immediate
Initial net yield	6.4%
Initial annual sum	£28,710
Indexation	RPI
Equivalent gross yield after higher rate tax	10.7%
Payable for	Life of plaintiff
Guarantee period	10 years

This was the first medical negligence structured settlement reached in Northern Ireland.

There was no discount on the damages.

McAllister v Lewisham and North Southwark Health Authority and Others

Causation: risk disclosure: surgeon: leg: operation: warning

Rougier J. [1994] 5 Med LR 343

In 1984 the plaintiff (Mrs McAllister) then in her mid-30s, noticed that her left foot was not behaving properly and that her shoe kept falling off. Her gait was ungainly and the foot could not be raised in the same way as her right foot. Consequently she tended to trip, particularly on stairs, although she had never actually fallen. Her symptoms got worse, and she had four episodes when her leg suddenly went numb and weak. She was divorcing her husband and was still in a probationary period of a desirable new job as a call director with Morgan Stanley when in June 1987 she consulted her general practitioner who referred her to Guy's Hospital where a CT brain scan and an angiogram were performed in September 1987. These investigations revealed that she had a large arteriovascular malformation (an AVM).

She was referred to Mr Strong, the senior consultant neurosurgeon at the Maudsley Hospital. When he saw her on 10 November 1987, his opening words were 'Now, about this operation'. He told her that if she did not have the operation her leg would not improve but, on the contrary, would get worse so that she would end in a calliper. He also stated that there was a 20% chance that the operation would make her leg worse rather than better. He made no mention of any of the general risks of brain surgery, and he did not convey to her that there was any risk that any increased deficit would extend beyond the leg. In particular, he did not communicate to her that there was any risk of the arm becoming impaired, still less of any left-sided hemiplegia.

On 3 December 1987 the operation commenced; it took 23 hours in all. When the plaintiff finally came round and was conscious, she discovered that she had not only a greatly increased weakness of her left leg but a complete hemiplegia on her left side involving her arm, which was totally useless and without voluntary movement. Her job was lost, and she had little realistic prospect of much gainful employment in future.

She sued the hospital authorities responsible for the Maudsley Hospital on the grounds that, first, Mr Strong was negligent in advising her to have the operation, and second, that he failed in his duty to give her sufficient information about the benefit-risk ratio. It was common ground that the operation had been performed with great skill.

Held:

   (i) the operation belonged in Group V under the Spetzler definitions. The plaintiff's condition was operable, but with a very considerable degree of risk. In deciding to operate, Mr Strong did not blunder or go outside a body of respectable medical opinion. There was a school of thought which would have condoned intervention, although that school was very much in the minority.

   (ii) apart from the considerable risk of the leg becoming worse, there was a 100% risk of further sensory deficit and a risk which was at least in the area of 5–10% of damage to the arm. Mr Strong's warnings to the plaintiff were inadequate; there was no reputable body of responsible opinion to the contrary. He should have disclosed the following:

      (a) that to some extent the plaintiff was bound to suffer sensory impairment to the leg at least;

      (b) that there was a considerable risk of the leg becoming worse – the plaintiff should not have been left with the impression that the chance was as low as 20%;

      (c) that there was a comparatively slight, but nevertheless more than minimal, risk of her present deficit;

      (d) although her leg would almost certainly be worse than if untreated, there was a slight chance that the deterioration would cease of its own accord.

   (iii) the plaintiff's evidence that, at the very least, she would have postponed the operation until such time as she had established herself in her new job, was accepted. Whilst she could not say what she would have done thereafter, she would probably have continued to decline the operation because she was a sensible and independent-minded woman, the deficit was not advancing rapidly, the slight chance of the progress of the deficit arresting itself spontaneously would still be there, the job and the independence it produced would still be just as precious later and, above all, she would very probably have taken a second opinion which would not have been in favour of the operation.

   (iv) the starting point for a subsequent assessment of damages must be the value of the plaintiff's present disability, knowing that there was no longer any risk of further disability from any cause associated with the AVM. The following features would all operate as deductions from this:

      (a) such neurological deficit as she possessed would have got worse and, subject to the slight possibility of spontaneous arrest, it would have put her in a calliper or similar device by about 2010;

      (b) there was the ever-present risk of haemorrhage which would be either fatal or disabling;

      (c) the anxiety which the knowledge of such a possibility would be bound to engender;

      (d) the possibility of haemorrhage less than instantly disabling, but of sufficient menace to drive her to seek the operation.

See pp 112, 113.

McAloon v Newcastle Health Authority

Dental: lingual nerve: operation

Court of Appeal. CAT, 28 February 1992

In November 1984 the plaintiff (Mrs Angela McAloon) underwent an operation for removal of her right wisdom tooth performed by Mr Prior, a newly qualified dentist at Newcastle Dental Hospital. As a result, she suffered numbness and loss of feeling in her mouth, particularly to her tongue. She sued the hospital authority.

Her expert testified that Mr Prior had been so clumsy that he had severed the buccal nerve when making an incision, and had thereafter severed the lingual nerve whilst using his burr as he cut bone away at the distal when the nerve was unprotected by a lingual retractor. The defence expert's theory was that the plaintiff's nerve damage was the result of major bleeding caused by the dental injection piercing an artery or a vein, which led to pressure on the blood supply to the nerves causing a state of bloodlessness which, in turn, led to the death of a limited portion of the tissue involved: a totally unforeseeable phenomenon. Mr Prior said in cross examination 'If I had given an injection and made such a severe slice, as you call it, to cut the buccal nerve or the main branch, and minutes later done much the same to the lingual nerve, I would have had some inkling, I would have known.' The trial judge dismissed the plaintiff's claim.

Held: the judge had been entitled to accept Mr Prior's testimony and to find, on the expert evidence, that both theories were improbable and that the plaintiff had not discharged the burden of proving her case.

See p 69.

McCormack v Redpath Brown & Co Ltd and Another

Diagnosis: casualty officer: x-rays: fracture: hospital administration: skull

Paull J. (1961) Times, 24 March

In April 1957 the plaintiff (Edward McCormack) was working as a steel erector at Vauxhall Motors in Luton for his then employers Redpath Brown & Co Ltd. He was hit on the head by a spanner accidentally dropped from above by a fellow workman. The spanner cut right through the plaintiff's cap and made a gash about one inch long well above the normal hair line but where he was was very nearly bald. He was taken to the Luton and Dunstable Hospital where he was attended to by the casualty officer, his wound cleaned and three or four stitches inserted. He was given a letter to his doctor and left.

He suffered from headaches and dizziness. In January 1958 he was examined by a neurologist attached to the West End Hospital for Nervous Diseases who diagnosed a depressed fracture of the skull. X-rays showed that there was a hole in his skull between a quarter and a half inch in diameter and that a piece of bone had been forced through into the brain itself. An operation took place in March 1958. He sued both his employers, who admitted liability, and the hospital authority who denied negligence.

Held: the casualty officer had been negligent in:

(i) failing to arrange for an X-ray to be taken; and

(ii) failing to discover the hole in the plaintiff's skull.

It appeared that he was overworked and unjustifiably assumed that this was just another cut head. The hospital authority was responsible for the consequences of his failure.

See pp 96, 133.

McCormick v O'Connor

Epilepsy: diagnosis: burden of proof: paranoia

Court of Appeal. 20 November 1978

The plaintiff (Alistair McCormick) had been a serving officer in the Royal Air Force. Air Vice-Marshal O'Connor diagnosed that he was suffering from epilepsy and paranoia. This put an end to his career in the RAF. He sued the Air Vice-Marshal for negligent diagnosis.

In 1966 the plaintiff had received a head injury in a road accident and had suffered at least two epileptic attacks in consequence. He had falsely alleged that his passenger Dr Drinkwater interfered with his driving. He had formed an obsessive desire to expose Dr Drinkwater and manifested other paranoid tendencies.

Held: all the medical evidence was one way, against the allegations of negligence. The trial judge (Mars-Jones J) had been correct to find that Air Vice-Marshal O'Connor was not liable.

McGrath v Kiely and Powell

Medical report: breach of contract: fracture: damages: shoulder: Ireland

Irish High Court. [1965] IR 497

In December 1959 the plaintiff (Margaret McGrath) was involved in a motor accident. She sustained injuries which included a fracture to her left clavicle. She instructed Mr Powell, a solicitor, to conduct her claim for damages against the drivers concerned and told him of the fracture. For the purposes of her claim, he commissioned and paid for a full medical report on her injuries from Professor Kiely, who had set the fractured clavicle in plaster. His report did not mention it.

She commenced High Court action against the two drivers. Her fractured clavicle was not pleaded. Counsel only learned of it on the morning of the hearing. A decision was taken to proceed without relying on it, since the alternative was an adjournment with substantial costs. The jury awarded £1,000 general damages.

The plaintiff then sued Professor Kiely and Mr Powell.

Held: (i)   each defendant was in breach of his contract with the plaintiff;

(ii)   if the fractured clavicle had been taken into account, the jury would have awarded the plaintiff a further £100 general damages, so she was entitled to judgment for £100 against both defendants.

See p 45.

McInnes v Bromley Health Authority

Operation: risk disclosure: surgeon: knee: consultant

Sir Michael Ogden QC. 17 January 1992

The plaintiff (Miss McInnes), was a 16-year-old girl in 1986. She was four feet seven inches in height, and suffered from congenital ligament laxity which caused recurrent knee-cap dislocation. Mr Lam, consultant surgeon at Orpington Hospital, examined her in 1985 and 1986. He recommended that both knee-caps be stabilised by an operation known as tibial tubercle transfer, with the left knee to be done first.

On 12 February 1986 he performed the tibial tubercle transfer operation on the left patella. He noted of his examination that day that these were the most dislocating knee-caps he had ever seen in almost 30 years of practice. The patellar tendon, known as the tibial tubercle, was lax and needed its lower end to be detached from the tibia, pulled down and reattached to the tibia. Mr Lam distalised or pulled down the tibial tubercle by five centimetres.

Following the operation, the plaintiff suffered from limitation of movement in her left leg and associated problems. She sued on the grounds that (i) Mr Lam did not warn her of this risk and (ii) he negligently conducted the operation. On (i), she and her mother testified that, since she intended to be a professional dancer, they were very concerned whether the operation might affect her ability to dance and Mr Lam assured them that it would not. Mr Lam denied that dancing was ever mentioned and stated that he warned them of the possibility of some restriction of movement. On (ii) her expert testified that the tibial turbercle should not have been pulled down by more than three centimetres, particularly bearing in mind the plaintiff's small stance, and that advancement by five centimetres led to tightness and limitation of movement. The defence expert, a teaching hospital professor, said that he taught his student surgeons that the patellar tendon should never be transferred so far distally that the knee could not be flexed to 90° during the procedure without disrupting the transferred insertions of the vastus medialis and the patellar tendon and to rely on this 90° flexion procedure alone, not the two to three centimetres injunction.

Held: (i)   Mr Lam's evidence about his conversations with the plaintiff and her mother were accepted. Nothing was said about dancing, and he warned them about the risk of restriction of movement following the operation.

   (ii)   the crucial point about the operation was the extreme nature of the plaintiff's disability. So bad was it that advancement of two to three centimetres would not have stabilised the knee. The defendant dealt with a most unusual and exceptional case in a reasonable and proper manner.

The plaintiff's case was dismissed.

See p 112.

McKay and Another v Essex Area Health Authority and Another

Wrongful birth: diagnosis: Congenital Disabilities (Civil Liability) Act 1976: striking out: rubella

Court of Appeal. [1982] QB 1166

In February 1975 the plaintiff (Mary McKay) was conceived. Her case was that while in her mother's womb she was infected with rubella (German measles). Her mother consulted Dr Gower-Jones who took blood samples that were submitted to a hospital laboratory. It was alleged that, despite this, Dr Gower-Jones informed her mother that she and her unborn child had not been infected with rubella during the pregnancy and that she need not consider an abortion. The plaintiff was born in August 1975 with severe congenital disabilities.

She sued Dr Gower-Jones and the hospital authorities. It was not disputed that she was entitled to bring a claim against the doctor for negligently causing her injuries by failing to inject globulins into her mother. She also claimed against both defendants for 'entry into a life in which her injuries are highly debilitating, and distress, loss and damage'.

Held: this latter claim was for 'wrongful life'. There was no duty to the foetus to cause its death. Such a proposition was wholly contrary to the sanctity of human life. Moreover the claim was impossible to value, since it involved a comparison with a state of non-existence. The Master was right to strike it out under RSC Ord 18, r 19(1) as disclosing no reasonable cause of action.

Per curiam: The effect of the Congenital Disabilities (Civil Liability) Act 1976 was that no child born after its passing could have a right of action for 'wrongful life'.

See pp 49, 53, 54, 126, 146, 168, 172.

McLellan* v Newcastle Health Authority

Risk disclosure: sterilisation (failed): registrar: senior house officer

Alliott J. [1992] 3 Med LR 215

The plaintiff (Mrs McLellan) had a daughter by her long divorced ex-husband. She and her partner of eleven years' standing decided upon sterilisation after a foetus conceived by them proved to be seriously deformed and was aborted. Consequently she was referred to Newcastle General Hospital where she was counselled by Dr Scott, a senior house officer, who arranged for her to sign the consent form below on 20 October 1987.

Newcastle Health Authority

NGH Hospital

I Judith McLellan
of 110 Linbridge Drive, West Dewton
hereby consent to undergo an operation for tubal ligation the
nature and effect of which have been explained to me by
Dr Scott.

I appreciate that the intention of the operation is to render me
sterile and incapable of parenthood. I understand the
operation is ~~usually~~ irreversible.

I also consent to such further operative measures as may be
found to be necessary at operation and to the administration
of a general, local or other anaesthetic.

No assurance has been given to me that the operation will be
performed by an particular surgeon.

Date 20/10/87   Signed J McLellan
                                       (Patient)

I confirm that I have explained to the patient the nature and
effect of this operation.

Date 20/10/87   Signed . . . . (illegible)
                               (Medical Practitioner)

Dr Gutteridge, a registrar, performed the operation and was satisfied that, after an initial difficulty, she had applied a Hulka clip to both tubes. Therefore she did not proceed to laparotomy. Nor did she offer the plaintiff a hysterosalpingogram. The operation was subsequently found to have been unsuccessful.

Held: (i)   although the plaintiff had no recollection that she was told that there was a small failure rate or that vasectomy had a better success rate, Dr Scott's note of these matters was clear and detailed. Moreover, although Dr Gutteridge had no recollection, she saw the plaintiff as was her invariable practice and made sure that she accepted that the procedure was irreversible and there was a failure rate of 1 in 200 and vasectomy had a smaller failure rate. The plaintiff's memory had failed her.

        (ii)   advising of irreversibility is different from advising of the risk of failure. The defendants were not liable for Dr Scott giving advice or signing the consent form with the word 'usually' deleted. Unlike the form used by the defendants in 1987, the modern consent form spells out the risk of possible failure. Dr Scott and Dr Gutteridge did the same in counselling the plaintiff.

(iii)   as Dr Gutteridge was genuinely and reasonably satisfied that the operation had been successful, there was no negligence in not offering a hysterosalpingogram. The defendants were not negligent in letting the plaintiff leave hospital with the impression she had undergone a successful sterilisation.

The plaintiff's claim was dismissed.

* The title of the Med LR report is *McLennan*, but the consent form refers to *McLellan*.

See pp 112, 128.

McLoughlin v Greenwich and Bexley Area Health Authority

Hospital administration: damages: fracture: femur: consent

McNeill J. (1984) 134 NLJ 383

The plaintiff (Mrs McLoughlin), aged 64, was a voluntary patient in a psychiatric hospital. She slipped on a wet patch of the ward floor.

She sustained a trochanteric fracture of the left femur, with bruising on the flank, and a Colles fracture of the right wrist. She underwent operative processes to repair her fractures, and the fracture of the left femur had to be dealt with by a pinning device. Her left leg was permanently shortened by nine centimetres and, even wearing a surgical boot, she was left with a severe limp. She relied on a tripod walking stick and a wheelchair for more than very short distances but had led a fairly immobile life out of preference before the accident. The left wrist had been her dominant wrist but had thickened and a 'dinner-fork' deformity had developed which slightly restricted movement so that, for example, she was unable to lift a teapot. No improvement was expected.

The plaintiff sued the health authority.

Held: general damages (July 1983) for pain, suffering and loss of amenities were assessed at £10,000.

See p 155.

Mahon v Osborne

Surgeon: operation: retained surgical product: nurse: fatal: res ipsa loquitur: ulcer

Court of Appeal. [1939] 2 KB 14

In March 1937 Thomas Mahon, a 24-year-old labourer, was operated on for a duodenal ulcer by Mr Osborne, resident surgeon at Park Hospital in Manchester. During the operation, swabs were used to pack off the adjacent areas in the patient's abdomen. At the end of the operation, Mr Osborne removed all the swabs of which he was aware. He asked the theatre sister whether the swab count was correct, and she told him that it was. He then sewed up the opening in Mr Mahon's body.

In June 1937 Mr Mahon again became acutely ill. A further operation became necessary. In the course of this a packing swab, left in at the first operation, was discovered lying just under the part of the liver which is close to the stomach. It had caused an abscess which led to Mr Mahon's death the next day.

His mother sued Mr Osborne and the theatre sister. The jury found that Mr Osborne had been negligent, but not the theatre sister.

Held: the trial judge had been wrong to direct the jury that there was a positive rule of English law, to be enforced in all abdominal operations, imposing on the surgeon a duty to search and make sure he has removed all the swabs. The issue was whether in all the circumstances of the operation the surgeon failed to exercise reasonable care with regard to the removal of packing swabs. A new trial was ordered.

Per Goddard LJ: 'I think it right to say that in my opinion the doctrine of *res ipsa loquitur* does apply in such a case as this, at least to the extent I mention below. The surgeon is in command of the operation, it is for him to decide what instruments, swabs and the like are to be used, and it is he who uses them. The patient, or, if he dies, his representatives, can know nothing about this matter. There can be no possible question but that neither swabs nor instruments are ordinarily left in the patient's body, and no one would venture to say that it is proper, although in particular circumstances it may be excusable, so to leave them. If, therefore, a swab is left in the patient's body, it seems to me clear that the surgeon is called on for an explanation, that is, he is called on to show not necessarily why he missed it but that he exercised due care to prevent it being left there.'

See pp 86, 125, 139.

Makino v Japanese Red Cross Society

Japan: cancer: risk disclosure: gall bladder: liver: fatal

High Court, Nagoya. (1990) Lancet 1309

In January 1983 Mrs Kazuko Makino, a 50-year-old nurse, was diagnosed as having cancer of the gall bladder. Deliberately disguising this from her, her doctor told her that her illness was due to gallstones. In the resultant belief that she was not seriously ill, Mrs Makino refused surgery and stopped visiting the hospital. By June 1983 the cancer had spread to her liver. She died in December 1983.

Four of her relatives sued the defendants in negligence, alleging that as she had not been told the true nature of her illness she had been unable to make an informed choice about surgery and follow-up.

Held: the defendants had not been negligent. Mrs Makino and her doctor did not share 'a relationship of mutual trust' that would have enabled him to disclose the true nature of her condition to her or to members of her family.

Malette v Shulman et al

Emergency: duty of care: consent: damages: blood transfusion: Canada: Jehovah's Witness

Ontario High Court of Justice. (1988) 47 DLR (4th) 18

On 30 June 1979 the plaintiff (Mrs Malette) was seriously injured in a road accident. She was taken to Kirkland District Hospital where she was treated by Dr Shulman. She showed signs of hypovolaemic shock, bled profusely and was becoming critically ill. As she was virtually unconscious and unable to speak, a nurse searched her purse and found a Jehovah's Witness card which (in an agreed English translation of the French) read as follows:

NO BLOOD TRANSFUSION!

As one of Jehovah's witnesses with firm religious convictions, I request that no blood or blood products be administered to me under any circumstances. I fully realise the implications of this position, but I have resolutely decided to obey the Bible command: Keep abstaining . . . from blood' (Acts 15: 28, 29). However, I have no religious objection to use the non-blood alternatives, such as Dextran, Haemacel, PVP, Ringer's Lactate or saline solution.

The contents of this card were communicated to Dr Shulman. When the plaintiff's condition deteriorated, he decided to administer blood and did so personally. When the plaintiff's daughter arrived, she objected to the administration of blood and expressed her conviction that the plaintiff wanted no blood. The daughter signed 'A Consent to Treatment and a Release of Liability Form' specifically prohibiting blood transfusions. Dr Shulman continued to administer them with a view to saving the plaintiff's life.

On 1 July the plaintiff was taken to Toronto General Hospital where the blood transfusions were discontinued. On 11 August she was discharged. She sued Dr Shulman, the hospital and four nurses for negligence and assault.

Held: (i)   there was no negligence in the diagnosis, and the treatment was carried out in a competent, careful and conscientious manner.

      (ii)   the card constituted a valid restriction of Dr Shulman's right to treat the plaintiff. The administration of blood by him constituted battery.

     (iii)   this was not a case for punitive damages. General damages payable by Dr Shulman for the plaintiff's mental distress were assessed at $20,000.

Per Donnelly J: 'A conscious, rational patient is entitled to refuse any medical treatment and the doctor must comply, no matter how ill advised he may believe that instruction to be.'

Note: Dr Shulman's subsequent appeal was dismissed by the Ontario Court of Appeal: [1991] 2 Med LR 162.

See p 7.

Mansouri v Bloomsbury Health Authority

Dismissal for want of prosecution: legal aid: counsel: solicitor

Court of Appeal. (1987) Times, 20 July

The plaintiff (Mrs Mina Mansouri) claimed damages for negligent medical treatment by Bloomsbury Health Authority in June 1979. In June 1982 she instructed solicitors, Duke-Cohan & Co, and a writ was issued. The writ was served in June 1983 and the Statement of Claim in July 1983. In August 1983 she was granted a legal aid certificate 'limited to preparation of papers for counsel and obtaining counsel's opinion upon merits and quantum after a conference which the assisted person should attend'.

She attended a conference with counsel, J Singh, in March 1984. He then left for India and in June 1984 the papers were transferred to his colleague Miss N Mathew. She wanted a further medical report which was received in February 1985 and sent to her. In March 1985 the defendant's solicitors decided to apply to strike out the action. Miss Mathew's opinion was received in May 1985 and sent to the Law Society in June 1985 when the limitation on the legal aid certificate was removed.

In July 1985 Master Waldman struck out the plaintiff's action for want of prosecution.

Held: it was well established that if there was a delay before the issue of the writ, it was all the more incumbent on the plaintiff's legal advisers to bring the action to trial speedily. It was not satisfactory for the solicitors simply to send chasers to counsel once a month. A situation in which counsel's opinion was received only in May 1985 constituted inordinate delay. The Master's order was correct.

See p 203.

Marchant v East Ham Borough Council and Another

Injection: needle breaking: causation: leg

Pearson J. (1955) 2 Lancet 973

The plaintiff, a 15-year-old schoolgirl, developed a blister on her heel which became septic. She went to a hospital clinic where a doctor advised an injection of penicillin. She was told to sit. While the nurse was giving her an intramuscular injection, using a No 16 needle, the plaintiff made a sudden movement. The needle broke and remained embedded in her thigh. The needle was 30/32 of an inch long and broke 1/32 of an inch from the mount.

The plaintiff was left with a three and a half inch scar on the thigh. She sued the hospital authority and the nurse.

Held: if a longer and thicker needle had been used, it would have caused more pain and thereby have been more likely to cause a convulsive reaction. It was not proved that the needle had been pushed in too far; the accident was due to an unexpected movement on the plaintiff's part. It would not be right to use a thicker needle and inflict extra pain on all patients to meet the possible contingency that one of them might flinch as this girl had. The nurse had not been negligent.

Judgment for the defendants.

See p 119.

Markham v Abrahams

Optician: representation: diagnosis: ophthalmic

Lord Chief Justice (with special jury). [1911] 1 BMJ 703

In 1907 the plaintiff (Miss Markham) was having trouble with her eyes and suffering from pain, dizziness and difficulty in reading. She went to the shop of Mr Thomas who practised in Manchester under the style of Wood Abrahams, describing himself as an 'eyesight and spectacle specialist' and a 'qualified optician'. One of his assistants prescribed spectacles. As these were unsatisfactory, the plaintiff returned more than once and in 1909 saw Mr Thomas. Later that year she consulted an ophthalmic surgeon who found that she was suffering from conical cornea of long standing.

She sued Mr Thomas, alleging that if he had exercised reasonable care and been possessed of sufficient skill he should have seen that it was a case of disease and not one of ordinary short sight. For Mr Thomas it was contended that he did not profess to be a person able to diagnose and cure diseases of the eye, but was simply a maker and seller of spectacles.

Held: the Lord Chief Justice told the jury that the plaintiff admitted she had not been influenced by Mr Thomas' description of himself as an eyesight specialist and that she knew an optician was not an oculist. Conical cornea was very rare. Could they say, in view of the fact that opticians carried on a well-known trade, that they were under any obligation to discover disease? He directed the jury that, to find in favour of the plaintiff, they must be satisfied that the defendant had been negligent as an optician, or had taken on himself and had not performed duties outside those of an optician.

The jury returned a verdict for the plaintiff.

See pp 47, 140.

Marram v North Tees Health Authority

Damages: hysterectomy: fistula

HH Judge Fox. [1992] CLY1665

In 1986 the plaintiff (Mrs Marram), aged 26, underwent a total hysterectomy with removal of the left cystic ovary. Seven days later she suffered a vesico-vaginal fistula. She was discharged home, apparently voiding satisfactorily, but immediately became incontinent of urine.

A catheter was inserted, but failed to control the leak satisfactorily. She underwent a cystoscopy, and it was decided that the catheter should remain in place for three months before surgical repair was attempted. She suffered pain associated with the urethral catheter. She underwent a further cystoscopy five weeks later and a suprapubic catheter was inserted. She was cystoscoped again before surgical closure of the fistula four and a half months after the fistula developed.

Whilst waiting for the surgical repair, full continence was not achieved with the catheters so she needed to wear pads. She also suffered problems from smell and excoriation of the vulva. This was embarrassing and upsetting, and she could not lead a normal life. Subsequent stress, incontinence and symptoms of frequency and urgency of micturition were not related to the fistula and subsequent operations.

Held (March 1992): the plaintiff was awarded £3,000 general damages for pain, suffering and loss of amenities. Special damages of £2,000 brought the total award up to £5,000.

Marsden v Bateman and Others

Brain damage: causation: childbirth: damages: general practitioner

Rose J. [1993] 4 Med LR 181

Ruth Marsden was born at home at 2.00pm on 20 April 1976 after a short period of labour. Dr Bateman, the family general practitioner, arrived immediately before delivery. At birth the baby was very pale and did not cry and, as to breathing, gave the odd gasp. She was obviously very poorly. Dr Bateman carried out mouth to mouth resuscitation for 20 minutes. The Apgar score recorded at the time by midwives was only four. After Dr Bateman and the midwives had left, Mrs Marsden noticed that her baby's breathing was accompanied by a grunting noise.

On 21 April she rang for Dr Bateman who called and looked at Ruth but did not undress her. She was still very pale, and her breathing was still very noisy. Dr Bateman thought that this might be due to damage to the throat while sucking out. When the pupil midwife attended later that day, Mrs Marsden told her that the baby was very slow to feed and not inclined to suck. Ruth's condition remained much the same during 22 April; she continued to breathe noisily and rapidly.

On 23 April a different midwife came and was immediately concerned about the breathing. A consultant paediatrician was called and came in the afternoon. He immediately rang for an ambulance and incubator. When he examined the baby, there was swelling all over the back from the shoulders to the buttocks. Ruth was taken to Maelor General Hospital, Wrexham, where four Dextrostix (blood sugar) readings of 45 mg/100ml were taken.

Ruth was thought to be suffering from hypoglycaemia. She was gravely mentally handicapped. Her father sued on her behalf Dr Bateman and the health authority that employed the midwives. They admitted negligence in failing to arrange for her prompt admission to hospital after her birth. The issue at trial was whether hypoglycaemia (low blood sugar) was the cause of Ruth's disabilities.

Held: (i)   there was no evidence that the baby ever went into a coma or suffered convulsions or had apnoea at any time. There was nothing in the expert evidence or the literature to show that, in the absence of coma, convulsions or apnoea, significant brain damage is capable of resulting from hypoglycaemia.

        (ii)   the four Dextrostix readings showed that Ruth was not hypoglycaemic in hospital. In conjunction with the other evidence about feeding and weight, they were inconsistent with there having been dangerously low blood sugar levels in the 24 hours following birth. They showed a stable, low normal blood sugar level from the early hours of 24 April. That was unlikely to have been achieved by a baby who three days or so before was so deprived of blood sugar that grave brain damage had been sustained.

        (iii)   Ruth's condition now was inconsistent with the type of damage to be accepted as a result of hypoglycaemia. There were no signs of spasticity from damage to the pyramidal tracts or involuntary movements from damage to the extra-pyramidal tracts.

        (iv)   the probability was that Ruth had a genetic disorder. The damage to the genes most probably occurred during the brain development stage of cell migration during the third to fifth month of gestation. Serious neonatal damage solely due to hypoglycaemia was very rare.

        (v)   the defendants' negligence did not cause Ruth's brain damage. This probably occurred during gestation, not after birth.

        (vi)   however if Ruth had been admitted to hospital immediately after the birth her scleroedema would have been avoided. There were no long term sequelae of this condition. £750 should be awarded for it.

See p 136.

Marshall v County Council of the Parts of Lindsey, Lincolnshire

Hospital administration: infection: tests: warning: vicarious liability: fever

House of Lords. [1937] AC 97

On 4 July 1933 Mrs Franklin, a patient at Cleethorpes Maternity Home, developed a high temperature and was taken to Grimsby General Hospital. On her removal, the ward in which she had been lying and the nurses who had been in contact with her were disinfected. The hospital diagnosed puerperal fever. On 5 July this diagnosis was communicated to the matron of the home and to Dr Stott, its medical superintendent. The normal precaution of taking swabs from the throats of all persons who had been in contact with Mrs Franklin, in order to ascertain whether any such person was a carrier, was not taken.

On 12 July the plaintiff (Mrs Mary Marshall) was admitted to the home. Neither she nor her husband was told about Mrs Franklin's case. On 13 July the plaintiff's child was born. On 17 July she herself suffered a very severe attack of puerperal fever. She sued the county council responsible for the nursing home.

Held: (i)   there was ample evidence to support the jury in finding that the nursing home was in breach of duty in admitting the plaintiff without ascertaining whether or not there was a carrier in the staff by taking swabs from all the nurses who had been in contact with Mrs Franklin, and that as the plaintiff had been admitted before this was ascertained, she or her husband or her doctor ought to have been informed of the facts in order to decide whether to enter the home and under what precautions.

            (ii)   the defendants were responsible for Dr Stott's negligence; it was no excuse in law for them to say they were misled by his advice.

See pp 21, 24, 131.

Marshall v Curry

Operation: consent: emergency: assault: interests of patient: Canada: hernia: testicle

Nova Scotia Supreme Court. [1933] 3 DLR 260

In 1929 the plaintiff (Mr Marshall), a master mariner, sent for Dr Curry. It was agreed that Dr Curry would perform an operation to remove a hernia in his left groin. When Dr Curry opened the inguinal canal, the plaintiff's left testicle appeared and was found grossly diseased. Dr Curry deemed it necessary to remove the testicle, not only to cure the hernia but also because if not removed the testicle might have become gangrenous and caused blood poisoning.

Dr Curry told the plaintiff of the removal of the testicle one or two days after the operation. The plaintiff sued him for negligence and assault.

Held: (i)   Dr Curry had performed the operation skilfully. The condition of the testicle could not reasonably have been anticipated before the operation. He had not been negligent.

            (ii)   where a great emergency that could not be anticipated arises, it is better to put consent altogether out of the case and to rule that it is the surgeon's duty to act in order to save the life or preserve the health of the patient. Despite the absence of express and possibly of implied consent on the plaintiff's part, Dr Curry had acted in the interest of his patient for the protection of his health and possibly his life. The removal was in that sense necessary. Dr Curry was not guilty of assault.

See p 16.

Matthews v Waltham Forest Health Authority

Brain damage: causation: childbirth: quadriplegia: caesarean

Pill J. 16 January 1991

On 9 June 1983 Mrs Matthews was admitted to Whipps Cross Hospital with spontaneous rupture of the membranes. There was a 'type 2 dip' as early as 8.55am on 10 June. The trace during the period from 3.45pm to 4.15pm indicated an impairment of blood supply to the cerebral cells. The note at 4.25pm read: 'Had one type 2 dip. Heart rate – 60 per 1½ minutes.' At about 6.53pm the heart beat rate dropped again to 60 and stayed at a level of 60 to 80 thereafter. Mrs Matthews was taken to theatre for emergency section at 7.20pm. Her son Oliver was born at 7.22pm. Though a full term baby, he weighed about 5 lbs, 6oz.

He was severely ill at birth. His Apgar score at one minute was three; he was resuscitated; Apgar at five minutes improved to five and at ten minutes to seven. A neurologically abnormal baby, he suffered from encephalopathy. Symptoms included seizures, abnormalities of muscle tone, irritability, floppiness, cycling movements of the arms and legs. He had cerebral palsy involving spastic quadriplegia with athetoid features.

Through his next friend, he sued the defendant hospital authority which accepted that the decision to deliver by caesarean section should have been taken by 4.25pm. The defendants accepted that there was considerable birth asphyxia after this time, but denied that it was the cause of the plaintiff's cerebral palsy.

Held: (i)   he suffered severe birth asphyxia. This was very severe indeed during the last period: the final anoxic insult.

   (ii)   it was common ground that he suffered a moderate degree of encephalopathy as a result of that birth asphyxia.

   (iii)   more congenital abnormalities, such as an accessory left nipple and an anomaly in hair patterning, did not reflect abnormalities in early brain development

   (iv)   on the balance of probabilities, the plaintiff's cerebral palsy was caused by the prolonged and severe birth asphyxia and was not predetermined. The palsy took the form of spastic quadriplegia which was most likely to result when birth asphyxia was the cause. Intelligence was unimpaired, whereas it is usually impaired where there is a predetermined cause.

The plaintiff was awarded agreed damages of £650,000.

See pp 69, 126.

Maynard v West Midlands Regional Health Authority

Tuberculosis: diagnosis: operation: standard of care

House of Lords. [1985] 1 All ER 635, [1984] 1 WLR 634

The plaintiff (Blondell Maynard), a West Indian lady, was treated at East Birmingham Hospital in 1970 by Dr Ross, a consultant physician, and Mr Stephenson, a consultant surgeon. They recognized that tuberculosis was the most likely diagnosis. But in their opinion there was an unusual factor, viz, swollen glands in the mediastinum unaccompanied by any evidence of lesion in the lungs, which meant that Hodgkin's disease was a possible danger. They therefore decided that she should undergo the diagnostic operation of mediastinoscopy. During the course of this the plaintiff's left laryngeal recurrent nerve was damaged, with resulting paralysis of the left vocal cord.

The plaintiff sued the hospital authority. No negligence in the performance of the operation was alleged. Her case was that the diagnosis of tuberculosis should have been so clear that the consultants were guilty of an error of judgement amounting to negligence in requiring the operation to be undertaken.

Held: the Court of Appeal had been right to reverse the trial judge's finding of negligence.

Per Lord Scarman: 'A case which is based on an allegation that a fully considered decision of two consultants in the field of their special skill was negligent clearly presents certain difficulties of proof. It is not enough to show that there is a body of competent professional opinion which considers theirs as a wrong decision, if there also exists a body of professional opinion, equally competent, which supports the decision as reasonable in the circumstances. It is not enough to show that subsequent events show that the operation need never have been performed, if at the time the decision to operate was taken it was reasonable in the sense that a responsible body of medical opinion would have accepted it as proper. I do not think that the words of Lord President (Clyde) in *Hunter* v *Hanley* 1955 SLT 213 at p 217 can be bettered:

In the realm of diagnosis and treatment there is ample scope for genuine difference of opinion and one man is not negligent merely because his conclusion differs from that of other medical men ... The true test for establishing negligence in diagnosis or treatment on the part of a doctor is whether he has been proved to be guilty of such failure as no doctor of ordinary skill would be guilty of if acting with ordinary care ...

I would only add that a doctor who professes to exercise a special skill must exercise the ordinary skill of his speciality. Differences of opinion and practice exist, and will always exist, in the medical as in other professions. There is seldom any one answer exclusive of all others to problems of professional judgement. A court may prefer one body of opinion to the other, but that is no basis for a conclusion of negligence.

... I have to say that a judge's "preference" for one body of distinguished professional opinion to another also professionally distinguished is not sufficient to establish negligence in a practitioner whose actions have received the seal of approval of those whose opinions, truthfully expressed, honestly held, were not preferred. If this was the real reason for the judge's finding, he erred in law even though elsewhere in his judgment he stated the law correctly. For in the realm of diagnosis and treatment, negligence is not established by preferring one respectable body of professional opinion to another. Failure to exercise the ordinary skill of a doctor (in the appropriate speciality, if he be a specialist) is necessary.'

See pp 57, 60, 64, 96.

Michael v Molesworth

Surgeon: breach of contract: trespass to person: damages: hernia

Singleton LJ. [1950] 2 BMJ 171

The plaintiff (Mr Michael) suffered from a hernia. He consulted Mr Molesworth, senior surgeon at the Royal Victoria Hospital, Folkestone. Mr Molesworth told the plaintiff that his minimum fee for a privately performed operation would be 25 guineas but that there were no private wards in Folkestone. He sought to make it clear to the plaintiff that he would be in a public ward in the Folkestone Hospital, and he did not undertake to carry out the operation personally.

On 23 March 1948, the operation was performed, with complete success, by the house surgeon, Mr Ribet. When the plaintiff discovered that Mr Ribet had operated, he sued Mr

Molesworth for breach of an alleged oral agreement to operate and for procuring a trespass upon him by Mr Ribet. He testified that he had been shocked that an apprentice had practised his skill on him without his consent when he had engaged a craftsman.

Held: (i)   there had been no breach of contract by Mr Molesworth. He had not agreed to carry out the operation himself, and he probably did not realise that the plaintiff expected him to do so.

         (ii)   Mr Ribet had operated without consent. The wording of the form that the plaintiff had signed did not debar him from bringing an action. There had been a technical trespass for which the plaintiff was awarded nominal damages of £1.

Note: Most modern consent forms state that no assurance has been given to the patient that the operation will be performed by any particular practitioner.

Miles v Wolverhampton Health Authority

Brain damage: childbirth: damages

Tucker J. *Halsbury's Laws Annual Abridgment* 1994, para 943

The plaintiff suffered serious brain damage at birth. This caused him to become severely handicapped and disabled. The defendant hospital authority admitted liability.

By the hearing 14 years later, damages were agreed under every head except for future loss of earnings. The plaintiff's case was that but for his disability, he would have gone into his father's profitable travel business. The defendants argued that it was impossible to predict how a child would see his future.

Held: (i)   the issue was not whether the plaintiff proved on a balance of probabilities that he would have gone into his father's business. The correct approach was to establish whether there was a significant chance that he would have joined the business or whether that chance was so speculative as to be disregarded.

         (ii)   in the present case, there was a 50% chance that he would have gone into his father's business so there should be a corresponding discount to reflect the chance that he might not have done so. It would be wrong to assume that the business would continue to generate the high profits that it had done in the past, so in assessing the plaintiff's likely amount of remuneration some reduction would be made for future uncertainties.

Mitchell v Hounslow and Spelthorne Health Authority

Childbirth: nurses: causation: brain damage: umbilical cord

Kenneth Jones J. (1984) 1 Lancet 579

In March 1979 Mrs Mitchell, expecting her first baby, was admitted to hospital in labour. After the admission procedure, she was given an enema and shown to the toilet. No one showed her the emergency bell. While she was there, the membranes ruptured and the umbilical cord prolapsed and emerged beyond the introitus.

She called out for help, but there was no one in the adjoining admission room. It was some minutes before she was found by her husband and another nurse. No pressure was applied, no warm saline gauze was wrapped round the protruding cord, and no other first-aid treatment was carried out until she reached the operating theatre. A caesarian section was performed, and a girl was born.

The infant plaintiff suffered spastic cerebral palsy caused by birth anoxia due to compression of the umbilical cord. She sued the health authority for failing to provide proper care after prolapse of the cord. The expert evidence was that if pressure had been applied to the foetus there was a sixty per cent chance that brain damage would have been avoided. All the specialists agreed that once the prolapse was discovered, first-aid treatment should have been given.

Held: the failure to apply pressure for about ten minutes constituted a failure of what should have been normal standard practice in the circumstances by a competent midwife. The hospital authority was liable for that negligence which was the probable cause of the plaintiff's condition.

See pp 78, 126.

Mitchell v Liverpool Area Health Authority (Teaching)

Arm: damages: amputation: child patient

Court of Appeal. CAT, 13 June 1985

The plaintiff (Anthony Mitchell) was born in August 1981. When one month old, he sustained damage to the circulation of his right arm. The defendants admitted liability.

The plaintiff's right arm had to be amputated at elbow level. Consequently he would be barred from certain manual and industrial trades requiring bi-manual digital skills, such as plumbing, and some types of intricate bench or assembly work. Occupations requiring work on ladders or scaffolding would be unsuitable. However, it seemed he would have very good power in his left hand and many jobs would be open to him.

In November 1984 the trial judge (Russell J) awarded him £30,000 general damages for pain, suffering and loss of amenities, but refused to add anything in relation to future loss of earnings or diminished potential in the labour market.

Held: (i) the court would not interfere with the award of £30,000 general damages for pain, suffering and loss of amenities, although it was very much at the top end of the range.

(ii) the judge had been in error in declining to make any award in respect of future financial loss. There was a real risk that the plaintiff would not be able to earn as much as if he had no disability. It was impossible to compute this arithmetically. After substantially discounting for acceleration, an award of £5,000 was appropriate under this head.

See pp 155, 160.

Mitchell v McDonald et al

Canada: informed consent: injection: res ipsa loquitur: shoulder

Alberta Court of Queen's Bench, Matheson J. (1987) 40 CCLT 266.

In September 1984 the plaintiff (Mrs Mitchell), a smoker in her early fifties, attended the Morinville Clinic of Dr McDonald, a general practitioner. She told him that her right shoulder was painful. Earlier conservative treatment having failed, he recommended a cortisone injection and she agreed to it: 'I thought he knew what he was doing.' He used a 22-gauge needle between one and a quarter and one and a half inches in length, to inject a mixture of cortisone and xylocane into her right rhomboid muscle. She exclaimed 'for God's sake, stop', but he completed the injection which took 30–60 seconds. Her right lung had been pierced, and she suffered a right side pneumothorax (collapsed lung).

She sued him, relying on the maxim res ipsa loquitur, and also pleading an absence of informed consent. Expert evidence was given that a two inch depth of muscle could be reasonably expected at the point of penetration, but that the defendant probably got in a little bit too deep – 'It was not a perfect shot'.

Held: (i) with regard to the suggestion that the plaintiff's consent might have been withdrawn by her exclamation, 'for God's sake, stop,' such a cry could well have been interpreted to mean, 'My God, stop hurting me'. Moreover the damage had already been done before her cry; the delivery of the cortisone into the rhomboid muscle, after the initial lung entry, did not contribute to the plaintiff's pneumothorax.

(ii) the doctrine of res ipsa loquitur did not apply. There was no mystery as to why the pneumothorax occurred. It did so when the needle entered the lung, because it hit a bleb or blister in the plaintiff's lung which had been caused by her smoking-induced emphysema.

(iii) the defendant was competent in performing the injection. He could have expected about two inches of muscle depth. He had used the proper 22-gauge needle and had only gone in about one inch. The probability of the lung puncture ensuing was utterly remote.

The plaintiff's claim was dismissed.

See pp 105, 121.

Moore v Lewisham Group Hospital Management Committee

Anaesthetics: consultant: spinal

Barry J. (1959) Times, 5 February

In January 1956 the plaintiff (Mrs Flora Moore) was a healthy and active woman aged 68 but for some 15 months she had been suffering from bouts of pain in the upper abdomen. She was admitted to Lewisham Hospital for a cholecystectomy operation. Dr Piney, the consultant anaesthetist, decided upon spinal anaesthesia supplemented by a light general anaesthetic. The next morning it was discovered that her left leg was paralysed and there was, for a time, acute urinary trouble. She made some improvement, but no further progress was expected.

The plaintiff sued the hospital authority for negligence. No criticism was made of the manner in which the anaesthetic was administered. Her case was that, owing to the known risk of permanent neurological damage, a spinal anaesthetic should not have been used for her operation. Some highly informed medical practitioners held the view that the risks involved in the use of spinal anaesthesia could never be justified; others justified its use for certain operations but not for those such as removal of the gall bladder; and there were yet others who denied the possibility of neurological damage in the absence of some contamination of the drug used.

Held: it was impossible to find that Dr Piney's decision to use spinal anaesthesia was negligent. It was one which could have been made by a competent and properly informed anaesthetist exercising a proper degree of skill and care.

See p 64.

Moore v Worthing District Health Authority

Operation: res ipsa loquitur: aural: consultant

Owen J. [1992] 3 Med LR 431

In January 1985 the plaintiff (Ronald Moore) underwent a left mastoidectomy at the defendants' hospital. The operation lasted about two hours. The consultant surgeon was Mr Topham, and the consultant anaesthetist was Dr Van Ryssen. In the course of the operation, the plaintiff suffered bilateral ulnar nerve lesions. EMG tests carried out between August 1985 and July 1989 showed that he was suffering from a polyneuropathy. The plaintiff sued the hospital authority and sought to rely on the maxim res ipsa loquitur.

It was common ground that there is a risk of damage to the ulnar nerve, if the lower part of the back of the upper arm is allowed to rest on a hard object for a long time. It was further agreed that the defendants had a duty to protect the ulnar nerve by wrapping it, or otherwise protecting it by material which would serve to absorb and disperse pressure from the weight of the arm and to protect the arm from other pressure.

Held:

    (i)   protection was afforded in the normal way to the plaintiff's elbows and upper arms by the insertion of pads beneath the elbows and on top of the plastic arm rests. The pads were properly positioned, cradling the arm above the elbow and protecting it from the uprights of the arm rest.

   (ii)   although criticised by the plaintiff's expert as too hard, the Eschmann pads in question were manufactured for this very purpose and were in very wide use. The defendants were not negligent in using these pads.

  (iii)   the plaintiff suffered from a polyneuropathy from before the operation. The cause of his bilateral ulnar lesions was his resultant susceptibility to injury.

  (iv)   res ipsa loquitur did not apply, in view of the evidence given by the surgeon and anaesthetist. Moreover the defendants had shown a way in which the injury occurred without negligence.

   (v)   there was no negligence of any kind on the part of Mr Topham, Dr Van Ryssen or any other member of the operating team.

See p 89.

Morgan v Gwent Health Authority

Diagnosis: blood transfusion: damages

Court of Appeal. CAT, 8 December 1987. (1988) 2 Lancet 519

The plaintiff (Caroline Morgan) was born in 1958. She did not know that her blood group was rhesus negative. In 1978 she underwent a small nasal operation at St Lawrence Hospital, Chepstow. She was given a transfusion of rhesus positive blood. The hospital authority admitted liability, since the hospital had negligently failed to ascertain what her blood group was.

The incompatibility produced a sensitivity to the rhesus antigen which could create very serious complications in pregnancy to the foetus, though not to the mother. The chances that any future husband would be compatible in the sense that no problem could arise was 17%; that any foetus would be rhesus positive (the foetus having rhesus positive blood causes the problem) was 59%; that the child would be severely affected was 20%.

Treatment of the child could avoid the consequences of stillbirth or serious disability in most cases, at the cost of her submitting to very tiring treatment during pregnancy.

The plaintiff discovered what had happened in 1980 when she had an abortion. In 1981 she became engaged, but in 1982 tests showed that there would be complications if any child was conceived by her fiancé, and in 1984 the engagement was broken off. Her choice of husband and thus her chances of marriage were restricted. She wanted a family and felt anxiety which would become acute during a pregnancy.

In November 1986 the trial judge (Boreham J) awarded her £8,000 general damages.

Held: the award should be increased to £20,000. The judge was mistaken in not holding that the negligent transfusion had been a major cause of the break-up of her engagement. A major factor was the reasonable anxiety which she would have to face about prospects of marriage, about prospects of telling the man concerned of her condition, and about problems of her reduced ability to bear a healthy child by a father not himself a rhesus negative.

See pp 133, 157.

Morris v Winsbury-White

Surgeon: retained surgical product: breach of contract: res ipsa loquitur: prostate

Tucker J. [1937] 4 All ER 494

In November 1933 the plaintiff (Arthur Morris) consulted Mr Winsbury-White, a surgeon specialising in genito-urinary diseases, who diagnosed prostate trouble. Mr Winsbury-White agreed to give the case his personal attention, and the plaintiff entered St Paul's Hospital. On 27 November there was performed the usual preliminary operation, which consisted of draining off the bladder, and on 18 December Mr Winsbury-White performed the main operation. The plaintiff remained in hospital until 10 February 1934.

He visited Mr Winsbury-White there on 28 March and 11 April when, as a result of an x-ray, Mr Winsbury-White performed an operation and found that a major part of a tube had been left in the bladder and a small portion in the perineum. The plaintiff continued to suffer great discomfort from periodical leaking. He sued Mr Winsbury-White for breach of contract and negligence.

Held: (i) the medical officers and nursing staff are not the agents of a specialist surgeon who comes in and performs an operation, in so far as they are performing their ordinary hospital duties.

(ii) the tube must have got in between 27 November and 10 February while the plaintiff was being dealt with and treated at the hospital by numerous nurses and sisters and two resident medical officers and being visited occasionally by Mr Winsbury-White. The doctrine of *res ipsa loquitur* was inapplicable to the facts of the case.

(iii) the agreement to give the case his personal attention did not place any additional material duty on Mr Winsbury-White who had carried out his obligations under the contract and was not guilty of negligence.

See pp 28, 29, 86, 125.

Mose v North West Hertfordshire Health Authority

Consultant: surgeon: operation: standard of care: knee

Court of Appeal. CAT, 26 November 1987

The plaintiff (Garrie Mose) was born in March 1976. In 1978 his parents noticed a lump behind his right knee. It increased in size. He was examined by Mr Hirschowitz, a consultant orthopaedic surgeon, at West Hertfordshire Hospital, who reasonably concluded that it was probably a cyst.

On 8 September 1980 Mr Hirschowitz performed an operation to excise the lump. In the process, he found that it was not a cyst but was either a schwannoma or a neurofibroma. He proceeded to remove it but in doing so also removed three inches of the lateral popliteal nerve. The plaintiff suffered a 'complete foot drop'.

He sued the hospital authority. The expert evidence at trial was that when a surgeon inexperienced in work on peripheral nerves comes inadvertently on a nerve expanded by a tumour, or apparently connected inextricably with a tumour, he or she should ideally restrict the procedure to a small biopsy or should close the wound without further action, and that the patient should then be sent to a surgeon experienced in work on peripheral nerves. Mr Hirschowitz testified that he operated on peripheral nerve lesions about once a week, although he had only occasionally treated a peripheral nerve tumour. The trial judge (Mr Anthony Hidden QC) held that he had been negligent in proceeding to remove the tumour which was found to be a plexiform neurofibroma.

Held: the central flaw in the judge's reasoning was that, contrary to what he thought, the description 'a surgeon inexperienced in work on peripheral nerves' did not apply to Mr Hirschowitz. The finding of negligence could not be justified.

See p 115.

Moser v Enfield and Haringey Area Health Authority

Operation: quadriplegia: damages: brain damage

Michael Davies J. (1982) 133 NLJ 105

In October 1976 the plaintiff (Robert Moser), then aged four, entered hospital for a minor operation. It went wrong and he was deprived of oxygen, thereby suffering irreversible brain damage. From being a bright child, he became severely mentally subnormal and was unlikely to have any insight into his condition. He also became quadriplegic and quite unable to look after himself. His life expectancy was a further twenty years to the age of thirty.

He sued the health authority who admitted liability.

Held (November 1982):   the plaintiff was awarded:

    (i)   general damages of £35,000 for pain, suffering and loss of amenities.

    (ii) £132,000 for future nursing care, based on a multiplicand of £12,000 and a multiplier of 11, and on the basis of his being indefinitely cared for at home, not in an institution.

    (iii) £21,480 for loss of earnings, based on a multiplicand of £5,370 and a multiplier of 4.

(iv)   £10,098 for equipment, based on a multiplicand of £918 and a multiplier of 11.

(v)   £13,750 for private physiotherapy: £1,250 × 11.

(vi)   £25,000 for the cost of having his house altered or of moving to a bungalow suitable for his long-term care.

(vii)   other items which resulted in a total award of £273,958 plus Court of Protection charges.

See pp 122, 155, 158, 160.

Mulla v Blackburn, Hyndburn and Ribble Valley Health Authority

After-care: damages: fractures: arm: child patient

District Judge Haythornwaite. [1992] CLY 1683

In August 1986 the plaintiff, aged five, sustained a supracondylar fracture of his left arm immediately above the elbow joint. He was admitted to the defendants' hospital. Their staff manipulated the fracture, but failed to take proper care thereafter and failed to observe the fracture subsequently slip.

As a result of that negligence, the plaintiff was required to undergo in June 1987 a further operation to correct the deformity of his elbow. His arm was put in plaster; later he underwent physiotherapy. In March 1988 the staple used to fix the bones was removed.

The plaintiff was left with a persisting, obvious, ugly 'gunstock' deformity of his left elbow with a four inch scar on the outer aspect. Movements of his elbow were restricted, and he was handicapped on the use of his arm. A further osteotomy operation was scheduled to be carried out in his elbow in his mid to late teens in an endeavour to remove the cosmetic deformity. It was unlikely that there would be any improvement in the functional disability.

Held (September 1991):   (i)   general damages of £12,500 were awarded for pain, suffering and loss of amenities.

(ii)   £3,500 was awarded for handicap on the future labour market, plus £2,400 for the cost of the future operation.

See p 155.

Mulloy v Hop Sang

Breach of contract: Canada: trespass to person: causation: damages: amputation

Alberta Supreme court, Appellate Division. [1935] 1 WWR 714

The defendant (Mr Hop Sang), who was Chinese, was badly injured in a car accident. It occurred near Cardston, and he was taken to hospital there. The plaintiff (Mr Mulloy), a physician and surgeon, was called to the hospital and saw the defendant who asked him to fix up his hand but not to cut it off as he wanted to have it looked after in his home city of Lethbridge. Later on, in the operating room, the defendant repeated his request that he did not want his hand cut off. The plaintiff, being more concerned in relieving the patient's suffering, replied that he would be governed by the conditions found when the anaesthetic had been administered. The defendant did not reply. As his hand was covered by an old piece of cloth, and it was necessary to administer an anaesthetic before doing anything, the plaintiff was not in a position to advise what should be done. On examination, he decided that an operation was necessary and the hand was amputated. The wounds indicated an operation, as the condition of the hand was such that delay would have meant blood poisoning with no possibility of saving it.

The plaintiff sued for his professional fees. The defendant counterclaimed for damages for trespass to the person, including $150 for an artificial hand.

Held: (i) the plaintiff disregarded the defendant's instructions which went to the root of the employment. He did not do the work he was hired to do, and he was not entitled to his professional fees.

(ii) the defendant was entitled to damages for trespass to the person.

(iii) however the operation was both necessary and ably performed. The damage and loss and cost of an artificial hand were the results of the accident, not the unauthorised operation. The defendant must have been shocked when he discovered the loss of his hand. His damages should be just sufficient to make them substantial rather than minimal. $50 was appropriate.

Per Jackson DCJ: 'I am, however, not satisfied that the defendant could not have been rushed to Lethbridge where he evidently wished to consult with a physician whom he knew and relied on. Dr Mulloy took it for granted when the defendant, a Chinaman without much education in English and probably not of any more than average mentality, did not reply or make any objection to his statement that he would be governed by conditions as he found them, that he had full power to go ahead and perform an operation if found necessary. On the other hand, the defendant did not, in my opinion, understand what the doctor meant, and he would most likely have refused to allow the operation if he did. Further, he did not consider it necessary to reply as he had already given explicit instructions.

Under these circumstances I think the plaintiff should have made full explanation and should have endeavoured to get the defendant to consent to an operation, if necessary.'

See pp 8, 103.

Munro v Oxford United Hospitals and Another

Operation: surgeon: teeth: tonsillectomy: child patient

Oxford County Court. [1958] 1 BMJ 167

When the plaintiff (Sheila Munro), then aged seven, was undergoing a tonsillectomy, the gag slipped. The surgeon was taken by surprise, and four of her front teeth were knocked out. Two of the teeth were second teeth, and as a result of their loss she had to wear a denture.

The plaintiff sued the surgeon and the hospital authority. Expert evidence was given that it was a matter of no difficulty to check and correct slipping of a gag.

Held: the defendants were liable. The operation was a normal one without complications, and it was a normal part of the surgeon's duty to prevent the gag from slipping. The only reasonable inference was that the surgeon had shown a lack of attention and alertness which fell short of the standard of care which it was reasonable to expect in the circumstances, and that the force required to dislodge the teeth had come from the surgeon's hands.

See p 117.

Murray v Kensington and Chelsea and Westminster Area Health Authority and Another

Childbirth: registrar: blindness: causation: premature baby

Court of Appeal. CAT, 11 May 1981

On Saturday 4 January 1975 the plaintiff (Robert Murray) was born in Westminster Hospital. He was a tiny baby, born prematurely after 28 weeks, and weighed two and a half pounds. He was placed in an incubator. In the evening the house doctor, Dr Murfitt, increased the oxygen in the incubator from 21% to 30%. When a registrar took over on the morning of Monday 6 January, the extra oxygen was discontinued.

On 7 January the baby became very poorly, suffering breathlessness and other symptoms. For the next three to four weeks, the oxygen content in the incubator was maintained at between 30 and 40%, and sometimes 100% oxygen was administered for short periods. The baby was kept alive, but it was later discovered that all the extra oxygen had left him totally blind.

His next friend sued the hospital authority. The trial judge (May J) found negligence proved but not causation.

Held: (i) as the baby did not initially suffer from breathing difficulties, it was negligent to subject him to an oxygen-enriched atmosphere for the first 36 hours; and harm from this was reasonably foreseeable. There was no subsequent negligence.

(ii) the trial judge was justified in concluding that the plaintiff had not discharged the onus of proving that this initial excess oxygen had materially contributed to his blindness.

See pp 72, 117.

Nash & Others v Eli Lilly & Co and Others

Limitation: drugs: Opren

Court of Appeal. [1993] 1 WLR 782, [1992] 3 Med LR 353, (1992) Times, 7 October

A non-steroidal anti-inflammatory drug, Benoxaprofen, was manufactured by Eli Lilly to relieve the pain caused by arthritis. In March 1980 it was licensed for use in the United Kingdom under the name Opren. Initially it was only available for use by consultant physicians in hospitals, but in October 1980 it was made available for prescription by general practitioners. It proved to have serious side effects, in particular photosensitivity and onycholysis. In August 1982 the English product licence was withdrawn and the drug was withdrawn by Eli Lilly throughout the world.

Later in August 1982 the Opren Action Committee was formed to encourage compensation claims by patients against Eli Lilly and others. Litigation commenced by many UK claimants in the United States was dismissed in June 1984 on the ground of forum non conveniens. Attention reverted to the United Kingdom. Well over 1,000 plaintiffs served writs by 1 October 1986 (Group A) and subsequently by 31 January 1987 (Group B). An offer of damages made around November 1987 was accepted by solicitors acting on behalf of Group A and B plaintiffs in January 1988.

Meanwhile further potential plaintiffs had come forward. Those who served their writs by 9 May 1988 were known as Group C. Hidden J. ordered that certain Group C plaintiffs should have their cases tried as lead actions on the preliminary issue of limitation. He held at the preliminary trial that with one exception these plaintiffs' actions were statute barred. They appealed.

Held: 1.   *Actual knowledge. s 14(1) of the Limitation Act 1980*

      (a)   suspicion, particularly if it is vague and unsupported, will clearly not be enough. However belief may amount to or become knowledge.

      (b)   knowledge is a condition of mind which imports a degree of certainty. The degree of certainty that is appropriate for this purpose is that which, for the particular plaintiff, may reasonably be regarded as sufficient to justify embarking upon the preliminaries to the making of a claim for compensation, such as the taking of legal or other advice.

      (c)   whether or not a state of mind for this purpose is to be treated as knowledge depends in the first place upon the nature of the information which the plaintiff has received, the extent to which he pays attention to the information as affecting him, and his capacity to understand it. There is a second stage at which the information, when received or understood, is evaluated: it may be rejected as unbelievable or regarded as unreliable or uncertain. The court must assess the intelligence of the plaintiff, consider and assess his assertions as to how he regarded such information as he had and determine whether he had knowledge of the facts by reason of his understanding of the information.

      (d)   the relevant date from which the limitation period runs is the date on which the plaintiff *first* had knowledge. Accordingly if a claimant is shown to have had knowledge that his injury is attributable to the act or omission of the defendant, the subsequent obtaining of expert advice, which states that his injury is not so attributable, does not retrospectively cause him never to have had such knowledge and does not prevent time from running.

      (e)   if a plaintiff held a firm belief which was of sufficient certainty to justify the taking of preliminary steps for proceedings by obtaining advice about making a claim for compensation, then such belief is knowledge and the limitation period runs from it.

      (f)   if a plaintiff, while believing that his injury is attributable to the act or omission of the defendant, realises that his belief requires expert confirmation before he acquires such a certainty of belief as amounts to knowledge, then he will not have knowledge until that confirmation is obtained.

      (g)   in any case where a claimant has sought legal advice and taken legal proceedings, it is difficult to perceive how it can rightly be held that he did not have relevant knowledge.

      (h)   it is important to remember where the onus of proof lies. If a writ is not issued within three years of the date when the cause of action arose, the onus is on the plaintiff to plead and prove a date within the three years preceding the date of the issue of the writ. If the defendant wishes to rely on a date prior to the three year period immediately preceding the issue of the writ, the onus is on the defendant to prove that the plaintiff had or ought to have had knowledge by that date.

  2.   *Significance of injury. s 14(1)(a), s 14(2)*

      (a)   the McCafferty (v Metropolitan Police Receiver) test is accepted as correct, involving a combination of the subjective and the objective. Taking *that* plaintiff, with *that* plaintiff's intelligence, would he have been reasonable in considering the injury not sufficiently serious to justify instituting proceedings for damages?

(b)   the distinction between an expected or accepted side-effect, and an injurious and unacceptable consequence, of taking a prescribed drug is valid. Thus until the degree of photosensitivity, for example, was sufficient to indicate that the drug was causing an effect completely outside that of an acceptable side-effect, it could not reasonably be said that the patient was aware of a significant injury.

3.   *Attributability of injury. s 14(1)(b)*

(a)   'attributable' means 'capable of being attributed'. The knowledge required is that attribution is possible, a real possibility and not a fanciful one, a possible cause as opposed to a probable cause of the injury.

(b)   there must be a degree of specificity, and not a mere global or catch-all character, about the act or omission which is alleged to constitute negligence or breach of duty. What is required is knowledge of the essence of the act or omission to which the injury is attributable.

(c)   the act or omission relevant in these cases is 'providing for the use of patients a drug which was unsafe in that it was capable of causing persistent photosensitivity in those patients and/or in failing to discover that this was the case so as properly to protect such patients'.

4.   *Identity of defendants. s 14(1)(c)*

(a)   in the case of a corporate entity, such as a group of companies, the law provides that the true position of the member companies of the group structure is ascertainable.

(b)   the identity of the servant of Eli Lilly who was in charge of clinical research and of submissions of applications for licences for drugs, was ascertainable on application to the Lilly defendants.

(c)   accordingly once attributability was established against one or more of these defendants, the identity of the remaining defendants was reasonably ascertainable.

5.   *Constructive knowledge. s 14(3)*

(a)   the proper approach under s 14(3)(a) is to determine what this plaintiff should have observed or ascertained, while asking of him no more than is reasonable.

(b)   it is under s 14(3)(a) that the position of a solicitor falls to be considered. Since his advice as to the law is irrelevant for this purpose, his contribution can only consist of factual information. Moreover, where constructive knowledge through a solicitor is in issue, this can only be relevant where it is established that the plaintiff ought reasonably to have consulted a solicitor.

(c)   s 14(3)(b) deals not only with medical advice but clearly extends to other experts whom it would be reasonable to expect the plaintiff to consult. In considering whether the enquiry is reasonable, the situation, character and intelligence of the plaintiff must be relevant.

(d)   in many of the cases, the general practitioner or specialist consulted by the plaintiff concentrated upon treatment, not attributability or fault. In these circumstances it would be unreasonable to attribute to a plaintiff knowledge possessed by a doctor, unless it would have been reasonable to expect the plaintiff to have sought advice which would have produced the information.

(e)   the mere announcement of the withdrawal of the drug, without more, did not necessarily put individual plaintiffs on notice. In many cases, all that happened is that the plaintiff was taken off the drug. This common experience might fall short of putting a plaintiff on notice that there was some act or omission on the part of the manufacturer or supplier to which the undesirable effect was attributable.

(f)   this did not dispose of the defendants' argument that the patients might well have been alerted by the extensive publicity given to the unacceptable side effects of the drug and the establishment of the Opren Action Committee. This was an area in which the onus of proving constructive knowledge was on the defendants.

6.   *Exercise of discretion. s 33*

(a)   the Court of Appeal will be very slow to interfere with the exercise of discretion under this section. Where, however, it is established that the judge either took into account factors which he should have ignored, or ignored factors which he should have taken into account, or was plainly wrong, then the Court of Appeal is under a duty to interfere and, in appropriate cases, to substitute a decision based on its own discretion.

(b)   provided that it is relevant, the judge may take into account a factor not specifically listed in the sub-paragraphs of s 33(3). On the other hand, if it is established that he failed to take into account any of the matters mentioned in s 33(3) which were relevant to the carrying out of the balancing exercise, then his judgement is susceptible to attack. However a judge is not under a duty specifically to refer to each and every fact which he has found and upon which he has exercised his discretion.

(c)   in the present cases, the judge fell into error in directing himself for the purposes of the s 33 issues with reference to cogency and prejudice to the defendants. As it was impossible to identify with certainty which of the possible grounds of prejudice the judge applied in any individual appeal, it was necessary to reconsider each case under s 33.

(d)   the consideration under s 33 must be broadly based. The primary purpose of the limitation period is to protect the defendant against the injustice of having to face a stale claim. Once the plaintiff has allowed the permitted term to elapse, the defendant is no longer subject to the disability of accepting without protest the limitation period itself. In such a situation, the court is directed to consider all the circumstances of the case, including conduct before the expiry of the limitation period, and to balance the prejudice to the parties.

(e)   it is not the case that wherever the ability of the defendants to contest the issue of liability has not been affected by the delay, the benefit of the limitation defence must be regarded as a windfall. It may be inequitable to secure to a dilatory plaintiff, who has let the limitation period pass without action, the power to claim from the defendants a sum in settlement of a poor case, which sum would reflect as much or more the risk in costs to the defendants as the fair value of the claim.

(f)   if the judge attached any weight to the settlement of the claims brought by plaintiffs in Groups A and B, he was wrong. The defendants could have accepted the approach made in August 1987 on behalf of the other plaintiffs. In so far as any prejudice was caused to the defendants by the presence of plaintiffs in later Groups, this was directly attributable to the conduct of the defendants and should be ignored.

(g)   'cogency' within s 33(3)(*b*) is directed to the degree to which either party is prejudiced in the presentation of the claim or defence because the evidence available to them is either no longer available or has been adversely affected by the passage of time. There is no room in this sub-section for the concept, apparently accepted by the judge, that lack of cogency in the case of a plaintiff could enure to the benefit of that plaintiff's case and thereby prejudice the defendant.

(h)   there cannot be a different method of applying the court's discretion in multi-partite cases from that in any ordinary individual claim. The judge was right to reject the submission that, were the court to exercise discretion in favour of all or a substantial number of the plaintiffs, the action would be contrary to public policy.

(A) *Mrs Nash*

Mrs Nash started to take Opren in April 1981. Soon afterwards, she began to suffer a painful scalding sensation on her skin whenever she went out into the sun. It got worse as the summer progressed. This skin sensitivity continued for about six months after she gave up Opren in June 1982. Her eye sensitivity had continued in very strong light ever since, but there was no contemporaneous record of any complaint over the years.

In June 1982 she saw a newspaper article which stated that Opren had caused significant side effects such as photosensitivity. Her doctor told her that Opren was to be withdrawn because of the side effects it had caused. She was convinced that Opren had caused her condition. In August 1982 her husband notified her claim to the manufacturers who disclaimed any responsibility for the side effects. Thereafter she did nothing until August 1987 when she read of and contacted the Opren Action Group. Her writ was issued in April 1988.

Held: (i)   the judge was right to hold that by August 1982 Mrs Nash had actual knowledge of the significance and attributability of her injury. She also had constructive knowledge of the identity of at least one of the defendants. Therefore her date of knowledge was more than three years before the issue of her writ.

     (ii) (a) the plaintiff, having advanced her claim in August 1982, laid it to rest for five years.
           (b) there was an absence of any contemporaneous record of complaint.
           (c) the judge regarded her claim as a weak case.
           (d) there would be significant prejudice to the defendants, and it would be inequitable to allow Mrs Nash's case to proceed.

(B) *Mrs Odam*

Mrs Odam started to take Opren in February 1981. In June 1982, on a holiday in Spain, she became aware of a burning and prickly sensation affecting her exposed skin. She became aware from a television programme in August 1982 that Opren had been withdrawn. Her general practitioner testified that he could not remember any complaint ever being made by her about skin and eye sensitivity up to 1987 but that, if she had asked him in August 1982, he would have told her that her symptoms were caused by Opren.

In August 1984 and October 1984 she wrote to Eli Lilly describing her symptoms and complaining of the embarrassment and expense incurred due to Opren. Their reply denied that the side effects suffered by her had been caused by Opren. A newspaper article prompted her to go to solicitors in 1987. Her writ was issued in January 1988.

Held: (i)   not only did she have actual knowledge of all relevant facts by August 1984 but also she had constructive knowledge by August 1982 because if she had asked her general practitioner, as reasonably she should have done, he would have told her that her symptoms were caused by Opren and she would have ascertained the rest. Her case was statute barred.

     (ii) (a) the judge found that the real reason for her delay was her worry over what legal action would cost.
           (b) the delay of 2 years had affected the cogency of her evidence, and there was no corroboration by contemporaneous record of her complaints.
           (c) the judge was right to hold that discretion should not be exercised in her favour.

(C) Mr Boxall

Mr Boxall took Opren from August 1981 until October 1981. Within two weeks of starting, he experienced serious symptoms of sensitivity to sunlight and to warmth. He was promptly referred back to the consultant rheumatologist who had prescribed the drug and was at once taken off it. He believed that his symptoms were caused by Opren and, from the withdrawal of the drug in August 1982, that it was unsafe. He did nothing until July 1987 when on advice from a Citizen's Advice Bureau he consulted solicitors. His writ was issued in November 1987.

Held: (i) the judge was right to find that Mr Boxall had knowledge of all relevant facts by August 1982. His case was statute barred in August 1985.

(ii) the judge could not be criticised for finding that:

(a) Mr Boxall had over the years from 1982 considered making a claim and decided against it on the ground of costs of litigation.

(b) the delay of more than two years made the evidence likely to be less cogent than would have been the case had the action been brought at the appropriate time.

(c) Mr Boxall had taken no steps to obtain medical or legal advice until 1987, although he had known by August 1982 that the drug was an unsafe product.

(d) the court's discretion should not be exercised so as to permit the claim to proceed.

(D) *Mrs Day*

Mrs Day began taking Opren in February 1981 but, due to the onycholysis which appeared to have resulted from it, she was taken off the drug in August 1981. She resumed taking it on prescription in November 1981, but in April 1982 she suffered severe photosensitivity and her general practitioner advised her not to take it any more. By early 1983 he was certain that Opren was the cause of her disability and communicated this to her. In February 1983 she wrote to Eli Lilly. There was no written record of any complaint of photosensitivity by her after December 1983. She did not obtain any medical or legal advice until 1987. Her writ was issued in November 1987.

Held: (i) the judge was entitled to find that Mrs Day had actual knowledge of the relevant facts by December 1982, or very shortly thereafter, in view of her letter to the defendants in February 1983 which demonstrated her prior knowledge. Accordingly her case was statute barred.

(ii) (a) the proper inference from the delay of nearly two years was that in 1983 her symptoms were such that she decided not to advance a claim.

(b) that inference was supported by the fact that there was no written record of any complaint of photosensitivity after December 1982.

(c) she had not established that it would be equitable to allow her claim to proceed.

(E) *Mrs Eaton*

Mrs Eaton first took Opren in April 1981. Within a few weeks, she suffered severe symptoms of photosensitivity. The symptoms continued throughout that summer. In May 1982, as a result of reading a newspaper article and seeing a television programme, she decided to halve her intake of Opren. When her supply ran out in July or August 1982, she did not go to her doctor for more. Each year her symptoms returned. In March 1986 she went to see her doctor. In May 1987 she went to the CAB who referred her to the Opren Action Committee. Her writ was issued in November 1987.

Held: (i) the judge was right to find that she had suffered a significant injury and that she had actual knowledge of the identity of Eli Lilly by May 1982. Further she had by August 1982 constructive knowledge of the relevant facts in that, if she had raised the matter with her general practitioner as would have been reasonable, he would have given her all the necessary answers.

(ii) (a) between 1982 and 1986 she did not seek medical or legal advice.

    (b)   the judge regarded this as a truly poor case in view of the lack of written record of complaints of photosensitivity, which was startling having regard to the severity of the symptoms as described.

    (c)   having regard to the prejudice to the defendants at being required to defend such a claim, it would not be equitable to allow the case to proceed.

(F) *Mrs O'Hara*

Mrs O'Hara began taking Opren in September 1980. In the summer of 1981 she began to suffer symptoms of photosensitivity all over her arms and face. She consulted her general practitioner who told her to continue to use skin cream and to take the drug. In August 1982 she saw that Opren was withdrawn from the market because of the side effects caused by it. Her general practitioner prescribed another drug in its place.

In February 1983 she wrote to the Opren Action Committee and filled in a questionnaire that they sent her. She felt that she lacked the money and the education to take the case further. From 1983 to 1988 she spent her time nursing her husband who was dying. The dim light indoors reduced the effects of her injury. In June 1987 she learned from a television programme that claims were being made for damages for the results of the side effects of Opren. She was referred by the CAB to solicitors. Her writ was issued in November 1987.

Held: (i)   it was acknowledged that the judge was justified in finding that by February 1983, when she wrote to the Opren Action Committee, she had both actual and constructive knowledge of all the relevant facts.

        (ii)   (a)   the relevant delay of some $1^{1}/_{2}$ years had been caused by financial constraints and domestic circumstances.

               (b)   the absence of any contemporaneous record of any complaint by her to her doctor might cast substantial doubt on the severity of her symptoms as now recalled by her.

               (c)   the judge was not regarding this as a poor case in the sense discussed above.

               (d)   upon the judge's findings of fact, the different conclusion should be reached that it would be equitable to allow Mrs O'Hara's action to proceed.

(G) *Mrs Higgins*

Mrs Higgins first took Opren in October 1981. Her case was that she began to suffer symptoms of photosensitivity in May 1982 and that she also had other symptoms such as growth of facial hairs, loss of head hair, and depression. In July 1982, having read reports of deaths caused by Opren, she was taken off the drug at her own request and her general practitioner commented that side effects were a normal consequence of taking drugs. Although she continued to see her doctor on a monthly basis, she did not complain of any further side effects and neither of them mentioned Opren again. In 1987, when she learned from a newspaper of claims being made, she went to the CAB, was referred to the Opren Action Committee and consulted solicitors. Her writ was issued in November 1987.

Held: (i)   the judge was justified in finding that by July 1982 she was aware of the significance of her injury, had actual knowledge of its attributability and constructive knowledge of the identity of the defendants. Her general practitioner's words to the effect that all drugs have side effects were said merely as a statement of fact when she mentioned press reports of Opren deaths. Her claim was therefore statute barred.

        (ii)   (a)   the main ground of the judge's refusal to exercise discretion was the total absence of record of any complaint of symptoms to her doctor when it was clear to the judge that, if she had been suffering these symptoms, she would have informed her doctor and sought advice and help.

(b) this was another case in which there would be disproportionate prejudice to the defendants if the action were allowed to proceed.

(H) *Mrs Forster*

Mrs Forster had suffered rheumatoid arthritis since 1976. She received a number of different treatments and experienced reactions to many, including rashes and skin irritation. In November 1980 she started to take Opren. She suffered symptoms of photosensitivity in April 1981. She thought this was due to Opren, but when she told her general practitioner he said that he did not know what had caused it. She also discussed the matter with a consultant, but he did not take it seriously and asked what was more important to her, being able to sit in the sun or being able to walk. She took his advice and carried on taking the drug until July 1982. She was aware of the withdrawal of Opren in August 1982 but had thought that this was because it caused liver problems in elderly patients. The reaction to sunlight recurred in the summer of 1983. She had had innumerable appointments with her general practitioner and various consultants, but they all seemed to believe that her continuing photosensitivity was just an unfortunate consequence of her body's reactions to drugs as a whole.

When she saw a television programme in June 1987, she was prompted to write to the Opren Action Committee. She instructed solicitors in July 1987, and her writ was issued in September 1987.

Held: the judge appeared to have accepted in general her evidence. If her account of her dealings with her doctor was correct, the judge erred in finding that she had only actual or constructive knowledge of the relevant facts under s 14 before September 1984. Accordingly her case was not statute barred.

(I) *Mr Cockburn*

Mr Cockburn was the only one of the so-called nine lead cases to succeed on limitation. The order for directions by Hirst J. had provided that, unless otherwise ordered, 'any costs which are ordered to be paid by, or which fall to be borne by, the plaintiff shall be paid or borne proportionately by each of the plaintiffs whose action is included in any Schedule III Action (including those plaintiffs who are legally aided) so that each such plaintiff shall bear an equal part thereof'. Hidden J. ordered the defendants to pay 1/338th of Mr Cockburn's costs. It was estimated that this would amount to about £90 out of £30,000.

Held: (i) the order for directions only provided for contribution between plaintiffs. It was not directed to orders for costs in favour of plaintiffs.

(ii) the trial judge's order was unjust in its effect and clearly wrong. There was no reason to make an exception to the general rule under RSC Ord 62, r 3(3) that costs should follow the event.

(iii) accordingly the order was set aside, and the precise terms of a fresh order left until after submissions from counsel.

(J) *Miss Jenkins*

Miss Jenkins started to take Opren in March 1981. She first suffered symptoms of photosensitivity in August 1981. Her general practitioner took her off Opren in May 1982 because it was making no impression on her arthritis. No further mention was made of it by him or her. In September 1982 she had a nervous breakdown with depression. In January 1983 her sister wrote to Jack Ashley MP about Miss Jenkins and Opren and received a letter with information from the Opren Action Group. In July 1987 Miss Jenkins herself wrote to Mr Ashley that 'I took Opren tablets for some time during 1981 and suffered as a result. I have not put in a claim as quite honestly I could not afford the cost'. Her writ was issued in April 1988.

Held: (i)   the judge was entitled to find that she had knowledge of significant injury at the end of 1982 or the beginning of 1983 at the latest. As to attributability, the information in her sister's January 1983 letter must have come from her. The identity of the defendants was ascertainable. Her case was statute barred.

       (ii)   the proper inference was that she decided that a claim was not worth pursuing. Her case was made weaker by her impaired memory, and she had made no contemporaneous complaint to her general practitioner of the onset and progress of her allegedly severe symptoms. The judge regarded this as a poor claim. The defendant would be prejudiced, and it would not be equitable to allow the action to proceed.

(K)   *Mr Stanley*

Mr Stanley started to take Opren in August 1981. His case was that from the late summer of 1981 onwards he suffered severe symptoms of photosensitivity. He ceased taking Opren in about June 1982 when another drug was prescribed. In August 1982 he told his general practitioner that he had been on Opren for several months and that he had noticed increasing stiffness in his ankles as a result. He knew of the withdrawal of Opren on the grounds of safety. In 1983 he wrote to the Opren Action Committee. In 1987 he consulted a doctor for the first time about his skin condition. After he saw a television programme about Opren, his writ was issued in November 1987.

Held: (i)   (a)   the judge found that Mr Stanley believed that his symptoms were caused by Opren by the time he applied to the Opren Action Committee for assistance. The finding that this belief amounted to actual knowledge was of uncertain validity, since his letter to the Committee was consistent with his holding the view that he needed further information and confirmation about the attributability of his symptoms.

            (b)   however the judge was entitled to hold that he had constructive knowledge by 1983, because if his account of his symptoms was correct he should reasonably have reported them to his doctors and would have acquired the knowledge available from them. His constructive knowledge was to be judged upon his evidence about his injury.

       (ii)   the judge's refusal to exercise his discretion under s 33 in Mr Stanley's favour was not referred to in the typed judgement.

The appeal was dismissed.

(L)   *Mr Sivyer*

Mr Sivyer started to take Opren in November 1980. He began to suffer symptoms of photosensitivity and light sensitivity in the summer of 1981. On 6 August 1982 his general practitioner recovered his remaining Opren tablets from him. Mr Sivyer did not complain to him about his problems, because he did not want to waste his time. Both his general practitioner and his consultant testified that, if he had asked, they would have told him that Opren was unsafe and the probable cause of his symptoms.

In June 1987 Mr Sivyer saw a newspaper article, as a result of which he consulted solicitors. His writ was issued in March 1988.

Held: (i)   the judge was justified in finding that Mr Sivyer had actual or/and constructive knowledge of all of the relevant facts by the end of 1983 at the latest. He was suffering allegedly severe symptoms, he must have known that Opren was the cause of them, that Opren had been withdrawn and that its nature had caused his general practitioner to call to recover from him all unused Opren tablets. Accordingly his case was statute barred.

       (ii)   this was another case of the judge not accepting evidence to the effect that complaints had been made of symptoms. If Mr Sivyer was suffering the symptoms which he now described, it was reasonable for him to report them to his doctors and seek advice. His appeal must be dismissed.

(M) *Mr Kirby*

Mr Kirby took Opren from 23 January 1981 to 3 February 1981. On the latter date his general practitioner noted: 'red hot needle feeling in the neck, sunlight, query skin sensitivity due to Opren.' Dr Myers told him that he thought that his skin symptoms were due to Opren. Indeed Mr Kirby believed this himself. In May 1983 Dr Myers referred him to a skin specialist, Dr McMillan, who advised that Opren was not the cause of the symptoms and Mr Kirby accepted what he was told.

In June 1987 his daughter sent him a newspaper article. He then saw three television programmes about Opren, which caused him to consult solicitors. In July 1987 Mr Kirby was referred again to Dr McMillan who again excluded Opren as the cause of his symptoms and advised that his skin complaint was a natural condition of seborrhoeic dermatitis. His writ was issued in January 1988.

Held: his appeal must be allowed.

Per Purchas LJ: 'The judge did not reject, and there was no apparent reason to reject, Mr Kirby's assertion that he had accepted and believed the advice of Dr McMillan. It seems to us that there was no sufficient evidence upon which Hidden J could properly hold that the belief held by Mr Kirby in 1981, that his skin condition had been caused by Opren, had become a state of mind of such degree of certainty or confidence that in 1982 or 1983 it was knowledge for the purposes of section 14 of the Act. The inescapable, or at least the better and safer, inference from his conduct is that, although he thought that Opren was the cause, he had sought advice from Dr Myers for confirmation of that belief and Dr Myers had advised him to obtain more expert advice; and Mr Kirby had accepted that advice from Dr Myers; and that Mr Kirby had accepted and acted upon the advice of Dr McMillan which was to the effect that Opren was not the cause of the symptoms. This is not a case of established knowledge being reversed or suspended by later advice but of the receipt of information by Mr Kirby in such a sequence and of such nature that, as it was understood by Mr Kirby, the information did not result at the relevant time in the acquisition of knowledge by him. It may be, in circumstances of this nature, that the actions of a plaintiff might provide safe grounds for inferring that, despite the receipt of adverse advice from a specialist, he still, upon the information which he had, believed that his symptoms constituted a significant injury attributable to the act or omission with such a degree of confidence that it must in those circumstances be regarded as knowledge for that purpose. We cannot regard this as such a case. The onus of proof is on the defendants and, in our judgment, it has not been discharged.'

(N) *Mrs Berger*

Mrs Berger started to take Opren in April 1981. Around July 1981 she developed a red rash over her face and suffered symptoms of photosensitivity. In August 1982 she saw a television programme as a result of which she consulted her general practitioner who told her to stop taking Opren. He testified that if she had complained of a photosensitive reaction, he could have told her that it might be due to Opren. Her specialist gave similar evidence. Mrs Berger mentioned in cross-examination not seeking advice because of cost. Her writ was issued in November 1987.

Held: the judge's conclusion that in 1982 she had attributed her symptoms to Opren, had known that the drug had been withdrawn on grounds of safety but had decided not to pursue the matter, could not be questioned. His conclusion that she had constructive knowledge of all relevant facts by the end of 1982 was open to him on the evidence. She described severe symptoms of photosensitivity, and it was reasonable for her to have sought advice about them from the doctors. Had she done so, she would probably have learned that such symptoms were a significant injury, not mere side-effects, and that they were attributable to the act or omission of the Lilly defendants of whom the identities were ascertainable.

She had not made an application under s 33. Her appeal was dismissed.

(O)   *Mrs Busuttil-Reynaud*

Opren was first prescribed to Mrs Busuttil-Reynaud in March 1982. A few weeks later, she suffered a painful burning sensation in her skin whenever it was exposed to bright sunlight. Her scalp was affected. In August 1982 she saw publicity about Opren and returned her tablets. An intelligent woman who kept herself informed about matters to do with arthritis, she did not complain to her doctor about photosensitive reactions between March 1982 and October 1986. Her writ was issued in January 1988.

Held: the judge's finding that she ought reasonably to have reported her symptoms to her doctor was unassailable. Had she done so in 1982 or early 1983, she would have acquired knowledge of the relevant facts. While she did not have actual knowledge of the identity of all defendants by the end of 1982, there was constructive knowledge at latest by the end of 1983. Her case was statute barred.

There was no mention of s 33. Her appeal was dismissed.

(P)   *Mrs Newell*

Mrs Newell started to take Opren in May 1982. She consulted her general practitioner about a photosensitive rash in July 1982, and she stopped her taking Opren then. From August 1982 she suffered painful burning and irritation of her skin when exposed to bright sunlight. Before the end of 1982 she attributed her symptoms to Opren which she knew had been withdrawn. She did not complain of them to her doctor until 1987. Her writ was issued in April 1988.

Held: upon the assumption that her description of her symptoms from August 1982 was accurate, she ought reasonably to have sought the advice of her doctor. If she had done so and had reported the continuation of her symptoms into 1983, she would have acquired all relevant knowledge from her doctor very strongly. The judge was justified in concluding that her sole reason for not pursuing the matter was the question of cost. Her case was statute barred.

There being no mention of s 33, her appeal was dismissed.

(Q)   *Mrs Fell*

Mrs Fell first took Opren on 18 May 1981 and stopped on 1 June 1981 because of a skin rash. She took it again from 11 December 1981 until 22 April 1982 when it was stopped because of photosensitivity. She continued to suffer photosensitivity and intolerance of heat. She attributed her condition to Opren, but did not return to her doctor to complain of it. In 1987 she saw a television programme involving Jack Ashley MP and was referred to a solicitor in December 1987. Her writ was issued in March 1988.

Held: on the assumption that her description of her symptoms from 1982 was accurate, it was reasonable for her to report them to her doctor and seek her advice. If she had done so, and thus made it clear to him that the symptoms were continuing after she had ceased to take the drug, he would have provided to her the requisite knowledge. The judge's findings as to her date of knowledge were justified by the evidence. Her case was statute barred.

There was no reference to s 33. Her appeal was dismissed.

See pp 32, 122, 181, 183, 187, 192, 193, 195.

Nash v Southmead Health Authority

Brain damage: childbirth: damages: interest

Alliott J. [1994] 5 Med LR 74

The plaintiff was born in September 1975. Owing to prolonged labour, he suffered from tachycardia, profound bradycardia, severe hypoxia and he was moribund. After prolonged resuscitation, he survived but was left with dyskinetic athetoid cerebral palsy. The defendants admitted negligence.

By trial when he was aged 17, he continued to manifest a continually varying increased muscle spasm and distortion of movement. This disrupted control of his limbs, trunk and face thereby caused a gross impairment of his physical disabilities. His speech was badly distorted. Hand movements were uncontrolled and carried out crudely. He could undress himself and go to the toilet on his own and could use a knife and fork. However he needed help with dressing, cutting up food and with washing and bathing. He could walk unsteadily and irregularly about the house, but he would often fall over. He could use one or two of his fingers to operate a powered wheelchair.

The plaintiff was pleasant and cheerful, persistent and determined. His intellectual ability had not been affected; he had achieved passes in eight GCSEs, was studying for two A levels and was expected to undertake a three year university course. The Department of Employment assessed him as capable of driving a suitably adapted standard production car. Much of the burden of looking after him at home had fallen on his parents and a younger sister.

Held (December 1992):

	£	£
1. General damages for pain, suffering and loss of amenity		90,000.00
2. Pre-trial loss:		
Cost of past parental care (a)	35,262.40	
Additional household costs (b)	7,000.00	
Travel expenses (agreed)	2,304.52	
Special needs (agreed)	9,781.92	54,348.84
Less deductions:		
Deductible benefits	(30,633.73)	
Interest on interim payment of £100,000	(1,628.67)	
		(32,262.40)
Sub-total (after deductions):		22,086.44
3. Future loss:		
Appliances, aids, equipment clothing etc.	159,816.98	
Home-based carer (c)	189,013.44	
Physiotherapy	11,312.00	
Travelling (agreed) (d)	18,700.00	
Holidays (agreed)	14,000.00	
Accommodation:		
Capital (agreed)	52,876.22	
Annual costs	18,812.54	
	(£1,106.62 x 17years)	
Lost earning capacity (e)	107,930.16	
		572,461.34
Less deductions for future benefits		(27,097.20)
Sub-total		545,364.14
Total award (before interest)		657,450.58
Interest on special damages (f)		9,022.14
Interest on general damages		8,028.00
Total award (inc interest)		674,500.72

(a) £5,314 pa (based on about five hours per day) when plaintiff living at home.

(b) reduced from total claimed of just over £11,000 to allow for enhanced capital value of house.

(c) based on total multiplier of 18.

(d) based on the Disability Allowance as provided for in a special scheme set up by Ford Motor Company.

(e) £14,635 net pa – £5,640 pa residual capacity = £8,995 pa x 12

(f) awarded over period of seven years only, due to 12-year delay in starting action.

See p 154.

Naylor v Preston Area Health Authority

Disclosure of experts' reports: duty of care: right to know treatment received: medical literature: epilepsy: fatal

Court of Appeal. [1987] 2 All ER 353, [1987] 1 WLR 958

Mrs Naylor was admitted to hospital in Preston for the birth of her child. She had a history of epilepsy. Four days after the birth she had an epileptic fit while taking a bath, and drowned. The administrator of her estate sued the health authority.

In this and three other cases, the plaintiffs appealed against the refusal of an order for the advance disclosure of the reports of all expert medical witnesses on liability issues which would be relied upon at the trial.

Held: in all four cases, the issues would be refined, costs would be saved and the chances of a consensual resolution of the dispute would be enhanced by an order for pre-trial disclosure of the substance of the expert evidence. This should be accompanied by an identification of any medical or scientific literature, published or unpublished, to which the experts intended to refer. In none of the four cases were there any grounds to depart from the norm of simultaneous disclosure.

Per Sir John Donaldson MR: 'I personally think that in professional negligence cases, and in particular in medical negligence cases, there is a duty of candour resting upon the professional man . . . In my judgement, still admittedly and regretfully obiter, it is but one aspect of the general duty of care, arising out of the patient-medical practitioner or hospital authority relationship and gives rise to rights both in contract and tort'.

Note: The subject matter of the appeals would now be governed by the revised RSC Ord 38, r 37.

See pp 30, 45, 114, 179, 182, 210.

Needham v Biograft Transplant Centre Ltd and Another

Surgeon: operation: retained surgical product: damages: hair

Hobhouse J. (1983) Times, 16 February

The plaintiff (Arthur Needham), aged 57, was a builder who was going bald. The Biograph Transplant Centre claimed that it could combat baldness with a new technique by which bald patches were removed and hair- bearing skin was drawn over them. In April 1981 Mr

Clamp, a surgeon, carried out the operation at Biograft's clinic. A swab of gauze was inadvertently left under the plaintiff's skin.

The plaintiff went straight to bed and stayed there for five days. He was in considerable pain and could not sleep. His face was badly swollen and he had black eyes. When he was on holiday in Majorca the next week, there appeared on his neck a lump which frequently wept and twice burst. The wound continued to discharge for the rest of the holiday, causing discomfort and embarrassment. A further operation was performed to remove the swab. The plaintiff made a good recovery but was left with scars on his head where hair did not grow.

He sued the Biograft Transplant Centre and Mr Clamp. Both admitted liability.

Held: general damages (February 1983) for pain, suffering and loss of amenities were assessed at £1,500. The plaintiff's total award was £3,903.

See p 476.

Newell and Newell v Goldenberg

Causation: risk disclosure: vasectomy

Mantell J. NLP 16 March 1995

The plaintiffs (Mr and Mrs Newell) consulted Mr Goldenberg about a vasectomy. He did not warn them that there was a 1 in 2300 risk of spontaneous refertilisation. In September 1985 Mr Goldenberg performed a vasectomy on Mr Newell. In December 1985 two follow up sperm tests proved negative. Subsequently Mrs Newell became pregnant.

It was accepted that Mr Goldenberg had performed the vasectomy operation competently. He testified that it had been his usual practice at the time to warn couples of the risk of spontaneous refertilisation, but that he had inadvertently failed to warn the plaintiffs. His defence was that in 1985 a responsible body of medical opinion preferred not to give such a warning.

Held: (i)   the defence in question existed as a potential justification for practitioners who are not aware of the correct practice. Its purpose was not to serve those who actually knew better. Mr Goldenberg had been negligent.

     (ii)   even if the plaintiffs had been warned of the risk of failure, they would not have declined the operation. Nor would they have adopted traditional methods of contraception and thereby avoided the pregnancy.

    (iii)   therefore they were only entitled to damages for the suffering and anxiety caused by the discovery that Mrs Newell was pregnant.

Newell v Eli Lilly & Co and Others

Limitation: drugs: Opren

Court of Appeal. [1992] 3 Med LR 398

See *Nash v Eli Lilly & Co* (P) (p 476).

Newnham and Another v Rochester and Chatham Joint Hospital Board

Child patient: hospital administration: supervision: nurses: fever

Talbot J (with jury). (1936) Times, 28 February

In December 1934 the plaintiff (Charles Newnham), aged 57, was suffering from scarlet fever. He was admitted to St William's Hospital in Rochester and placed in a ward on the ground floor. During the late afternoon of his second day he was in bed a few feet from a window, the lower part of which was open. In the absence of a nurse, he fell out of the window and dropped about seventeen feet on to the ground below. As a result, his forehead was badly disfigured and both feet became flat, requiring special supports.

Held: the hospital staff were negligent in leaving the boy unattended near the open window.

See p 132.

Newton v Newton's Model Laundry Ltd and Others

Fracture: diagnosis: hospital doctor: examination: knee

Salmon J. (1959) Times, 3 November

On 29 September 1954 the plaintiff (Vernon Newton) went up to inspect tanks in the roof of the laundry which he managed. He slipped and fell twelve feet on to the concrete floor below. He was taken to Acton Hospital where he was seen by Dr Potasnick who did not diagnose the broken patella in his left knee. The plaintiff suffered excruciating pain until the fracture was diagnosed on 16 October 1954. When an operation was performed, it was found that the bone was broken into eleven pieces.

Held: Dr Potasnick had been negligent. He had failed to examine the plaintiff's left knee properly.

See p 96.

Nickolls v Ministry of Health and Another

Surgeon: operation: cancer: larynx

Gorman J. (1955) Times, 4 February

In December 1944 the plaintiff (Mrs Winifred Nickolls) underwent an operation by Mr Joll at the Royal Free Hospital. He was suffering from cancer at the time and knew that he had the disease. Her recurrent laryngeal nerves were damaged in the operation. Mr Joll died a few weeks later.

The plaintiff sued the Ministry of Health and the Royal Free Hospital alleging that Mr Joll was unfit for the task.

Held: Mr Joll was fit to perform the operation. The evidence did not make out a case of negligence against him.

See p 60.

Nicoleau v Brookhaven Memorial Hospital

Blood transfusion: consent: Jehovah's Witness: USA

US Court of Appeals. (1990) 300 BMJ 491

In December 1988 Mrs Denise Nicoleau gave birth to a son in Brookhaven Memorial Hospital in Long Island. She suffered a severe postpartum haemorrhage and required a blood transfusion which, as a Jehovah's Witness, she refused on religious grounds.

Lawyers for the hospital contacted the Supreme Court of New York which decided that a hearing was unnecessary since the newborn child was alive and healthy, needing a mother's care, and a transfusion was necessary for treatment. Consequently Mrs Nicoleau was given a transfusion despite her objections.

Afterwards she appealed, alleging inter alios that the absence of a hearing denied her family and her the opportunity to show that other family members could have cared for her child had she died.

Held: the Supreme Court should have held a hearing. The presence of minor children is not an overriding reason to prevent a patient from refusing necessary medical treatment.

See p 8.

Nutbrown v Sheffield Health Authority

After-care: brain damage: damages: prostate

Potts J. [1993] 4 Med LR 187

In November 1987 the plaintiff (Lawrence Nutbrown) was a happy, energetic 72-year-old man leading a full life. Then he underwent a prostatectomy for a benign prostatic hypertrophy at the Royal Hallamshire Hospital. Owing to a failure of post operative care there, he sustained grievous brain damage. The hospital authority accepted liability.

He could dress himself, keep himself clean and just about manage to live on his own near his daughter who visited him frequently and did all his shopping and much of the preparation of his meals. However he suffered from visual agnosia, had problems with tasks involving spatial orientation, was forgetful, could not manage money, pay rent, collect his pension or go shopping. Furthermore he frequently got lost, was unable to write, and could not cope with those tasks which he previously performed on a regular basis. He had dyslexic, agnostic and discalulic difficulties: for example, he could not correctly name a toothbrush or a thimble. He had some insight into his disabilities.

His mother summarised his condition by noting: 'My son, Lawrence, went into hospital for a simple stomach operation and came out a simple cabbage.' His life expectancy was ten years from the operation to the age of 82. The only issue in dispute was general damages.

Held: (i)   the correct approach in this case was to assess what damages would be appropriate for a man in the prime of life and then to reduce that figure to reflect the age of the plaintiff at the date of injury and his life expectancy.

        (ii)   if he had been aged 30 when he sustained his injuries, an appropriate sum to compensate him for his pain, suffering and loss of amenity would have been £50,000.

> (iii) it was necessary to consider the plaintiff as he was before his injury and as he had become, and to have regard throughout to his age and life expectancy. The court must also remember that at the age of 72 this man, in apparent good health, had been deprived of the enjoyment of his last years.
>
> (iv) the appropriate award of general damages for pain, suffering and loss of amenities was £25,000.

See p 152.

Re O (a minor) (medical treatment)

Blood transfusion: Jehovah's Witness: parental objection

Johnson J. [1993] 4 Med LR 272; 137 Sol Jo LB 107, [1993] 2 FLR 149, (1993) Times, 19 March

JO was born on 18 January 1993. Her arrival was premature by 12 weeks. She weighed just 2 lbs 13 oz. She suffered respiratory distress syndrome. Her parents were Jehovah's Witnesses.

Dr B was the consultant paediatrician in charge of J's care. By 22 January he became concerned that J's condition might at any minute deteriorate to the point where blood transfusion was a matter of immediate necessity. Since her parents objected, he turned for guidance to the local authority who obtained an emergency protection order that afternoon. The order recited that: 'The reasons for making this order are that there is reasonable cause to suspect that the child is suffering or is likely to suffer significant harm because the parents are withholding their permission to give urgent medical treatment and unless this treatment is received the child may die.' Pursuant to this, blood transfusions were given to J in the early hours of 25 January and again during the night of 27 January.

Next the local authority applied for a care order on the basis that there was an urgent and continuing need for medical treatment, including blood transfusion, to which the parents were refusing to give consent. Dr B testified that J was on a ventilator and that her red blood cell count was critical with potential threat to her vital organs: if she was to survive, there was no alternative to blood transfusion.

Held: (i)   it was appropriate to pay every respect and give great weight to the family's religious principles. Having done that, the court must 'act as the judicial reasonable parent'.

(ii) this required the giving of directions to ensure that, whenever medical need arose, J would receive the transfusion of blood or blood products that medical advice dictated.

(iii) such matters should ordinarily be dealt with under the inherent jurisdiction of the High Court. Emergency protection orders and interim care orders were inappropriate in these circumstances.

See pp 12, 13.

O'Bonsawin v Paradis

Battery: Canada: consent: operation: interests of patient: fistula

Judge Disalle, Ontario Court of Justice. [1994] 5 Med LR 399

The plaintiff (Ms O'Bonsawin), who suffered from chronic renal failure, was referred by her nephrologist to the defendant (Ms Paradis), a general surgeon specialising in vascular access for potential dialysis patients. The defendant was asked to create an arteriovenous fistula in the plaintiff's non-dominant arm, in order to facilitate dialysis until a transplant could be performed.

Access for dialysis could be obtained by either of two methods: arteriovenous fistula (AVF) or by a gortex graft. The defendant told the plaintiff that she preferred to do the fistula, but that her veins were too small and that the fistula would probably not succeed. Consequently it was agreed to do a graft. The plaintiff signed a consent which was for a gortex graft and also allowed for such 'additional or alternative treatment or operative procedures as in the opinion of (the defendant) are immediately necessary'.

When the plaintiff was under anaesthetic, the defendant concluded that the veins were adequate to enable her to do the fistula. She attempted to perform this but failed (through no negligence on her part). Eventually the plaintiff did receive access by gortex graft, but developed a neuroma caused by the cutaneous nerve being transected or cut.

She claimed damages for battery, but abandoned her allegations of negligence.

Held: (i) it would have been foolish for the defendant to stop and later obtain a consent for the fistula. Her decision to continue with it was reasonable under the circumstances and in the best interests of the patient.

(ii) it was not a situation where the plaintiff had consented to one treatment and another radically different treatment had been performed. Both procedures accomplished the same purpose of providing access for dialysis.

(iii) in all the circumstances, including the consent signed, the arteriovenous fistula performed did not go beyond the plaintiff's consent. The defendant was entitled to infer consent to the fistula in this situation.

See p 105.

O'Donnell v South Bedfordshire Health Authority

Brain damage: childbirth: damages: quadriplegia: caesarean: diagnosis

Drake J. [1991] CLY 1578

An emergency caesarian section to deliver the infant plaintiff was abandoned when he was diagnosed as being dead in utero. Seventeen hours later he was born vaginally with severe disabilities.

He suffered from cerebral palsy and spastic quadriplegia. He was immobile and unable to speak, but had at least some insight into his condition. Life expectancy was up to 28 years.

Held (November 1990): general damages for pain, suffering and loss of amenities were assessed at £105,000 out of a total award of £346,476 including interest.

See p 154.

O'Hara v Eli Lilly & Co and Others

Limitation: drugs: Opren

Court of Appeal. [1992] 3 Med LR 384

See *Nash v Eli Lilly & Co* (F) (p 472).

O'Malley-Williams v Governors of National Hospital for Nervous Diseases

Registrar: operation: diagnosis: risk disclosure: res ipsa loquitur: ophthalmic: artery: hand

Bridge J. [1975] 1 BMJ 635

In 1968 the plaintiff (Mr O'Malley-Williams), an accomplished pianist, sought treatment at the National Hospital for Nervous Diseases. He had been afflicted by recurrent episodes of loss of vision in the right eye. Stenosis of the right carotid artery was diagnosed. To confirm the diagnosis, the hospital decided to perform an aortagram. The plaintiff was not informed of any risk.

The operation was performed under local anaesthetic by a registrar, Dr Bland. He successfully punctured the femoral artery in the patient's right groin with the Seldinger needle, but then met an obstruction before the guide wire had travelled more than five or six inches up the artery. Therefore he abandoned the femoral route and decided to insert the catheter by way of the right axillary artery. Before that artery was successfully punctured, Dr Bland had to make a number of passes and the plaintiff suffered great pain.

Thereafter, the trouble with the vision in the plaintiff's right eye was successfully treated with anti-coagulants. However he suffered neurological complications which led to partial paralysis of his right hand. He sued the hospital.

Held: (i) even severe pain was by no means uncommon with aortagrams under local anaesthesia, so it was not negligent of Dr Bland to continue trying to get into the artery.

(ii) *res ipsa loquitur* did not apply, since the injury sustained was recognized as an inherent risk of the treatment undergone.

(iii) a failure to warn of remote risks, where the patient had not raised the question, was not negligence.

Judgment for the defendants.

See pp 89, 111, 116.

O'Neill v Kelly

Dental: fracture: causation: jaw

Davies LJ. (1961) Times, 15 December

On 4 September 1957 the plaintiff (Mrs Patricia O'Neill) attended the surgery of Mr Kelly, a young dentist who had just qualified. In trying to remove a tooth in her lower jaw, he took the crown off. He told her that he must take out the root and gave her a local injection. After he failed to remove the root with forceps, the plaintiff wanted to go home but finally consented to remain. He proceeded to use an elevator three or four times. During its use the plaintiff was jumping, and the nurse had to hold her head down. Mr Kelly then felt a movement of the elevator and something gave. In consequence the plaintiff was taken to Guy's Hospital where it was discovered that she had fractured a jaw bone. She sued Mr Kelly for using the elevator negligently.

Held: the plaintiff had failed to make out a case of negligence. There had been nothing abnormal about Mr Kelly's use of the elevator. The plaintiff, being excitable and nervous, had jerked her head at the last moment and this had caused the fracture.

See p 130.

O'Toole v Mersey Regional Health Authority

Damages: structured settlement

May J. 21 August 1992

The plaintiff (Sian O'Toole) was born in January 1982 and was ten years old when his case was settled on a conventionally assessed basis of £675,000. Just over £225,000 was paid as a contingency sum to the family and into the Court of Protection. In addition, Mersey Health Authority agreed to pay regular sums of:

(i)   £20,000 pa, retail price index linked, payable for life with a guaranteed minimum payment period of 20 years;

(ii) £5,000 every five years, retail price index linked, payable for life.

Sian's solicitor was given very specific instructions as to what was required in terms of periodic payments. Accordingly, the agreement to structure was based directly on the requirements, rather than negotiated on the basis of a discount for the defendants.

The novel feature of the case was the agreement of the Mersey Health Authority to make payments under a structured settlement without purchasing an annuity to match its obligations. This followed detailed discussions with the Department of Health and the Treasury. A significant cash saving for the National Health Service was achieved.

In August 1992 the settlement was approved by Mr Justice May.

See p 152.

Obembe and Others v City and Hackney Health Authority

Brain damage: childbirth: limitation

Drake J. Lexis, 9 June 1989.

The first plaintiff (Geoffrey Obembe) was born on 8 July 1979. The second and third plaintiffs (his parents) alleged that immediately after his birth he was left unattended for ten to fifteen minutes, during which time he ceased to breathe, in consequence of which he suffered irreversible brain damage. The parents claimed damages for themselves as well as him.

In July 1984 they instructed solicitors who set out the plaintiffs' allegations of negligence in a letter to the hospital in which they requested the medical records. The hospital produced these in October 1984, and another hospital produced records in December 1984. A conference with counsel was held in July 1986. Further notes were obtained. After another conference in February 1988, the writ was issued on 21 July 1988.

A preliminary trial was held on the issue of whether the parents' claim was statute-barred. The plaintiffs conceded that at a very early stage they knew that the injury in question was significant. The defendants produced affidavit evidence that certain nurses or midwives could not be traced and that a doctor who had gone to Australia had not been traced either.

Held: (i) (a) the fact that the parents were dealing with a severely handicapped child did not provide a good reason, viewed objectively, why nothing was done by them to seek legal advice at an earlier stage.

(b) nor did the fact that they had 21 years in which to bring an action on behalf of the first plaintiff provide a good reason for their not seeking legal advice and pursuing their own claim earlier.

(c) their solicitors' letter in July 1984 suggested that they knew that they had a good cause of action for the injuries that they had sustained arising out of their infant's injuries.

     (d)   their state of knowledge was greatly increased by the prompt production of hospital records in October and December 1984.

     (e)   accordingly, time began to run against them well before 21 July 1985, and their writ issued on 21 July 1988 was statute barred.

(ii) (a)   the parents had not shown good reason for the delay which had occurred.

     (b)   the cogency of the defendants' evidence had been reduced by their inability to find certain witnesses.

     (c)   there was a completely inexplicable and inexcusable delay on the plaintiffs' side between December 1984 and July 1988.

     (d)   the parents would be prejudiced by not being able to pursue their action for their own injuries.

     (e)   the long delay since the birth greatly prejudiced the defendants, even though they would still have to meet the claim of the infant first plaintiff.

     (f)   it would not be equitable to allow the parents' claim to proceed.

See p 197.

Odam v Eli Lilly & Co and Others

Limitation: drugs: Opren

Court of Appeal. [1992] 3 Med LR 380

See *Nash v Eli Lilly & Co* (B) (p 470).

Re P (a minor)

Consent: abortion: minor: wardship: parental objections

Butler-Sloss J. (1986) 80 LGR 301

In August 1966, Shirley was born. In 1979 she was convicted of theft and committed to the care of Lewisham Borough Council. In 1980 she conceived and gave birth to a baby boy. She lived with him in a single room in a mother and child unit. In 1981, at the age of 15, she became pregnant again. She wanted an abortion and understood the implications. Her general practitioner and hospital consultant were in favour of an abortion. Her father, a Seventh Day Adventist, opposed it, partly on religious grounds.

The Lewisham Borough Council applied to make Shirley a ward of court and sought an order that the pregnancy, which had lasted eleven weeks, be terminated.

Held: (i)   it was appropriate for the local authority to have placed the problem before the court under wardship proceedings.

        (ii)   the case came within the Abortion Act 1967. The continuance of the pregnancy would involve injury to the mental health of Shirley and her existing child, and that risk was undoubtedly much greater than the risk of the pregnancy being terminated.

        (iii)   the parents' feelings must be considered as a factor in the case, and their religious objections must be taken into account. However Shirley's welfare must be paramount. The parents' objections could not weigh against her needs so as to prevent the termination.

The applications were granted.

See p 12.

Palmer and Palmer v Eadie

Vasectomy (failed): warning: risk disclosure: state of knowledge

Court of Appeal. CAT, 18 May 1987

By 1980 the plaintiffs (Mr and Mrs Palmer) had had four children and three aborted pregnancies. Mr Palmer consulted Mr Eadie, a consultant urologist, about a vasectomy. Mr Eadie warned him that the operation, though likely to be successful, carried with it the risk of failure. He performed the vasectomy. Mr Palmer had two successive zero sperm counts. However in 1983 the plaintiffs had another child.

They sued Mr Eadie. The evidence was that in 1980 the vasectomy operation could be carried out in two ways, either by three to four centimetre excisions, or by 1.5 centimetre excisions with other steps. If three to four centimetres were excised, it was more difficult to reverse the operation. However in 1980 it was thought that, if after either method was used, there were two successive zero sperm counts, then there was no chance that the operation had failed. The trial judge (Hollings J) dismissed the plaintiffs' claim.

Held: (i) as the trial judge accepted that Mr Eadie had warned Mr Palmer of the risk of failure, there was no breach of contract;

(ii) it was not negligent of Mr Eadie not to discuss with Mr Palmer the choice between the two methods of excision, at a time when nobody thought there was a risk provided that there were two consecutive zero counts.

See p 128.

Pargeter v Kensington and Chelsea and Westminster Health Authority

Injection: drugs: after-care: nurses: standard of care: burden of proof: ophthalmic

Forbes J. (1979) 2 Lancet 1030

The plaintiff (Mr Pargeter) was admitted to hospital for the removal of a cataract in his left eye. At 2.00pm on the day of the operation he received an injection of 15 mg of papaveretum, with an anti-emetic drug, as pre-operative medication. Further injections of 10 mg of papaveretum, without an anti-emetic drug, were administered by nursing staff after the operation at 4.35pm, when the plaintiff was in some pain, and at 11.30pm, to "settle" him. When he awoke the next morning at 7.15, he was offered a cup of tea, drank it and vomited immediately. His left eye burst open and he lost the sight in it.

The plaintiff sued the hospital authority. Evidence was given at trial that everything must be done to stop the patient from coughing or vomiting after an open eye operation. Evidence was also given that it was wholly wrong nursing practice to give tea to a patient recovering from an anaesthetic, unless it was first established that he could tolerate liquid by giving him controlled sips of water.

Held: (i) as there was a respectable body of medical opinion which took the view that papaveretum should be administered, even though there was an opposing school of thought, the hospital staff were not negligent in using it;

(ii) if a patient were given tea without trial sips, especially after having had papaveretum without an anti-emetic, that would be negligent nursing practice. However it was highly improbable that this precaution was not taken.

Judgment for the defendants.

See p 139.

Parkinson v West Cumberland Hospital Management Committee and Another

Diagnosis: hospital doctor: cardiac: error of judgment: fatal

Ashworth J. [1955] 1 BMJ 977

Soon after 4.00 am on 11 July 1973 Mr Parkinson, aged 39, went to the Workington Infirmary and complained of chest pains. Dr Graham, a newly qualified doctor in his fourth day there, examined him for nearly an hour. Then he discharged Mr Parkinson, giving him two tablets of codeine and telling him to return later for x-ray examination. A quarter of an hour later, Mr Parkinson was found dead in a street near the hospital. He had died of a massive coronary thrombosis.

The plaintiff (his widow) sued the hospital authority and Dr Graham.

Held: Dr Graham made a mistake, but he had not been negligent. His examination had been careful, and there were signs and symptoms pointing away from a serious condition.

See p 99.

Parry v North West Surrey Health Authority

Causation: cerebral palsy: childbirth: nurse: registrar

HH Judge Curtis. [1994] 5 Med LR 259

Jill Dickson, the mother of the plaintiff (Edward Parry) was admitted to St Peter's Hospital at Chertsey at 11.10am on 19 December 1989, after her membranes had ruptured spontaneously on 18 December. She was abdominally and vaginally examined by Dr Anthony who wrote '5/5' which indicated a high head. She underlined her marking of 5/5 thrice, since it was unusual to discover a baby so high at that stage of labour. She reported this to Dr Ahmed, an acting registrar. He did not examine Ms Dickson but gave instructions for her to be left for a few hours until the head descended a little. When she was last abdominally palpated at 4.45pm, she was 3/5 palpable. At 8.30pm the top of the baby's head on vaginal examination was at the level of the ischial spines, so he was at station zero. An episode of bradycardia occurred then. He made no further progress in his descent.

When the midwife, Mrs Moss, came on duty at 9.30pm, she carried out a vaginal examination but not an abdominal palpation. Full dilatation occurred at 10.30pm. At 10.40pm she left Ms Dickson in the care of a student midwife with whose encouragement she started to push. When Mrs Moss returned about 11.20pm, she allowed the pushing to continue. At midnight a further episode of fetal stress occurred.

At 00.35am Mrs Moss alerted Dr Ahmed who carried out a hurried examination but did not abdominally palpate Ms Dickson. He then attempted to deliver the baby by ventouse. After this failed, he attempted an extraction by Kielland's forceps. At 1.10am the fetal heart rate fell. When the plaintiff was eventually born, he was found to be suffering from cerebral palsy caused by a fairly short period of hypoxia close to the time of birth.

Held: (i) for Mrs Moss to omit abdominal palpations was outside the bracket of acceptable practice. The establishment of the position of the vertex of the baby as precisely as possible was most important. It is difficult for this to be done by vaginal examination due to caput and moulding. The accepted practice was to do an abdominal palpation first and then a vaginal examination.

(ii) instead of discounting the pushing that had occurred before her return at 11.20pm, Mrs Moss should have sent for a doctor. The acceptable limit of time for maternal pushing was one hour. It was wholly wrong to make Ms Dickson go on pushing, since she had been in labour one and a half hours and pushing well for one hour, with no descent since 8.30pm.

(iii) Dr Ahmed was negligent not to have abdominally palpated Ms Dickson. This led to him mistakenly thinking that the plaintiff's head was lower than it was.

(iv) he failed to obtain and/or properly consider all of the available information.

(v) his attempt at the extraction by Kielland's forceps was done at an unacceptably high level.

(vi) what he ought to have done instead was to proceed to a caesarean section. This would have resulted in the plaintiff being delivered undamaged.

(vii) the attempt by Dr Ahmed to deliver the foetus by Kielland's forceps when it was too high in the mother's pelvis at least materially contributed to, if it did not solely cause, the episode of bradycardia which in turn caused the acute hypoxia-ischaemia.

See p 138.

Pask v Bexley Health Authority

Retained surgical product: scarring: damages

Court of Appeal. [1988] CLY 1098

In July 1981 the plaintiff, then aged twenty-three, having taken tablets and alcohol, was admitted to hospital to have her stomach pumped out. A year later it was discovered that two and a half feet of plastic tubing had been left in her body. The tubing had worked its way into the bottom of her left lung.

When the plaintiff was discharged in July 1981, she suffered severe breathlessness and dreadful pains in her body, coughed violently and brought up blood and phlegm. She endured appalling discomfort and pain for the next year. The operation to remove the tube left a very large scar running from underneath her left breast and up her back almost to the base of her neck. It was 36 centimetres long, ugly and permanent. It was also tender, causing pain and discomfort if she should knock it or wear tight clothing. The plaintiff's health improved after the operation but she still suffered from breathlessness and had repeated chest infections. The infections would recur, and she would suffer discomfort for the rest of her life. She needed help from her mother with housework.

She sued the health authority who admitted liability. In October 1987 the trial judge (Caulfield J) awarded her £25,000 for her pain and suffering, to include an element to enable her to pay those who help her in future, and £17,500 for the disfigurement and discomfort resulting from her scar.

Held: the court would not interfere with the total award of £42,500 general damages, although it might have been preferable not to split it up into two constituents.

See p 125.

Patel v Adyha

General practitioner: examination: diagnosis

Court of Appeal. CAT, 2 April 1985

In September and October 1975 the plaintiff (Mrs Patel) went three times to her general practitioner, Dr Adyha, and complained of pains in her back. He only examined her once when he inserted his hand underneath her dress and placed it on her back. He did not ask her to take her dress off. She was given analgesics on each visit. In March 1976 there was a collapse of her spine. She was found to be suffering from a tubercular condition and there was kyphus.

The plaintiff sued Dr Adyha. There was expert evidence that a suitable examination would have found either local spinal deformity or local stiffness detectable on palpation or bending. The trial judge found in her favour.

Held: (i) the trial judge was right to accept that Dr Adyha negligently failed to carry out a proper examination which would have revealed the need to obtain specialist advice and led to treatment;

(ii) the plaintiff could not be criticised for not seeking further medical advice before March 1976, since she did not know that she had a serious condition and the mere prescription of analgesics signalled that her's was a case for patience and fortitude rather than treatment.

See p 98.

Patel v Patel

Asthma: damages: pharmacist: drugs

HH Judge Edwards. [1993] CLY 1589

The plaintiff (Mrs Patel) was aged 47 when her general practitioner prescribed Prednisolome and Uniphyllin for her severe asthmatic condition. The pharmacist mixed up the labels on the bottles. The plaintiff took the drugs as instructed on the labels. In consequence, she suffered from an excessive dose of Uniphyllin equivalent to five or six times over the prescribed amount.

Later that evening, she suffered the toxic side-effects. She became unwell, with vomiting that continued all night, four episodes of loose watery diarrhoea, cramping pains in the epigastrium, a headache and some pain in the chest and back. The next morning, she was taken to hospital where medical examination revealed shortage of breath, wheeziness, widespread rhonchi, poor air entry, crepitations in the upper lobe area, and tenderness in the abdomen, especially in the epigastic area. The plaintiff remained in hospital where her condition improved after three days. She was discharged another four days later. She was off work for a further three months.

Held (March 1993): (i) general damages of £3,000 were awarded for her pain, suffering and loss of amenities.

(ii) £3.50 per hour was awarded for the time spent by her husband and others in travelling to and from the hospital and for their attendance on the plaintiff in hospital.

Paterson v Chadwick

Anaesthetics: injection: discovery: solicitor's negligence: dental: hand

Boreham J. [1974] 1 WLR 890

In February 1969 the plaintiff (Mrs Sarah Paterson) attended Northampton Hospital for dental treatment. An anaesthetic injection was given to her. She sustained a serious and permanent disability of her left hand. She alleged that this was due to the injection having been negligently carried out.

She instructed solicitors to claim damages for her. They did not start court action, so her claim became statute barred in February 1972. Thereafter she consulted other solicitors and in February 1973 a writ was issued against her former solicitors for negligence and breach of contract.

The plaintiff applied by summons pursuant to s 32(1) of the Administration of Justice Act 1970 and RSC Ord 24, r 7A for an order for disclosure by the hospital authority of medical records and other documents relating to her treatment at Northampton Hospital.

Held: there was a clear and firm connection between her professional negligence claim and her personal injuries. Thus she was 'a person who is a party to proceedings in which a claim in respect of personal injuries to a person is made' within the words of s 321(1) of the 1970 Act. As such, she was entitled to the order for disclosure.

Note: Section 32(1) of the Administration of Justice Act 1970 has been replaced by s 34(2) of the Supreme Court Act 1981.

See pp 179, 207.

Paton v British Pregnancy Advisory Service Trustees and Another

Abortion: father's status: foetus' rights: parental objections: injunction

Sir George Baker P. [1979] 1 QB 276, [1978] 2 All ER 987, [1978] 3 WLR 687

On 8 May 1978 Mrs Joan Paton's general practitioner confirmed that she was pregnant. She applied for and obtained the necessary medical certificate entitling her to an abortion within the terms of the Abortion Act 1967. On 16 May she left the matrimonial home. On 17 May she filed a petition for divorce.

The plaintiff, her husband William Paton, applied for an injunction to restrain the British Pregnancy Advisory Service and Mrs Paton from causing or permitting an abortion to be carried out on her. It was accepted that there had been correct compliance with the provisions of the Abortion Act 1967.

Held: (i)   the foetus cannot have a right of its own until it is born and has a separate existence from its mother;

(ii)   personal family relationships in marriage cannot be enforced by the order of a court. The Abortion Act 1967 gives no right to a father to be consulted in respect of a termination of a pregnancy. The plaintiff, whether as husband or father, had no legal right to stop his wife having the abortion or to stop the doctors from carrying it out.

Per Sir George Baker P: 'It would be quite impossible for the courts in any event to supervise the operation of the Abortion Act 1967. The great social responsibility is firmly placed by the law upon the shoulders of the medical profession.'

Note: Mr Paton's subsequent application to the European Commission of Human Rights was also dismissed: *Paton v United Kingdom* (1980) 3 EHRR 408.

See p 55.

Patten v Birmingham Regional Hospital Board and Others

House surgeon: operation: fingers: amputation

Stable J. (1955) 2 Lancet 1336

The plaintiff (Mrs Lily Patten), a factory operative, was injured at work when a power press suddenly descended and caught her right hand. An orthopaedic surgeon at the hospital advised that part of the middle finger should be amputated. The operation was carried out by a house surgeon who by mistake removed the tip of the little finger. Also, an operation for the suture of a severed tendon in the injured finger was performed too late, and all three middle fingers were bent in towards the palm. Nineteen months after the operation the whole of the middle finger was amputated.

The plaintiff sued her employers, the hospital authority and the house surgeon.

Held: the hospital authority was liable with the house surgeon who made the grave blunder for substantially the whole of the condition of the plaintiff's injured hand.

See p 117.

Patterson v Rotherham Health Authority

Diagnosis: hospital doctor: fracture: damages: knee: sports injury

Court of Appeal. CAT, 20 May 1987

On 29 August 1982 the plaintiff (Angela Patterson), then aged 22, fell from her horse in a show-jumping competition. She suffered a fracture of the tibia within her left knee joint. She was immediately taken to Rotherham District General Hospital where they failed to diagnose the fracture until she returned there on 13 September. An operation was carried out on 14 September.

The plaintiff suffered acute pain in the fortnight after the accident. The delay made it impracticable to attempt to repair the medial collateral ligament. There was continuing pain and discomfort in her knee, and worsening osteoarthritic changes which would eventually require an arthroplasty. If the operation had been immediately performed, her disability would have been 20%; instead it was 50%.

She sued the health authority who admitted negligently failing to diagnose the fracture. In July 1986 the trial judge (French J) awarded her £24,000 general damages including the cost of arthroplasty.

Held: (i) the judge was entitled to conclude that the future need for an arthroplasty had been caused by the delay in treatment; £2,500 was appropriate as a discounted sum of this future cost.

(ii) £1,000 was appropriate for the needless pain and suffering during the fortnight after the accident.

(iii) the award for the subsequent extra suffering and loss of amenities caused by the defendant's negligence could not properly exceed £15,000.

(iv) the total award for general damages should be £18,500.

See p 96.

Payne v St Helier Group Hospital Management Committee and Another

Diagnosis: casualty officer: second opinion: peritonitis: fatal

Donovan J. (1952) Times, 12 November

On 10 July 1950 Reginald Payne was kicked in the abdomen by a horse. His general practitioner sent him for examination to the Sutton and Cheam Hospital. He was examined there nine and a half hours after the accident by Dr Perkins, the hospital's casualty officer. Dr Perkins noted a bruise about the size of a man's hand on Mr Payne's abdomen but concluded that there was no internal injury. He sent Mr Payne home and told him to go to bed and to call his own panel doctor if he should experience pain.

By 28 July 1950 Mr Payne was very ill and was admitted to hospital where two operations were later performed on him; first a lumbar incision, and then a laparotomy which revealed a condition of general peritonitis. Mr Payne died from this condition nine days later on 30 August 1950. His widow sued Dr Perkins and the hospital authority.

Held: (i) the hospital was not negligent in respect of the system that it provided for the examination of abdominal injury.

(ii) Dr Perkins ought to have found that Mr Payne was suffering from pain, shock and rigidity of the abdomen. It was wholly unreasonable for him to send Mr Payne home and not to detain him for observation and examination by a consultant. Dr Perkins had failed to exercise reasonable care in his diagnosis and treatment. He was negligent and the hospital authority was vicariously liable.

(iii) the hospital authority was granted an indemnity against Dr Perkins in respect of the whole of the damages and two-thirds of the costs.

See pp 60, 98.

Perionowsky v Freeman and Another

Consultant: nurses

Cockburn CJ (with jury). (1866) 4 F & F 977

In May 1865 the plaintiff (Mr Perionowsky) suffered a disease and became a patient at St George's Hospital. Mr Freeman and Mr Holmes, two surgeons there, ordered that he should have a hot hip bath. They went on to attend other patients in the ward and were not present when nurses put the plaintiff into the bath. He was somewhat scalded.

The plaintiff sued the two surgeons. Evidence was given that it was usual hospital practice for doctors to leave it to nurses to see to the baths.

Held: such matters should be left to nurses. The surgeons would not be liable for the negligence of the nurses, unless near enough to be aware of it and to prevent it.

The jury returned a verdict for the defendants.

See p 129.

Phelan v East Cumbrian Health Authority

Anaesthetic awareness: damages: leg: operation

Schiemann J. [1991] 2 Med LR 419

The plaintiff (Mr Phelan) went to the operating theatre with a bad leg injury requiring surgery under general anaesthesia. He was told he would have an injection and that, when he woke up, the operation would be over. He did have an injection and lost consciousness. He then woke up in the operating theatre. He heard nurses talking and had a tube down his throat. At this stage, he was relaxed. However, he wiggled his toes to let them know as best he could he was awake. He heard the nurses refer to the fact that his toes were moving. He heard a man say that it was 'just reflexes' and to ignore it. He then felt somebody get hold of his leg and apply a rubber tourniquet to his groin. He heard the man say to the nurse to remove after five and three quarter minutes. The plaintiff then realised that the operation was not over, but about to start but he was unable to move. He then went through the operation. He felt a burning pain to his leg which was the scalpel being applied to his leg. He felt his leg being drilled. As a carpenter, he had a graphic idea of what was going on. Four holes were drilled into the bone. The pain was like an electric shock to the head or drilling through a nerve by the dentist. All the while, the plaintiff was being artificially ventilated. He felt very sick and stopped breathing in the hope that this would indicate that he was awake but the machine started breathing for him.

Immediately after the operation the plaintiff was convulsed by anger and relived his experience again and again when asked about it by friends or his wife. He thought about the operation when in bed. Although the hospital authority admitted liability, the failure to agree damages led to his concentrating on his operation in a way in which he would not otherwise have done had agreement been reached.

Held (October 1991): £5,000 was awarded for the experience on the operating table. A further £10,000 was awarded for pain, suffering and loss of amenity. The total award was £15,000.

See p 123.

Pickering v Governors of the United Leeds Hospital

Operation: after-care: nurses: consultant: bedsores: femur: gangrene

Slade J. (1954) 1 Lancet 1075

The plaintiff (Mrs Pickering), aged 82, was admitted to hospital after falling and fracturing a femur. She was mentally alert and in no way senile, but weighed about fifteen stone and suffered from a mild form of Parkinson's disease. Her operation lasted one and a half hours, and she needed a subsequent blood transfusion lasting ten hours. The surgeon forbade the turning of the plaintiff on to her side in the early stages after the operation. Later he directed that she should be moved on to her right side. She developed severe bedsores while in hospital, and two operations had to be performed in a nursing home for removal of gangrenous tissue.

The plaintiff sued the hospital authority, alleging that the nursing staff failed to keep the bed dry and failed to change her position. The orthopaedic officer testified that he examined the bed at least once every day and always found it dry. The only direct evidence of the bed being wet was that of the plaintiff's daughter who said she did nothing about it.

Held: the plaintiff had failed to make out her allegations. The question of changing the plaintiff's position was one for the surgeon, not the nurses. There had been no negligence on the part of the nursing staff.

See p 138.

Pimm v Roper

Diagnosis: duty of care: settlement of claim

Bramwell B. (1862) 2 F&F 783

The plaintiff (Mr Pimm) was injured while a passenger in a train that collided. At the station the railway company's staff sent him to Mr Roper, the railway company's surgeon. The plaintiff, whose face was bleeding, told Mr Roper that he was injured in his face and arm. Mr Roper made the usual applications for these visible wounds. On the plaintiff's next visit, considering that he was more frightened than hurt, Mr Roper sent him to the railway company's authorities who gave him £5 which he accepted in settlement.

Next day the plaintiff came again and got Mr Roper to examine his abdomen. It was discovered that it was ruptured. The plaintiff's claim against the railway company for further damages failed due to the settlement. He then sued Mr Roper.

Held: there was no proof of any injury sustained by the plaintiff as a result of any neglect on the part of Mr Roper to examine him. Examination was the only duty that had been proved. There was no further ground of action.

See p 18.

Pimpalkhare v North West Hertfordshire Health Authority

Brain damage: childbirth: quadriplegia: structured settlement

Otton J. *Halsbury's Laws Annual Abridgment* 1993, para 924

The plaintiff was born in 1983 by emergency caesarean section, after trial of scar to the point that his mother's uterus ruptured. He was severely asphyxiated and, as a result of the brain damage sustained at the time of his birth, suffered from a mixture of dyskinetic cerebral palsy and spastic quadriplegia. He had involuntary movements of all four limbs and head, coupled with generally increased muscle tone. He was severely physically handicapped. His vision, hearing and intelligence were normal. He was able to make some sounds but no words. He was totally dependent on others for feeding, toileting, dressing and mobility. He needed constant care and attention together with specialist help from a paediatric physiotherapist, occupational therapist and speech therapist, as well as appropriate electronic and communication aids. His life expectancy was assessed at 40–50 years from trial. Liability was admitted. The value of his claim was agreed at £1,270,000 including general damages of £130,000 for pain, suffering and loss of amenities.

The case was then adjourned in order to explore the possibility of a structured settlement. After payment out of sums due to the plaintiff's mother, and purchase of a suitable home and certain other incidental expenses, the sum remaining for a possible structured settlement was approximately £900,000. The hospital authority sought a discount of between £60,000 and £95,000. This left approximately £800,000 of which it was proposed that £150,000 should be invested in a contingency fund. This would have left £650,000 to purchase an annuity producing an annual tax free retail price index-linked income of £27,795 pa for life.

This was compared to the alternative of a conventional lump sum award. On the basis of a model portfolio obtained from the Public Trustee, a fund of £900,000 invested as to 15% in gilts, 5% on deposit and 80% in equities was expected to produce an income of £30,768 net of tax. Accountants advised that on past performance it was reasonable to assume that an appropriately invested portfolio of equities would produce a net return after inflation of one to two per cent per annum over a lifetime, that the plaintiff would be better placed financially with a conventional award than with a structured settlement and that, provided the fund was managed appropriately, it would not be exhausted before the plaintiff's death.

Held: the conventional lump sum award of £1,270,000 was approved.

Note: The discount sought by the health authority was very large, compared with subsequent cases. See for instance *Flynn v Maidstone Health Authority* (p 344).

See p 152.

Pippin and Wife v Sheppard

Surgeon: duty of care

Court of Exchequer. (1822) 11 Price 400

The declaration stated that the defendant, Mr Sheppard, followed and carried on the art, mystery and occupation of a surgeon – that defendant, afterwards, and etc at Bristol aforesaid, was retained and employed as such surgeon for a certain reasonable reward to be to him therefore paid, to treat, attend to, and cure divers grievous hurts, cuts and etc just before then by the plaintiff Mrs Pippin had and received: and the said defendant then and there entered upon the treatment and cure of her; yet defendant afterwards so carelessly, negligently, improperly and unskilfully, conducted himself in that behalf, and then and there so carelessly and etc applied his care and treatment in and upon a certain wound and etc of the said wife, that by means thereof the said wound became and was grievously aggravated and made worse, and was thereby then and there made and rendered violently and dreadfully inflamed and etc to the danger of the wife, and that her life was greatly despaired of, and that by means thereof she suffered great pain and etc and was forced to submit to painful surgical operations in and about the treatment of the said wound by other and more skilful surgeons.

Held: the declaration was a sufficient pleading. It was not necessary to state by whom the defendant was retained and employed. Nor did the declaration need to allege that it was the duty of the defendant, or that he undertook or engaged, properly or skilfully to conduct himself in the treatment and cure of the said wounds.

See pp 18, 43.

Powell v Streatham Manor Nursing Home

After-care: nurses: hysterectomy: bladder

House of Lords. [1935] AC 243

In January 1930 the plaintiff (Helena Powell) entered the defendants' nursing home as a paying patient. Dr Kirkland performed the operation of hysterectomy on her. Soon afterwards it was found that her bladder had been punctured.

The plaintiff sued the defendants in the name of the nursing home. She testified at trial that one of the nurses there, in attempting to relieve her of urine after the operation, used a rigid catheter and passed it not into the urethra (as she ought to have done) but into the vagina, and continued forcing the catheter through the suture, which had been made to complete the operation, until it perforated the bladder.

The trial judge (Horridge J) believed her evidence and decided the case in her favour. The Court of Appeal reversed his judgment.

Held: it was impossible to say that the trial judge was wrong in believing the plaintiff and therefore finding that the defendants had negligently punctured her bladder. His judgment should be restored.

Per Viscount Sankey LC: 'the judge of first instance is not the possessor of infallibility and, like other tribunals, there may be occasions when he goes wrong on a question of fact; but first and last and all the time, he has the great advantage, which is denied to the Court of Appeal, of seeing the witnesses and watching their demeanour.'

See p 138.

Prendergast v Sam & Dee Ltd and Others

General practitioner: pharmacist: prescription: foreseeability: apportionment of liability: brain damage

Court of Appeal. [1989] 1 Med LR 36, (1989) Times, 14 March

In December 1983 the plaintiff (James Prendergast), an asthmatic who was starting to get a cold, consulted his general practitioner, Dr Miller. Dr Miller wrote out a prescription for three drugs including twenty-one 250 mg Amoxil tablets to be taken three times a day. The word Amoxil was written, not very legibly, in lower case. The plaintiff took the prescription to the pharmacy of Sam & Dee Limited where Mr Kozary misread the prescription and dispensed twenty-one 5 mg tablets of Daonil, a drug to control diabetes by reducing the sugar content of the blood. After taking six Daonil tablets, the plaintiff suffered hypoglycaemia which led to unconsciousness and irreparable brain damage.

He sued Sam & Dee Limited, Mr Kozary and Dr Miller. The trial judge (Auld J) found all the defendants liable and apportioned liability of 75% to Sam & Dee Limited and Mr Kozary, and 25% to Dr Miller. Dr Miller appealed.

Held: (i) a prescription which is so written as to invite or reasonably permit misreading by a pharmacist under ordinary working conditions (which may be less than ideal) falls below the necessary standard. Dr Miller's poor writing came within this category;

(ii) although other aspects of the prescription, such as the dosage and number of tablets, should have put Mr Kozary on inquiry as being inconsistent with Daonil, the chain of causation was not broken and it was reasonably foreseeable that Daonil would be prescribed;

(iii) the trial judge did not err in his allocation of liability between the defendants.

See pp 80, 121, 135.

Prescott v Basildon Health Authority

Damages: diagnosis: fracture: arm

Henry J. (1991) AVMA Journal, April, p 12.

In March 1987 the plaintiff (Stephen Prescott), then working as a doorman at Flicks Discotheque in Dartford, was injured during a disturbance. He was taken to West Hill Hospital in Dartford where a displaced fracture of the right ulna was diagnosed. He was advised to attend the nearest hospital to his home the following day,

He attended Basildon Hospital where a further x-ray was thought to show a displaced fracture of the right ulna. A plaster was applied and his arm was x-rayed again on 3 April 1987. In fact the plaintiff had sustained a Monteggia fracture which should have been treated immediately by open reduction of the ulna and relocation of the radial head. The Monteggia fracture was not diagnosed until November 1987. Nothing was done about it until June 1989 after he had re-fractured his arm whilst playing with his daughter.

As a result of the failure to diagnose and treat, the plaintiff had restricted range of elbow and wrist movement, both movements being painful at their extremes. Before the assault, he was a HGV lorry driver. The injuries prevented him from continuing his chosen occupation and he had to set up his own business as a van driver. The prognosis was that there was likely to be a deterioration in function of his right arm and increasing discomfort in his right wrist. It was likely that beyond ten years his symptoms would become too severe for him to manage as a van driver. If properly treated, he could reasonably have expected to have been back at work as a HGV lorry driver, roping and sheeting, within six to nine months of the injury.

The hospital authority admitted liability.

Held (February 1991):   general damages of £15,000 were awarded for pain, suffering and loss of amenities. Special damages were £18,995 and future loss was £47,016.

See pp 96, 155.

Prout v Crowley and Another

Injection: standard of care: arm

G Glynn Blackledge QC. [1956] 1 BMJ 580

In June 1952 the plaintiff (Mrs Catherine Prout) was being treated for anaemia as an in-patient at Walton Hospital, Liverpool. On three previous occasions Dr Crowley had successfully injected ferrivenin into a vein of the antecubital fossa of her right arm. On the fourth occasion the plaintiff complained of pain after he had injected about 1 ml. He realised that the point of the needle had come out of the vein, so he immediately withdrew the needle and ordered poultices to be applied to her arm. A small quantity of the ferrivenin had entered the tissues surrounding the vein. This caused an abscess to develop.

The plaintiff sued Dr Crowley and the hospital authority.

Held: the extravenous injection of a small quanitity of solution could happen without any negligence on the part of the operator. Dr Crowley had followed the correct technique and had stopped the injection as soon as he realised that the point of the needle was outside the vein. He had not been negligent.

See p 120.

Pudney v Union-Castle Mail SS Co Ltd and Another

Ship's doctor: diagnosis: standard of care: rheumatism

Devlin J. [1953] 1 Lloyd's Rep 73

In April 1948 the plaintiff (David Pudney), then aged 25, was an assistant pantryman in the defendant's ship travelling from London to Cape Town. On 9 April he was taken ill with rheumatic pains and was treated by Dr Fairley, the ship's surgeon. He developed a high temperature and suffered a sore throat. There was no swelling of his joints, the fever subsided, but his pains remained. Dr Fairley advised the plaintiff to be discharged from the ship at Cape Town on 24 April and repatriated. His diagnosis was one of a mild rheumatic complaint.

The plaintiff deteriorated thereafter. In October 1949, after he had been examined by a number of doctors, it was discovered that he was suffering from acute rheumatoid arthritis. This left him a permanent cripple. He sued Dr Fairley and the shipping company, alleging that Dr Fairley should have guarded against potential dangers, of which rheumatoid arthritis was one, and advised immediate rest until the diagnosis was complete.

Held: Dr Fairley had not been negligent. It was impossible to diagnose a mild rheumatic atttack as rheumatoid arthritis until swellings in the joints appeared. Following an apparently mild attack of rheumatism with a high temperature, it was not practicable to insist on the patient remaining in bed or going to hospital.

See p 99.

R v Adomako

Anaesthetics: manslaughter: operation: cardiac arrest: criminal liability: locum

House of Lords. [1994] NLJR 936; (1994) Times, 4 July, [1994] 5 Med LR 277

In January 1987 Alan Loveland, aged 33, underwent a detached retina operation at Mayday Hospital in Croydon. The defendant (Dr Adomako) was a locum anaesthetist at the hospital for that weekend. He took over as sole anaesthetist during the operation. The tube from the ventilator supplying oxygen to the patient's mouth became disconnected. By 11.10am the patient's pulse was 40/min and his blood pressure was low. The defendant's initial response to the signals of distress was to assume that the monitor was faulty and to obtain another blood pressure cuff. He administered atropine at 11.15am. The surgeon began cardiac massage and it was he, not the defendant, who noticed that the tube was disconnected, which must have been the case for about six minutes. Although the ventilator was reconnected and the patient's lungs ventilated manually with oxygen, he had suffered a cardiac arrest which caused irreversible brain damage. He subsequently died of hypoxia in July 1987.

The defendant was charged with manslaughter. The expert evidence at his trial was that any competent anaesthetist who was looking at his patient should have realised total disconnection within seconds.

Held: (i)   in cases of manslaughter by criminal negligence involving a breach of duty, the test is whether the defendant was guilty of gross negligence. It is not necessary to refer to recklessness, although it is perfectly open to the trial judge to do so.

(ii)   the summing up of the trial judge in this case was a model of clarity: The defendant's appeal must be dismissed.

Note: Alliott J had sentenced Dr Adomako to 6 months' imprisonment suspended for 12 months.

Per Lord Mackay: 'On this basis in my opinion the ordinary principles of the law of negligence apply to ascertain whether or not the defendant has been in breach of a duty of care towards the victim who has died. If such breach of duty is established the next question is whether that breach of duty caused the death of the victim.

If so, the jury must go on to consider whether that breach of duty should be characterised as gross negligence and therefore as a crime. This will depend on the seriousness of the breach of duty committed by the defendant in all the circumstances in which the defendant was placed when it occurred. The jury will have to consider whether the extent to which the defendant's conduct departed from the proper standard of care incumbent upon him, involving as it must have done a risk of death to the patient, was such that it should be judged criminal.

It is true that to a certain extent this involves an element of circularity, but in this branch of the law I do not believe that is fatal to its being correct as a test of how far conduct must depart from accepted standards to be characterised as criminal. This is necessarily a question of degree and an attempt to specify that degree more closely is I think likely to achieve only a spurious precision.

The essence of the matter, which is supremely a jury question, is whether, having regard to the risk of death involved, the conduct of the defendant was so bad in all the circumstances as to amount in their judgment to a criminal act or omission.'

See p 122.

R v Bateman

Childbirth: general practitioner: criminal liability: manslaughter: second opinion: fatal: uterus

Court of Appeal. (1925) 94 LJKB 791

On 23 July Dr Bateman, a general practitioner, was called in by the midwife to attend Mary Ann Harding on her confinement. He administered chloroform and attempted, properly but unsuccessfully, to effect delivery by the use of instruments. He then proceeded with his hands to perform the operation known as 'version', using of necessity considerable force. He worked at this operation for an hour and then delivered the child which was dead. In removing the placenta, he mistakenly removed with it a portion of the uterus. He visited the patient twice daily, but despite requests by the husband and the midwife, did not remove her to the infirmary until 28 July. She grew gradually weaker and died on 30 July.

On a post-mortem examination, the bladder was found to be ruptured, the colon was crushed against the sacral promontory, there was a small rupture of the rectum, and the uterus was almost entirely gone. Dr Bateman was prosecuted for manslaughter. The charges of negligence made against him were, in substance: (i) causing the internal ruptures in performing the operation of 'version'; (ii) removing part of the uterus along with the placenta; (iii) delay in sending the patient to the infirmary. He was convicted and sentenced to six months' imprisonment.

Held: in order to establish criminal liability, the facts must be such that, in the opinion of the jury, the negligence of the accused went beyond a mere matter of compensation between subjects and showed such disregard for the life and safety of others as to amount to a crime against the State and conduct deserving punishment.

The conviction was quashed, as there was no evidence to support the first charge, and it was uncertain whether the jury would have convicted on the second and third charges alone.

See p 58.

R v Bingley Magistrates' Court, ex p Morrow

Discontinuance of life-preserving treatment: murder: criminal liability

Queen's Bench Divisional Court. (1993) Times, 28 April.

Dr James Howe had discontinued all treatment sustaining the life of Anthony James Bland, pursuant to the House of Lords' decision in *Airedale National Health Service Trust v Bland*. Consequently Mr Bland died on 3 March 1993.

The Reverend Morrow applied to the Bingley Magistrates' Court to issue a summons charging Dr Howe with murder. The magistrates refused to do so.

Held: the House of Lords had declared that, if death occurred due to the removal of life support and nutrition, it should be attributed to natural causes and that anything done in good faith should be without criminal or civil liability. The magistrates were right to refuse to issue the summons.

See *Airedale National Health Service Trust v Bland* (p 222).

R v Cambridge Health Authority, ex p B

Hospital resources: judicial review: child patient: leukaemia

Court of Appeal. [1995] 2 All ER 129, (1995) Times, 15 March

B, a girl aged ten, had contracted non-Hodgkins lymphoma with common acute lymphoblastic leukaemia at the age of 5. Despite initially successful treatment, in 1993 she developed acute myeloid leukaemia. After further chemotherapy and an allogenic bone marrow transplant, the disease went into remission. However in January 1995 she suffered a relapse. Doctors who had treated her considered that a further course of chemotherapy followed by a second transplant would not be in her best interests. They gave her six to eight weeks to live, and said that they could not treat her further.

Her father applied to the hospital authority for funding for such treatment. He found a doctor who was willing to offer further chemotherapy and, if that proved successful, a further transplant. As a bed was unavailable on the National Health Service, the treatment would have to be carried out privately. The chances of a complete remission following chemotherapy were assessed at around 10%, at a cost of £15,000; while the chances for the transplant, costing £60,000, which would be performed if the chemotherapy were completed successfully, were put in the same region. The authority declined the father's application to fund the treatment.

B's father as her next friend applied for an order of certiorari quashing the authority's decision not to fund any further treatment for her, and applied for an order of mandamus to direct the authority to fund the treatment.

Held: (i) difficult and agonising judgments had to be made as to how the limited budget could best be allocated for the maximum advantage for the maximum number of patients. That was not a judgment for the court.

(ii) the authority had not exceeded its powers or acted unreasonably. The powers of the Court of Appeal were not such that it could substitute its own decision for that of the authority.

(iii) the decision by the hospital authority not to fund specific treatment for B on the grounds that the proposed treatment, described as experimental, would not be in her best interests and that the expenditure would not be an effective use of its limited resources, was not unlawful.

(iv) accordingly the court could not intervene by way of judicial review.

See pp 25, 47.

R v Central Birmingham Health Authority, ex p Collier

Judicial review: hospital resources: duty of care: cardiac

Court of Appeal. CAT, 6 January 1988

Matthew Collier was born in June 1983 with a missing heart valve: 'a hole in his heart'. By-pass surgery did not achieve the desired progress. In September 1987 his surgeon at the Children's Hospital advised that Matthew 'desperately needed' open heart surgery. He was placed at the top of the waiting list but, due to a shortage of intensive care beds and nurses, months passed without the operation being performed.

His father, Barry Collier, sought leave to apply for judicial review in respect of an alleged 'decision of the Central Birmingham Health Authority . . . not to conduct an operation and/or provide proper medical care for his baby boy Matthew Collier'.

Held: it was not for the court to allocate financial resources. There was no evidence that the health authority had acted unreasonably or in breach of any public duty. It would not be right for the court to intervene by means of judicial review.

See pp 25, 47.

R v Central Birmingham Health Authority, ex p Walker

Judicial review: duty of care: hospital resources: baby

Court of Appeal. (1987) Independent, 26 November

The applicant's baby required an operation. On 20 October 1987 the Central Birmingham Health Authority accepted this, but decided that it was unable to conduct the operation at that time.

Leave to apply for judicial review of this decision was refused by Macpherson J. The applicant appealed.

Held: the decisions of National Health Service authorities were amenable to judicial review, but the court's discretion to intervene must be used extremely sparingly. Leave was refused.

Per Sir John Donaldson MR: 'It is not for this court, or indeed any court, to substitute its own judgment for the judgment of those who are responsible for the allocation of resources. This court could only intervene where it was satisfied that there was a prima-facie case, not only of failing to allocate resources in the way in which others think that resources should be allocated, but of a failure to allocate resources to an extent which was "Wednesbury unreasonable" (see *Associated Provincial Picture Houses v Wednesbury Corporation* [1948] 1 KB 223, [1947] 2 All ER 680), to use the lawyers' jargon or, in simpler words, which involves a breach of a public law duty. Even then, of course, the court has to exercise a judicial discretion. It has to take account of all the circumstances of the particular case with which it is concerned.'

See pp 25, 47.

R v Cheshire

Causation: murder: novus actus interveniens

Court of Appeal. [1991] 3 All ER 670, [1991] 1 WLR 844, (1991) The Times, 24 April

The defendant (David Cheshire) shot a man in the thigh and the stomach. After treatment of the wounds, the victim developed breathing difficulties and chest infections. He died nine weeks after the shooting. It was alleged that negligent treatment was the immediate cause of death. The defendant appealed against his conviction for murder.

Held:　(i)　where the jury had to consider whether negligence in the treatment of injuries inflicted by an accused was the cause of death, it was sufficient for the judge to tell the jury that they had to be satisfied that the Crown had proved that the acts of the accused caused the death of the deceased, adding that the accused's acts need not be the sole or even the main cause of death, it being sufficient that his acts contributed significantly to that result.

(ii)　even though negligence in the treatment of a victim was the immediate cause of death, the jury should not regard it as excluding the responsibility of the accused, unless the negligent treatment was so independent of his acts and in itself so potent in causing death that they regarded the contribution made by his acts as insignificant.

(iii)　although the trial judge erred in inviting the jury to consider the degree of fault in the medical treatment rather than its consequences, no miscarriage of justice had occurred. On the evidence, it was inconceivable that any jury would have found otherwise than that the defendant's acts remained a significant cause of the death.

R v Cox

Consultant: attempted murder: euthanasia: criminal liability: rheumatism

Winchester Crown Court. (1992) 340 Lancet, 782

A 70-year-old woman had had acute rheumatoid arthritis for 20 years with serious complications, including internal bleeding and abscesses. She was admitted to the Royal Hampshire County Hospital, Winchester, for regular inpatient treatment under Dr Cox, a consultant rheumatologist, whose patient she was from 1978. Until about two weeks before her death, she had endured an 'appalling catalogue' of pain and disability with courage and good humour. However, after a family bereavement, her condition deteriorated. Her pain was constant and grindingly severe and she made it clear to her sons and her doctors that she wished to be allowed to die and would accept no more treatment other than painkillers. She asked Dr Cox for a fatal injection, which he refused. She remained alive. Two days before she died Dr Cox wrote in her notes: 'She still wants out and I don't think we can reasonably disagree.' The severe, continuous pain did not respond to the increasingly large dose of opioids. Dr Cox had reassured her that she would not be allowed to suffer terrible pain during her final days. He was unable to honour that pledge by giving conventional drugs, including diarmorphine and diazepam. As an act of compassion, he injected two ampoules of potassium chloride and recorded this in the notes. The patient died peacefully a few minutes later in the presence of her sons. The cause of death was recorded as bronchopneumonia and the body was cremated.

The case was investigated when a Roman Catholic nurse not usually on that ward read the notes. She eventually reported the matter to the hospital authorities, who in turn informed the police. Dr Cox was charged with attempted murder: because there was no body, it was not possible to prove that the potassium chloride had caused the patient's death.

Held:　(i)　the jury found Dr Cox guilty of attempted murder as charged.

(ii)　Ognall J gave him a suspended sentence of 12 months' imprisonment.

See p 17.

R v Crick

Alternative practitioner: prescription: overdose: criminal liability: child patient: fatal

Pollock CB (with jury). (1859) 1 F & F 519

Mrs Orpin took a child named William Hardwicke to Mr Crick, a herb doctor. He examined the child and gave Mrs Orpin a bottle of infusion of lobelia inflata. He advised her to give the child two teaspoonfuls of the infusion three times a day. She gave the child some doses of the infusion for several days. Then she ceased, as she thought that he had got better. The child died, three weeks after Mr Crick saw him, and more than a week after the last dose had been administered.

Mr Crick was prosecuted. Medical witnesses testified that the child had died of overdoses of lobelia.

Held: Pollock CB directed the jury: 'it is no crime for anyone to administer medicine, but it is a crime to administer it so rashly and carelessly as to produce death; and in this respect there is no difference between the most regular practitioner and the greatest quack . . . on the evidence it appeared that the child got better while the medicine was being administered to it. If the prisoner had been a medical man I should have recommended you to take the most favourable view of his conduct, for it would be most fatal to the efficiency of the medical profession if no one could administer medicine without a halter around his neck; and although I cannot speak of a person in the prisoner's position in language as strong, still he ought not to be responsible unless it has been proved with reasonable certainty that he caused the death by the careless administration of the drug.'

The jury returned a verdict of not guilty.

See p 140.

R v Gaud

Criminal liability: hepatitis: registrar: surgeon

Blofield J. (1994) Times, 30 September

In 1985 Umesh Gaud qualified as a doctor in his native India. In 1990, whilst he was working as a senior house officer at Killingbeck Hospital in Leeds, it was discovered that he was a carrier of the hepatitis B virus when he sought treatment for an unrelated condition. In January 1991, after supplying falsified employment details which did not mention Killingbeck Hospital and stated that his last post was in Calcutta, he became a senior house officer at the Royal London Hospital. In April 1992, after telling similar lies and claiming that he had been inoculated against hepatitis B, he became a registrar in cardio-thoracic surgery at the London Chest Hospital where he carried out 323 operations. In February 1993, after a hepatitis outbreak at the Royal London Hospital, Dr Gaud was asked for a blood sample and supplied one taken from a patient instead of himself. In August 1993, after a hepatitis outbreak at London Chest Hospital, a blood sample was taken from Dr Gaud under supervision. He was suspended and later dismissed for gross misconduct. In October 1993 he was arrested after five patients had shown hepatitis symptoms. It was suspected, but not proved, that he might have infected up to 24 patients at the Royal London Hospital and the London Chest Hospital.

He pleaded guilty to a common law charge of causing a public nuisance by endangering the health of the public between August 1990 and October 1993.

Held: he had contracted hepatitis B during his work. No conclusive link had been proved between his condition and those of the patients on whom he had operated. Nevertheless he had done a 'terrible thing' in putting his interests before the lives of his patients. He was sentenced to 12 months' imprisonment.

The case is believed to be unique in British legal history. Its closest parallel is perhaps the 1815 case of a woman who wheeled her smallpox-infected baby around the streets.

R v Harris and Harris

Alternative practitioner: diabetes: manslaughter: parental objection: homeopathy: criminal liability: fatal

Tucker J. (1993) 307 BMJ 1232

Nakhira Harris, aged nine, was diagnosed as having diabetes at the Queen's Medical Centre in Nottingham. Her devout Rastafarian parents discharged her from hospital, after refusing to accept doctors' insistent advice that insulin was the only treatment.

For the next six weeks Mr Harris tried to cure her at home with homeopathic medicine, but Nakhira lost one third of her body weight. On 29 January 1992 the Harrises telephoned Dr Hammond, a homeopathic doctor who originally qualified as a general practitioner. They consulted him three times that day, asking him to suggest a homeopathic remedy for Nakhira's cough and possible bronchitis. He emphasised on the telephone the need to monitor Nakhira's blood glucose, and told the parents to contact their general practitioner if her condition worsened.

Dr Hammond first saw Nakhira on the morning of 31 January when her father carried her into his surgery in a diabetic coma. He spent 90 minutes with the couple before sending Nakhira to hospital, later explaining that he had to bridge the 'yawning gap' between them and staff at Queen's Medical Centre.

Mr Harris objected to the nursing sister injecting Nakhira with insulin, saying: 'We are vegans. We can't have pork or beef.' When one of the doctors told him it was human insulin, he agreed to the injection. It was too late. Nakhira died shortly afterwards.

Held: Mr and Mrs Harris were jailed for manslaughter of their daughter. He was sentenced to 2¹/₂ years imprisonment, and she to 18 months.

See p 13.

R v Jones

Alternative practitioner: diabetes: criminal liability: fatal

Charles J. [1938] 1 BMJ 1401

A 23 year old school teacher, who had suffered from diabetes for four years, was on a strict diet and was taking insulin. On the advice of a friend she consulted an 'osteopath and radiologist' named Herbert Jones. He told her that she had not got diabetes and had never had it, but that she was suffering from anaemia. He advised her to starve herself for four days and take nothing but orange juice. This she did, discontinuing her insulin, and within three days she had lost seven pounds. Her father telephoned Mr Jones who replied that she should continue with her treatment until he saw her in a few weeks' time. On that day she went into a coma and, despite hospital treatment, she died a week after the consultation.

Mr Jones was committed for trial at the Gloucestershire Assizes. He testified that he had taken up the science of healing 23 years ago, when he had cured by the laying of hands a man who was dying of consumption, but admitted that he had no experience in diabetes.

Held: Charles J remarked that Mr Jones' conduct was a danger to the State and the public. If it had not been for his good character he would have been bound to send him to prison for a long term, not only to correct him but also to deter others who might be likely to undertake the treatment of sick folk without proper knowledge. A sentence of six months' imprisonment was imposed.

R v Larah

Assault: benzodiazepine: dental: sexual abuse: criminal liability

Hodgson J. (1990) 335 Lancet 403

The defendant (George Larah), a dentist, was charged with sexually assaulting seven women who had been given diazepam for dental treatment. The assaults were alleged to have taken place over a number of years. None was corroborated or confirmed, and some of the complaints were not made until months or years afterwards. He could not recall the individual patients, but denied all the charges.

Professor Healey testified that he accepted the findings of Professor Dundee that one woman in 200 given large doses of benzodiazepine experienced sexual fantasies, including fantasies of sexual assault in circumstances where this could not have happened. The first case of benzodiazepine-induced sexual fantasy to be recorded in the UK was in 1981. By the end of the decade Dundee had been notified of 43 such cases, and the number was mounting.

Held: the jury was directed to enter a verdict of not guilty. The women had given what they believed to be accurate accounts, but the danger was that they were mistaken – 'that their recollection honestly believed is of an unreal and not a real experience ... It is clear that there is a mounting body of evidence that patients under sedation from this class of drugs do sometimes experience erotic fantasies.'

R v Legal Aid Area (No 8) (Northern) Appeal Committee, ex p Angell and Others

Causation: legal aid: vaccine damage: product liability: group litigation

Simon Brown J. [1990] 1 Med LR 394

The seven applicants all suffered from brain damage. They alleged that their injuries had been caused by vaccination with DTP vaccine. They wished to bring actions for damages. Each applicant required legal aid support to proceed.

In *Loveday v Renton and Wellcome Foundation Ltd* (see p 435) Lord Justice Stuart-Smith held, as a preliminary issue, that it had not been established that pertussis vaccine could cause permanent brain damage in young children. Following that decision the two leading and two junior counsel representing the plaintiff in *Loveday* gave a joint opinion in three parts. Part I, signed only by leading counsel, emphasised the difficulties in proving negligence and causation and advised against an appeal. Part II contained a critique of the judgment in *Loveday*. Part III advised that that judgment was unsound and that it should not be treated as a ground for refusing legal aid in suitable cases.

Following the *Loveday* decision the deputy area director of the No 8 area legal aid office, to whom all vaccine damage litigation had been delegated, discharged the legal aid certificates of five of the applicants and refused the applications for legal aid by two of the applicants.

On appeal by the applicants, the respondent appeal committee gave as their reasons for discharging the appeal inter alia that, following upon *Loveday* and in the absence of any new medical evidence, there did not appear to be any realistic prospect of establishing to the required standard of proof any causative link between pertussis vaccine and the assisted person's illness and present condition.

According to one of the affidavits in the proceedings, the committee assessed the *Loveday* judgment as an impressive and well-reasoned work and recognised that the decision was not binding but,

'[paragraph 10] ... we recognised that in order to justify a further significant commitment of public money we had to be satisfied that there was likely to be further evidence available which would give some real prospect of a different decision [from *Loveday*] being reached on general causation if another case was brought to trial.

[paragraph 11] we also felt entitled to rely on Part I of the joint opinion signed by leading counsel . . . junior counsel clearly felt far more bullish about an appeal, but both leading counsel were very much more circumspect both on the subject of an appeal and the prospect of any future cases succeeding.'

Held: (i) adequacy of reasons

    (a) although a legal aid area committee could not be expected to give the fullest and most detailed reasons, a short succinct statement being all that was required, the original reasons provided by the respondent committee were inadequate;

    (b) what was required in the way of reasoning would vary according to the circumstances; these were cases clearly calling for something out of the ordinary in the way of reasons;

    (c) despite the inadequacy of the original reasons, the respondents' affidavits in the proceedings could be invoked and, therefore, proper and adequate reasons had been provided and the appeal on the grounds of inadequate reasons would be dismissed.

  (ii) regard to all material considerations

    (a) the respondents' affidavits established that the doctors' 'evidence' was adequately considered by the respondents;

    (b) as to the joint opinion: the opinion held out a realistic prospect that in a future case a different judge would come to a different conclusion on the issue of general causation; it seemed that the respondents had either rejected the joint opinion or misunderstood its true purport, yet the inference from the affidavits was that (1) the joint opinion had been accepted; (2) the respondents understood leading counsel in Part I to be qualifying what was said in Part II; in fact, Part I of the opinion did not bear upon prospects of success at a future trial on the issue of general causation; accordingly, the absence of any reasons even touching on the effect of Part II of the joint opinion showed a misplaced reliance on Part I and indicated a want of proper consideration of the matter such as to constitute an error of law; on that ground alone the decisions should be quashed;

  (iii) the relevant seven determinations of the respondent appeal committee must be quashed. The appeals would have to be re-heard by a differently constituted legal aid committee.

See p 40.

R v Legal Aid Board and Department of Social Security, ex p Clark

Legal aid: operation: thyroidectomy

McPherson J. [1993] 9 PMILL 5

The plaintiff (Ms Clark) underwent a partial thyroidectomy in 1987. She suffered a progressive and severe loss of her voice. In 1991 she retired from her employment on medical grounds directly due to the surgery of which she complained. As a result of this retirement, she received a pension including a lump sum retiring allowance. But for the surgery, she would not have received this until retiring due to age in 1995.

Initially the plaintiff was granted legal aid to pursue a claim for damages for medical negligence. However the Legal Aid Assessment Office of the DSS decided that the lump sum retiring allowance would disentitle her to legal aid on grounds of excess capital.

Paragraph 14B of Schedule 3 to the Civil Legal Aid (Assessment of Resources) Regulations 1989 provides: 'In computing the amount of capital of the person concerned, there should be wholly disregarded any capital payment received from any source which is made in relation to the incident giving rise to the dispute in respect of which the Legal Aid application has been made.'

Held: this applied to the lump sum retiring allowance. The decision to reassess the plaintiff's financial circumstances in the light of it was erroneous. Judicial review of the decision was granted.

R v Mid Glamorgan Family Health Services Authority and Another, ex p Martin

Discovery: patient's history: interests of patient: depression

Court of Appeal. [1995] 1 All ER 356, [1995] 1 WLR 110, (1994) Times, 16 August

The applicant (Trevor Martin), aged 45, had suffered depression and psychological problems since 1966. He requested disclosure of his medical records (which were not on computer) for information about his past and formative years. The first respondent refused disclosure of his general practitioner's records to him. The second respondent (the South Glamorgan Health Authority) would consider disclosure of hospital records on the condition that no potential litigation was contemplated by the applicant. Both respondents offered disclosure to a medical adviser nominated by the applicant. He refused the offers and applied for judicial review of their decisions.

Held: (i) the Access to Health Records Act 1990, which established a patient's right of access to health records, did not apply since the Act generally excluded access to records which existed before its commencement on 1 November 1991.

(ii) the Data Protection Act 1984 gave an individual a right to access of information held about him in computerised form, but did not apply where access would be likely to cause serious harm to the physical or mental health of the patient.

(iii) the above statutes were only passed to give a right of access to records which otherwise the patient did not have. There was no right at common law for the applicant to have access to any records before 1 November 1991.

(iv) at common law a doctor, likewise a health authority, had an absolute right to deal with medical records in any way that it chose and a duty to act at all times in the best interests of the patient. They might deny the patient access to medical records if this was in his best interests, for example if their disclosure would be detrimental to his health.

(v) the judge had been entitled to refuse the applicant the relief that he sought. His decision should be affirmed.

R v North West Thames Regional Health Authority and Another, ex p Daniels

Judicial Review: hospital resources: operation

Queen's Bench Division (Divisional Court). [1993] 4 Med LR 364

The applicant (Rhys Daniels) was born in December 1990. Early in 1992 he was diagnosed as suffering from Batten's disease. There was a chance that, if given a bone marrow transplant (BMT) before the age of three, he could live beyond the age of seven. In July 1992 he was examined at the Bone Marrow Transplant Unit at Westminster Children's Hospital. The transplant operation was approved, and in February 1993 a donor was found.

In April 1992 a review team had published a report concluding that the BMT unit was not viable. In February 1993 the applicant's father was told that the operation could not be performed because of the number of staff who had left the unit. In April 1993 the BMT unit was finally closed down.

The applicant through his father commenced legal proceedings challenging the closure.

Held: (i) there had been a material failure on the part of the district health authority to consult the Community Health Council in May or June 1992 about the prospective closure.

(ii) there was insufficient evidence to show that the decision to close the unit was irrational.

(iii) the court would not quash the decision to close the unit. Such an order would not in any event directly affect the applicant's future care and treatment.

See pp 25, 47.

R v Prentice and Sullman

House officer: injections: manslaughter: leukaemia: criminal liability

Court of Appeal. [1993] 4 Med LR 304

Malcolm Savage, aged 16, suffered from leukaemia. He came regularly to Peterborough General Hospital for treatment with cytotoxic drugs. Once a month, he was injected intravenously (IV) with Vincristine. Every other month, he was injected intrathecally (IT) with Methotrexate into his spine.

He was due for both injections on 28 February 1990. On 27 February the drugs were duly prepared by the pharmacy. They were put in a red box bearing labels that they were cytotoxic drugs. Also on the outside of the box were two labels bearing the patient's name, the name of the drug and the route by which it was to be injected (IT or IV). Inside the box

509

were two syringes containing the drugs, also bearing labels containing the same information as the labels on the outside of the box. It is not certain whether, as usually occurred, the drugs chart showing the consultant's prescription was put with the patient's medical notes which went on the trolley with the drugs.

On 28 February the box of cytotoxic drugs was put on a trolley in the ward. Normally cytotoxic drugs are put on a special cytotoxic trolley which also contains the manufacturer's data sheet. On this occasion, the lumbar-puncture trolley was used because it was large and could hold all the necessary equipment. The data sheet was not transferred from the cytotoxic trolley to the lumbar-puncture. The medical notes were on the trolley, but it is not clear whether the drugs chart was there.

Dr Prentice, a pre-registration houseman, told the registrar that he was reluctant to do the cytotoxic injection because of his inexperience. The registrar asked him to get Dr Sullman, the senior house officer, to supervise him. Dr Sullman had once previously attempted to do a lumbar puncture, and that attempt had failed; he had previously injected Vincristine intravenously on one occasion. An important misunderstanding took place. Dr Prentice thought that Dr Sullman was to supervise the whole procedure, including the administration of the cytotoxic drugs; whereas Dr Sullman thought he was there only to supervise the use of the needle to make a lumbar puncture, but that he had no responsibility over the administration of the cytotoxic drugs.

After administering a local anaesthetic, Dr Prentice successfully inserted the lumbar puncture needle into the spine. He put on a pair of goggles, the normal procedure for dealing with cytotoxic drugs, and then asked for the drugs themselves. Dr Sullman opened the red box, took out the first syringe and handed it to Dr Prentice who then fitted the syringe onto the needle and injected it into the patient's spine. He then unscrewed that syringe and took the second syringe from Dr Sullman and injected that also into the spine. Neither doctor checked the labels on the box or the labels on the syringes. So it was that the Vincristine was injected wrongly into the spine.

On arriving later, the consultant discovered that a terrible mistake had been made. Dr Prentice went to the preparation room and looked at the data chart on the cytotoxic trolley. He was extremely upset and said 'Oh my God. It can be fatal', which he had not realised before. A wash-out procedure operation was commenced. It was unsuccessful and damaged the base of the brain and the spinal cord. Malcolm Savage died.

At the Birmingham Crown Court Dr Prentice and Dr Sullman were both convicted of manslaughter and sentenced to nine months' imprisonment suspended for 12 months. They appealed.

Held: (i) except in motor manslaughter, the ingredients of involuntary manslaughter by breach of duty which need to be proved are:

      (a) the existence of the duty.

      (b) the breach of the duty causing death.

      (c) gross negligence which the jury considers justifies a criminal condition.

    (ii) if the jury had been given the gross negligence test, then in deciding whether the necessary high degree of gross negligence had been reached they could properly have taken into account 'excuses' or mitigating circumstances.

   (iii) there were many of these. Dr Prentice was inexperienced and reluctant to give the treatment, he did not have the data chart on the cytotoxic trolley, and he believed that Dr Sullman (who had handed him the syringes) was supervising the administration of the drugs. Dr Sullman believed that he was simply required to supervise the insertion of the lumbar puncture needle by an inexperienced houseman, and he did not have special experience or knowledge of cytotoxic drugs.

   (iv) had the directions to the jury left it open to them to take those matters into account, they might have reached a different verdict.

The defendants' convictions were quashed.

R v Saha and Salim

Benzodiazepine: manslaughter: police surgeon: criminal liability: fatal

Court of Appeal. (1992) 340 Lancet 1462; CAT, 20 December 1994

Graham Rawlinson was a 23-year-old former heroin addict. The defendants (Dr Saha and Dr Salim) were general practitioners who acted as police surgeons in Grimsby.

On 19 July 1990 Mr Rawlinson was arrested when spotted in the street in the early hours carrying two wrapped lavatory seats. He was remanded in custody. Because of the closure of Strangeways Prison, Manchester, in May of that year, he had been detained in a succession of police cells in Blackpool, Rochdale, and Preston before being transferred to a police cell in Grimsby on 7 September 1990. By this time, the four GPs who had managed his care had weaned him off heroin and all other drugs and he seemed fit and cheerful.

Allegedly, however, Mr Rawlinson asked for tranquillisers on the day of his arrival at Grimsby, where several violent prisoners were being detained and prescribed tranquillising medication. He was seen by Dr Saha who initiated a heavy regimen of benzodiazepines. On 10 September, Dr Salim added chlorpromazine (300mg, daily from 11 September) to a daily ingestion of 80mg diazepam and 160mg temazepam at night. On 13 September, Saha added 30mg methadone and on 15 September 130mg co-proxamol.

Drug name	Main properties and uses	Usual daily dose range	Maximum daily dose on its own	Dose prescribed
Temazepam ('Normison')	Long acting benzodiazepine tranquilliser and hypnotic; used for insomnia; habit-forming; in overdose and in combination with other central nervous system depressants it may depress the cardio-respiratory system; similar to diazepam	10mg–20mg	60mg	100mg (7/9) 120mg (8/9) 160mg (9/9) 160mg (10/9) 160mg (11/9) 160mg (12/9) 160mg (13/9) 160mg (14/9) 160mg (15/9) – (16/9)
Diazepam ('Valium')	Long-acting tranquilliser; used to treat anxiety and insomnia; habit-forming; in overdose and in combination with other central nervous system depressants it may depress the cardia-respiratory system; similar to temazepam; is converted to active metabolites which include temaxepam	2mg–30mg	30mg	44mg (8/9) 80mg (9/9) 80mg (10/9) 80mg (11/9) 80mg (12/9) 80mg (13/9) 80mg (14/9) 80mg (15/9) 80mg (16/9)

Drug name	Main properties and uses	Usual daily dose range	Maximum daily dose on its own	Dose prescribed
Chlorpromaxine ('Largactil')	Very potent tranquilliser; used for treatment of major psychotic illnesses, eg. schizophrenia; exaggerates the effects of other central nervous system depressants including temazapam, diazepam, methadone and d-propoxyphene taken at the same time	75mg– 300mg	300mg	100mg (10/9) 300mg (11/9) 300mg (12/9) 300mg (13/9) 300mg (14/9) 300mg (15/9) 225mg (16/9)
Methadone	Very long-acting potent narcotic painkiller; used for terminal care treatment of cancer patients and for heroin addicts; has most of the properties of heroin	5mg– 30mg	30mg	30mg (13/9) 30mg (14/9) 30mg (15/9) 30mg (16/9)
Co-proxamol	Long-acting narcotic painkiller combining paracetamol and dextropropoxyphene – a potent narcotic painkiller, similar to methadone	195mg– 260mg of d-propocy- phene	260mg of d-propoxy- phene	130mg (15/9) 65mg (16/9)

Chart prepared for the prosecution from prescribing notes.

Saha prescribed on 7–9 and 13 September, Salim on 10, 12, 14 and 16 September.

During this time, Mr Rawlinson's condition deteriorated so that he was described as shambling about with glazed eyes in a zombie-like state. On the evening of Sunday 16 September he was found to be comatose and was taken to the casualty department at Grimsby and District Hospital, where he was examined by a casualty officer, who discussed the case with Salim and discharged Rawlinson back to the cells. At 7.30am on 17 September he was found to be unrousable and sent back to hospital, where he died about an hour later from pulmonary oedema.

The jury convicted both defendants of manslaughter. Curtis J sentenced them to 21 months' and 12 months' imprisonment respectively. Dr Saha did not appeal against conviction, and his application for leave to appeal against sentence was refused. Dr Salim appealed against his conviction.

Held: (i) following the House of Lord's ruling in *R v Adomako* (p 499), the correct test in a case of involuntary manslaughter by breach of duty was gross negligence, not recklessness. Accordingly the trial judge had misdirected the jury.

(ii) there were a number of circumstances which might have led the jury to acquit, if the gross negligence test had been left to them. Unlike Dr Saha who prescribed and increased the drugs in the first place, Dr Salim inherited an established regime of prescribed drugs. To alter or cancel another doctor's prescription would have put him in a difficult position. Finally, Dr Salim did reduce the dosage on 16 November, and arguably it was not unreasonable for him to observe the deceased on 14 and 15 November, before making the reduction.

    (iii)   therefore Dr Salim's appeal against conviction should be upheld.

See *R v Adomako* (p 499).

R v Sargent

Anaesthetics: manslaughter: operation: fatal: criminal liability

(1990) 336 Lancet 430

The defendant (Dr Norman Sargent), aged 66, was a licentiate of the Worshipful Society of Apothecaries but had no higher specialist qualification. He was working as a locum anaesthetist at Royal Doncaster Infirmary in June 1988.

The patient was a 55-year-old woman who was admitted for laryngoscopy, pharyngoscopy and oesophagoscopy. The defendant connected a 'No 5' Portex microlaryngeal tube, which was cuffed, to a high pressure oxygen source and not a ventilating machine via an intravenous three-way tap attached to a hose via a pistol grip with an inflating lever. The source was a cylinder containing oxygen at 2000 pounds per square inch (psi) which was three-quarters full. That pressure was stepped down to 15–20 psi.

When the patient, who had been given a muscle relaxant, was put on the operating table, signs of cyanosis were noted but the defendant reassured the surgeon that all was well. The surgeon had just inserted an instrument into the patient's throat when a theatre nurse saw the patient becoming bloated and blue, her arm swelling alarmingly. The surgeon stopped the procedure, only to witness the patient become so rapidly inflated that her skin was taut and translucent. She suffered fatal barotrauma and died in the operating theatre.

The defendant was charged with manslaughter. The prosecution claimed that he had inserted the tube into the patient's throat and emptied the entire contents of the cylinder (ie 1020) litres into her, inflating her until she resembled the 'Michelin man' advertisements. The defendant did not give evidence.

Held: he was convicted of manslaughter and sentenced to six months' imprisonment suspended for a year.

See p 122.

R v Stuart

Anaesthetics: criminal liability: dental: manslaughter: cardiac arrest: fatal: drugs

Garland J. (1995) Guardian, 24 January, (1995) Daily Telegraph, 1 February

Mrs Marie Everett, aged 68, attended Mr Stuart's surgery in Market Drayton in order to have all 28 of her remaining teeth extracted. She suffered from angina and arthritis, and she was taking tablets for her heart condition. She said that she was terrified, and Mr Stuart tried to reassure her. He injected her with more than four times the recommended maximum of the pain killing drug lignocaine, and he also gave a her a huge dose of meprivocaine. She started to twitch, which turned into her having convulsions. Mr Stuart called an ambulance, and he and his partner administered oxygen. Mrs Everett's general practitioner arrived and gave her cardiac massage, put an airway into her mouth and tried mouth-to-mouth resuscitation. Ambulance men tried electric shock treatment and attempted to stimulate her heart three times, but there was no positive effect. She died due to heart failure precipitated by local anaesthetic. Mr Stuart was convicted of manslaughter.

Held: no deterrent sentence was required, because Mr Stuart faced being struck off by the General Dental Council. He was given a nine month prison sentence, suspended for one year.

R v Vaccine Damage Tribunal, ex p Loveday

Vaccine damage: causation: baby

Court of Appeal. (1985) 2 Lancet 1137

In 1970 a seven week old baby was seen at a clinic, where notes were made referring to 'hypotonia' and 'a miserable little baby'. On 16 April, when she was medically examined for the purposes of adoption, a general practitioner found no abnormality. On 13 May he gave her a first DTP vaccination. On 22 June a squint was observed. On 1 July 1970 and 1 January 1971 she was given two more doses of DTP. Subsequently she was found to be seriously brain damaged.

She claimed compensation under the Vaccine Damage Payments Act 1979. Her claim was rejected by a vaccine damage tribunal whose members did not accept that vaccination had caused her disability. A High Court judge quashed the tribunal's decision and remitted the case for further review by another tribunal. He refused to direct the tribunal to find as a matter of law that the child was entitled to a payment. The mother appealed to the Court of Appeal.

Held: the appeal was dismissed. It was impossible for the court to conclude that the child's condition resulted inevitably from vaccination. The state of her health before vaccination was not established on the evidence. The court was not prepared to direct the tribunal to pronounce in favour of the claimant, although in principle it might be possible to do so in a different case in the future.

See pp 40, 78.

Re R (a minor) (blood transfusion)

Parental objections: Jehovah's Witness: consent: blood transfusion: child patient: interests of patient

Booth J. (1993) Times, 8 June, (1993) Independent, 9 June

R, aged ten months, suffered from B-cell lymphoblastic leukaemia and was in hospital receiving treatment. She had already been given blood products as a life-saving measure on her admission, and was likely to need more. Her medical consultants believed that this was the only treatment likely to succeed. R's parents, Jehovah's Witnesses, refused to consent to it.

In order to obtain the court's authorisation for the use of blood products the London Borough of Camden, as local authority, applied for a specific issue order under s 8 of the Children Act 1989. The parents submitted that they should instead have applied to invoke the inherent jurisdiction of the High Court.

Held: (i) in such cases, the most strenuous efforts should always be made to achieve an inter partes hearing. Such issues should also be determined wherever possible by a High Court judge. But these prerequisites could as well be met by an application for a specific issue order under section 8 as by an application for the exercise of the court's inherent jurisdiction. A section 8 application could, and in such circumstances undoubtedly should, be made to a High Court. All necessary directions for a speedy hearing could be given.

(ii) the welfare of the girl was the court's permanent consideration. So overwhelming was the need for blood and so much was it in her best interests to have it that, for her welfare, the parents' wishes were bound to be overridden and the use of blood products authorised, enabling the doctors to give her transfusions.

(iii) accordingly there should be a specific issue order in respect of the child, namely that:

(a) in any imminently life-threatening situation where it was the professional opinion of those medically responsible for the child that she was in need of the administration of blood products, she should be given such blood products without the consent of her parents;

(b) in any situation which was less than imminently life-threatening, those medically responsible for the child should consult with her parents and would consider at every opportunity all alternative forms of management suggested by the parents. In the event of those medically responsible for the child concluding, after such consultation, that there was no reasonable alternative to the administration of blood products, they should be at liberty to administer blood products without the consent of the parents.

Re R (a minor) (wardship: medical treatment)

Consent: minors: psychiatric patient: wardship

Court of Appeal. [1992] Fam 11, [1991] 4 All ER 177

R was born in September 1975. After a fight with her father in March 1991, she was received into local authority care and placed in a children's home. Her mental health deteriorated. She began to suffer visual and auditory hallucinations and to express suicidal thoughts. On one occasion she left the home and was found by the police on a bridge threatening suicide.

During May 1991 her behaviour became increasingly disturbed. On 24 May she returned to her parents' home where, in addition to seriously damaging the contents, she attacked her father with a hammer. On 2 June a direction was given for her compulsory admission to hospital. On 7 June she was transferred to an adolescent psychiatric unit.

R's condition deteriorated further there. She became increasingly defiant. Furthermore she denied her past experience of hallucinations and voices, alleging that she had made it all up. On 28 June a senior consultant at the unit diagnosed a psychotic state. He telephoned a social worker at the local authority to request permission to administer anti-psychotic medication to R. He said that she was acting extremely paranoid and becoming extremely hostile and accusative.

Later that evening R telephoned the social worker, informed her that the unit were trying to give her drugs and lucidly stated that she did not need them and she did not want to take them. The local authority withdrew permission for the drugs to be administered. When a consultant child psychiatrist saw her on 3 July, she behaved calmly and was rational but still entertained suicidal ideas and suffered from visual and auditory hallucinations. He reported that without treatment her florid psychotic behaviour might return and she might become a suicidal risk again.

The local authority took wardship proceedings and applied to the court to give leave to the unit to administer such medication as was medically necessary, including anti-psychotic drugs without R's consent. Waite J granted the application. The Official Solicitor appealed.

Held: (i) the Gillick test of a child's competence, ie whether the child has sufficient understanding of what is involved to give a valid consent in law, is not apt to a situation where the understanding and capacity of the child varies from day to day according to the effect of mental illness;

(ii) the court in the exercise of its wardship or statutory jurisdiction has power to override the decisions of a 'Gillick competent' child as much as those of parents and guardians;

(iii) the judge was right to hold that R was not 'Gillick competent' and, even if she had been, was right to consent to her undergoing treatment which might involve compulsory medication.

See *Gillick v West Norfolk and Wisbech Area Health Authority* (p 353).

See p 10.

Raleigh Fitkin-Paul Morgan Memorial Hospital v Anderson and Anderson

USA: blood transfusion: consent: Jehovah's Witness: femur: leg

Supreme Court of New Jersey (1964) 201 A 2d 537

The plaintiff hospital sought authority to administer blood transfusions to Mrs Willimina Anderson, in the event that such transfusions should be necessary to save her life and the life of her unborn child. The pregnancy was beyond the 32nd week. Mrs Anderson had notified the hospital that she did not wish blood transfusions, since they would be contrary to her religious conviction as a Jehovah's Witness. The evidence established a probability that at some point in the pregnancy Mrs Anderson would haemorrhage severely and that both she and the unborn child would die unless a blood transfusion was administered.

Held: the unborn child was entitled to the law's protection. An appropriate order should be made to ensure blood transfusions to the mother, in the event that they are necessary in the opinion of the physician in charge at the time.

Per Curiam: 'We have no difficulty in so deciding with respect to the infant child. The more difficult question is whether an adult may be compelled to submit to such medical procedures when necessary to save his life. Here we think it is unnecessary to decide that question in broad terms because the welfare of the child and the mother are so intertwined and inseparable that it would be impracticable to attempt to distinguish between them with respect to the sundry factual patterns which may develop. The blood transfusions (including transfusions made necessary by the delivery) may be administered if necessary to save her life or the life of her child, as the physician in charge at the time may determine.'

See pp 8, 13.

Ralph v Riverside Health Authority and another

Diagnosis: psychiatric patient: striking out: paranoia

Court of Appeal. CAT 10 September 1990

The plaintiff (Alistair Ralph) was referred for assessment to St Mary Abbots Hospital where he was seen by a psychiatric registrar who subseqently wrote to his general practitioner as follows:

'Thank you for referring this . . . man for assessment at the Psychiatric Outpatient Department . . .

Mr Ralph attended his interview and presented his situation as if it were a legal brief, in a rigid and anxious manner. He felt quite clearly that he was seeing us with regard to an issue of United Nations law regarding an incident in which his rights were infringed in 1993. He stated that he was currently suing the Australian Government for this. He stated that in 1983 he was given a bone graft to his left maxilla, in which a device was planted in his left cheek-bone. He states that this is a microphone which is connected to his left and right ears and that this results in "accoustic emissions" coming from him, an example of which is if he wears a walkman radio the music emanating from himself is amplified. He states that his privacy has gone now and that the microphone enables people to listen to conversations he has of a private and personal nature, and this information is later used to annoy and harass him . . .

Mr Ralph presents a very interesting picture of a very well systemised paranoid delusion, which is without doubt unchallengable in his mind. He appeared mildly agitated. He is completely without insight into his present situation and refused any offers of help, either of further interviews or any form of medication . . .'

I feel that he is suffering from a paranoid psychosis for which neuroleptic medication is indicated but unfortunately at present, unable to be administered . . .'

The plaintiff asserted that these conclusions were wrong. He commenced court proceedings which were struck out as disclosing no cause of action. Considering that this action had failed because he had misunderstood the relevance of international law to a private law claim in the UK against the health authority, he started new proceedings alleging that the letter was false and malicious and that it was written without proper care. On the defendants' application, the judge struck out the action as 'it disclosed no reasonable cause of action, is frivolous and vexatious and otherwise an abuse of the court process.' The plaintiff applied for leave to appeal.

Held: (i)   the allegation of falsity by itself meant nothing. A doctor does not warrant that he will diagnose accurately in every case. He merely undertakes to use proper professional care and skill and to act honestly.

(ii)   it is not sufficient to allege malice in order to require the court to consider the case on its merits. Some particular must be given; none was in this case.

(iii)   the claim had no conceivable chance of success and had been correctly struck out.

See p 100.

Rance v Mid-Downs Health Authority and Storr

Abortion: pregnancy: radiographer: spina bifida

Brooke J. [1990] 2 Med LR 27

On 20 January 1983 the plaintiff (Mrs Lorna Rance), a solicitor, attended St Richard's Hospital in Chichester for an ultrasonic scan which confirmed that she was six to seven weeks pregnant. Having moved house in the meantime, she attended Cuckfield Hospital on 9 May when Mrs Karle, the radiographer, measured the bi-parietal diameter (BPD) at 57 mm and recorded a maturity estimate of 21½ weeks.

On 9 June Mrs Karle performed another ultrasound scan, recorded the BPD as 69.4 mm and estimated the gestation period at 25½ weeks. When she used the Diasonograph scanner she saw nothing untoward. When she used the real time scanner, however, she saw something in the region of the lumbar spine which did not look right; it came and went in a flash. She took a polaroid photograph which failed to recapture what she had seen. She had seen leg movement, so she ticked the appropriate entry on the report form and wrote on it '??F spine'. She discussed the case with Dr Storr, the consultant in charge of the radiology department, who wrote 'no conclusive evidence of abnormality on these polaroids.' He thought that there was a possibility that the foetus was abnormal, but considered that it was far too late for an abortion. This view accorded with the practice of three obstetric consultants at the hospital. The suspicion of abnormality was communicated to the consultant obstetrician but not to the plaintiff.

On 21 July Mrs Karle carried out another ultrasound scan and recorded the BPD at 86.4 mm and the estimated gestational period as 32 weeks. She could not see what she thought she had seen on 9 June and wrote 'F spine appears normal' on the report form. On 13 September 1993 the plaintiff's son John was born. He suffered from spina bifida associated with hydrocephalus. The plaintiff was shocked, not only by his condition, but also by subsequently learning from a community midwife that a scanner had raised a question over the state of the foetal spine at 25½ weeks.

She sued the hospital authority and Dr Storr, contending that if she had been told that her baby had a severe abnormality at 26 weeks she would have had an abortion up to 28 weeks and that Dr Storr should have arranged an early rescan after 10 June. Experts testified that the first scan on 20 January was the most reliable, that the gestation period was about 22 weeks on 9 May and about 26 weeks, 2 or 3 days, on 9 June, which was consistent with the birth on 13 September.

Held: (i)   it is probable that John was 26 weeks and two days old on 9 June, subject to a margin for uncertainty.

        (ii)   if the defendants had referred the plaintiff to a tertiary referral centre before the weekend of 11–12 June, it is highly probable that spina bifida would have been detected and that termination would have been performed on 14 or 15 June, when John would have been about 27 weeks and one day old.

       (iii)   if born at 27 weeks' gestation, he would certainly have been born alive in the sense that he could have breathed unaided for at least two–three hours and probably longer. Thus he would have been 'capable of being born alive' within the meaning of s 1 of the Infant Life (Preservation) Act 1929. Any abortion would therefore have been unlawful.

       (iv)   when he took the view that after 9 June it was too late to contemplate a termination, Dr Storr was both legally correct and adopting an approach which was accepted as proper by a responsible body of medical men skilled in radiology and obstetrics. The defendants had not been negligent.

See pp 49, 99, 171.

Ratty v Haringey Health Authority and Another

Cancer: damages: operation: surgeon: bladder: ureter

Court of Appeal. [1994] 5 Med LR 410

In 1983 the plaintiff (Leslie Ratty) was referred to the North Middlesex Hospital. Dr Woolf, a consultant physician, found on rectal examination a mass in the abdomen anteriorly to the rectum. Although a biopsy proved negative, both he and Mr Payne, a consultant general surgeon, reasonably concluded that the plaintiff had cancer of the bowel at the recto-sigmoid junction.

When Mr Payne started to operate, he found a large mass in the pelvis with infiltration of the bladder, and puckering of the peritoneum over the right ureter spreading out into the pelvis; there was also infiltration of the left lateral ligament of the rectum, and the whole mass extended down into the hollow of the sacrum. He performed an abdomino-perineal resection (APR), removing the whole of the sigmoid colon from the highest point affected by the disease, the whole of the rectum, the anal sphincter and the anus, together with surrounding skin. As that put an end to normal anal function, he provided a colostomy.

It was discovered on the evening of the operation that there was a hole in the bladder. A further major operation had to be performed to repair that hole, and to deal with the ureters which were found to have been severed. Pathological examination of the tissue which had been extracted revealed that it was non-malignant. The plaintiff had only been suffering from diverticulitis.

The plaintiff's two experts at trial testified that it was wrong in any circumstances to undertake an APR without histological proof of cancer, a rule that they attributed to Sir Ralph Marnham. The defendants' two experts regarded this as a useful guideline, but considered that if on incision the mass was found to be as described by Mr Payne then it was appropriate to proceed to an APR without histological proof. The trial judge found in favour of the plaintiff and awarded him £127,933 damages and interest.

Held: (i) there was no evidence on which the judge could find that the mass was not as large as recorded by Mr Payne. All the experts agreed that what Mr Payne found strengthened the diagnosis of cancer. Two reputable consultants, whose own standing and credibility were never in dispute, both considered that he had been right to perform an APR. This made it impossible for the judge correctly to hold that he had been negligent.

(ii) however the judge was justified in concluding that Mr Payne's repair of the bladder was inadequate. The clear inference from the evidence was that a properly repaired bladder would not have broken down as early as the evening of the operation.

(iii) although the evidence was that damage to ureters could happen in the course of an APR without negligence, none of the experts testified that they had ever overlooked such damage themselves. The judge was entitled to conclude that Mr Payne's failure to discover this damage by the end of the operation signified a lack of reasonable care and skill.

(iv) therefore the plaintiff was entitled to be compensated for the pain, suffering and loss of amenity which he endured as a result of his bladder not being properly repaired, and as a result of the damage to his ureters not being discovered before the end of the operation. An award of £5,000 damages was appropriate.

See pp 64, 116.

Reay v South Tees Health Authority

Damages: nasal

Middlesbrough District Registry. Unreported

The plaintiff, aged three, sustained an injury to his nose whilst on holiday. This resulted in a septal haematoma. An operation was immediately performed.

A week after his return from holiday, the plaintiff was taken to hospital because his nose had again become painful, it was throbbing and he had a fever. He was not treated for a week as measles was suspected.

The delay caused him to develop necrosis of the cartilage, due to a return of the septal haematoma. As a result, he suffered saddle deformity of his nose which could not be treated by plastic surgery until he was 18.

Held (November 1990): general damages of £7,500 were awarded.

See pp 97, 155.

Redmayne v Bloomsbury Health Authority

Diagnosis: tropical disease

Garland J. QBD transcript, 31 January 1992

The plaintiff (Ms Redmayne) was a social anthropologist who lived in Tanzania from 1965 to 1967, visited East Africa in 1968 and 1969 and lived in Nigeria from 1971 to 1974. After she returned to Oxford, her health caused her concern. In August, September and October 1975 she attended the Hospital for Tropical Diseases in London. Dr Cole, who examined her there found:

(1) lassitude, aches and pains, various swollen glands;
(2) no complaint of itching;
(3) no complaint of rashes save for an old one on the neck - dry and scaly;
(4) no raised eosinophil count at any stage;
(5) negative CFT;
(6) on examination of whole skin, no evidence of onchodermatitis;
(7) no onchokeratitis;
(8) no palpable lymph glands;
(9) no nodules.

In 1982 the plaintiff sued the hospital authority. Her case was that she had been suffering from onchocerciasis (known as river blindness), that this was diagnosed elsewhere in 1979 and that the negligent failure to diagnose and treat caused her suffering and debilitation to the detriment of her academic career. She relied on the following:

(1) restlessness which became lethargy and inability to concentrate;
(2) itching;
(3) rashes;
(4) musculo-skeletal pain;
(5) hip pain;
(6) swollen lymph glands;
(7) nodules (cervical spine and between the legs);
(8) Mazzotti reaction to DE;
(9) exposure to the river fly Simulium damnosum.

Held: (i) the plaintiff did not tell Dr Cole about itching or rashes (save to the neck). He carried out a proper examination. His findings of 'no onchodermatitis' and 'no onchokeratitis' were reliable, as were his failure to find any glands or enlarged spleen.

(ii) the plaintiff never had onchocerciasis. Her history of itching and rashes was unreliable, her hip pains had an orthopaedic explanation and eosinophilia was absent throughout. The diagnosis of onchocerciasis was unsustainable.

(iii) even if she had been suffering from onchocerciasis, the hospital doctors had not failed to discharge their duty to exercise the due care and skill to be expected of those specialising not in filarial infections only, but in tropical medicine generally.

See p 60.

Reed v Oswal and Cleveland Area Health Authority

Operation: consultant: fresh evidence: aural: face

Court of Appeal. CAT, 22 November 1979

In June 1970 the plaintiff (Mrs Mary Reed) underwent a stapedectomy operation by Mr Oswal at the North Riding Infirmary, Middlesbrough. Following the operation, which was intended to improve the hearing of her right ear, she suffered from almost complete paralysis of the facial muscles on the right side of her face. She sued Mr Oswal and the hospital authority. In November 1978 the trial judge (Jones J) gave judgment for the defendants.

As a result of local publicity about the trial, the plaintiff learned afterwards about Mrs Addison on whom Mr Oswal performed a mastoidectomy in July 1970. This left Mrs Addison with total paralysis of the right side of her face. The plaintiff appealed, applying for leave to adduce fresh evidence about Mrs Addison's operation.

Held: the fresh evidence was credible and could not have been obtained with reasonable diligence for use at the trial. However if given, it would probably not have had an important influence on the result. The drill used by Mr Oswal cut Mrs Addison's facial nerve, which was not how the plaintiff's injuries were caused. The facts of the two operations were not similar enough for evidence about Mrs Addison's operation to be of probative value in the plaintiff's case. The plaintiff's appeal and application were dismissed.

See p 148.

Reibl v Hughes

Operation: risk disclosure: informed consent: battery: prudent patient test: causation: Canada: artery: stroke

Supreme Court of Canada. (1980) 114 DLR (3d) 1

The plaintiff (John Reibl) suffered from headaches and high blood pressure. He was referred to Dr Hughes, a neurosurgeon, and an arteriogram was taken. This showed that his left carotid artery had narrowed so as to permit only 15% of the normal blood flow through the artery, which leads to the brain. Dr Hughes advised an operation and told the plaintiff that he would be better off to have the operation than not to have it. Dr Hughes did not tell him that the operation involved a four per cent risk of death and a further ten per cent risk of having a stroke.

The plaintiff consented to the operation which was intended to remove an occlusion in the left carotid artery. Dr Hughes performed it competently in March 1970, but the plaintiff suffered a massive stroke which left him paralysed on the right side of his body and also impotent. Alleging that his was not an 'informed consent', he sued Dr Hughes for damages in battery and negligence.

Held: (i) the facts did not justify the imposition of liability for battery. An action for battery does not arise where there has been consent to the very surgical procedure carried out upon the patient, and the only failure is a breach of the duty of disclosure of attendant risks. Actions for battery in respect of surgical or other medical treatment should be confined to cases where there has been no consent at all or where, emergency situations aside, the surgery or treatment has gone beyond that to which there was consent.

    (ii) the relationship between surgeon and patient gives rise to a duty of the surgeon to make disclosure to the patient of all material risks attending the recommended surgery. A surgeon, generally, should answer any specific questions posed by the patient as to the risk involved and should, without being questioned, disclose to him the nature of the proposed operation, its gravity, any material risks and any special or unusual risks attendant upon the performance of the operation. Even if a certain risk is a mere possibility which ordinarily need not be disclosed, yet if its occurrence carries serious consequences, for example, paralysis or even death, it should be regarded as a material risk requiring disclosure. The risks attending the surgery in question of a stroke, of paralysis, and indeed of death, were without question material risks. Dr Hughes had been negligent in not disclosing them.

    (iii) the objective standard is the preferable one on the issue of causation. It must take into account any special considerations affecting the particular patient. The test is what the average prudent person, the reasonable person in the plaintiff's particular position, would agree to or would not agree to, if all material and special risks of going ahead with the surgery or forgoing it were made known to him. As the plaintiff was at no immediate risk without the operation and was within one and a half years of earning pension benefits if he continued at his job, a reasonable person in his position would probably have opted against surgery at that time. The plaintiff succeeded on causation.

See pp 62, 107.

Rhodes v Rowbotham

Prescription: asthma: drugs

Hilbery J. [1935] 1 BMJ 622

The plaintiff (Kenneth Rhodes) was treated by Dr Rowbotham for asthma for six weeks from June 1933. Dr Rowbotham attempted to stop his asthma spasms by spraying the plaintiff's nose on six occasions with ten per cent solution of cocaine. On one occasion, when the plaintiff was going away, Dr Rowbotham filled his atomiser with cocaine to spray his nose, warning him that it was not to be used indiscriminately but only for the relief of asthma. Dr Rowbotham also once left a bottle of percaine at his house. The cocaine sprays relieved the asthma.

The plaintiff sued Dr Rowbotham alleging that as a result of the treatment he had become a cocaine addict.

Held: the plaintiff had not become a drug addict. Dr Rowbotham's treatment was perfectly sound and up to date. He had not been negligent.

Rich v Pierpont

Childbirth: duty of care: causation

Earle CJ. (with jury). [1862] 3 F & F 35

In December 1861 the plaintiff (Mrs Rich) was pregnant. Her husband hired Mr Pierpont to attend to her as accoucheur. Mr and Mrs Rich were teetotallers and expressly desired Mr Pierpont not to give spirits. On 11 and 12 December the plaintiff retained nothing in her stomach and suffered from nausea and exhaustion. Mr Pierpont did not then direct stimulants and support, due to Mr Rich's aversion to the use of spirits. When he saw the plaintiff again in the early hours of 13 December, he desired to give her a little gin in warm water. The nurse brought him a bottle containing some colourless fluid of which, supposing it to be gin, he gave the plaintiff half a drachma in warm water. When it was discovered that the fluid was not gin but tartaric acid, Mr Pierpont again suggested the use of a little gin and water. Mr Rich still objected and said that he would rather his wife should die than take it. Disagreement ensued, the result of which was that the plaintiff did not have the spirits. The delivery on 14 December proved abortive, the child being dead.

Held: Earle CJ directed the jury that it was not enough to make Mr Pierpont liable because some medical men, of far greater experience and ability, might have used a greater degree of skill, nor even that he might possibly have used some greater degree of care. The question was whether there had been a want of competent care and skill to such an extent as to lead to the bad result. The mistake about the tartaric acid turned out to have been of no consequence.

The jury delivered a verdict for the defendant.

See p 58.

Richardson v Kitching

Causation: fatal: general practitioner: deafness

Mance J. N.L.P. 28 March 1995

On 19 September 1983 Mark Richardson first complained of deafness to his general practitioner, Dr Kitching. In September 1984 he was referred to an ear, nose and throat specialist. On 1 February 1985 an acoustic neuroma was discovered by a cranial scan. On 21 February 1985 Mr Richardson died following an operation to remove this neuroma.

The plaintiff (his widow) alleged that in September 1983 Dr Kitching had recommended that Mr Richardson be referred to an ear, nose and throat specialist but had failed to implement this recommendation or, in the alternative, that he had failed to appreciate the seriousness of the condition or to make such a recommendation at all. She further alleged that, but for this delay, his true condition would have been diagnosed sooner and an operation carried out which would have saved his life.

Held: (i)   the delay had not been proved to be a result of Dr Kitching's acts or omissions, as opposed to some other factors such as Mr Richardson's reluctance to seek specialist advice.

       (ii)   as this case involved injury arising due to concurrent causes, it was not sufficient to show that the delay 'materially contributed' to Mr Richardson's death. The plaintiff had to prove both liability and causation on the balance of probability. She had failed to discharge that burden.

Riddett v D'Arcy

General practitioner: diagnosis: examination: fatal: baby

Southampton County Court. [1960] 2 BMJ 1607

On Sunday 18 January 1960 the plaintiff (Mr Riddett) called Dr D'Arcy, a general practitioner, to see his month old baby. The baby was icy cold, displayed a mauve colour and swelling about the eyes, and was breathing irregularly. Dr D'Arcy discerned only a runny nose, diagnosed that the baby had a cold and recommended a dose of castor oil.

In the evening of the next day, Dr Nally, a partner of Dr D'Arcy, called and saw the baby. He immediately sent for an ambulance. The baby died in hospital of staphylococcal pneumonia.

Held: it should have been apparent to Dr D'Arcy that the baby was sick. Symptoms of heart failure had been present, but Dr D'Arcy's examination was insufficiently close to enable him to notice them. He had been negligent.

See p 97.

Riggs v East Dorset Health Authority

Damages: diagnosis: pregnancy: fallopian tubes: ovaries

HH Sir Gervase Sheldon. [1991] CLY 1417

The plaintiff (Ms Rigg), aged 19, had an ectopic pregnancy. Owing to the delay in its diagnosis, she underwent laparotomy and excision of both fallopian tubes and her right ovary. She was thereby rendered infertile, save for the possibility of conception by in vitro fertilisation.

Held (October 1990): (i) general damages of £7,500 were awarded for loss of fertility.

(ii) the defendants were to discharge the costs of the plaintiff, aged 25 at trial, undergoing up to 12 cycles in invitro fertilisation plus one incomplete cycle, if any, for the purpose of giving birth to a maximum of three infants surviving to be capable of being taken home from hospital. They were to pay the plaintiff £100 towards personal expenses for each cycle. The treatment was to cease on medical advice, save that the plaintiff might obtain a second opinion with provision for an independent medical arbitrator in the event of disagreement.

Ritter v Godfrey

Childbirth: communication: costs: breech delivery: diagnosis

Court of Appeal. (1919) 2 Lancet 1163

Mrs Ritter was pregnant with her first child. Dr Godfrey, an obstetrician, had to deal with a double breech presentation, requiring quick action on his part. The nurse in attendance did not inform him of a material fact on his arrival. Consequently he made a mistaken diagnosis. The baby died at birth.

The plaintiff (Mr Ritter), a barrister, complained. Dr Godfrey wrote in response a heated and argumentative fifteen page letter containing a detailed reply and an emphatic repudiation of liability.

The plaintiff sued Dr Godfrey. The trial judge (McCardie J) found that he had not been negligent. He dismissed the plaintiff's claim but, referring to the letter with disapproval, refused to order the plaintiff to pay Dr Godfrey his costs. Dr Godfrey appealed.

Held: the discretion to disallow costs was not absolute but must be exercised in accordance with certain principles. A judge should give costs to a successful defendant, unless he had either brought about the litigation, or had done something connected with the institution or conduct of the suit calculated to cause unnecessary litigation, or had done some wrongful act in the course of the transaction of which the plaintiff complained. Dr Godfrey's letter accurately explained what had occurred and did not give the plaintiff any reasonable grounds for believing that he had a good cause of action. It would be a negation of justice to hold that Dr Godfrey was disentitled to his costs merely because he had retaliated with some warmth. His appeal was allowed.

See p 126.

Ritchie v Chichester Health Authority

Anaesthetics: child birth: paraplegia: twins: injection: registrar: spinal

HH Judge Anthony Thomson QC. [1994] 5 Med LR 187

On 26 September 1989 the plaintiff (Mrs Michelle Ritchie), aged 32, entered St Richard's Hospital in Chichester for a confinement. She was in the 30th week of her pregnancy, and was known to be carrying twins. Labour was successfully induced during the afternoon of 29 September. Around midnight the anaesthetic registrar, Dr Berelian, set up the epidural. The plaintiff was required to lie on her left side with her knees up as far as they would go.

She testified that Dr Berelian went to work behind her on her back and that he spent some time feeling it before she felt an injection. Immediately she felt a dreadful pain shoot down into her legs, principally her left leg, and she screamed about the pain and asked Dr Berelian to stop. Although she continued to scream about the awful pain in her legs, he just told her to keep still. Eventually he said that he would take the needle out and after a rest would put it in again. After the needle came out, the pain eased a little but the plaintiff was left with an awful ache in her legs. Shortly afterwards the needle was reinserted, and again she felt the awful pain shoot down into her leg as before. She protested as before, but her treaties were ignored. The needle was withdrawn again, and a third injection successfully eased the pain.

Dr Berelian, who was unable to attend the trial, testified by affidavit that he prepared the plaintiff's back with antiseptic solution and surgical drapes and, having identified the site of the injection, gave her a local anaesthetic of lignocaine into the skin and deeper tissues using an orange needle, followed by a blue needle. He noticed that the local injections seemed to cause more pain than usual. He waited for about three minutes for the local anaesthetic to take effect before inserting the 18 gauge epidural needle in the midline between the third and fourth lumbar vertebrae using loss of resistance to air to detect the epidural space. The needle insertion was uneventful, and no blood or fluid was seen to issue from the needle. When however he threaded the catheter through the needle, the plaintiff complained of very sharp pains shooting down her left leg. He then withdrew the needle and catheter together completely, and the pain went off. After her pains had reduced, he reinserted the needle after further local anaesthetic infiltration in the same space and this time inserted the epidural catheter without difficulty. He did not recall the plaintiff screaming.

Subsequent top ups of the epidural were administered. Eventually a caesarean section under general anaesthetic proved necessary. This was performed soon after midday on 30 September. Both twins were born healthy. However the plaintiff was found to have suffered permanent and total paralysis of the saddle area, incontinence and loss of vaginal sensation.

The plaintiff sued the hospital authority, alleging that a toxic substance was administered to her during the epidural. The defence was that her injury was due to ischaemia caused by either a fibrocartilaginous embolus (FCE) or spontaneous infarction.

Held: (i) the lesion was in the cauda equina and not the conus. FCE would have to be in the conus or above and could not be in the cauda equina. That ruled out FCE as a cause.

    (ii) the site of the lesion effectively disposed of the defence of spontaneous infarction as well. This was exceedingly rare in a young woman and, if there had been a lesion in the spinal cord due to infarction, that would be expected to show up on the MRI scans.

    (iii) there was a spinal tap at the time of the setting up of the epidural. This was indicated by the plaintiff's raised protein level and the presence of xanphochronia. Either there was total penetration into the subarachnoid space by the needle, or there was just penetration of the dura which was then completed when the catheter was introduced.

    (iv) the plaintiff's account of the pain which she suffered at the time when the epidural was set up was substantially accurate.

    (v) her neurological deficit was a cauda equina lesion which was caused by the inadvertent injection of a neurotoxic substance in the labour ward of St Richard's Hospital shortly after midnight on 30 September 1989.

    (vi) accordingly the plaintiff had established negligence and succeeded on the issue of liability.

See p 122.

Roach v Oxfordshire Health Authority

Limitation: costs: ophthalmic

Court of Appeal. Lexis, 16 January 1990.

The plaintiff (Ian Roach) alleged negligence by the defendants in treating his eyes between 1961 and 1981. His writ was issued on 24 March 1988. The defendants denied negligence and pleaded limitation.

At the preliminary trial on limitation, Drake J dismissed the case as statute barred. The plaintiff appealed. On 19 October 1989 the Court of Appeal Registrar ordered the plaintiff to provide security in the sum of £2,500 by 16 November 1989. The plaintiff appealed against that decision. He made it clear that he was not in a position to meet the defendants' costs if he should continue with his appeal and lose it.

Held: (i) the position with regard to costs in the Court of Appeal differs from the position in the court of first instance in that if an appellant, by reason of impecuniosity, is unable to satisfy the Court of Appeal that he will be able to pay the costs of the other party should he lose the appeal, that is a valid ground upon which the Court of Appeal may order security for costs and perhaps thus effectually debar him from continuing his appeal.

    (ii) an exception to this rule arises where the plaintiff alleges that his impecuniosity is the result of the very actions of the defendants about which he is complaining. As the plaintiff alleged that the defendants' negligence had caused him to lose his earning capacity, it was appropriate to consider what were the prospects of the appeal succeeding.

    (iii) the judge's finding that there was no allegation that the defendants had been negligent within three years of the issue of the writ was clearly correct.

(iv) the plaintiff's case was that he first had knowledge of some relevant facts when he received an experts' report in February 1986, but the registrar was right to conclude that all the report did was to provide the plaintiff with evidence in support of allegations that he had already made prior to 24 March 1985.

(v) there was no reason to disagree with the conclusion that the limitation period should not be disapplied under s 33 of the Limitation Act 1980.

(vi) accordingly the appeal against the requirement of security for costs must be dismissed. The registrar's order would be varied to allow 28 days from this dismissal for the security to be raised.

Roberts v Johnstone and Another

Blood transfusion: damages

Court of Appeal. [1989] QB 878, [1988] 3 WLR 1247

The plaintiff (Sandra Roberts) was born in November 1981. Her mother's blood group was rhesus negative. In 1975 she had erroneously received a blood transfusion of rhesus positive blood. The father's blood group was rhesus positive. The defendants knew about these matters. Nevertheless they failed to give appropriate treatment to the mother during pregnancy. Consequently the plaintiff was born with a severe form of haemolytic disease.

From May 1984 the plaintiff's care was entrusted to Mr and Mrs Woodward who legally adopted her. Their cottage was unsuitable for her, so it was sold for £18,000 and a bunglow purchased for £86,500. The conversion cost of the bungalow was £38,284 of which £10,000 was due to 'betterment' rather than the plaintiff's needs.

Mrs Woodward cared for the plaintiff full time and would continue to do so. Mr Woodward assisted and served as a relief for her.

The plaintiff sued the obstetrician and the health authority who admitted liability. In July 1986 the trial judge (Alliott J) awarded her £335,000 damages and interest, including £75,000 general damages for pain, suffering and loss of amenities.

Held: (i) the damages to be awarded in respect of the specially purchased accommodation should be the additional annual cost of providing it. A rate of 2 per cent should be applied to the full difference of £68,500, a figure of £1,370 which, applying the multiplier of 16, equals £21,920. To this should be added the net conversion costs of £28,284.

(ii) the judge was arithmetically correct in awarding £9,152 in respect of Mrs Woodward's care to trial: 2.2 years at £80 per week over 52 weeks. This head, relating to the notional cost of services performed by someone else, was recoverable as special and not general damages. Interest should have been awarded at the rate appropriate to special damages.

(iii) there was no need for two people to care for the plaintiff all the time, but Mr Woodward was entitled to some recompense for the services he had to provide if his wife was to be engaged or on call for 24 hours a day. These should be assessed at £20 per week for 46.5 weeks a year.

(iv) some relief one night a week should be allowed to enable both Mr & Mrs Woodward to be absent from home together if they so wished, so £20 per week should be allowed for night-sitting relief.

The total award was increased to around £400,000 damages and interest.

See pp 155, 162, 166.

Roberts v West Midland Health Authority and Others

Assault: consent: limitation: operation: foot

Court of Appeal. CAT 25 November 1993

The plaintiff (Mr Roberts) had long standing trouble with his right heel. From 1964 onwards, many operations were carried out upon it and on the achilles tendon in that area. On 16 September 1980 the plaintiff issued a High Court writ alleging medical negligence and other matters. In December 1980 a master ordered that it be set aside. In January 1981, during an appointment in chambers, Comyn J adjourned his appeal against this and suggested that he ought to see a solicitor to get his tackle in order. In February 1981 the plaintiff's appeal was dismissed. Nevertheless in March 1986 the plaintiff issued a summons in the same action. On his appeal in June 1986 against a further master's order, Alliott J who had ascertained that this order was a nullity because the action had already died, suggested that the right step to get the case running again would be to commence a fresh court action.

Pursuant to this, the plaintiff issued a second writ on 17 June 1986. He alleged surgical negligence from 1964 to 1980, pernicious discrimination due to homosexual nature, intimidation to drop litigation, and three other matters. The endorsement of the statement of claim on the second writ added a seventh allegation that 'Mr Porter . . . operated on my . . . achilles tendon without my permission on 6 November 1985 and was negligent because he did not eradicate bursitis. . . The operation of 6 November 1985, I agreed to be performed by Mr Cotterill . . . and not Mr Porter.' In November 1990 a circuit judge, sitting as a deputy High Court judge, struck out the initial six allegations as statute-barred. In November 1991 another judge tried the seventh allegation, namely the endorsement of the statement of claim which was not statute-barred; he found that the plaintiff had read, understood and signed the consent to operation form, and dismissed the claim. The plaintiff appealed against both judges' decisions.

Held: (i) the plaintiff's complaint on the limitation issue, that it was wrong for the circuit judge trying it to overrule a High Court judge, was misconceived since neither Comyn J nor Alliott J had made any order.

        (ii) his complaint on the consent issue, that although he signed the consent form he did not read it because he had not taken his spectacles with him to the hospital, was negatived by the finding of fact which the trial judge had justifiably made.

The plaintiff's appeals were dismissed.

Robinson v Post Office and Another

General practitioner: injection: brain damage: causation: foreseeability: novus actus interveniens: departing from orthodox practice: foot

Court of Appeal. [1974] 2 All ER 737, [1974] 1 WLR 1176

On 15 February 1968 the plaintiff (Keith Robinson), a joiner employed by the Post Office, was descending an oily ladder at work when he slipped and sustained a laceration some three inches long on his left shin. About eight hours later he saw his general practitioner, Dr McEwan, who enquired what anti-tetanus injections he had previously had. Dr McEwan sent the plaintiff to a chemist for anti-tetanus serum (ATS) and, on his return, gave him an injection of it. On 25 February the plaintiff became delirious and suffered brain damage. As a result of the injection, he had contracted encephalitis.

He sued the Post Office and Dr McEwan. Evidence was given at the trial that there was a reputable school of thought which considered that administration of ATS was appropriate in the case of a non-immunised patient with a contaminated wound over six hours old. However it was common ground that in the case of a patient who had already had an injection of ATS the correct procedure was to administer just below the skin a test dose and wait half an hour to see whether the patient showed any reaction. Dr McEwan knew that the plaintiff had had an ATS injection in 1955 but did not follow this procedure.

Held: (i) Dr McEwan had not been negligent in injecting ATS, since in doing so he had acted in accordance with a practice accepted as proper by a responsible body of medical men.

  (ii) he had negligently diverged from proper practice in respect of administration of the test dose.

  (iii) as an adverse reaction would not have manifested itself in the standard half hour, Dr McEwan's negligence had not caused or contributed to the encephalitis, so he was not liable to pay damages to the plaintiff.

  (iv) since the accident and the need for an anti-tetanus prophylactic were reasonably foreseeable, the Post Office could not rely on the doctor's negligence as a *novus actus interveniens* and were liable to the plaintiff both for the skin wound and the encephalitis.

See pp 65, 68, 82, 99, 121.

Robinson v Salford Health Authority

Damages: sterilisation (failed): wrongful birth

Morland J. [1992] 3 Med LR 270

On 1 July 1986 the plaintiff (Mrs Lona Robinson), the mother of three young daughters, underwent a laparoscopic sterilisation operation. It was negligently performed with the result that on 8 April 1987 she gave birth to a son, Jonathan. The defendants admitted liability.

The plaintiff had a difficult pregnancy, during which she had to be admitted to hospital for short periods. After the birth, she had to undergo surgery for the removal of her fallopian tubes. This left her with unsightly scarring and residual discomfort.

Jonathan was born prematurely and was seriously underweight and underdeveloped. He had to remain in hospital for 15 weeks. His problems included vomiting in his first year, troublesome asthma, ear and eye trouble. His residual problems were speech difficulty and behavioural problems. However he was expected to develop within the normal range.

Before his birth, the plaintiff had worked for two days a week as a cashier at a department store in Manchester, employing a child minder when she did so. She and her husband separated in September 1989. Jonathan needed her full time care until he went to school in September 1991.

Held (January 1992): (i) if the sterilisation operation had been successful, the plaintiff would have returned to work in December 1986 when her youngest daughter was eight months old and would have continued working there until the breakdown of her marriage in September 1989. Thereafter she would not have found comparable part time work until December 1989. Throughout she would have required a paid childminder on the days when she worked. Damages under this head were £2,800.

(ii)   although her husband transferred to lower paid work in October 1988, he only occasionally took the children to the park and did little more than before. The claim for his loss of earnings should be disallowed.

(iii)   the basic allowance assessed by the National Foster Care Association was inappropriate in assessing the cost of Jonathan's upkeep to date, as details of the family income and expenditure were available. Excluding child benefit, £30 net per week should be allowed as the average weekly cost of Jonathan's upkeep over 250 weeks, a total of £7,500.

(iv)   £50 per week should be allowed for the future cost of Jonathan's upkeep, again putting out of the calculation child benefit, but bearing in mind that he was a boy who could not inherit clothes from his sisters and who would need a room of his own. Nine years was the appropriate multiplier. £50 x 52 weeks x 9 years = £23,400 under this head.

(v)   £350 should be allowed in respect of the cost of travel to his psychologist and speech therapist.

(vi)   there should also be awarded agreed general damages of £10,000.

The total award was £44,050 plus interest.

See pp 168, 171.

Robitaille et al v Vancouver Hockey Club Ltd

Canada: contributory negligence: exemplary damages: vicarious liability: sports injury: spinal

British Columbia Court of Appeal. (1981) 16 CCLT 225

In 1976–77 the plaintiff (Mike Robitaille) was a professional ice hockey player for Vancouver Hockey Club. Though a good player, he was subject to anxiety attacks. The club's general manager was Philip Maloney, and the trainer was Patrick Dunn. At the beginning of the season, the club made arrangements for three new team doctors (including Dr Piper) to look after the players.

In late October 1976 the plaintiff suffered a shoulder injury and was out of the line up for a short time on the instructions of Dr Piper. On 1 November 1976, Mr Maloney was quoted in the Vancouver Daily Province as saying: '. . . of course, we were short a defenceman with (Mike) Robitaille out (sore shoulder). I don't know exactly how bad it is but I tell you he'd better start playing.'

On 2 January 1977, in a game against New York, the plaintiff was checked and suffered what he described as 'shocking sensations' and a 'rubbery feeling' in his right leg. He also complained of a painful neck. When the team returned to Vancouver, Dunn telephoned Dr Piper who undertook that a doctor would examine the plaintiff at the next home game on 12 January.

Although the plaintiff arrived early on 12 January, no doctor saw him before the game. Towards the end of it, he collided with an opposing player and fell to the ice. He suffered 'electric shock' sensations. His right leg jerked uncontrollably for a few minutes. He was helped off the ice. In the dressing room Dr Piper walked past him, spoke to Dunn, and then walked out without examining him.

On 19 January 1977 the plaintiff played again. During the game, he was checked heavily by an opposing player and suffered a spinal cord injury. Yet no stretcher was brought to him. Instead Dunn and another player pulled him to his feet and with difficulty brought him off the ice to a waiting stretcher. Dr Piper examined him in the dressing room and told him to go home, advising him to take a couple of shots of Courvoisier cognac.

The plaintiff subsequently saw other doctors, was hospitalised for ten days and was told that he had a 'bruised spinal cord'. Whilst he was in hospital, the club tried to trade him to Calgary without disclosing his disability. Maloney still persisted in believing that the plaintiff could play, ordered him to practise, and in late February threatened him with suspension.

It subsequently emerged that he had sustained a spinal cord contusion on 12 January, which was seriously aggravated in the game on 19 January. He was left permanently disabled and sued the defendant club. The trial judge found negligence to be established, awarded him both compensatory and exemplary damages, but deducted 20% for contributory negligence.

Held: (i) the defendant club was under a duty to exercise reasonable care to ensure the safety, fitness and health of its players. It breached that duty by failing to react reasonably to the injury of 12 January 1977 and by failing to keep the plaintiff from playing on 19 January.

(ii) the defendants had the power of selecting, controlling and dismissing the team doctors who were hired to further their business purposes. They were vicariously liable for Dr Piper's negligence.

(iii) the harm to the plaintiff's physical and mental health, his professional standing and pride, was a foreseeable result of the defendants' behaviour which was high-handed and arrogant as well as negligent. The award of $35,000 exemplary damages should stand.

(iv) there was evidence upon which the judge was entitled to find that the plaintiff was 20% at fault because his failure to take any action to protect his own interest was less than reasonable. He was a highly paid, experienced, modern-day, professional athlete.

(v) however this did not contribute towards the defendants' conduct which gave rise to the exemplary damages, so the 20% deduction for contributory negligence should not apply to the exemplary award but only to the compensatory damages.

See p 83.

Roe v Minister of Health and Another; Woolley v Same

Anaesthetics: res ipsa loquitur: vicarious liability: medical literature: state of knowledge

Court of Appeal. [1954] 2 QB 66

On 13 October 1947 the plaintiffs (Cecil Roe and Albert Woolley) were operated on at Chesterfield and North Derbyshire Royal Hospital for minor complaints. The anaesthetist, Dr Graham, had been appointed as visiting anaesthetist to the hospital. He carried on a private anaesthetic practice, but with another anaesthetist he was under an obligation to provide a regular anaesthetic service for the hospital.

In each case phenol, in which the glass ampoules containing the anaesthetic had been immersed, percolated through invisible cracks in each ampoule. It contaminated the spinal anaesthetic that was given to the plaintiffs. The risk of this happening was first drawn to the attention of the medical profession by a book published in 1951.

Each plaintiff developed a condition of spastic paraplegia and was perman ently paralysed from the waist down. Each sued Dr Graham and the hospital authority. The trial judge found for the defendants.

Held: (i) the hospital authority was liable for Dr Graham's acts.

(ii) the maxim *res ipsa loquitur* applied.

(iii) the hospital had explained how the accident occurred; applying the standard knowledge to be imputed to competent anaesthetists in 1947, Dr Graham was not negligent in failing to appreciate the risk.

Per Lord Denning: (i) 'I think that the hospital authorities are responsible for the whole of their staff, not only for the nurses and doctors, but also for the anaesthetists and surgeons. It does not matter whether they are permanent or temporary, resident or visiting, whole-time or part-time. The hospital authorities are responsible for all of them. The reason is because even if they are not servants, they are the agents of the hospital to give the treatment. The only exception is the case of consultants or anaesthetists selected and employed by the patient himself.'

(ii) 'The judge has said that those facts do not speak for themselves, but I think that they do. They certainly call for an explanation. Each of these men is entitled to say to the hospital: "While I was in your hands something has been done to me which has wrecked my life. Please explain how this has come to pass" . . . I approach this case, therefore, on the footing that the hospital authorities and Dr Graham were called on to give an explanation of what has happened.'

(iii) 'But I think that they have done so . . . I do not think that their failure to foresee this was negligence. It is so easy to be wise after the event and to condemn as negligence that which was only a misadventure . . . We must not look at the 1947 accident with 1954 spectacles. The judge acquitted Dr Graham of negligence and we should uphold his decision.'

See pp 19, 22, 24, 58, 59, 61, 78, 87, 123.

Rogers v Whittaker

Australia: causation: risk disclosure: ophthalmic: advice: blindness

Supreme Court of New South Wales, Court of Appeal. [1992] 3 Med LR 331

In May 1984 the plaintiff (Mrs Maree Whittaker), aged 48, who had suffered a penetrating injury from a piece of wood in 1946, was almost totally blind in her right eye. Her left eye was normal. Dr Rogers, an ophthalmic surgeon, advised her that he could operate on her right eye to remove scar tissue and to improve the sight in that eye. She incessantly questioned him about possible complications, to the point of irritating him, but did not ask him whether the operation could cause damage to her left eye. There was a 1 in 14,000 chance of sympathetic ophthalmia developing. Dr Rogers did not mention it.

Consequently the plaintiff agreed to submit to the surgery. The operation was performed in August 1984. Sympathetic ophthalmia resulted, and she lost the sight of her left eye. By 1986 she had become virtually totally blind.

Held: (i) the standard of care required of Dr Rogers by law could not be conclusively determined by the evidence given by some of the experts that only a direct question about complications to the good eye could call for any mention of the risk of sympathetic ophthalmia;

(ii) there was no therapeutic reason for not disclosing the risk. The surgery proposed was purely elective. The alternative was the status quo with which the plaintiff had lived for nearly forty years;

    (iii) the trial judge was correct in finding that Dr Rogers failed to exercise reasonable skill and care in answering her general question about possible complications, when he failed to mention the remote risk of sympathetic ophthalmia in her good eye leading to total blindness;

    (iv) but for the negligent advice, the plaintiff would not have accepted the risk and undergone surgery. The defendant's negligence was a cause of her sympathetic ophthalmia.

Per Mahoney JA: 'For myself, I think it should be clear that if a patient makes it plain to her medical practitioner that she desires to be told or warned of a particular thing, it is in principle a breach of duty by the medical practitioner not to tell her. There are, of course, obvious limits and qualifications to this. There are some questions to which the answer may be: "I do not know". There may be cases in which the condition of the patient, eg, in the emotional or the psychiatric sense, is such that there is a compelling medical reason why the answer should not be given. It is not necessary to pursue the circumstances in which this may be so. And there may be other reasons why it would not be a breach of duty for the answer not to be given, for example, the urgent need of treatment, the real likelihood of misunderstanding or failure to understand, and matters of that kind. But, in my opinion, the position remains in principle that subject to appropriate qualifications, the patient is entitled to be told what she asks to be told.'

Note: This decision was upheld on appeal by the High Court of Australia, as reported in [1993] 4 Med LR 79.

See pp 110, 113.

Rosen v Edgar

Operation: consultant: registrar: vicarious liability: foot

Tucker J. (1986) 293 BMJ 552

The plaintiff (Mrs Margaret Rosen) was referred by her general practitioner for treatment of a bunion as a National Health Service patient to the clinic of Mr Edgar, consultant, at the Middlesex Hospital. In February 1977 she saw a senior registrar in out-patients. In June 1978 the same senior registrar operated on her.

Acting without solicitors, she issued a writ against Mr Edgar. She claimed that the operation was negligently performed and indeed deliberately done to cripple her. She considered that Mr Edgar was liable because he was in charge of the senior registrar.

Held: Mr Edgar was not liable. He had no responsibility in law for what was done in the operation. An employee is not vicariously liable for the acts of another employee, even if that other employee is junior to him and in some senses answerable to him.

Note: The appropriate defendants were the senior registrar and the local health authority.

See p 21.

Rosen v Marston

Surgeon: operation: limitation: striking out for want of prosecution: varicose veins: leg

Court of Appeal. CAT, 15 March 1984

In March 1977 the plaintiff (Mrs Margaret Rosen) was operated on for varicose veins in both legs by Mr Marston at the Middlesex Hospital. She alleged that this left her with a scar from the middle of her right leg to the ankle.

In early 1980 she issued a writ endorsed with a Statement of Claim. A Defence was served. The pleadings were closed in October 1980. The plaintiff consulted solicitors at the Mary Ward Legal Centre. No further steps in the action were taken until February 1983 when Mr Marston's solicitors, on learning that a request had been made to the hospital for release of the operation case notes, applied for the case to be struck out for want of prosecution. Hirst J reversed the Master's decision to strike out.

Held: (i) the delay of two and a half years in a case in which the writ was issued shortly before the expiry of the limitation period was excessive. The judge was in error in so far as he took the view that the plaintiff had a good excuse because she entrusted her case to persons who claimed legal qualifications who failed her;

(ii) there was prejudice to Mr Marston, not only because his recollection was likely to be significantly impaired, but also because the action with its potential threat to reputation and the attendant anxiety and distress would be hanging over his head for more than two years longer than it should have been.

The case was struck out for want of prosecution.

See p 203.

Rothwell et al v Raes et al

Canada: causation: general practitioner: locum: product liability: vaccine damage: vicarious liability

Ontario High Court of Justice, Osler J. (1988) 54 DLR (4th) 193

On 17 January 1979 the plaintiff (Patrick Rothwell) was born. He was one of a pair of male twins, the other of which was stillborn and macerated. On 20 April, 25 May and 26 June 1979, he received immunisation doses of DPTP, which was manufactured by Connaught Laboratories Ltd: a vaccine known as a quadrigen, and which was intended to give protection against diphtheria, pertussis, tetanus and poliomyelitis. The vaccines were administered either by Dr Raes, a medical doctor with a family practice, or by Dr Hall, a family physician at that time filling in for Dr Raes occasionally as a locum, or by a nurse acting under the instructions of Dr Raes or Dr Hall.

Although the plaintiff was healthy before the vaccinations, by August 1979 serious development abnormality was suspected. He was found to have suffered very severe brain damage and became to all intents and purposes, blind and largely deaf. His purposive movements were limited, he could not speak, and he was dependent in virtually every activity of life.

Held: (i) Dr Raes was not negligent, either in recommending the vaccination or in failing to warn of possible damaging effects. It was at the time the practice to recommend vaccination without reference to the rare possibility of harmful consequences.

(ii) nor was Dr Raes negligent in his choice of Dr Hall as locum tenens. No evidence of negligence on her part was offered. Even if Dr Hall had been negligent as a locum, she was exercising her own professional skill and judgment and Dr Raes, the family physician, could not be vicariously liable for her.

(iii) the manufacturer's leading researchers were familiar with the literature postulating encephalopathy and grave brain damage as possible consequences of administration of the vaccine. Had the manufacturer warned the physician, the court could not presume that he would have failed to discuss the possibilities or at least mention them. Therefore the manufacturer was negligent in this respect.

(iv) the burden was on the plaintiffs to establish on a balance of probabilities that the brain damage was caused by the vaccine. They had failed to discharge this burden. It had not been shown that the vaccine could cause brain damage. Even if it had been established that brain damage might be due to the vaccine, the evidence suggested that the plaintiff suffered from neurological deficiencies from the beginning and that his condition was idiopathic.

The actions were dismissed.

Note: The decision was affirmed on appeal (1990) 76 DLR (4th) 280.

Rouse v Kensington and Chelsea and Westminster Area Health Authority

Diagnosis: casualty officer: warning: foot: sports injury

Court of Appeal. CAT, 26 January 1982

On 16 May 1976 the plaintiff (Mr Rouse) injured his left foot playing football. The next day he was seen at the Casualty Department at Westminster Hospital by Dr Roskovek, who noted 'Tender over upper part of Achilles tendon and pain there on flexion of ankle. Treatment. Elastoplast for 10 days.' On 1 June he returned to the Casualty Department where Dr Mirza removed the elastoplast and noted 'Pain in the tendon Achilles on walking. Treatment: Crepe bandage'.

When the plaintiff was seen at the Orthopaedic Clinic on 1 October, Mr Andrews diagnosed a ruptured Achilles tendon. The plaintiff needed three operations. His left foot was seriously disfigured and partly deformed.

He sued the health authority, alleging negligence by the two casualty officers on 17 May and 1 June. The trial judge (Boreham J) dismissed his claim.

Held: (i)   the trial judge was entitled to conclude that the initial injury was a partially ruptured Achilles tendon and that the casualty officers had not been negligent in their diagnosis.

(ii) there was no reason to interfere with his finding that their treatment was the proper treatment.

(iii) there was no evidence that they failed to give the plaintiff a warning, if such was needed, to be careful with his injured foot.

See p 99.

Routledge v Mackenzie and Shires

Cauda equina syndrome: damages: spinal

Otton J. [1994] PIQR Q49, [1992] CLY 1666

In July 1988 the plaintiff (Mrs Margaret Routledge), aged 37 at trial, experienced increasing back pain. She consulted doctors and underwent treatment, including surgery. Owing to the defendants' admitted negligence, she suffered cauda equina syndrome. Had she been appropriately treated, a laminectomy would have been carried out and she would have made a complete recovery, resuming her career in autumn 1988.

She sustained a cauda equina lesion affecting the nerve roots L5, S1, 2, 3, 4 and 5. Both the motor and sensory nerves were impaired. She had weakness of the calves, feet and buttocks, and was only able to walk a few yards. She was virtually paralysed below the knees. She was unable to develop pressure sores. She got cramps in the calves and right toes. Her bladder function had been severely impaired. She had urgency, odorous urine and occasional fever. She was frequently incontinent of both urine and faeces. She suffered a diminution of sexual function which proved a severe deprivation in marital relations and led to some depression. She had severe pain in her buttocks, rectum, bladder and in her back; it was continuous, acute and debilitating. Her condition was permanent. Her life expectancy had been shortened by five years.

Her ability to look after her husband, who had post-traumatic head injury syndrome following a fall from a horse, was much impaired. She needed permanent care herself. If fit she would have continued as a successful solicitor specialising in commercial conveyancing, working from home as a sole practitioner.

Held (May 1992):   (i)   the appropriate award for general damages for pain, suffering and loss of amenities was £55,000.

(ii)   the defendants were obliged to compensate the plaintiff for (a) the cost of the services which she could no longer perform for her husband and three children and (b) the care which was directly attributable to her injury, subject to credit for the cost of such help (eg a nanny) that she would have employed if not injured. The appropriate future multiplier was 17. £12,500 was awarded for past care and £277,494 for future care.

(iii)   the base figure for loss of future earnings should be £35,000 x 2 plus £41,456 x 12, rounded up to £660,000 to reflect the value of the firm's car and the possibility of her transferring to higher paid work at a local firm, but giving credit for a residual earning capacity of £60,000 (£7,500 pa x 8). The award for loss of future earnings was £600,000. The award for past loss of earnings was £103,378.

(iv)   the cost of investment advice on managing the damages was not recoverable.

(v)   the addition of agreed items resulted in a total award to the plaintiff of £1,185,612, including interest of £30,205.

Routley v Worthing Health Authority and Others

Psychiatric patient: leave to sue: negligent certification: duty of care: false imprisonment

Court of Appeal. CAT, 14 July 1983

The plaintiff (David Routley), then aged 20, was extremely distressed following the death of his mother in May 1979. The family general practitioner, Dr Lewis, referred him to Dr Vaudrey, a consultant psychiatrist at the Graylingwell Hospital, who saw the plaintiff in December 1979 and February 1980.

As a result of letters from the plaintiff's father, Dr Lewis requested Dr Vaudrey to make a domiciliary visit which he did late in the evening of 15 July 1981. The plaintiff returned from the opera at 10.30pm. Dr Vaudrey was waiting for him. The plaintiff refused to see him and rushed past him up the stairs to his room. Dr Vaudrey stated that he was 'making strange noises'. The plaintiff's father told him that the plaintiff had fought with his younger brother, broken furniture and threatened to kill both the father and the brother. Dr Vaudrey decided that the plaintiff should be admitted to a psychiatric hospital for treatment under s 26 of the Mental Health Act 1959 and completed the s 26 recommendation papers.

On 16 July Dr Vaudrey telephoned Dr Lewis with his advice, and reported what had happened. Dr Vaudrey also telephoned a mental welfare officer to ask him and Dr Lewis to make arrangements for the plaintiff's admission. On 17 July Dr Lewis and the mental welfare officer went to the plaintiff's home, with police and ambulance in attendance. They talked to the plaintiff, mostly through locked doors. When he tried to run out of the back door, three police constables jumped on him and forcibly strapped and handcuffed him to the stretcher. Dr Lewis signed the s 26 recommendation.

The plaintiff was detained at Graylingwell Hospital for 18 days. It subsequently transpired that he was not suffering from any mental illness. He sought leave to sue Dr Vaudrey, Dr Lewis and others for negligence and false imprisonment. Wood J refused his application.

Held: the plaintiff had substantial grounds for contending that the recommendations which led to his admission were made by both doctors without reasonable care. He should be granted leave to bring court action against them.

Ruddock v Lowe

Alternative practitioner: representations

Crompton J (with jury). (1865) 4 F & F 519

In the early 1860s Mr Lowe was the proprietor of an 'anatomical museum' in the Strand. He circulated among those who entered the museum a pamphlet in which he had held himself out as a master in the art of healing sexual disorders. He denounced the use of mercury or mineral medicines and stated 'I never undertake a case unless I can guarantee a perfect cure'. To which he added his address, 'Dr' Lowe, at the 'Strand Museum'.

In December 1865 the plaintiff (Mr Ruddock) was induced by the pamphlet to consult 'Dr' Lowe who said it was a 'very bad case' and gave him medicine and charged him two guineas. After many further visits, medicines and fees, the plaintiff found that he was getting worse instead of better, his mouth becoming sore and his teeth loose in his head.

He sued Mr Lowe. The expert evidence was that the medicine contained a great deal of mercury and that the plaintiff was suffering under excessive salivation. Mr Lowe, who was not a duly qualified doctor, denied that he had ever seen or treated the plaintiff.

Held: Crompton J directed the jury that the substantial issue was whether Mr Lowe did undertake to and did treat the plaintiff, since there was no doubt that the supposed treatment was grossly improper.

The jury returned a verdict for the plaintiff.

See pp 30, 47.

Re S (adult: refusal of treatment)

Consent: declaration: interests of patient: pregnancy: caesarian

Sir Stephen Brown P. [1993] Fam 123, [1992] 4 All ER 671, [1992] 3 WLR 806, 136 [1993] 4 Med LR 671, Sol Jo 299, [1992] 1450.

Mrs S, aged 30, and her husband were both 'born again Christians' who were against anything other than a natural childbirth. In October 1992, whilst in her third pregnancy, she was admitted to hospital with ruptured membranes and in spontaneous labour. Six days beyond the expected date of birth, she refused on religious grounds to submit herself to a caesarian section operation.

The hospital authority sought a declaration permitting it to carry out an emergency caesarian operation despite her objection. A doctor testified that her situation was desperately serious, as was also that of the unborn child. The child was in a position of 'transverse lie', with an elbow protruding through the cervix and the head being on the right side. There was the gravest risk of a rupture of the uterus. The doctors were concerned with 'minutes rather than hours'; it was a 'life and death' situation. He had unsuccessfully attempted to persuade the mother that the only means of saving her life, and also the life of her unborn child, was to carry out a caesarian section operation.

Held: this medical evidence was accepted. It was ordered and declared 'that the operation of caesarian section and all necessary consequential treatment which the plaintiff by its servants or agents proposes to perform on the defendant at the .... hospital is in the vital interests of the defendant and of the child she is carrying and can lawfully be performed despite the defendant's refusal to give her consent thereto.'

See p 12.

Re S (hospital patient: court's jurisdiction)

Declaration: injunction: interests of patient

Court of Appeal. (1995) Times, 6 March

In 1945 S, a Norwegian citizen, married his present wife; in 1947 their son was born. In 1989 S met the plaintiff with whom he formed a close friendship; in 1991 he set up house with her in England. In 1993, when S suffered a stroke, the plaintiff secured immediate treatment for him and subsequently his admission to a private hospital, whose account she paid from funds in bank accounts operated under the power of attorney he had given her. She visited him regularly, showing close interest in his welfare.

S's wife and son also visited and, considering that he should be removed for care to Norway, took him away from hospital. The plaintiff alerted the police who intercepted the ambulance taking S to the airport. He was returned to hospital. The plaintiff obtained an interlocutory injunction restraining his removal.

Held: (i) the law respected the right of adults of sound mind to physical autonomy. It was up to them to give or withhold consent as they wished, for reasons good or bad.

(ii) that simple rule could not be applied in cases of minors and those subject to serious mental illness, so in such situations the law provided for parents or next friends or guardians to speak for them.

(iii) those rendered unconscious or inarticulate by accident or sudden illness, such as afflicted S, posed a less familiar problem. They could not express preferences like rational conscious adults.

(iv)   the consequence of that inability was that, in cases of controversy and in cases involving momentous and irrevocable decisions, the courts had treated as justiciable any genuine question as to what the best interest of the patient required or justified.

(v)   where such a serious justiciable issue was brought before the court by a party with a genuine and legitimate interest in obtaining a decision against an adverse party, the court would not impose nice procedural tests to determine the precise legal standing of that claimant.

(vi)   the evidence did not suggest that S was immune from pain and incapable of emotion, so it was not safe to assume that he had no preferences about his future care and residence. There was a serious justiciable issue, potentially involving the happiness and welfare of a helpless human being.

(vii)   when S suffered his stroke, it was clear that the plaintiff had assumed the duty of ensuring that he was properly cared for. If, as was probable, she had made the contract with the private hospital as S's agent, deriving her authority from necessity, then she remained as agent authorised to safeguard the performance of the contract unless and until S's best interests were shown to require a change in the arrangements. If it was necessary for the plaintiff to demonstrate in herself a specific legal right which was liable to be infringed by the wife's and son's proposed action, then she had done so.

(viii)   however to insist on demonstration of such a right in the present sensitive and socially important area of the law was to confine the court's inherent jurisdiction within an inappropriate straitjacket. The plaintiff was far from being a stranger or an officious busybody, and that was enough to give the court jurisdiction.

(ix)   although S's wife and son had ties of affinity and blood with him which the plaintiff lacked, those ties conferred no legal right to determine the course of his treatment.

(x)   if the law were powerless to give practical help in cases such as the present, the invitation to others similarly placed in future to take the law into their own hands, with the risk at least of unseemly tussles and at worst of violence, would be obvious. It was pre-eminently an area in which the common law should respond to social needs as they were manifested, case by case.

Re SG (adult mental patient: abortion)

Abortion: declaration: interests of patient

Sir Stephen Brown P. [1993] 4 Med LR 75, [1991] 2 FLR 329, [1991] FCR 753.

The applicant (Miss SG), aged 26, was a severely mentally handicapped woman with a mental age equivalent to an eight year old child. She was 17 weeks pregnant. Her general practitioner referred her to a consultant gynaecologist. Both considered that it would be in the best interests of Miss SG for her pregnancy to be terminated.

The applicant through her father and next friend applied for a declaration that the termination would be lawful despite her inability to consent due to mental incapacity.

Held: (i)   even in these circumstances, a formal declaration from the High Court was not needed before the pregnancy could be terminated.

(ii)   the matter was governed by the Abortion Act 1967. Provided that there was compliance with the conditions of s 1, it provided fully adequate safeguards for the doctors involved.

S and Another v Distillers Co (Biochemicals) Ltd; J and Another v Same

Drugs: thalidomide: damages: duty of care: product liability

Hinchcliffe J. [1969] 3 All ER 1412, [1970] 1 WLR 114

The drug thalidomide was first marketed in the UK in 1958. It was withdrawn in December 1961, after it had been shown that if taken during the fifth and eighth weeks of pregnancy the drug could cause damage to the embryo. Writs were issued on behalf of about sixty deformed infants and their parents. The issue of liability was settled, with approval of the court, on the basis that the defendant would pay forty per cent of the appropriate figure for damages.

DJ, aged eight, was born without any viable limbs and was in the category of those children who had been most badly affected by the drug.

RS, aged seven, was born without arms and was in the middle of the category of injuries.

Mrs S, his mother, had been depressed, anxious and worried.

Held (1969): (i) the appropriate figure for DJ's general damages for pain, suffering and loss of amenities was £28,000. Total award £52,000 less 60%.

(ii) the award for RS' pain, suffering and loss of amenities was £18,000. Total award £32,000 less 60%.

(iii) Mrs S was awarded general damages of £5,000 for grievous shock, future travelling expenses, special clothes for the boy and loss of wages. Total award £7,250 less 60%.

See p 52.

Sabapathi v Huntley

Fractures: diagnosis: x-ray: libel/slander: Sri Lanka

Privy Council. [1938] 1 WWR 817

On 27 January 1933 Mr Huntley, a planter, and his wife were involved in a serious road accident in Ceylon. They were taken to the Government Hospital at Karawanella where they were treated by Dr Sabapathi, the district Medical Officer. Dr Sabapathi examined them on admission and visited them twice on 28 January. They left hospital on 29 January, and Mr Huntley wrote a letter of gratitude to Dr Sabapathi on 1 February.

On 7 February Mr and Mrs Huntley visited a doctor in Colombo who did not make a diagnosis but arranged for them to be x-rayed. The x-rays showed that they had suffered fractures in the accident. Mr Huntley wrote a letter of complaint, alleging negligence and incompetence against Dr Sabapathi. This letter was publicly discussed at a meeting of the Planters' Association and was published in the Ceylon Daily News.

Dr Sabapathi sued Mr Huntley for damages for libel and slander. Mr Huntley pleaded justification. The Supreme Court reversed on appeal the trial judge's finding in favour of Dr Sabapathi.

Held: it is not necessarily the case that, after a road accident, the attending physician must advise resort to a radiologist and that, if he omits to do so, he displays both incompetence and negligence. The advisability of an x-ray examination must always depend on the circumstances, in particular the condition of the patient, the character of the injuries and the accessibility of the apparatus. Dr Sabapathi's treatment had been competent and careful. He was entitled to damages.

Sa'd v Robinson and Dunlop; Sa'd v Ransley and Mid Surrey Health Authority

General practitioner: diagnosis: communication: damages: costs: child patient: brain damage

Leggatt J. [1989] 4 PMILL 25

Around 5.45am on 18 July 1980 the plaintiff (Zeena Sa'd), then aged 19 months, put her mouth to the spout of a teapot which had just been placed on a low table. Her mother was absent answering the telephone, but four other adults were present. The resulting pain and screams caused Mrs Sa'd to take Zeena to the doctor's surgery within ten minutes.

Dr Robinson examined the child who was trying to vomit and had mucus in her mouth. He noted a scalded lip, recorded 'swallowed hot tea', prescribed a painkiller together with an antacid, and said that the child would be 'OK'.

By about 8.00pm she had not significantly improved, so Mrs Sa'd telephoned the surgery where her call was redirected to Dr Dunlop, a partner of Dr Robinson. She related the facts. He told her that the previous medication would take about two hours to work and did not seem unduly concerned.

About two hours later, following a further telephone call from Mrs Sa'd, Dr Dunlop promptly attended and examined the child, checking her respiration and pulse. He advised that she should be in hospital where she could be observed. He telephoned the hospital to warn that she had drunk something hot some hours before, had a possibility of respiratory problems and should be kept in.

Around 10.45pm the hospital SHO in paediatrics recorded the child's condition as grave. Dr Ransley, the consultant paediatrician, was summoned by telephone. He managed to insert an intravenous line, but the obstruction was becoming more complete due to the mucus. The child then had an anoxic fit. As soon as the fit was over, Dr Ransley inserted an endotracheal tube, but by that time apnoea had persisted for an indefinite period. The plaintiff suffered gross and irreversible brain damage.

The plaintiff through her father sued Dr Robinson and Dr Dunlop. Dr Robinson issued Third Party proceedings against Mrs Sa'd on the grounds that she allowed the child to reach the teapot and failed to give him a full and proper history. Mrs Sa'd in turn served a Second and Third Party Notice on Dr Ransley and the hospital authority. The plaintiff added the three Third Parties as defendants. A fortnight before the trial Dr Robinson discontinued the Third Party proceedings against Mrs Sa'd but declined to grant an indemnity.

Held: (i) Dr Robinson had been negligent. He had failed to appreciate the significance of ingestion of tea and potential damage to the oesophagus leading to the obstruction. He should have referred the plaintiff to hospital immediately.

(ii) Dr Dunlop was also liable. The telephone call and subsequent visit should have prompted admission of the plaintiff to hospital. His subsequent examinations were also inadequate, as was his description to the hospital of the plaintiff's condition.

(iii) neither Mrs Sa'd, Dr Ransley nor the hospital authority had been negligent.

(iv) the plaintiff was awarded total damages of £535,000 which included general damages, future schooling and care and Court of Protection costs.

(v) Dr Robinson and Dr Dunlop were ordered to pay on the standard basis the plaintiff's costs of proceeding against them and also to indemnify the plaintiff, under a Sanderson Order, in respect of the costs of the other three defendants.

541

(vi) Dr Robinson was ordered to pay on an indemnity basis the whole of the costs of the Third Party proceedings, the costs of the proceedings against Dr Ransley and the hospital authority up to discontinuance of the Third Party proceedings, and the costs subsequently incurred by Mrs Sa'd continuing to and including trial.

See p 97.

Sadler v Henry

General practitioner: diagnosis: meningitis: fatal: aural

Cassels J. [1954] 1 BMJ 1331

On 25 April 1952 Kathleen Sadler, aged 26, went to see Dr Henry at his surgery. She gave a history of having had a cold earlier and complained of earache. Dr Henry examined her right ear with an auriscope, took her temperature (99°F), looked and felt behind her ear, and saw partial inflammation of the right eardrum. He saw no discharge or sign of perforation, diagnosed 'catarrhal drum' and prescribed drops to relieve the pain and a sedative.

He was called on 26 April, and was told that she had a headache and some vomiting, and that she heard 'rushing noises like the sea' in her head. He examined her ear through the auriscope, thought it slightly improved and ordered glucose and codeine tablets.

At 6.30pm on 27 April Dr Henry called and made a thorough examination. He could find nothing clinically wrong. Her temperature was again 99°F, and she was worried and emotional. He thought she had acute hysteria. At 8.45pm she became irrational, and he arranged for her admission to hospital. At 11.50pm she died from acute meningitis due to suppurative otitis media.

Her father sued Dr Henry.

Held: there were no signs or symptoms which could reasonably have led Dr Henry to suspect localised meningitis. His diagnosis of hysteria was a mistake, but one which others might well have made. He had failed in the difficult circumstances of the case to diagnose the real condition, which the necropsy disclosed. However he had not been negligent.

See p 99.

Salih v Enfield Health Authority

Damages: wrongful birth: rubella: diagnosis: pregnancy

Court of Appeal. [1991] 2 Med LR 235

The plaintiffs (Mr and Mrs Salih) had two healthy children. In April 1983 their daughter was diagnosed as suffering from rubella (German measles). On it being confirmed that she was pregnant again, Mrs Salih attended an antenatal clinic run by the defendants and expressed concern about contact with rubella. After tests, she was told that she was free from infection and she proceeded with the pregnancy. In December 1983 her third child, a boy called Ali, was born suffering from congenital rubella syndrome with serious impairment to both eyes and both ears.

The defendants admitted liability for failing to diagnose and warn Mrs Salih of the danger that the child she was carrying might be affected by rubella syndrome. Had she known this, she would have had the pregnancy terminated. Previously the plaintiffs had planned to have a total of four children. After Ali's birth they decided not to have another one, and when Mrs Salih became pregnant again that pregnancy was terminated.

In November 1989 Drake J awarded the plaintiffs £68,000 including interest. Three issues arose on appeal.

Held: (i) the general rule was to place the injured party in the same financial position as he would have been in if the negligent act had not occurred. Accordingly the decision of the plaintiffs not to have a fourth child, with the consequential saving of future expenditure, was a relevant consideration. Thus the basic cost of maintaining Ali should be disallowed, and only the additional costs due to his condition were recoverable.

(ii) general damages are peculiarly well suited to be dealt with by the trial judge. There was no reason to interfere with his award of £5,000 for Mrs Salih's pain, suffering and loss of amenity.

(iii) in view of the risk of deterioration to Ali's eyes, £1,500 should be added to the damages for the risk of the plaintiff's becoming involved in further expenditure should this occur.

See pp 128, 168.

Salisbury v Gould

Diagnosis: public health officer: damages: smallpox: negligent certification: fever: child patient

Grantham J (with jury). [1904] 1 BMJ 282

The plaintiff (Mrs Salisbury) was a dressmaker in Lambs Conduit Street, Holborn. In September 1901 her child was taken ill. Dr Gould was sent for and diagnosed smallpox. The next day he returned with Dr Bond, the Medical Officer of Health for Holborn and, following a further examination, notified the authorities that the child was suffering from smallpox. In consequence, a magistrate's order was obtained, pursuant to which the child was forcibly removed to the 'sheds' at Rotherhithe. The child was detained there for three days and then returned as suffering from chickenpox only.

The plaintiff sued Dr Gould, claiming that she had lost customers due to it being known amongst them that an ambulance had taken away her child from the house in which she carried on her business. For the defence it was contended that Dr Gould acted bona fide and that he was compelled under the provisions of the Public Health Acts to notify the case as soon as he was of opinion that it was one of smallpox.

Held: the jury found that Dr Gould had acted properly in giving the notification certificate, and returned a verdict in his favour.

See p 132.

Sammut v South Lincolnshire Health Authority

Discovery: fatal: inquest

Rougier J. [1992] 3 Med LR 284, [1993] PIQR P259.

See *Stobart v Nottingham Health Authority* (p 567).

Samuels v Davis

Breach of contract: dental

Court of Appeal. [1943] 1 KB 526

The plaintiff (Edgar Samuels), a registered dental surgeon, claimed from the defendant (Mr Davis) the sum of 12 guineas for making a denture for his wife. The denture was unsatisfactory, and Mrs Davis was unable to use it. Mr Davis refused to pay. The plaintiff sued for payment.

The trial judge acquitted the plaintiff dentist of negligence, but found that the denture was not reasonably fit for Mrs Davis' use.

Held: the trial judge found as a fact that the dentures were not reasonably fit for the purpose for which they were intended. There was no error of law in his judgment. The plaintiff was not entitled to payment.

Per Scott LJ: 'In my view, it is a matter of legal indifference whether the contract was one for the sale of goods or one of service to do work and supply materials. In either case, the contract must necessarily, by reason of the relationship between the parties, and the purpose for which the contract was entered into, import a term that, given reasonable co-operation by the patient, the dentist would achieve reasonable success in his work, or, in other words, that he would produce a denture which could be used by the patient for the purpose of eating and talking in the ordinary way. I appreciate that, in doing work of that kind, a dentist must rely greatly on the active assistance, co-operation and patience of the patient. A good patient helps a good dentist enormously in the success of his work. On the other hand, if a patient makes it impossible for the dentist to complete his work successfully, the fault must rest with the patient and leave the dentist entitled to recover the agreed remuneration for the work which he has done, or would have done, but for the failure of co-operation on the part of the patient. In this case, however, there is no issue on this point.'

See pp 28, 129.

Sandell v Worthing Health Authority

Damages: operation: surgeon

Blofield J. [1994] 10 PMILL 31

In 1986 the plaintiff (Mr Sandell) aged 18, felt tired and listless. His general practitioner referred him to a specialist for a cervical lymph node biopsy operation which was inconclusive. In November 1987, during a further operation of this type, the surgeon severed a branch of the left spinal accessory nerve. The hospital authority admitted liability.

The plaintiff's trapezius muscle, on the left side, was deprived of 90% of motor function. He was left-handed. In August 1988 he underwent a partially successful nerve repair operation, restoring about 50% function of the left trapezius. He suffered numbness in the part of the forearm where a nerve graft had been taken to mend the severed nerve, and a scar under the armpit from where the nerve transplant was taken. He experienced continuing pain when using the trapezius muscle. He found house decoration difficult and driving painful. He was unable to play racquet sports, and found it hard to pick up his child. The pain affected his temper.

The injury resulted in his not being able to perform his work as a craftsman/carpenter as quickly as his colleagues. He lost pay of £10 gross per day in consequence.

Held (February 1994):   (i)   general damages for pain, suffering and loss of amenities were assessed at £11,000.

(ii)   special damages were £5,483. Future loss of earnings, based on a multiplier of 16, were £25,355.

The total award was £44,299 including interest.

See p 118.

Sankey v Kensington and Chelsea and Westminster Area Health Authority

Hospital doctors: operation: consent: risk disclosure: duty of care to third party: skull: epilepsy

Tudor Evans J. QBD 2 April (1982)

The plaintiff (Mr Sankey), who suffered from hypertension, had had left-sided headaches for seveal years. An x-ray of his skull showed that the pituitary fossa was grossly eroded. H was admitted to Westminster Hospital for further tests. On 3 July 1975 Dr Gibberd advised an arteriogram to identify the nature of the lesion in the pituitary fossa. He explained the procedure and told the plaintiff that the main risks were because of his high blood pressure which could be made worse; he told him that the procedure was risky because of the hypertension and the vascular disease associated with it. Dr Gibberd separately saw the plaintiff's wife and advised her that the arteriogram should be done but that it would be risky. He left a junior doctor, Dr Truter, to obtain the plaintiff's signed consent to the operation. Dr Truter told the plaintiff that, because of his raised blood pressure, the risks were a little greater than normal. After the arteriogram was performed, the plaintiff became highly disturbed and then lapsed into coma; he had a number of major epileptic fits.

The plaintiff sued the hospital authority. By the end of the hearing, his case was solely that his consent to the arteriogram had been negligently obtained without his having been given any or adequate warning of the risks involved. Evidence was given that the arteriogram involved a risk of a stroke which in a normal patient was well under two per cent and was not substantially increased in the plaintiff's case. The majority of experts testified that they would mention risks without using the word 'stroke'.

Held: (i)   the question of warning had to be judged by competent responsible medical opinion. Dr Gibberd gave the plaintiff a very full and wholly acceptable description of what was involved in the procedure and a warning of the risks involved.

(ii)   Dr Gibberd very properly left the signing of the consent form to be obtained by a junior doctor. Competent medical practice does not require a second warning, although in fact Dr Truter gave one.

(iii)   there is no duty in law to give warning of risks to the relative of an adult patient, certainly if the patient himself has been warned. Even so, Dr Gibberd warned Mrs Sankey.

Judgment for the defendants.

See p 111.

Saumarez v Medway and Gravesend Hospital Management Committee

Fracture: diagnosis: hospital doctor: x-rays: fingers

Havers J. [1953] 2 BMJ 1109

In July 1949 the plaintiff (Julie Saumarez), a violinist, fell and sustained a fracture of the base of the proximal phalanx of the left thumb and a chip fracture of the base of the distal phalanx of the middle finger of the left hand. From 15 July to 1 October she was treated by Dr Theobalds at the Sheppey General Hospital. She complained several times about her finger and told him that an x-ray examination at the London Hospital had revealed a chip fracture. Nevertheless he only treated her for the thumb fracture and did not discover or diagnose the chip fracture to the finger.

As a result the bone set in a crooked position, making it impossible for her to play the violin properly. She sued the hospital authority.

Held: Dr Theobalds should have discovered the injury on his first examination. If he had discovered it, his duty would have been to make a further clinical and x-ray examination. It was even more incumbent upon him to make further enquiries, since the plaintiff had complained of injury to the finger. He had been negligent.

See p 97.

Saunders v Leeds Western Health Authority and Another

Operation: anaesthetics: cardiac arrest: res ipsa loquitur: hip: quadriplegia

Mann J. [1993] 4 Med LR 355, 129 Sol Jo 225, [1986] 1 PMILL 82

The plaintiff, (Nicola Saunders) when four years old, underwent an operation to correct a congenitally dislocated hip. During the operation she suffered a cardiac arrest lasting thirty to forty minutes. In consequence her brain was permanently damaged by hypoxia, and she became permanently quadriplegic, mentally retarded and blind.

She sued the health authority and the anaesthetist. At trial she relied on *res ipsa loquitur*. Evidence was given that the heart of a fit child did not arrest under anaesthesia if proper care was taken in the anaesthetic and surgical processes. The defendants sought to explain the cardiac arrest by the effect of a paradoxical air embolism travelling from the site of the operation to block a coronary artery.

Held: *res ipsa loquitur* applied, so the plaintiff need not show the specific cause of the arrest. The defendants' explanation was rejected. The inevitable inference was that proper monitoring would have disclosed significant signs, including a forewarning of the arrest. The defendants had been negligent.

See pp 90, 117, 122.

Saunders v West Suffolk Health Authority

Childbirth: diagnosis: episiotomy: consultant

Phillips J. (1994) AVMA Journal, Spring, p 12

On 6 July 1987 the plaintiff (Mrs Saunders) was admitted to Newmarket General Hospital for the delivery of her first child. At 6.50am the senior house officer telephoned the consultant obstetrician at home and advised her that the foetal heart rate had dropped to 60, that there had been meconium staining, and that there was an anterior lip that the two midwives had been unable to reduce. The consultant requested that the staff prepare for a forceps delivery. On arriving at the hospital at approximately 7.10am, she performed a vaginal examination of the plaintiff and established that the baby was lying in a transverse position. She elected to perform a forceps delivery.

Before doing so, the consultant performed a large episiotomy. Either by the subsequent application of the forceps blades or the actual rotation, the episiotomy extended in a large vaginal tear, necessitating five litres of blood replacement for the plaintiff. Substantial perineal damage was caused. This required two subsequent operations and prevented the plaintiff from having sexual intercourse for eight months.

Medical experts testified that, in a low or mid-cavity forceps delivery, there is no need to perform an episiotomy before the application of the forceps. However at least three text books up to 1981 referred to this practice.

Held: (i)   the consultant obstetrician was not negligent in having decided to perform an episiotomy before applying the forceps.

(ii)   however she was negligent in misdiagnosing the position of the baby and consequently rotating it into the OP position instead of the favoured and intended OA position.

(iii)   she applied repeated excessive force in the delivery, first with the Kiellands forceps then with Neville Barnes forceps and finally through axis traction.

(iv)   the plaintiff was awarded damages which had been agreed at £10,000 for the perineal damage, £2,500 for the extended episiotomy and £800 special damages.

Savill v Southend Health Authority

Appeal: extension of time: striking out

Court of Appeal. (1994) The Times, 28 December

The plaintiff (Violet Savill) alleged that she had been negligently treated at one of the defendants' hospitals between October 1985 and May 1986. In January 1988 her solicitors wrote to request the hospital records. A writ was then issued, and it was served on 11 October 1988. The defendants' solicitors acknowledged service on 16 October 1988. A statement of claim was not served until 13 November 1992. The defendant solicitors issued a summons to dismiss the action for want of prosecution. This was granted by the district judge on 15 November 1993.

The deadline for the plaintiff to appeal against this order, as calculated under RSC Ord 58, rr 1 and 3, was 24 November 1993. Her notice of appeal was issued five days later on 29 November 1993. No explanation for the delay was given. The plaintiff's application to extend time for service of the notice of appeal was dismissed.

Held: (i)   in order to justify a court in extending the time during which some procedure requires to be taken, there must be some material in which the court can exercise its discretion.

(ii)   that applied as much to a minimal delay as to a delay which was substantial.

(iii)   there was no such material before the judge, so he did not act contrary to principle in refusing to exercise his discretion to extend time.

The plaintiff's appeal was dismissed.

Sayer v Kingston and Esher Health Authority

Childbirth: caesarian: pleadings: after-care

Court of Appeal. CAT, 9 March 1989

On 19 February 1980 the plaintiff (Pauline Sayer) gave birth to her second child by caesarian section in one of the defendants' hospitals. There were various complications, and two further operations were necessary.

In January 1983 she sued the health authority. Her writ and Statement of Claim were limited to complaints of what happened on 18–19 February, the period of the operation itself. In September 1988, on the eve of her trial, she applied to amend her Statement of Claim.

The amendment, which she obtained leave from the judge to make, deleted the complaints about the caesarian section operation altogether. It substituted three new complaints:

(i) that she was allowed to spend too long in the second stage of labour before the operation;

(ii) that her condition was not monitored closely enough after the operation; and

(iii) that a follow-up operation on 26 February should have been performed by a specialist urologist.

The defendants appealed against the judge's order granting leave to amend.

Held: (i) the amendments arose out of substantially the same facts, although not the same facts, as those already pleaded, so the judge had discretion to allow the amendment under s 35(5) of the Limitation Act 1980 and RSC Ord 20, r 5(5),

(ii) the judge acted within his discretion in allowing the amendment, since the defendants' main witnesses were still available and full and detailed medical records were in existence.

Scuriaga v Powell

Abortion: wrongful birth: breach of contract: damages: public policy

Court of Appeal. CAT, 24 July 1980. (1979) 123 Sol Jo 406

In April 1972 the plaintiff (Miss Florence Sciuraga), a polio sufferer then aged 22, contracted with Dr Powell that he would terminate her pregnancy for a fee of £150. He failed to remove the foetus which she had been carrying for some seven weeks, and he did not tell her what had happened. When she found out, he repaid her the £150 and offered to try again. She refused and in December 1972 was delivered of a baby boy by caesarian section.

The plaintiff sued Dr Powell for breach of contract. In May 1979 the trial judge (Watkins J) found that he had performed the operation negligently and in breach of contract and rejected the defence that no damages were recoverable on the ground of public policy. He awarded the plaintiff £7,000 for loss of earnings to date of trial, £7,500 for future loss of earning capacity, £3,500 for impairment of her marriage prospects and £750 for her pain and distress. Dr Powell appealed on quantum.

Held: (i) her loss of future earnings should be assessed by deducting from her figure of £4,000 per annum for a full-time audio-typist the £2,000 per annum that she could earn in the part-time work to which her young son's presence limited her, reducing the gross loss of £2,000 to £1,400 net of tax and applying a multiplier of 3. To the resultant figure of £4,200 should be added payments of £550 for child minder, a total of £4,750.

(ii) as the presence of the child impaired her marriage prospects to some extent, but not greatly, in view of other factors, the judge's award under this head should be reduced to £1,500.

See pp 55, 80, 81, 114, 168, 169, 196.

Scott v Bloomsbury Health Authority and Others

Spinal: x-rays

Brooke J. [1990] 1 Med LR 214

The plaintiff (Mr Scott) was born in 1928. In 1957 he was involved in a road traffic accident, in which he suffered a fracture dislocation of his D 12 and L 1 vertebrae. He developed urinary and faecal incontinence, and paralysis of the lower limbs. By 1961 he had only minor residual symptoms.

In October 1977 the plaintiff again started to experience urinary incontinence. In May 1978 he started to experience trouble with his legs. His right knee hyper-extended. In 1979 these problems were accompanied by weakness, foot-drop, a sensory level at D12 and sciatica. His problems of incontinence and weakness occurred throughout 1980. In March 1981 a consultant orthopaedic surgeon performed an extensive decompression laminectomy from D12 to L4 to relieve spinal cord stenosis. This led to some subjective improvement, though with little objective evidence.

The plaintiff sued a number of those who had care of him between 1977 and 1981. The single foundation for all his allegations of medical negligence was the belief of a retired neuro-surgeon that the cause of his troubles from 1977 onwards was the growth of new bone at the original fracture site at D12/L1, or possibly a disc protrusion at that site. The belief was based, in part, on the radiologist's report on September 1979 x-rays which the retired neurosurgeon did not examine before the trial started.

Held: (i) the plaintiff's deterioration was due to avascular fibrosis in his spinal cord (the formation of scar tissue caused by a deficient blood supply), inflammation of the subarachnoid space also resulting in scarring of the cord, and angulation of the spine following the original accident, putting unnatural pressures on the spinal canal in the lumbar region. His problems were familiar long-term consequences of a spinal injury.

(ii) the alleged new compression of the spine anteriorly at the fracture site at D12/L1, on which the plaintiff based his whole case, did not in fact exist. Any reasonably careful reading of the 1979 x-ray report and the 1981 operation note would have led any reasonably competent witness to this conclusion.

(iii) none of the defendants had been negligent.

Per Brooke J: 'I received a submission that the evidence of three of the defendants' expert witnesses should be viewed with particular caution since it might be coloured by the fact that they were members of the council of the Medical Defence Union, which had a financial interest in the outcome of the case. Any wise judge will approach with care, as I did, the evidence of any professional man or woman who gives evidence in support of a fellow-member of the same profession who is charged with negligence, in case professional objectivity is imperilled by personal sympathy . . . But a member of the council of the union stands in no different position from any other defence witness in this regard. As Dr Pollock pointed out, a council member will know how expensive these cases are to contest and the frequent occasions on which they advise that cases should not be contested because a member of the union has in their view been negligent. I would be sorry if the time ever came when members of the council of the union felt inhibited from furnishing evidence to a court in the fields in which they had particular expertise because they felt a court would accede to the type of submission I received in this case.

In my judgment, even if the reference to "hospital records" is appropriate in the first instance to describe paper records in a list of documents, special care must be taken by those preparing such a list to identify relevant x-rays and myelograms and other photographic records and to list them in the appropriate section of the list, depending on whether they are or are not still in existence. I was told, incidentally, by Mr Wilson that it is now possible to make copies of x-rays. In a case in which particular x-rays are of obvious significance to the outcome of the litigation, copies should be made. This will at the same time speed the process by which each side's experts comment on the x-rays and will avoid the danger of crucial x-rays getting lost or, as happened at a critical moment in this case, getting locked up in the boot of somebody's car when they are needed for the litigation...

In my judgment the Legal Aid Board should review this judgment carefully in order to see what steps can be taken, perhaps in consultation with the General Medical Council and the Royal Colleges, to prevent complex claims from being supported in future at public expense on the uncorroborated evidence of a consultant who has retired from practice so long ago.'

Seare v Prentice

Fracture: surgeon: diagnosis: arm

Ellenborough CJ. (1807) 8 East 348

In April 1805 the plaintiff (Mr Seare) fell from a horse. He dislocated his elbow and fractured his arm. He attended the village surgeon, Mr Prentice, and told him that his arm was broken. Mr Prentice said that he thought the arm, which was swollen, was not broken. He applied vinegar to it and bound it with tape. About nine days later Mr Prentice set the elbow. The plaintiff continued in a crippled state until July 1805 when another surgeon instituted a cure.

The plaintiff sued Mr Prentice for negligent, ignorant and unskilful treatment. The trial judge directed the jury to consider the issue of negligence and that unskilfulness alone would not suffice. They returned a verdict for the defendant.

Held: an ordinary degree of skill is necessary for a surgeon. A surgeon could also be liable for crass ignorance. However as the plaintiff's expert specifically imputed the failure of the cure to negligence and the jury duly considered this, the court could not order a new trial.

Note: The distinction between carelessness, unskilfulness and ignorance is no longer pertinent. They simply constitute different ways of failing to achieve a proper standard of care.

See p 58.

Secretary of State for the Home Department v Robb

Consent: force feeding: prison inmate

Thorpe J. [1995] 1 All ER 677, [1995] 2 WLR 722, (1994) Times, 21 October

After being convicted of wounding with intent, robbery and theft, Derek Robb was detained in the segregation unit of Whitemoor Prison. There he indicated that he no longer wished to eat or drink. He had been advised of the clinical consequences of his decision.

The Home Office applied for a declaration for an order that prison officials, responsible attending physicians and nursing staff might lawfully observe and abide by his refusal to receive nutrition and might lawfully abstain from providing hydration and nutrition to him by artificial means or otherwise for as long as he retained the capacity to refuse this.

Held: (i) the fundamental principle was that a person's body was inviolate and was protected from molestation. Every adult of sound mind has a right to determine what should be done to his body.

(ii) that principle of self-determination required respect to be given to the wishes of the patient. If an adult of sound mind refused to consent to treatment which might prolong life, his doctors had to give effect to that wish even though it was not in his best interest.

(iii) a patient who died following a refusal to accept treatment did not commit suicide; and a doctor who had complied with the patient's wish in such circumstances did not aid or abet suicide.

(iv) the right of an adult of sound mind to self-determination prevailed over any countervailing interest of the state. Therefore the declaration sought should be made.

See p 47.

Selfe v Ilford and District Hospital Management Committee

Suicide risk: nurses: supervision: paraplegia

Hinchcliffe J. (1970) 114 Sol Jo 935, (1970) Times, 26 November

In June 1966 the plaintiff (Alan Selfe), then aged 17, left for work but could not face it and took an overdose of sleeping pills. He told his mother that he had done so, and the family doctor arranged for him to be admitted to King George's Hospital, Ilford. He was put in a ward on the ground floor with an unlocked window behind him. There were 27 patients in the ward. He was grouped together with the three other suicide risks at one end.

There were three nurses allocated to the ward. Each knew that the plaintiff was a suicide risk and was to be kept under constant supervision. One nurse was in charge of the ward. Without a word to the nurse in charge, another nurse went to the lavatory and a nursing auxiliary went to the kitchen. Neither could see into the main ward. The charge nurse answered a call for assistance by a patient and went to him.

The plaintiff then climbed through the window, walked along a grass path and climbed up some steps on to a roof from which he threw himself to the ground. He became a paraplegic and sued the hospital authority.

Held: the hospital's duty of reasonable care demanded adequate supervision, which included continuous observation by duty nurses in the ward. To leave unobserved a 17-year-old youth with suicidal tendencies and an unlocked window behind his bed was asking for trouble. The hospital had been negligent.

See pp 24, 44, 132, 137.

Sellers v Cooke and Others (preliminary issue)

Abortion: fresh evidence: diagnosis: pregnancy

Court of Appeal. [1990] 2 Med LR 13

On 16 February 1983 the plaintiff (Mrs Christine Sellers) was admitted to the Royal Victoria Hospital at Bournemouth. She had been suffering from vaginal bleeding. A threatened miscarriage of her 18 week pregnancy was diagnosed. She was in the care of the first defendant consultant Mr Cooke, his registrar Dr Salimi and houseman Dr Kennedy.

On 17 February an alpha-fetoprotein test recorded 81, the upper limit of normal being 77. On 18 February an ultrasonic scan recorded a fair reading for foetal development; foetal movement and heartbeat were seen. On 21 February, Dr Salimi examined the plaintiff and it was noted: 'Os still closed, little PV bleeding. The patient was advised to get up and about.' On 23 February Mr Cooke saw the plaintiff. An alpha-fetoprotein test gave a reading of 114. Over the next five days some blood loss was recorded.

On 1 March a further scan gave a 'good reading' for foetal development. The placenta was recorded as 'extending down bladder wall but not apparently reaching Os (ie unlikely to be praevia).' Dr Salimi examined the plaintiff and recorded '. . . a slight red loss. Pain in the lower abdomen.' A vaginal examination showed the Os closed and the cervix long.

On 2 March, Mr Cooke recorded vaginal tenderness in the lower abdomen. He concluded that all the symptoms were consistent with placental separation and bleeding from the placental site. He advised the plaintiff that he expected her to miscarry within 48 hours. Rejecting her request for an amniocentesis, he proposed a wait for 48 hours to see whether miscarriage occurred and, if not, then putting up a drip to assist it.

On 4 March, the plaintiff signed a consent to termination of her pregnancy. Dr Kennedy prescribed the drip. The drip set up began before 2pm. The drug composition of the drip was wrong. In consequence, the plaintiff suffered severely for several hours before the foetus was expelled at 10.40pm.

The plaintiff sued the first defendant and two hospital authorities for alleged unlawful termination of pregnancy or negligent diagnosis. Her statement of claim was amended at trial to allege negligence in the drug composition of the drip, which it was agreed was a massive dose certain to abort a live foetus.

Caulfield J found all three defendants liable in negligence in respect of the composition of the drip, saying that Dr Salimi was 'the real culprit' for the drug dosage and awarded the plaintiff £2,500 general damages for pain and suffering. However he dismissed the rest of her claim, not finding that Mr Cooke's diagnosis had been either wrong or negligent and holding that, in any event, the plaintiff's claim would have failed on causation because the foetus would not have survived due to chorioamnionitis and the resultant post-partum pneumonia.

Dr Salimi was abroad when the trial started, but returned to England before judgment was given. He later furnished an affidavit to the plaintiff's solicitors, stating that it was not he who had advised on the nature of the drip and dealing with the question of whether the plaintiff had been told by Mr Cooke and Dr Kennedy that the foetus which she was carrying was likely to be deformed. The plaintiff applied for this evidence to be adduced at the hearing of the appeal.

Held: (i) the plaintiff's solicitors had no reason to suppose that the evidence which Dr Salimi would give would contradict the evidence of Mr Cooke and Dr Kennedy as to the customary use of this drug regime in the hospital. As Mr Cooke had ordered the regime and Dr Kennedy had prescribed it, it was not until they gave evidence that Dr Salimi was responsible that the plaintiff's solicitors had any grounds for thinking that there might be any conflict or dispute about the matter. This emerged during the trial when Dr Salimi was abroad. The fresh evidence could not have been obtained for use at the trial by the exercise of reasonable diligence.

(ii) whether the fresh evidence would have an important bearing on the outcome of the case would depend on the appeal court's decision on causation. Thus the decision whether to admit the fresh evidence must be left until the full appeal hearing.

See p 69.

Sellers v Cooke and Others

Abortion: causation: fresh evidence

Court of Appeal. [1990] 2 Med LR 16

The facts are set out in the above report of the preliminary issue hearing. The Court of Appeal at the main hearing heard argument on the issue of causation alone since, unless the plaintiff could prove that the foetus would have survived, the rest of her appeal could not succeed.

Held: (i) the judge was entitled to accept the defence expert evidence that there was intra-uterine infection of the interstitial tissues of the foetal lung, indicated by the abnormal presence of lymphocytes in the lung, and that the foetus would in all probability not have survived.

(ii) as the plaintiff had failed to establish that the judge had erred on the causation issue, her application to adduce fresh evidence would be dismissed since the evidence, if given, would not have affected the outcome of the case.

See p 69.

Sergeant v Lewisham Health Authority

Childbirth: limitation

Phillips J. 6 July 1990

The plaintiff (Mr Sergeant) claimed damages in respect of a muscle injury. His case was that this was caused by excessive traction at delivery. His expert medical report was received when he was nearly 21. His writ was issued when he was 21 years and 3 months old. The defendants pleaded limitation.

Held: (i) the plaintiff only acquired actual knowledge of the relevant facts when the expert's report was received;

(ii) a minor was not required to take 'reasonable steps' to obtain such evidence, and he should not be fixed with any failure of his parents to take them. Accordingly there was no earlier date of constructive knowledge.

The plaintiff's case was allowed to proceed.

Shallard v Arline and Another

Alternative practitioner: burns: representations: breach of contract: fraud: post traumatic stress-disorder

Cassels J. (1939) 2 Lancet 215

The plaintiff (Mrs Shallard) was a middle-aged lady whose husband had died in December 1937. Miss Arline persuaded her to try the Gustavson treatment at her Knightsbridge clinic. She was given a pamphlet about his facial and other rejuvenation treatment which was described as absolutely harmless and certain in its effects. She was told that her condition was good except for toxins in her body, which toxins the Gustavson treatment would remove. His fee would be 200 guineas.

On 14 March 1938 the plaintiff entered the clinic. Mr Gustavson administered the treatment. She was put to bed, and there was applied to her face some substance which burned her.

She was given tablets which made her vomit. Next day there was similar treatment. Her eyes became painful. She was placed in a bath of Epsom salts. On 18 March bandages were taken off, which tore the skin from her forehead and neck, leaving them sore and bleeding. She was in pain until 28 March when she insisted on being driven home.

Her skin was thickened and had a mask-like appearance. She suffered a nervous breakdown. She sued Miss Arline and Mr Gustavson. Mr Gustavson, a Swede, left the country and did not return for the trial.

Held: the defendants were liable for negligence, breach of contract and fraud. They had divided the proceeds of a fraudulent scheme for extracting money from a middle-aged woman in indifferent health.

Note: Miss Arline's appeal to the Court of Appeal was dismissed.

See pp 30, 141.

Sidaway v Board of Governors of Bethlem Royal Hospital and the Maudsley Hospital and Others

Surgeon: operation: risk disclosure: foreseeability: spinal

House of Lords. [1985] AC 871, [1985] 1 All ER 643, [1985] 2 WLR 480

The plaintiff (Mrs Amy Sidaway) was complaining of very persistent pain in the right arm and shoulder and also pain in the left forearm. In October 1974 she was admitted to the Maudsley Hospital where a myelogram was performed. Mr Falconer decided that pressure on the fourth cervical nerve root was the cause of her pain and decided to operate. The operation consisted of a laminectomy of the fourth cervical vertebra and a facetectomy or foraminectomy of the disc space between the fourth and fifth cervical vertebrae. Mr Falconer freed the fourth cervical nerve root by removing the facets from the fourth vertebra and used a dental drill to free the nerve within the foramen. The plaintiff's spinal cord was damaged. She suffered severe disability.

She sued the hospital authority and the surgeon's estate. The operation had not been negligently performed. Her claim was based on failure to warn her of the risk of damage to the spinal cord. The two specific risks were damage to a nerve root and damage to the spinal cord. Evidence at trial was that the combined risk was between one and two per cent, and that the risk of damage to the spinal cord alone, the more serious risk, was less than one per cent. The trial judge found that Mr Falconer mentioned the possibility of disturbing a nerve root and the consequences of doing so but not the danger of spinal cord damage. The medical witnesses agreed that they would mention that there was a small risk of untoward consequences and of an increase of pain instead of relief. It was a practice accepted as proper by a responsible body of competent neuro-surgeons not to frighten a patient by talking about death or paralysis. The trial judge dismissed the plaintiff's claim.

Held: as there was a responsible body of medical opinion which would have warned the plaintiff in substantially the same terms as Mr Falconer had done, her claim failed.

Per Lord Diplock: 'What we do know, however, and this is in my view determinative of this appeal, is that all the expert witnesses specialising in neurology . . . agreed that there was a responsible body of medical opinion which would have undertaken the operation at the time the neuro-surgeon did and would have warned the patient of the risk involved in the operation in substantially the same terms as the trial judge found on the balance of probabilities the neuro-surgeon had done, ie without specific reference to risk of injuring the spinal cord . . .

No doubt if the patient in fact manifested this attitude by means of questioning, the doctor would tell him whatever it was the patient wanted to know; but we are concerned here with volunteering unsought information about risks of the proposed treatment failing to achieve the result sought or making the patient's physical or mental condition worse rather than better. The only effect that mention of risks can have on the patient's mind, if it has any at all, can be in the direction of deterring the patient from undergoing the treatment which in the expert opinion of the doctor it is in the patient's interest to undergo. To decide what risks the existence of which a patient should be voluntarily warned and the terms in which such warning, if any, should be given, having regard to the effect that the warning may have, is as much an exercise of professional skill and judgement as any other part of the doctor's comprehensive duty of care to the individual patient, and expert medical evidence on this matter should be treated in just the same way. The *Bolam* test should be applied.'

Per Lord Bridge: 'I should perhaps add at this point, although the issue does not strictly arise in this appeal, that, when questioned specifically by a patient of apparently sound mind about risks involved in a particular treatment proposed, the doctor's duty must, in my opinion, be to answer both truthfully and as fully as the questioner requires . . .

The issue whether non-disclosure in a particular case should be condemned as a breach of the doctor's duty of care is an issue to be decided primarily on the basis of expert medical evidence, applying the *Bolam* test. But I do not see that this approach involves the necessity "to hand over to the medical profession the entire question of the scope of the duty of disclosure, including the question whether there has been a breach of that duty". Of course, if there is a conflict of evidence as to whether a responsible body of medical opinion approves of non-disclosure in a particular case, the judge will have to resolve that conflict. But even in a case where, as here, no expert witness in the relevant medical field condemns the non-disclosure as being in conflict with accepted and responsible medical practice, I am of opinion that the judge might in certain circumstances come to the conclusion that disclosure of a particular risk was so obviously necessary to an informed choice on the part of the patient that no reasonably prudent medical man would fail to make it. The kind of case I have in mind would be an operation involving a substantial risk of grave adverse consequences, as, for example, the ten per cent risk of a stroke from the operation which was a subject of the Canadian case of *Reibl* v *Hughes* (1980) 114 DLR (3d) 1. In such a case, in the absence of some cogent clinical reason why the patient should not be informed, a doctor, recognizing and respecting his patient's right of decision, could hardly fail to appreciate the necessity for an appropriate warning.'

Per Lord Templeman: 'In my opinion a simple and general explanation of the nature of the operation should have been sufficient to alert Mrs Sidaway to the fact that a major operation was to be performed and to the possibility that something might go wrong at or near the site of the spinal cord or the site of the nerve root causing serious injury. If, as the judge held, Dr Falconer probably referred expressly to the possibility of damage to a nerve root and to the consequences of such damage, this warning could only have reinforced the possibility of something going wrong in the course of a delicate operation performed in a vital area with resultant damage. In view of the fact that Mr Falconer recommended the operation, Mrs Sidaway must have been told or could have assumed that Mr Falconer considered that the possibilities of damage were sufficiently remote to be ignored. Mrs Sidaway could have asked questions. If she had done so, she could and should have been informed there was an aggregate risk of between one per cent or two per cent risk of some damage either to the spinal cord or to a nerve root resulting in injury which might vary from irritation to paralysis. But to my mind this further information would only have reinforced the obvious, with the assurance that the maximum risk of damage, slight or serious, did not exceed two per cent. Mr Falconer may reasonably have taken the view that Mrs Sidaway might have been confused, frightened or misled by more detailed information which she was unable to evaluate at a time when she was suffering from stress, pain and anxiety. A patient may prefer that the doctor should not thrust too much detail at the patient.'

See pp 6, 28, 57, 60, 61, 105, 107, 109, 113, 126, 128, 210.

Sindell v Abbott Laboratories et al

USA: cancer: DES: product liability: bladder

Supreme Court of California. 607 P 2d 924 (1980)

The mother of the plaintiff (Judith Sindell) took DES during pregnancy for the purpose of preventing miscarriage. As a result of the DES ingested by her mother, the plaintiff developed a malignant bladder tumour which was removed by surgery. She suffered from adenosis and needed to be constantly monitored by biopsy or colposcopy to insure early warning of further malignancy.

She pursued proceedings against several drug companies, on behalf of herself and other women similarly situated. The defendants manufactured and marketed DES, a drug which was a synthetic compound of oestrogen, until 1971 when the Food and Drug Administration ordered them to cease marketing and promoting DES for the purpose of preventing miscarriages.

The plaintiff was unable to identify which defendant had manufactured the drug responsible for her injuries. There were approximately 200 companies that might have done so. One of the defendants was dismissed from the action, upon filing a declaration that it had not manufactured DES until after the plaintiff's birth.

Held: each defendant would be held liable for the proportion of the judgment represented by its share of the market, unless it demonstrated that it could not have made the product which caused the plaintiff's injuries.

See p 32.

Sion v Hampstead Health Authority

Amendment: post traumatic stress disorder: striking out: renal

Court of Appeal. [1994] 5 Med LR 170

On 2 September 1988 Lionel Sion, aged 23, was injured in a motor-cycle accident. He was taken to the Royal Free Hospital. The plaintiff (his father) stayed at his son's bedside for 14 days, watching him deteriorate and fall into a coma. On 16 September 1988 the son died. The plaintiff suffered a very severe and prolonged grief reaction, characterised by profound depression.

The plaintiff's case was that the hospital staff negligently failed to diagnose substantial and continuing bleeding from the left kidney, which resulted in his son entering a coma on 5 September 1988. He commenced court proceedings on 28 August 1991. His original claims under the Law Reform (Miscellaneous Provisions) Act 1934 and the Fatal Accidents Act 1976 were not pursued. There remained his claim for damages for his own psychiatric illness.

The defendant hospital authority applied for his action to be struck out under RSC Ord 18, r 19, as disclosing no cause of action. At the hearing of this application in December 1992, the plaintiff sought to amend the statement of claim under RSC Ord 20, r 5. The judge granted the defendants' application and struck out the claim.

Held: (i) if a statement of claim fails to disclose a cause of action, but by some amendment can be made to do so on the same facts or substantially the same facts as those already pleaded, the court has a discretion to allow the amendment even after the limitation period has expired.

(ii) on an application to strike out a case as disclosing no reasonable cause of action, the appropriate test is whether it is obviously doomed to fail.

(iii) there was no trace in the medical report served with the statement of claim of 'shock', no sudden appreciation by sight and sound of a horrifying event. On the contrary, the report described a process continuing for some time. In particular, the son's death was not surprising but expected.

(iv) whilst the proposed amendment to the statement of claim twice mentioned nervous shock, the medical report made it plain that the case was not one of nervous shock as required by established law. It was obviously doomed to fail.

The plaintiff's appeal was dismissed.

See p 51.

Sivyer v Eli Lilly & Co and Others

Limitation: drugs: Opren

Court of Appeal. [1992] 3 Med LR 393

See *Nash v Eli Lilly & Co* (I) (p 473).

Size v Shenley Hospital Group Management Committee

Psychiatric patient: supervision: nurses: foreseeability

Court of Appeal. (1970) 1 Lancet 313

In January 1962 the plaintiff (Mr Size) was a detained patient in Shenley Hospital where the treatment was permissive. M, who was suffering from manic depressive psychosis, was a patient in the same open ward, his bed being near the nurse's desk. M had relapsed into a hypomanic phase and was due to be tranferred to a closed ward at 6.00pm. Between 4.30 pm and 5.00pm he assaulted and injured the plaintiff. The nurse was just too late to prevent this.

The plaintiff sued the hospital authority, alleging that M had made attacks on two previous occasions. The trial judge dismissed his case, finding that the hospital did not know of any previous attacks.

Held: (i) the judge was entitled to conclude that the foreseeable risk was minimal. Thus the hospital was not to be blamed for not transferring M sooner or for not giving him more sedation.

(ii) nor should M have been more closely supervised. He was a bed patient close to the nurse's desk, and the nurse was only just too late to stop the damage. The plaintiff had suffered a misfortune for which the hospital was not liable.

See p 133.

Slater v Baker and Stapleton

Surgeon: departing from orthodox practice: fractures: experimentation: leg: trespass to person

Wilmot CJ. (1767) 2 Wils KB 359, 95 ER 860

The plaintiff (Mr Slater) broke one of his legs. It was set and started to heal. He then consulted Mr Stapleton, an apothecary, who called in Mr Baker, a surgeon from St Bartholomew's Hospital. Mr Baker put on the plaintiff's leg a heavy steel contraption with teeth intended to stretch and extend his leg. He took up the plaintiff's foot in both his hands and nodded to Mr Stapleton. Mr Stapleton took the plaintiff's leg on his knee and the leg cracked.

The plaintiff's leg had been fractured again and for the next three to four months he suffered gravely. He sued Mr Baker and Mr Stapleton. The trial jury found in his favour.

Held: (i)   there was a joint undertaking by both the defendants.

(ii)   the objection that the action ought to have been brought in trespass was rejected.

(iii)   in performing on the plaintiff the first experiment with this new instrument, the defendants had acted ignorantly and unskilfully contrary to the known rule and usage of surgeons.

The judgment for the plaintiff was upheld.

See pp 7, 65.

Slater v Maidstone Health Authority

Childbirth: adjournment of trial

Michael Davies J. (1987) Times, 2 December

The infant plaintiff was born in 1980. Medical negligence was alleged to have occurred during the birth. The health authority was sued. In June 1986 the trial date was fixed for 7 December 1987. On 1 December 1987 the plaintiff's application for an adjournment was heard.

Held: (i)   the application for an adjournment was granted in view of the health authority's consent. If the case were tried in December 1987, that would have been bad enough because of the delay. The case was now said not to be ready. If the health authority had opposed the application, it would have been refused. The doctors against whom the negligence was alleged had had the case hanging over them for seven years. It was an appalling situation.

(ii)   where an application was made in the High Court by one party to an action to stand the case out of the date fixed for the trial, the lay parties to the particular case should attend court when the application was made so that the reason for the need to defer the case could be explained to them by the court and not, subsequently, by their legal representatives.

Smith v Barking, Havering and Brentwood Health Authority

Surgeon: risk disclosure: causation: damages: quadriplegia: spinal

Hutchison J. [1989] 5 PMILL 26, [1994] 5 Med LR 285

In April 1970, when the plaintiff (Sharon Smith) was nine years old, Mr Fairburn performed on her at the Oldchurch Hospital an operation to drain a cyst in the upper cervical canal. In 1979 she began to experience a recurrence of her symptoms of weakness and loss of sensation in her limbs. Mr Fairburn reluctantly decided that a further operation was advisable, although he regarded it as difficult. On the one hand, if nothing was done, the plaintiff could well become tetraplegic within a year. On the other hand, the operation itself carried an inherent risk of up to 25% of immediate tetraplegia. He did not inform the plaintiff of the risks or discuss the dilemma with her. When he carried out the second operation in January 1981, she suffered damage to the spinal cord resulting in immediate and permanent tetraplegia.

The plaintiff sued the hospital authority on the grounds of Mr Fairburn's failure to warn her of the risks inherent in the operation.

Held (July 1988):   (i) the situation obviously called for careful explanation to the plaintiff. Mr Fairburn negligently omitted to tell her either of the inherent risk of immediate tetraplegia or that she was destined to become tetraplegic if she did not have the operation.

(ii) the strong probability was that the plaintiff, if suitably informed, would have agreed to the operation, since it was her only chance of avoiding tetraplegia in the near future.

(iii) she was therefore only entitled to £3,000 general damages to compensate her for her shock and depression upon discovering – without prior warning – that she had been rendered tetraplegic.

See pp 68, 112.

Smith v Brighton and Lewes Hospital Management Committee

Prescription: nurse: injections: overdose: causation

Streatfield J. (1958) Times, 2 May

In May 1954 the plaintiff (Mrs Florence Smith) had a severe attack of boils and was admitted to hospital. On 13 May Dr Vickery, the house surgeon, ordered a course of thirty streptomycin injections to be administered at intervals of eight hours. The last injection should have been given at 10.00pm on 23 May. In fact the plaintiff received four more injections than had been ordered. Her final injection was at 6.00am on 25 May.

On 26 May she experienced a sense of giddiness and suffered a permanent loss of balance. She sued the hospital authorities.

Held: (i) the two nurses who administered the last four injections had no reason at the time to suppose that the doses were other than those prescribed by a doctor, so they had not been negligent.

(ii) the blame lay with the ward sister who alone had known that the injections had exceeded the prescribed dose. It would have been simple for her to draw a red line, a star or some other red danger signal in a diary or treatment sheet, indicating the time when the prescription was to end. The injury was foreseeable. She had been negligent.

(iii) it was the last injection which probably did the damage. The hospital authority was liable.

See pp 121, 138.

Smith v Lewisham Group Hospital Management Committee

Hospital administration: supervision: femur

Gorman J (with jury). (1955) Times, 21 June

In March 1953 the plaintiff (Mrs Emma Smith then aged 86, was admitted to Lewisham Hospital. She was suffering from acute cholecystitis, was in a frail condition and was in considerable pain. On admission she was placed on a four-wheeled trolley, about two feet wide and two and a half feet high, the top of which had no edge or rail or other protection. The nurse attending her in her cubicle left her in order to answer the telephone. The plaintiff fell off the trolley and broke a thigh. She sued the hospital authority.

Held: the jury found that the hospital staff had been negligent in leaving the plaintiff unattended on the trolley.

See p 132.

Smith v Lowry

Alternative practitioner: osteopath: X-ray: fractures: child patient: femur: masseur: rheumatism

Talbot J (with jury). [1935] 1 BMJ 743

The plaintiff (Sheila Smith) had rheumatic fever when she was five. Four years later she complained of pains in her leg, which were attributed to rheumatism. In August 1931, when she was aged eleven, her parents consulted Captain Lowry, a blind osteopath and masseur. When he was manipulating her under anaesthetic, a cracking noise was heard. She was sent to hospital where it was found that the neck of her left thigh had been fractured. She was left with permanent disability in her left hip.

The plaintiff sued Captain Lowry. An x-ray taken a year earlier in 1930 had revealed a displacement of the neck of the thigh-bone on both sides. Expert evidence was given that a manipulation which would cause no injury to a normal child might fracture the thigh of a child suffering from displacement, and that if an x-ray had been taken before the treatment it would have disclosed the dangers of manipulation to a man who knew his work.

Held: (i) the jury found that Captain Lowry had been negligent, so the plaintiff was awarded damages for her injuries.

(ii) they dismissed Captain Lowry's counterclaim for the balance of his fee.

See p 140.

Smith v Pare

Cancer: burns: x-rays: assault: consent: breast

Lawrence J (with special jury). [1904] 1 BMJ 1227

In 1899 Mrs Pare underwent an operation for a non-cancerous growth on her left breast. In March 1903 she consulted Dr Smith who thought that she was suffering from cancer and advised a combined treatment by x-rays and high- frequency currents. Mr Pare told him that he would not agree to any treatment which caused his wife pain. Dr Smith was supposed to obtain the consents of her regular doctor and the surgeon who had operated earlier, but these were never forthcoming. Nevertheless the treatment was pursued. X-rays were applied over the whole of Mrs Pare's body and caused burns to her skin. In June 1903 her husband assaulted Dr Smith on the steps of his private hospital.

Dr Smith sued Mr Pare for damages for assault. Mr Pare counterclaimed damages for negligence. Expert evidence was given that Mrs Pare was in fact suffering from septic pneumonia and that the x-rays should have been stopped as soon as damage to the skin commenced. Mr Pare testified that he had decided to assault Dr Smith after he had seen the burns from which his wife was suffering.

Held: (i)   the jury found that Mr Pare did not consent to the x-ray part of the treatment, which was improper, negligent and unskilful.

  (ii) they awarded Dr Smith £2 damages for the assault (which had already been paid into court) and Mr Pare £100 damages on the counterclaim.

See p 129.

Smith v Rae

Canada: childbirth: fatal: breach of contract: duty of care: breech delivery

Ontario Supreme Court, Appellate Division. [1919] 51 DLR 323

In October 1918 the plaintiff (Mrs Rae), who was pregnant with her first child, called with her husband upon the defendant, a physician and surgeon practising in Toronto. Her husband contracted with the defendant that he would attend her. The confinement was expected to take place about the middle of November.

On 2 December 1918 Mrs Roberts, a midwife of some experience, was with the plaintiff. During the afternoon Mrs Roberts arranged for a neighbour to leave a telephone message asking the doctor to call. This was received by him on his return home at 6.30pm. Between 7.10pm and 7.30pm the plaintiff's husband telephoned the defendant, told him that she was in labour and asked him to come and see her. The defendant asked how frequent the labour pains were, and was informed that they were every three to five minutes. He then told the husband that he had several patients in his office, and had an appointment for 8pm with another patient coming from a distance, and that he could not conveniently attend before 8.30pm. The birth actually commenced at 7.30pm and was complete by 8.20pm. It was a breech presentation, and the baby died.

Held: (i)   the defendant knew that an experienced midwife was in attendance. The medical information did not indicate that his attendance would be necessary until after 8.30pm. His failure to attend before that time did not amount to negligence.

  (ii) the plaintiff could not sue for breach of contract to attend, because the contract had been made with her husband and she was not a party to it.

Per Middleton J: 'I do not think that the plaintiff is right in the contention that when a doctor undertakes to attend a case of this description he thereby undertakes to drop all other matters in hand to attend the patient instanter upon receiving a notification. The doctor must, having regard to all circumstances, act reasonably. Here the first message received did not indicate any urgency. It was a request for him to call some time during the evening, and the message received from the husband did not then indicate any extreme urgency. The doctor had other patients who had some claim upon his time and attention. Had he been given to understand that the plaintiff's situation was critical, undoubtedly he should, and I think he would, have dropped everything and gone to her assistance; but, in view of the information that he had, I do not think it could possibly be said that he acted negligently or unreasonably.'

See p 28.

Smith v Tunbridge Wells Health Authority

Causation: impotence: medical literature: rectal: risk disclosure: surgeon

Morland J. [1994] 5 Med LR 334

The plaintiff (Mr Smith) was a 28-year-old married man with two young children. On 23 September 1988 his consultant surgeon, Mr Cook, diagnosed and observed a full thickness rectal prolapse on straining. This problem was an aspect of the bowel syndrome from which the plaintiff had suffered since 1980. Despite the embarrassment, distress and inconvenience of his condition, involving very frequent and pressing urges to defecate, the worry of the discharge of blood and mucus and the occasional pain and discomfort, he was able to lead a normal life. The condition was not life threatening.

Mr Cook recommended an ivalon sponge rectopexy, known as the Wells operation. This was performed exceedingly rarely upon sexually active men, since they tend to have narrower pelvises than women and that creates a difficulty in the surgery. Mr Cook explained that there was a possibility of some nerves being bruised in the operation and that there was a 10% chance of the plaintiff becoming sterile. The plaintiff immediately consented to the operation.

On 7 November 1988 the plaintiff underwent the Wells operation at the Kent and Sussex Hospital. The surgery was competently conducted and was successful in the sense that the rectum was repositioned in its correct anatomical place. However, due to nerve damage caused during the surgery, the plaintiff was rendered impotent and suffered from significant bladder malfunction.

He sued the hospital authority on the grounds that Mr Cook had failed to explain to him the particular risks of impotence and bladder dysfunction which could arise through mishap in a Wells operation. Mr Cook said in evidence that although he had no recollection or note of giving the plaintiff a warning of the risk of impotence, he would have done so because he saw it as his duty. Professor Golligher, the author of a leading textbook which did not specifically refer to this risk in its 1982 and 1984 editions, testified that he regretted this omission with hindsight and that he became convinced of the risk in 1985 or 1986 and would have warned of it thereafter.

Held: (i) Mr Cook's personal view as to his duty to warn the risk of impotence was not definitive evidence that in law he owed that duty. It was however cogent evidence to this effect. Although by 1988 some surgeons might still not have been warning patients in similar situations of the risk of impotence, that omission was neither reasonable nor responsible. Mr Cook, in stating that he considered that he owed a duty to warn, was reflecting not only the accepted proper practice, but also the only reasonable and responsible standard of care to be expected from a consultant in his position faced with the plaintiff's situation.

(ii) Mr Cook accepted that he did not mention the risk to bladder function. He was mistaken in thinking that he had specifically mentioned the risk of impotence. The plaintiff had established on the balance of probabilities that Mr Cook failed to explain the risk of impotence with sufficient clarity to be expected in 1988 of a consultant general surgeon with his interest in colorectal surgery. He had been negligent on this occasion.

(iii) if the risk of impotence had been explained to the plaintiff, he would have refused the operation. It is unlikely that a happily married 28-year-old man would have immediately consented to the operation, if impotence had been mentioned.

Judgment was entered in favour of the plaintiff for the agreed sum of £130,000 damages.

See pp 112, 113.

Snell v Carter

Alternative practitioner: burns: gangrene: masseur: fatal

HH Judge Scobell Armstrong. (1941) 2 Lancet 321

Miss Winifred Snell, aged thirty-two, suffered from disseminated sclerosis. She consulted Mr Carter who described himself as a masseur and medical electrician. He agreed to carry out four treatments a week at 7s 6d per treatment. Two treatments were given on successive days; Miss Snell's back was massaged with oil, and ray lamps were used. Soon after the second treatment, the skin began to come off her back which was severely burned. The burns became gangrenous and, after suffering great pain, Miss Snell died of toxaemia.

The plaintiff (her mother) sued Mr Carter. Expert evidence was given that ray treatment was inadvisable and useless; the disease made the skin sensitive to heat. It was said that anyone with medical knowledge would realise the danger of ray treatment in such a case.

Held: Mr Carter had been negligent.

See pp 129, 140.

Sones v Foster

Alternative practitioner: naturopath: foot: amputation: causation: gangrene

Atkinson J (with jury). [1937] 1 BMJ 250

The plaintiff (Mr Sones) had a corn on the little toe of his left foot. When this became septic, he consulted Mr Foster, a naturopath, and spent nine weeks in Mr Foster's house under treatment at eight guineas a week. On 17 August, when he arrived, an attendant sprayed the foot with antiseptic and administered a hot compress, applying a poultice at about midnight. During the first six days Mr Foster used a nail brush, which caused intense pain, about five times a day, and had then sprayed the foot and applied hot compresses. On one occasion Mr Foster inserted the foot in antiseptic and cut off a quantity of skin, afterwards pressing the foot by force into almost boiling water. Other operations were performed for cutting off mortified skin under the foot and toes, and a little toe which had become necrotic. On 22 October the plaintiff was taken to St Bartholomew's Hospital where his left leg was amputated above the knee.

He sued Mr Foster for negligence. Expert evidence was given that he was suffering from arteriosclerosis and had gangrene as far back as the ankle. If an operation had been performed when the plaintiff first went to Mr Foster, it would probably have been safe to amputate seven inches below the knee. The nail brush was not good treatment and was likely to do harm.

Held: Atkinson J directed the jury that, although the orthodox medical profession liked to think itself the sole repository of knowledge of the art of healing, there were undoubtedly unorthodox practitioners who rendered great public service. Professional osteopaths were an example, and the same might be said of naturopaths, who combined herbalism and nature treatment, and the more reputable of them had formed themselves into associations which did their best to create standards. No one need consult these practitioners unless he liked; a patient who consulted one had the right to expect the average skill, knowledge and efficiency of the body of naturopaths to which the practitioner belonged.

The jury found that Mr Foster had been negligent in his advice and treatment. The plaintiff was awarded general damages for his pain, suffering and loss of amenities, plus a return of most of the fees he had paid.

See pp 47, 140.

Spinola v South Glamorgan Health Authority

Casualty officer: causation: diagnosis: leg: knee

Brooke J. (1991) AVMA Journal, January p11.

The plaintiff was a 30 year old woman who received serious leg injuries in a road traffic accident in 1975. The injuries primarily involved fractures to the left femur and tibia, but also damage to the anterior cruciate ligament of the knee. Signs of this ligament damage were missed in the casualty department in 1975. The knee was treated conservatively.

By 1978 the ligament damage was noticed. Various attempts were made to repair it through carbon fibre treatment. Four operations ensued, but these were unsuccessful. The plaintiff was left with instability in the knee, severe risk of osteoarthritis and the probability of a future arthrodesis.

Her personal injury claim arising out of the road traffic accident had been settled for a modest sum in 1978. She sued the hospital authority.

Held: (i)   the hospital doctors had negligently failed to diagnose the ligament damage. Conservative management of the injury was inadequate.

           (ii)   had suitable treatment been effected, the plaintiff's knee would have been 'workable'. She was awarded £108,000 including interest.

See p 97.

Stamos v Davies

Canada: biopsy: duty of care: right to know treatment received: surgeon

Ontario High Court of Justice, Krever J. (1985) 21 DLR (4th) 507

The plaintiff (Mr Stamos) consulted the defendant, a hospital internist, about a disease which the defendant suspected was fibrosing alveolitis. As the plaintiff refused to undergo a thoracotomy, the defendant on 9 November 1977 performed a trephine needle lung biopsy.

The trephine pierced the plaintiff's left hemidiaphragm and spleen. The defendant learned from the pathology report on 11 November that the biopsy had been taken from the spleen, not the lung, and that it had caused a serious haemorrhage. He did not tell the plaintiff this. Instead he informed him that he had no result from the biopsy, because he had not obtained what he wanted. When asked by the plaintiff what he had obtained, he replied 'something else'.

On 12 November the plaintiff was discharged home. On 15 November he was rushed to hospital as an emergency with severe pain. A splenectomy was performed.

Held: (i)   there was a duty in law on the defendant to inform the plaintiff that he had entered his spleen. The plaintiff asked the defendant what he had obtained at the biopsy. The defendant's failure to answer candidly was a breach of duty.

      (ii)   however there was no causal connection between the failure to inform the plaintiff about the splenic injury and the loss of the spleen. The spleen was doomed from the moment it was injured.

     (iii)   the cumulative effect of a series of errors of judgment was that the defendant had been negligent in the performance of the biopsy itself, and the plaintiff was entitled to damages on that basis.

See p 114.

Stanley v Eli Lilly & Co and Others

Limitation: drugs: Opren

Court of Appeal. [1992] 3 Med LR 390

See *Nash v Eli Lilly & Co* (K) (p 474).

Stephen v Riverside Health Authority

Limitation: radiographer: x-rays: breast: skin complaint

Auld J. [1990] 1 Med LR 261, (1989) Times, 29 November.

On 11 March 1977 the plaintiff (Mrs Sheila Stephen), who had worked as an unqualified radiographer in the 1950s, underwent a mammography at Charing Cross Hospital. The radiographer handled the equipment poorly and took ten films instead of four to six. The plaintiff suffered erythema in her upper chest for some three months. Her consultant at the hospital told her that she had received in the mammography a total of 34 roentgen to each breast. On 22 April 1977 she wrote a letter of complaint to the hospital administrator. On 23 May 1977 the administrator replied that the radiation dose of 34 roentgen to each breast could not cause erythema or any other adverse effects. During the next month she saw three other doctors, all of whom reassured her that she was in no danger from the effects of radiation.

The plaintiff was not unduly concerned about the erythema, but continued to worry over the possibility that she had received an overdose of radiation that might cause her harm in future. In early 1979 she instructed solicitors who wrote to the hospital. Its solicitors replied denying negligence. In October 1979 she instructed a second firm which obtained negative expert advice, issued a protective writ on 6 March 1980 but took no further steps. In 1983 she instructed a third firm which consulted Professor Berry. He raised in March 1984 the possibility that she could have received a very much higher dose of radiation than the 34 roentgen to each breast. His opinions during 1984 were very cautious, referring to the possibility of an excessive dose and the lack of supporting evidence. However on 20 February 1985 he advised in conference that the 34 roentgen reading would not be reliable if the radiographer was unreliable, that to judge from her erythema the dosage was 300 to 1000 roentgen to each breast and that this would have increased the risk of cancer developing.

The writ was issued on 15 February 1988. A preliminary trial on limitation was ordered.

Held: (i)   despite all the contrary medical opinion, the plaintiff suspected that she was at an increased risk of cancer. However her anxiety about this did not amount to knowledge of injury.

(ii)   she undoubtedly knew about her erythema and associated anxiety, but she did not regard these alone as warranting a claim for damages and she was reasonable in not regarding them as sufficiently serious to justify her instituting proceedings.

(iii)   since she had been told that she had been exposed to 34 roentgen to each breast and that hundreds or even thousands of roentgen would be needed to cause her symptoms, she did not know that her symptoms were capable of being attributed to the mammography until the conference on 20 February 1985.

(iv)   her past experience in radiography did not constitute her an expert in the field so as to characterise her suspicion as knowledge of attributability, to set off against the chorus of negative opinion by highly qualified experts.

(v)   as her writ was issued on 15 February 1988, within three years of her date of knowledge on 20 February 1985, her case was not statute-barred.

See pp 181, 182.

Stevens v Bermondsey and Southwark Group Hospital Management Committee and Another

Diagnosis: casualty officer: x-ray: settlement: duty of care: back

Paull J. (1963) 107 Sol Jo 478

In May 1957 the plaintiff (Mr Stevens) sustained injury when he was thrown off his bicycle after a borough council roadsweeper had pushed his broom into the plaintiff's bicycle wheel. He was examined at hospital by a casualty officer. The plaintiff told him that he was suffering severe pain in his back and asked for an x-ray. He was not x-rayed, however, because the doctor thought that there was nothing seriously wrong. On his fourth visit to the hospital he still complained of the pain in his back, and the doctor prescribed a course of physiotherapy.

On the strength of this medical advice, the plaintiff settled his claim for negligence against the borough council at £125. Later, when he was seen by another doctor at another hospital, he was diagnosed as suffering from spondylolisthesis, a congenital affliction hitherto free of symptoms, which had been activated by the fall from his bicycle.

The plaintiff sued the casualty officer and the health authority. One head of claim was that, but for their negligence, he would have claimed and recovered a much larger sum from the borough council.

Held: the plaintiff was not entitled to damages under this head. A doctor's duty was limited to the sphere of medicine, and he had nothing to do with the sphere of legal liability unless he examined with an eye to liability. Unless there were special circumstances, he was not required to contemplate or foresee any question connected with a third party's liability to his patient.

See p 45.

Stobart v Nottingham Health Authority; Sammut v South Lincolnshire Health Authority; Yafi v North Lincolnshire Health Authority

Discovery: fatal: inquest

Rougier J. [1992] 3 Med LR 284, [1993] PIQR P259.

Three children died in different hospitals. In each case, it was alleged that this was due to breaches of care by the hospitals and their staff. Applications were made pursuant to s 33 (2) of the Supreme Court Act 1981 for pre-action discovery. The defendants accepted that the three plaintiffs were entitled to this at some stage. The issue in dispute was whether such discovery should take place before the inquests.

Held: (i)   it is a principle that discovery can only be used in relation to the proper conduct of the action, not for any collateral or ulterior purpose. Proper conduct includes investigation at an early stage.

(ii) the coroner's remit was to ascertain the cause of death. This was not a collateral purpose, but a purpose well within the reasons for granting pre-action discovery.

(iii) if the Access to Health Records Act 1990 had governed the present cases, the children's representatives would have been entitled to their medical records within 40 days of their deaths. Parliament cannot have thought that the obtaining of medical records before an inquest was injurious to the public interest.

(iv) therefore discovery before the inquests should be ordered.

Per Rougier J: 'Any attempt to use material disclosed for any purpose other than the narrow purpose of ascertaining the cause of death would, in my judgment, be departing from the implied undertaking not to use the material for collateral purposes. Not only would the coroner be obliged to nip any such attempt in the bud, but the further safeguard would be provided by the fact that those who appeared at the inquest for the potential defendants would no doubt be quick to rise to their feet and object.'

See p 208.

Stockdale v Nicholls

Brain damage: causation: child patient: general practitioner: baby (premature): nurse

Otton J. [1993] 4 Med LR 190

In June 1980 the plaintiff (Caroline Stockdale) was born six weeks premature. She had feeding problems. On 1 August it was recorded that she was vomiting her feeds.

On Sunday 3 August 1980, when Caroline was seven weeks old, she cried and whimpered all day. Around 7pm her mother rang Dr Nicholls' surgery. He sent the practice nurse who visited around 7.30pm. The nurse found the rectal temperature to be 36.6F, fed Caroline 3 oz from the bottle and told Mrs Stockdale that she was not feeding the baby correctly and advised her to give boiled water only. Half an hour after her departure, Caroline vomited copiously.

Mrs Stockdale rang and spoke to Dr Nicholls at his home at 11pm that night. He reached her home around midnight. He wrote up his notes during the visit and recorded: '23.30 visited. Baby vomited food. Has been vomiting intermittently ?1–3½ days. Worse one and a half days. Restless, crying. Last feed 15.30. Bowels opened yesterday not today? Vomiting projectile. Helped by Merbentyl. Mother said baby has snuffles no cough. OE T 99.6 A 140 chest ears throat no discharge. Tongue coated. Abdo NAD Rx Paedofed 5mls. Fontanelle normal not bulging Kernigs (sic).' He concluded that it was not necessary to admit Caroline to hospital.

After he left, the baby became restless, cried more, would not take water and vomited 'brown mucus'. Mr Stockdale rang Dr Nicholls around 4am on 4 August, and he arrived by 4.30am. She struck him as slightly more unwell than before. Her apex beat was raised to 160 which was clear tachycardia for a baby of her age. He decided that she ought to go into hospital and wrote a referral letter. He asked if Mr Stockdale had a car and was told that he had not, but was assured that the Stockdales would get either a lift from a friend or a taxi. Dr Nicholls left at about 5am.

In the result, it was not until after 7am that Caroline was taken by ambulance to the casualty department at Yeovil Hospital. She was admitted to the paediatric ward at about 8am. Shortly afterwards the senior house officer noted dehydration, suspected septicaemia and planned hourly observation. Near 10am Caroline had two convulsions and needed resuscitation. Tests later in the day led to a diagnosis of septicaemia shock which had caused the convulsions.

The effects were devastating and permanent. The plaintiff sustained substantial damage to her brain, leading to severe physical disability and mental incapacity. She sued Dr Nicholls through her mother and next friend.

Held: (i)   it was reasonable, not negligent, to send an experienced practice nurse in response to the first call. There was nothing in the report from the nurse that would have caused concern to a competent general practitioner.

   (ii)   although at Dr Nicholls' first visit the temperature of 99.6F and the 140 apex heartbeat were signs to be considered, a child who is fretful and has cried a lot can produce such readings which were within the limits of normality. There was no symptom of septicaemia. Dr Nicholls was not negligent in failing to arrange a hospital admission then.

   (iii)   nor was there any sign of septicaemia on his second visit. He decided that the baby should be admitted to hospital for observation and checked that the Stockdales had means of transport. There was no basis for a finding of negligence against him.

   (iv)   nor was there any such sign recorded on admission to the hospital casualty department at 7.20am. The first manifestation was at 10am when the collapse occurred. Admission three hours earlier would not have made any difference. Causation was not established.

See pp 69, 136.

Stokes v Guest, Keen and Nettlefold (Bolts and Nuts) Ltd

Works doctor: state of knowledge: warning: duty of care: causation: skin complaint: fatal: cancer

Swanwick J. [1968] 1 WLR 1776

From 1950 to 1965 Sidney Stokes worked as a tool setter/operator at GKN's Darlaston factory. His job involved him in intermittently leaning over machines in such a way as to bring the lower part of his stomach and the top of his thighs into contact with a film of cooling or cutting oil (of the type accepted as containing carcinogenic elements) which escaped on to the part of the machine over which a tool-setter would lean. His boilersuits got soaked with oil down the front, his trousers underneath got oily, and his underpants often had discoloured oil patches down the front. He developed an epithelioma of the scrotum from which he died in 1966.

In July 1960 the Factory Inspectorate had issued a leaflet, Form 295, entitled 'The Effects on the Skin of Mineral Oil', specifically describing warts on the scrotum, indicating that they might develop into skin cancer and should therefore be reported to a doctor without delay, warning against putting oily rags in trouser pockets, and contemplating that there might be periodical examinations by works doctors of which workers should avail themselves. In January 1961 Dr Lloyd, the full-time factory medical officer, learned that Mr Ward, another tool setter operator at the same works, was suffering from scrotal cancer and traced the cause as heavy contamination of overalls at work by mineral oil.

Dr Lloyd rejected the suggestion of periodical medical examinations, even when made by the coroner at the inquest on Mr Ward's death in 1963. Nor did he circulate Form 295. His only measure was to address the Works Council later in 1963, stressing personal hygiene and mentioning cancer, but not mentioning the scrotum or warts or reporting.

Held: (i)   a factory doctor is to be judged by the standards of a physician in the medical aspects of his work; the economic and administrative aspects are covered by the general principles of employers' liability.

(ii)   the defendants were responsible for Dr Lloyd's negligence in:

(a)   not instituting after the discovery of Mr Ward's condition and *a fortiori* after his death six-monthly periodic medical examinations of tool-setters at the Darlaston works; and

(b)   not issuing at these same times direct to the workers either Form 295 or an equivalent notice calling attention to the existence of a risk of cancer of the scrotum, describing the symptoms and recommending immediate reference to the factory doctor or general practitioner.

(iii)   these measures would probably have saved Mr Stokes' life.

See p 65.

Strangways-Lesmere v Clayton

Prescription: overdose: nurse: vicarious liability: fatal

Horridge J. [1936] 2 KB 11

In May 1935 Mrs Strangways-Lesmere was admitted to the Weymouth and District Hospital for an operation. The house surgeon wrote out on the bed card that six drachms of paraldehyde were to be administered. A piece of paper with the instructions that the paraldehyde was to be six drachms in nine ounces of water was handed to Nurse Miles. She poured out a dose of six ounces of paraldehyde and Nurse Chapman checked this. Neither of them looked at the bed card. Consequently six ounces, rather than six drachms, of paraldehyde were administered to Mrs Strangways-Lesmere. She died without recovering consciousness.

The plaintiff (her husband) sued the nurses Miles and Chapman and the hospital authority.

Held: the nurses were guilty of negligence. Nurse Miles misread the note that was handed to her. Both the nurses ought to have looked at the bed card when measuring out a dose.

Note: Following the cases of *Cassidy* v *Ministry of Health* and *Roe* v *Minister of Health*, the judge's further finding that the hospital authority was not liable for the nurses' negligence would not be good law today.

See pp 21, 121, 139.

Sullivan v Manchester Regional Hospital Board and Another

Operation: after-care: nurse: diagnosis: surgeon

Lynskey J. [1957] 2 BMJ 1442

In September 1953 the plaintiff (Mrs Sullivan) underwent an operation by Mr Evans at Accrington Victoria Hospital for the removal of nasal polypi. When she recovered from the anaesthetic, her right eye was swollen and remained so for several days. She asked the ward sister several times if her eye 'would be all right' and accepted reassurance that it would be. Two days after the operation, she noticed that her eyeball had the appearance of red jelly and that she could not see. Four days after the operation, the ward sister asked the resident surgical officer to examine her because the swelling still persisted. This led to her transfer to the care of an eye specialist.

The plaintiff had suffered damage to the optic nerve with loss of sight. She sued Mr Evans and the hospital authority, alleging that Mr Evans had been negligent in the performance of the operation and that the nursing staff had failed for four days to act on her complaints. Expert evidence was given that the occurrence of such bleeding behind the eye did not signify lack of skill on the part of the surgeon.

Held: (i)   Mr Evans had not been guilty of any lack of reasonable skill and care.

(ii)   the nursing staff had not been negligent in failing to recognize the significance of the plaintiff's appearance and her complaint that she could not see.

Judgment for the defendants.

See p 138.

Sutton v Population Services Family Planning Programme Ltd and Another

Cancer: diagnosis: nurse: damages

McCowan J. (1981) Times, 7 November, (1981) 2 Lancet 1430

The plaintiff suffered cancer. The negligence of a nurse employed by the first defendants caused the cancerous growth to be detected and removed too late. Since the cancer was highly malignant, an earlier removal would not have eradicated it. However its recurrence would have been delayed for four years during which the plaintiff would have led a normal life and worked full-time. In addition, her menopause was prematurely brought forward.

Held: (i)   the plaintiff was awarded damages for four years' loss of future earnings plus the conventional figure for four years' expectation of life.

(ii) she was further awarded £1,000 for the suffering caused by the premature arrival of her menopause.

(iii) since she would have undergone the same operations and treatment four years later, there could be no extra award of damages for pain and suffering.

See pp 44, 98, 138.

Swindon and Marlborough NH Trust v S

Consent: discontinuance of life-supporting treatment: interests of patient: PVS

Ward J. (1994) Guardian, 10 December

In June 1992 Mrs S went into a persistent vegetative state (PVS) after neurosurgery to remove a brain tumour. From December 1992 she had been at home where her family and friends, assisted by district nurses and the general practitioner, cared for her. She was fed by a gastrostomy tube inserted through her stomach wall. On 25 November 1994 her husband (Mr S) discovered that the tube had become blocked internally. Neither he, the district nurse nor the GP was able to dislodge the obstruction. After anxious deliberation, the family decided that it was a propitious moment when no more should be done. They opposed Mrs S, then aged 48, being admitted to hospital to undergo surgery to remove and replace the tube.

The health authority applied for directions. The case was heard on 26 November. Mr S testified that both he and Mrs S had shared religious convictions and did not regard earthly life as all that could be expected. They did not believe in euthanasia, but neither did they believe in preserving life at all costs. He specifically recalled a discussion with his wife, not long before her neurosurgical operation, when they were visiting a disabled patient. She then said that if she were ever in that position she would rather go to sleep and die, in order to await her resurrection. Their adult son also supported the decision not to reinsert the tube.

Clarification was sought and given on two matters. First, evidence that Mrs S sometimes responded quite agitatedly to certain familiar voices; the medical evidence was that this was a purely reflex reaction and the fact that it was a known voice was insignificant. The second was some facial twitching which led to speculation about a possibility that Mrs S might be suffering from epilepsy; the medical evidence was that this was not the case.

Held: (i) all appropriate steps had been taken to eliminate other possibilities before making a diagnosis of PVS.

(ii) the family's wishes were the product of full and informed thought and had been expressed after careful, probably prayerful, mature reflection over a period of time.

(iii) the stark sincerity of their views were relevant as matters appropriately to be taken into account by the medical team in accordance with BMA guidelines.

(iv) it was lawful for a patient in a persistent vegetative state who was being cared for at home by her family to be allowed to die.

(v) it was in her best interests to discontinue all life-sustaining treatment, despite her inability to consent.

(vi) the nurses were authorised to furnish appropriate treatment of nursing care to ensure that she suffered the least distress and retained the greatest dignity until her life came to an end.

Note: This is thought to be the first such application made in respect of a patient cared for at home.

Re T (consent to medical treatment: adult patient)

Blood transfusion: consent: Jehovah's Witness: interests of patient: caesarian

Court of Appeal. [1993] Fam 95, [1992] 4 All ER 649, [1992] 3 WLR 782, [1992] 3 Med LR 306, [1992] 2 FLR 458, [1992] NLJR 1125, [1992] 2 FCR 861

T's parents separated in 1975; her mother was a fervent Jehovah's Witness, whereas her father emphatically rejected the faith. Her mother brought her up with a view to her becoming a Jehovah's Witness, but in May or June 1992 she told her father that she had not done so.

On July 1992, when T was 19 years old and 34 weeks pregnant by the man with whom she was living, she was injured in a road traffic accident and diagnosed as suffering from pleurisy or pneumonia. By 5 July she was very ill and receiving oxygen; the Pethidine and antibiotics made her drowsy and detached. For some time before 5pm she was alone with her mother; when a staff nurse joined them, T told her 'out of the blue' that she did not want a blood transfusion.

Soon afterwards T went into labour. After 11pm she was transferred to the maternity unit; during the ambulance journey, she was again alone with her mother. A decision was made on arrival that the delivery should be by caesarian section. T told the midwife that she did not want a blood transfusion. Dr F then saw her and asked 'do you object to the blood transfusions?'; T replied 'yes'. Dr F asked 'does that mean that you do not want a blood transfusion?'; T replied 'no'. She asked 'you can use the other things though, can't you, like sugar solutions?'; attempting to reassure her, Dr F falsely answered in the affirmative. T signed a form refusing consent to blood transfusions; contrary to what was stated in the form, it was not explained to her 'that it may be necessary to give a blood transfusion as to prevent injury to my health or even to preserve my life'.

The caesarian section was performed on 6 July; the baby was stillborn. T's condition deteriorated to the point where on 7 July the consultant in charge of the intensive care unit would have administered a blood transfusion, had he felt able to do so. On 8 July, after an emergency hearing, Ward J ruled in his lodgings that it would not be unlawful for the hospital to administer a blood transfusion to T. On 9 July she received a transfusion of blood or plasma. On 10 July Ward J confirmed his order after a full hearing.

Held: (i)   there was abundant evidence that T was not in a fit physical or mental condition to reach a valid decision to imperil her life by refusing a blood transfusion.

        (ii)   even if she had been, it was hard to suppose that the influence of her mother did not sap her will or destroy her volition. There was abundant evidence that she was subjected to the undue influence of her mother which vitiated the decision.

        (iii)   as there had been no valid refusal by T to a blood transfusion, the appeal against the judge's order should be dismissed.

Per Lord Donaldson MR:

The right to choose

'An adult patient who, like Miss T, suffers from no mental incapacity has an absolute right to choose whether to consent to medical treatment, to refuse it or to choose one rather than another of the treatments being offered. The only possible qualification is a case in which the choice may lead to the death of a viable foetus. That is not this case and, if and when it arises, the courts will be faced with a novel problem of considerable legal and ethical complexity. This right of choice is not limited to decisions which others might regard as sensible. It exists notwithstanding that the reasons for making the choice are rational, irrational, unknown or even non-existent (*Sidaway v Board of Governors of the Bethlem Royal Hospital and Maudsley Hospital* [1985] AC 871, pp 904F–905A).

But just because adults have the right to choose, it does not follow that they have in fact exercised that right. Determining whether or not they have done so is a quite different and sometimes difficult matter. And if it is clear that they have exercised their right of choice, problems can still arise in determining what precisely they have chosen. This appeal illustrates both these problems.

The role of consent

The law requires that an adult patient who is mentally and physically capable of exercising a choice must consent if medical treatment of him is to be lawful, although the consent need not be in writing and may sometimes be inferred from the patient's conduct in the context of the surrounding circumstances. Treating him without his consent or despite a refusal of consent will constitute the civil wrong of trespass to the person and may constitute a crime. If, however, the patient has made no choice and, when the need for treatment arises, is in no position to make one – eg the classic emergency situation with an unconscious patient – the practitioner can lawfully treat the patient in accordance with his clinical judgment of what is in the patient's best interest.

There seems to be a view in the medical profession that in such emergency circumstances the next of kin should be asked to consent on behalf of the patient and that, if possible, treatment should be postponed until that consent has been obtained. This is a misconception because the next of kin has no legal right either to consent or to refuse consent. This is not to say that it is an undesirable practice if the interests of the patient will not be adversely affected by any consequential delay. I say this because contact with the next of kin may reveal that the patient has made an anticipatory choice which, if clearly established and applicable in the circumstances – two major "ifs" – would bind the practitioner. Consultation with the next of kin has a further advantage in that it may reveal information as to the personal circumstances of the patient and as to the choice which the patient might have made if he or she had been in a position to make it. Neither the personal circumstances of the patient nor a speculative answer to the question 'What would the patient have chosen?' can bind the practitioner in his choice of whether or not to treat or how to treat or justify him in acting contrary to a clearly established anticipatory refusal to accept treatment but they are factors to be taken into account by him in forming a clinical judgment as to what is in the best interests of the patient. For example, if he learnt that the patient was a Jehovah's Witness, but had no evidence of a refusal to accept blood transfusions, he would avoid or postpone any blood transfusion as long as possible.

The vitiating effect of outside influence

A special problem may arise if at the time the decision is made the patient has been subjected to the influence of some third party. This is by no means to say that the patient is not entitled to receive and indeed invite advice and assistance from others in reaching a decision, particularly from members of the family. But the doctors have to consider whether the decision is really that of the patient. It is wholly acceptable that the patient should have been persuaded by others of the merits of such a decision and have decided accordingly. It matters not how strong the persuasion was, so long as it did not overbear the independence of the patient's decision. The real question in each such case is 'Does the patient really mean what he says or is he merely saying it for a quiet life, to satisfy someone else or because the advice and persuasion to which he has been subjected is such that he can no longer think and decide for himself?' In other words 'Is it a decision expressed in form only, not in reality?'

When considering the effect of outside influences, two aspects can be of crucial importance. First, the strength of the will of the patient. One who is very tired, in pain or depressed will be much less able to resist having his will overborne than one who is rested, free from pain and cheerful. Second, the relationship of the 'persuader' to the patient may be of crucial importance. The influence of parents on their children or of one spouse on the other can be, but is by no means necessarily, much stronger than would be the case in other relationships. Persuasion based upon religious beliefs can also be much more compelling and the fact that arguments based upon religious beliefs are being deployed by someone in a very close relationship with the patient will give them added force and should alert the doctors to the possibility – no more – that the patient's capacity or will to decide has been overborne. In other words the patient may not mean what he says.

Misinformed refusal

As Ward J put it in his judgment, English law does not accept the transatlantic concept of 'informed consent' and it follows that it would reject the concept of 'informed refusal'. What is required is that the patient knew in broad terms the nature and effect of the procedure to which consent (or refusal) was given. There is indeed a duty on the part of doctors to give the patient appropriately full information as to the nature of the treatment proposed, the likely risks (including any special risks attaching to the treatment being administered by particular persons), but a failure to perform this duty sounds in negligence and does not, as such, vitiate a consent or refusal. On the other hand, misinforming a patient, whether or not innocently, and the withholding of information which is expressly or impliedly sought by the patient may well vitiate either a consent or a refusal.

The role of the courts

If in a potentially life-threatening situation or one in which irreparable damage to the patient's health is to be anticipated, doctors or hospital authorities are faced with a refusal by an adult patient to accept essential treatment and they have real doubts as to the validity of that refusal, they should in the public interest, not to mention that of their patient, at once seek a declaration from the courts as to whether the proposed treatment would or would not be lawful. This step should not be left to the patient's family, who will probably not know of the facility and may be inhibited by questions of expense. Such cases will be rare, but when they do arise, as was the case with Miss T, the courts can and will provide immediate assistance'.

Per Butler-Sloss LJ: '. . . I can see circumstances in which a patient is unwilling to have certain procedures carried out and says so under the impression that in any event the emergency which would bring those procedures into play will not happen. If the patient has been misled or misinformed, he may not have given a genuine consent or refusal. This is not to bring in the doctrine of informed consent which is not the law of this country. But on the present facts, Miss T did not want a blood transfusion but she did ask whether there was a substitute treatment and was told, erroneously, I believe, that there was. She was also told in order to calm her down that a blood transfusion was most unlikely and she did not have to face, it appears, the possible serious or even fatal consequences of her decision. Had she been making a genuine decision to refuse the treatment, it would be necessary in a case such as this to find out if the patient had received any advice as to the consequences of a refusal to accept treatment.'

See pp 89, 103.

T v D

Brain damage: childbirth: structured settlement: damages

FTSB, Spring 1994

The plaintiff (T) suffered severe cerebral palsy and Erb's palsy due to negligent procedures at birth. When he was seven years of age, medical reports suggested that 'his life expectancy is reasonably good and not reduced below normal by more than a few years'.

The following settlement was agreed.

Interim payments	£225,000
Capital cost of structure	£743,000
Damages held in trust	£232,000
Other damages	£50,000
Total	£1,250,000

The structured sum was applied to purchase an annuity of £30,000 pa, increasing each year in line with the retail price index, and payable for life with a 10-year guarantee period. There was no discount on the damages.

The structured settlement was approved.

Tanswell v Nelson and Others

Dentist: general practitioner: diagnosis: x-rays: standard of care: jaw

McNair J. (1959) Times, 11 February

On 26 October 1954 the plaintiff (Mrs Gwendoline Tanswell) had ten teeth removed by her dentist Mr Nelson. Consequently she suffered a locking of the jaws accompanied by intense pain and swelling of the cheek and face. Mr Nelson treated her with irrigation of the mouth and hot washes. Her condition did not improve.

On 5 November Mr Nelson sent the plaintiff to her doctor Dr Cree, who diagnosed dental abscess with infection spreading up into the parotid gland, and treated her with antibiotics. On 9 November Dr Cree told Mr Nelson that he was satisfied the abscess was coming to a head. Dr Cree continued to treat her until 29 November when he arranged for her to go into hospital.

It emerged that the plaintiff had suffered trismus, a locking of the jaws, and osteomyelitis of the jaw. She became a frail and sick person. She sued Mr Nelson and Dr Cree on the grounds that each in turn failed to have x-ray films taken of her jaw and to send her to hospital until it was too late.

Held: (i) the taking of x-rays by Mr Nelson probably would not have told him anything he did not know already. A dentist was entitled to rely upon a doctor's opinion of the patient's general response to antibiotic treatment, unless that opinion was clearly inconsistent with facts observed by the dentist;

(ii) many of the symptoms shown by the plaintiff were inconsistent with developing osteomyelitis. They were not such as should have led Dr Cree to suspect it.

See pp 130, 133.

Tarasoff et al v Regents of the University of California et al

Psychiatric patient: duty of care to third party: warning: confidentiality: USA

Supreme Court of California. 551 P 2d 334 (1976)

In August 1969 Prosenjit Poddar was a voluntary outpatient receiving therapy at Cowell Memorial Hospital in the University of California at Berkeley. The plaintiffs' case was that

Poddar informed Dr Moore, his therapist there, that he was going to kill an unnamed girl, readily identifiable as Tatiana Tarasoff, when she returned home from spending the summer in Brazil; that Dr Moore decided that Poddar should be committed for observation in a mental hospital and requested the assistance of the police department in securing Poddar's confinement; that police officers took Poddar into custody but, satisfied that he was rational, released him on his promise to stay away from Tatiana; that Dr Powelson, Dr Moore's superior, then directed that no further action be taken to detain Poddar; and that Dr Moore did not warn Tatiana or her parents.

On 27 October 1969, shortly after her return from Brazil, Poddar went to Tatiana Tarasoff's home and killed her there. The plaintiffs (her parents) sued, *inter alia*, Dr Moore, Dr Powelson and the university. These defendants had statutory immunity from liability for failing to confine Poddar. The plaintiffs alleged that they were negligent in failing to warn of the danger.

Held: (i) the defendant therapists could not escape liability merely because Tatiana herself was not their patient. When a therapist determines, or pursuant to the standards of his profession should determine, that his patient presents a serious danger of violence to another, he incurs an obligation to use reasonable care to protect the intended victim against such danger. The discharge of his duty may require the therapist to take one or more of various steps, depending upon the nature of the case. Thus it may call for him to warn the intended victim or others likely to apprise the victim of the danger, to notify the police, or to take whatever other steps are reasonably necessary under the circumstances. Thus the plaintiffs' causes of action could be amended to allege that Tatiana's death proximately resulted from the defendants' negligent failure to warn Tatiana or others likely to apprise her of the danger;

(ii) the broad rule of privilege protecting confidential communications between patient and psychotherapist does not apply if the psychotherapist has reasonable cause to believe that the patient is in such a mental or emotional condition as to be dangerous to himself or to the person or property of another, and that disclosure of the communication is necessary to prevent the threatened danger. The protective privilege ends where the public peril begins.

See pp 19, 51.

Tate v West Cornwall and Isles of Scilly Health Authority

Bed sore: cauda equina syndrome: damages: injection: spinal: impotence: depression

HH Judge Thompson QC. [1994] 4 CL 229

In 1987 the plaintiff (Mr Tate), aged 64, who had already undergone an above-knee amputation of his right leg, developed a circulatory problem in his left leg which limited his mobility. In September 1987 he underwent chemical sympathectomy injection to improve his circulation. Injection of phenol into the subarachnoid space damaged the cauda equina, leaving him paralysed from the waist downwards.

He also developed a bed sore. The defendant's hospital provided no treatment for this. Moreover, they permitted him to be transferred to a wheelchair, thus preventing healing. The defendants concluded that nothing could be done for it. The plaintiff used part of his interim payment to provide private treatment for the bed sore which eventually healed.

The plaintiff was not able to return home until November 1992. For practical purposes, he was a paraplegic. He retained slight residual power and sensation in his left leg. He also retained some sensation in his buttocks which was a source of permanent discomfort. He was left doubly incontinent and prone to bowel accidents. He was rendered impotent, and suffered severe depression during his five years of hospitalisation. His condition was such that he could not be left unattended. He needed to be turned three times per night. His life expectancy was seven years.

Held (January 1994): (i) general damages of £85,000 for pain, suffering and loss of amenities were awarded. These were higher than otherwise due to inadequate care from the defendants, as a result of which the plaintiff spent four and a half years unnecessarily in hospitals.

(ii) other items brought the total award up to £484,976 before appropriate deduction of DSS benefit.

See p 121.

Taylor v Glass

Vaccine damage: meningitis: adjournment of trial

Court of Appeal. CAT, 23 May 1979

The plaintiff (David Taylor) was born in June 1970. When he was one year old, Dr Glass gave him a vaccination against diphtheria and other illnesses. A little later he was taken ill with meningitis. This illness left him permanently incapacitated.

The plaintiff sued Dr Glass who admitted liability. There was a major issue as to his expectation of life, which his own experts suggested was normal, but which Dr Glass' experts said was limited to fifteen years. Only one of his five experts had seen the plaintiff.

The case had been on the warned list at the Newcastle District Registry two or three times. It reached the top of the list, with the result that it was expected to be heard on 26 April 1979. A vacation judge granted the defendant's application for an adjournment on the ground that his expert witnesses could not attend court then.

Held: the vacation judge had been under a misapprehension as to the listing arrangements in Newcastle. By making suitable arrangements the defendant could either obtain the attendance of his original medical experts or, as only one of them had seen the plaintiff, could get substitute doctors who would be equally capable of helping the court in matters of theoretical opinion. The original date in the list should be restored.

Taylor v Somerset Health Authority

Damages: fatal: post traumatic stress disorder: cardiac

Auld J. [1993] 4 Med LR 34, [1993] PIQR P262

In 1986 a hospital run by the defendants failed to diagnose and treat Eric Taylor's serious heart disease. On 19 January 1987 he had a fatal heart attack at work. He was taken to hospital where at about 3pm he was certified dead.

Shortly afterwards the plaintiff (Mrs June Taylor) was informed that he had become ill and had been taken to hospital. She arrived there at about 3.20pm. After a wait of 15 to 20 minutes, a doctor had informed her that her husband had died. She was shocked and distressed by that news, and could not believe it. A few minutes later, she identified her husband's body in the hospital mortuary. She did so, partly because she was requested to do so, but mainly because she could not believe that what she had been told was true. The sight of his dead body caused her further shock and distress. As a result of all these circumstances, she suffered a psychiatric illness.

The hospital authority admitted that its negligence had caused Mr Taylor's death and settled the plaintiff's claim relating to this for £54,000. She also claimed damages for her nervous shock as a result of her presence at the hospital shortly after his death.

Per Auld J: 'The immediate aftermath principle is one which has been introduced as an exception to the general principle established in accident cases that a plaintiff can only recover damages for psychiatric injury when the accident and the primary injury or death caused by it occurred within his sight or hearing. There are two notions implicit in this exception cautiously introduced and cautiously continued by the House of Lords. They are of:

(1) an external, traumatic, event caused by the defendant's breach of duty which immediately causes some person injury or death; and

(2) a perception by the plaintiff of the event as it happens, normally by his presence at the scene, or exposure to the scene and/or to the primary victim so shortly afterwards that the shock of the event as well as of its consequence is brought home to him.'

Held: (i) there was no such external event here apart from the final consequence of Mr Taylor's progressively deteriorating heart condition which the hospital authority, by its negligence many months before, had failed to arrest. His death at work, and the subsequent transfer of the body to the hospital where the plaintiff was told of what had happened and where she saw the body, did not constitute such an event.

(ii) even if Mr Taylor's fatal heart attack was an event to which the 'immediate aftermath' principle applied, the doctor's communication to the plaintiff of that fact, even within an hour of the death, would not come within the extension. The law does not compensate for shock induced by communication from a third party.

(iii) the main purpose of the plaintiff's visit to the mortuary was to settle her disbelief as to her husband's reported death. His body bore no marks that would have conjured up the circumstances of his fatal attack. Her visit went to the fact of death, not the circumstances in which death occurred, and was not capable of being part of any possible immediate aftermath.

(iv) accordingly the plaintiff was not entitled to damages for her nervous shock.

See p 51.

Taylor v Worcester and District Health Authority

Anaesthetic awareness: caesarean: post-traumatic stress disorder

McKinnon J. [1991] 2 Med LR 215

On 11 January 1985 the plaintiff (Mrs Sandra Taylor), aged 22, underwent a caesarean section operation for delivery of her first child at Ronkswood Hospital in Worcester. The anaesthetist was Dr Hussain. When she examined the plaintiff at 7am, just before anaesthesia, the plaintiff's blood pressure was 140/100, heart normal. Induction, beginning with administration of 250mg thiopentone followed by 100mg suxamethonium, began at 7.15am. The plaintiff was then intubated and given 50:50 nitrous oxide, oxygen and 0.5%

halothane, at a six litre minute volume. Alcuronium in a 15mg dose was given just after five minutes from induction. As soon as the widest part of the baby was delivered, the plaintiff was given five units syntocinon plus a further five units after 14mg of omnopon was administered when the cord was clamped. On delivery of the baby by fundal pressure at 7.30am, the nitrous oxide was increased to 70%, oxygen decreased to 30% and then the halothane was turned off, about four to five minutes after the omnopon. Blood pressure was 130, pulse normal. At 7.45am an extra dose of alcuronium was given, and at 7.50 to 7.55 am an extra dose of 2mg omnopon. At 8.10am reversal commenced by administering atropine and neostigmine. Dr Hussain saw no signs of awareness during the operation.

The plaintiff contended that she was awake during the operation. Her testimony was as follows. She was taken to the operating theatre, given a mask to breathe through, somebody started to count and she became unconscious after a few seconds. She felt an increasingly acute pain, like a burning sensation, across her abdomen, followed by a strong sensation of something pressing down inside. She could not open her eyes or move. She could hear a hissing sound. She felt as if the whole of her body was moving with a tugging sensation. There was also a constant pressure and release of pressure on her chest. She was terrified and felt as if she was going to die. She lost consciousness again and then gradually heard voices. After the conclusion of the operation, she said, she still felt as if she was paralysed. She did not tell anyone other than her mother of her experience. She started having nightmares when she returned home. The extreme pain and terror which she suffered had a lasting effect on her.

Held: (i) Dr Hussain's anaesthetic technique was generally accepted as suitable for a caesarean section in 1985. It was taught and widely used then. It was a perfectly responsible technique with an incidence of awareness of less than 0.35%.

(ii) Dr Hussain carried out the technique in a careful and competent manner. There was no evidence of any substance to the contrary. She had not been negligent.

(iii) the plaintiff's episode of awareness did not occur during the operation at all. It occurred afterwards, at the reversal stage. The plaintiff's description was consistent with this. It contained nothing exclusively referable to a time about the time of birth. There were no clinical signs of pain or distress during the operation. Dr Hussain's anaesthetic technique would have provided sufficient anaesthetic cover throughout.

The plaintiff's claim was dismissed.

See p 123.

Thake and Another v Maurice

Vasectomy (failed): breach of contract: wrongful birth: risk disclosure: damages: public policy

Court of Appeal. [1986] QB 644, [1986] 1 All ER 497, [1986] 2 WLR 337

In 1975 the plaintiffs (Mr and Mrs Thake) had four children with a fifth on the way. They arranged with Mr Maurice that he would carry out a vasectomy operation on Mr Thake for £20. Mr Maurice told them that the vasectomy operation was irreversible, subject to a possible operation to restore fertility, and did not warn them that there was a chance of the vasectomy failing to sterilise Mr Thake. He performed it in October 1975. Late recanalisation occurred, and in autumn 1978 Mrs Thake was informed to her surprise that she was five months' pregnant. She declined a late abortion, and a daughter Samantha was born to her in April 1979.

Thake and Another v Maurice

The plaintiffs sued Mr Maurice for breach of contract and negligence. The trial judge (Peter Pain J) found for them on liability and awarded £6,677 agreed damages for the cost of the layette and of Samantha's upkeep to the age of seventeen, plus an agreed sum of £2,000 to Mrs Thake for loss of earnings, but he refused to make any award of general damages for pain and suffering.

Held: (i) sterility was the expected result of the operation, but that did not mean that a reasonable person would have understood the defendant to be giving a binding promise that the operation would achieve its purpose. Accordingly there was no breach of contract.

(ii) in the absence of expert evidence of standard practice, the judge was entitled to conclude that Mr Maurice's failure to warn amounted to an inadvertent breach of his duty of care to the plaintiffs. The consequence that Mrs Thake would not appreciate that she had become pregnant at an early enough stage to enable her to have an abortion was reasonably foreseeable. Mr Maurice was liable in negligence.

(iii) the joy of having the child should be set off against the time, trouble and care inevitably involved in her upbringing. But the pre-natal distress, pain and suffering stood in a separate category and she should be compensated for this by the agreed sum of £1,500.

See pp 27, 55, 81, 111, 127, 168, 169, 179.

Ter Neuzen v Korn

Canada: HIV: infection: state of knowledge

British Columbia Court of Appeal. *Halsbury's Laws Annual Abridgment* 1993, para 1767, (1993) 103 DLR (4th) 473

The plaintiff contracted the HIV virus as a result of an artificial insemination procedure (AI) carried out by the defendant doctor. Knowledge of the transmission of HIV via AI was not widespread at that time. A jury found the defendant negligent. He appealed.

Held: (i) the jury ought to have been instructed to decide whether the defendant had conducted himself as a reasonable doctor would have done in similar circumstances. In so doing, the jury had to confine itself to prevailing standards of practice.

(ii) the defendant had acted in accordance with the standards of AI practice current at the time. He was therefore not negligent in being unaware of the risk of HIV infection.

(iii) the only issue was whether the defendant had taken reasonable steps to protect his patients against sexually transmitted diseases in general. If he had failed to do so, he would be liable even if the specific virus of HIV was one which he did not foresee.

(iv) accordingly the defendant's appeal was allowed, and a new trial was ordered.

Thomas v North West Surrey Health Authority

Abortion: brain damage: damages: receiver

Tucker J Lexis, 9 November 1989

In February 1981 the plaintiff (Miss Julia Thomas), aged 27, was admitted to St Peter's Hospital in Chertsey for an abortion. As part of the termination procedure, the hospital staff administered an intravenous solution to her in increasing amounts. They failed to monitor the process properly. As a result, the plaintiff suffered acute water intoxication causing a chronic encephalopathy. The hospital authority admitted liability.

The plaintiff sustained very substantial brain damage, resulting in severe dysphasia and fairly severe behavioural abnormalities. She was unconscious for three weeks. During the first year she was very violent, was continually screaming and was doubly incontinent. Subsequently she improved, but she would never be able to speak to any meaningful extent or to lead an independent existence. She had little insight into her condition. She did not suffer from any significant physical handicap. Her life expectancy was normal. Except for three months in 1983, she remained at St Peter's Hospital for eight years. The care and stimulation she needed could not be supplied in the National Health Service. In March 1989 she entered Worlton Hall near Barnard Castle, a private establishment that suited her needs well. In November 1990 she was to be transferred to a sister establishment, Victoria House in Darlington.

Held (November 1989):
    (i)   general damages for pain, suffering and loss of amenities were assessed at £75,000.

    (ii)   although Worlton Hall and Victoria House were expensive, the expense was justified because, when someone has suffered as catastrophically as this, then, unless the cost is outrageous and unacceptable, she should be given the best chance of clinging to these shreds of enjoyment which remain. It was appropriate to deduct from this what the plaintiff, if fit, would have spent on her own upkeep. As she was aged 36 at trial, a multiplier of 17 was taken for future care.

    (iii)   the appropriate multiplier for future loss of earnings was 13.

    (iv)   receivership fees shall be awarded (contrary to the defendant's contention).

With other items included, the total award was £576,595 plus receivership fees and interest.

See pp 127, 159.

Thomas v Wignall and Another

Anaesthetics: damages: brain damage: tonsillectomy: paraplegia

Court of Appeal. [1987] QB 1098, [1987] 1 All ER 1185, [1987] 2 WLR 930

In March 1976 the plaintiff (Linda Thomas), then aged 16, underwent a routine operation for removal of her tonsils in the University Hospital of Wales in Cardiff. The anaesthetic went wrong. She sued the health authority and the anaesthetist who admitted liability for negligence.

The plaintiff suffered permanent brain damage. She became very seriously disabled. She was confined to a wheelchair and would need constant care and attention for the rest of her life. She was not aware of what had happened to her. She was incontinent and had serious behavioural problems. She was not expected to live beyond the age of 55.

In December 1985 the trial judge (Hutchison J) awarded the then record sum of £679,264 damages. The principal items were agreed general damages of £60,000 for pain, suffering and loss of amenities, £49,000 for past and future loss of earnings, £25,000 for conversion of a house to her requirements and £502,500 for the past and future cost of the plaintiff's care.

Held: the award was affirmed and the defendant's appeal dismissed.

See pp 122, 154, 159, 162.

Thompson v South Tees Area Health Authority

Brain damage: damages: diagnosis: quadriplegia: baby: general practitioner

French J. [1990] CLY 1576, [1990] 6 PMILL 37

The plaintiff (Suzanne Thompson) was six months old and developing normally when her general practitioner failed to diagnose an intestinal obstruction due to intussusception. She remained at home for 48 hours, vomiting continually. When eventually referred to hospital, she was grossly dehydrated. There was a delay at the hospital before the correct diagnosis was made. No efforts were made to rehydrate her before the operation to remove the blockage, making cerebral irritation and fits more likely. In the early hours of the next day, she suffered a major fit which was not controlled for 45 minutes.

Cerebral anoxia led to spastic quadriplegia and severe mental handicap. At the time of the trial, when she was aged nine, she was unable to crawl, roll or move around in any way. She was unable to sit unsupported. The spasticity had resulted in a dislocation of the left hip. She had a primitive grasp and could transfer objects from one hand to the other. She had no speech but could be happy and distressed. She made a moaning noise a good deal of the time. She also screamed and cried. She was unable to feed herself but did not appear to have any difficulty in swallowing. She was still in nappies and unable to indicate her toilet needs. She was aware of her two younger sisters and responded to affection. She had microcephaly. Developmentally she showed no responses beyond the six to seven month baby level. The maximum level of development she would ever attain with hard work by those around her would be about 12 to 15 months. She would need regular physiotherapy, and multi-disciplinary reports and evidence from her school identified many specific needs – including her need for 'one-to-one' attention throughout virtually all her waking hours. Life expectancy was at the top end of the bracket of 25 to 30 years old.

Held (April 1990): (i) general damages for pain, suffering and loss of amenities were assessed at £100,000.

(ii) special damages, including parents past care but deducting DSS benefits, totalled £54,449.

(iii) £33,605 was awarded for future aids and equipment, including a computer with a touch-screen.

(iv) £244,141 was awarded for the cost of future professional and parents' care, deducting future DSS benefits.

(v) £26,000 was awarded for future costs of physiotherapy.

(vi) £27,137 was awarded for future travel requirements.

(vii) her parents had built a bungalow at a cost of £169,460. 2% of this cost was awarded for 12.5 years, a sum of £42,365.

(viii) £16,062 was awarded for extra household expenses.

(ix) £20,000 was awarded for the plaintiff's future loss of earnings.

(x) £12,500 was awarded for additional holiday costs.

(xi) £13,475 was awarded for Court of Protection costs.

(xii) interest on general damages was £10,000. Interest on special damages was £14,000.

The total award including interest was £613,734.

See p 98.

Thomsen v Davison

Australia: army doctor: duty of care: pathologist: tests: kidney: communication

Supreme Court, Brisbane. [1975] Qd R 93

The plaintiff (Trooper Thomsen) was requested by his superiors to present himself for examination to the defendant (Dr Davison), the regimental medical officer, for the purpose of gaining admission to an officer's cadet training unit. Urine tests carried out by the defendant caused him to have doubts about the plaintiff's state of health. Therefore he requested him to have blood and urine tests at the laboratory of microbiology and pathology within the State Health Department. The defendant failed to ascertain the results, although it would have been easy for him to do so. Had he been aware of them, he would have advised the plaintiff to seek medical treatment because of the likelihood of his suffering from serious kidney disease.

Held: the defendant owed a duty of care to the plaintiff. He negligently failed to discharge this by ascertaining and communicating the test results.

Per W. B. Campbell J: 'Although the relationship of doctor and patient in the ordinary sense may not have existed between the first defendant and the plaintiff, and assuming for present purposes that it did not, it seems to me that a doctor who undertakes the examination of a person in order to assess his state of health has a duty of care (not merely to the Army, the insurance company or other employer as the case may be), to that person to conduct the examination competently. He is also under a duty to the examinee not to do anything, or to omit to do anything, in the course of performing the examination, which is likely to cause the latter damage. Dr Davison set in motion the taking of further tests and there is ample evidence to establish that it was understood by both parties that the doctor would follow up these tests. In effect, the jury have found that the doctor did not complete the examination upon which he had entered and, in the circumstances, this omission was such as to justify a finding that the doctor should reasonably have foreseen that it may cause harm to the plaintiff; the doctor had the task of watching over the health of the soldiers when they were in camp and on army duties, and should have been aware of the confidence and trust they were likely to place in him . . .

. . . In my opinion, a pathologist to whom samples of blood or urine or other specimens are referred for testing or analysis is under a duty to the patient not only to see that the tests are performed in a proper manner but also to take reasonable steps to ensure that the results are communicated to the referring doctor. The requirement to report or to communicate may be categorised as an administrative or ministerial duty rather than one appertaining to the performance of professional skills. In ordinary circumstances it is reasonably foreseeable by any pathologist that, should he omit to make known the results of the tests to the referring doctor, the patient may suffer damage. Dr Davison admitted that one of his functions as an employee of the Health Department was to ensure that information as to the tests performed in the laboratory was sent to the referring medical authority – in this instance to himself as the regimental medical officer of the 2/14th Queensland Mounted Infantry. In this respect no distinction should be drawn between the duty of a private pathologist, that of a pathologist in the employ of a public body or that of the proprietor (private or public) of the testing laboratory. It is not to the point that there was a corresponding duty upon the referring doctor to take steps to find out the results.'

Thorne v Northern Group Hospital Management Committee

Suicide risk: supervision: nurse: causation: fatal

Edmund Davies J. (1964) 108 Sol Jo 484

Mrs Thorne was a patient in a general hospital. The plaintiff (her husband) told the ward sister that she had threatened suicide. She was a suspected depressive. The hospital transferred her to one wing of two in a convalescent ward.

On 16 August 1960 she was due to be removed at 10.00am to an outside neurosis unit for further investigation. At 8.45am a nurse saw her sitting by her bed. At 9.00am the nurse and ward sister left the wing temporarily. Mrs Thorne walked out of the hospital, went to her home and committed suicide. The plaintiff sued the hospital authority.

Held: the degree of care and supervision required of hospital staff in relation to a patient with known or, perhaps, even suspected suicidal tendencies was greater than that called for in relation to patients generally. However, Mrs Thorne was set upon making her escape for the purposes of self-destruction and it was highly conceivable that she kept a wary eye on the nurses and seized her opportunity immediately their backs were turned and had absented themselves temporarily. That did not connote negligence on the part of the nurses.

Judgment for the defendants.

See pp 24, 132, 137.

Thornton and Others v Nicol

Baby: diagnosis: general practitioner: meningitis

Macpherson J. [1992] 3 Med LR 41

At 9am on 19 June 1984 Dr Nicol examined the plaintiff (Fiona Thornton), aged ten weeks, at her home. Her mother Mrs Thornton said 'look at her eye'. It was very badly swollen. He used suitable force to open it. The left eye was red in the conjunctiva. Some pus was present in it. Later in the consultation, Mrs Thornton told Dr Nicol about other matters including a 'swooshing' sickness which happened at 8.40am. He did not take off Fiona's clothes to examine her, but he weighed her, touched her forehead and flexed her neck. He diagnosed conjunctivitis, accompanied by 'oedema of lids' and prescribed sulphacetamide drops for her eye.

Dr Nicol called again at 9.15am on 20 June. The left eye had improved; the swelling was less. He put his hand on her head and fontanelle. Fiona's earlier projectile vomiting had improved, and her overall condition had not deteriorated. Dr Nicol was concerned about her, because she still had a bad eye and was unwell, but he did not think that she was particularly ill or that it was right to refer her to hospital. He noted 'Imp' for improved and resolved to see her again in two days' time.

At 4am on 21 June, Dr Jayasena, a deputising doctor, was called to the Thorntons' home. He was told that Fiona had been crying, and had been listless and moaning 'since last night'. He found that the anterior fontanelle was bulging and that Kernig's sign (rigidity in the lower limbs) was present. He provisionally diagnosed meningitis and sent the baby to Farnborough Hospital where the diagnosis was confirmed.

The original accusation against Dr Nicol was that he had missed the diagnosis of meningitis. It was subsequently accepted that meningitis did not develop before about 5pm on 20 June. The case against him at trial was that he failed to diagnose periorbital cellulitis or to refer the plaintiff to hospital by 9.30am on 20 June.

Held: (i)   upon a balance of probabilities, Dr Nicol was justified in concluding that she suffered from conjunctivitis. The improvement in her eye would have been remarkable in a case of periorbital cellulitis.

         (ii)   the plaintiff was not so ill that no reasonable doctor could have failed to send her to hospital. Violent vomiting was not a feature on 20 June. Dr Nicol's touching of the head and fontanelle did not show that the temperature was a matter for concern.

         (iii)   Dr Nicol had not been negligent.

See pp 99, 136.

Tombs v Merton and Sutton Area Health Authority

Anaesthetics: brain damage: damages: structured settlement

McPherson J. 11 December 1991

In August 1987, when aged 27, the plaintiff (Alan Tombs) was treated at Sutton General Hospital for anal dilatation and injection of haemorrhoids. In the process of administering anaesthesia, carbon dioxide was given by mistake. He suffered very severe brain damage in consequence.

Damages on the conventional basis amounted to £1,644,252. Interim payments of £244,252 had been made. £273,000 was paid over immediately for the purchase and adaptation of accommodation for Mr Tombs. £17,300 was paid to his wife and the balance to the Court of Protection. £950,000 was placed into the structure. The defendants received a discount of £100,000.

Interim payments	£244,252
Other lump sum payments	£335,000
Structured sum	£965,000
Defendant's discount	£100,000
Total	£1,644,252

A single annuity was purchased of £85,075 pa, retail price index-linked, payable for Mr Tombs' life or for ten years, whichever was the longer. This was considered sufficient to cover not only annual expenses but also the replacement cost of the capital items.

Mr Justice Macpherson approved the settlement in February 1992.

See p 122.

Tredget and Tredget v Bexley Health Authority

Childbirth: post-traumatic stress disorder: fatal

HH Judge White. [1994] 5 Med LR 178

The plaintiffs (Mr and Mrs Tredget) married in the mid-1980s. In August 1987 their first child was born at their local Farnborough Hospital by caesarean section, since, as an insulin dependant diabetic, Mrs Tredget was suffering from polyhydramnios. When she became pregnant again in 1989, she was very anxious to have a vaginal delivery. Since the obstetrician at Farnborough Hospital would not have agreed to this she was referred to Mrs Hannah, the consultant obstetrician and gynaecologist at Queen Mary's Hospital in Sidcup, who understood her wish to have a normal birth and was prepared to accept her as a patient on this basis.

On 5 November 1989, when she was just under 38 weeks pregnant, Mrs Tredget entered this hospital for labour to be induced. Strong contractions started during the evening of 7 November, so she was admitted to the labour ward just before midnight. No excessively high hydramnios was present, but scans had revealed that the baby was larger than average. Her waters broke about 1.00am on 8 November. Labour progressed normally until 2.00am when the cervix was noted to be seven centimetres dilated. Thereafter labour slowed. A decision to perform or at least strongly advise a caesarean section should have been taken at about 4.45am.

Mrs Tredget's condition was giving cause for concern by 8.30am when an attempt was made to stimulate the uterus. The fetal heart having shown deceleration, oxygen was administered. At 9.45am Mrs Hannah saw Mrs Tredget and, observing that there had been no progress since 9.30am, pushed the anterior lip of the cervix over the baby's head to allow it to come down. In accordance with her instructions, Mrs Tredget started pushing at 10.30am for half an hour, but without success. A vacuum extraction was then begun. When the baby's head appeared, the umbilical cord was found tied around its neck and had to be clamped and cut. The baby's shoulders then became caught within the pelvis, and it was necessary for a shoulder bone to be broken to allow the birth process to be completed. When the baby boy (Callum) was finally delivered at 11.32am on 8 November, he was in a severely asphyxiated condition with no heart beat detectable. He was resuscitated in the labour room behind where Mrs Tredget was lying and then placed in an incubator. His weight at birth was 9lbs 10oz.

Mrs Tredget found the birth of Callum with its immediate aftermath a long, painful and traumatic experience. After she had been trying to force the baby down, she said there came a time when 'all hell was let loose'. At the point which her husband described as 'pandemonium taking place', she became aware of a difficulty in getting the baby out. It took four minutes from the moment the head was out to deliver the rest of the body. Exhausted after 15 hours' labour, she did not see the baby when it was delivered. Mr Tredget witnessed the birth and saw that Callum was discoloured – black and mauve. A doctor came a little later to say – 'the good news is that he is alive, but the bad news is that he has a 60/70% chance of brain damage.'

On 9 November both Mr and Mrs Tredget saw Callum who was in an incubator in the special care unit. He deteriorated overnight. On 10 November his parents were advised that there was no hope for him, and the decision was taken to turn off the life support equipment. Arrangements were made for him to be christened, and Mrs Tredget held him in her arms before he died at 1.00pm.

Both Mr and Mrs Tredget suffered psychiatric illnesses which took the form of a complicated grief reaction riddled with grievance. The relationship was immediately adversely affected by Callum's death and, although a daughter was born by elective caesarean section in January 1992, the marriage finally broke down in June 1993. Mr Tredget had a nervous breakdown in 1992 and he continued to be a full time psychiatric patient thereafter.

The plaintiff sued the hospital authority who admitted negligence in respect of the failure to decide upon a caesarean section delivery by 4.45am. The authority accepted that the plaintiffs had suffered psychiatric illness, but argued that this resulted from grief rather than shock and was not compensatable.

Held: (i) as the plaintiffs were the parents of Callum, the requirement of proximity was clearly satisfied.

(ii)   so was that of reasonable foreseeability. Neo-natal death is a potent cause of psychiatric disturbance of the kind suffered by the plaintiffs.

(iii) each suffered a form of psychiatric illness. This was more than mere grief, distress or sorrow.

(iv)   the actual birth with its chaos or pandemonium, the difficulties that the mother had on delivery, the sense in the room that something was wrong on the arrival of the child in a distressed condition requiring immediate resuscitation was extremely frightening for the parents. It constituted a horrifying external event.

(v)   what happened was in full sight of the father. It would be unrealistic to distinguish the mother because she in labour, pain, sedated and suffering from exhaustion, was not fully conscious of what was happening about her. It would also be unrealistic to separate out and isolate the delivery as an event, from the other sequence of happenings from the onset of labour to Callum's death two days later.

(vi)   therefore the defendants were liable to pay damages to the parents for their psychiatric illnesses and consequential losses. (There had been no dispute over their liability to pay the bereavement award of £3,500 plus funeral expenses).

Note: The plaintiffs' cases were subsequently settled for £300,000.

See pp 51, 173.

Tomkins v Bexley Health Authority

Dental: lingual nerve: operation: senior house officer

HH Judge Wilcox. [1993] 4 Med LR 235

In March 1985 the plaintiff (Mrs Tomkins) was admitted to Queen Mary's Hospital in Sidcup for the removal of all four wisdom teeth. x-rays showed that three of the teeth were straightforwardly positioned. However, the lower left wisdom tooth was a deep horizontal impaction and uneruptive into the mouth; there was bone overlying the distal part of the crown.

Mr Byrne, a senior house officer, used the lingual split technique. He inserted a Howarth elevator between the bone of the mandible and the membrane of the bone. The three straightforward teeth were extracted. However, he was unable to extract the lower left wisdom tooth. Therefore he decided to use a drill with a burr end and to carry out a vertical section of the tooth. He did this by placing the round burr in the centre of the tooth and cutting vertically between the crown and the root. The tooth was thus divided into three pieces and removed. Then he carried out a debridement of the rough bone, washed out the cavity and stitched it with one stitch. The lingual nerve was 90% severed in that process.

The plaintiff suffered permanent pain and numbness in her tongue. She sued the hospital authority.

Held: (i)   it was appreciated in 1985 that the lingual nerve could be damaged when wisdom teeth were being removed. Mr Byrne knew of this risk.

(ii)   the procedures for sectioning a tooth, properly carried out by an experienced and careful operator, should not involve penetration of the lingual plate and the lingual tissues and severance of the lingual nerve. The fact that all these structures had been penetrated meant that the operator had been negligent.

The plaintiff was awarded agreed damages of £28,000 inclusive of interest.

Trew v Middlesex Hospital

Nurse: burns

Gerrard J. (1953) 1 Lancet 343

The plaintiff (Mr Trew), a private patient, was sitting in bed in the Middlesex Hospital. He had one leg in a sling and the other on a pillow. Considering this, he was sitting as upright as he comfortably could. A nurse, who was a small brisk woman in a hurry, placed a tea tray on his lap. The tray tilted and hot water from the jug was spilt on to the plaintiff.

He sustained burns and sued the hospital.

Held: the nurse had been negligent. She 'breezed into the room, put down the tray and went out, giving the patient no time to protest'.

See p 139.

Turner v N S Hair Treatment Clinic

Damages: hair: scarring

HH Judge Roberts. [1994] 10 CL 133

The plaintiff (Mr Turner), aged 41, underwent a hair replacement treatment known as 'interplant'. 6,500 artificial hairs were injected into his scalp under local anaesthetic over the course of 15 treatment sessions. His scalp became infected during the latter part of the treatment, but it was continued with the sole precaution of an anti-dandruff shampoo.

The plaintiff's scalp became increasingly painful. Soon after the end of the treatment, the artificial hair fell out and the infection remained producing pus. He was so embarrassed by the appearance of his scalp that he gave up work and effectively opted out of social life, which led to a permanent split from his girlfriend. He was left with noticeable scars and pitting on his scalp, with a distinct ridge extending from his hairline over his scalp, some areas of which remained sensitive. Although he gradually became more confident, he continually wore a hat when out in public and avoided bright lights which highlighted his scarring.

Held (September 1994): general damages of £4,500 were awarded for his pain, suffering and loss of amenities. Special damages were £7,100.

See p 141.

Tyndall v Alcock

Fracture: hospital doctor: child patient: arm

Court of Appeal. [1928] 1 BMJ 528

In July 1926 the plaintiff (Phyllis Tyndall), then aged eight, fell from a donkey and sustained a fracture of the lower end of the left humerus. She was taken to Gloucester where she was treated by Dr Alcock, first at a nursing home and later in the Gloucester Infirmary. He manipulated the bones into position and was satisfied that the fracture had been properly reduced. The arm was then suspended from the shoulder, and an x-ray was taken. The next day the hand was a little swollen, so the bandages were loosened. By the fifth day there was more discolouration. Dr Alcock realised that the circulation was obstructed, so the bandages were loosened further and the strapping removed. The plaintiff developed Volkmann's contracture. Her left arm became fixed at the elbow, resulting in permanent impairment of movement.

Her claim against Dr Alcock was heard before Shearman J and a special jury. The jury found that Dr Alcock had been negligent in failing to set the bone properly and in his subsequent treatment. He appealed to the Court of Appeal.

Held: the jury were the persons put there by the constitution to try actions involving questions of negligence. Since there was evidence before them on which they were entitled to find either way, it was impossible for a Court of Appeal to interfere with the result.

Udale v Bloomsbury Area Health Authority

Sterilisation (failed): wrongful birth: damages: public policy: fallopian tube

Jupp J. [1983] 2 All ER 522, [1983] 1 WLR 1098

By 1977 the plaintiff (Mrs Muriel Udale) and her husband had four children, all daughters. In October 1977 she underwent an operation for laparoscopic sterilisation. The operation failed. In June 1978 she was told that she was pregnant. In November 1978 she gave birth to a healthy baby boy.

She sued the hospital authority. The surgeon, who should have placed a metal clip on each fallopian tube in order to close it, in fact placed the right-hand clip, not on the fallopian tube but on a nearby ligament. The defendants admitted liability.

Held: (i) the plaintiff was awarded (February 1983) £8,000 general damages to compensate her for:

    (a) the shock and anxiety of an unwanted pregnancy;

    (b) her anger at the thwarting of her decision not to have further children;

    (c) the ordinary symptoms of pregnancy during the first three and a half months to June 1978, thought by her to be illness or disease, and the taking of unnecessary drugs to overcome them;

    (d) the subsequent symptoms of pregnancy and the fear after its diagnosis that the drugs may have harmed or deformed the child;

    (e) an operation for resterilisation two or three days after the birth;

    (f) an operation in September 1982 to remove the sterilisation clip on the left side.

(ii) she was also awarded £1,025 agreed damages in respect of her loss of earnings for eleven months, made necessary by the pregnancy and birth.

Note: In view of the Court of Appeal decisions in *Emeh v Kensington and Chelsea and Westminster Area Health Authority* and *Thake v Maurice*, the judge's decision to reject the cost of the child's upbringing on the ground of public policy is not good law.

See pp 55, 81, 128, 168, 169.

Upton v North Tees Health Authority

Deafness: diagnosis: meningitis: deafness

Court of Appeal. CAT 26 February 1993

On 17 August 1982 the plaintiff (Christopher Upton), aged 13, fell or rolled down a cliff near the beach at Whitby. The fall caused obvious and painful injuries to his left wrist, which was fractured, and to the left side of his face, in particular his nose. There was no loss of consciousness. He was taken to Whitby General Hospital where he was later recorded as having a good recall of the accident and was well orientated. x-rays were taken of the wrist and head. No basal fracture of the skull was shown on the x-ray. There was then no leak of CSF. He was allowed home and told to report to North Tees Hospital the next day.

On 18 August his mother took him to North Tees Hospital with the x-rays and a transfer letter from Whitby. He was seen by Mr Stothard, an orthopaedic surgeon in the fracture clinic, and was kept in hospital due to a complication from the way in which the fractured wrist had been carried in the sling. The ward sister, because he had suffered facial injuries, decided to keep four hourly observations on him and to that end provided a head chart. A nurse then, rather inaccurately, recorded in the nursing notes – 'Admitted for head injury observations, four hourly, elevation of arm'. The plaintiff did not have a visible drip of CSF from his nose. No test to detect a CSF leak was carried out. Dr Baliga and Dr Das Gupta examined him after his admission to the ward in the morning. Dr Das Gupta examined him upon his discharge home that evening.

By 20 August the plaintiff was ill: he complained of a violent headache and being unable to hear. On 22 August he was referred back to North Tees Hospital and found to be suffering from meningitis, which was treated with penicillin. He was sent home on 8 September 1982. By then irreversible damage had been done to his hearing. His deafness had been caused by CSF rhinorrhea following the fall.

The trial judge rejected the plaintiff's primary case that the doctors and nurses failed to observe an obvious CSF leak by intermittent dripping from his nose on 18 August. The judge's conclusion that Mr Stothard's failure to examine for a CSF leak and to exclude the risk by means of the test was reasonable, having regard to the known facts and signs, was accepted. The plaintiff's case on appeal was that Dr Baliga and Dr Das Gupta failed by use of a simple pressure test to discover the presence of a lesion or leak, despite the absence of any observable drip.

Held: the judge's findings that there was no visible CSF leak and that the admission was for the wrist injury were accepted. The notes made by Dr Baliga demonstrated beyond peradventure that he either formed his own view that this was not a serious head injury case or that he had been told of Mr Stothard's opinion that it was not. On either basis there was no negligence. The mere presence of the head chart did not constitute an instruction to Dr Baliga or Dr Das Gupta to carry out the tests there listed. The plaintiff's appeal must be dismissed.

Urbanski v Patel et al; Firman et al v Patel

Surgeon: duty of care to third party: Canada: kidney: foreseeability

Manitoba Queen's Bench (Wilson J). (1978) 84 DLR (3d) 650

In April 1975 Mrs Shirley Firman entered the Gimli Hospital for a tubal ligation. As she had felt occasional abdominal discomfort, it was agreed that Mr Patel, the surgeon, should explore for and if necessary remove any ovarian cyst causing this. Instead, by mistake, he removed her only kidney.

Mrs Firman's father, Victor Urbanski, donated one of his own kidneys. This was implanted in May 1976. Unfortunately Mrs Firman's body rejected the kidney, and she had to go back on to dialysis.

Mr and Mrs Firman and Mr Urbanski sued Mr Patel who admitted negligence. He conceded liability to the Firmans but not to Mr Urbanski.

Held: in the light of today's medicine, kidney transplant is an accepted remedy in renal failure. The transplant must be viewed as an expected result, something to be expected as a consequence of loss of normal kidney function. It was entirely foreseeable that one of Mr Firman's family would be invited, and would agree, to donate a kidney for transplant: an act according with the principle developed in the many 'rescue' cases. Mr Patel was liable to Mr Urbanski as well as the Firmans.

See p 51.

Urry v Bierer and Another

Childbirth: caesarian: retained surgical product: surgeon: nurses

Court of Appeal. (1955) Times, 15 July

The plaintiff (Mrs Ellen Urry) underwent an operation by Mr Bierer, a gynaecological surgeon, for delivery of a child by lower caesarian section. The Harley Street Nursing Home Limited provided the surgical packs which were about ten inches square. The sister counted them before and after use. One was left in the plaintiff's body.

The plaintiff sued the nursing home and Mr Bierer. The nursing home admitted liability for the sister's count having been wrong. The trial judge (Pearson J) found Mr Bierer and the nursing home liable in equal shares. Mr Bierer appealed.

Held: the patient was entitled to expect that the surgeon would do what is reasonable to ensure that packs were removed from the body before he asked the sister if the count was correct. The one was independent of the other. The sister's count was an additional check for the protection both of the patient and of the surgeon. That it failed occasionally only emphasised the need for diligence on the part of the surgeon in that respect. Mr Bierer had insisted that he was entitled to rely on the sister's count, and his technique did not include any particular effort to remember or have himself reminded of the location of particular packs. He fell far short of the standard of care required of him and was equally liable with the sister.

See pp 125, 139.

Vancouver General Hospital v McDaniel and Another

Hospital administration: duty of care: infection: smallpox: Canada: fever

Privy Council. (1934) 152 LT 56, (1934) WN 171

On 17 January 1932 Annabelle McDaniel, aged nine, who was then suffering from diphtheria, was admitted to the Infectious Diseases Hospital in Vancouver. At that time there was smallpox in Vancouver. Between 18 and 29 January seven smallpox patients were admitted and placed in rooms on the same floor. The hospital's policy was to deal with this by a system of sterilisation rather than isolation. Nevertheless on 29 January Annabelle was removed to another floor on her doctor's request.

On 12 February she was diagnosed as suffering from smallpox. She suffered personal disfigurement and sued the hospital, alleging negligence in juxtaposing the smallpox patients on the same floor as her and in allowing nurses who also nursed the smallpox patients to attend on her. The trial judge found in her favour.

Held: the system adopted by the hospital was in accord with general if not universal practice in Canada and the United States. A defendant charged with negligence can clear himself if he shows that he has acted in accord with general and approved practice. The hospital had established this and was not liable.

See p 131.

Vaughan v Paddington and North Kensington Area Health Authority

Cancer: diagnosis: scarring: mastectomy: damages: breast

Boreham J. [1987] 3 PMILL 66

In July 1981 the plaintiff (Mrs Vaughan), a middle aged woman with two adult children, had a lump in her right breast. She was referred to St Mary's Hospital where after a biopsy she was told that she had cancer of the breast. In September both her breasts were removed in a mastectomy operation. There was persistent bleeding. In October the prosthesis in the right breast was removed, and in December 1981 the left prosthesis was removed. She underwent unsuccessful plastic surgery to reconstitute the nipples. A further operation was required in February 1984 to insert a larger prosthesis in her left breast.

It was then discovered that she had never had cancer at all. She sued the health authority who admitted that they had been negligent.

The plaintiff was left with scars which had once been very unsightly but had been substantially improved by cosmetic surgery. She suffered permanent pain and restriction of movement of her back and arms. She was very sensitive to the removal of her breasts. For two and a half years she had been led to believe that she had cancer, and there were times when she thought that she was going to die.

Held: (i) she was awarded (October 1986) £25,000 general damages for pain, suffering and loss of amenities.

(ii) she was also awarded £3,000 in respect of her inability to do her housework, £15,000 for the cost of future help, £13,870 for wages lost to date of trial, £36,000 for future loss of earnings as a chambermaid and miscellaneous expenses of £105.32.

See pp 99, 156.

Venner v North East Essex Area Health Authority and Another

Sterilisation (failed): pregnancy: advice

Tucker J. (1987) Times, 21 February, (1987) 1 Lancet 638

The plaintiff (Mrs Venner) was a married woman born in August 1954. She had four children aged at trial between five and fourteen. She sued the first defendants (North East Essex AHA) and the second defendant (Mr Donald Morrison, a gynaecologist) arising out of the birth of the youngest child.

The plaintiff used the contraceptive pill and conceived on withdrawal from it. In 1978 she became pregnant when she forgot to take the pill. The second defendant terminated that pregnancy. He declined to sterilise her at the time in view of her age (then 24).

In 1980 the second defendant agreed to sterilise the plaintiff. Owing to the risk of thrombosis, he told her to come off the pill one month before the operation. He advised her that either she should abstain from sex or her husband should use a sheath. Neither precaution was taken.

On the morning of the operation the second defendant checked that the plaintiff still wanted the operation. He told her that the operation would not terminate any pregnancy and asked whether she might be pregnant; she replied that she was certain that she was not. The operation took place on the twenty-seventh day of her menstrual cycle. No dilatation and curettage (D and C) was performed.

In fact the plaintiff was pregnant. She later gave birth to a healthy child. An expert called on her behalf at the trial said that he always performed a D and C and that, if this had been done, the plaintiff would probably not have remained pregnant.

Held: the defendants were not negligent. The second defendant was justified in advising the plaintiff to come off the pill before the operation. It was neither necessary nor desirable for a D and C to be performed as a matter of course.

See p 128.

Vernon v Bloomsbury Health Authority

Prescription: tests: causation: Taiwan and Australia

Tucker J. [1986] 3 MLJ 190

In the summer of 1982 the plaintiff went on holiday to Taiwan and Australia where she contracted two infections. She continued to feel unwell and was admitted to hospital. On 16 and 17 November her condition was diagnosed as subacute bacterially negative endocarditis. All attempts to grow an organism from blood culture failed. She was given a nineteen day course of 1.2g of intravenous benzylpenicillin four-hourly plus a loading dose of gentamicin (160mg intravenously) followed by 120mg eight-hourly (360mg) per day. She weighed 64kg. The treatment lasted from 17 November to 6 December. The hospital monitored the trough levels of her blood up to 29 November but did not monitor the peak levels at all. Her temperature remained normal throughout.

Soon after the end of the treatment, the plaintiff suffered symptoms of irreversible bilateral vestibular damage. She sued the hospital authorities, alleging that she had been given excessive amounts of gentamicin for too long and that they had not monitored her blood levels adequately.

Held: the dose given was a proper one, and the hospital had acted in the plaintiff's best interests by continuing treatment for nineteen days. Extra monitoring would have had no effect on the outcome, since probably no danger would have been revealed. The hospital doctors had conformed with a proper standard of treatment. The defendants were not liable.

See pp 69, 121.

Voller v Portsmouth Corpn

Injection: infection: hospital administration: meningitis: res ipsa loquitur: femur: paraplegia

Birkett J. (1947) 203 LTJ 264

In April 1944 the plaintiff (Edwin Voller) fractured a femur while playing football and was admitted to St Mary's Hospital, Portsmouth. Dr Hans, senior resident medical officer, gave him a spinal injection of Nupercaine in the ward with a needle and syringe. A few days later the plaintiff was diagnosed as suffering from meningitis. Owing to the injection, he became permanently disabled, both legs being paralysed.

The plaintiff sued the hospital authority and three of the hospital doctors.

Held: (i)   the surface skin of the plaintiff was properly cleansed before the operation and Dr Hans prepared himself in the approved way by washing his hands and did all that was required. There was no evidence of negligence against the three doctors.

         (ii)   as the bacillus entered the plaintiff's body from without at the moment of the injection, there must have been some breach of the aseptic technique at the hospital. The only remaining source of infection was in the apparatus used for the operation. This was within the control of the hospital and its staff. The infection would not have arisen without negligence on their part and must have been due to a breach of the aseptic technique. The hospital authority was liable.

See pp 122, 131.

Waghorn v Lewisham and North Southwark Area Health Authority

Surgeon: operation: limitation

SN McKinnon QC. QBD 23 June 1987

The plaintiff (Mrs Waghorn) went to Guy's Hospital because she had a very short perineum which was causing marital problems. Her case was that she requested an operation which would lengthen the perineum and tighten the introitus, whereas instead on 31 March 1977 Mr Thomkinson performed an operation which shortened the perineum and opened the introitus further. On 4 April 1977, upon examining herself, she ascertained what had happened.

In May 1978 the plaintiff complained to Guy's Hospital through the Community Health Council. In September 1978 she notified the hospital health authority of her claim for damages. In May 1979 she instructed solicitors who commissioned a report from Mr Coden, a consultant obstetrician and gynaecologist. Following Mr Coden's report, counsel was instructed in December 1979 and advised that there had been no negligence in the 1977 operation.

In July 1980 Mr Coden performed a further operation on the plaintiff. In January 1982 he advised that if her narrative was correct the hospital might have been at fault. In February 1982 her solicitors advised her that she could have a claim. In April 1983 she changed her solicitors. Sometime in 1983 Mr Coden operated again. In April 1984 the writ was issued. It was not served until nearly a year later. There was a preliminary trial of the limitation defence.

Held: (i) the plaintiff knew that her injury was significant in April 1977. Time began to run against her then. It was immaterial that she did not have supporting expert medical advice until 1982. Accordingly her action had been brought outside the primary period specified by s11 of the Limitation Act 1980.

(ii) part of the delay (from early 1982 onwards) was inexcusable. However, the defendants knew about the plaintiff's complaints in 1978, and all the hospital records except for the nursing notes had been preserved. Further surgery in 1980 and 1983 had obscured the surgical procedures that were undertaken in 1977. Even so, the evidence had been rendered only marginally less cogent by the delay since 1980. The potential prejudice to the plaintiff, who would be left effectively without a remedy, outweighed that to the defendant. The court's discretion under s 33 of the Limitation Act 1980 was exercised in the plaintiff's favour to allow her action to proceed.

See pp 118, 195.

Walker v Eli Lilly & Co

Discovery: drugs: Opren

Hirst J. [1986] NLJ Rep 608

The plaintiff was claiming damages against Eli Lilly & Co and others for personal injuries resulting from alleged side-effects of the drug Opren. She applied under s 34(2) of the Supreme Court Act 1981 against a health authority, which was not a party to the action, seeking discovery of her hospital and medical notes and records of the relevant treatment carried out. During extensive correspondence, which had lasted nearly a year, the health authority had been reluctant to release these documents.

Held: the plaintiff's application for discovery was granted.

Per Hirst J: 'Availability of such notes and records is, of course, essential both to the plaintiff and defendants and, indeed, to the court itself, for the proper conduct and disposal of the litigation . . .

Where, as in the present case, no special consideration of confidentiality is invoked, the court will almost certainly order disclosure if a summons should become necessary. It is, therefore, very much to be hoped that in future health authorities and medical practitioners will respond readily and promptly to any requests for disclosure in such cases, so that unnecessary expense and delay can be avoided.

Needless to say, where in any case special considerations arise, such as a particular reason for confidentiality, the authority or medical practitioner would be fully justified in having the matter tested in court.

One problem which arose in the present case, and which may arise elsewhere, was the anxiety on the part of the health authority that any documents disclosed might subsequently be used against them; it will, I hope, be some reassurance on this score for me to emphasise that, under well- established principles, there is an implied undertaking by a party seeking discovery in legal proceedings that documents so obtained will be used only for the purpose of those proceedings and for no other purpose'.

See p 209.

Walker v Semple

Causation: diagnosis: psychiatric patient: depression: schizophrenia

Court of Appeal. CAT, 30 March 1993

The plaintiff (Mr Walker) was employed as a clerk by the Liverpool City Council. His history had been blighted by nervous problems. He was depressed, and in May 1980 he took an overdose. From November 1980 to March 1981 he was a psychiatric in-patient at St Catherine's Hospital in Liverpool. Professor Semple, an occupational health physician with experience of psychiatry, examined the plaintiff at the Council's request. He found that he was untidy in appearance, jumped from one topic to another during conversation, talked repetitively, was irrational and manifested a sense of persecution. These factors led him to diagnose the plaintiff as suffering from schizophrenia and hypomania. He communicated this diagnosis to the Council, together with a recommendation that the plaintiff be retired from his post. The Council dismissed him with effect from November 1981.

The plaintiff sued Professor Semple. His medical expert, a consultant psychiatrist at one of the hospitals where he had been treated, testified that from first to last the plaintiff had been suffering from a mental disorder, namely depression, but that he had never suffered from either schizophrenia or hypomania. The trial judge accepted this, but noted that other doctors had concluded that the plaintiff had suffered from a schizophrenic form of illness earlier in his life or suspected schizophrenia at the material time. He dismissed the plaintiff's claim.

Held: (i) the judge was plainly entitled to find that the defendant's error in diagnosis did not amount to negligence, for it was reached upon information which might well have misled the ordinary, competent doctor.

(ii) equally the judge was entitled to find that, even if the defendant had diagnosed depression, he would still have advised that the plaintiff was permanently unfit and should be retired, so the mistaken diagnosis had not caused any damage or loss.

See pp 46, 100.

Walker v South West Surrey District Health Authority

Childbirth: injection: nurse: leg: damages

Court of Appeal. CAT, 17 June 1982

On 22 March 1978 the plaintiff (Mrs Danielle Walker) went into St Luke's Hospital to have her third child. At about 11.00pm on 23 March she was given an injection of pethidine by the midwife, Sister Dyer. Dr Champion noted on 24 March: 'also complaining of paraesthesia of the right leg. L1, L2. distribution distal to the injection site of pethidine', with a drawing showing an area of paraesthesia extending from around the middle of the thigh down to the ankle and an arrow pointing to an injection site on the inner side of the right thigh.

The injection damaged a superficial nerve, leaving the plaintiff with an area of numbness in her right leg. She sued the hospital authority. The trial judge (HH Judge Vick) found in her favour and awarded £1,000 damages.

Held: the judge had been right to accept the plaintiff's evidence that the injection was given to her on the inner side of the right thigh. No careful nurse or doctor would give an injection there in the absence of some compelling reason. It was clearly negligent.

See pp 120, 138.

Walkin v South Manchester Health Authority

Limitation: sterilisation (failed)

Court of Appeal NLP, 27 June 1995

In 1986 the plaintiff (Ms Walkin) underwent a sterilisation operation carried out by the defendants' surgeon. In 1987 she became pregnant. In 1989 her first writ was issued, but it was never secured. Her second writ in 1991 claimed damages only for financial loss resulting from the alleged negligence. The defendants pleaded limitation.

Held: an unwanted pregnancy does not create two different causes of action according to the damages claimed. The personal injury is the impairment of the mother's physical condition by the unwanted pregnancy. The birth and its subsequent costs were caused by this personal injury. The plaintiff could not avoid the three year limitation period by claiming only damages in respect of financial loss. Her case was statute-barred.

Note: The Court of Appeal reserved the question of whether the position in cases of failed male sterilisation is different.

See pp 29, 128, 168, 172, 179.

Waller and Waller v Canterbury and Thanet Health Authority

Damages: post-traumatic stress disorder: suicide: supervision: fatal

HH Judge Peppitt QC. Unreported

Mark Waller, aged 20, was admitted as a voluntary patient to St Augustine's Hospital. The plaintiffs (his parents) had warned the hospital of his suicidal tendencies; they were assured that he would not be let out of the ward. A few days later, they found that he had been able to enter a disused building on the hospital site; they were given a similar assurance. On the fifth day, when Mark was again found to be missing from the ward, the plaintiffs suggested that he might have gone to the same disused building. The hospital staff failed to carry out any proper search, and Mark was not found. At 9pm the plaintiffs conducted their own search. They went to the disused building where they found their son's body hanging dead by a rope from a pipe. The hospital authority admitted liability.

Mr Waller, aged 43, felt depressed and cried when thinking of his son. His sleep was disturbed, and he had dreams of his son hanging. During the day he had unpleasant images of what had occurred. He was generally lacking in energy and interest, and could see little point in going on with life. He had become forgetful and his concentration was poor. Occasional headaches experienced previously had become much worse. At the time of the hearing he was still receiving counselling from a community psychiatric nurse as well as medication from his general practitioner. Nine months after his son's death he was certified unfit to work and he was still unfit to work at the time of the hearing. He had been in partnership with his son in a fishing boat which was now uneconomic to run and the boat had to be sold. By reason of his depressive illness he was unable to follow other work. The prognosis was that he would recover slowly over the course of one to two years after the conclusion of litigation and at best after one year.

The condition of Mrs Waller, aged 44, was similar. She felt low, had no interest in doing anything, was impatient and irritable, and was frequently tearful. She had disturbed sleep and dreams of losing babies. She had been drinking excessively to help her sleep. When awake she had images of her son hanging or in his coffin. She was also receiving medication and counselling. The prognosis was the same as her husband. Before her son's death she had planned to take in foreign language students as additional income when they had succeeded in buying a bigger property, but this plan was abandoned.

Held (September 1993):   (i)   general damages of £8,500 for pain, suffering and loss of amenities were awarded to each plaintiff.

                       (ii)   for loss of earnings, Mr Waller was awarded £19,850 and Mrs Waller £1,000.

Walton v Lief and Another

Alternative practitioner: representations: naturopath: osteopath: breach of contract: causation: damages

Lord Chief Justice (with special jury). (1933) 1 BMJ 132, (1933) 2 Lancet 147

The plaintiff (Mrs Eleanor Walton) suffered from lupus erythematosus. In February 1932 Mr Stanley Lief MNCA, an osteopath and naturopath, warranted that he would cure her completely if she undertook his treatment. She spent five weeks at his sanatorium in Champneys where she was subjected to a starvation diet and repeated light treatment from a mercury vapour lamp. She then underwent further treatment from him at Park Lane. Her face and scalp became permanently disfigured.

The plaintiff sued Mr Lief and his company, Natural Healing Ltd, for breach of warranty and negligence. He explained in evidence that MNCA meant 'Member Nature Cure Association' of which he was president. Expert testimony was that starvation treatment was a bad preface to any local treatment and that ultra-violet rays were irritating unless applied in very small doses. Lupus erythematosus had an inherent tendency to flare up, and it was doubted whether ultra-violet rays would cause it to do so.

Held: (i)   the jury found that Mr Lief was in breach of his warranty to effect a complete cure of her disease, and assessed her damages under this head as the amount of the bill.

        (ii)   the jury also found that he had been negligent in his treatment and awarded one farthing damages (possibly because they decided that the negligence had little causative effect).

See pp 30, 141.

Ward v Wakefield Health Authority

Damages: diagnosis: fracture: femur

HH Judge Herrod. [1993] CLY 1558

The plaintiff (Mrs Ward), aged 92, presented at hospital with an undisplaced inter-trochanteric fracture of the left femur. There was a failure to diagnose this. She was admitted into a geriatric ward for mobilisation. Nursing staff spent three days attempting to cajole her into using her leg. Eventually she was discharged home to the care of her daughter.

She suffered continual pain and discomfort and needed continuous nursing. She was visited by a consultant whose handling of her leg caused traumatic discomfort, and the fracture became displaced. After 17 days, the fracture was finally diagnosed and was repaired by insertion of enders nails. The delayed diagnosis prolonged her recovery by three months.

Held (July 1993): (i) general damages were assessed at £100 per day for the first 17 days plus £1,000 for prolonged recovery, a total of £2,700 for pain, suffering and loss of amenities.

                (ii) special damages for nursing care were assessed at £2.77 per hour × 24 hours for the first 17 days, a total of £1,130, plus £2,494 for nursing during the three month period.

Warren v Greig; Warren v White

Dental: general practitioner: diagnosis: teeth: leukaemia: fatal

McKinnon J. (1935) 1 Lancet 330

Mr Warren was under treatment for lumbago and sciatica. His doctor, observing the presence of pyorrhoea, advised a dental examination. A dentist was called in and, on the joint advice of doctor and dentist, Mr Warren consented to the extraction of his teeth. All 28 teeth were extracted in one operation at 2.00pm with the doctor administering the anaesthetic. Bleeding persisted despite remedial measures.

At 5.55pm Mr Warren was removed to hospital where he died within 24 hours. Post-mortem examination revealed acute leukaemia. The plaintiff (his widow) sued the dentist and the doctor.

Held: (i) the mere performance of a mass extraction was not negligence. When a dentist was acting in conjunction with a doctor, it was no part of the dentist's duty to discover the general health of the patient or to search for abnormal signs. The dentist had not been negligent.

      (ii) having regard to the rarity of acute leukaemia, it was not necessary to carry out a blood test as a safeguard against the possibility of the patient suffering from it. The doctor failed to find the disease without having been negligent.

Judgment for the defendants.
See pp 98, 130.

Waters and Another v Park

Sterilisation (failed): risk disclosure

Havers J. (1961) Times, 15 July

The plaintiff (Mrs Waters) had a weak heart and was advised that she should have an operation for hysterectomy and sterilisation. An operation for sterilisation (but not for hysterectomy) was performed on 29 May 1956 by Mr Park at Selly Oak Hospital, Birmingham. In view of her cardiac trouble, he used a less efficient method of sterilisation that carried a slight risk of failure.

Mr Park's standard practice was to tell a patient of this risk. However, he did not tell the plaintiff in hospital because she was in an extremely congested ward with beds down the middle and no source of privacy. Instead he gave her an appointment to see him about six weeks after her discharge from hospital so that he could tell her then. She never kept the appointment.

On 3 July 1957 the plaintiff gave birth to a still-born child and had to undergo a further operation for sterilisation. She sued Mr Park.

Held: there was no generally approved practice at the time about telling patients of the risk; there were two schools of thought. In the light of current medical practice and opinion, a surgeon did not fall short of the proper standards of his profession if, in circumstances such as these, he did not tell the patient that there was a slight risk or did not advise her to use contraceptives. The risk of pregnancy within six weeks was very slight, and the chances were generally only about six in one thousand. There were reasons which made it impracticable for Mr Park to tell the plaintiff in the ward. He had not committed any breach of duty by not telling her afterwards of the slight risk of failure.

See p 106.

Wells v Surrey Area Health Authority

Sterilisation: consent: advice: damages: loss of chance

Croom Johnson J. (1978) Times, 29 July

The plaintiff (Mrs Doreen Wells), a Roman Catholic, was thirty-five years of age and having trouble with her third pregnancy. It was the defendant hospital's practice, if a woman who already had two or three children needed a caesarian operation, to offer to sterilise her at the same time. Sterilisation had not been mentioned during the antenatal period and was first suggested to the plaintiff when she was in labour. There was no medical necessity. The hospital did not counsel her about the sterilisation, and she was in a state of some exhaustion when she consented.

The baby was born alive and well, but the plaintiff bitterly regretted the sterilisation. She sued the hospital authority.

Held: (i)   the plaintiff understood the implication of the operation when she signed a consent form authorising the hospital to carry it out. Her claim for assault failed.

  (ii)   counselling is an important preliminary to sterilisation. The hospital had been negligent in failing to give her proper advice about it.

  (iii)   she was awarded (July 1978) £3,000 general damages, covering the loss of a 'somewhat remote chance' of having another baby.

See p 106.

Westaway v South Glamorgan Health Authority

Dismissal for want of prosecution: diagnosis: fracture: ankle

Court of Appeal. CAT, 9 June 1986

On 29 May 1976 the plaintiff (Brian Westaway) fell in his garden and injured his left ankle. On the same day he attended Cardiff Royal Infirmary. In March 1977 he wrote to the health authority to complain of his treatment. His writ was issued in April 1979 and served in June 1979. The Statement of Claim was served in April 1980. The defendants' solicitors persistently indicated a willingness to settle the case. They served the Defence in May 1983. In October 1983 the plaintiff amended his Statement of Claim to allege failure to diagnose a Pott's fracture and the consequent provision of inappropriate treatment. The amended

Defence was served in January 1984. The defendants' solicitors still indicated that they regarded it as a case for full liability settlement. The plaintiff's solicitors failed to respond to a request for quantification. In June 1985 the defendants issued a summons to dismiss the action for want of prosecution.

Held: (i)   the delay was inordinate and parts of it were inexcusable.

          (ii)   as the only negligence now relied upon was the failure to diagnose the Pott's fracture at the plaintiff's original attendance at Cardiff Royal Infirmary, which must be substantially if not entirely a question of the medical records and expert evidence, there was no particular prejudice to the defendants. The general principle that all delay is prejudicial was not enough to require the drastic step of dismissing the action.

See p 203.

Whichello v Medway and Gravesend Hospital Management Committee and Another

Surgeon: operation: tests: appendicitis

Ashworth J. (1963) 108 Sol Jo 55

In 1958 the plaintiff (Mr Whichello) underwent an operation for appendicitis and was discharged from hospital. Four days later he was readmitted for a second operation as the wound was infected. The surgeon in charge of the case did not order a culture to be taken. The wound did not heal properly and a third operation was performed. Still the wound did not heal. A fourth operation was undertaken and antibiotics were administered, after which the wound healed and the plaintiff was discharged from hospital.

He sued the health authority and the surgeon, alleging that they were negligent in failing to take a culture or administer antibiotics earlier than they did. Expert evidence was given at trial that a culture would have been an essential step, had a decision then been made to treat the infection by administering antibiotics, but was not a necessary prerequisite of the treatment followed, namely an operation to reopen and drain the wound. It was realised that antibiotics, in some circumstances, had disadvantages greater than those the antibiotics were intended to cure.

Held: it would have been wise to take a culture before the second operation. The surgeon had, however, decided to dispose of the case by surgery and, in view of the state of medical opinion then, he was not negligent in doing that. It was one thing to say that it was wiser to take a step, quite another to say that it was negligent not to do so. The defendants were not liable.

See p 134.

White v Board of Governors of Westminster Hospital and Another

Surgeon: operation: ophthalmic

Thompson J. (1961) Times, 26 October

The plaintiff (Robert White) suffered from an inveterate squint in his right eye. In June 1955, when he was nine years old, Mr McAuley performed a cosmetic operation on him at the Westminster Hospital. In the course of the operation, while cutting muscle and tendon attached by scar tissue, Mr McAuley unintentionally cut through to the retina. The eye became shrunken and useless and had to be removed.

The plaintiff sued Mr McAuley and the hospital authority.

Held: the plaintiff was the victim of mischance. The scale of the parts involved was very small, and Mr McAuley exercised due skill, care and judgment. He had not been negligent.

See p 116.

White et al v Turner et al

Canada: informed consent: mammoplasty: plastic surgery: breast: operation: scarring

Ontario High Court of Justice, Linden J. (1981) 120 DLR (3d) 269

The plaintiff (Mrs Nancy White) a legal secretary, was unhappy with the size of her breasts. Although she was only 5' 1" tall and weighed 135lbs, her breasts measured 41" around, as contrasted with her waist which measured 32" and her hips which measured 39". When she bent forward her breasts measured 45" which she agreed could be described as 'pendulous'. She had deep grooves in her shoulders from the straps of her brassiere.

In August 1976 she consulted the defendant (Dr Turner) about breast reduction surgery. He told her about the risks of fat necrosis, infection and haematoma and indicated, in a general way, that the incisions would leave some scarring. He did not tell her about the possibility that the shape of her breasts after surgery might not be perfect. Nor did he say anything about the possibility that her nipples might be asymmetrical. He did not inform her that the scars on her breasts might be two to three inches wide. She decided to have the operation, the main purpose of which was cosmetic.

In October 1976 Dr Turner performed the mammoplasty at the Sudbury Memorial Hospital. He employed the Strombeck method and altogether removed 705gr of tissue from both breasts. He did not tack the flaps of skin together with a few sutures at the end of the surgery, in order to make a judgment about the bulk of the breasts. The operation took one hour and 35 minutes.

Although the plaintiff's breasts finally healed, their shape was not a success. The bottoms of her breasts had a box-like appearance. The nipples were too high on the breasts, and they looked in. There were scars two to three inches wide from her nipples to the bottoms of her breasts. There were also two z-shaped scars, nearly three inches long, below the folds of both breasts. Her husband was 'disgusted' by them. Dr Turner admitted that the result of the operation was 'not 100%'.

In February 1977 he commenced a corrective operation under local anaesthetic but he had to abort it when the plaintiff noticed blood running down her body and fainted. In May 1978 another plastic surgeon performed a 'Clouthier operation' on her in Toronto, removing another 350gr from both breasts together. The plaintiff was relatively pleased with the end result.

Held: (i)   the poor outcome of the October 1976 mammoplasty was the result of the defendant's negligent execution of the surgery. The reason for the bad result was that he removed insufficient tissue; he should have taken out an additional 300 to 350gr. His failure to do so resulted from two factors connoting negligence: (a) the operation was done too quickly, and (b) the suturing was started before a proper check was made of whether enough tissue had been removed.

(ii) the information given to a patient was to be analysed, not by the professional medical standard, but by the reasonable patient standard. The test was what a reasonable patient in the position of the plaintiff would consider to be 'material risks' or 'special or unusual risks' about which he would want to receive information.

(iii) where an operation is elective, as this one was, even minimal risks must be disclosed to patients. A fortiori in a case where the predominant aim is cosmetic, possible risks affecting the appearance of the breasts such as undue scarring, the box-like appearance and the poor position of the nipples must be classified as material. The defendant's failure to disclose these risks was negligent. Had he done so, the plaintiff would not have undergone the operation.

See p 108.

Whiteford v Hunter

Surgeon: operation: diagnosis: cancer: tests: prostate: bladder

House of Lords [1950] WN 553, 94 Sol Jo 758

In March 1942 the plaintiff (Mr Whiteford), a consulting engineer, entered an English hospital and was seen by Mr Hunter, a consulting surgeon. The plaintiff's bladder was emptied and drained. In April Mr Hunter operated on him, with a view to removing his prostate. Near the base of the bladder he saw what he described as an indurated mass about the size of a palm of a man's hand. At no stage did he use a cystoscope or make a biopsy. He concluded that the plaintiff was suffering from inoperable cancer and so informed his wife, intimating that his life could only last a matter of months.

In this belief, the plaintiff closed down his practice, sold his home and went to the United States. A cystoscope examination there, followed by pathological analysis, showed the presence of chronic cystitis and a benign prostate hypertrophy. There was no trace of cancer.

The plaintiff sued Mr Hunter. His two main criticisms were:

(i) that no cystoscope was used before the opening of the bladder; and
(ii) no specimen of the growth was taken in order to test microscopically whether it was cancerous or not.

All the English medical witnesses testified that it was against approved practice in England to use a cystoscope where there was acute urinary retention, and that when the bladder was drained and collapsed, it was difficult if not impossible to use one effectively unless it were of the flushing type, an instrument which was rare in England in 1942 and which Mr Hunter did not possess. Mr Hunter testified that a biopsy would have involved a serious risk of perforating the bladder wall and that, if the condition were cancerous, an unhealing ulcer would supervene.

Held: a defendant charged with negligence can clear himself if he shows that he acted in accord with general and approved practice. Mr Hunter was not negligent in not using a cystoscope. He explained why he did not make a biopsy. His actions conformed to the proper professional practice of the time. He was not liable.

See pp 98, 179.

Whitehouse v Jordan and Another

Childbirth: registrar: brain damage: error of judgment: senior registrar

House of Lords. [1981] 1 All ER 267, [1981] 1 WLR 246

Mrs Whitehouse had been seen during her pregnancy by a number of doctors at Queen Elizabeth Hospital, Edgbaston. She was a small woman aged thirty and had been identified as a difficult case. On 31 December 1969 Professor McLaren recorded that he thought the outlet was tight and that a trial labour would be needed. When she was admitted to hospital on 6 January 1970 it was noted that she was carrying a 'fair-sized baby'.

Mr Jordan, a senior registrar of near consultant status, embarked on a trial of forceps delivery at 11.45pm on 6 January. He was trying to see whether, with the use of forceps, a delivery *per vaginam* was possible. After pulling with five or six contractions, he decided that a vaginal delivery would be too traumatic. Consequently he proceeded to perform a caesarian section.

The baby (Stuart Whitehouse) was born apnoeic. He was made to breathe after 35 minutes, by which time irreversible brain damage had occurred. He sued Mr Jordan and the hospital authority. The trial judge (Bush J) concluded that Mr Jordan had negligently pulled too long and too hard with the forceps, thereby causing the brain damage. The Court of Appeal reversed the finding of negligence.

Held: the view of the judge who saw and heard the witnesses as to the weight to be given to their evidence is always entitled to great respect. However in this case the important facts were almost all inferences from the primary facts and, in determining what inferences should be drawn, an appellate court is just as well placed as a trial judge. There was not sufficient evidence to justify a finding that Mr Jordan had been negligent.

Per Lord Edmund-Davies: 'to say that a surgeon committed an error of clinical judgment is wholly ambiguous, for, while some such errors may be completely consistent with the due exercise of professional skill, other acts or omissions in the course of exercising clinical judgement may be so glaringly below proper standards as to make a finding of negligence inevitable... Doctors and surgeons fall into no special category and, to avoid any future disputation of a similar kind, I would have it accepted that the true doctrine was enunciated and by no means for the first time, by McNair J in *Bolam v Friern Hospital Management Committee*... The test is the standard of the ordinary skilled man exercising and professing to have that special skill. If a surgeon fails to measure up to that standard in any respect ('clinical judgment' or otherwise), he has been negligent and should be so adjudged'.

Per Lord Wilberforce: 'While some degree of consultation between experts and legal advisers is entirely proper, it is necessary that expert evidence presented to the courts should be, and should be seen to be, the independent product of the expert, uninfluenced as to form or content by the exigencies of litigation. To the extent that it is not, the evidence is likely to be not only incorrect but self-defeating.'

See pp 56, 57, 59, 115, 118, 126.

Whitfield v North Durham Health Authority

Limitation: operation: pathologist: surgeon: shoulder: arm: solicitors

Court of Appeal. [1995] 6 Med LR 32

In April 1985 the plaintiff (Ms Whitfield) was found to have a swelling in the area of her shoulder. A sample was aspirated from this lesion by Mr Cook, a general surgeon of the Dryburn Hospital, and sent for cytological analysis by a consultant histopathologist,

Dr Robinson. On 21 May Dr Robinson reported that the lesion was malignant. In consequence Mr Cook proceeded to try to remove it surgically on 31 May 1985. He discovered that the lump was inextricably involved in the bundle of nerves known as the brachial plexus and, because he believed it to be malignant, he proceeded to remove the lump in its entirety, despite the fact that such a radical surgery was likely to cause injury to the nerves. As a result, the plaintiff's arm sustained permanent neurological injury.

A subsequent histopathological analysis of the material removed from the shoulder showed that it was benign. A few days later, Mr Cook informed the plaintiff and her parents that a mistake had been made. Acting on this, the plaintiff's father wrote on 18 June 1985 to AVMA. By then the plaintiff knew that she had developed a growth on her right shoulder; that the cytology test made upon the aspirate taken from the growth had been misread, and that this was a mistake; that as a result of that mistake the surgeon had deliberately severed the nerve (rather than chipping away at risk of leaving some of the growth behind); that the subsequent histology test showed conclusively that the growth was benign; and that but for this mistake the disability with which he was left would never have been suffered.

Pursuant to that letter, the plaintiff was put in touch with her first firm of solicitors. After obtaining the hospital records in 1986, they issued a writ on 21 December 1987 against Mr Cook and the hospital authority but they never served it. The endorsement on the writ alleged negligence by Mr Cook but not by Dr Robinson. In May 1988 the plaintiff attended a conference with counsel, her first solicitors and the medical expert, pursuant to which her first solicitors wrote to her later that month to inform her that Mr Cook had not been negligent and to advise her to drop her claim or to seek a second opinion. In November 1988 she instructed second solicitors who received the file from her first solicitors in February 1989. Three experts' reports were obtained between November 1990 and February 1992. The plaintiff attended a conference with her lawyers and experts, following which a writ against the hospital authority in respect of negligence by both Mr Cook and Dr Robinson was issued on 19 March 1992.

Held: (i) (a) in assessing the date of knowledge, the court should look to the essence of the complaint and enquire how far the plaintiff had knowledge in broad terms of the facts on which it was based. It was wrong to look beyond the basic essentials and to try to anticipate how the case might be put in terms of positive act or negligent omission. The issue of the 1987 writ was not determinative of the date of knowledge. The plaintiff had knowledge of the facts underlying her complaint against the hospital authority in respect of the acts or omissions of both doctors by the date of her father's letter to AVMA on 18 June 1985. Therefore her action had been commenced six years and nine months out of time.

(b) the issue of the 1987 writ against Mr Cook precluded the exercise of the court's discretion in the plaintiff's favour in respect of his alleged negligence. Although the 1987 action had not been discontinued, the reality was that it had become defunct through passing the point at which there was any possibility of a successful application being made for renewal of the 1987 writ.

(c) (i) had the first solicitors acted properly, Dr Robinson would have been named in the 1987 writ and the exercise of the court's discretion would have been precluded in respect of his negligence as well. The fact that the plaintiff would be gaining a windfall advantage from the failures of her first solicitors was a highly relevant consideration.

(ii) affidavit evidence filed by the defendant asserted that diligent prosecution of the claim would have reached a concluded hearing before 31 December 1989 at the latest with the result that any damages awarded (being well below £300,000) would have been met by the doctors' medical defence organisations rather than by the defendant hospital authority.

(iii)   the delay was bound to have had some degree of prejudicial effect. The fair trial of the claim had required a court to reconstruct the scene as it was in Dr Robinson's laboratory in 1985, in the light of medical opinion as it then obtained, and that reconstruction was a process which became more difficult with the passing of time, not only in terms of the doctor's own powers of recollection as to his processes of thought and interpretation in 1985, but also upon the ability of the experts to carry out a clear retrospective reconstruction of the impression which was or should have been made on his mind when he carried out his inspection.

(iv)   the overriding question under s 33 of the Limitation Act 1980 was one of equity: would it be equitable for the action to be allowed to proceed on a balance of prejudice weighed with due regard to all the circumstances. It was not to be determined on comparative scales of hardship alone.

(v)   in the process of assessing equity and balancing prejudice, a party's action or inaction cannot be divorced from the acts or omissions of his legal representative.

(vi)   it would be inequitable to allow the plaintiff's action to proceed.

Willett v North Bedfordshire Health Authority

Brain damage: childbirth: damages: quadriplegia

Hobhouse J. [1993] CLY 1422

During the plaintiff's birth, her mother suffered an intra-uterine infection and the plaintiff became severely anoxic. The hospital authority admitted liability.

The plaintiff was born with severe disabilities. She suffered from cerebral palsy and spastic quadriplegia. Her life expectancy was 30 years.

Held (November 1992):   general damages were assessed at £105,000 for pain, suffering and loss of amenities out of a total award of £612,773 including interest.

See p 154.

Williams v Imrie

Sterilisation (failed): wrongful birth: damages: school fees: scarring

Hutchison J. [1988] 4 PMILL 22

In July 1979 the plaintiff, then aged 32, underwent a sterilisation operation which was unsuccessful. She subsequently became pregnant. This caused her considerable distress, as she did not know the reason for the symptoms she was suffering. Her medical advisers believed that a clip had worked free from her fallopian tube. This in turn caused the plaintiff to worry for the well-being of the child she was carrying. Nevertheless she gave birth to a healthy daughter. Immediately after the birth she had to undergo a further sterilisation operation which led to a four to five inch-long scar across her abdomen. The pregnancy and birth caused financial worries and problems, particularly as the plaintiff, who already had two young children, felt unable to continue her part-time work.

Held: (i) (April 1987) general damages for pain, suffering and loss of amenities were assessed at £4,000.

(ii) the remaining damages consisted of £485 for the costs attributable to the birth to the end of the first year, £676 for the costs of maintaining the child to the end of its fourth year, £6,065 for the costs of maintaining the child from its fifth to seventeenth year, and £5,970 for loss of earnings to when the plaintiff was able to resume work.

The total award was £17,197.

See pp 128, 170.

Williams v North Liverpool Hospital Management Committee and Others

Anaesthetics: injection: varicose veins

Court of Appeal. (1959) Times, 17 January

In October 1955 the plaintiff (Mrs Alice Williams) was to undergo an operation for varicose veins at Bootle Hospital. Dr Pratt attempted to induce anaesthesia by means of intravenous injections of pentothal into one of her arms. She was exceedingly fat. This made the veins more difficult to find; a further handicap was that fat was not sensitive to pain. Dr Pratt found the vein on either the first or second prick and aspirated by withdrawing the plunger to check that there was blood in the cylinder. He then injected up to 5 cc of pentothal. A substantial part of the pentothal went into the tissues, which were injured. When Dr Pratt appreciated that he had not succeeded in anaesthetising her with the pentothal, he injected a saline solution into the tissues to counteract the irritant effect of the pentothal.

The plaintiff suffered from an abscess which was caused by the first or second injection of pentothal. She sued the hospital authority and Dr Pratt. The trial judge (Elwes J) found in her favour.

Held: Dr Pratt could not have taken any further steps to ensure that the needle was in the lumen of the vein. The plaintiff did not manifest any pain to put him on enquiry. There was no basis for a finding of negligence against him.

See p 120.

Williams v Ward

Works doctor: diagnosis: fracture: arm

Grantham J (with special jury). [1901] 2 BMJ 505

The plaintiff (Mr Williams) was an Aberdare collier. On 25 August 1900, while he was working in the pit, his left arm was fractured between the wrist and the elbow by the fall of a heavy stone. He was seen by Dr Ward, the works doctor, who put the injured limb in splints and bandages. On 17 September the plaintiff went to the works surgery with his father who was getting anxious due to the appearance of certain swellings on the arm. They saw Dr Ward who said it would be all right and promised to put the limb in plaster, which he did on 24 September. When the limb was subsequently freed, the swelling was still apparent. Dr Ward suggested that plaster of Paris should be used again. Instead the plaintiff was taken by his father to Liverpool where he was placed under the care of Dr Jones who operated.

The plaintiff sued Dr Ward, alleging negligence in that the bones of the arm had not been placed in position and could not, therefore, be properly set. The Works Committee approached Dr Ward and suggested that he should pay some compensation.

Dr Ward made a promise of some kind at the time, but later wrote to the Committee to say that anything he should give would be quite voluntary, as Dr Jones' report completely exonerated him from blame. Dr Jones testified that Dr Ward's treatment was perfectly proper and denied that he had ever mentioned the existence of negligence to the plaintiff or his father.

Held: the jury returned a verdict for the defendant.

Willson v McKechnie

Surgeon: operation: advice: back: paraplegia

Thesiger J. (1973) 2 Lancet 163

In May 1968 the plaintiff (Mr Willson) was suffering from back pain. It improved during bed rest from 4 May to 21 May, but worsened on mobilisation from 21 May to 2 June. Between 2 June and 13 June his symptoms improved. The myelogram showed a disc protrusion at L3–L4 level. A lumbar puncture revealed a high protein count in the cerebro-spinal fluid of 160 mg per 100 ml. Some functional overlay was suspected.

On 14 June Mr McKechnie operated on the plaintiff for what turned out to be a minor lumbar disc protrusion. Within three hours the plaintiff developed low paraplegia. He suffered permanent partial incapacity in the use of his legs and sued Mr McKechnie.

Held: Mr McKechnie had been too quick to advise an operation. Conservative treatment by bed rest had not been sufficiently tried. He had not given enough weight to the plaintiff's improvement in the one and a half weeks before the operation. The disastrous result was the kind of damage to be feared. Operating in these circumstances amounted to negligence.

Wilsher v Essex Area Health Authority

Hospital administration: registrar: causation: burden of proof: baby (premature): blindness

House of Lords. [1988] AC 1074, [1988] 1 All ER 871, [1988] 2 WLR 557

At 11.25pm on 15 December 1978 the plaintiff (Martin Wilsher) was born at the Princess Alexandra Hospital, Harlow. He was a tiny baby, and his birth was nearly three months early. He could not breathe effectively and needed extra oxygen.

In order to monitor the partial pressure of oxygen (PO22) in the arterial blood of a young baby, it is standard practice to pass a catheter through the umbilical artery into the aorta. Some time after 1.00am on 16 December Dr Wiles, a senior house officer, inserted the catheter into a vein instead of an artery. The monitor was then connected, and a blood sample was drawn through the catheter. This and subsequent samples were mixtures of arterial and venous blood instead of pure arterial blood, so they gave false readings of the level of PO22 in the arterial blood.

Dr Wiles arranged for an x-ray and called Dr Kawa, a registrar, to inspect what he had done. Neither doctor realised that the configuration of the catheter disclosed by the x-ray meant that it must be following the line of a vein. At about 10.00am on 16 December Dr Kawa decided to change the catheter. Dr Wiles withdrew the old catheter, and Dr Kawa inserted the new one. Again it was inserted in a vein. A further x-ray was taken and inspected, but again the error in placing the catheter was not realised.

The misplaced catheters gave readings of PO22 well below the true level of PO22 in the arterial blood. This led to increased levels of oxygen being administered in an attempt to raise the PO22 level. Consequently, by the time, around 8.00am on 17 December, that Dr Wiles realised that the catheter was in the wrong place and it was duly changed and inserted in an artery, the baby's PO22 levels had been excessive for about eight to twelve hours.

He needed extra oxygen for another eleven weeks. He suffered unduly high levels of PO22 in his arterial blood on five subsequent occasions between 20 December 1978 and 23 January 1979.

The plaintiff contracted retrolental fibroplasia (RLF) and was nearly blind. He sued the health authority, alleging that this was due to an excess of oxygen in his bloodstream during the early weeks. The trial judge (Peter Pain J) found in his favour.

The Court of Appeal affirmed the judge's decision, in so far as it was based on negligence affecting the first period (16–17 December) though not any subsequent period. The majority held that a hospital doctor's duty of care is to be assessed in relation to the post which he occupies. It was not suggested that inserting the catheter into a vein instead of an artery amounted to negligence. The Court of Appeal held that the trial judge was right to find that Dr Kawa had been negligent in failing to appreciate that the catheter was not situated in an artery, but that Dr Wiles was entitled to rely on his work being checked by Dr Kawa and that Dr Wiles had not been negligent.

The defendant health authority appealed. There was no dispute on negligence before the House of Lords. The sole issue for their decision was causation.

Held: (i) the onus of proving causation was on the plaintiff who had to establish that the raised level of PO22 in his arterial blood before 8.00am on 17 December 1978 probably caused or materially contributed to his RLF. The mere fact that excess oxygen was one of a number of different factors which could have caused the RLF raised no presumption that it caused or contributed to it in this case;

(ii) as the primary conflict of opinion between the experts as to whether excess oxygen during the relevant period probably caused or materially contributed to the plaintiff's RLF could not be resolved by reading the transcript of their evidence, there was no alternative but to order a retrial.

See pp 24, 36, 44, 57, 60, 65, 71, 117, 126, 131, 212.

Wilson v Tomlinson

Fracture: wrist

Ashworth J. (1956) 2 Lancet 1154

The plaintiff, a 62-year-old woman, visited Dr Tomlinson for a course of treatment for her neck and right arm. On about the sixth visit, when she was still suffering from considerable pain, he asked her to lie on a couch in a cubicle for manipulative treatment to her neck. On the couch, which was covered in Rexine, there was a blanket which was not tied with tapes but was to some extent kept in position on the right side by a flange along the side of the cubicle against which it was pressed. The top of the couch was 2ft 9½ in. from the floor, and it was impossible for the patient to reach the floor when in a sitting position.

When the treatment was finished, Dr Tomlinson indicated that she should get off the couch. The plaintiff had reached a sitting position and was swinging her legs around to the left, when the blanket came away and both she and the blanket fell to the floor. She sustained a fractured wrist and sued Dr Tomlinson.

Held: where there was a displaced or loose blanket on Rexine, a person on top of it who moved her legs around on it was likely to slip. Dr Tomlinson was dealing with a lady aged sixty-two who was not well and whose right arm was giving her trouble. He should have known that a patient of that age and in that condition required assistance in getting off the couch. In the exercise of reasonable care, he should have placed himself at the side of the couch to help her. He had been negligent.

See p 132.

Winch v Jones and Others

Psychiatric patient: leave to sue: negligent certification: paranoia

Court of Appeal. [1986] QB 296, [1985] 3 All ER 97, [1985] 3 WLR 729

In October 1978 the applicant (Mary Winch) was admitted to the North Wales Hospital for treatment pursuant to recommendations under s 26 of the Mental Health Act 1959. Such an admission authorised the detention of the patient for up to twelve months. The necessary recommendations were made by Dr Hayward, the medical officer of Risley Remand Centre, and Dr Bishop, a general practitioner. On admission to North Wales Hospital, the applicant came under the care of Dr Jones. She spent twelve months subject to the s 26 admission either at the hospital or on leave from it.

She applied to the High Court for leave to sue the doctors and their employers. She complained that Dr Hayward and Dr Bishop failed to exercise reasonable care in diagnosing that she suffered from paranoia and in recommending that she be admitted to a mental hospital. Her complaint against Dr Jones was that he failed to give any or adequate consideration to discharging her before the order came to an end twelve months after her admission. Otton J refused her application for leave under s 139 Mental Health Act 1983.

Held: her applications should be granted, as her complaints deserved fuller investigation.

Per Sir John Donaldson MR: 'The section is intended to strike a balance between the legitimate interest of the applicant to be allowed, at his own risk as to costs, to seek the adjudication of the courts upon any claim which is not frivolous, vexatious, or an abuse of process, and the equally legitimate interests of the respondent to such an application not to be subjected to the undoubted exceptional risk of being harassed by baseless claims by those who have been treated under the Acts. In striking such a balance, the issue is not whether the applicant has established a prima-facie case or even whether there is a serious issue to be tried, although that comes close to it. The issue is whether, on the material immediately available to the court, which, of course, can include material furnished by the proposed defendants, the applicant's complaint appears to be such that it deserves the further investigation which will be possible if the intended applicant is allowed to proceed.'

See p 100.

Winterbone v West Suffolk Health Authority

Bladder: damages: operation: fistula: scarring

H H Judge Bromley. [1994] 1 CL 135

In 1988, the plaintiff (Mrs Winterbone), aged 44, underwent an operation at the defendant's hospital for the removal of an ovarian cyst. Her bladder was accidentally stitched to the vaginal vault. In addition, the surgeons correctly performed a total abdominal hysterectomy and bilateral salpingo-oophorectomy.

On the seventh day after the operation, the plaintiff suddenly found herself totally incontinent of urine. After two months, a diagnosis of vesica-vaginal fistula was made. After a further month, surgical repair was successfully undertaken under general anaesthetic. Until this repair, she suffered considerable discomfort and inconvenience, including one month's continuous catheterization, abstinence from sexual intercourse and social embarrassment. For a few weeks after the repair, she experienced some further discomfort and irritation. Post operative scarring was greater as a result of the need for a second operation.

Held (November 1993):   (i)   in the absence of difficulty in separating the bladder, the surgical stitching of the bladder to the vaginal vault was negligent.

                                  (ii)   general damages of £4,500 were awarded for pain, suffering and loss of amenities. Special damages were £480.

See pp 117, 156.

Wood v Thurston and Others

Fractures: diagnosis: casualty officer: examination: fatal

Pritchard J. (1951) Times, 25 May

On 6 August 1948 John Wood had been drinking with friends after work. After leaving a public house, he crawled on all fours underneath a lorry. As he did so the lorry started to move and one of its rear wheels pinned Mr Wood to the ground, although he was released before it went completely over him.

He walked to the casualty department of Charing Cross Hospital where he was examined by Dr Thurston. He was intoxicated but not drunk. He told Mr Thurston what had happened and said that there was nothing wrong with him and that he wanted to go home. Dr Thurston treated him for a nose bleed. He felt Mr Wood's chest but in a cursory manner, and allowed him to travel in a taxi to his home.

In the early hours of 7 August, Mr Wood was admitted to West Middlesex Hospital where he died at about 7.00am. Post-mortem examination showed that he had a broken collar bone, 18 fractured ribs and badly congested lungs. The plaintiff (his widow) sued Dr Thurston and the hospital authority.

Held: (i)   Dr Thurston did not examine Mr Wood with the care that was demanded in the circumstances. If a stethoscope had been used, it was almost inevitable that Mr Wood's true condition would have been discovered.

             (ii)   Mr Wood would not have died if he had been kept immobile. His death was caused by Dr Thurston's negligence.

See p 96.

Woodhouse v Yorkshire Regional Health Authority

Surgeon: operation: res ipsa loquitur: damages: hysteria: fingers

Court of Appeal. CAT, 12 April 1984. (1984) 1 Lancet 1306

On 28 January 1976 the plaintiff (Elizabeth Woodhouse), a keen pianist, was admitted to Scarborough General Hospital with a subphrenic abscess. On 31 January and 10 February she was operated on under general anaesthetics by Mr Fletcher, a consultant surgeon. Her left ulnar nerve was damaged during the first operation and her right ulnar nerve during the second. She was left with severe contraction deformities of her fingers. She also suffered from a hysterical condition.

The plaintiff sued the hospital authority. It was agreed that ulnar nerve damage is a well recognized hazard of operating under anaesthesia and great care must be taken to ensure that it does not occur. The trial judge (Russell J) found that the defendants had been negligent.

Held: (i) the plaintiff had suffered injuries which ought not to occur if standard precautions had been taken. The judge inferred that these precautions could not have been taken and, in the absence of any explanation for failing to take them, he was entitled to conclude that such a failure was negligent.

          (ii) the defendants were liable for the plaintiff's hysteria as well as her organic injuries. The tortfeasor takes the victim as he finds her. The defendants had damaged a plaintiff with a hysterical personality. As a result they had caused greater damage than might have been expected, but in law they were responsible for it.

See pp 89, 146.

Worster v City and Hackney Health Authority

Sterilisation: consent: risk disclosure: representation

Garland J. (1987) Times, 22 June

The plaintiff signed a consent form for a sterilisation operation. It included the words: 'This is to certify that we, the undersigned, agree to this operation of sterilisation being performed on. . . . . and we understand this means we can have no more children.'

The defendant health authority's consultant gynaecologist, Mr John Woolf, did not warn the plaintiff that a sterilisation operation by the Pomeroy method was subject to a small possibility of failure.

Held: the wording on the consent form was not a negligent representation capable of being understood as an assurance of success. The plaintiff's claim was dismissed.

See pp 28, 111.

X v France

AIDS: blood transfusion: damages: France: costs

European Court of Human Rights. (1991) 12 BMLR 25

Mr X, born in 1963, was a French haemophiliac who lived in Paris. Between September 1984 and January 1985 he received several blood transfusions at the Saint-Antoine Hospital. In June 1985 it was discovered that he was HIV positive. Attempts by the French

Association of Haemophiliacs to obtain compensation for him and others from the state were unsuccessful.

On 1 December 1989, X made a preliminary claim for compensation to the Minister for Solidarity, Health and Social Protection, alleging negligent delay by the minister in implementing appropriate rules for the supply of blood products. 649 similar claims were made. On 30 March 1990, the Director General for Health rejected X's claim.

In May 1990 X filed an application in the Paris Administrative Court for annulment of the ministerial decision. In September and October 1990 he required in-patient hospital treatment for the first time. In a memorial on 29 October 1990, he stressed the urgency of his case. In February 1991 the Minister lodged a memorial in reply, asking the court to appoint an expert with a view to establishing whether X's injury was attributable to the state's negligence. At the court's behest, certain investigations were carried out over the next six months. In September 1991 X submitted further memorials stating that he had developed AIDS. In December 1991 the Paris Administrative Court dismissed his claim, holding that the state had only been negligent between 12 March 1985 and 1 October 1985, after the transfusions in question. In January 1992, X appealed to the Paris Administrative Court of Appeal. He died in February 1992.

In February 1991, X had lodged an application with the European Commission, alleging that his case had not been heard within a reasonable time. His parents continued the proceedings. Article 6(1) of the European Convention for the Protection of Human Rights and Fundamental Freedoms provides that: 'In the determination of his civil rights and obligations . . . everyone is entitled to a . . . hearing within a reasonable time by (a) . . . tribunal . . .'

Held: (i)   Article 6(1) applied to the present case. It was sufficient that the outcome of the proceedings should be decisive for private rights and obligations.

    (ii)   the case was one of some complexity, and investigations could have been necessary to determine the state's liability. However, the government had probably been aware for a long time that proceedings were imminent. It could have obtained much of the relevant information, and ought to have commissioned an objective report on liability, immediately after the commencement of the cases.

    (iii)   although X could have decided to sue the blood transfusion centres in the ordinary courts, his action was intended to challenge the state on which he considered that responsibility really fell. He had displayed normal diligence and had attempted to galvanise the investigation.

    (iv)   the proceedings were of crucial importance to X, having regard to his incurable disease and reduced life expectancy. Exceptional diligence was required. Yet the administrative court did not use its powers to make orders to accelerate the proceedings, although from 29 October 1990 it was aware of the deterioration in X's health.

    (v)   a reasonable time had already been exceeded when the judgment was delivered in December 1991. The subsequent proceedings in the Paris Administrative Court of Appeal could not redress this failure, whatever the outcome as to the merits. There had been a violation of Article 6(1).

    (vi)   X had claimed in the first place 150,000 francs for non-pecuniary damage. The length of the proceedings had prevented him from obtaining the compensation for which he had hoped, and thus from being able to live independently and in better psychological conditions for the remaining period of his life. Pursuant to Article 50, his parents should be awarded the entire 150,000 francs sought.

    (vii)   X had also claimed 30,000 francs for costs and expenses incurred before the Commission and the court. This should also be awarded in its entirety.

X v NHS Trust

Blood transfusion: consent: injunction: Jehovah's Witness: living will

Court of Appeal. [1995] HCRR Vol 1, Issue 3, p 3

X, an elderly Jehovah's Witness, was admitted to hospital for a left transabdominal nephrectomy. Before the operation he signed a standard form of advance directive, indicating that under no circumstances did he wish to receive blood or blood products. Accordingly during the operation a cell-saver was used; no blood or blood products were administered.

Within 24 hours after the operation X's condition deteriorated and his haemoglobin level dropped to approximately half the normal level. During an interview between X, his consultant surgeon, the registrar and staff nurse, it was explained that without a blood transfusion he would die very soon. Although X was incapable of speech, the others present believe that he had clearly indicated consent to receiving a blood transfusion by nodding his head in answer to specific questions. Accordingly instructions were left with the hospital staff that four units of blood should be given immediately.

Approximately 36 hours after the operation, X's family obtained an ex parte injunction that no blood or blood products could be administered to him. The judge granting this was ignorant of the interview which had taken place between X and the hospital staff. The hospital authority immediately appealed to the Court of Appeal.

Held: the earlier injunction should be stayed, in view of X's apparent consent during the post operative interview with the hospital staff.

Note: Very soon afterwards a blood transfusion was given.

Yafi v North Lincolnshire Health Authority

Discovery: fatal: inquest

Rougier J. [1992] 3 Med LR 284, [1993] PIQR P59.

See *Stobart v Nottingham Health Authority* (p 567).

Yerex v Bloomsbury Health Authority

After-care: fatal: operation: peritonitis

Court of Appeal. CAT, 26 July 1990

At 5pm on 26 May 1983 Lincoln Yerex, aged 91, a patient at Athlone House Long Stay Unit, was diagnosed as suffering from sigmoid volvulus. At 7pm Dr Wahal inserted a sigmoidoscope into Mr Yerex's rectum and perforated the wall of the sigmoid colon with it. The perforation took place within the volvulus and about three to five centimetres beyond the recto-sigmoid junction. It was not perceived at the time.

At 9pm Dr Hacking examined Mr Yerex and noted – 'Flatus tube passed through sigmoid volvulus with good success. Still has some colicky pain. Mucus and red blood per rectum. ? trauma. Abdomen less tense, bowel sounds normal.' When he telephoned Dr Wahal at

10pm, the possibility of a perforation and peritonitis was considered. Dr Wahal, who did not visit Mr Yerex, concluded that the risk of operating was greater than the risk of not operating. Mr Yerex died the next day of peritonitis.

Held: (i) the judge was entitled to conclude that the perforation of the bowel wall did not necessarily indicate negligence.

(ii) it was not negligent of Dr Wahal to fail to visit Mr Yerex between 10pm and midnight. Even if he had done so, the clinical signs would have at most suggested the possibility of a perforation. Moreover the patient was a poor operative risk, and it would not have been negligent to decide not to carry out a laparatomy which might have been fatal.

The plaintiff's appeal was dismissed.

See p 116.

Zimmer et al v Ringrose

Canada: after-care: battery: departing from orthodox practice: informed consent: sterilisation (failed): fallopian tubes

Alberta Court of Appeal. (1981) 124 DLR (3d) 215

The plaintiff (Mrs Zimmer) told the defendant (Dr Ringrose) that she wished to be sterilised following the birth of her second child in January 1973. He informed her of a new technique which utilized silver nitrate paste as a means of blocking the passages of the fallopian tubes. He told her that the procedure could be performed in an office setting, but did not say that it was not generally accepted in the medical community.

On 1 March 1973 she submitted to the silver nitrate treatment, primarily because it did not require a stay in hospital. Dr Ringrose told her to return for an x-ray (hysterosalpingogram) in two months, in order to enable him to assess whether the fallopian tubes were blocked, and in the meantime to exercise birth control. She consulted him on 31 May because she had not had a menstrual period since January; a pregnancy test proved negative. On 14 June he performed the hysterosalpingogram but, due to his misapplication of the die, the test gave an unreliable reading as to the effect of silver nitrate on the fallopian tubes. However he advised her that the procedure had proved effective.

On 13 September 1973 she again attended Dr Ringrose, because she was concerned by the absence of her menstrual periods. He diagnosed her as pregnant, conception having occurred in May. She travelled to Seattle where she was aborted by means of a saline injection. In October 1974 he successfully sterilised her.

Held: (i) the plaintiff understood the nature of the silver nitrate technique and agreed to undergo the method of sterilisation. Consequently the defendant was not liable for battery.

(ii) he did not give the plaintiff any comparison between his silver nitrate method and other methods of effecting sterilisation. Moreover he failed to appraise her of the fact that the silver nitrate technique had not been approved by the medical profession. In view of these failures, his conduct was negligent.

(iii) however, considering the plaintiff's desire to avoid going into hospital when she had a new baby at home to look after, combined with the fact that all the alternative methods of sterilisation required hospitalization, a full disclosure at the particular time would not have induced a reasonable person in her particular position to forego the silver nitrate procedure. That branch of her action failed.

(iv) despite the defendant's awareness that the silver nitrate technique required further evaluation, he negligently failed to follow the plaintiff's progress by conducting regular medical examinations during the summer of 1993. Such conduct was inconsistent with good clinical practice. Had she received proper follow-up care, her pregnancy would most certainly have been diagnosed at an earlier stage, thereby reducing the seriousness of the subsequent abortion.

See pp 65, 113.

Index of case subjects in Part II

Deafness
Atkinson (p 230); Baig (p 235); Richardson (p 523); Upton (p 590).

Declaration
Fox (p 337); Johnstone v Bloomsbury (p 404).

Departing from orthodox practice
Clark (p 279); Coughlin (p 289); Henderson (p 376); Landau (p 425); Robinson (p 528); Slater v Baker (p 558).

Depression
Ackers (p 221); Bagley (p 234); Bolam (p 250); Buckle (p 263); Gale (p 345); Grayson (p 359); Hatwell (p 372); Hooper (p 387); Hyde (p 396); Kerby (p 412); R v Mid Glamorgan (p 508); Tate (p 576).

Diabetes
R v Harris (p 505); R v Jones (p 505).

Diagnosis
Barker (p 237); Bayliss (p 240); Bova (p 254); Braisher (p 258); Burridge (p 266); Champion (p 273); Chapman (p 274); Clarke v City (p 280); Colegrove (p 282); Colston (p 284); Connelly (p 284); Connolly v Rubra (p 285); Crivon (p 293); Cunningham (p 297); Edler (p 319); Elkan (p 320); Evason (p 324); Farquhar (p 330); Furstenau (p 343); Gardiner (p 345); Haines (p 364); Herskovits (p 378); Hogg v Ealing (p 383); Holland (p 385); Horner (p 388); Hotson (p 389); Hucks (p 392); Hughes (p 392); Hulse (p 394); Hunter (p 396); Hyde (p 396); Junor (p 407); Kenyon (p 411); Kilburn (p 414); Kinnear (No 2) (p 417); Langley (p 425); Lanphier (p 426); Lock (p 432); Luke v South Glamorgan (p 437); McCormack (p 445); McCormick (p 446); McKay (p 447); Markham (p 452); Maynard (p 456); Morgan (p 461); Newton (p 480); O'Donnell (p 483); O'Malley-Williams (p 484); Parkinson (p 488); Patel v Adyha (p 490); Payne (p 493); Pimm (p 495); Prescott (p 497); Pudney (p 498); Ralph (p 517); Redmayne (p 520); Riddett (p 523); Riggs (p 524); Ritter (p 524); Rouse (p 535); Sabapathi (p 540); Sa'd (p 541); Sadler (p 542); Salisbury (p 543); Saumarez (p 546); Saunders v West Suffolk (p 546); Seare (p 550); Sellers (p 550); Spinola (p 564); Stevens (p 566); Sullivan (p 570); Sutton (p 570); Tanswell (p 575); Thompson (p 582); Thornton (p 584); Upton (p 590); Vaughan (p 592); Walker v Semple (p 596); Warren (p 599); Westaway (p 600); Whiteford (p 603); Williams v Ward (p 607); Wood (p 611).

Disclosure of experts' reports
Naylor (page 478).

Disconnection from ventilator
Re A (p 217).

Discontinuance of life-preserving treatment
R v Bingley Magistrates (p 501).

Discontinuance of life-supporting treatment
Airedale (p 222); Frenchay (p 339); Clarke v Hurst (p 281); Re G (p 343); Swindon (p 571).

Discovery
Boothe (p 253); Cunningham (p 297); Davies v Eli Lilly (p 300); Dunning (p 315); Hall v Wandsworth (p 366); Harris (p 370); Jacob (p 399); Lask (p 426); Lee (p 428); Locke (p 433); M v Plymouth (p 440); Paterson (p 491); R v Mid Glamorgan (p 508); Stobart (p 567); Summut (p 543); Walker v Eli Lilly (p 595); Yafi (p 614).

Dismissal for want of prosecution
Biss (p 248); Joseph (p 407); Mansouri (p 451); Westaway (p 600).

Down's Syndrome
Re B (a minor) (p 233); Gregory (p 361).

Hospital resources

R v Cambridge (p 501); R v Central Birmingham (ex parte Collier) (p 502); R v Central Birmingham (ex parte Walker) (p 502); R v NW Thames (p 509).

House surgeon (qv **Hospital doctor**)

Christie (p 277); Collins (p 283); Junor (p 407); Patten (p 492).

HIV Discovery

AB v Scottish Blood Transfusion Service (p 220); Australian Red Cross Society (p 232); Re HIV (p 394).

Hysterectomy

Breen (p 259); Chaunt (p 276); Cull (p 296); Re E (a minor) (medical treatment) (p 317); F v F (p 326); Re G F (p 344); Gascoine (p 346); Grayson (p 359); Hendy (p 377); Hendy (No 2) (p 378); Hooper (p 387); Jacobs (p 399); Marram (p 453); Powell (p 496).

Hysteria

Woodhouse (p 612).

Impotence

Smith v Tunbridge Wells (p 562); Tate (p 576).

Infection

Bayliss (p 240); Fletcher (p 333); Heafield (p 375); Marshall v Lindsey CC (p 454); Ter (p 580); Vancouver General Hospital (p 591); Voller (p 594).

Informed consent

Canterbury (p 269); Coughlin (p 289); Karp (p 409); Reibl (p 521); Zimmer (p 615).

Injections

Akerele (p 223); Allan (p 224); Brazier (p 259); Caldeira (p 269); Chin Keow (p 276); Ciarlariello (p 278); Corner (p 289); Daly (p 298); Davidson (p 298); Freeman (p 339); Gale (p 345); Gerber (p 351); Hayward (p 373); Hunter (p 396); Jacobs (p 399); Kay (p 470); Kidd (p 413); King (p 415); Marchant (p 452); Mitchell v McDonald (p 459); Pargeter (p 487); Paterson (p 491); Prout (p 498); R v Prentice (p 509); Robinson v Post Office (p 528); Smith v Brighton (p 559); Tate (p 576); Voller (p 594); Walker v South West Surrey (p 596); Williams v North Liverpool (p 607).

Interests of patient

Airedale (p 222); Devon (p 309); Re E (a minor) (medical treatment) (p 317); F (p 326); F v F (p 326); Frenchay (p 339); Re G (p 343); Re G F(p 344); Re J (a minor) (p 398); Marshall v Curry (p 455); R v Mid Glamorgan (p 508); Re R (p 514); Ritchie (p 525); Re S (adult: refusal of treatment) (p 538); Re S (hospital treatment) (p 538); Re SG (adult) (p 539); Swindon (p 571); Re T (p 572).

Interrogatories

Ali (p 223).

Inquest

Stobart (p 567); Yafi (p 614).

Ireland

Brogan (p 262).

Japan

Makino (p 450).

Jaw

Ashton (p 230); Bridges (p 260); Fish (p 332); Fletcher (p 333); Hatwell (p 372); Lock (p 432).

Jehovah's Witness

Devon (p 309); Malette (p 450); Nicoleau (p 481); Re O (a minor) (p 482); Re R (p 514); Raleigh (p 516); Re T (p 572); X v NHS Trust (p 614).

Judicial review

R v Cambridge (p 501); R v Central Birmingham Health Authority (ex p Collier) (p 502); R v Central Birmingham Health Authortiy (ex p Walker) (p 502).

Jurisdiction

Distillers v Thompson (p 309).

Kidney

Antcliffe (p 227); Hooper (p 387); Thomsen (p 583); Urbanski (p 590).

Knee

Broadley (p 261); Gladwell (p 354); Kilburn (p 414); McInnes (p 446); Mose (p 463); Newton (p 480); Patterson (p 492); Spinola (p 564).

Laparotomy

Carter (p 270).

Laryngeal

Nickolls (p 480).

Leave to sue

Re Frost (p 340); Furber (p 341); Routley (p 536); Winch (p 610).

Leg

Daly (p 298); Driscoll (p 313); Hartley (p 371); Marchant (p 452); Phelan (p 494); Raleigh (p 516); Slater v Baker (p 558); Spinola (p 564).

Legal aid

Hunt (p 395); Jacob v Wessex (p 399); Lockley (p 434); R v Legal Aid (p 507).

Legal negligence

Gascoine v Ian Sheridan (p 348).

Leukaemia

R v Cambridge (p 501); R v Prentice (p 509); Warren v Greig (p 599); Warren v White (p 599).

Libel/Slander

Sabapathi (p 540).

Limitation

Atkinson (p 230); Baig (p 235); Bentley (p 244); Berger (p 244); Bowers (p 257); Boxall (p 258); Broadley (p 261); Busutill (p 267); Cockburn (p 281); Colgrove (p 282); Dobbie (p 310); Driscoll (p 313); Eaton (p 318); Fletcher v Sheffield (p 334); Forster (p 336); Gascoine (p 348); Grenville (p 361); Hall v Eli Lilly (p 366); Hands (p 368); Hendy (p 377); Higgins (p 372); Jenkins (p 403); Khan (p 413); Kidd (p 413); Kirby (p 418); Nash v Eli Lilly (p 466); Newell v Eli Lily (p 479); O'Hara (p 483); Obembe (p 485); Odam (p 486); Roach (p 526); Sergeant (p 553); Sivyer (p 557); Stanley (p 565); Stephen (p 565); Waghorn (p 594); Walkin (p 597); Whitfield (p 604).

Lingual nerve

Christie (p 277); Heath (p 375); McAloon (p 443); Tomkins (p 587).

Liver

Carter (p 270); Luke (p 437); Makino (p 450).

Living will

Clarke v Hurst (p 281); X v NHS Trust (p 614).

Locum

Farquhar (p 330).

Loss of chance

Herskovits (p 378); Hotson (p 389); Kenyon (p 411); Langley (p 425); Wells (p 600).

Index

639